T0091462

HANDBOOK ON COMPUTER LEARNING AND INTELLIGENCE

Volume 1: Explainable AI and Supervised Learning

HANDBOOK ON COMPUTER LEARNING AND INTELLIGENCE

Volume 1: Explainable AI and Supervised Learning

Editor

Plamen Parvanov Angelov

Lancaster University, UK

 **World Scientific**

NEW JERSEY · LONDON · SINGAPORE · BEIJING · SHANGHAI · HONG KONG · TAIPEI · CHENNAI · TOKYO

Published by

World Scientific Publishing Co. Pte. Ltd.

5 Toh Tuck Link, Singapore 596224

USA office: 27 Warren Street, Suite 401-402, Hackensack, NJ 07601

UK office: 57 Shelton Street, Covent Garden, London WC2H 9HE

Library of Congress Cataloging-in-Publication Data

Names: Angelov, Plamen P., editor.

Title: Handbook on computer learning and intelligence / editor,
  Plamen Parvanov Angelov, Lancaster University, UK.

Other titles: Handbook on computational intelligence.

Description: New Jersey : World Scientific, [2022] | Includes bibliographical references and index. |
  Contents: Volume 1. Explainable AI and supervised learning --
  Volume 2. Deep learning, intelligent control and evolutionary computation.

Identifiers: LCCN 2021052472 | ISBN 9789811245145 (set) | ISBN 9789811246043 (v. 1 ; hardcover) |
  ISBN 9789811246074 (v. 2 ; hardcover) | ISBN 9789811247323 (set ; ebook for institutions) |
  ISBN 9789811247330 (set ; ebook for individuals)

Subjects: LCSH: Expert systems (Computer science)--Handbooks, manuals, etc. |
  Neural networks (Computer science)--Handbooks, manuals, etc. | Systems engineering--
  Data processing--Handbooks, manuals, etc. | Intelligent control systems--Handbooks, manuals, etc. |
  Computational intelligence--Handbooks, manuals, etc.

Classification: LCC QA76.76.E95 H3556 2022 | DDC 006.3/3--dc23/eng/20211105

LC record available at https://lccn.loc.gov/2021052472

British Library Cataloguing-in-Publication Data

A catalogue record for this book is available from the British Library.

For any available supplementary material, please visit
https://www.worldscientific.com/worldscibooks/10.1142/12498#t=suppl

Desk Editors: Nandha Kumar/Amanda Yun

Typeset by Stallion Press
Email: enquiries@stallionpress.com

Printed in Singapore

Preface

The Handbook aims to be a one-stop-shop for the various aspects of the broad research area of *Computer learning and Intelligence*. It is organized in two volumes and five parts as follows:

Volume 1 includes two parts:

    Part 1   Explainable AI

    Part II Supervised Learning

Volume 2 has three parts:

    Part III Deep Learning

    Part IV Intelligent Control

    Part V   Evolutionary Computation

The Handbook has twenty-six chapters in total, which detail the theory, methodology and applications of *Computer Learning and Intelligence*. These individual contributions are authored by some of the leading experts in the respective areas and often are co-authored by a small team of associates. They offer a cocktail of individual contributions that span the spectrum of the key topics as outlined in the titles of the five parts. In total, over 67 authors from over 20 different countries contributed to this carefully crafted final product. This collaborative effort brought together leading researchers and scientists form USA, Canada, Wales, Northern Ireland, England, Japan, Sweden, Italy, Spain, Austria, Slovenia, Romania, Singapore, New Zealand, Brazil, Russia, India, Mexico, Hong Kong, China, Pakistan and Qatar.

    The scope of the Handbook covers the most important aspects of the topic of *Computer Learning and Intelligence*.

    Preparing, compiling and editing this Handbook was an enjoyable and inspirational experience.

    I hope you will also enjoy reading it, will find answers to your questions and will use this book in your everyday work.

Plamen Parvanov Angelov

Lancaster, UK

3 June 2022

About the Editor

 **Professor Plamen Parvanov Angelov** holds a Personal Chair in Intelligent Systems and is Director of Research at the School of Computing and Communications at Lancaster University, UK. He obtained his PhD in 1993 and DSc (Doctor of Sciences) degree in 2015 when he also become Fellow of IEEE. Prof. Angelov is the founding Director of the Lancaster Intelligent, Robotic and Autonomous systems (LIRA) Research Centre which brings together over 60 faculty/academics across fifteen different departments of Lancaster University. Prof. Angelov is a Fellow of the European Laboratory for Learning and Intelligent Systems (ELLIS) and of the Institution of Engineering and Technology (IET) as well as a Governor-at-large of the International Neural Networks Society (INNS) for a third consecutive three-year term following two consecutive terms holding the elected role of Vice President. In the last decade, Prof. Angelov is also Governor-at-large of the Systems, Man and Cybernetics Society of the IEEE. Prof. Angelov founded two research groups (the Intelligent Systems Research group in 2010 and the Data Science group at 2014) and was a founding member of the Data Science Institute and of the CyberSecurity Academic Centre of Excellence at Lancaster.

Prof. Angelov has published over 370 publications in leading journals and peer-reviewed conference proceedings, 3 granted US patents, 3 research monographs (by Wiley, 2012 and Springer, 2002 and 2018) cited over 12300 times with an h-index of 58 (according to Google Scholar). He has an active research portfolio in the area of computer learning and intelligence, and internationally recognized results into online and evolving learning and algorithms. More recently, his research is focused on explainable deep learning as well as anthropomorphic and empirical computer learning.

Prof. Angelov leads numerous projects (including several multimillion ones) funded by UK research councils, EU, industry, European Space Agency, etc. His research was recognized by the 2020 Dennis Gabor Award for "outstanding contributions to engineering applications of neural networks", '*The Engineer Innovation and Technology 2008 Special Award'* and *'For outstanding Services'* (2013) by IEEE and INNS. He is also the founding co-Editor-in-Chief of Springer's journal on *Evolving Systems* and Associate Editor of several leading international journals, including *IEEE Transactions on Cybernetics, IEEE Transactions on Fuzzy Systems, IEEE Transactions on AI*, etc. He gave over 30 dozen keynote/plenary talks at high profile conferences. Prof. Angelov was General Co-Chair of a number of high-profile IEEE conferences and is the founding Chair of the Technical Committee on Evolving Intelligent Systems, Systems, Man and Cybernetics Society of the IEEE. He is also co-chairing the working group (WG) on a new standard on Explainable AI created by his initiative within the Standards Committee of the Computational Intelligent Society of the IEEE which he chaired from 2010–2012. Prof. Angelov is the founding co-Director of one of the funded programs by ELLIS on Human-centered machine learning. He was a member of the International Program Committee of over 100 international conferences (primarily IEEE conferences).

Acknowledgments

The Editor would like to acknowledge the unwavering support and love of his wife Rositsa, his children (Mariela and Lachezar) as well as of his mother, Lilyana.

Contents

Handbook on Computer Learning and Intelligence

Introduction by the Editor

You are holding in your hand the second edition of the handbook that was published six years ago as *Handbook on Computational Intelligence*. The research field has evolved so much during the last five years that we decided to not only update the content with new chapters but also change the title of the handbook. At the same time, the core chapters (15 out of 26) have been written and significantly updated by the same authors. The structure of the book is also largely the same, though some parts evolved to cover new phenomena better. For example, the part Deep Learning evolved from the artificial neural networks, and the part Explainable AI evolved from fuzzy logic. The new title, *Computer Learning and Intelligence*, better reflects the new state-of-the-art in the area that spans machine learning and artificial intelligence (AI), but is more application and engineering oriented rather than being theoretically abstract or statistics oriented like many other texts that also use these terms.

The term *computer learning* is used instead of the common term *machine learning* deliberately. Not only does it link with the term *computational intelligence* but it also reflects more accurately the nature of learning algorithms that are of interest. These are implemented on computing devices spanning from the Cloud to the Edge, covering personal and networked computers and other computerized tools. The term *machine* is more often used in a mechanical and mechatronic context as a physical device contrasting the (still) electronic nature of the computers. In addition, the term *machine learning*, the genesis of which stems from the research area of AI, is now used almost as a synonym for *statistical learning*. In fact, *learning* is much more than function approximation, parameter learning, and number fitting. An important element of learning is reasoning, knowledge representation, expression and handling (storage, organization, retrieval), as well as decision-making and cognition. Statistical learning is quite successful today, but it seems to oversimplify some of these aspects. In this handbook, we aim to provide all perspectives, and therefore, we combine computer learning with intelligence.

Talking about intelligence, we mentioned *computational intelligence*, which was the subject of the first edition of the handbook. As is well known, this term itself came around toward the end of the last century and covers areas of research that are inspired and that "borrow"/"mimic" such forms of natural intelligence as the human brain (artificial neural networks), human reasoning (fuzzy logic and systems), and natural evolution (evolutionary systems). Intelligence is also at the core of the widely used term AI. The very idea of developing systems, devices, algorithms, and techniques that possess characteristics of *intelligence* and are computational (not just conceptual) dates back to the middle of the 20th century or even earlier, but only now it is becoming truly widespread, moving from the labs to the real-life applications.

In this handbook, while not claiming to provide an exhaustive picture of this dynamic and fast-developing area, we provide some key directions and examples written in self-contained chapters, which are, however, organized in parts on topics such as:

- Explainable AI
- Supervising Learning
- Deep Learning
- Intelligent Control
- Evolutionary Computation

The primary goal of *Computer Learning and Intelligence* is to provide efficient computational solutions to the existing open problems from theoretical and application points of view with regard to the understanding, representation, modeling, visualization, reasoning, decision, prediction, classification, analysis, and control of physical objects, environmental or social phenomena, etc., to which the traditional methods, techniques, and theories (primarily so-called first principles based, deterministic, or probabilistic, often expressed as differential equations, regression, and Bayesian models, and stemming from mass and energy balance) cannot provide a valid or useful/practical solution.

Another specific feature of *Computer Learning and Intelligence* is that it offers solutions that bear characteristics of *intelligence*, which is usually attributed to humans only. This has to be considered broadly rather than literally, as is the area of AI. This is, perhaps, clearer with fuzzy logic, where systems can make decisions very much like humans do. This is in a stark contrast to the deterministic-type expert systems or probabilistic associative rules. One can argue that artificial neural networks, including deep learning, process the data in a manner that is similar to what the human brain does. For evolutionary computation, the argument is that the population of candidate solutions "evolves" toward the optimum in a manner similar to the way species or living organisms evolve in nature.

The handbook is composed of 2 volumes and 5 parts, which contain 26 chapters. Eleven of these chapters are new in comparison to the first edition, while the other 15 chapters are substantially improved and revised. More specifically,

Volume 1 includes Part I (Explainable AI) and Part II (Supervised Learning).

Volume 2 includes Part III (Deep Learning), Part IV (Intelligent Control), and Part V (Evolutionary Computation).

In Part I the readers can find six chapters on explainable AI, including:

- *Explainable AI and Computational Intelligence: Past and Present*

  This new chapter provides a historical perspective of explainable AI. It is written by Dr. Mojtaba Yeganejou and Prof. Scott Dick from the University of Alberta, Canada.

- *Fundamentals of Fuzzy Sets Theory*

  This chapter is a thoroughly revised version of the chapter with the same title from the first edition of the handbook. It provides a step-by-step introduction to the theory of fuzzy sets, which itself is anchored in the theory of reasoning and is one of the most prominent and well-developed forms of explainable AI (the others being decision trees and symbolic AI). It is written by one of the leading experts in this area, former president of the International Fuzzy Systems Association (IFSA), Prof. Fernando Gomide from UNICAMP, Campinas, Brazil.

- *Granular Computing*

  This chapter is also a thoroughly revised version from the first edition of the handbook and is written by two of the pioneers in this area, Profs. Witold Pedrycz from the University of Alberta, Canada, and Andrzej Bargiela. Granular computing became a cornerstone of the area of explainable AI, and this chapter offers a thorough review of the problems and solutions that granular computing offers.

- *Evolving Fuzzy and Neuro-Fuzzy Systems: Fundamentals, Stability, Explainability, Useability, and Applications*

  Since its introduction around the turn of the century by Profs. Plamen Angelov and Nikola Kasabov, the area of evolving fuzzy and neuro-fuzzy systems has been constantly developing as a form of explainable AI and machine learning. This thoroughly revised chapter, in comparison to the version in the first edition, offers a review of the problems and some of the solutions. It is authored by one of the leading experts in this area, Dr. Edwin Lughofer from Johannes Kepler University Linz, Austria.

- *Incremental Fuzzy Machine Learning for Online Classification of Emotions in Games from EEG Data Streams*

This new chapter is authored by Prof. Daniel Leite and Drs. Volnei Frigeri Jr and Rodrigo Medeiros from Adolfo Ibáñez University, Chile, and the Federal University of Minas Gerais, Brazil. It offers one specific approach to a form of explainable AI and its application to games and EEG data stream processing.

- *Causal Reasoning*

  This new chapter is authored by Drs. Ramin Ramezani and Wenhao Zhang and Prof. Arash Naeim). It describes the very important topic of causality in AI.

Part II consists of six chapters, which cover the area of supervised learning:

- *Fuzzy Classifiers*

  This is a thoroughly revised and refreshed chapter that was also a part of the first edition of the handbook. It covers the area of fuzzy rule-based classifiers, which combine explainable AI and intelligence, more generally, as well as the area of machine or computer learning. It is written by Prof. Hamid Bouchachia from Bournemouth University, UK.

- *Kernel Models and Support Vector Machines*

  This chapter offers a very skillful review of one of the hottest topics in research and applications related to supervised computer learning. It is written by Drs. Denis Kolev, Mikhail Suvorov, and Dmitry Kangin and is a thorough revision of the version that was included in the first edition of the handbook.

- *Evolving Connectionist Systems for Adaptive Learning and Knowledge Discovery: From Neuro-Fuzzy to Spiking, Neurogenetic, and Quantum Inspired: A Review of Principles and Applications*

  This chapter offers a review of one of the cornerstones of computer learning and intelligence, namely the evolving connectionist systems, and is written by the pioneer in this area, Prof. Nikola Kasabov from the Auckland University of Technology, New Zealand.

- *Supervised Learning Using Spiking Neural Networks*

  This is a new chapter written by Drs. Abeegithan Jeyasothy from the Nanyang Technological University, Singapore; Shirin Dora from the University of Ulster, Northern Ireland, UK; Sundaram Suresh from the Indian Institute of Science; and Prof. Narasimhan Sundararajan, who recently retired from the Nanyang Technological University, Singapore. It covers the topic of supervised computer learning of a particular type of artificial neural networks that holds a lot of promise—spiking neural networks.

- *Fault Detection and Diagnosis based on LSTM Neural Network Applied to a Level Control Pilot Plant*

This is a thoroughly revised and updated chapter in comparison to the version in the first edition of the handbook. It covers an area of high industrial interest and now includes long short-term memory type of neural networks and is authored by Drs. Emerson V. de Oliveira, Yuri Thomas Nunes, and Malison Ribeira Santos and Prof. Luiz Affonso Guedez from the Federal University of Rio Grande du Nord, Natal, Brazil.

- *Conversational Agents: Theory and Applications*

This is a new chapter that combines intelligence with supervised computer learning. It is authored by Prof. Mattias Wahde and Dr. Marco Virgolin from the Chalmers University, Sweden.

The second volume consist of three parts. The first of these, part III, is devoted to deep learning and consists of five chapters, four of which are new and specially written for the second edition of the handbook:

- *Deep Learning and Its Adversarial Robustness: A Brief Introduction*

This new chapter, written by Drs. Fu Wang, Chi Zhang, PeiPei Xu, and Wenjie Ruan from Exeter University, UK, provides a brief introduction to the hot topic of deep learning to understand its robustness under adversarial perturbations.

- *Deep Learning for Graph-Structured Data*

This new chapter written by leading experts in the area of deep learning, Drs. Luca Pasa and Nicolò Navarin and Prof. Alessandro Sperduti, describes methods that are specifically tailored to graph-structured data.

- *A Critical Appraisal on Deep Neural Networks: Bridge the Gap from Deep Learning to Neuroscience via XAI*

This new chapter, written by Anna-Sophia Bartle from the University of Tubingen, Germany; Ziping Jiang from Lancaster University, UK; Richard Jiang from Lancaster University, UK, Ahmed Bouridane from Northumbria University, UK, and Somaya Almaadeed from Qatar University, provides a critical analysis of the deep learning techniques trying to bridge the divide between neuroscience and explainable AI

- *Ensemble Learning*

This is a thoroughly revised chapter written by the same authors as in the first edition (Dr. Yong Liu and Prof. Qiangfu Zhao) and covers the area of ensemble learning.

- *A Multistream Deep Rule-Based Ensemble System for Aerial Image Scene Classification*

  This is a new chapter contributed by Dr. Xiaowei Gu from the University of Aberystwyth in Wales, UK, and by Prof. Plamen Angelov. It provides an explainable-by-design form of deep learning, which can also take the form of linguistic rule base and is applied to aerial image scene classification.

Part IV consists of four chapters covering the topic of intelligent control:

- *Fuzzy Model-Based Control: Predictive and Adaptive Approach*

  This chapter is a thorough revision of the chapter form the first edition of the handbook and is co-authored by Prof. Igor Škrjanc and Dr. Sašo Blažič from Ljubljana University, Slovenia.

- *Reinforcement Learning with Applications in Automation Control and Game Theory*

  This chapter written by renowned world leaders in this area, Dr. Kyriakos G. Vamvoudakis from the Georgia Institute of Technology, Prof. Frank L. Lewis from the University of Texas, and Dr. Draguna Vrabie from the Pacific Northwest National Laboratory in the USA. In this thoroughly revised and updated chapter in comparison to the version in the first edition, the authors describe reinforcement learning that is being applied not only to systems control but also to game theory.

- *Nature-Inspired Optimal Tuning of Fuzzy Controllers*

  This chapter is also a thorough revision from the first edition by the same authors, Prof. Radu-Emil Precup and Dr. Radu-Codrut David, both from the Politehnica University of Timisoara, Romania.

- *Indirect Self-Evolving Fuzzy Control Approaches and Their Applications*

  This is a new chapter and is written by Drs. Zhao-Xu Yang and Hai-Jun Rong from Xian Jiaotong University, China.

Finally, part V includes five chapters on evolutionary computation:

- *Evolutionary Computation: History View and Basic Concepts*

  This is a thoroughly revised chapter from the first edition of the handbook, which sets the scene with a historical and philosophical introduction of the topic. It is written by one of the leading scientists in this area, Dr. Carlos A. Coello-Coello from CINVESTAV, Mexico, and co-authored by Carlos Segura from the Centre of Research in Mathematics, Mexico, and Gara Miranda from the University of La Laguna, Tenerife, Spain.

- *An Empirical Study of Algorithmic Bias*

  This chapter is written by the same author as in the first edition, Prof. Dipankar Dasgupta from the University of Memphis, USA, and co-authored by his associate Dr. Sanjib Sen, but it offers a new topic: an empirical study of algorithmic bias.

- *Collective Intelligence: A Comprehensive Review of Metaheuristic Algorithms Inspired by Animals*

  This chapter is a thoroughly revised version of the chapter by the same author, Dr. Fevrier Valdez from the Institute of Technology, Tijuana, Mexico, who contributed to the first edition.

- *Fuzzy Dynamic Parameter Adaptation for Gray Wolf Optimization of Modular Granular Neural Networks Applied to Human Recognition Using the Iris Biometric Measure*

  This chapter is a thoroughly revised version of the chapters contributed by the authors to the first edition of the handbook. It is written by the leading experts in the area of fuzzy systems, Drs. Patricia Melin and Daniela Sanchez and Prof. Oscar Castillo from the Tijuana Institute of Technology, Mexico.

- *Evaluating Inter-task Similarity for Multifactorial Evolutionary Algorithm from Different Perspectives*

  The last chapter of this part of the second volume and of the handbook is new and is contributed by Lei Zhou and Drs. Liang Feng from Chongqing University, China, and Min Jiang from Xiamen University, China, and Prof. Kay Chen Tan from City University of Hong Kong.

In conclusion, this handbook is a thoroughly revised and updated second edition and is composed with care, aiming to cover all main aspects and recent trends in the *computer learning and intelligence* area of research and offering solid background knowledge as well as end-point applications. It is designed to be a one-stop shop for interested readers, but by no means aims to completely replace all other sources in this dynamically evolving area of research.

Enjoy reading it.

Plamen Parvanov Angelov
Editor of the Handbook
Lancaster, UK
3 June 2022

Part I

Explainable AI

https://doi.org/10.1142/9789811247323_0001

Chapter 1

Explainable Artificial Intelligence and Computational Intelligence: Past and Present

Mojtaba Yeganejou* and Scott Dick†

Department of Electrical and Computer Engineering
University of Alberta, 9211 116 Street, Edmonton, AB, Canada, T6G 1H9
*yeganejo@ualberta.ca
† sdick@ualberta.ca

Explainable artificial intelligence is a very active research topic at the time of writing this chapter. What is perhaps less appreciated is that the concepts behind this topic have been intimately connected to computational intelligence for our field's entire decades-long history. This chapter reviews that long history and demonstrates its connections to the general artificial intelligence literature. We then examine how computational intelligence contributes to modern research into explainable systems.

1.1. Introduction

At the time of this writing in 2021, artificial intelligence (AI) seems poised to fundamentally reshape modern society. One estimate finds that half of all the tasks the workers perform during their jobs in North America could be automated (although only about 5% of jobs can be *totally* automated). This automation is expected to raise productivity growth back above 2% annually and add between $3.5 and $5.8 trillion dollars of value per year to the economy [1]. We have reached the point where modern algorithms (e.g., deep learning) can exceed human performance in certain domains. However, they are "black boxes," and their decision-making process is opaque; sometimes to the point of being incomprehensible to even human experts in the area. A famous example is the 19th move in the second game of the historic 2016 Go match between Lee Sedol, a grandmaster at the game, and AlphaGo [2] built by DeepMind. "It's a creative move," commented Go expert Michael Redmond. "It's something that I don't think I've seen in a top player's game" [3].

It is human nature to distrust what we do not understand, and this leads us to a profound, even existential question for the field of AI: *Why should humans trust these algorithms with so many important tasks and decisions?* Simply put, if human users do not trust AI algorithms, *they will not be used.* Unless the question of trust is resolved, all of the progress of AI in the last several decades could be utterly wasted, as humanity at large simply walks away from the "AI revolution."

Research into trusted AI has shown that providing users with interpretations and explanations of the decision-making process is a vital precondition for winning users' trust [4, 5], and numerous studies have linked trust and explanation with each other [6]. Various forms of intelligent systems are trusted more if their recommendations are explained (see [7–10] for more details). In this sense, interpretability can be defined as the degree to which humans comprehend the process by which a decision is reached. It can also be considered the degree to which a human expert could consistently predict the model's result [11, 12].

From a philosophical standpoint, what does it mean for an AI to be opaque or transparent? One viewpoint, originating from [13], is that opacity of an algorithm refers to a stakeholder's lack of knowledge, at a point in time, of "epistemically relevant elements." Zednik [14] proposes that the epistemically relevant elements for AI are any portion of the AI algorithm, its inputs, outputs, or internal calculations that *could* be cited in an explanation. Zednik further points out that this definition of opacity is agent-specific and that different stakeholders (such as the stakeholder groups in [15]) may have different needs for understanding those elements. Plainly, opacity is also a matter of degree, as many stakeholders do have knowledge of at least the architecture and learning algorithm of even the largest deep neural network. We thus see that AI opacity could be defined as the degree of a given stakeholder's lack of knowledge, at a point in time, of all possible explanatory elements for a given AI model. Explanations, then, are a means of redressing opacity for a given stakeholder by communicating an "adequate" set of those explanatory elements.

The above suggests that one route to generating explanations might be to provide a trace of the inferential processes by which the AI reaches its decisions. However, researchers as far back as the 1970s have strongly argued that this is *not* adequate and that instead, explanations must provide the user with insight into the problem domain and corresponding justifications for the AI's decisions. Furthermore, this also means that merely presenting an "interpretable" AI model to the user (e.g., a rulebase) is also insufficient; creating and presenting an explanation is a major system task in itself and needs a suitable interface [16]. In the remainder of this chapter, we will refer to this capability (and the component/modules and user experience elements supporting it) as the explanation interface (EI).

As Miller points out, explanation is a social act; an *explainer* communicates knowledge about an *explanandum* (the object of the explanation) to the *explainee*;

this knowledge is the *explanans* [11]. In XAI, a decision or result obtained from an AI model is the explanandum, the explainee is the user who needs more information, the explainer is the EI of the AI, and the explanans is the information (explanation) communicated to the user [17]. Thus, the EI must interact with the user to communicate an explanans. Research into EIs also shows that they are generally designed to respond to only a few question types: *what, how, what if, why*, and *why not*. *What* questions ask for factual statements; these are fairly simple in nature. The others involve causal reasoning (relating causes and effects). The literature on education and philosophy also views the cognitive process of explanation as a close relative of causal reasoning; explanations often refer to causation, and causal analyses have been found to have explanatory value [18–23]. A number of researchers treat explanation as the development of a causal analysis for why some event occurred or how some system operates, e.g., [24, 25].

Miller contends that causal analyses answering *how, what if, why*, and *why not* questions are best approached using *contrastive* explanations; a counterfactual (something that did not occur) is chosen as the explanandum, and an explanans is generated [11]. (Note that counterfactuals for *what if* and *why not* questions are specified by the user.) A further analysis of counterfactuals is conducted in [26], where four fundamental usages of counterfactuals were identified. First, one could add or remove a fact from the current world state, and reason about the outcomes. Second, one could select a "better" or "worse" world state, and reason about how these might be reached. Third, they can be used to investigate possible causes of the current world state. Finally, they can aid in apportioning blame for the current world state.

As above, the goal of an EI is to foster user trust; this obviously implies that XAI researchers must measure the extent to which their explanations improve user trust. However, the issue of *accurately* measuring user trust is a familiar problem from the information sciences literature. In technology adoption studies particularly, the *act* of trusting consists of using the technology. This is very difficult to study in the field, and laboratory experiments are necessarily limited in their fidelity to the real world. Hence, many studies employ an antecedent to actual use (the construct of *Intent to Use*, measured by psychometric scales), as a proxy for use of the technology [27, 28]. However, when the subjects' trusting behaviors are compared against their responses on the scales, the two are often inconsistent. A relatively small number of XAI papers have also begun using a similar proxy, where trust in the AI is measured via psychometric scales [29]. These too have repeatedly been found to be inconsistent with users' actual behaviors [30, 31]. Drawing these points together, Papenmeier [32] proposes three design requirements for empirical studies of user trust in AI: the experiment must present a realistic, relatable scenario for the subjects; there must be negative consequences for the AI's errors; and the experiment must require the subjects to perform an action, either following the AI's recommendation or not. Paez also points out that in many situations, the decision to trust an AI or not must be made under time pressure, which should be simulated in an experiment [33].

An EI will also be necessary to achieve other AI system objectives, including [34]:

- *Verifiability:* An AI model will reproduce biases in the knowledge it is provided or the data it is trained on [35]; the model may also contain errors. Models must therefore be verified as being fit for purpose. However, this is only possible when the reviewers performing the verification can understand the AI models.
- *Comparative judgments:* Different models might perform equally well, but via very different decision-making processes. It is quite possible that some of those processes might be socially unacceptable, *even though they might perform better on some benchmarks.* It is only through the EI that those different processes can be revealed and evaluated.
- *Knowledge discovery:* AI models often identify relationships that humans would not be able to find. However, these discoveries can only have an impact beyond that AI if they can be comprehensibly presented to human analysts (as in the KDD framework [36]).
- *Legal compliance:* The European Union's General Data Protection Regulation includes a "right to explanation," granting any data subject the right to an explanation concerning any decision made about them by an algorithm [37, 38]. We find it unlikely that an EU judge and jury would accept "the neural network said so" as an adequate explanation if data subjects challenge those decisions in court.

Numerous scholars have also examined the impact of uninterpretable AI models on social justice and equity [39–51]. Unjust outcomes from AI decisions have repeatedly been observed in fields as diverse as criminal sentencing decisions, loan and insurance approvals, and hiring practices. If the AI in these cases provided an explanans for these decisions, these outcomes may well have been changed. Data bias is another pernicious, significant issue; social problems such as gender and racial inequality can influence a corpus of primary sources used to train an AI in unexpected ways (see [42, 49, 58, 59] for more details). Sometimes these are blatant, other times more subtle; but review of the AI by experts using an EI seems to be one of the few defenses against this form of bias.

The focus of this chapter is on the history of explanations in AI systems, and in particular how computational intelligence is bound up with that history. One point we wish to emphasize at the outset is that "explainable" AI—despite the recent flurry of activity under the banner of XAI—is in fact a research topic that has been studied for over 50 years. This is a large body of work that should be studied and appreciated, lest hard-won lessons from those earlier years be lost. We need only look to the history of independent component analysis to appreciate that this is entirely possible [52]. In fact, the importance of interpretability has been recognized from the earliest days of intelligent system research [53], and one can easily identify multiple generations of approaches to the interpretability problem in the literature.

The remainder of this chapter is organized as follows. In Section 1.2, we survey the history of expert systems and machine learning (including neural networks), and how explanation systems developed in concert with them. In Section 1.3, we examine several contemporary XAI approaches in depth. In Section 1.4, we examine how soft computing contributed to XAI in the past and present. We offer a summary and conclusions in Section 1.5.

1.2. History of XAI

At the AAAI conference in 2017, a panel discussed the history of expert systems, which had seen vast enthusiasm in the 1980s, before their limitations led to disappointment and the "AI Winter" of the 1990s [54, 55]. One of the panelists, Peter Dear, was a historian of science specializing in the Scientific Revolution of the 16th and 17th centuries. In his 2006 treatise, he describes science (in its present conception) as a hybrid of two goals, intelligibility and instrumentality. *Intelligibility* refers to the discovery of the fundamental nature of the universe, and the accounting of how this results in the world we experience around us. *Instrumentality*, on the other hand, is the search for a means to affect the world around us, manipulating it for our own purposes [56]. The difference between these two goals seems strikingly similar to a divide that has plagued XAI for decades. In the AI field, intelligibility is interpreted to mean *explainability*; it should be possible to understand why an AI came to the conclusion it did. Instrumentality, meanwhile, is interpreted as the AI's quantified performance (via accuracy, ROC curves, etc.). One of the panel findings about expert systems—and AI in general, past and present—is that intelligibility and instrumentality are currently *not* complementary to each other in our field. Indeed, they are seen as conflicting goals, for which improvements in one must come at the expense of the other (this is also known as the interpretability/accuracy trade-off [57]). AI experts such as Randall Davis recounted their experiences supporting this viewpoint during the panel [54].

A considerable amount of the history of XAI can be seen as a vacillation between systems emphasizing intelligibility and those focused solely on instrumentality. The former are largely made up of "symbolic" approaches to AI (e.g., expert systems, theorem provers, etc.), what Nilsson refers to as "good old-fashioned AI" [55]. Such systems are commonly designed around a known base of expert knowledge, which is strongly leveraged in building solutions. Instrumentality is not neglected

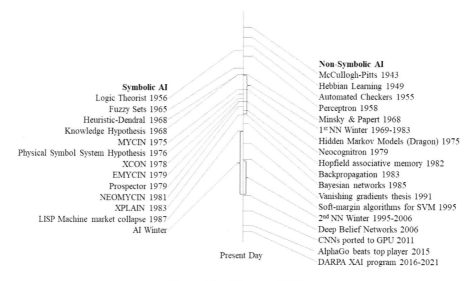

Symbolic AI
Logic Theorist 1956
Fuzzy Sets 1965
Heuristic-Dendral 1968
Knowledge Hypothesis 1968
MYCIN 1975
Physical Symbol System Hypothesis 1976
XCON 1978
EMYCIN 1979
Prospector 1979
NEOMYCIN 1981
XPLAIN 1983
LISP Machine market collapse 1987
AI Winter

Present Day

Non-Symbolic AI
McCullogh-Pitts 1943
Hebbian Learning 1949
Automated Checkers 1955
Perceptron 1958
Minsky & Papert 1968
1st NN Winter 1969-1983
Hidden Markov Models (Dragon) 1975
Neocognitron 1979
Hopfield associative memory 1982
Backpropagation 1983
Bayesian networks 1985
Vanishing gradients thesis 1991
Soft-margin algorithms for SVM 1995
2nd NN Winter 1995-2006
Deep Belief Networks 2006
CNNs ported to GPU 2011
AlphaGo beats top player 2015
DARPA XAI program 2016-2021

Figure 1.1: History of XAI.

in these systems, but neither is it their sole objective; they are relatively transparent to the human user. The latter, on the other hand, are largely composed of "non-symbolic" approaches such as statistical learning and neural networks, which figure prominently in pattern recognition and signal processing. These systems emphasize excellence in performing a task, but are not easily intelligible (and may in fact be *un*intelligible), thus requiring a post hoc accounting of their decision processes. In Figure 1.1, we summarize some highlights the development of these two approaches to AI, and their effect on explainability research. The remainder of this section will discuss this material in depth.

1.2.1. *Symbolic AI and Expert Systems*

A symbol in the AI sense is a meaningful entity, in and of itself. It can also be combined into more complex aggregations with other symbols following regular rules; entities of this type were also sometimes referred to as *physical* symbols [58]. Symbolic processing has been at the heart of AI from the very beginning; e.g., the Logic Theorist (the first automated theorem prover, published in 1956) was a symbolic system [59]. Indeed, one of the most famous conjectures in AI, the Physical Symbol System hypothesis, holds that

> A physical symbol system has the necessary and sufficient means for general intelligent action [60].

In this hypothesis, a physical symbol system is an abstract machine that operates on collections of symbols and, over time, modifies them or produces new ones.

Thus, this hypothesis asserts that symbolic processing is the necessary and sufficient condition to produce what we refer to as "intelligence" [55].

A variety of symbolic AI systems were produced following the development of the Logic Theorist (see [55] for an in-depth review). One of these, the Dendral system, became the forerunner of the expert systems field. It was originally designed to assist chemists in interpreting mass spectrometer data. In its original form, Dendral simply generated all the possible (acyclical) sub-structures of a molecule from its chemical formula and some other basic information. An expert chemist could then compare that dictionary of structures against actual mass spectrometer data to determine which structures were most likely being caught by the instrument [55]. Feigenbaum et al. suggested that this dictionary could be augmented with knowledge elicited from expert chemists to constrain the search to the most likely sub-structures. This knowledge was encoded in inference rules with an IF–THEN structure, potentially with a fairly complex antecedent expression. The resulting program was called Heuristic-Dendral [61], and is widely considered the first expert system to have been developed; its descendants are still used by chemists today. This research led Feigenbaum to advance the *knowledge principle*: that the problem-solving power in an expert system arises principally from the quality of the elicited knowledge it contains, and has little to do with the inference mechanisms applied to it [55].

Interestingly, the Dendral project also incorporated an explicit test of the instrumentality of its predictions. A simulation of a mass spectrometer was designed, which accepted predicted structures as its inputs. The simulation results for each structure were then compared with the actual output of a mass spectrometer; a close match indicated that the predicted structures were probably correct. This was the first time that such a confirmatory step was included in an AI system [55].

Following on from the Dendral project, work began on an AI system that would use expert knowledge to diagnose bacterial infections and recommend treatment plans. This was the MYCIN system, which laid down several design approaches that deeply influenced subsequent research. Firstly, knowledge to be stored in the system was elicited from known experts in the field, in the form of IF–THEN rules (inspired by their successful use in Dendral) for diagnosing infections and treating them. Second, uncertainty was explicitly represented in the system (using the ad hoc construct of "certainty factors"). Third, inferences were executed by backwards chaining. Fourth, the IF–THEN rules were separated from the inference routines (unlike in Dendral), dividing the architecture into a *knowledge base* and an *inference engine* [62].

This last point would help spawn an entire industry. If the knowledge in an expert system is entirely modularized into the knowledge base, then applying the expert system to a different problem would simply require changing out the knowledge base. The EMYCIN project [63] attempted just this, using a single inference engine and rules elicited from domain experts to construct expert systems in a range of different fields of study. By the late 1980s, a wide variety of commercial expert systems were in use, some based on EMYCIN and others not; 130 such systems are identified in [64].

Now let's examine how these symbolic systems provide explanations to the user about a decision they reached. As discussed earlier, while it seems simple to just output the set of rules that affected the system's decision, such traces have been found to be ineffective as an explanans; in the end, the explainee does not gain an adequate grasp of the explanandum. Expert system designers were well aware of this point; MYCIN was designed with an *explanation system* that could respond to "how" and "why" questions with English-language answers [55, 65]. This intuitively seems like a step forward, but what does it tell us about XAI in general? Indeed, one of the principal theoretical questions for XAI is just what constitutes a "good explanation"; a great many answers have been proposed over the years. Swartout and Moore [66] proposed five desirable characteristics for explainable AI:

(1) *Fidelity*: An explanans must reflect the actual processes used to reach the decision.
(2) *Understandability*: An explanans must be comprehensible to the system's users.
(3) *Sufficiency*: The explanans must provide enough detail to justify and defend the decision.
(4) *Low Overhead*: The design effort expended on the EI should be proportionate to the total design effort needed for the whole AI system.
(5) *Efficiency*: The execution time of the AI system should not be substantially increased due to the EI.

Plainly, some of these desired characteristics are conflicting. For instance, if our standard of sufficiency is adequate detail to withstand a lawsuit, then the explanation will be very lengthy and detailed; but it is known that lengthy, detailed explanations are less understandable [66]. High-fidelity explanations can also be poorly understandable; again, due to the complexity of the explanation. Chakraborty et al. [67] argue that interpretability is multidimensional, incorporating, e.g., explainability, accountability, fairness, transparency, and functionality. The authors also consider the need to rationalize, justify, and understand systems and users' confidence in their results. Doshi-Velez and Kim [68] distinguish explanation from formal interpretability, and suggest fairness, privacy, reliability, robustness, causality, usability, and trust as core characteristics of XAI.

Some authors divide expert systems from the 1970s and '80s into a first and second generation, based principally on how explanations are created and communicated to the user. In the first generation, systems such as MYCIN re-expressed the set of rules used to reach a decision as statements in natural language. However, the results (especially when a number of rules were invoked) became linguistically unnatural. Moreover, this was only a "surface" explanation; the explanation subsystem had no ability to provide deeper insight or the general principles governing the decision [66].

In second-generation systems, researchers sought to address both shortcomings. They focused on making explanations sensitive to knowledge about the user, their history and goals, and the problem domain. Some second-generation systems were also self-improving [69]. Thus, instead of merely parroting the expert system rules, the EI drew upon computational linguistics and natural language understanding (itself a field of AI) to formulate a more responsive and personalized explanans. To do so, additional information about the world model that the rules represent was also added; this may take the form of metarules (as in NEOMYCIN [70]); abstract strategies for problem-solving (as in Generic Tasks [71]), explicitly representing the system's design in a knowledge base (as in the Explainable Expert System [72]), or by designing a second, separate knowledge base specifically for the explanation subsystem (as in the Reconstructive Explanation system [73]) [66]. The XPLAIN system [74, 75] incorporated both additional domain knowledge and system design knowledge. An interesting point about these last two systems is that an explanans might not exhibit fidelity to the AI's decision process. This might be unintentional in Reconstructive Explanations, but the use of "white lies" to "improve" the explanans was an observed outcome in the XPLAIN system.

1.2.2. *Non-Symbolic Learning and XAI*

Non-symbolic approaches, such as machine learning, have been a part of AI for at least as long as symbolic ones. The McCullogh–Pitts artificial neuron, often cited as the beginning of the neural networks field, was developed in 1943 [76]. The first learning rule for neural networks, due to Hebb, was proposed in 1949 [77], and Rosenblatt's perceptron architecture was published in 1958 [78]. Separately, Samuel's automated checkers program was enhanced with machine learning concepts, including the minimax search of a move tree and an early exploration of what would become temporal difference learning, in 1955 [79].

Statistical machine learning has also established itself as a key part of artificial intelligence. Statistical methods for pattern recognition have been a part of AI since the 1950s, principally centered around Bayesian reasoning. Later, there were also limitations observed with the certainty factors used in MYCIN. As rulebases grew larger, it became clear that the ad hoc assignment of these factors was creating inconsistencies and conflicts within a rulebase, which had to be tediously hand corrected. The addition of another rule would, furthermore, often undo the delicate balance of the existing rules. In response, AI designers began incorporating statistical concepts (and Bayes' rule in particular) in the design of expert systems [55]. Additional proposals for dealing with uncertainty, around this time period, included the Dempster–Schafer theory of evidence [80] and fuzzy logic [55, 81].

An important elaboration of these first methods in the 1970s was the development of graph structures that encode causal links between different events in an AI system. The so-called Bayesian networks allowed AI designers to encode their knowledge of a domain in a graph structure; with the links denoting causality, one can then simplify the use of Bayes' rules. A Bayesian network can also be inductively learned from data. One notable point is that Bayesian networks were designed for tabular (i.e., static) data, rather than a data stream. Time-varying data, on the other hand, was the focus of the hidden Markov models first designed for the DRAGON speech-recognition system [55].

This period in the 1970s was also the first neural network "winter," after interest in the perceptron algorithm collapsed following Minsky and Papert's analysis that it could only ever solve linearly separable problems [82]. However, some work did continue. In particular, Fukushima's Neocognitron architecture [83] laid the foundations for the convolutional neural networks developed by Lecun [84], which, in their various elaborations, currently dominate signal-, image-, and video-processing research. Interest in neural networks also began picking up in the late 1970s and quickened after Rumelhart et al. published their backpropagation algorithm [85], which demonstrated a general solution to the credit assignment problem that had bedeviled previous research into multilayer neural networks. At roughly the same time, Hopfield's associative memory [86] invigorated research into recurrent neural networks [55].

The resurgence of interest in neural networks led to a flowering of new ideas. Numerous approaches to speeding up the basic backpropagation algorithm were proposed, from simple approaches such as adding *momentum* terms to the back-propagation weight update [87], to more complex proposals involving computing second derivatives of the error surface (e.g., conjugate gradient algorithms [88], the Levenberg–Marquardt algorithm [89]). Domain knowledge was used to initialize NNs to place them near a strong local minimum in, e.g., the KBANN system [90], while trained networks were pruned to improve their generalization performance, e.g., the Optimal Brain Surgeon algorithm [91]. Entirely different approaches to NN design, often dealing with completely different problems, were also proposed; kernel-based approaches such as radial basis function networks [92] might compete with multilayer perceptrons in classification or function-approximation tasks, but neither addresses the blind-source separation problem that independent components analysis [93] tackles. Information-theoretic learning also gives us the Infomax principle [94], while Q-learning networks [95] and Boltzmann machines [96] grow out of statistical learning theory and Markov processes [87].

While NN algorithms generally were the state-of-the-art in machine learning during the late 1980s and early '90s, the black-box nature of NNs made the problem of user trust substantially worse [55]. Simultaneously, it also made the problem of generating an explanans significantly harder; there was now no knowledge base of expert rules to begin from, only an unintuitive weighted graph. Thus, XAI in this period focused on post hoc explanations, under the banner of *knowledge extraction*. An influential 1995 survey [97] proposed a taxonomy for this field of study based on five criteria. They were originally oriented toward rule extraction, as opposed to other representational formats, but were later generalized to capture others. The criteria were [98]:

(1) *Rule Format.* This originally captured the distinction between a rulebase based on Boolean propositional logic, one based on Boolean first-order logic, and one based on fuzzy logic. In the more general form, this criterion distinguishes between representational forms for the knowledge extracted from the network.

(2) *Rule Quality.* This is a multidimensional quantity, capturing the (out-of-sample) accuracy of the rulebase, its fidelity to the NN, its consistency, and its comprehensibility (through the proxy of counting the number rules and rule antecedents). This is perhaps the most controversial of the five criteria, and there have been multiple alternative proposals for defining and measuring the "quality" of extracted rules (e.g., [99, 100]), to say nothing of evaluating other representations.

(3) *Translucency.* This criterion focuses on the granularity of the knowledge extraction algorithm. At one extreme, the decompositional level extracts rules from each individual neuron; at the other, only the input/output behavior of the whole network is studied. Approaches falling between these extremes were originally labeled "eclectic," although later work on alternative representations suggested "compositional" instead [101].

(4) *Algorithmic Complexity.* As with earlier criteria, the complexity of an EI is a vital concern.

(5) *Portability.* This criterion is something of a misnomer, as the EIs at this time were not truly portable between one NN and another. Rather, it captures the degree to which the NN itself employed an idiosyncratic learning algorithm, or alternatively, was trained following one of the dominant approaches such as backpropagation. More generally, this criterion focuses on the assumptions underlying an extraction algorithm.

Despite investigations of other representations, in this period the dominant form of an explanans for a trained NN remained IF–THEN rules (be they based on propositional, first-order, or fuzzy logic). This is ascribed to the popularity of feedforward networks and the familiarity of rule-based expert systems [98].

Furthermore, the bulk of these rule-extraction algorithms were decompositional (extracting rules for individual neurons and then pruning the resulting rule set), and produced rules expressed in Boolean logic [98, 101]. Some of the earliest rule-extraction algorithms, e.g., [102–104] (the latter two focusing on specialized NN architectures), belonged to this group. In particular, the KBANN algorithm [103] employed "M of N" rules, which fire if at least M out of a total of N antecedents are true. Decompositional algorithms continued to be developed, including [105–108]. Other authors, in the meantime, focused on the "pedagogical" approach: treating the NN as a black box and deriving rules by observing the NN's overall transfer function. The first of these [109] even predates the decompositional papers, but encountered a rule explosion problem even with heuristics to limit the search space. It is extremely difficult to constrain the search space of antecedent combinations for rules without additional information from the structure of the network. As the number of rules is based on the power set of antecedent clauses, and realistic neural networks have a substantial number of input dimensions, a rule explosion results (i.e., we again run into the curse of dimensionality). One important note is that these algorithms generally induced rules that correspond to an axis-parallel hyperbox in feature space. While such structures are computationally easier to generate, they do tend to be inefficient at capturing concepts (i.e., clusters in feature space) that are not conveniently in an axis-parallel orientation [97, 98, 110].

Rule refinement is a variation of rule extraction, in which the NN is first initialized using a rulebase and then trained on a dataset from that domain. The rules then extracted from the trained NN are expected to be a more "refined" model compared to the rules used to initialize it. Obviously, this requires a neural network architecture that can be initialized using rules; KBANN [90] is a classic example. Others include feedforward networks [111] and the refinement of regular grammars in recurrent neural networks [112].

A number of other representations for an explanans have also been explored, although not in as great a depth. For feedforward networks, the next most important representation appears to have been decision trees [97, 113, 114]. There was also work on extracting rules covering polyhedral regions in feature space (allowing for concepts that are not axis-parallel) [115]. One variation on this work was Maire's algorithm for backpropagating a classification *region* from the network's output domain back to the input domain [116]; there is substantial conceptual similarity between this work and the more modern approach of generating saliency maps as an explanans (as will be discussed in Section 3). Sethi et al. [117] generated decision tables as the explanans in [117]. Recurrent networks require different representations in order to capture the effect of their feedback loops (which IF–THEN rules do not represent efficiently). The dominant representation in this case appears to have been either deterministic or fuzzy finite state automata [112, 118]. We should also mention an early work that directly treats XAI as a visualization problem [119]. Visualizations (and again, saliency maps in particular) are today a common representation of an explanans.

Returning to the five criteria from [97] discussed above, the question of algorithmic complexity in rule extraction has been investigated in more depth. A number of results show that conceptually useful algorithms in this area are NP-hard, NP-complete, or even exponentially complex. A sampling of these results includes:

- Searching for rule subsets in a decompositional approach is exponentially complex in the number of inputs to each node [120]. This is a crucial step for this class of algorithms, as the fundamental approach of decomposition is to first generate rules at the level of each neuron and then aggregate them into a more compact and understandable rulebase.
- Finding a minimal Disjunctive Normal Form expression for a trained feedforward network is NP-hard [120].
- The complexity of the query-based approach in [121] is greater than polynomial [120]. That algorithm attempted to *improve* upon the runtime of search-based algorithms with pedagogical translucency (black-box algorithms) by using queries.
- Determining if a perceptron is symmetrical with respect to two inputs is NP-complete [106]. This technique would allow the weights on the two inputs to be revised to their combined average, simplifying rule extraction from that node.
- Extracting M-of-N rules from single-layer NNs is NP-hard [120].

These are general results, and NNs specifically designed for rule extraction can have far more tractable complexity. For instance, the DIMPL architecture, and ensembles thereof, supported rule extraction in polynomial time by modifying the structure and activation functions of a multilayer perceptron to force all learned concepts to form axis-parallel hyperboxes [122]. A more recent variation of DIMPL that creates an explainable convolutional NN was proposed in [123].

1.2.3. *The AI Winter and XAI*

In the late 1980s, there was a sudden, rapid decline in the funding support for, and industrial application of, expert systems generally. The underlying cause is widely agreed to have been disillusionment with AI when it could not meet the lofty promises being made by AI researchers [124]. We can see this as the trough of a *hype cycle*; this is a concept advanced by Gartner Research that sees technology adoption as a five-phase process. After a technological development or discovery, the second phase is intense publicity and interest, with a significant boost in funding; proponents often offer speculative statements on the ultimate potential of the technology during this period. The third phase is the *trough of disillusionment*, where the interested audience from phase 2 loses faith in the technology because it does not achieve the lofty goals being promised by its proponents. Industrial adoption stagnates or falls, and research funding is sharply reduced. Successful technologies weather this trough, and more practical and effective applications are developed, eventually winning the technology a place of acceptance in science and engineering.[1]

Funding for AI in the early to mid-1980s was driven by major national technology development efforts: Japan's Fifth Generation Computing initiative, the USA's Strategic Computing Initiative, and the UK's Alvey project all focused on AI as a core technology for achieving their goals [55]. At the same time, major industrial investments were made in AI following Digital Equipment Corporation's successful use of the XCON expert system in its operations. One particular aspect of this investment was the *LISP Machine*, a specialized computer architecture for executing programs in the LISP programming language, which was the dominant approach for programming expert systems at the time. In 1987, the LISP Machine market abruptly collapsed, as less expensive general-purpose workstations from, e.g., Sun Microsystems were able to run LISP programs faster; LISP Machine vendors were simply not able to keep pace with the advance of Moore's law. The expert systems themselves were also proving to be brittle and extremely difficult to maintain and update; even XCON had to be retired as it did not respond well to the changing markets that Digital was addressing [124]. Simultaneously, the Fifth Generation project and the Strategic Computing Initiative were wound down for not achieving their goals [55].

Neural networks research also suffered a major slowdown, beginning several years after the LISP Machine collapse. The first major blow came in a 1991 PhD dissertation [125] that comprehensively examined the *vanishing gradient* problem (and its dual of *exploding* gradients). NN researchers had for years noted that backpropagation networks with more than two hidden layers performed quite poorly, even though biological neural networks had a large number of layers. It seemed that the magnitude of the error gradients at each successive layer was dropping significantly. Hochreiter [125] confirmed this observation and revealed that an exponential decay of gradient magnitudes was a consequence of the backpropagation algorithm itself. Being limited to just a shallow network of about two hidden layers was a significant constraint for the field, made critical by the emergence of the soft-margin algorithm for training support vector machines (SVMs) in 1995 [126]. From this point forward, SVMs and related kernel-based methods became the dominant

---

[1]https://www.gartner.com/en/research/methodologies/gartner-hype-cycle

learning algorithms for pattern recognition in the late 1990s and early 2000s, with Random Forests a close competitor; see, for instance, [127, 128].

The research into explanations for expert systems and NNs also declined during their winter periods. However, there was a continued interest in explanations for kernel-based learning and SVMs in particular. The reason is simple: while the learning algorithm at the heart of the SVM is just another linear separation, the separation takes place in the induced feature space arising from a nonlinear kernel transform of the input space (commonly to a higher dimensional space in which Cover's theorem tells us that patterns are more likely to be linearly separable). The transform is, furthermore, never explicitly computed, but implicitly represented in the pairwise distances between observations recorded in the Gram matrix [87]. Thus, a trained SVM is as much a black box as a trained NN. A review in 2010 [129] found that explanations for SVMs was still an active research topic at that time, even as the deep learning revival was already bringing the neural network and AI winters to an end—and re-igniting the need for explanations of NNs [130]. Explanations for other forms of machine learning, such as probabilistic reasoning [131] and Bayesian networks [132], also remained active. Results from second-generation expert systems were also applied in agent-based systems [133, 134], explainable tutoring systems [135, 136], and case-based reasoning [137, 138].

1.2.4. *XAI Resurgence*

Since the mid-2010s, a new generation of XAI systems—now actually called XAI—has emerged in response to the renewed interest in NNs and particularly deep neural networks (DNNs). A large and growing literature now exists on visualizing, comparing, and understanding the operation of DNNs [12, 139–145]. As one might expect, a driving force in these developments is (*again!*) the need to engender trust from AI users [4, 146–151]. Once again, the U.S. government (through the Defense Advanced Research Projects Agency [DARPA]) is funding substantial volumes of research in this field, launching their 4-year *Explainable Artificial Intelligence* program in 2017 [152]. Modern XAI is expected to take advantage of the huge strides made in computing power and technology, data visualization, and natural language processing to produce superior explanans. For example, argumentative dialogues are a class of EI that simply did not exist in first- and second-generation systems, but are possible now [146, 153]. Contrastive explanations also seem much more common today, be they occlusions in an image rather than saliency maps [145], model ablation [141], comparisons across datasets [140], or counter-examples [154, 155].

For all these advances, however, there seems to have been a forgetting of much of the progress made in previous generations of XAI. Pedagogical approaches seem to be the norm, with saliency maps from the original input domain presently a dominant representation. Compositional and decompositional approaches, on the other hand, are much rarer [156]. Likewise, the goals of the current EIs often appear to be simply accounting for the current decision made by an AI (the literature refers to this as a *local* explanation). By contrast, *global* explanations account for the sum total of knowledge learned by a DNN and can help tie together individual decisions into an appreciation of the DNN's world model [4, 73, 157]. This also assists with other possible goals for an EI: understanding future decisions, trust formation, and debugging and validating the AI, among others. Critically, an EI must respond to the needs of the stakeholders it is designed for; in other words, it must be *engineered* for human users [158]. Furthermore, in the modern world, users must expect to interact with AIs over an extended period of time; hence, the AI will need to be cognizant of not only the user's goals, knowledge, and experience, but also of how these have been affected by the AI and its prior explanations [159].

1.3. Methods for XAI

We now examine modern XAI. We first examine the issue of trust in an XAI, and in particular, the formation and maintenance of user trust; after all, gaining user trust is the raison d'etre of the XAI field. We then examine four current approaches to generating an explanans in depth. Our discussion covers layer-wise relevance propagation (LRP) [160], local interpretable model-agnostic explanations (LIME) [4], testing with concept activation vectors (TCAV) [161], and rule extraction with meta-features [162].

1.3.1. *Trust in XAI Systems*

The starting point for our discussion is necessarily to define what *trust* means for an AI. This is nontrivial, as trust is a vague and mercurial concept that many fields have grappled with [163]. There are thus a number of definitions of "trust" in the XAI literature, which are more or less similar to the better-studied constructs of "trust in automation" or "trust in information technology." There is of course the classic meaning of trust as a *willingness to be vulnerable to another entity* [164]; as pointed out by Lyons et al. [165], there is a correlation between how vulnerable the user is to the entity (i.e., the level of risk) and how reliant they are on it [166, 167]. There also seems to be a tendency for the most automated systems to pose the greatest risk [168].

In a definition more directly aimed at autonomous systems, Lee and See define trust as an "attitude that an agent will help achieve an individual's goals in a situation characterized by uncertainty and vulnerability" [169, 170]; this seems to be the most commonly adopted definition in the XAI literature. Other papers make use of more traditional definitions of trust, such as from Mayer et al.'s 1995 work on organizational trust: "the willingness of a party to be vulnerable to the actions of another party based on the expectation that the other will perform a particular action important to the trustor, irrespective of the ability to monitor or control that other party" [164]. Israelsen and Ahmed define it as "a psychological state in which an agent willingly and securely becomes vulnerable, or depends on, a trustee (e.g., another person, institution, or an autonomous intelligent agent), having taken into consideration the characteristics (e.g., benevolence, integrity, competence) of the trustee" [171]. Others take a more behaviorist slant; trust was "the extent to which a user is confident in, and willing to act on the basis of, the recommendations, actions, and decisions of an artificially intelligent decision aid" in [172].

Trust, as an attitude or belief, does not exist in a vacuum, and is not extended willy-nilly. Trust formation is, instead, a complex psychological process. The information systems literature conceives trust as being a psychological state that is influenced by a number of precursors. Researchers studying trust in some specific situations must therefore define the conceptual framework of factors that influence trust within that context. For XAI specifically, an explanans is then hypothesized to influence one or more of those antecedents to trust. One of the most commonly used frameworks in XAI research postulates *ability, benevolence,* and *integrity* (the so-called ABI model) as major factors influencing user trust in AI [164, 173] (the ABI+ variant adds the fourth factor of *predictability* [27]). The constructs of the technology adoption model (TAM) [28], particularly *ease of use* and *usefulness*, are also frequently used to frame XAI research [174]. Trust is also influenced by *usefulness of the explanation* and *user satisfaction* in, e.g., [174]. A few other models have been put forward; for instance, Ashoori and Weisz propose seven factors influencing trust in an AI; trust itself was a multidimensional construct, measured by five psychometric scales [170].

We also need to consider how humans interact with, and develop trust in, AI systems. Dennet proposed that people treat unknown entities as objects whose properties can be abstracted at various levels; he proposes three distinct ones. The Physical level applies to relatively simple concrete objects that we can understand via the laws of physics. The design level is for highly complex objects (living creatures, intricate machinery, etc.) that humans simply cannot analyze in enough depth to reduce the actions to physical laws. Instead, understanding must come from an abstracted model of how the object functions. The intentional level presumes that the object has beliefs and/or desires and will deliberately act to satisfy them. Understanding is thus achieved from the comprehension of these beliefs and desires [175].

Now let us apply the above framework to AI. An AI is not driven by the laws of physics at any level beyond computing hardware; indeed, the layered architecture of modern computer systems means that physical-level understanding of a program is simply nonsensical. Similarly, the design of an AI is simply too complex to produce a useful understanding. Thus, by default, people choose to treat it as an *intelligence* (as its name implies) and seek to understand and develop trust in the AI at the intentional level. They will seek to determine its beliefs and desires and extend trust based on that understanding [176]. A considerable amount of research bears out this conclusion. Participants in user studies treated autonomous systems as intentional beings in, e.g., [177–180]. People were found to respond to a robot's *social presence* ("*a psychological state in which virtual (para-authentic or artificial) actors are experienced as actual social actors*" [181]) in [182]. It seems reasonable to say that the main goal of studies of emotion and affect in robotics is to improve user trust in the robot; the underlying assumption must therefore be that users are again treating the robot as an intentional being. Furthermore, as pointed out in [183], "humans have a tendency to over interpret the depth of their relationships with machines, and to think of them in social or moral terms where this is not warranted." However, these findings are not universal. For instance, the results from [184] indicate that employees prefer co-workers who are real, trustworthy human beings. AI is only entrusted with low-risk, repetitive work [170, 184]. As one study participant stated, "I don't think that an AI, no matter how good the data input into it, can make a moral decision" [170].

1.3.2. *Layer-wise Relevance Propagation*

In the last half-decade, saliency maps have become a preferred explanans for problem domains in which DNNs are applied to image data. A saliency map is a transform of a digital image X, which has been classified by a trained DNN, into a new image SM of equal dimensions with the property that, for every pixel $X(i, j)$ of the original image, $SM(i, j)$ represents how "important" that pixel is in generating the overall classification of A. In other words, SM is a heat map indicating the importance of each pixel in reaching a classification decision. For a wide variety of datasets, researchers have found that the pixels that are "important" to a DNN classifier tend to group together into patches covering significant, meaningful regions or objects in the image A. Thus, presenting the heat map to a user provides an intuitively comprehensible rationale for the DNN's classification decision.

LRP [160] is perhaps the best known of the algorithms for generating saliency maps. Consider an input image X consisting of V pixels. The transfer function f of a trained DNN maps the image X to an output y

$$f : \mathbb{R}^v \rightarrow \mathbb{R}^1, \ f(X) \geq 0,$$
$$y = f(X). \tag{1.1}$$

Without loss of generality, we will assume that y is a real-valued scalar. Given the predicted values $f(X)$, LRP defines an ad hoc measure of "importance," termed

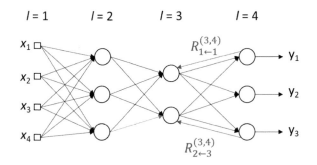

Figure 1.2:   Illustration of layer-wise relevance propagation.

relevance in [160]. The idea is that, for a given input image, there is a total amount of relevance, which remains constant as the input image is transformed in each layer. The outputs of the network thus contain the same total amount of relevance that the input image contained, albeit more concentrated. LRP thus initializes the relevance at the output layer as the network output (or the sum of all outputs $\sum_j y_j$ for the multiple-output case). Relevance is then propagated to the input layer, under the constraint that the total relevance at each layer is an identical constant to that of every other layer. The basic concept is depicted in Figure 1.2.

In this simple dense feedforward network, each layer is fully connected to its predecessor and successor layers. Each connection is weighted, with weights being real-valued. The inputs (pixels) are assumed to be flattened rather than in their row–column configuration. We depict a network with three outputs y_i, which we assume will be one-hot encoded to represent three output classes. The red arrows denote *messages*, which combine the relevance from their source node with the weight on the connection between the source and sink nodes. Superscripts denote the source and sink layers, and subscripts denote the source and sink neurons. The total relevance at each layer is given by

$$f(x) = \sum_{d \in output} R_d^{(output)} = \sum_{d \in l} R_d^{(l)} = \cdots \sum_d R_d^{(1)} \tag{1.2}$$

where d denotes a neuron within the l-th layer, and R_d is the relevance for that neuron. $R_d < 0$ is interpreted to mean that the neuron contributes evidence against the network's classification, while $R_d > 0$ contributes evidence favoring it.

LRP proceeds by propagating relevance values from the output layer toward the input. The relevance of any neuron, except an output neuron, is defined as the weighted sum of incoming relevances from all connected neurons in the succeeding layer, represented by messages [160]:

$$R_i^{(l)} = \sum_{k:i \ is \ input \ for \ neuron \ k} R_{i \leftarrow k}^{(l,l+1)} \tag{1.3}$$

LRP defines the message $R_{i \leftarrow k}^{(l,l+1)}$ from neuron k to neuron i as follows [160]:

$$R_{i \leftarrow k}^{(l,l+1)} = R_k^{(l+1)} \frac{a_i w_{ik}}{\sum_h a_h w_{hk}} \tag{1.4}$$

where $R_k^{(l+1)}$ is the relevance value for neuron k at layer $l+1$, a_i is the activation value of neuron i, and w_{ik} is the weight between neuron i and neuron k, and h iterates through all the neurons of layer l. Hence, the message sent from neuron k at layer $l + 1$ to neuron i at layer l is a portion of the relevance of neuron k. For an output neuron, relevance can be defined using $R^{(l)} = f(x) = y$, the known network output.

A point to consider is that neuron activations and weights can be zero or nearly so, and this can possibly create numerical instabilities. LRP thus defines a *stabilizer* constant ϵ and adds it to the messages, yielding [160]:

$$z_{ij} = a_i w_{ij} \tag{1.5}$$

$$z_j = \sum_i z_{ij} + b_j \tag{1.6}$$

$$R_{i \leftarrow j}^{(l,l+1)} = \begin{cases} \dfrac{z_{ij}}{z_j + \epsilon} . R_j^{(l+1)} & \text{if } z_j \geq 0 \\[2ex] \dfrac{z_{ij}}{z_j - \epsilon} . R_j^{(l+1)} & \text{if } z_j < 0. \end{cases} \tag{1.7}$$

Once the relevances for each neuron in the input layer are determined, they define the pixel values for the saliency map *SM* [160].

1.3.2.1. *Quantitative analysis of visual interpretations*

With saliency maps being one of the most common modern representations of an explanans [160, 185–188], the question naturally arises of how to measure their *quality*. Where a rulebase can be evaluated using predictive accuracy or complexity measures, these are not available for a saliency map. While it is possible to request human raters to evaluate different maps and one could, in theory, obtain reliable results with a large enough pool of raters, in practice such approaches are not scalable in time or resources. A quantitative, computable measure of saliency map quality is thus called for.

Perturbation analysis [189] is an approach that examines the impact of particular regions of an image on the overall classification mechanism. Consider a pixel p in a saliency map generated for an image x; we assign it the saliency value h_p. We sort the pixels in descending order by their h_p values, yielding [189]:

$$O = (r_1 r_2, \ldots, r_L) \tag{1.8}$$

where r_i is the ith largest value h_p out of a total of L pixels. We then apply a sequence of random pixel perturbations (denoted Most Relevant First, MoRF) to the image x, following the ordering O [189]. This has the effect of iteratively removing the information associated with the most salient pixels from the image. We can then compare the performance of a fixed classifier on the original image versus the progressively perturbed ones to determine how swiftly the classification decays. The faster the decay, the more important the lost information is—and the better the estimated saliencies are. The sequence of perturbations is given by [189]

$$x_{MoRF}^{(0)} = x \tag{1.9}$$

$$\forall\, 1 \le k \le L : x_{MoRF}^{(k)} = g\left(x_{MoRF}^{(k-1)}, r_k\right) \tag{1.10}$$

where $g(xr)$ is a function that removes information from image x at location r, r_k is the kth entry in O, and L is the number of regions perturbed. A perturbation consists of replacing pixel r_k and its immediate neighbors with random values, thus nulling out the information contained at that location. The MoRF sequences for two saliency methods can then be compared over a dataset using the area over the perturbation curve (AOPC), given by [189]:

$$AOPC = \frac{1}{L+1}\left\langle \sum_{k=0}^{L} f\left(x_{MoRF}^0\right) - f\left(x_{MoRF}^k\right)\right\rangle_{px} \tag{1.11}$$

where $\langle\cdot\rangle_{px}$ indicates averaging over all images in a dataset, and f is a class discriminant function (e.g., logits in the softmax layer of a trained DNN). A toy example is provided in Table 1.1.

The AOPC are computed as:

$$Method\ 1 = \frac{[(25-20)+(25-10)+(25-2)+(25-0)]}{5} = \frac{68}{5}$$

$$Method\ 2 = \frac{[(25-21)+(25-13)+(25-2)+(25-0)]}{5} = \frac{64}{5}$$

Table 1.1:   Illustration of a comparison between two MoRF sequences.

Remove windows per Saliency Map 1	Value of $f(x)$	Remove windows per Saliency Map 2	Value of $f(x)$
Original image	25	Original image	25
Remove r_1^1	20	Remove r_1^2	21
Remove r_2^1	10	Remove r_2^2	13
Remove r_3^1	2	Remove r_3^2	2
Remove r_4^1	0	Remove r_4^2	0

We would thus conclude that Saliency Map 1 was more effective in highlighting the pixels having the greatest influence on the classifier.

Some recent criticisms also highlight other weaknesses of the saliency map as an explanans. For example, a recent work has demonstrated that saliency maps generated from randomized networks are similar to those from well-trained ones [190]. Simple data processing steps, such as mean shifts, may also substantially change the saliencies, even though no new information is added [191]. Ghorbani et al. [192] showed that small changes to input images, if carefully chosen, could significantly alter the resulting saliency maps, even though the changes were invisibly small to a human observer. Wang et al. [193] found that the bias term in neurons had a substantial correlation with the neuron's relevance; as a bias does not respond to any input, such a correlation is certainly questionable. The expressiveness of Integrated Gradients [194] and Taylor decomposition [195] have been found to be highly dependent on the chosen reference point. Adebayo et al. [196] found that some gradient-based saliency algorithms created saliency maps that seemed to come from trained networks, even when these networks contained only randomly selected weights.

1.3.3. *Local Interpretable Model-Agnostic Explanations*

Local interpretable model-agnostic explanations (LIME) [4] are, as the name implies, focused solely on individual predictions as the explanandum. Fundamentally, LIME constructs an auxiliary model relating each prediction to the system input features and identifies the features that most strongly influence (positively or negatively) the classification in that auxiliary model (see e.g. [197]).

To illustrate the LIME representation of an explanans, consider the example of an algorithm trained for medical diagnosis in Figure 1.3. For a diagnosis of "Flu," LIME will construct a model (from some highly-interpretable class of models) that relates the observed features to the class "Flu." The features that most strongly support the class (headache and sneezes are reported), and those

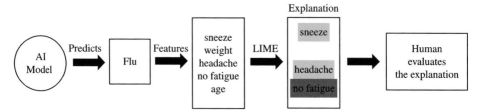

Figure 1.3: The AI model predicts that a patient has the flu. LIME highlights the important symptoms. Sneeze and headache support the "flu" prediction, while "no fatigue" is evidence against it.

which most strongly contradict it (a lack of fatigue is reported) are highlighted as such.

In LIME an explanans is denoted as $g \in G$, where G is a set of models widely held to be interpretable, e.g., decision trees, linear regressions, etc. [198] These models are made up of components (tree nodes, terms in the regression, etc.), and the domain of g is $\{0, 1\}^{d'}$, indicating the existence of a given component. However, it common that not all possible $g \in G$ are simple enough to be easily interpretable; a decision tree may be too deep, a regression may have too many terms, etc. $\Omega(g)$ is defined as a measurement of the complexity of the model (tree depth, number of terms, etc.) [197].

Now let us denote the classifier generating the prediction to be explained as $f : \mathbb{R}^d \rightarrow \mathbb{R}$, with a real-valued dependent variable $f(x)$ treated as the probability that instance x is assigned to a given class. Define $\pi_x(z)$ as a distance between an instance z and the instance x. The loss function $\mathcal{L}(f, g, \pi_x)$ measures the error that g makes in approximating f in the neighborhood π_x. The goal of LIME is to simultaneously minimize this loss function and the complexity $\Omega(g)$ [197]:

$$\xi(x) = \begin{matrix} argmin \\ g \in G \end{matrix} \mathcal{L}(f, g, \pi_x) + \Omega(g) \tag{1.12}$$

A key goal of LIME is to perform this minimization without information concerning f, thus making LIME model-agnostic. To do so, we draw uniform samples z without replacement from the domain of f, and use the trained classifier to produce $f(z)$. Each of these samples is then weighted by their distance $\pi_x(z)$ to instance x; samples closer to x will more strongly influence the loss function L. Once a collection of these samples is obtained, the minimization above is carried out.

In [199], Mohseni et al. evaluated the explanans from the LIME algorithm by comparing it to a collection of 10 human-created explanans. Elements of the LIME explanans seemed irrelevant compared to the human explanations, leading to a low precision of the LIME explanans. In a similar experiment concerning the SHAP XAI algorithm [200], Weerts et al. studied adding explanations to AI decisions. The human users were found to simply prefer to check the class posterior probabilities, rather than engage with the SHAP explanations.

1.3.4. *Testing with Concept Activation Vectors (TCAV)* [161]

Testing with concept activation vectors (TCAV) [32] would be categorized as a compositional approach to explanation, which probes how layers in a DNN *respond*

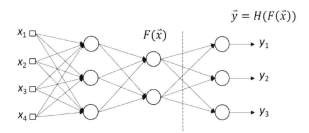

Figure 1.4:   A neural network with one of the hidden layers selected for TCAV analysis.

to concepts selected by the EI. It is thus a different approach from LRP or LIME, which seek to *re-express* concepts that are implicit within the DNN in a more comprehensible form. TCAV examines how a layer in a trained network would respond to a set of examples P that belong to a user-selected concept, versus a set Q of randomly selected ones that do not belong to the concept. The concepts are presented to the trained network's inputs, and proceed through the network to the designated layer l. Denote the transfer function of the network up to and including layer l as F, and the transfer function of the remaining layers as H. For all $p \in P$ and $q \in Q$, a concept activation vector (CAV) is determined by first training a linear classifier to discriminate between the classes $F(p)$ and $F(q)$, and then taking the gradient of the separating hypersurface between them. This CAV now points in the "direction" of the activations representing the concept.

To illustrate this concept, consider a neural network with inputs $\vec{x}$ and outputs $\vec{y}$ as in Figure 1.4. Outputs are assumed to be one-hot encoded as usual. We identify a hidden layer L in the network to be analyzed using TCAV. The transfer function of the network up to and including that layer is denoted as $F(\vec{x})$, and the transfer function for the remainder of the network is $\vec{y} = H(F(\vec{x}))$. To probe the response of L to a user-defined concept P, we present input examples $p \in P$ containing that concept to the network and observe the results $F(p)$. We also present randomly selected input examples $q \in Q$ that do *not* contain the concept P and observe the outputs $F(q)$. For example, in Figure 1.5, we present examples of the desired concept "circle," contrasted with inputs that are not circles. The next step is to train a linear classifier to separate the $F(p)$ and $F(q)$. This produces a separating hyperplane in the input space of that layer; the gradient of that hyperplane is of course a vector orthogonal to it. Denote that vector as the *CAV* (shown in red in Figure 1.5).

With a CAV in hand, we can now inquire how class K relates to that concept. Take the directional derivative of H with respect to the CAV as [161]

$$S_{CAV,k,l}(x) = \lim_{\varepsilon \to 0} \frac{H(F(x) + \varepsilon CAV) - H(F(x))}{\varepsilon} = \nabla H(F(x)) \cdot CAV \quad (1.13)$$

where x is an element of the training dataset belonging to class K, and $H()$ is restricted to the output representing class K. $S_{CAV,k,l}(x)$ thus represents how sensitive

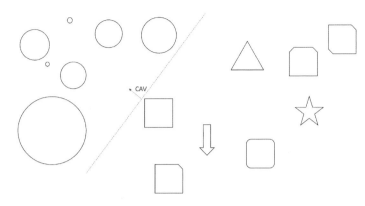

Figure 1.5: Determining a CAV for the concept "circle".

class K is to the concept in P. Now suppose that X_k represents all of the examples in the dataset that belong to class K. One can then calculate what fraction of them have a positive sensitivity S versus the concept in P; this will be the TCAV figure of merit, representing how strongly the concept influences class K [161]:

$$TCAV_{Q_{CAV,k,l}} = \frac{|\{x \in X_k : S_{CAV,k,l}(x) > 0\}|}{|X_k|} \tag{1.14}$$

By probing the different classes and layers in a DNN with multiple concepts, we will discover which concepts most strongly influence which classes at different layers. The highly influential concepts together become the explanans for the decisions made by the DNN [161].

1.3.5. *Meta-Features and Rule Extraction*

Meta-features are abstracted feature representations, used to improve the fidelity, stability, and sometimes accuracy of an explanans. The meta-feature approach focuses on global explanations in the *pedagogical* approach (the DNN is a black box) [97, 201, 202]. It is particularly appropriate for sparse, high-dimensional data, as a rule-based explanation for such data will either have poor coverage [203], or a large number of narrow, highly specific rules. In neither case will the explanans be robust. Instead, we can map input-domain features to more abstract, less sparse meta-features. Clustering is a classic example, as is treating a patch of a digital image as a *superpixel* [161, 204]. Key characteristics of effective meta-features include [162, 205]

- Low dimensionality
- Low sparsity
- High fidelity
- Statistical independence
- Comprehensibility

One example of the meta-feature approach is data-driven meta-features (DDMFs), in which meta-features are found using dimensionality reduction algorithms; for instance, Ramon et al. [162] employ the non-negative matrix factorization (NMF) algorithm. Consider an $n \times m$ data matrix X with n unique data items composed of m features. NMF factors X into two non-negative matrices U and W such that $X \approx UW$ and $\|X - UW\|^2$ is minimized with respect to U and W, with $U, W \geq 0$. To evaluate DDMFs, the authors in [162] propose three measures: accuracy (in the classic sense); fidelity (the accuracy of labels from the explanans compared only to the predicted labels from the DNN); and stability (the rulebases from different training sessions of an explanans will consistently repeat the same label predictions on out-of-sample data). While the first two are quite easily computed, measuring stability required a Monte Carlo algorithm [162].

1.3.6. *Discussion*

The XAI field exists because human users (often for a good reason) do not extend the same level of trust to an AI that they would to a human. Explanations are thus a means to improve user trust in the AI; the assumption is that increased trust will then lead to increased acceptance and usage of AI systems. Experience with other types of automated or internet-based systems has borne this out. Life in the COVID-19 pandemic, for example, was very strongly influenced (most would probably say positively) by internet-based e-commerce; this is despite the fact that e-commerce essentially did not exist prior to 1995.

In this section, we reviewed four modern techniques for generating an explanans, which are all meant to be problem- and architecture-agnostic. They are intended as generalized explanation algorithms, which therefore assumes that "explanation" is an independent phenomenon. On the other hand, Miller's review showed that "explanation" is a social act [11], and therefore dependent on context. One might therefore ask if an EI, rather than being a generalizable system component, might need to be engineered to respond to the needs of a particular stakeholder group. One example would be explanations of AI decisions in the banking sector (e.g., granting or refusing a loan), which must satisfy the government's banking regulators. Anecdotal discussions have indicated that some regulators may want to see a mathematical formula by which these decisions are made. Contrast this with AI developers who would be more interested in the execution trace of a DNN.

1.4. XAI and Fuzzy Logic

Fuzzy sets were first introduced by Lotfi A. Zadeh at the University of Berkeley in 1965 [81]. One of the pioneers of modern control theory, Zadeh had for some years been considering the question of vagueness in human language and reasoning. Tolerating that vagueness appeared to be a key reason why humans could forge ahead in uncertain environments, when computer programs simply reached an error state [206]. His 1965 formalization of this idea was to extend the definition of the characteristic function of a classical set from having a codomain consisting of the binary set {0, 1} to the closed real interval [0,1]. This new construct is the *fuzzy set*, defined by its *membership function*. Formally, a fuzzy set $A = \{(x, \mu_A(x))|x \in X\}$ where A is a *fuzzy subset* of X, and $\mu_A(x)(\mu:X \rightarrow [0,1])$ is the membership function (MF) for the fuzzy set A Several set-theoretic operations (including union, complement, and intersection) were also extended to fuzzy sets [81]. Later research has shown that "fuzzy set theory" is a family of theories differentiated by the set-theoretic operations in each one; fuzzy intersections can be any member of the class of *triangular norm* functions, and unions can be any *triangular conorm*. Fuzzy set complements do not conveniently map to a specific class of functions, but they are usually chosen so that the DeMorgan laws of Boolean logic will hold with the particular choice of intersection and union. Fuzzy logic is a family of many-valued logics that are isomorphic to the family of fuzzy set theories. Specifically, fuzzy logic normally denotes the class of logics having an uncountably infinite truth-value set (the real interval [0,1] is dense and thus has an uncountably infinite cardinality). Again, conjunctions may be any triangular norm, and disjunctions may be any triangular conorm. A survey of over 30 such logics may be found in [207]. A thorough introduction to fuzzy sets and fuzzy logic is provided in other chapters of this handbook, and we will not repeat that material here save for what is essential to our discussion.

Fuzzy logic is most commonly operationalized via a fuzzy inferential system (FIS), which employs linguistic fuzzy rules (based on the *linguistic variable* construct discussed in Section 4.1) to create an input-output mapping. An FIS is thus highly transparent, in the sense of [13]; the fuzzy rules are IF–THEN structures with linguistic predicates, usually chosen to be intuitively meaningful. A second common operationalization is to hybridize neural networks with fuzzy logic. This produces a network that is more interpretable (either at the decompositional or the pedagogical level, depending on the precise hybridization performed). Hence, we see that fuzzy logic has been employed in generating explanans since the 1970s, and research into hybrid deep fuzzy networks is ongoing today.

Our review in this section begins with the first major application of an FIS to practical problems, in the area of automated control. We will then explore the similarities and differences between FIS and fuzzy expert systems, which were contemporaneous with second-generation expert systems. We then turn our attention to neuro-fuzzy and genetic fuzzy hybrid systems, and close with a discussion of current research into deep neuro-fuzzy systems.

1.4.1. *Fuzzy Logic and Control Systems*

By the early 1970s, research into fuzzy logic was garnering interest from multiple researchers. The early focus was mainly on the mathematical properties of fuzzy sets. Zadeh introduced a theory of state equations for describing the behavior of fuzzy systems in 1971 [208], and in 1972 began suggesting that fuzzy sets could be used for automatic control [209]. From the perspective of XAI, one of the most vital developments was the introduction of the *linguistic variable* (LV) construct in [210–212]. This is the use of fuzzy sets to provide a mathematical meaning to linguistic terms such as *small* or *cold*. A linguistic variable is a 5-tuple (X, U, T, S, M) where X is the name of the variable, U is its universe of discourse (the universal set that X belongs to), T is the set of linguistic terms for the variable, S is a syntactic rule for generating additional linguistic terms (S is usually a context-free grammar whose terminal symbols are the terms in set T), and M is a semantic rule that associates a fuzzy subset of U with each term in S [210, 212]. The grammar S is needed to accommodate linguistic hedges in a variable (e.g., *very*, or *more or less*); a term generated by S (referred to as a composite term) will normally consist of a single base term, and an arbitrary number of hedges. The semantic rule M assigns a fuzzy subset of U to the base term, and a function $h: [0, 1] \to 0, 1$ to each hedge. The functions h are applied to the fuzzy set for the base term, in the order defined by the parse tree of the entire composite term [210, 212, 213].

As mentioned above, an FIS is composed of linguistic fuzzy rules. Specifically, these are IF–THEN rules much like in a traditional expert system, but with the antecedent predicates (and possibly the consequent predicates) defined as linguistic variables over each input (and output) dimension in the system feature space. The first application of the FIS to real-world problems was the design of an automated controller by Mamdani [214] (see [215, 216] as well). The first well-known commercial application was the cement kiln controller developed by Holmblad and Ostergaard [217]. Pappis and Mamdani's traffic controller [218], Flanagan's sludge process controller [219], and the first fuzzy inference chip developed by AT&T Bell Laboratories [220] are other well-known industrial applications. A good review of this initial development can be found in [221].

Mamdani's system rapidly prototyped a control algorithm by elucidating the knowledge of experienced human operators (in the form of *if–then* rules), and representing that knowledge as an FIS. When it was evaluated, the FIS algorithm (discussed in more detail below) proved to be immediately effective [214]. This has become a hallmark of fuzzy control; ongoing research and industrial experience have shown that the FIS is, in fact, a swift and intuitive means to devise a control surface (the response function of a control algorithm) of essentially arbitrary shape. They have in fact been shown to outperform classical PID controllers in many instances.

Figure 1.6:   Feedback control system.

One of the most famous examples is use of fuzzy control for a fully automated subway in the Japanese city of Sendai [222–224]. Fuzzy control algorithms are usually referred to as a fuzzy logic controller (FLC).

1.4.1.1. *Mamdani's FLC*

Automated feedback control systems follow the general design in Figure 1.6. The *plant* is the system being controlled, which is actually performing some useful work as measured by the output vector $\vec{y}$. The controller is the system that determines and applies control inputs $\vec{u}$ to affect the plant, and thereby alter the output $\vec{y}$. The input to the controller is an error vector $\vec{e}$, which represents the deviation of the output $\vec{y}$ from a desired *reference signal*. In modern control theory, the plant is represented as a vector of *state variables* $\vec{x}$, which measure specific, important characteristics of the plant. The time evolution of those state variables, as well as the control input vector $\vec{u}$, and their effect on the plant's outputs, are represented as differential equations [225]:

$$\frac{d\vec{x}}{dt} = \vec{F}(\vec{x}(t), \vec{u}(t)) \tag{1.15}$$

$$\vec{y}(t) = G(\vec{x}(t)) \tag{1.16}$$

where $\vec{x}$, $\vec{u}$ and $\vec{y}$ are (vector-valued) functions of time.

Conventional controllers are thus based on a mathematical model of the plant being controlled. They work extremely well for linear plants whose state variables are easily and precisely observed. However, this clearly describes only a minority of the circumstances in which automatic control is desirable; indeed many high-value, high-risk plants exhibit significant nonlinearities and poor observability of state variables. Nonetheless, trained human operators are able to safely operate such plants. It thus becomes highly desirable to create an automatic controller that can mimic those operators' performance. One possibility is to elicit condition–response rules from those operators, and deploy them as the controller of a plant; the FLC developed by Mamdani and Assilian [214] was the first practical example of employing fuzzy logic, which we discuss in more detail below.

The plant in [214] is a steam engine (a highly nonlinear system) whose observed state variables are the speed error (difference from the set point), pressure error, and the derivatives of each error. The two control variables are the heat input to the boiler and the throttle opening at the input of the engine cylinder. The control unit's goal is thus to determine the proper value of the two control variables, given the four inputs. For each input, a linguistic variable was defined over that universe of discourse. Each LV contained only base linguistic terms (no hedges); these are Positive Big (PB), Positive Medium (PM), Positive Small (PS), Negative Big (NB), Negative Medium (NM), Negative Small (NS), and Nil.

Mamdani and Assilian's design approach followed an earlier suggestion by Gaines [226] that a general learning procedure for an intelligent controller could consist of initializing the controller using *priming*, *coding*, and *training* approaches, followed by reinforcement learning to optimize the controller. Priming refers to the *communication* of a control strategy to the controller (e.g., as a rulebase); coding refers to establishing a representational format common to the controller and plant components; and *training* refers to adapting the controller to take a known optimal action for selected scenarios. As discussed in [214], the FLC was intended to perform the priming function only; however, the resulting algorithm was consistently superior to the digital controller used as an experimental contrast. Thus, the additional step of optimizing via reinforcement learning was not undertaken, and the results of just the FLC were reported.

In designing the FLC, Mamdani and Assilian needed to solve multiple challenges:

1. Firstly, how are the IF–THEN rules represented? If linguistic variables are employed as the predicates of the rules, then two further challenges arise:

   a. How are linguistic predicates from different universes of discourse to be combined within a rule?
   b. How are observations from sampled-data sensors to be interpreted in rules with linguistic predicates?

2. How will a conclusion be inferred from the set of IF–THEN rules and sensor observations?
3. How will this conclusion (itself a linguistic value) be interpreted into a control action for the physical plant?

As we know, the FLC [214] was designed with linguistic variables as the predicates to make the control rules as intuitive as possible (i.e., transparent). The solutions to these challenges were as follows (we will discuss only a two-input, single-output system for clarity of presentation). Given input variables X, Y and control variable Z, fuzzy rules were of the form

$$\text{IF } x \text{ is } A \text{ and } y \text{ is } B \text{ THEN } z \text{ is } C$$

for $x \in X$, $y \in Y$, $z \in Z$, and A, B, C being linguistic values that map to fuzzy subsets of X, Y, Z, respectively. Challenge (1a) is solved using the Cartesian product of fuzzy sets; for example, if we consider the two fuzzy sets A and B, the Cartesian product is given by [214]

$$\mu_{A \times B}(x, y) = min(\mu_A(x), \mu_B(y)) \tag{1.16}$$

applied to the fuzzy sets defined by the semantic rule of each linguistic variable. To solve challenge (1b), we can combine this product with a real-valued observation (x_0, y_0) using Zadeh's compositional rule of inference. The one step that is needed is to convert (x_0, y_0) into a fuzzy membership value; this was done by evaluating $\mu_{A \times B}(x, y)$ at the point (x_0, y_0). This leads us to the solution of challenge (2): Mamdani and Assilian combine the antecedent and consequent predicates of a fuzzy rule together using the Cartesian product again, producing a fuzzy relation R. This R, and the memberships of the observation vector $\vec{x}$, produce the output fuzzy set C' via the compositional rule of inference. (Note that this is not equivalent to a *fuzzy implication*.) Thus the inference result of one rule is produced by [214]

$$\mu_{C'}(z) = max \; min(\mu_{A \times B}(x_0, y_0), min(\mu_{A \times B}(x, y), \mu_C(z))) \tag{1.17}$$

Multiple rules are combined via fuzzy union [214]:

$$\mu_{out} = \bigcup_i \mu_{C'i}(z) \tag{1.18}$$

where the index i ranges over the whole set of fuzzy rules, and the fuzzy union is implemented by the *max()* t-conorm. Finally, for challenge (3), the control action output was chosen to be the unique element of Z with the highest membership in the output fuzzy set, if such exists; an expected value was taken if there were multiple elements with the maximal membership [214].

Mamdani and Assilian's work in [214] has been tremendously influential on the fuzzy systems community. Indeed, their approach to designing the FLC has, with some generalizations, become one of the de facto standards of the community. Figure 1.7 illustrates the general architecture of a modern FIS. Firstly, the IF–THEN rule format above has become the "canonical" form of fuzzy rules having linguistic consequents (we discuss alternative consequents later). Secondly, observations (assumed to be numeric quantities) undergo *fuzzification* as the first stage of an FIS, which converts them into fuzzy sets (commonly with only a single object-membership pair, known as a fuzzy singleton). The fuzzified observations are then passed to the inference engine, which combines them with a stored database of fuzzy linguistic rules (the *rulebase*) to determine an inferred conclusion. This inference engine still uses Mamdani's inference algorithm instead of a fuzzy implication function; the algorithm is visualized in Figure 1.8. The conclusion then commonly needs to be converted back into a numeric output, a process termed *defuzzification*.

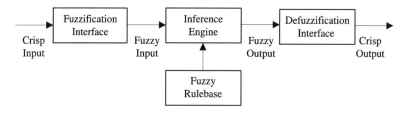

Figure 1.7: Basic architecture of a fuzzy expert system.

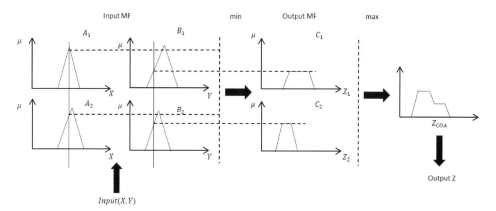

Figure 1.8: Mamdani fuzzy inference system using min and max for T-norm and T-conorm operators [227].

Defuzzification is most commonly implemented by the centroid method, i.e., determining the z value for the centroid of the output fuzzy set via the familiar equation from physics [227]:

$$Z_{COA} = \frac{\int_z^\square \mu_A(z)z\,dz}{\int_z^\square \mu_A(z)\,dz} \tag{1.19}$$

where $\mu_A(z)$ is the aggregated output MF.

While the Mamdani architecture was the first FLC published, the Takagi–Sugeno–Kang (TSK) FLC, first published in 1985 [228], is also very widely used. The principal difference between the two is that consequents in the TSK FLC are always numeric functions of the inputs, rather than fuzzy sets. A basic TSK fuzzy inference system, with linear consequent functions, is illustrated in Figure 1.9. In this system, the canonical form of the rules is *IF x is A_1 and y is B_1, THEN* $z_1 = f(x, y)$. The system output is then a sum of the output functions, weighted by the firing strength of each rule.

Considering the FLC from the perspective of XAI, it seems clear that a linguistic rulebase is more comprehensible than a differential equation in several variables!

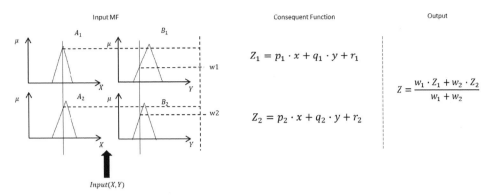

Figure 1.9:   Takagi–Sugeno fuzzy inference system using a min or product as T-norm operator [227].

Specifically, a human would be able to understand those rules *without* having to first learn the topic of differential equations. However, neither Mamdani nor Takagi et al. actually designed an EI for their FLC, and so the explanans for an FLC is just the fuzzy rulebase. Recalling the EI of MYCIN and other conventional expert systems, the rules of the expert system were not deemed a sufficient explanation. Nor does the literature on FLCs commonly attempt a more formal evaluation of the comprehensibility of an FLC.

A further point arises when we consider the differences between the Mamdani and TSK fuzzy systems. The TSK systems have attractive numerical properties; specifically, the linear coefficients (p, q, and r in Figure 1.9) afford additional degrees of freedom, allowing for a more precise control law—or more accurate predictions when the TSK system is used for classification or other tasks. Furthermore, design rules for building TSK controllers with guaranteed stability have long been known [229]. However, a linear function is, on its face, less transparent than a single linguistic term as produced by Mamdani controllers. This is a first example of the interpretability/accuracy trade-off that will be discussed in more depth later in this section [230].

1.4.2. *Expert Systems and Fuzzy Logic*

As discussed, researchers quickly realized that expert systems such as MYCIN and PROSPECTOR could be reused in different problem domains by swapping out their rulebase; the rest of the system was considered a reusable expert system *shell*. These shells generally employed the *production system* architecture, depicted in Figure 1.10.

The EI and rulebase components have been previously discussed. The *working memory* contains all data that have been input to the system, conclusions inferred from all rules fired to this point (we can collectively call these *facts*), and the set of

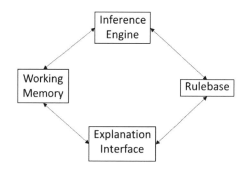

Figure 1.10:   Production system architecture for expert systems [231].

all rules whose antecedents may yet be matched to the available facts (the *conflict set*). The *inference engine* is either a forward- or backwards-chaining approach. In forward chaining, the engine will iteratively select a rule from the conflict set whose antecedents are fully matched by available facts, and then execute any actions in the THEN part of the rule; this may include adding new facts to the working memory. The conflict set is then updated (rules might be added or deleted), and the process repeats, until the conflict set is empty [232]. In backwards chaining, the inference engine treats the possible outcomes of rules as statements that need to be proved by reasoning from the facts and rules in working memory. If a fact directly proves the statement, it is selected. Otherwise, rules whose consequents match the statement are selected, and their antecedents are added to working memory as new statements to be proven. The process continues recursively until either facts proving the entire sequence of statements are identified, or no more facts and rules that continue the chain can be found [233].

One of the key steps in the production system is identifying the conflict set; this is generally called the many-pattern–many-object matching problem. As its name implies, the problem is to take a collection of objects, and a collection of patterns, and find every object that matches any of the patterns. The brute-force approach to this problem has an exponential time complexity, and so other alternatives are needed. The Rete network algorithm is generally used in practical expert systems. The Rete network organizes the rulebase into a tree structure, based on testing single features at each node. Then, once a new fact enters the working memory, it can be quickly passed through the Rete network to arrive at a set of rules compatible with that fact. Once all antecedents in a rule have been matched to facts in the working memory, the rule can fire. The complexity of this algorithm has been shown to be polynomial in the number of rules [232, 234].

As discussed earlier, the developers of MYCIN quickly realized that their expert system needed some way to tolerate vagueness and imprecision in its inputs and rules. Their solution, ad hoc certainty factors, worked initially but was found to be extremely fragile; certainty factors throughout the rulebase might have to be manually re-tuned whenever a new rule was added [55]. It is thus unsurprising that researchers in the 1970s and 1980s began to study fuzzy expert systems as a potentially more robust means of accommodating imprecision and vagueness. Early systems included Sphinx, Diabeto, and CADIAG-2 for medical diagnostic support [235–237]. Zadeh's 1983 article [238] described how uncertainty in a production system-based shell can be accounted for by using possibility distributions and the compositional rule of inference. He expanded on these points in his discussion of fuzzy syllogistic reasoning in [239]. An alternative approach is outlined by Negoita in [240]. Buckley et al. present a fuzzy expert system where the facts are fuzzy numbers in addition to the rulebase being fuzzy [241]; a refinement of this system is discussed in [242]. An expert system for military target classification is proposed in [243]. A fuzzy expert system based on backwards chaining is proposed in [244]; notably, this system includes an EI that can respond to *why*, *how*, and *what if* questions. The Fuzzy CLIPS shell[2] is a modification of the CLIPS shell (for traditional forward-chaining expert systems) that incorporates fuzzy logic.

Of all the fuzzy expert systems discussed, only Fuzzy CLIPS employs a Rete network for the many-pattern/many-object problem; the others simply use a brute-force search. However, Fuzzy CLIPS overlooks a key difference between fuzzy and traditional expert systems. In fuzzy forward rule chaining, a rule containing a given predicate in its antecedents must not fire until all rules in the conflict set that assert that predicate in their conclusions have fired [245]. This attention to ordering is needed because, unlike in the Boolean logic, the proposition $(p \rightarrow q) \wedge (q \rightarrow s) \rightarrow (p \rightarrow s)$ (sometimes called the chaining syllogism) is not generally a tautology in fuzzy logic (i.e., it is not a tautology in all possible fuzzy logics) [246]. Thus, ignoring the ordering constraint can lead to incorrect results. FuzzyShell is an alternative fuzzy forward-chaining shell, with a modified Rete network that does account for this ordering constraint [247].

In reviewing fuzzy expert system shells, one once again finds the same pattern that was present in FLC designs: a linguistic rulebase again seems to improve the transparency of the expert system, but the EI seems to have been neglected. With the exception of [244], none of the reviewed systems have a way of responding to any user queries, or a means to construct counterfactuals. The potential is clearly there, and causal reasoning is a topic of interest in the fuzzy community (e.g., [248, 249]). The extra step of building an EI, however, seems to seldom be taken.

---

[2]https://github.com/garydriley/FuzzyCLIPS631

1.4.3. *Hybrid Fuzzy Systems*

One of the signature characteristics of computational intelligence is that hybrid system designs combining its major core disciplines (neural networks, fuzzy logic, and evolutionary computing) are very commonly superior to designs using only one approach [250]. Specifically, the hybrids involving fuzzy logic are usually considered more "intuitive" or "understandable," due to their incorporation of "interpretable" fuzzy sets. This is much the same argument that is made for fuzzy systems in general. In the next two subsections, we will review neuro-fuzzy and evolutionary fuzzy systems, respectively, and examine what kinds of explanans are being offered by these systems.

1.4.3.1. *Neuro-fuzzy systems*

Hybrids of neural networks and fuzzy logic were first investigated in the early 1970s, during the neural network winter. Lee and Lee designed a generalization of the McCullogh–Pitts neuron which operated with fuzzy inputs and outputs [251]. Later, Keller and Hunt designed a perceptron that created a fuzzy hyperplane instead of a crisp one as the decision boundary (an idea that presaged the soft-margin algorithm for support vector machines some 10 years later) [252]. Wang and Mendel proposed a gradient-descent algorithm for inductively learning fuzzy rulebases in [253]. Then in 1988, NASA organized the 1st Workshop on Neural Networks and Fuzzy Logic, which catalyzed developments in this area [254]. In the years since, thousands of theory and application papers have explored the design space of neuro-fuzzy systems. We can divide this design space into two major approaches: fuzzifying neural networks, and neural architectures that mimic fuzzy systems (authors often define the term neuro-fuzzy systems to only mean this latter subclass). We discuss each in turn below.

The term "fuzzy neural network" has come to mean a traditional neural network architecture that has been modified to incorporate fuzzy sets and logic in some fashion for the purpose of improving the transparency of the NN. This quite commonly takes the form of modifying individual neurons to employ fuzzy quantities in their computations. A good example is Hayashi's fuzzified multilayer perceptron, in which neuron inputs, outputs, and weights are all fuzzy numbers (fuzzy sets with unimodal, convex membership functions, which represent a real number that is not precisely known) [255]. Another example is Pal and Mitra's Fuzzy MLP [256], in which only the network inputs and outputs are fuzzy; internally the network is a basic MLP with backpropagation. The network inputs are the memberships from each fuzzy set in a linguistic variable covering the actual input dimensions of a dataset, while the outputs are fuzzy class labels (permitting each object x to belong to more than one class). These two examples also illustrate

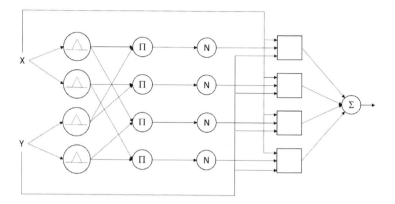

Figure 1.11:   ANFIS architecture [257].

a significant parallel to the knowledge extraction algorithms for shallow networks discussed in [98]; after all, the intent of those works was also to make the knowledge stored in NNs more transparent. Hayashi's work can be seen as fuzzification at the *decompositional* level, which Pal and Mitra's might be considered fuzzification at the *pedagogical* level. As a very general statement, fuzzy neural networks tend to be more transparent than traditional NNs, but without sacrificing a great deal of accuracy.

Mimicking a fuzzy system using a neural network has a somewhat different purpose. If a 1:1 correspondence between the neural architecture and an FIS can be shown, then the knowledge in the NN is highly transparent; the problem lies in *acquiring* that knowledge. This class of neuro-fuzzy systems is commonly used to design and optimize an FIS, using observed data rather than knowledge elicitation from experts. Perhaps the best-known example is Jang's ANFIS architecture [257], which is provably equivalent to a TSK fuzzy system. As shown in Figure 1.11, this NN is radically different from an MLP. Each layer of the network executes one stage of computations that together form a TSK fuzzy system. The first layer computes the membership of the numeric inputs in each fuzzy set from a linguistic variable over that dimension. The second layer combines the linguistic predicates from the first layer into rules; note that this layer is not fully connected to the first. The pattern of connections from layer 1 to layer 2 defines the rules of the fuzzy system. Layer 3 normalizes the firing strength of each rule, and then layer 4 computes a linear function of the inputs as the TSK consequent to each rule, weighted by the normalized firing strength of the rule. The outputs of layer 4 are then summed to produce the network output. There have been a wide variety of modifications and extensions proposed for ANFIS in the last three decades. For more details on both approaches to neuro-fuzzy systems, we direct the reader to the recent review in [258].

When we compare fuzzy neural networks with the FIS mimics, we again observe the interpretability/accuracy trade-off; there is a tendency for the former to be more accurate, while the latter are more transparent as they directly translate into an FIS [227]. Note, however, that the latter statement has its limits; ANFIS, for instance, treats the parameters of the layer 1 fuzzy sets as adaptive parameters to be learned. It is thus entirely possible for the fuzzy sets in a trained ANFIS to diverge from an "intuitive" meaning associated with a linguistic term they may have been assigned [250]. Furthermore, these architectures once again focus on transparency, but generally do not actually follow up with designing an EI.

1.4.3.2. *Evolutionary fuzzy algorithms*

Evolutionary algorithms are a class of iterative optimization techniques based on the metaheuristic of selection pressure. In each iteration, a population of solutions is generated, and ranked according to their "fitness" (the value of an objective function). Those with the highest fitness are used to form the next population that will be evaluated; those with low fitness are discarded. The algorithms might closely follow the ideas of mate competition and genetic reproduction; crystal formation in an annealing process; foraging behaviors of ants; and many others [250]. As with neuro-fuzzy systems, the goal of an evolutionary fuzzy algorithm (EFA) is to design an intelligent system to model a dataset with both high accuracy and interpretability. However, while EFAs have a shorter history than neuro-fuzzy systems (the first articles [259–261] describing genetic fuzzy systems appeared in 1991), they are generally accepted today as producing more accurate systems. Moreover, multi-objective genetic fuzzy systems can simultaneously optimize the accuracy *and* interpretability of an FIS [57].

Multiple elements of an FIS might be designed/optimized in an EFA. The rulebase, the inference engine, and the fuzzy sets of the semantic rules for each LV can all be learned in the EFA. Fundamentally, there are two different learning approaches used in an EFA: it might either be used to fine-tune an initial FIS, or alternatively the EFA can inductively learn the whole FIS from a dataset. In the former case, the initial FIS is likely hand-crafted by the system designer, possibly including knowledge elicitation from experts on the system being modeled. The rulebase thus developed will be highly interpretable. The FIS is then fine-tuned by the evolutionary algorithm to improve its accuracy on observed data. In particular, such systems often focus on fine-tuning membership function parameters, e.g., [262], although some proposals also adapt the inference engine of the FIS [57].

Alternatively, an FIS might be inductively learned from a dataset. Again, this can take multiple forms. One might, for example, use an EFA to select an optimal subset of rules from a larger set of rule candidates [263]; or one might directly generate the fuzzy rules. In the latter case, the linguistic variables for each predicate are usually pre-defined, and the EFA only considers the rules arising from their different combinations, e.g., [264]. A much smaller number of papers do consider the much wider design space of learning both the linguistic variables and the rules inductively (e.g., [265]) [57]. Note that generally, as in the previous discussions of this section, the explanans offered by EFA algorithms is again just the fuzzy rulebase.

1.4.4. *Fuzzy Logic and XAI: Recent Progress*

Hybridizations of fuzzy logic and DNNs have received little attention until very recently. Much like the shallow neuro-fuzzy systems discussed above, *deep* neuro-fuzzy systems are designed to improve the transparency of a DNN, while retaining as much of the accuracy offered by a DNN as possible. As with their shallow-network counterparts, deep neuro-fuzzy systems can be divided into two groups: fuzzy DNNs and FIS mimics. One key difference with deep FIS mimics, however, is that the architectures usually create multiple, stacked FIS layers instead of one single FIS. Furthermore, we also note that deep neuro-fuzzy system architectures again do not commonly include a dedicated EI.

Fuzzy DNNs include the fuzzy deep MLP in [266] and the fuzzy restricted Boltzmann machine in [267]. The latter is stacked into a fuzzy deep belief network in [268]. Echo state networks were modified with a second reservoir employing fuzzy clustering for feature reinforcement in [269], and then stacked into a DNN. Rulebases are learned using the Wang–Mendel algorithm [253], and then stacked, in [270]. Stacked autoencoders are merged with fuzzy clustering in [271]. A deep version of the Fuzzy MLP is proposed in [272]. Similarly, fuzzy C-means clustering was used to preprocess images for stacked autoencoders in [273], and for CNNs in [274]. ResNet is fuzzified in [275]. The Softmax classification layer at the output of a DNN was replaced with a fuzzy decision tree in [276]. There are also papers that build a fuzzy DNN using *extensions* to type-1 fuzzy sets. The fuzzy restricted Boltzmann machine of [267] was redesigned in [277] to employ Pythagorean fuzzy sets [278], and to employ interval type-2 fuzzy sets in [279]. Pythagorean fuzzy sets were used to fuzzify stacked denoising autoencoders in [280].

FIS mimics include a hybrid of ANFIS and long short-term memory in [281], a network for mimicking the fuzzy Choquet integral in [282], and stacked TSK fuzzy systems in [283–285]. A CNN was pruned using fuzzy compression in [286]. A solver for polynomial equations with Z-number coefficients is proposed in [287]. In [288] and [289], the convolutional and deep belief components of a DNN, respectively, are employed as feature extractors prior to building a model via clustering. This is quite similar to the approach in [290, 291]: the densely connected layers at the end of a deep network are replaced with an alternative classifier built from a clustering algorithm. The latter two, however, employ the fuzzy C-means and Gustafson–Kessel fuzzy clustering algorithms, respectively.

1.4.5. *Discussion*

Interpretability has been a desideratum of fuzzy sets since Zadeh's initial development of the topic, but truly became a defining characteristic with the development of the *linguistic variable* construct. Fuzzy control systems and fuzzy expert systems both grew out of Zadeh's approximate reasoning framework, which is founded on LVs. The success of fuzzy control in particular seems to have provided the impetus for researchers to study hybridizations of neural networks with fuzzy logic. It's worth noting that neuro-fuzzy systems began to gain traction just as the AI Winter was setting in, while EIs for neural networks were again becoming a major concern. By exploring the limits of the interpretability/accuracy trade–off, neuro-fuzzy system research is thus an important historical facet of XAI. In recent works, researchers have again returned to these roots, examining how various hybrids of neural networks and fuzzy logic fare in that trade-off. These include fuzzy deep neural networks and stacked fuzzy system mimics, paralleling earlier work on shallow neuro-fuzzy systems.

1.5. Summary and Conclusions

In this chapter, we examined current and historical approaches to XAI and their relationships with computational intelligence. We examined the motivations behind XAI, and how the historical development of symbolic and non-symbolic approaches to AI influenced research into explainability, and vice versa. We then reviewed the research into trust and AI in more depth, along with four major modern approaches to generating an explanans. Our final major topic was the historical and current research into XAI and computational intelligence, in which fuzzy sets and logic play a central role in making AI more explainable. This normally takes the form of algorithms hybridizing machine learning and fuzzy logic (e.g., neuro-fuzzy evolutionary fuzzy systems).

We found that AI systems based on fuzzy sets and logic, in particular, produce highly transparent models, through the use of the linguistic variable construct. It appears that this advantage can carry over to hybrid neuro-fuzzy systems (particularly the fuzzy system mimics) and evolutionary fuzzy systems as well. However, the design of dedicated explanation interfaces for all modern AI systems seems to have received far less attention than they did during the heyday of traditional expert systems. In future work, we believe that EI design should again become a major focus for AI and machine learning in general, including in computational intelligence. In particular, recent progress in natural language processing seems to be a particularly ripe area for creating more effective explanations.

References

[1] J. Manyika and K. Sneader, AI, automation, and the future of work: ten things to solve for, (2018). [Online]. Available at: https://www.mckinsey.com/featured-insights/future-of-work/ai-automation-and-the-future-of-work-ten-things-to-solve-for#.

[2] D. Silver et al., Mastering the game of Go with deep neural networks and tree search, *Nature*, vol. 529 (2016), doi: 10.1038/nature16961.

[3] C. Metz, Google's AI wins pivotal second game in match with Go grandmaster, *WIRED*, Mar. 10 (2016).

[4] M. T. Ribeiro, S. Singh, and C. Guestrin, Why should I trust you?: Explaining the predictions of any classifier, in *Proceedings of the 22nd ACM SIGKDD International Conference on Knowledge Discovery and Data Mining*, pp. 1135–1144 (2016).

[5] R. Caruana, Y. Lou, J. Gehrke, P. Koch, M. Sturm, and N. Elhadad, Intelligible models for healthcare: predicting pneumonia risk and hospital 30-day readmission (2015), doi: 10.1145/2783258.2788613.

[6] R. R. Hoffman, S. T. Mueller, G. Klein, and J. Litman, Metrics for explainable AI: challenges and prospects, *arXiv*. (2018).

[7] S. Antifakos, N. Kern, B. Schiele, and A. Schwaninger, Towards improving trust in context-aware systems by displaying system confidence (2005), doi: 10.1145/1085777.1085780.

[8] P. Dourish, Accounting for system behaviour: representation, reflection and resourceful action, *Third Decenn. Conf. Comput. Context (CIC '95)* (1995).

[9] H. J. Suermondt and G. F. Cooper, An evaluation of explanations of probabilistic inference, *Comput. Biomed. Res.* (1993), doi: 10.1006/cbmr.1993.1017.

[10] J. Tullio, A. K. Dey, J. Chalecki, and J. Fogarty, How it works: a field study of non-technical users interacting with an intelligent system (2007), doi: 10.1145/1240624.1240630.

[11] T. Miller, Explanation in artificial intelligence: insights from the social sciences, *Artif. Intell.*, vol. 267, pp. 1–38 (2019).

[12] B. Kim, R. Khanna, and O. Koyejo, Examples are not enough, learn to criticize! Criticism for interpretability (2016).

[13] P. Humphreys, The philosophical novelty of computer simulation methods, *Synthese*, vol. 169, no. 3, pp. 615–626 (2008).

[14] C. Zednik, Solving the black box problem: a normative framework for explainable artificial intelligence, *Philos. Technol.* (2019), doi: https://doi.org/10.1007/s13347-019-00382-7.

[15] R. Tomsett, D. Braines, D. Harborne, A. Preece, and S. Chakraborty, Interpretable to whom? A role-based model for analyzing interpretable machine learning systems, *arXiv*. (2018).

[16] J. D. Moore and W. R. Swartout, Explanation in expert systems: a survey, *ISI Res. Rep.* (1988).

[17] J. A. Overton, 'Explain' in scientific discourse, *Synthese* (2013), doi: 10.1007/s11229-012-0109-8.

[18] J. Y. Halpern and J. Pearl, Causes and explanations: a structural-model approach. Part I: causes, *Br. J. Philos. Sci.* (2005), doi: 10.1093/bjps/axi147.

[19] J. Y. Halpern and J. Pearl, Causes and explanations: a structural-model approach. Part II: explanations, *Br. J. Philos. Sci.* (2005), doi: 10.1093/bjps/axi148.

[20] J. Pearl, *Probabilistic Reasoning in Intelligent Systems: Networks of Plausible Inference* (Morgan Kaufmann Series in Representation and Reasoning) (1988).

[21] L. R. Goldberg, *The Book of Why: The New Science of Cause and Effect*. Judea Pearl and Dana Mackenzie (2018). Hachette UK.

[22] J. D. Trout, Scientific explanation and the sense of understanding, *Philos. Sci.* (2002), doi: 10.1086/341050.

[23] T. Lombrozo, Explanation and abductive inference, in *The Oxford Handbook of Thinking and Reasoning* (2012).

[24] S. Sigurdsson, P. A. Philipsen, L. K. Hansen, J. Larsen, M. Gniadecka, and H. Christian Wulf, Detection of skin cancer by classification of Raman spectra, *IEEE Trans. Biomed. Eng.* (2004), doi: 10.1109/TBME.2004.831538.

[25] K. T. Schütt, F. Arbabzadah, S. Chmiela, K. R. Müller, and A. Tkatchenko, Quantum-chemical insights from deep tensor neural networks, *Nat. Commun.* (2017), doi: 10.1007/s13351-018-7159-x.

[26] R. M. J. Byrne, Counterfactuals in explainable artificial intelligence (XAI): evidence from human reasoning, in *IJCAI*, pp. 6276–6282 (2019).

[27] G. Dietz and D. N. Den Hartog, Measuring trust inside organisations, *Pers. Rev.*, vol. 35, no. 5, pp. 557–588 (2006).

[28] F. D. Davis, Perceived usefulness, perceived ease of use, and user acceptance of information technology, *MIS Q.*, vol. 13, no. 3, pp. 319–340 (1989).

[29] X. Deng and X. Wang, Incremental learning of dynamic fuzzy neural networks for accurate system modeling, *Fuzzy Sets Syst.*, vol. 160, no. 7, pp. 972–987 (2009).

[30] N. Wang, D. V. Pynadath, and S. G. Hill, Trust calibration within a human-robot team: comparing automatically generated explanations, in *International Conference on Human-Robot Interaction (HRI)*2, 16AD, pp. 109–116.

[31] Z. Buçinca, P. Lin, K. Z. Gajos, and E. L. Glassman, Proxy tasks and subjective measures can be misleading in evaluating explainable AI systems, in *International Conference on Intelligent User Interfaces 2*, pp. 454–464 (2020).

[32] A. Papenmeier, Trust in automated decision making: how user's trust and perceived understanding is influenced by the quality of automatically generated explanations, University of Twente (2019).

[33] A. Paez, The pragmatic turn in explainable artificial intelligence (XAI), *Minds Mach.*, vol. 29, pp. 441–459 (2019).

[34] Samek, Wojciech, T. Wiegand, and K.-R. Müller, Explainable artificial intelligence: understanding, visualizing and interpreting deep learning models, *arXiv Prepr. arXiv1708.08296* (2017).

[35] S. Hajian, F. Bonchi, and C. Castillo, Algorithmic bias: from discrimination discovery to fairness-aware data mining, (2016), doi: 10.1145/2939672.2945386.

[36] U. M. Fayyad, G. Piatetsky-Shapiro, and P. Smyth, Knowledge discovery and data mining: towards a unifying framework, in *International Conference on Knowledge Discovery and Data Mining*, Portland, OR, United States (1996).

[37] B. Goodman and S. Flaxman, European Union regulations on algorithmic decision-making and a 'right to explanation,' *arXiv Prepr. arXiv1606.08813* (2016).

[38] B. Goodman and S. Flaxman, European Union regulations on algorithmic decision making and a 'right to explanation,' *AI Mag.*, (2017), doi: 10.1609/aimag.v38i3.2741.

[39] P. Adler et al., Auditing black-box models for indirect influence, *Knowl. Inf. Syst.*, (2018), doi: 10.1007/s10115-017-1116-3.

[40] V. Bellotti and K. Edwards, Intelligibility and accountability: human considerations in context-aware systems, *Hum.-Comput. Interact.*, (2001), doi: 10.1207/S15327051HCI16234_05.

[41] N. Bostrom and E. Yudkowsky, The ethics of artificial intelligence, in *The Cambridge Handbook of Artificial Intelligence* (2014).

[42] C. Dwork, M. Hardt, T. Pitassi, O. Reingold, and R. Zemel, Fairness through awareness, (2012), doi: 10.1145/2090236.2090255.

[43] C. K. Fallon and L. M. Blaha, Improving automation transparency: addressing some of machine learning's unique challenges, (2018), doi: 10.1007/978-3-319-91470-1_21.

[44] B. Hayes and J. A. Shah, Improving robot controller transparency through autonomous policy explanation, (2017), doi: 10.1145/2909824.3020233.

[45] M. Joseph, M. Kearns, J. Morgenstern, S. Neel, and A. Roth, Rawlsian fairness for machine learning, *arXiv Prepr. arXiv1610.09559* (2016).

[46] M. Joseph, M. Kearns, J. Morgenstern, and A. Roth, Fairness in learning: classic and contextual bandits, *arXiv, abs/1605.07139* (2016).

[47] J. A. Kroll et al., Accountable algorithms, *University of Pennsylvania Law Review* (2017).

[48] C. Otte, Safe and interpretable machine learning: a methodological review, *Studies in Computational Intelligence*, (2013), doi: 10.1007/978-3-642-32378-2_8.

[49] L. Sweeney, Discrimination in online ad delivery: google ads, black names and white names, racial discrimination, and click advertising, *Queue*, (2013), doi: 10.1145/2460276.2460278.

[50] K. R. Varshney and H. Alemzadeh, On the safety of machine learning: cyber-physical systems, decision sciences, and data products, *Big Data*, (2017), doi: 10.1089/big.2016.0051.

[51] S. Wachter, B. Mittelstadt, and C. Russell, Counterfactual explanations without opening the black box: automated decisions and the GDPR, *arXiv*. 2017, doi: 10.2139/ssrn.3063289.

[52] P. Comon, Independent component analysis: a new concept?, *Signal Process.*, (1994), doi: 10.1016/0165-1684(94)90029-9.

[53] G. Montavon, W. Samek, and K. R. Müller, Methods for interpreting and understanding deep neural networks, *Digital Signal Proces.*, (2018), doi: 10.1016/j.dsp.2017.10.011.

[54] D. C. Brock, Learning from artificial intelligence's previous awakenings: the history of expert systems, *AI Mag.*, (2018), doi: 10.1609/aimag.v39i3.2809.

[55] N. Nilsson, *The Quest for Artificial Intelligence: A History of Ideas and Achievements*. New York, NY, USA: Cambridge University Press (2009).

[56] P. Dear, *The Intelligibility of Nature: How Science Makes Sense of the World*. Chicago, IL, USA: The University of Chicago Press (2006).

[57] M. Fazzolari, R. Alcala, Y. Nojima, H. Ishibuchi, and F. Herrera, A review of the application of multiobjective evolutionary fuzzy systems: current status and further directions, *IEEE Trans. Fuzzy Syst.*, (2013), doi: 10.1109/TFUZZ.2012.2201338.

[58] D. Poole and A. Mackworth, *Artificial Intelligence: Foundations of Computational Agents*, 2nd edn. New York, NY, USA: Cambridge University Press (2017).

[59] A. Newell and H. A. Simon, The logic theory machine: a complex information processing system, *Proc. IRE Trans. Inf. Theory*, vol. IT-2, pp. 61–79 (1956).

[60] A. Newell and H. A. Simon, Computer science as empirical inquiry: symbols and search, *Commun. ACM*, vol. 19, no. 3, pp. 113–126, Sep. 1976, doi: 10.1145/1283920.1283930.

[61] R. K. Lindsay, B. G. Buchanan, E. A. Feigenbaum, and J. Lederberg, *Applications of Artificial Intelligence for Organic Chemistry: The Dendral Project*. New York, NY, USA: McGraw-Hill (1980).

[62] B. G. Buchanan and E. H. Shortliffe, Rule-based expert systems: the MYCIN experiments of the Stanford Heuristic Programming Project. Addison-Wesley, Reading (1984).

[63] W. van Melle, A Domain-independent system that aids in constructing knowledge-based consultation programs, Stanford University (1980).

[64] E. A. Feigenbaum, P. McCorduck, and H. P. Nii, *The Rise of the Expert Company: How Visionary Companies are Using Artificial Intelligence to Achieve Higher Productivity and Profits*. New York, NY, USA: Times Books (1988).

[65] L. K. Hansen and L. Rieger, Interpretability in intelligent systems: a new concept?, in *Lecture Notes in Computer Science (including subseries Lecture Notes in Artificial Intelligence and Lecture Notes in Bioinformatics)* (2019).

[66] W. R. Swartout and J. D. Moore, Explanation in second generation expert systems, in *Second Generation Expert Systems*, J. M. David, J. P. Krivine, and R. Simmons (eds.), Berlin, Germany: Springer (1993), pp. 543–585.

[67] S. Chakraborty et al., Interpretability of deep learning models: a survey of results (2018), doi: 10.1109/UIC-ATC.2017.8397411.

[68] F. Doshi-Velez and B. Kim, A roadmap for a rigorous science of interpretability, *arXiv Prepr. arXiv1702.08608v1* (2017).

[69] J. Psotka, L. D. Massey, S. A. Mutter, and J. S. Brown, Intelligent tutoring systems: lessons learned, Psychology Press (1988).

[70] D. W. Hasling, W. J. Clancey, and G. Rennels, Strategic explanations for a diagnostic consultation system, *Int. J. Man. Mach. Stud.*, vol. 20, no. 1, pp. 3–19 (1984).

[71] B. Chandrasekaran, Generic tasks in knowledge-based reasoning, *IEEE Expert*, vol. 1, no. 3, pp. 23–30 (1986).

[72] W. R. Swartout, C. L. Paris, and J. D. Moore, Design for explainable expert systems, *IEEE Expert*, vol. 6, no. 3, pp. 58–64 (1991).

[73] M. R. Wick and W. B. Thompson, Reconstructive expert system explanation, *Artif. Intell.*, (1992), doi: 10.1016/0004-3702(92)90087-E.

[74] W. R. Swartout, XPLAIN: a system for creating and explaining expert consulting programs, *Artif. Intell.*, (1983), doi: 10.1016/S0004-3702(83)80014-9.

[75] R. Neches, W. R. Swartout, and J. D. Moore, Enhanced maintenance and explanation of expert systems through explicit models of their development, *IEEE Trans. Software Eng.* (1985), doi: 10.1109/TSE.1985.231882.

[76] W. S. McCulloch and W. Pitts, A logical calculus of the ideas immanent in nervous activity, *Bull. Math. Biophys.*, vol. 5, pp. 115–133 (1943).

[77] D. O. Hebb, *The Organization of Behavior: A Neuropsychological Theory*. New York, NY, USA: Wiley (1949).

[78] F. Rosenblatt, The Perceptron: a probabilistic model for information storage and organization in the brain, *Psychol. Rev.*, vol. 65, pp. 386–408 (1958).

[79] J. J. Williams et al., AXIS: generating explanations at scale with learnersourcing and machine learning, (2016), doi: 10.1145/2876034.2876042.

[80] G. Shafer, *A Mathematical Theory of Evidence*. Princeton, NJ, USA: Princeton University Press (1976).

[81] L. a. Zadeh, Fuzzy sets, *Inf. Control* (1965), doi: 10.1016/S0019-9958(65)90241-X.

[82] M. L. Minsky and S. A. Papert, *Perceptrons: An Introduction to Computational Geometry*. Cambridge, MA, USA: MIT Press (1969).

[83] K. Fukushima, Neural network model for a mechanism of pattern recognition unaffected by shift in position: neocognitron, *Trans. IECEans.*, vol. J62-A, no. 10, pp. 655–658 (1979).

[84] Y. LeCun, L. Bottou, Y. Bengio, and P. Haffner, Gradient-based learning applied to document recognition, *Proc. IEEE* (1998), doi: 10.1109/5.726791.

[85] D. E. Rumelhart, G. E. Hinton, and R. J. Williams, Learning representations by back-propagating errors, *Nature*, vol. 323, pp. 533–536 (1986).

[86] J. J. Hopfield, Neural networks and physical systems with emergent collective computational abilities, *Proc. Natl. Acad. Sci.*, vol. 79, no. 8, pp. 2554–2558 (1982).

[87] S. Haykin, *Neural Networks and Learning Machines*. Prentice Hall (2008).

[88] E. M. Johansson, F. U. Dowla, and D. M. Goodman, Back-propagation learning for multi-layer feedforward neural networks using the conjugate gradient method, *Int. J. Neural Syst.*, vol. 2, no. 4, pp. 291–301 (1991).

[89] D. Marquardt, An algorithm for least-squares estimation of non-linear parameters, *J. Soc. Indus. Appl. Math.*, vol. 11, no. 2, pp. 431–441 (1963).

[90] G. G. Towell, Symbolic knowledge and neural networks: insertion, refinement, and extraction, University of Wisconsin, Madison (1991).

[91] B. Hassibi and D. G. Stork, Second-order-derivatives for network pruning: optimal brain surgeon, in *Advances in Neural Information Processing Systems*, pp. 164–171 (1993).

[92] D. S. Broomhead and D. Lowe, Multivariable functional interpolation and adaptive networks, *Complex Syst.*, vol. 2, pp. 321–355 (1988).

[93] A. Bell and T. J. Sejnowski, An information-maximization approach to blind separation and blind deconvolution, *Neural Comput.*, vol. 6, pp. 1129–1159 (1996).

[94] R. Linsker, Self-organization in a perceptual network, *IEEE Comput.*, vol. 21, no. 3, pp. 105–117 (1988).

[95] G. Tesauro, Temporal difference learning and TD-gammon, *Commun. ACM*, vol. 38, no. 3, pp. 58–68 (1995).

[96] D. H. Ackley, G. E. Hinton, and T. J. Sejnowski, A learning algorithm for Boltzmann machines, *Cogn. Sci.*, vol. 9, no. 1, pp. 147–169 (1985).

[97] R. Andrews, J. Diederich, and A. B. Tickle, Survey and critique of techniques for extracting rules from trained artificial neural networks, *Knowledge-Based Syst.* (1995), doi: 10.1016/0950-7051(96)81920-4.

[98] A. B. Tickle, F. Maire, G. Bologna, R. Andrews, and J. Diederich, Lessons from past, current issues, and future research directions in extracting the knowledge embedded in artificial neural networks, *Lect. Notes Artif. Intell.*, vol. 1778, pp. 226–239 (2000).

[99] M. J. Healy, A topological semantics for rule extraction with neural networks, *Conn. Sci.*, vol. 11, no. 1, pp. 91–113 (1999).

[100] R. Krishnan, G. Sivakumar, and P. Battacharya, A search technique for rule extraction from trained neural networks, *Pattern Recognit. Lett.*, vol. 20, pp. 273–280 (1999).

[101] A. B. Tickle, R. Andrews, M. Golea, and J. Diederich, The truth will come to light: directions and challenges in extracting the knowledge embedded within trained artificial neural networks, *IEEE Trans. Neural Networks* (1998), doi: 10.1109/72.728352.

[102] L. M. Fu, Rule learning by searching on adapted nets, in *National Conference on Artificial Intelligence*, pp. 590–595 (1991).

[103] G. Towell and J. Shavlik, The extraction of refined rules from knowledge based neural networks, *Mach. Learn.*, vol. 131, pp. 71–101 (1993).

[104] C. McMillan, M. C. Mozer, and P. Smolensky, The connectionist scientist game: rule extraction and refinement in a neural network (1991).

[105] R. Krishnan, A systematic method for decompositional rule extraction from neural networks, in *NIPS'96 Rule Extraction From Trained Artificial Neural Networks Wkshp*, pp. 38–45 (1996).

[106] F. Maire, A partial order for the M-of-N rule extraction algorithm, *IEEE Trans. Neural Networks*, vol. 8, pp. 1542–1544 (1997).

[107] K. Saito and R. Nakano, Law discovery using neural networks, in *Proc. NIPS'96 Rule Extraction from Trained Artificial Neural Networks*, pp. 62–69 (1996).

[108] R. Setiono, Extracting rules from neural networks by pruning and hidden unit splitting, *Neural Comput.*, vol. 9, pp. 205–225 (1997).

[109] K. Saito and R. Nakano, Medical diagnostic expert system based on PDP model, in *IEEE International Conference on Neural Networks1*, pp. 255–262 (1988).

[110] A. Bargiela and W. Pedrycz, *Granular Computing: An Introduction*. Boston, MA, USA: Kluwer Academic (2003).

[111] R. Andrews and S. Geva, RULEX & cebp networks as the basis for a rule refinement system, in *Hybrid Problems, Hybrid Solutions*, J. Hallam and P. McKevitt (eds.), Amsterdam, The Netherlands: IOS Press (1995), p. 12pp.

[112] C. L. Giles and C. W. Omlin, Rule refinement with recurrent neural networks, in *IEEE International Conference on Neural Networks*, pp. 801–806 (1993).

[113] M. W. Craven, Extracting Comprehensible Models from extraction algorithms from an artificial neural network, Univ. Wisconsin (1996).

[114] S. Thrun, Extracting rules from artificial neural networks with distributed representations (1995).

[115] R. Setiono and L. Huan, NeuroLinear: from neural networks to oblique decision rules, *Neurocomputing*, vol. 17, pp. 1–24 (1997).

[116] F. Maire, Rule-extraction by backpropagation of polyhedra, *Neural Networks*, vol. 12, pp. 717–725 (1999).

[117] K. K. Sethi, D. K. Mishra, and B. Mishra, Extended taxonomy of rule extraction techniques and assessment of KDRuleEx, *Int. J. Comput. Appl.*, vol. 50, no. 21, pp. 25–31 (2012).

[118] C. L. Giles and C. W. Omlin, Rule revision with recurrent networks, *IEEE Trans. Knowl. Data Eng.*, vol. 8, no. 1, pp. 183–188 (1996).

[119] M. Humphrey, S. J. Cunningham, and I. H. Witten, Knowledge visualization techniques for machine learning, *Intell. Data Anal.*, vol. 2, no. 4, pp. 333–347 (1998).

[120] J. Diederich, Rule extraction from support vector machines: an introduction, *Studies in Computational Intelligence* (2008), doi: 10.1007/978-3-540-75390-2_1.

[121] M. W. Craven and J. W. Shavlik, Using sampling and queries to extract rules from trained neural networks, in *Machine Learning Proceedings 1994* (1994).

[122] G. Bologna, A study on rule extraction from several combined neural networks, *Int. J. Neural Syst.*, vol. 11, no. 3, pp. 247–255 (2001).

[123] G. Bologna and S. Fossati, A two-step rule-extraction technique for a CNN, *Electronics*, vol. 9, no. 6 (2020).

[124] D. Crevier, *AI: The Tumultuous History of the Search for Artificial Intelligence*. New York, NY, USA: BasicBooks (1993).

[125] J. Hochreiter, Untersuchungen zu dynamischen neuronalen Netzen, Technische Universität Munchen (1991).

[126] C. Cortes and V. Vapnik, Support-vector networks, *Mach. Learning*, vol. 20, pp. 273–397 (1995).

[127] R. Díaz-Uriarte and S. A. de Andrés, Gene selection and classification of microarray data using random forest, *BMC Bioinf.*, vol. 7, no. 3, 2006.

[128] A. Statnikov and C. F. Aliferis, Are random forests better than support vector machines for microarray-based cancer classification?, in *AMIA Annual Symposium* (2007), pp. 686–690.

[129] N. Barakat and A. P. Bradley, Rule extraction from support vector machines: a review, *Neurocomputing*, vol. 74, pp. 178–190 (2010).

[130] D. Erhan, A. Courville, and Y. Bengio, Understanding representations learned in deep architectures, *Network* (2010).

[131] M. J. Druzdzel and M. Henrion, Using scenarios to explain probabilistic inference, *Proc. AAAI–90 Work. Explan.* (1990).

[132] C. Lacave and F. J. Díez, A review of explanation methods for Bayesian networks, *Knowl. Eng. Rev.*, vol. 17, no. 2, pp. 107–127 (2002), doi: 10.1017/S026988890200019X.

[133] W. L. Johnson, Agents that learn to explain themselves, *AAAI-94 Proceedings* (1994).

[134] M. van Lent, W. Fisher, and M. Mancuso, An explainable artificial intelligence system for small-unit tactical behavior, *IAAI-04 Proceedings* (2004).

[135] V. A. W. M. M. Aleven and K. R. Koedinger, An effective metacognitive strategy: learning by doing and explaining with a computer-based Cognitive Tutor, *Cogn. Sci.*, (2002), doi: 10.1207/s15516709cog2602_1.

[136] H. C. Lane, M. G. Core, M. Van Lent, S. Solomon, and D. Gomboc, Explainable artificial intelligence for training and tutoring, *Proc. 12th Int. Conf. Artif. Intell. Educ.* (2005).

[137] F. Sørmo, J. Cassens, and A. Aamodt, Explanation in case-based reasoning-perspectives and goals, *Artif. Intell. Rev.* (2005), doi: 10.1007/s10462-005-4607-7.

[138] A. Kofod-Petersen, J. Cassens, and A. Aamodt, Explanatory capabilities in the CREEK knowledge-intensive case-based reasoner, in *Proceedings of the 2008 conference on Tenth Scandinavian Conference on Artificial Intelligence: SCAI 2008*, pp. 28–35 (2008).

[139] Y. Goyal, T. Khot, D. Summers-Stay, D. Batra, and D. Parikh, Making the V in VQA matter: elevating the role of image understanding in visual question answering (2017), doi: 10.1109/CVPR.2017.670.

[140] Y. Goyal, A. Mohapatra, D. Parikh, D. Batra, and V. Tech, Interpreting visual question answering models (2016).

[141] F. Sadeghi, S. K. Divvala, and A. Farhadi, VisKE: visual knowledge extraction and question answering by visual verification of relation phrases (2015), doi: 10.1109/CVPR.2015.7298752.

[142] R. R. Selvaraju, M. Cogswell, A. Das, R. Vedantam, D. Parikh, and D. Batra, Grad-CAM: why did you say that? Visual explanations from deep networks via gradient-based localization, *arXiv:1610.02391* (2016).

[143] J. Yosinski, J. Clune, A. Nguyen, T. Fuchs, and H. Lipson, Understanding neural networks through deep visualization, *arXiv Prepr. arXiv1506.06579* (2015).

[144] T. Zahavy, N. Ben-Zrihem, and S. Mannor, Graying the black box: understanding DQNs, in *Proceedings of The 33rd International Conference on Machine Learning*, 2016, pp. 1899-1908.

[145] M. D. Zeiler and R. Fergus, Visualizing and understanding convolutional networks, in *European Conference on Computer Vision*, pp. 818–833 (2014).

[146] L. A. Hendricks, Z. Akata, M. Rohrbach, J. Donahue, B. Schiele, and T. Darrell, Generating visual explanations (2016), doi: 10.1007/978-3-319-46493-0_1.

[147] T. Kulesza, M. Burnett, W. K. Wong, and S. Stumpf, Principles of explanatory debugging to personalize interactive machine learning (2015), doi: 10.1145/2678025.2701399.

[148] T. Kulesza, S. Stumpf, M. Burnett, and I. Kwan, Tell me more? The effects of mental model soundness on personalizing an intelligent agent (2012), doi: 10.1145/2207676.2207678.

[149] M. Lomas, R. Chevalier, E. V. Cross, R. C. Garrett, J. Hoare, and M. Kopack, Explaining robot actions (2012), doi: 10.1145/2157689.2157748.

[150] D. H. Park et al., Attentive explanations: justifying decisions and pointing to the evidence (extended abstract), *arXiv.* (2017).

[151] S. Rosenthal, S. P. Selvaraj, and M. Veloso, Verbalization: narration of autonomous robot experience, in *Proceedings of the Twenty-Fifth International Joint Conference on Artificial Intelligence (IJCAI-16)* (2016).

[152] D. Gunning and D. W. Aha, DARPA's explainable artificial intelligence program, *AI Mag.*, vol. Summer, pp. 44–58 (2019).

[153] A. Arioua, P. Buche, and M. Croitoru, Explanatory dialogues with argumentative faculties over inconsistent knowledge bases, *Expert Syst. Appl.* (2017), doi: 10.1016/j.eswa.2017.03.009.

[154] P. Shafto and N. D. Goodman, Teaching games: statistical sampling assumptions for learning in pedagogical situations, in *Proceedings of the 30th annual conference of the Cognitive Science Society*, pp. 1632–1637 (2008).

[155] A. Nguyen, J. Yosinski, and J. Clune, Deep neural networks are easily fooled: high confidence predictions for unrecognizable images (2015), doi: 10.1109/CVPR.2015.7298640.

[156] R. Sheh and I. Monteath, Defining explainable AI for requirements analysis, *KI - Kunstl. Intelligenz* (2018), doi: 10.1007/s13218-018-0559-3.

[157] P. Lipton, Contrastive explanation, *R. Inst. Philos. Suppl.* (1990), doi: 10.1017/s1358246100005130.

[158] J. A. Glomsrud, A. Ødegårdstuen, A. L. St. Clair, and Ø. Smogeli, Trustworthy versus explainable AI in autonomous vessels, in *International Seminar on Safety and Security of Autonomous Vessels* (2019), p. 11.

[159] F. Nothdurft, F. Richter, and W. Minker, Probabilistic human-computer trust handling, in *SIGDIAL*, pp. 51–59 (2014).

[160] S. A. Binder, G. Montavon, F. Klauschen, K. R. Müller, and W. Samek, On pixel-wise explanations for non-linear classifier decisions by layer-wise relevance propagation, *PLoS One* (2015), doi: 10.1371/journal.pone.0130140.

[161] B. Kim et al., Interpretability beyond feature attribution: quantitative testing with concept activation vectors (TCAV), in *Proc. ICML*, pp. 2673–2682 (2018).

[162] Y. Ramon, D. Martens, T. Evgeniou, and S. Praet, Metafeatures-based rule-extraction for classifiers on behavioral and textual data: a preprint, *arXiv*. (2020).

[163] P. Beatty, I. Reay, S. Dick, and J. Miller, Consumer trust in e-commerce web sites, *ACM Comput. Surv.*, vol. 43, no. 3, pp. 14.1–14.46 (2011).

[164] R. C. Mayer, J. H. Davis, and F. D. Schoorman, An integrative model of organizational trust, *Acad. Manag. Rev.*, vol. 20, no. 3, pp. 709–734 (1995).

[165] J. Lyons, N. Ho, J. Friedman, G. Alarcon, and S. Guznov, Trust of learning systems: considerations for code, algorithms, and affordances for learning, in *Human and Machine Learning*, J. Zhou and F. Chen (eds.), Cham, Switzerland: Springer International Publishing AG, pp. 265–278 (2018).

[166] J. D. Lee and B. D. Seppelt, Human factors in automation design, in *Springer Handbook of Automation*, S. Y. Nof (ed.), Berlin, Germany: Springer-Verlag, pp. 417–436 (2009).

[167] J. B. Lyons and C. K. Stokes, Human–human reliance in the context of automation, *Hum. Factors*, vol. 54, no. 1, pp. 112–121 (2011).

[168] L. Onnasch, C. D. Wickens, H. Li, and D. Manzey, Human performance consequences of stages and levels of automation: an integrated meta-analysis, *Hum. Factors J. Hum. Factors Ergon. Soc.*, vol. 56, no. 3, pp. 476–488 (2014).

[169] J. D. Lee and K. A. See, Trust in automation: designing for appropriate reliance, *Hum. Factors*, vol. 46, no. 1, pp. 50–80 (2004).

[170] M. Ashoori and J. D. Weisz, In AI we trust? Factors that influence trustworthiness of AI-infused decision-making processes (2019). [Online]. Available at: https://arxiv.org/abs/1912.02675.

[171] B. Israelsen and N. Ahmed, 'Dave...I can assure you ...that it's going to be all right ...' A definition, case for, and survey of algorithmic assurances in human-autonomy trust relationships, *ACM Comput. Surv.*, vol. 51, no. 6, pp. 1–37 (2019).

[172] J. Drozdal et al., Trust in AutoML: exploring information needs for establishing trust in automated machine learning systems (2020). [Online]. Available at: https://arxiv.org/abs/2001.06509.

[173] E. Toreini, M. Aitken, K. Coopamootoo, K. Elliott, C. G. Zelaya, and A. van Moorsel, The relationship between trust in AI and trustworthy machine learning technologies (2020). [Online]. Available at: https://arxiv.org/abs/1912.00782.

[174] S. Mohseni, N. Zarei, and E. D. Ragan, A multidisciplinary survey and framework for design and evaluation of explainable AI systems (2020). [Online]. Available at: https://arxiv.org/abs/1811.11839.

[175] D. C. Dennett, *The Intentional Stance*. Cambridge, MA, USA: MIT Press (1996).

[176] P. Cofta, Trusting the IoT: there is more to trust than trustworthiness, in *IFIP International Conference on Trust Management*, pp. 98–107 (2019).

[177] M. Desai et al., Effects of changing reliability on trust of robot systems, in *International Conference on Human-Robot Interaction (HRI)*, pp. 73–80 (2012).

[178] A. Freedy, E. DeVisser, G. Weltman, and N. Coeyman, Measurement of trust in human-robot collaboration, in *International Symposium on Collaborative Technologies and Systems*, pp. 106–114 (2007).

[179] R. C. Arkin, J. Borenstein, and A. R. Wagner, Competing ethical frameworks mediated by moral emotions in HRI: motivations, background, and approach, in *ICRES 2019: International Conference on Robot Ethics and Standards*, London, UK (2019).

[180] K. Weitz, D. Schiller, R. Schlagowski, T. Huber, and E. Andre, 'Do you trust me?': Increasing user-trust by integrating virtual agents in explainable AI interaction design, in *International Conference on Intelligent Virtual Agents*, pp. 7–9 (2019).

[181] K. M. Lee, Presence, explicated, *Commun. Theory*, vol. 14, no. 1, pp. 27–50 (2004).

[182] W. A. Bainbridge, J. W. Hart, E. S. Kim, and B. Scassellati, The benefits of interactions with physically present robots over video-displayed agents, *Int. J. Soc. Robot.*, vol. 3, pp. 41–52 (2011).

[183] P. Andras et al., Trusting intelligent machines: deepening trust within socio-technical systems, *IEEE Technol. Soc. Mag.*, vol. 37, no. 4, pp. 76–83 (2018).

[184] K. Lazanyi, Readiness for artificial intelligence, in *International Symposium on Intelligent Systems and Informatics (SISY)*, pp. 235–238 (2018).

[185] M. D. Zeiler, D. Krishnan, G. W. Taylor, and R. Fergus, Deconvolutional networks (2010), doi: 10.1109/CVPR.2010.5539957.

[186] K. Simonyan, A. Vedaldi, and A. Zisserman, Deep inside convolutional networks: visualising image classification models and saliency maps, *arXiv1312.6034 [cs]* (2013).

[187] J. T. Springenberg, A. Dosovitskiy, T. Brox, and M. Riedmiller, Striving for simplicity: the all convolutional net, *arXiv Prepr. arXiv1412.6806* (2014).

[188] M. D. Zeiler, G. W. Taylor, and R. Fergus, Adaptive deconvolutional networks for mid and high level feature learning (2011), doi: 10.1109/ICCV.2011.6126474.

[189] W. Samek, A. Binder, G. Montavon, S. Lapuschkin, and K. R. Müller, Evaluating the visualization of what a deep neural network has learned, *IEEE Trans. Neural Networks Learn. Syst.* (2017), doi: 10.1109/TNNLS.2016.2599820.

[190] J. Adebayo, J. Gilmer, I. Goodfellow, and B. Kim, Local explanation methods for deep neural networks lack sensitivity to parameter values, *arXiv:1810.03307* (2018).

[191] P. J. Kindermans et al., The (un)reliability of saliency methods, in *Lecture Notes in Computer Science (including subseries Lecture Notes in Artificial Intelligence and Lecture Notes in Bioinformatics)* (2019).

[192] A. Ghorbani, A. Abid, and J. Zou, Interpretation of neural networks is fragile (2019), doi: 10.1609/aaai.v33i01.33013681.

[193] S. Wang, T. Zhou, and J. A. Bilmes, Bias also matters: bias attribution for deep neural network explanation, in *Proceedings of the 36th International Conference on Machine Learning*, Long Beach, California (2019).

[194] M. Sundararajan, A. Taly, and Q. Yan, Axiomatic attribution for deep networks, in *Proceedings of the 34th International Conference on Machine Learning*, Sydney, Australia (2017).

[195] G. Montavon, S. Lapuschkin, A. Binder, W. Samek, and K. R. Müller, Explaining non-linear classification decisions with deep Taylor decomposition, *Pattern Recognit.* (2017), doi: 10.1016/j.patcog.2016.11.008.

[196] J. Adebayo, J. Gilmer, M. Muelly, I. Goodfellow, M. Hardt, and B. Kim, Sanity checks for saliency maps, *NeurIPS* (2018).

[197] C. Szegedy et al., Going deeper with convolutions, in *Proceedings of the IEEE Conference on Computer Vision and Pattern Recognition*, pp. 1–9 (2015).

[198] F. Wang and C. Rudin, Falling rule lists, in *Proceedings of the 18th International Conference on Artificial Intelligence and Statistics (AISTATS) 2015*, San Diego, CA, USA (2015).

[199] S. Mohseni and E. D. Ragan, A human-grounded evaluation benchmark for local explanations of machine learning, *arXiv.* (2018).

[200] H. J. P. Weerts, W. Van Ipenburg, and M. Pechenizkiy, A human-grounded evaluation of SHAP for alert processing, *arXiv.* (2019).

[201] D. Martens, B. Baesens, T. Van Gestel, and J. Vanthienen, Comprehensible credit scoring models using rule extraction from support vector machines, *Eur. J. Oper. Res.* (2007), doi: 10.1016/j.ejor.2006.04.051.

[202] W. Chen, M. Zhang, Y. Zhang, and X. Duan, Exploiting meta features for dependency parsing and part-of-speech tagging, *Artif. Intell.* (2016), doi: 10.1016/j.artint.2015.09.002.

[203] M. Sushil, S. Šuster, and W. Daelemans, Rule induction for global explanation of trained models, *arXiv.* (2018), doi: 10.18653/v1/w18-5411.

[204] Y. Wei, M. C. Chang, Y. Ying, S. N. Lim, and S. Lyu, Explain black-box image classifications using superpixel-based interpretation (2018), doi: 10.1109/ICPR.2018.8546302.

[205] D. Alvarez-Melis and T. S. Jaakkola, Towards robust interpretability with self-explaining neural networks, *arXiv:1806.07538* (2018).

[206] R. Seising, *The Fuzzification of Systems: The Genesis of Fuzzy Set Theory and Its Initial Applications - Developments Up to the 1970s.* Berlin, Germany: Springer (2007).

[207] E. Turunen, Algebraic structures in fuzzy logic, *Fuzzy Sets Syst.*, vol. 52, pp. 181–188 (1992).

[208] L. A. Zadeh, R. E. Kalman, and N. DeClaris, *Aspects of Network and System Theory* (1971).

[209] L. A. Zadeh, A rationale for fuzzy control, *J. Dyn. Syst. Meas. Control. Trans. ASME* (1972), doi: 10.1115/1.3426540.

[210] L. A. Zadeh, Outline of a new approach to the analysis of complex systems and decision processes, *IEEE Trans. Syst. Man Cybern.* (1973), doi: 10.1109/TSMC.1973.5408575.

[211] L. A. Zadeh, On the analysis of large-scale systems, in H. Gottinger (ed.), *Systems Approaches and Environment Problems*, Gottingen: Vandenhoeck and Ruprecht, pp. 23–37 (1974).

[212] L. A. Zadeh, The concept of a linguistic variable and its application to approximate reasoning-I, *Inf. Sci. (Ny)* (1975), doi: 10.1016/0020-0255(75)90036-5.

[213] L. A. Zadeh, Quantitative fuzzy semantics, *Inf. Sci. (Ny)*, vol. 3, no. 2, pp. 159–176 (1971).

[214] E. H. Mamdani and S. Assilian, An experiment in linguistic synthesis with a fuzzy logic controller, *Int. J. Man. Mach. Stud.* (1975), doi: 10.1016/S0020-7373(75)80002-2.

[215] E. H. Mamdani, Application of fuzzy algorithms for control of simple dynamic plant, *Proc. Inst. Electr. Eng.* (1974), doi: 10.1049/piee.1974.0328.

[216] E. H. Mamdani, Advances in the linguistic synthesis of fuzzy controllers, *Int. J. Man. Mach. Stud.* (1976), doi: 10.1016/S0020-7373(76)80028-4.

[217] L. P. Holmblad and J. J. Ostergaard, Control of a cement kiln by fuzzy logic, in M. M. Gupta and E. Sanchez (eds.), *Fuzzy Information and Decision Processes*, Amsterdam: North-Holland, pp. 389–399 (1982), doi: 10.1016/b978-1-4832-1450-4.50039-0.

[218] C. P. Pappis and E. H. Mamdani, A fuzzy logic controller for a traffic junction, *IEEE Trans. Syst. Man Cybern.* (1977), doi: 10.1109/TSMC.1977.4309605.

[219] M. J. Flanagan, On the application of approximate reasoning to control of the activated sludge process, *J. Environ. Sci. Heal. Part B Pestic. Food Contam. Agric. Wastes* (1980), doi: 10.1109/JACC.1980.4232059.

[220] M. Togai and H. Watanabe, A VLSI implementation of a fuzzy-inference engine: toward an expert system on a chip, *Inf. Sci. (Ny)* (1986), doi: 10.1016/0020-0255(86)90017-4.

[221] R. M. Tong, An annotated bibliography of fuzzy control, *Ind. Appl. Fuzzy Control*, pp. 249–269 (1985).

[222] S. Yasunobu, S. Miyamoto, and H. Ihara, Fuzzy control for automatic train operation system, *IFAC Proc.* (1983), doi: 10.1016/s1474-6670(17)62539-4.

[223] S. Miyamoto, Predictive fuzzy control and its application to automatic train operation systems, *First Int. Conf. Fuzzy Inf. Process.*, pp. 22–26 (1984).

[224] S. Yasunobu, Automatic train operation by predictive fuzzy control, *Ind. Appl. Fuzzy Control* (1985).

[225] P. D. Hansen, Techniques for process control, in *Process/Industrial Instruments and Controls Handbook*, pp. 2.30–2.56 (1999).

[226] B. R. Gaines and J. H. Andreae, A learning machine in the context of the general control problem, in *IFAC Congress*, pp. 342–349 (1966).

[227] G. J. Klir and B. Yuan, *Fuzzy Sets and Fuzzy Logic: Theory and Applications.* Upper Saddle River, NJ: Prentice Hall PTR (1995).

[228] T. Takagi and M. Sugeno, Fuzzy identification of systems and its applications to modeling and control, *IEEE Trans. Syst. Man Cybern.* (1985), doi: 10.1109/TSMC.1985.6313399.

[229] K. Tanaka and H. O. Wang, *Fuzzy Control Systems Design and Analysis: A Linear Matrix Inequality Approach.* New York, NY, USA: John Wiley & Sons, Inc. (2001).

[230] O. Cordon, A historical review of evolutionary learning methods for Mamdani-type fuzzy rule-based systems: designing interpretable genetic fuzzy systems, *Int. J. Approx. Reason.*, vol. 52, pp. 894–913 (2011).

[231] J. Durkin, Expert system development tools, in *The Handbook of Applied Expert Systems*, J. Liebowitz (ed.), Boca Raton, FL, USA: CRC Press (1998).

[232] C. L. Forgy, Rete: a fast algorithm for the many pattern/many object pattern match problem, *Artif. Intell.*, vol. 19, pp. 17–37 (1982).

[233] S. Russell and P. Norvig, *Artificial Intelligence: A Modern Approach*, 4th edn. Hoboken, NJ, USA: Pearson Education (2020).

[234] J. Pan, G. N. DeSouza, and A. C. Kak, FuzzyShell: a large-scale expert system shell using fuzzy logic for uncertainty reasoning, *IEEE Trans. Fuzzy Syst.*, vol. 6, no. 4, pp. 563–581 (1998).

[235] M. Fieschi, M. Joubert, D. Fieschi, and M. Roux, SPHINX: a system for computer-aided diagnosis, *Methods Inf. Med.*, vol. 21, no. 3, pp. 143–148 (1982).

[236] J.-C. Buisson, H. Farreny, and H. Prade, The development of a medical expert system and the treatment of imprecision in the framework of possibility theory, *Inf. Sci. (Ny)*, vol. 37, no. 1–3, pp. 211–226 (1985).

[237] K.-P. Adlassnig, G. Kolarz, and W. Scheithauer, Present state of the medical expert system CADIAG-2, *Methods Inf. Med.*, vol. 24, no. 1, pp. 13–20 (1985).

[238] L. A. Zadeh, The role of fuzzy logic in the management of uncertainty in expert systems, *Fuzzy Sets Syst.*, vol. 11, no. 1–3, pp. 199–227 (1983).

[239] L. A. Zadeh, Syllogistic reasoning in fuzzy logic and its application to usuality and reasoning with dispositions, *IEEE Trans. Syst. Man Cybern.*, vol. 15, no. 6, pp. 754–763 (1985).

[240] C. Negoita, *Expert Systems and Fuzzy Systems.* Menlo Park, CA, USA: Benjamin-Cummings Pub. Co. (1985).

[241] J. J. Buckley, W. Siler, and D. Tucker, A fuzzy expert system, *Fuzzy Sets Syst.*, vol. 20, pp. 1–16 (1986).

[242] J. J. Buckley and D. Tucker, Second generation fuzzy expert system, *Fuzzy Sets Syst.*, vol. 31, pp. 271–284 (1989).

[243] P. Bonissone, S. S. Gans, and K. S. Decker, RUM: a layered architecture for reasoning with uncertainty, in *Proc. IJCAI*, pp. 891–898 (1987).

[244] K. S. Leung, W. S. F. Wong, and W. Lam, Applications of a novel fuzzy expert system shell, *Expert Syst.*, vol. 6, no. 1, pp. 2–10 (1989).

[245] L. O. Hall, Rule chaining in fuzzy expert systems, *IEEE Trans. Fuzzy Syst.*, vol. 9, no. 6, pp. 822–828 (2001).

[246] C. Igel and K.-H. Temme, The chaining syllogism in fuzzy logic, *IEEE Trans. Fuzzy Syst.*, vol. 12, no. 6, pp. 849–853 (2004).

[247] J. Pan, G. N. DeSouza, and A. C. Kak, FuzzyShell: a large-scale expert system shell using fuzzy logic for uncertainty reasoning, *IEEE Trans. Fuzzy Syst.*, vol. 6, no. 4, pp. 563–581 (1998).

[248] D. Dubois and H. Prade, Fuzzy relation equations and causal reasoning, *Fuzzy Sets Syst.*, vol. 75, no. 2, pp. 119–134 (1995).

[249] L. J. Mazlack, Imperfect causality, *Fundam. Inform.*, vol. 59, no. 2–3, pp. 191–201 (2004).

[250] J.-S. R. Jang, C.-T. Sun, and E. Mizutani, *Neuro-Fuzzy and Soft Computing: A Computational Approach to Learning and Machine Intelligence.* Upper Saddle River, New Jersey: Prentice Hall (1997).

[251] S. C. Lee and E. T. Lee, Fuzzy sets and neural networks, *J. Cybern.*, vol. 4, pp. 83–103 (1974).

[252] J. M. Keller and D. J. Hunt, Incorporating fuzzy membership functions into the perceptron algorithm, *IEEE Trans. Pattern Anal. Mach. Intell.*, vol. 7, no. 6, pp. 693–699 (1985).

[253] L.-X. Wang and J. M. Mendel, Generating fuzzy rules by learning from examples, *IEEE Trans. Syst. Man Cybern.*, vol. 22, no. 6, pp. 1414–1427 (1992).

[254] H. Takagi, Fusion technology of fuzzy theory and neural networks - survey and future directions, in *Proc. Int. Conf. on Fuzzy Logic and Neural Networks*, pp. 13–26 (1990).

[255] Y. Hayashi, J. J. Buckley, and E. Czogala, Fuzzy neural network with fuzzy signals and weights, *Int. J. Intell. Syst.*, vol. 8, pp. 527–537 (1993).

[256] S. K. Pal and S. Mitra, Multilayer perceptron, fuzzy sets, and classification, *IEEE Trans. Neural Networks* (1992), doi: 10.1109/72.159058.

[257] J. S. R. Jang, ANFIS: adaptive-network-based fuzzy inference system, *IEEE Trans. Syst. Man Cybern.* (1993), doi: 10.1109/21.256541.

[258] P. V. de C. Souza, Fuzzy neural networks and neuro-fuzzy networks: a review the main techniques and applications used in the literature, *Appl. Soft Comput.*, vol. 92, p. 26 (2020).

[259] M. Valenzuela-Rendón, The fuzzy classifier system: motivations and first results, in *Int. Conf. Parallel Problem Solving from Nature*, pp. 330–334 (1991).

[260] P. Thrift, Fuzzy logic synthesis with genetic algorithms, in *Int. Conf. on Genetic Algorithms*, pp. 509–513 (1991).

[261] D. T. Pham and D. Karaboga, Optimum design of fuzzy logic controllers using genetic algorithms, *J. Syst. Eng.*, vol. 1, pp. 114–118 (1991).

[262] A. Botta, B. Lazzerini, F. Marcelloni, and D. C. Stefanescu, Context adaptation of fuzzy systems through a multi-objective evolutionary approach based on a novel interpretability index, *Soft Comput.*, vol. 13, no. 5, pp. 437–449 (2009).

[263] H. Ishibuchi and T. Yamamoto, "Fuzzy rule selection by multi-objective genetic local search algorithms and rule evaluation measures in data mining, *Fuzzy Sets Syst.*, vol. 141, no. 1, pp. 59–88 (2004).

[264] M. Cococcioni, P. Ducange, B. Lazzerini, and F. Marcelloni, A Pareto-based multi-objective evolutionary approach to the identification of Mamdani fuzzy systems, *Soft Comput.*, vol. 11, no. 11, pp. 1013–1031 (2007).

[265] R. Alcala, P. Ducange, F. Herrera, B. Lazzerini, and F. Marcelloni, A multiobjective evolutionary approach to concurrently learn rule and data bases of linguistic fuzzy-rule-based systems, *IEEE Trans. Fuzzy Syst.*, vol. 17, no. 5, pp. 1106–1122 (2009).

[266] A. Sarabakha and E. Kayacan, Online deep fuzzy learning for control of nonlinear systems using expert knowledge, *IEEE Trans. Fuzzy Syst.* (2020), doi: 10.1109/TFUZZ.2019.2936787.

[267] C. L. P. Chen, C. Y. Zhang, L. Chen, and M. Gan, Fuzzy restricted boltzmann machine for the enhancement of deep learning, *IEEE Trans. Fuzzy Syst.* (2015), doi: 10.1109/TFUZZ.2015.2406889.

[268] S. Feng, C. L. Philip Chen, and C. Y. Zhang, A fuzzy deep model based on fuzzy restricted Boltzmann machines for high-dimensional data classification, *IEEE Trans. Fuzzy Syst.* (2020), doi: 10.1109/TFUZZ.2019.2902111.

[269] S. Zhang, Z. Sun, M. Wang, J. Long, Y. Bai, and C. Li, deep fuzzy echo state networks for machinery fault diagnosis, *IEEE Trans. Fuzzy Syst.* (2020), doi: 10.1109/TFUZZ.2019.2914617.

[270] L. X. Wang, Fast training algorithms for deep convolutional fuzzy systems with application to stock index prediction, *IEEE Trans. Fuzzy Syst.* (2020), doi: 10.1109/TFUZZ.2019.2930488.

[271] Q. Feng, L. Chen, C. L. Philip Chen, and L. Guo, Deep fuzzy clustering: a representation learning approach, *IEEE Trans. Fuzzy Syst.* (2020), doi: 10.1109/TFUZZ.2020.2966173.

[272] P. Hurtik, V. Molek, and J. Hula, Data preprocessing technique for neural networks based on image represented by a fuzzy function, *IEEE Trans. Fuzzy Syst.* (2020), doi: 10.1109/TFUZZ.2019.2911494.

[273] L. Chen, W. Su, M. Wu, W. Pedrycz, and K. Hirota, A fuzzy deep neural network with sparse autoencoder for emotional intention understanding in human-robot interaction, *IEEE Trans. Fuzzy Syst.* (2020), doi: 10.1109/TFUZZ.2020.2966167.

[274] V. John, S. Mita, Z. Liu, and B. Qi, Pedestrian detection in thermal images using adaptive fuzzy C-means clustering and convolutional neural networks (2015), doi: 10.1109/MVA. 2015.7153177.

[275] C. Guan, S. Wang, and A. W.-C. Liew, Lip image segmentation based on a fuzzy convolutional neural network, *IEEE Trans. Fuzzy Syst.* (2019).

[276] Y. Wang et al., Deep fuzzy tree for large-scale hierarchical visual classification, *IEEE Trans. Fuzzy Syst.* (2020), doi: 10.1109/TFUZZ.2019.2936801.

[277] Y.-J. Zheng, W.-G. Sheng, X.-M. Sun, and S.-Y. Chen, Airline passenger profiling based on fuzzy deep machine learning, *IEEE Trans. Neural Networks Learn. Syst.* (2016), doi: 10.1109/TNNLS.2016.2609437.

[278] R. R. Yager, Pythagorean membership grades in multicriteria decision making, *IEEE Trans. Fuzzy Syst.* (2014), doi: 10.1109/TFUZZ.2013.2278989.

[279] A. K. Shukla, T. Seth, and P. K. Muhuri, Interval type-2 fuzzy sets for enhanced learning in deep belief networks (2017), doi: 10.1109/FUZZ-IEEE.2017.8015638.

[280] Y. J. Zheng, S. Y. Chen, Y. Xue, and J. Y. Xue, A pythagorean-type fuzzy deep denoising autoencoder for industrial accident early warning, *IEEE Trans. Fuzzy Syst.* (2017), doi: 10.1109/ TFUZZ.2017.2738605.

[281] A. I. Aviles, S. M. Alsaleh, E. Montseny, P. Sobrevilla, and A. Casals, A deep-neuro-fuzzy approach for estimating the interaction forces in robotic surgery (2016), doi: 10.1109/FUZZ-IEEE.2016.7737812.

[282] M. A. Islam, D. T. Anderson, A. J. Pinar, T. C. Havens, G. Scott, and J. M. Keller, Enabling explainable fusion in deep learning with fuzzy integral neural networks, *IEEE Trans. Fuzzy Syst.* (2020), doi: 10.1109/TFUZZ.2019.2917124.

[283] S. Rajurkar and N. K. Verma, Developing deep fuzzy network with Takagi Sugeno fuzzy inference system (2017), doi: 10.1109/FUZZ-IEEE.2017.8015718.

[284] T. Zhou, F. L. Chung, and S. Wang, Deep TSK fuzzy classifier with stacked generalization and triply concise interpretability guarantee for large data, *IEEE Trans. Fuzzy Syst.* (2017), doi: 10.1109/TFUZZ.2016.2604003.

[285] S. Gu, F. L. Chung, and S. Wang, A novel deep fuzzy classifier by stacking adversarial interpretable TSK fuzzy sub-classifiers with smooth gradient information, *IEEE Trans. Fuzzy Syst.* (2020), doi: 10.1109/TFUZZ.2019.2919481.

[286] W. R. Tan, C. S. Chan, H. E. Aguirre, and K. Tanaka, Fuzzy qualitative deep compression network, *Neurocomputing* (2017), doi: 10.1016/j.neucom.2017.04.023.

[287] R. Jafari, S. Razvarz, and A. Gegov, Neural network approach to solving fuzzy nonlinear equations using Z-numbers, *IEEE Trans. Fuzzy Syst.* (2020), doi: 10.1109/TFUZZ.2019.2940919.

[288] Y. De la Rosa, Erick, Wen, Data-driven fuzzy modeling using deep learning, *arXiv Prepr. arXiv1702.07076* (2017).

[289] Z. Zhang, M. Huang, S. Liu, B. Xiao, and T. S. Durrani, Fuzzy multilayer clustering and fuzzy label regularization for unsupervised person reidentification, *IEEE Trans. Fuzzy Syst.* (2020), doi: 10.1109/TFUZZ.2019.2914626.

[290] M. Yeganejou and S. Dick, Classification via deep fuzzy c-means clustering (2018), doi: 10.1109/FUZZ-IEEE.2018.8491461.

[291] M. Yeganejou, S. Dick, and J. Miller, Interpretable deep convolutional fuzzy classifier, *IEEE Trans. Fuzzy Syst.* (2020), doi: 10.1109/TFUZZ.2019.2946520.

https://doi.org/10.1142/9789811247323_0002

Chapter 2

Fundamentals of Fuzzy Set Theory

Fernando Gomide

School of Electrical and Computer Engineering,
University of Campinas, 13083-852 Campinas, SP, Brazil
gomide@unicamp.br

The goal of this chapter is to offer a comprehensive, systematic, updated, and self-contained tutorial-like introduction to fuzzy set theory. The notions and concepts addressed here cover the spectrum that contains, we believe, the material deemed relevant for computational intelligence and intelligent systems theory and applications. It starts by reviewing the very basic idea of sets, introduces the notion of a fuzzy set, and gives the main insights and interpretations to help intuition. It proceeds with characterization of fuzzy sets, operations and their generalizations, information granulation and its key constituents, and ends discussing the issue of linguistic approximation and extensions of fuzzy sets.

2.1. Sets

A set is a fundamental concept in mathematics and science. Classically a set is defined as "any multiplicity which can be thought of as one ... any totality of definite elements which can be bound up into a whole by means of a law" or being more descriptive "any collection into a whole M of definite and separate objects m of our intuition or our thought" [1, 2].

Intuitively, a set may be viewed as the class M of all objects m satisfying any particular property or defining condition. Alternatively, a set can be characterized by an assignment scheme to define the objects of a domain that satisfy the intended property. For instance, an indicator function or a characteristic function is a function defined on a domain $\mathbf{X}$ that indicates membership of an object of $\mathbf{X}$ in a set A on $\mathbf{X}$, having the value 1 for all elements of A and the value 0 for all elements of $\mathbf{X}$ not in A. The domain can be either continuous or discrete. For instance, the closed interval [3, 7] constitutes a continuous and bounded domain whereas the set $\mathbf{N} = \{0, 1, 2, \ldots\}$ of natural numbers is discrete and countable, but with no bound.

In general, a characteristic function of a set A defined in $\mathbf{X}$ assumes the following form:

$$A(x) = \begin{cases} 1, & \text{if } x \in A \\ 0, & \text{if } x \notin A \end{cases} \tag{2.1}$$

The empty set $\varnothing$ has a characteristic function that is identically equal to zero, $\varnothing(x) = 0$ for all x in $\mathbf{X}$. The domain $\mathbf{X}$ itself has a characteristic function that is identically equal to one, $\mathbf{X}(x) = 1$ for all x in $\mathbf{X}$. Also, a singleton $A = \{a\}$, a set with only a single element, has the characteristic function $A(x) = 1$ if $x = a$ and $A(x) = 0$ otherwise.

Characteristic functions $A{:}\mathbf{X} \to \{0, 1\}$ induce a constraint with well-defined boundaries on the elements of the domain $\mathbf{X}$ that can be assigned to a set A.

2.2. Fuzzy Sets

The fundamental idea of a fuzzy set is to relax the rigid boundaries of the constraints induced by characteristic functions by admitting intermediate values of class membership. The idea is to allow assignments of intermediate values between 0 and 1 to quantify our perception on how compatible the objects of a domain are with the class, with 0 meaning incompatibility, complete exclusion, and 1 compatibility, complete membership. Membership values thus express the degrees to which each object of a domain is compatible with the properties distinctive to the class. Intermediate membership values mean that no natural threshold exists and that elements of a universe can be a member of a class and, at the same time, belong to other classes with different degrees. Gradual, less strict membership degrees are the essence of fuzzy sets.

Formally, a fuzzy set A is described by a membership function mapping the elements of a domain $\mathbf{X}$ to the unit interval [0,1] [3].

$$A: \mathbf{X} \to [0, 1] \tag{2.2}$$

Membership functions fully define fuzzy sets. Membership functions generalize characteristic functions in the same way as fuzzy sets generalize sets. Fuzzy sets can be also seen as a set of ordered pairs of the form $\{x, A(x)\}$, where x is an object of $\mathbf{X}$ and $A(x)$ is its corresponding degree of membership. For a finite domain $\mathbf{X} = \{x_1, x_2, \ldots, x_n\}$, A can be represented by a n-dimensional vector $A = (a_1, a_2, \ldots, a_n)$ with each component $a_i = A(x_i)$.

Being more illustrative, we may view fuzzy sets as elastic constraints imposed on the elements of a universe. Fuzzy sets deal primarily with the concepts of elasticity, graduality, or absence of sharply defined boundaries. In contrast, sets are concerned with rigid boundaries, lack of graded belongingness, and sharp binary constraints. Gradual membership means that no natural boundary exists and that some elements

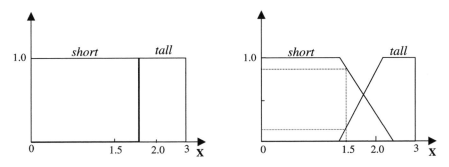

Figure 2.1: Two-valued membership in characteristic functions (sets) and gradual membership represented by membership functions (fuzzy sets).

of the domain can, contrary to sets, coexist (belong) to different fuzzy sets with different degrees of membership. For instance, in Figure 2.1 (left), $x_1 = 1.5$ belongs to the category of *short* people, and $x_2 = 2.0$ belongs to the category of *tall* people, but in Figure 2.1 (right), x_1 simultaneously is 0.8 *short* and 0.2 *tall*, and x_2 simultaneously is 0.4 *short* and 0.8 *tall*.

2.2.1. *Interpretation of Fuzzy Sets*

In fuzzy set theory, fuzziness has a precise meaning. Fuzziness primarily means lack of precise boundaries of a collection of objects and, as such, it is a manifestation of imprecision and a particular type of uncertainty.

First, it is worth noting that fuzziness is both conceptually and formally different from the fundamental concept of probability. In general, it is difficult to foresee the result of tossing a fair coin as it is impossible to know if either head or tail will occur for certain. We may, at most, say that there is a 50% chance to have a head or tail, but as soon as the coin falls, uncertainty vanishes. On the contrary, when we say that a person is tall we are not being precise, and imprecision remains independently of any event. Formally, probability is a set function, a mapping whose universe is a set of subsets of a domain. In contrast, fuzzy sets are membership functions, mappings from some given universe of discourse to the unit interval.

Secondly, fuzziness, generality, and ambiguity are distinct notions. A notion is general when it applies to a multiplicity of objects and keeps only a common essential property. An ambiguous notion stands for several unrelated objects. Therefore, from this point of view, fuzziness means neither generality nor ambiguity and applications of fuzzy sets exclude these categories. Fuzzy set theory assumes that the universe is well defined and has its elements assigned to classes by means of a numerical scale.

Applications of fuzzy sets in areas such as data analysis, reasoning under uncertainty, and decision-making suggest different interpretations of membership grades in terms of similarity, uncertainty, and preference [4, 5]. Membership value

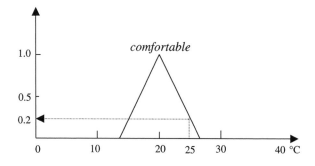

Figure 2.2:   Membership function for a fuzzy set of *comfortable* temperature.

$A(x)$ from the point of view of similarity means the degree of compatibility of an element $x \in \mathbf{X}$ with representative elements of A. This is the primary and most intuitive interpretation of a fuzzy set, one that is particularly suitable for data analysis. An example is the case when we question on how to qualify an environment as *comfortable* when we know that the current temperature is $25°$C. Such quantification is a matter of degree. For instance, assuming a domain $\mathbf{X} = [0, 40]$ and choosing $20°$C as representative of *comfortable* temperature, we note that $25°$C is comfortable to the degree of 0.2 (Figure 2.2). In the example, we have adopted piecewise linearly decreasing functions of the distance between temperature values and the representative value $20°$C to determine the corresponding membership degree.

Now, assume that the values of a variable x is such that $A(x) > 0$. Then given a value v of $\mathbf{X}$, $A(v)$ expresses a possibility that $x = v$ given that x is in A is all that is known. In this situation, the membership degree of a given tentative value v to the class A reflects the degree of plausibility that this value is the same as the value of x. This idea reflects a type of uncertainty because if the membership degree is high, our confidence about the value of x may still be low, but if the degree is low, then the tentative value may be rejected as an implausible candidate. The variable labeled by the class A is uncontrollable. This allows assignment of fuzzy sets to possibility distributions as suggested in possibility theory [6]. For instance, suppose someone said he felt comfortable in an environment. In this situation, the membership degree of a given tentative temperature value, say $25°$C, reflects the degree of plausibility that this value of temperature is the same as the one under which the individual felt comfortable. Note that the actual value of the temperature value is unknown, but there is no question if that value of temperature did occur or not. Possibility concerns whether an event may occur and to what degree. On the contrary, probability concerns whether an event will occur.

Finally, assume that A reflects a preference on the values of a variable x in $\mathbf{X}$. For instance, x can be a decision variable and fuzzy set A a flexible constraint characterizing feasible values and decision-maker preferences. In this case, $A(v)$

denotes the grade of preference in favor of v as the value of x. This interpretation prevails in fuzzy optimization and decision analysis. For instance, we may be interested in finding a comfortable value of temperature. The membership degree of a candidate temperature value v reflects our degree of satisfaction with the particular temperature value chosen. In this situation, the choice of the value is controllable in the sense that the value being adopted depends on our choice.

2.2.2. Rationale for Membership Functions

Generally speaking, any function $A: \mathbf{X} \rightarrow [0, 1]$ is qualified to serve as a membership function describing the corresponding fuzzy set. In practice, the form of the membership functions should reflect the environment of the problem at hand for which we construct fuzzy sets. They should mirror our perception of the concept to be modeled and used in problem solving, the level of detail we intend to capture, and the context in which the fuzzy sets are going to be used. It is essential to assess the type of fuzzy set from the standpoint of its suitability when handling the design and optimization issues. Keeping these reasons in mind, we review the most commonly used categories of membership functions. All of them are defined in the universe of real numbers, that is $\mathbf{X} = \mathbf{R}$.

Triangular membership function: It is described by piecewise linear segments of the form

$$A(x, a, m, b) = \begin{cases} 0 & \text{if } x \leq a \\ \dfrac{x - a}{m - a} & \text{if } x \in [a, m] \\ \dfrac{b - x}{b - m} & \text{if } x \in [m, b] \\ 0 & \text{if } x \geq b. \end{cases}$$

Using more concise notation, the above expression can be written down in the form $A(x, a, m, b) = \max\{\min[(x - a)/(m - a), (b - x)/(b - m)], 0\}$ (Figure 2.3). The meaning of the parameters is straightforward: m is the modal (typical) value of the fuzzy set while a and b are the lower and upper bounds, respectively. They could be sought as those elements of the domain that delineate the elements belonging to A with nonzero membership degrees.

Triangular fuzzy sets (membership functions) are the simplest possible models of grades of membership as they are fully defined by only three parameters. The semantics of triangular fuzzy sets reflects the knowledge of the typical value of the concept and its spread. The linear change in the membership grades is the simplest possible model of membership one could think of. If the derivative of the

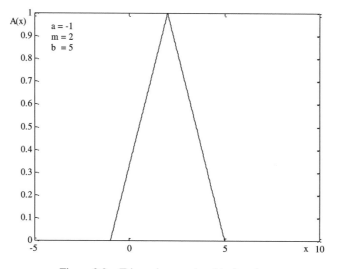

Figure 2.3:   Triangular membership function.

triangular membership function could be sought as a measure of sensitivity of A, then its sensitivity is constant for each of the linear segments of the fuzzy set.

Trapezoidal membership function: A piecewise linear function characterized by four parameters, a, m, n, and b each of which defines one of the four linear parts of the membership function (Figure 2.4). It has the following form:

$$A(x) = \begin{cases} 0 & \text{if } x < a \\ \dfrac{x-a}{m-a} & \text{if } x \in [a, m] \\ 1 & \text{if } x \in [m, n] \\ \dfrac{b-x}{b-n} & \text{if } x \in [n, b] \\ 0 & \text{if } x > b \end{cases}$$

We can rewrite A using an equivalent notation as follows:

$$A(x, a, m, n, b) = \max\{\min\left[(x-a)/(m-a), 1, (b-x)/(b-n)\right], 0\}$$

Γ-membership function. This function has the form

$$A(x) = \begin{cases} 0 & \text{if } x \leq a \\ 1 - e^{-k(x-a)^2} & \text{if } x > a \end{cases} \quad \text{or} \quad A(x) = \begin{cases} 0 & \text{if } x \leq a \\ \dfrac{k(x-a)^2}{1 + k(x-a)^2} & \text{if } x > a, \end{cases}$$

where $k > 0$ (Figure 2.5).

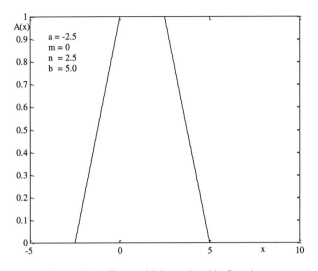

Figure 2.4: Trapezoidal membership function.

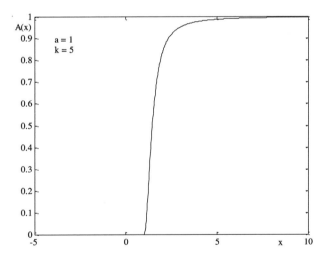

Figure 2.5: Γ-membership function.

S-membership function: The function is expressed by

$$
A(x) = \begin{cases}
0 & \text{if } x \leq a \\
2\left(\dfrac{x-a}{b-a}\right)^2 & \text{if } x \in [a, m] \\
1 - 2\left(\dfrac{x-b}{b-a}\right)^2 & \text{if } x \in [m, b] \\
1 & \text{if } x > b.
\end{cases}
$$

The point $m = (a + b)/2$ is the crossover point of the S-function (Figure 2.6).

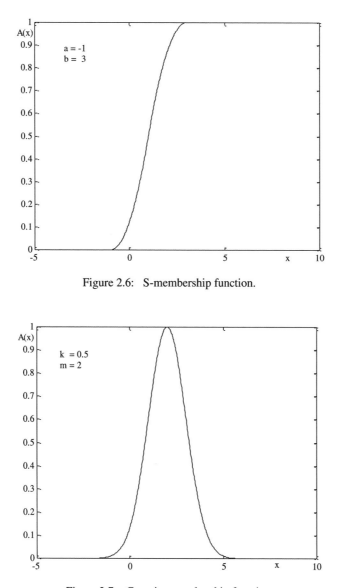

Figure 2.6:   S-membership function.

Figure 2.7:   Gaussian membership function.

Gaussian membership function: This membership function is described by the following relationship:

$$A(x, m, \sigma) = \exp\left(-\frac{(x - m)^2}{\sigma^2}\right).$$

An example of the membership function is shown in Figure 2.7. Gaussian membership functions have two important parameters. The modal value m represents

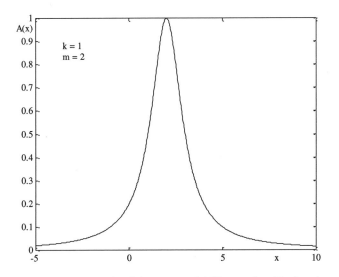

Figure 2.8: An example of the exponential-like membership function.

the typical element of A while σ denotes a spread of A. Higher values of σ corresponds to larger spreads of the fuzzy sets.

Exponential-like membership function: It has the following form (Figure 2.8):

$$A(x) = \frac{1}{1 + k(x - m)^2}, \quad k > 0. \tag{2.3}$$

The spread of the exponential-like membership function increases as the value of k gets lower.

2.3. Characteristics of Fuzzy Sets

Given the diversity of potentially useful and semantically sound membership functions, there are certain common characteristics or descriptors that are conceptually and operationally useful to capture the essence of fuzzy sets. We provide next a list of the descriptors commonly encountered in practice.

Normality: We say that the fuzzy set A is *normal* if its membership function attains 1, that is,

$$\sup_{x \in \mathbf{X}} A(x) = 1 \tag{2.4}$$

If this property does not hold, we call the fuzzy set *subnormal*. An illustration of the corresponding fuzzy set is shown in Figure 2.9. The supremum (sup) in the

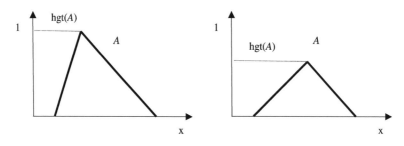

Figure 2.9: Examples of normal and subnormal fuzzy sets.

above expression is also referred to as a height of the fuzzy set A. Thus, the fuzzy set is normal if $hgt(A) = 1$. The normality of A has a simple interpretation: by determining the height of the fuzzy set, we identify an element of the domain whose membership degree is the highest. The value of the height being equal to 1 states that there is at least one element in $\mathbf{X}$ that is fully typical with respect to A and that could be sought as entirely compatible with the semantic category presented by A. A subnormal fuzzy set has height lower than 1, viz. $hgt(A) < 1$, and the degree of typicality of elements in this fuzzy set is somewhat lower (weaker) and we cannot identify any element in $\mathbf{X}$ that is fully compatible with the underlying concept. In practice, while forming a fuzzy set we expect its normality.

Normalization: The normalization, demoted by *Norm*(.), is a mechanism to convert a subnormal nonempty fuzzy set A into its normal counterpart. Dividing the original membership function by its height can do this

$$Norm(A) = \frac{A(x)}{hgt(A)}. \tag{2.5}$$

While the height describes the global property of the membership grades, the following notions offer an interesting characterization of the elements of $\mathbf{X}$ regarding their membership degrees.

Support: Support of a fuzzy set A, *Supp*(A), is a set of all elements of $\mathbf{X}$ with nonzero membership degrees in A

$$Supp(A) = \{x \in \mathbf{X} \mid A(x) > 0\}. \tag{2.6}$$

In other words, support identifies all elements of $\mathbf{X}$ that exhibit some association with the fuzzy set under consideration (by being allocated to A with nonzero membership degrees).

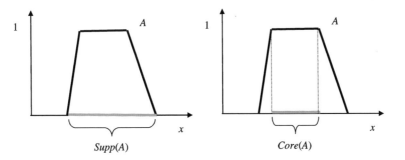

Figure 2.10: Support and core of A.

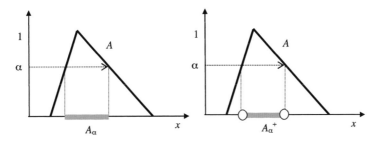

Figure 2.11: Example of α-cut and of strong α-cut.

Core: The core of a fuzzy set A, *Core(A)*, is a set of all elements of the universe that are typical to A: they come with unit membership grades

$$Core(A) = \{x \in \mathbf{X} \mid A(x) = 1\}. \tag{2.7}$$

The support and core are related in the sense that they identify and collect elements belonging to the fuzzy set yet at two different levels of membership. Given the character of the core and support, we note that all elements of the core of A are subsumed by the elements of the support of this fuzzy set. Note that both support and core are sets, not fuzzy sets. In Figure 2.10, they are intervals. We refer to them as the set-based characterizations of fuzzy sets.

While core and support are somewhat extreme, in the sense that they identify the elements of A that exhibit the strongest and the weakest links with A, we may be also interested in characterizing sets of elements that come with some intermediate membership degrees. The notion of α-cut offers here an interesting insight into the nature of fuzzy sets

α-cut: The α-cut of a fuzzy set A, denoted by A_α, is a set consisting of the elements of the domain whose membership values are equal to or exceed a certain threshold

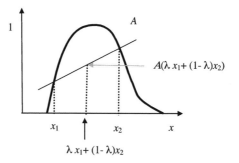

Figure 2.12: Convex fuzzy set A.

level $\alpha \in [0, 1]$. Formally, $A_\alpha = \{x \in \mathbf{X} \,|\, A(x) \geq \alpha\}$. A strong α-cut identifies all elements in $\mathbf{X}$ for which $A_\alpha^+ = \{x \in \mathbf{X} \,|\, A(x) > \alpha\}$. Figure 2.11 illustrates the notion of α-cut and strong α-cut. Both support and core are limit cases of α-cuts and strong α-cuts. From $\alpha = 0$ and the strong α-cut, we arrive at the concept of the support of A. The value $\alpha = 1$ means that the corresponding α-cut is the core of A.

Representation theorem: Any fuzzy set can be viewed as a family of fuzzy sets. This is the essence of a result known as the representation theorem. The representation theorem states that any fuzzy set A can be decomposed into a family of α-cuts

$$A = \bigcup_{\alpha \in [0,1]} \alpha A_\alpha,$$

or, equivalently in terms of membership functions,

$$A(x) = \sup_{\alpha \in [0,1]} \alpha A_\alpha(x).$$

Convexity: We say that a fuzzy set is convex if its membership function satisfies the following condition:

$$A[\lambda x_1 + (1 - \lambda)x_2] \leq \min\,[A(x_1), A(x_2)], \quad \forall x_1, x_2 \in \mathbf{X}, \lambda \in [0, 1]. \qquad (2.8)$$

Relationship (2.8) says that, whenever we choose a point x on a line segment between x_1 and x_2, the point $(x, A(x))$ is always located above or on the line passing through the two points $(x_1, A(x_1))$ and $(x_2, A(x_2))$ (Figure 2.12). Note that the membership function is not a convex function in the conventional sense [7].

The set S is convex if, for all $x_1, x_2 \in S$, then $x = \lambda x_1 + (1 - \lambda)x_2 \in S$ for all $\lambda \in [0,1]$. Convexity means that any line segment identified by any two points in S is contained in S. For instance, intervals of real numbers are convex sets. Therefore, if a fuzzy set is convex, then all of its α-cuts are convex, and conversely, if a fuzzy set has all its α-cuts convex, then it is a convex fuzzy set (Figure 2.13). Thus, we may say that a fuzzy set is convex if all its α-cuts are convex.

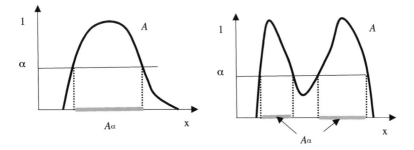

Figure 2.13: Convex and non-convex fuzzy sets.

Fuzzy sets can be characterized by counting their elements and using a single numeric quantity as a descriptor of the count. While in the case of sets this sounds clear, with fuzzy sets we have to consider different membership grades. In the simplest form this counting comes under the name of cardinality.

Cardinality: Given a fuzzy set A defined in a finite or countable universe $\mathbf{X}$, its cardinality, denoted by $Card(A)$ is expressed as the following sum:

$$Card(A) = \sum_{x \in \mathbf{X}} A(x) \tag{2.9}$$

or, alternatively, as the integral

$$Card(A) = \int_{\mathbf{X}} A(x)dx, \tag{2.10}$$

assuming that the integral is well-defined. We also use the alternative notation $Card(A) = |A|$ and refer to it as a sigma count (σ-count).

The cardinality of fuzzy sets is explicitly associated with the concept of granularity of information granules realized in this manner. More descriptively, the more the elements of A we encounter, the higher the level of abstraction supported by A and the lower the granularity of the construct. Higher values of cardinality come with the higher level of abstraction (generalization) and the lower values of granularity (specificity).

So far, we discussed properties of a single fuzzy set. Next, we look at the characterizations of relationships between two fuzzy sets.

Equality: We say that two fuzzy sets A and B defined in $\mathbf{X}$ are equal if and only if their membership functions are identical, that is,

$$A(x) = B(x) \quad \forall x \in \mathbf{X}. \tag{2.11}$$

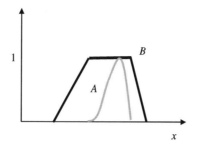

Figure 2.14: Inclusion $A \subset B$.

Inclusion: Fuzzy set A is a subset of B (A is included in B), $A \subseteq B$, if and only if every element of A also is an element of B. This property expressed in terms of membership degrees means that the following inequality is satisfied

$$A(x) \leq B(x) \quad \forall x \in X. \tag{2.12}$$

An illustration of these two relationships in the case of sets is shown in Figure 2.14. To satisfy the relationship of inclusion, we require that the characteristic functions adhere to Eq. (2.12) for all elements of **X**. If the inclusion is not satisfied even for a single point of **X**, the inclusion property does not hold. See Pedrycz and Gomide [8] for an alternative notion of inclusion that captures the idea of the degree of inclusion.

Specificity: Often, we face the issue to quantify how much a single element of a domain could be viewed as a representative of a fuzzy set. If this fuzzy set is a singleton, then

$$A(x) = \begin{cases} 1 & \text{if } x = x_0 \\ 0 & \text{if } x \neq x_0 \end{cases},$$

and there is no hesitation in selecting x_o as the sole representative of A. We say that A is very *specific* and its choice comes with no hesitation. On the other extreme, if A covers the entire domain **X** and has all elements with the membership grade equal to 1, the choice of the only one representative of A becomes more problematic once it is not clear which element to choose. These two extreme situations are shown in Figure 2.15. Intuitively, we see that the specificity is a concept that relates with the cardinality of a set. The higher the cardinality of the set (the more evident its abstraction) is, the lower its specificity.

One approach to quantify the notion of specificity of a fuzzy set is as follows [9]: The specificity of a fuzzy set A defined in **X**, denoted by $Spec(A)$, is a mapping from a family of normal fuzzy sets in **X** into nonnegative numbers such that the following conditions are satisfied (Figure 2.16).

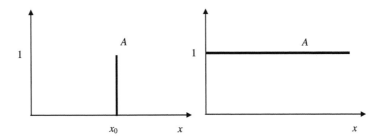

Figure 2.15: Two extreme cases of sets with distinct levels of specificity.

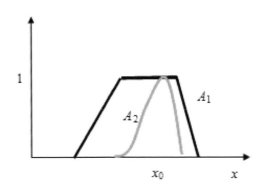

Figure 2.16: Specificity of fuzzy sets: fuzzy set A_1 is less specific than A_2.

1. $Spec(A) = 1$ if there exists only one element x_o of $\mathbf{X}$ for which $A(x_o) = 1$ and $A(x) = 0 \; \forall x \neq x_o$ (A is a singleton);
2. $Spec(A) = 0$ if $A(x) = 0 \; \forall x \in \mathbf{X}$ (A is the empty set $\emptyset$);
3. $Spec(A_1) \leq Spec(A_2)$ if $A_1 \supset A_2$.

A particular instance of specificity measure is [10]

$$Spec(A) = \int_0^{\alpha_{max}} \frac{1}{Card(A_\alpha)} d\alpha,$$

where $\alpha_{max} = hgt(A)$. For finite domains, the integration is replaced by the sum

$$Spec(A) = \sum_{i=1}^{m} \frac{1}{Card(A_{\alpha_i})} \Delta\alpha_i,$$

where $\Delta\alpha_i = \alpha_i - \alpha_{i-1}$ with $\alpha_o = 0$; m stands for the number of the membership grades of A.

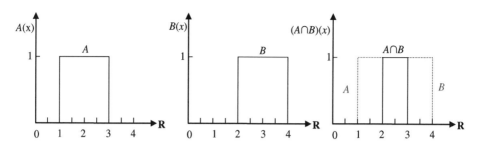

Figure 2.17:   Intersection of sets in terms of their characteristic functions.

2.4. Operations with Fuzzy Sets

As in set theory, we may combine fuzzy sets to produce new fuzzy sets. Generally, combination must possess properties to match intuition, to comply with the semantics of the intended operation, and to be flexible to fit application requirements. Next, we provide an overview of the main operations and their generalizations, interpretations, and examples of realizations.

2.4.1. *Standard Operations on Sets and Fuzzy Sets*

To start, we review the familiar operations of intersection, union, and complement of set theory. Consider two sets $A = \{x \in \mathbf{R} \mid 1 \leq x \leq 3\}$ and $B = \{x \in \mathbf{R} \mid 2 \leq x \leq 4\}$, closed intervals of the real line. Their intersection is the set $A \cap B = \{x \in \mathbf{R} \mid 2 \leq x \leq 3\}$. Figure 2.17 shows the intersection operation in terms of the characteristic functions of A and B. Looking at the values of the characteristic function of $A \cap B$ that results when comparing the individual values of $A(x)$ and $B(x)$ for each $x \in \mathbf{R}$, we note that they correspond to the minimum between the values of $A(x)$ and $B(x)$.

In general, given the characteristic functions of A and B, the characteristic function of their intersection $A \cap B$ is computed using

$$(A \cap B)(x) = \min\left[A(x), B(x)\right] \quad \forall x \in \mathbf{X}, \cdot \tag{2.13}$$

where $(A \cap B)(x)$ denotes the characteristic function of the set $A \cap B$.

The union of sets A and B in terms of the characteristic functions proceeds similarly. If A and B are the same intervals as above, then $A \cup B = \{x \in \mathbf{R} \mid 1 \leq x \leq 4\}$. In this case, the value of the characteristic function of the union is the maximum of corresponding values of the characteristic functions $A(x)$ and $B(x)$ taken pointwise (Figure 2.18).

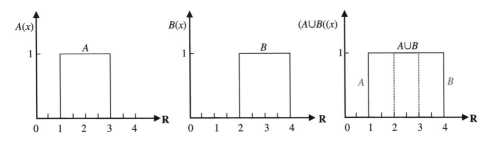

Figure 2.18: Union of two sets in terms of their characteristic functions.

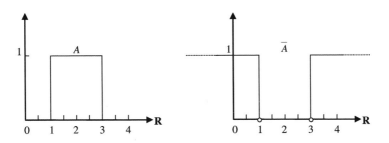

Figure 2.19: Complement of a set in terms of its characteristic function.

Therefore, given the characteristic functions of A and B, we determine the characteristic function of the union as

$$(A \cup B)(x) = \max [A(x), B(x)] \quad \forall x \in \mathbf{X}, \tag{2.14}$$

where $(A \cup B)(x)$ denotes the characteristic function of the set $A \cup B$.

Likewise, as Figure 2.19 suggests, the complement $\overline{A}$ of A, expressed in terms of its characteristic function, is the one-complement of the characteristic function of A. For instance, if $A = \{x \in \mathbf{R} \mid 1 \leq x \leq 3\}$, then $\overline{A} = \{x \in \mathbf{R} \mid 4 < x < 1\}$.

Thus, the characteristic function of the complement of a set A is

$$\overline{A}(x) = 1 - A(x), \quad \forall x \in \mathbf{X}. \tag{2.15}$$

Because sets are particular instances of fuzzy sets, the operations of intersection, union and complement should equally well apply to fuzzy sets. Indeed, when we use membership functions in Eq. (2.2) to (2.15), these formulae serve as standard definitions of intersection, union, and complement of fuzzy sets. Examples are shown in Figure 2.20. Standard set and fuzzy set operations fulfill the properties of Table 2.1.

Figures 2.19 and 2.20 show that the laws of non-contradiction and excluded middle hold for sets, but they do not hold by fuzzy sets with the standard operations (see Table 2.2). Particularly worth noting is a violation of the non-contradiction law

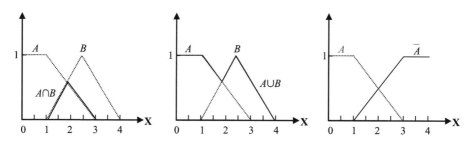

Figure 2.20:　Standard operations on fuzzy sets.

Table 2.1:　Properties of operations with sets and fuzzy sets.

1. Commutativity	$A \cup B = B \cup A$
	$A \cap B = B \cap A$
2. Associativity	$A \cup (B \cup C) = (A \cup B) \cup C$
	$A \cap (B \cap C) = (A \cap B) \cap C$
3. Distributivity	$A \cup (B \cap C) = (A \cup B) \cap (A \cup C)$
	$A \cap (B \cup C) = (A \cap B) \cup (A \cap C)$
4. Idempotency	$A \cup A = A$
	$A \cap A = A$
5. Boundary conditions	$A \cup \phi = A$ and $A \cup \mathbf{X} = \mathbf{X}$
	$A \cap \phi = \phi$ and $A \cap \mathbf{X} = A$
6. Involution	$\overline{\overline{A}} = A$
7. Transitivity	if $A \subset B$ and $B \subset C$ then $A \subset C$

Table 2.2:　Non-contradiction and excluded middle for standard operations.

	Sets	Fuzzy sets
8. Non-contradiction	$A \cap \overline{A} = \phi$	$A \cap \overline{A} \neq \phi$
9. Excluded middle	$A \cup \overline{A} = \mathbf{X}$	$A \cup \overline{A} \neq \mathbf{X}$

once it shows the issue of fuzziness from the point of view of the coexistence of a class and its complement, one of the main source of fuzziness. This coexistence is impossible in set theory and means a contradiction in conventional logic. Interestingly, if we consider a particular subnormal fuzzy set A whose membership function is constant and equal to 0.5 for all elements of the universe, then from Eqs. (2.2)–(2.15) we see that $A = A \cup \overline{A} = A \cap \overline{A} = \overline{A}$, a situation in which there is no way to distinguish the fuzzy set from its complement and any the fuzzy set that results from standard operations with them. The value 0.5 is a crossover point representing a balance between membership and non-membership at which we attain the highest level of fuzziness. The fuzzy set and its complement are indiscernible.

As we will see next, there are types of operations for which non-contradiction and excluded middle are recovered. While for sets these types produce the same result as the standard operators, this is not the case with fuzzy sets. In addition, $A = A \cup \overline{A} = A \cap \overline{A} = \overline{A}$ does not hold for any choice of intersection, union and complement operators.

Operations on fuzzy sets concern manipulation of their membership functions. Therefore, they are domain dependent and different contexts may require their different realizations. For instance, since operations provide ways to combine information, they can be performed differently in image processing, control, and diagnostic systems applications for example. When developing realizations of intersection and union of fuzzy sets it is useful to require commutativity, associativity, monotonicity, and identity. The last requirement (identity) has different forms depending on the operation. For instance, the intersection of any fuzzy set with domain **X** should return the fuzzy set itself. For the union, identity implies that the union of any fuzzy set and an empty fuzzy set returns the fuzzy set itself. Thus, in principle any two place operator $[0, 1] \times [0, 1] \rightarrow [0, 1]$ that satisfies the collection of the requirements can be regarded as a potential candidate to realize the intersection or union of fuzzy sets, identity acting as boundary conditions meaning. In general, idempotency is not strictly required, but the realizations of union and intersection could be idempotent as are the minimum and maximum operators ($\min [a, a] = a$ and $\max [a, a] = a$).

2.4.2. *Triangular Norms and Conorms*

Triangular norms and conorms constitute general forms of operations for intersection and union. While t-norms generalize intersection of fuzzy sets, t-conorms (or s-norms) generalize the union of fuzzy sets [11].

A triangular norm is a two-place operation t: $[0, 1] \times [0, 1] \rightarrow [0, 1]$ that satisfies the following properties:

1. Commutativity: $a \, t \, b = b \, t \, a$
2. Associativity: $a \, t \, (b \, t \, c) = (a \, t \, b) \, t \, c$
3. Monotonicity: if $b \leq c$ then $a \, t \, b \leq a \, t \, c$
4. Boundary conditions: $a \, t \, 1 = a \, a \, t \, 0 = 0$

where $a, b, c \in [0, 1]$.

There is a one-to-one correspondence between the general requirements outlined above and the properties of t-norms. The first three reflect the general character of set operations. Boundary conditions stress the fact all t-norms attain the same values at boundaries of the unit square $[0, 1] \times [0, 1]$. Thus, for sets, any t-norm produces the same result.

Examples of t-norms are

Minimum:　　　　$at_m\, b = \min(a, b) = a \wedge b$

Product:　　　　　$at_p\, b = ab$

Lukasiewicz:　　　$at_l\, b = \max(a + b - 1, 0)$

Drastic product:　$at_d\, b = \begin{cases} a & \text{if } b = 1 \\ b & \text{if } a = 1 \\ 0 & \text{otherwise} \end{cases}$

The minimum (t_m), product (t_p), Lukasiewicz (t_l), and drastic product (t_d) operators are shown in Figure 2.21, with examples of the union of the triangular fuzzy sets on $\mathbf{X} = [0,8]$, $A = (x, 1, 3, 6)$ and $B = (x, 2.5, 5, 7)$.

Triangular conorms are functions s: $[0, 1] \times [0, 1] \rightarrow [0, 1]$ that serve as generic realizations of the union operator on fuzzy sets.

One can show that s: $[0, 1] \times [0, 1] \rightarrow [0, 1]$ is a t-conorm if and only if there exists a t-norm, called dual t-norm, such that for $\forall a, b \in [0,1]$ we have

$$a\,s\,b = 1 - (1 - a)\,t\,(1 - b). \tag{2.16}$$

For the corresponding dual t-norm we have

$$a\,t\,b = 1 - (1 - a)\,s\,(1 - b). \tag{2.17}$$

The duality expressed by Eq. (2.16) and Eq. (2.17) can be viewed as alternative definition of t-conorms. Duality allows us to deduce the properties of t-conorms on the basis of the analogous properties of t-norms. From Eq. (2.16) and Eq. (2.17), we get

$$(1 - a)\,t\,(1 - b) = 1 - a\,s\,b$$

$$(1 - a)\,s\,(1 - b) = 1 - a\,t\,b\,.$$

These two relationships can be expressed symbolically as

$$\overline{A} \cap \overline{B} = \overline{A \cup B}$$

$$\overline{A} \cup \overline{B} = \overline{A \cap B}\,.$$

which are the De Morgan laws. Commonly used t-conorms includes

Maximum:　　　　$a\, s_m\, b = \max(a, b) = a \vee b$

Algebraic sum:　$as_p\, b = a + b - ab$

Lukasiewicz:　　$as_l\, b = \min(a + b, 1)$

Drastic sum:　　$as_d\, b = \begin{cases} a & \text{if } b = 0 \\ b & \text{if } a = 0 \\ 1 & \text{otherwise} \end{cases}$

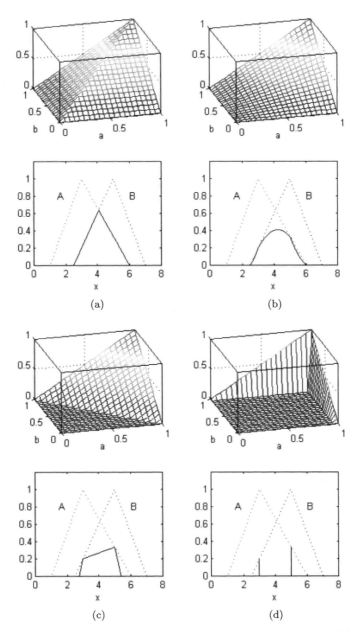

Figure 2.21:   The (a) min, (b) product, (c) Lukasiewicz, (d) drastic product t-norms and the intersection of fuzzy sets A and B.

The maximum (s_m), algebraic sum (s_p), Lukasiewicz (s_l), and drastic sum (s_d) operators are shown in Figure 2.22, which also includes the union of the triangular fuzzy sets on $[0, 8]$, $A = (x, 1, 3, 6)$ and $B = (x, 2.5, 5, 7)$.

The properties $A \cup \overline{A} = \mathbf{X}$ and the excluded middle hold for the drastic sum.

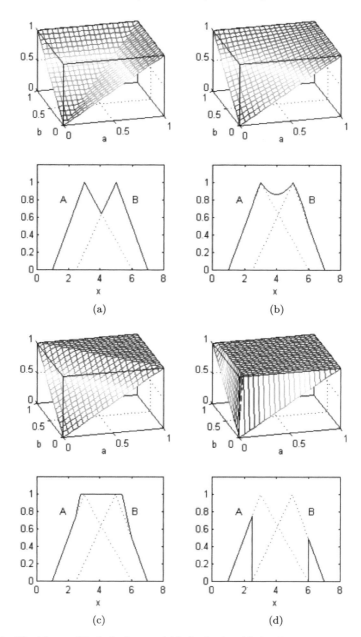

Figure 2.22:   The (a) max, (b) algebraic sum, (c) Lukasiewicz, (d) drastic sum s-norms and the union of fuzzy sets A and B.

2.4.3. *Triangular Norms as Categories of Logical operators*

Fuzzy propositions involve combinations of linguistic statements (or their symbolic representations) such as in

1. temperature is *high* and humidity is *low*;
2. velocity is *low* or noise level is *high*.

These sentences use logical operations $\wedge$ (*and*), $\vee$ (*or*) to combine linguistic statements into propositions. For instance, in the first example we have a conjunction (*and*, $\wedge$) of linguistic statements while in the second there is a disjunction (*or*, $\vee$) of the statements. Given the truth values of each statement, the question is how to determine the truth value of the composite statement or, equivalently, the truth value of the proposition.

Let $truth(P) = p \in [0,1]$, the truth value of proposition P. Thus, $p = 0$ means that the proposition is false while $p = 1$ means that P is true. Intermediate values $p \in (0,1)$ indicate partial truth of the proposition. To compute the truth value of composite propositions coming in the form of $P \wedge Q$, $P \vee Q$ given the truth values p and q of its components, we have to come up with operations that transforms truth values p and q into the corresponding truth values $p \wedge q$ and $p \vee q$. To make these operations meaningful, we require that they satisfy some basic requirements. For instance, it is desirable that $p \wedge q$ and $q \wedge p$ (similarly, $p \vee q$ and $q \vee p$) produce the same truth values. Likewise, we require that the truth value of $(p \wedge q) \wedge r$ is the same as the following combination $p \wedge (q \wedge r)$. In other words, the conjunction and disjunction operations are commutative and associative. In addition, when the truth value of an individual statement increase, the truth values of their combinations also increase. Moreover, if P is absolutely false, $p = 0$, then $P \wedge Q$ should also be false no matter what the truth value of Q is. Furthermore the truth value of $P \vee Q$ should coincide with the truth value of Q. On the other hand, if P is absolutely true, $p = 1$, then the truth value of $P \wedge Q$ should coincide with the truth value of Q, while $P \vee Q$ should also be true. Triangular norms and conorms are the general families of logic connectives that comply with these requirements. Triangular norms provide a general category of logical connectives in the sense that t-norms are used to model conjunction operators while t-conorms serve as models of disjunctions.

Let $L = \{P, Q, \ldots\}$ be a set of single (atomic) statements $P, Q, \ldots$ and truth: $L \rightarrow [0,1]$ a function which assigns truth values $p, q, \ldots \in [0,1]$ to each element of L. Thus, we have

$$truth(P \, and \, Q) \equiv truth(P \wedge Q) \rightarrow p \wedge q = p \, t \, q$$

$$truth(P \, or \, Q) \equiv truth(P \vee Q) \rightarrow p \vee q = p \, s \, q.$$

Table 2.3 shows examples of truth values for $P, Q, P \wedge Q$, and $P \vee Q$, when we selected the min and product t-norms, and the max and algebraic sum t-conorms, respectively. For $p, q \in \{0, 1\}$, the results coincide with the classic interpretation of conjunction and disjunction for any choice of the triangular norm and conorm. The differences are present when $p, q \in (0, 1)$.

Table 2.3: Triangular norms as generalized logical connectives.

p	q	$\min(p, q)$	$\max(p, q)$	pq	$p + q - pq$
1	1	1	1	1	1
1	0	0	1	0	1
0	1	0	1	0	1
0	0	0	0	0	0
0.2	0.5	0.2	0.5	0.1	0.6
0.5	0.8	0.5	0.8	0.4	0.9
0.8	0.7	0.7	0.8	0.56	0.94

A point worth noting here concerns the interpretation of set operations in terms of logical connectives. By being supported by the isomorphism between set theory and propositional two-valued logic, the intersection and union can be identified with conjunction and disjunction, respectively. This can also be realized with triangular norms viewed as general conjunctive and disjunctive connectives within the framework of multivalued logic [7, 12]. Triangular norms also play a key role in different types of fuzzy logic [13].

Given a continuous t-norm t, let us define the following φ operator

$$a \varphi b = sup\{c \in [0, 1] | a \, t \, c \leq b\} \text{ for all } a, b \in [0, 1].$$

This operation can be interpreted as an implication induced by some t-norm,

$$a \varphi b = a \Rightarrow b,$$

and therefore it is, like implication, an inclusion. The operator φ generalizes the classic implication. As Table 2.4 suggests, the two-valued implication arises as a special case of the φ operator in case when $a, b \in \{0, 1\}$.

Note that $a \varphi b$ ($a \Rightarrow b$), returns 1 whenever $a \leq b$. If we interpret these two truth values as membership degrees, we conclude that $a \varphi b$ models a multivalued inclusion relationship.

Table 2.4: φ operator for binary values of its arguments.

a	b	$a \Rightarrow b$	$a \varphi b$
0	0	1	1
0	1	1	1
1	0	0	0
1	1	1	1

2.4.4. *Aggregation of Fuzzy Sets*

Several fuzzy sets can be combined (aggregated) to provide a single fuzzy set forming the result of such an aggregation operation. For instance, when we compute intersection and union of fuzzy sets, the result is a fuzzy set whose membership function captures the information carried by the original fuzzy sets. This fact suggests a general view of aggregation of fuzzy sets as a certain transformations performed on their membership functions. In general, we encounter a wealth of aggregation operations [14–18].

Aggregation operations are n-ary functions $g\colon [0, 1]^n \to [0, 1]$ with the following properties:

1. Monotonicity $\qquad g(x_1, x_2, \ldots, x_n) \geq g(y_1, y_2, \ldots, y_n) \text{ if } x_i > y_j$
2. Boundary conditions $\quad g(0, 0, \ldots\ldots, 0) = 0$

$$g(1, 1, \ldots\ldots, 1) = 1$$

Since triangular norms and conorms are monotonic, associative, satisfy the boundary conditions, they qualify a class of associative aggregation operations whose neutral elements are equal to 1 and 0, respectively. The following operators constitute important alternative examples:

Averaging operations: In addition to monotonicity and the satisfaction of the boundary conditions, averaging operations are idempotent and commutative. They can be described in terms of the generalized mean [19]

$$g(x_1, x_2, \ldots, x_n) = \sqrt[p]{\frac{1}{n}\sum_{i=1}^{n}(x_i)^p} \quad p \in \mathbf{R}, p \neq 0$$

Generalized mean subsumes well-known averages and operators such as

$$p = 1 \quad g(x_1, x_2, \ldots, x_n) = \frac{1}{n}\sum_{i=1}^{n}x_i \qquad \text{arithmetic mean}$$

$$p \to 0 \quad g(x_1, x_2, \ldots, x_n) = \sqrt[n]{\prod_{i=1}^{n}x_i} \qquad \text{geometric mean}$$

$$p = -1 \quad g(x_1, x_2, \ldots, x_n) = \frac{n}{\sum\limits_{i=1}^{n}1/x_i} \qquad \text{harmonic mean}$$

$$p \to -\infty \quad g(x_1, x_2, \ldots, x_n) = \min(x_1, x_2, \ldots, x_n) \qquad \text{minimum}$$

$$p \to \infty \quad g(x_1, x_2, \ldots, x_n) = \max(x_1, x_2, \ldots, x_n) \qquad \text{maximum}$$

The following relationship holds

$$\min(x_1, x_2, \ldots, x_n) \leq g(x_1, x_2, \ldots, x_n) \leq \max(x_1, x_2, \ldots, x_n)$$

Therefore, generalized means ranges over the values not being covered by triangular norms and conorms.

Ordered weighted averaging operations: Ordered weighted averaging (OWA) is a weighted sum whose arguments are ordered [20]. Let $\mathbf{w} = [w_1 w_2 \ldots w_n]^T$, $w_i \in [0, 1]$, be weights such that

$$\sum_{i=1}^{n} w_i = 1.$$

Let a sequence of membership values $\{A(x_i)\}$ be ordered as follows $A(x_1) \leq A(x_2) \leq \ldots \leq A(x_n)$. The family of ordered weighted averaging OWA$(A, \mathbf{w})$ is defined as

$$\text{OWA}(A, \mathbf{w}) = \sum_{i=1}^{n} w_i A(x_i)$$

By choosing certain forms of $\mathbf{w}$, we can show that OWA includes several special cases of aggregation operators mentioned before. For instance:

1. if $\mathbf{w} = [1, 0, \ldots, 0]^T$ then OWA$(A, \mathbf{w}) = \min(A(x_1), A(x_2), \ldots, A(x_n))$
2. if $\mathbf{w} = [0, 0, \ldots, 1]^T$ then OWA$(A, \mathbf{w}) = \max(A(x_1), A(x_2), \ldots, A(x_n))$
3. if $\mathbf{w} = [1/n, \ldots, 1/n]^T$ then OWA$(A, \mathbf{w}) = \dfrac{1}{n} \sum_{i=1}^{n} A(x_1)$ arithmetic mean.

Varying the values of the weights w_i results in aggregation values located in-between between min and max,

$$\min(A(x_1), A(x_2), \ldots, A(x_n)) \leq \text{OWA}(A, \mathbf{w}) \leq \max(A(x_1), A(x_2), \ldots, A(x_n)),$$

and OWA behaves as a compensatory operator, similar to the generalized mean.

Uninorms and nullnorms: Triangular norms provide one of possible ways to aggregate membership grades. By definition, the identity elements are 1 (t-norms) and 0 (t-conorms). When used in the aggregation operations, these elements do not affect the result of aggregation (that is, $a\,t\,1 = a$ and $a\,t\,0 = a$).

Uninorms generalize and unify triangular norms by allowing the identity element to be any value in the unit interval, that is, $e \in (0, 1)$. Uninorms become t-norms when $e = 1$ and t-conorms when $e = 0$. They exhibit some intermediate characteristics for all remaining values of e. Therefore, uninorms share the same properties as triangular norms with the exception of the identity [21].

A uninorm is an operation u: $[0,1] \times [0,1] \rightarrow [0,1]$ that satisfies the following:

1. Commutativity: $a \, u \, b = b \, u \, a$

2. Associativity: $a \, u \, (b \, u \, c) = (a \, u \, b) u \, c$

3. Monotonicity: if $b \leq c$ then $a \, u \, b \leq a \, u \, c$

4. Identity: $a \, u \, e = a, \forall a \in [0,1]$

where $a, b, c \in [0,1]$.

Examples of uninorm include conjunctive u_c and disjunctive u_d forms of uninorms. They can be obtained in terms of a t-norm t and a conorm s as follows:

a) if $(0 \, u \, 1) = 0$, then

$$
a \, u_c \, b =
\begin{cases}
e\left(\dfrac{a}{e}\right) t \left(\dfrac{b}{e}\right) & \text{if } 0 \leq a, b \leq e \\[2ex]
e + (1-e)\left(\dfrac{a-e}{1-e}\right) s \left(\dfrac{b-e}{1-e}\right) & \text{if } e \leq a, b \leq 1 \\[2ex]
\min(a, b) & \text{otherwise}
\end{cases}
$$

b) If $(0 \, u \, 1) = 1$, then

$$
a \, u_d \, b =
\begin{cases}
e\left(\dfrac{a}{e}\right) t \left(\dfrac{b}{e}\right) & \text{if } 0 \leq a, b \leq e \\[2ex]
e + (1-e)\left(\dfrac{a-e}{1-e}\right) s \left(\dfrac{b-e}{1-e}\right) & \text{if } e \leq a, b \leq 1 \\[2ex]
\max(a, b) & \text{otherwise}
\end{cases}
$$

2.5. Fuzzy Relations

Relations represent and quantify associations between objects. They provide a mechanism to model interactions and dependencies between variables, components, modules, etc. Fuzzy relations generalize the concept of relation in the same manner as fuzzy set generalizes the fundamental idea of set. Fuzzy relations have applications especially in information retrieval, pattern classification, modeling and control, diagnostics, and decision-making.

2.5.1. *Relations and Fuzzy Relations*

Fuzzy relation is a generalization of the concept of relations by admitting the notion of partial association between elements of domains. Intuitively, a fuzzy relation can be seen as a multidimensional fuzzy set. For instance, if **X** and **Y** are two domains of interest, a fuzzy relation R is any fuzzy subset of the Cartesian product of $\mathbf{X}$ and $\mathbf{Y}$ [22]. Equivalently, a fuzzy relation on $\mathbf{X} \times \mathbf{Y}$ is a mapping

$$R: \mathbf{X} \times \mathbf{Y} \to [0, 1].$$

The membership function of R for some pair (x, y), $R(x, y) = 1$, denotes that the two objects x and y are fully related. On the other hand, $R(x, y) = 0$ means that these elements are unrelated while the values in-between, $0 < R(x, y) < 1$, underline a partial association. For instance, if d_{fs}, d_{nf}, d_{ns}, d_{gf} are documents whose subjects concern mainly fuzzy systems, neural fuzzy systems, neural systems, and genetic fuzzy systems whose keywords are denoted by w_f, w_n and w_g, respectively, then a relation R on $\mathbf{D} \times \mathbf{W}$, $\mathbf{D} = \{d_{fs}, d_{nf}, d_{ns}, d_{gf}\}$ and $\mathbf{W} = \{w_f, w_n, w_g\}$ can assume the matrix form with the following entries:

$$R = \begin{bmatrix} 1 & 0 & 0.6 \\ 0.8 & 1 & 0 \\ 0 & 1 & 0 \\ 0.8 & 1 & 0 \end{bmatrix}$$

Since the universes are discrete, R can be represented as a 4×3 matrix (four documents and three keywords) and entries are degrees of memberships. For instance, $R(d_{fs}, w_f) = 1$ means that the document content d_{fs} is fully compatible with the keyword w_f whereas $R(d_{fs}, w_n) = 0$ and $R(d_{fs}, w_g) = 0.6$ indicate that d_{fs} does not mention neural systems, but does have genetic systems as part of its content. As with relations, when $\mathbf{X}$ and $\mathbf{Y}$ are finite with $\mathrm{Card}(\mathbf{X}) = n$ and $\mathrm{Card}(\mathbf{Y}) = m$, then R can be arranged into a certain $n \times m$ matrix $R = [r_{ij}]$, with $r_{ij} \in [0,1]$ being the corresponding degrees of association between x_i and y_j.

The basic operations on fuzzy relations, union, intersection, and complement, are analogous to the corresponding operations on fuzzy sets once fuzzy relations are fuzzy sets formed on multidimensional spaces. Their characterization and representation also mimics fuzzy sets.

2.5.2. Cartesian Product

A procedure to construct fuzzy relations is through the use of Cartesian product extended to fuzzy sets. The concept closely follows the one adopted for sets once they involve pairs of points of the underlying universes, added with a membership degree.

Given fuzzy sets A_1, A_2, ... A_n on the respective domains $\mathbf{X}_1$, $\mathbf{X}_2$, ..., $\mathbf{X}_n$, their Cartesian product $A_1 \times A_2 \times \ldots \times A_n$ is a fuzzy relation R on $\mathbf{X}_1 \times \mathbf{X}_2 \times \ldots \times \mathbf{X}_n$

with the following membership function

$$R(x_1, x_2, \ldots, x_n) = \min\{A_1(x_1), A_2(x_2), \ldots, A_n(x_n)\},$$

$$\forall x_1 \in \mathbf{X}_1, \forall x_2 \in \mathbf{X}_2, \ldots, \forall x_n \in \mathbf{X}_n.$$

In general, we can generalize the concept of this Cartesian product using t-norms:

$$R(x_1, x_2, \ldots, x_n) = A_1(x_1) \, t \, A_2(x_2) t \ldots t A_n(x_n) \; \forall x_1 \in \mathbf{X}_1,$$

$$\forall x_2 \in \mathbf{X}_2, \ldots, \forall x_n \in \mathbf{X}_n.$$

2.5.3. *Projection of Fuzzy Relations*

Contrasting with the concept of the Cartesian product, the idea of projection is to construct fuzzy relations on some subspaces of the original relation.

If R is a fuzzy relation on $\mathbf{X}_1 \times \mathbf{X}_2 \times \ldots \times \mathbf{X}_n$, its projection on $X = \mathbf{X}_i \times \mathbf{X}_j \times \ldots \times \mathbf{X}_k$, is a fuzzy relation R_X whose membership function is [23]

$$R_{\mathrm{X}}(x_i, x_j, \ldots, x_k) = \mathrm{Pr} \, oj_{\mathrm{X}} R(x_1, x_2, \ldots, x_n) = \sup_{x_t, x_u, \ldots, x_v} R(x_1, x_2, \ldots, x_n),$$

where $I = \{i, j, \ldots, k\}$ is a subsequence of the set of indexes $N = \{1, 2, \ldots, n\}$, and $J = \{t, u, \ldots, v\}$ is a subsequence of N such that $I \cup J = N$ and $I \cap J = \emptyset$. Thus, J is the complement of I with respect to N. Notice that the above expression is computed for all values of $(x_1, x_2, \ldots, x_n) \in \mathbf{X}_1 \times \mathbf{X}_2 \times \ldots \times \mathbf{X}_n$. Figure 2.23 illustrates projection in the two-dimensional $\mathbf{X} \times \mathbf{Y}$ case.

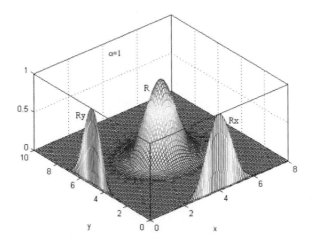

Figure 2.23: Fuzzy relation R and its projections on $\mathbf{X}$ and $\mathbf{Y}$.

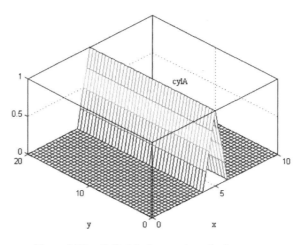

Figure 2.24: Cylindrical extension of a fuzzy set.

2.5.4. *Cylindrical Extension*

The notion of cylindrical extension aims to expand a fuzzy set to a multidimensional relation. In this sense, cylindrical extension can be regarded as an operation complementary to the projection operation [23].

The cylindrical extension on $\mathbf{X} \times \mathbf{Y}$ of a fuzzy set of $\mathbf{X}$ is a fuzzy relation *cylA* whose membership function is equal to

$$cyl\,A(x, y) = A(x) \quad \forall x \in \mathbf{X}, y \in \mathbf{Y}.$$

Figure 2.24 shows the cylindrical extension of a triangular fuzzy set A.

2.6. Linguistic Variables

One frequently deals with variables describing phenomena of physical or human systems assuming a finite, quite small number of descriptors.

In contrast to the idea of numeric variables as commonly used, the notion of linguistic variable can be understood as a variable whose values are fuzzy sets. In general, linguistic variables may assume values consisting of words or sentences expressed in a certain language [24]. Formally, a linguistic variable is characterized by a quintuple $<$X, T(X), $\mathbf{X}$, G, M $>$, where X is the name of the variable, T(X) is a term set of X whose elements are labels L of linguistic values of X, G is a grammar that generates the names of X, and M is a semantic rule that assigns to each label L∈T(X) a meaning whose realization is a fuzzy set on the universe $\mathbf{X}$ with base variable x. Figure 2.25 shows an example.

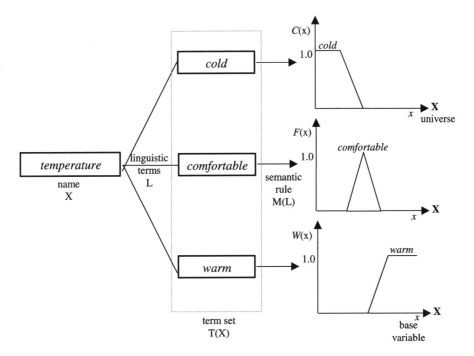

Figure 2.25: An example of the linguistic variable *temperature*.

2.7. Granulation of Data

The notion of granulation emerges as a need to abstract and summarize data to support the processes of comprehension and decision-making. For instance, we often sample an environment for values of attributes of state variables, but we rarely process all details because of our physical and cognitive limitations. Quite often, just a reduced number of variables, attributes, and values are considered because those are the only features of interest given the task under consideration. To avoid all necessary and highly distractive details, we require an effective abstraction procedure. Detailed numeric information is aggregated into a format of information granules where the granules themselves are regarded as collections of elements that are perceived as being indistinguishable, similar, close, or functionally equivalent.

There are different formalisms and concepts of information granules [25]. For instance, granules can be realized as sets (intervals), rough sets, probability densities [26]. Typical examples of the granular data are singletons and intervals. In these two special cases, we typically refer to discretization and quantization (Figure 2.26). As the specificity of granules increases, intervals become singletons and in this limit case the quantization results in a discretization process.

Fuzzy sets are examples of information granules. When talking about a family of fuzzy sets, we are typically concerned with fuzzy partitions of **X**. Given the nature

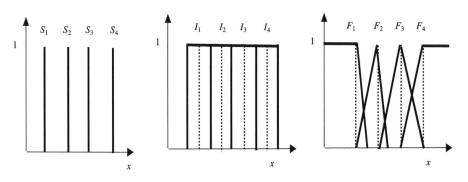

Figure 2.26:   Discretization, quantization, and granulation.

of fuzzy sets, fuzzy granulation generalizes the notion of quantization (Figure 2.26) and emphasizes a gradual nature of transitions between neighboring information granules [27]. When dealing with information granulation we often develop a family of fuzzy sets and move on with the processing that inherently uses all the elements of this family. The existing terminology refers to such collections of data granules as frames of cognition [8]. In what follows, we briefly review the concept and its main properties.

Frame of cognition: A frame of cognition results from information granulation when we encounter a finite collection of fuzzy sets—information granules that represent the entire universe of discourse and satisfy a system of semantic constraints. The frame of cognition is a notion of particular interest in fuzzy modeling, fuzzy control, classification, and data analysis.

A frame of cognition consists of several labeled, normal fuzzy sets. Each of these fuzzy sets is treated as a reference for further processing. A frame of cognition can be viewed as a codebook of conceptual entities. We may view them as a family of linguistic landmarks, say *small*, *medium*, *high*, etc. More formally, a frame of cognition Φ

$$\Phi = \{A_1, A_2, \ldots, A_m\}, \tag{2.18}$$

is a collection of fuzzy sets defined in the same universe **X** that satisfies at least two requirements, coverage and semantic soundness.

Coverage: We say that Φ covers **X** if any element $x \in \mathbf{X}$ is compatible with at least one fuzzy sets A_i in Φ, $i \in I = \{1, 2, \ldots, m\}$ meaning that it is compatible (coincides) with A_i to some nonzero degree, that is

$$\forall_{x \in \mathbf{X}} \ \exists_{i \in I} \ A_j(x) > 0 \tag{2.19}$$

Being stricter, we may require a satisfaction of the so-called δ-level coverage, which means that for any element of **X**, fuzzy sets are activated to a degree not lower than $\boldsymbol{\delta}$

$$\forall_{x \in X} \; \exists_{i \in I} \; A_j(x) > \delta \qquad (2.20)$$

where $\delta \in [0,1]$. From application perspective, the coverage assures that each element of **X** is represented by at least one of the elements of Φ, and guarantees any absence of gaps, that is, elements of **X** for which there is no fuzzy set being compatible with it.

Semantic soundness: The notion of semantic soundness is more complicated and difficult to quantify. In principle, we are interested in information granules of Φ that are meaningful. While there is far more flexibility in a way in which a number of detailed requirements could be structured, we may agree upon a collection of several fundamental properties:

1. Each A_i, $i \in I$, is a unimodal and normal fuzzy set.
2. Fuzzy sets A_i, $i \in I$, are disjoint enough to assure that they are sufficiently distinct to become linguistically meaningful. This imposes a maximum degree λ of overlap between any two elements of Φ. In other words, given any $x \in X$, there is no more than one fuzzy set A_i such that $A_i(x) \geq \lambda$, $\lambda \in [0,1]$.
3. The number of elements of Φ is low; following the psychological findings reported by Miller and others we consider the number of fuzzy sets forming the frame of cognition to be maintained in the range of 7 ± 2 items.

Coverage and semantic soundness [28]are the two essential conditions that should be fulfilled by the membership functions of A_i to achieve interpretability. In particular, δ-coverage and λ-overlapping induce a minimal (δ) and maximal (λ) level of overlap between fuzzy sets (Figure 2.27).

Considering the families of linguistic labels and associated fuzzy sets embraced in a frame of cognition, several characteristics are worth emphasizing.

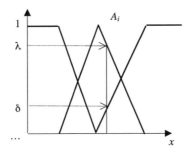

Figure 2.27: Coverage and semantic soundness of a cognitive frame.

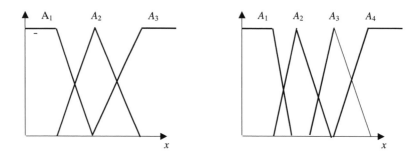

Figure 2.28:   Two frames of cognition; Φ_1 is coarser (more general) than Φ_2.

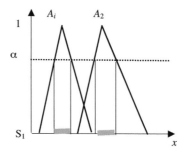

Figure 2.29:   Focus of attention; two regions of focus of attention implied by the corresponding fuzzy sets.

Specificity: We say that the frame of cognition Φ_1 is more specific than Φ_2 if all the elements of Φ_1 are more specific than the elements of Φ_2 (Figure 2.28). Here the specificity $Spec(A_i)$ of the fuzzy sets that compose the cognition frames can be evaluated as suggested in Section 2.3. The less specific cognition frames promotes granulation realized at the higher level of abstraction (generalization). Subsequently, we are provided with the description that captures fewer details.

Granularity: Granularity of a frame of cognition relates to the granularity of fuzzy sets used there. The higher the number of fuzzy sets in the frame, the finer the resulting granulation is. Therefore, the frame of cognition Φ_1 is finer than Φ_2 if $|\Phi_1| > |\Phi_2|$. If the converse holds, Φ_1 is coarser than Φ_2 (Figure 2.28).

Focus of attention: A focus of attention induced by a certain fuzzy set $A = A_i$ in Φ is defined as a certain α–cut of this fuzzy set. By moving A along $\mathbf{X}$ while keeping its membership function unchanged, we can focus attention on a certain selected region of $\mathbf{X}$, as shown in Figure 2.29.

Information hiding: Information hiding is closely related to the notion of focus of attention and manifests through a collection of elements that are hidden

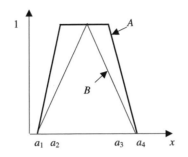

Figure 2.30:   A concept of information hiding realized by the use of trapezoidal fuzzy set A. Points in $[a_2, a_3]$ are made indistinguishable. The effect of information hiding is not present in case of triangular fuzzy set B.

when viewed from the standpoint of membership functions. By modifying the membership function of $A = A_i$ in Φ we can produce an equivalence of the elements positioned within some region of $\mathbf{X}$. For instance, consider a trapezoidal fuzzy set A on $\mathbf{R}$ and its 1-cut (core), the closed interval $[a_2, a_3]$, as depicted in Figure 2.30.

All points within the interval $[a_2, a_3]$ are made *indistinguishable* and through the use of this specific fuzzy set they are made equivalent. Hence, more detailed information, a position of a certain point falling within this interval, is *hidden*. In general, by increasing or decreasing the level of the α–cut we can accomplish a so-called α–information hiding through normalization.

2.8. Linguistic Approximation

In many cases we are provided with a finite family of fuzzy sets $\{A_1, A_2, \ldots, A_c\}$ (whose membership functions could have been determined earlier) using which we would like to represent a certain fuzzy sets B. These fuzzy sets are referred to as a vocabulary of information granules. Furthermore, assume that we have at our disposal a finite collection of linguistic modifiers $\{\tau_1, \tau_2, \ldots, \tau_p\}$. There are two general categories of the modifiers realizing operations of concentration and dilution. Their semantics relates to the linguistic adjectives of the form *very* (concentration) and *more or less* (dilution). Given the semantics of Ai's and the linguistic modifiers, the aim of the representation process is to capture the essence of B. Given the nature of the objects and the ensuing processing being used here, we refer to this process as a linguistic approximation. There are many ways to attain linguistic approximation. For instance, the scheme shown in Figure 2.31 comprises of two steps: the first finds the best match between B and Ai's. The quality of matching can be expressed in terms of some distance or similarity measure. The next step refines the best match by applying one of the linguistic modifiers. The result of the linguistic approximation is $B \approx \tau_i(A_j)$ with the indexes i and j determined by the matching mechanism.

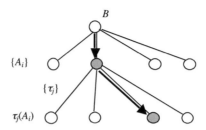

Figure 2.31: Linguistic approximation of B using a vocabulary and modifiers.

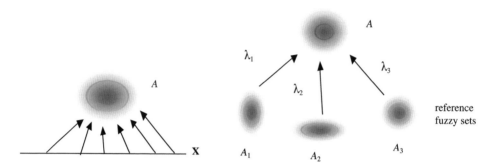

Figure 2.32: Fuzzy sets of order 1 (left), and order 2 (right).

2.9. Generalizations and Extensions of Fuzzy Sets

The essential notion of fuzzy set can be generalized into more abstract constructs such as second order fuzzy sets and interval fuzzy sets. Various construction and conceptual issues arise concerning values of membership, inducing a collection of views of granular membership grades. The simplest construct is interval-valued fuzzy sets. More refined versions of the construct produce fuzzy sets of higher type and type-2 fuzzy sets.

2.9.1. *Higher Order Fuzzy Sets*

To make it simple, the notion of fuzzy sets discussed so far could be referred to as fuzzy sets of order 1. The essence of a fuzzy of order 2 is that it is defined over a collection of some other fuzzy sets. Figure 2.32 shows the difference between fuzzy sets, which in this context is referred to as fuzzy sets of order 1, and fuzzy sets of order 2. For the order 2 fuzzy set, one can use the notation $A = [\lambda_1, \lambda_2, \lambda_3]$ given the reference, fuzzy sets are A_1, A_2, and A_3. In a similar way, fuzzy sets of higher order, say order 3 or higher, can be formed in a recursive manner. While conceptually appealing and straightforward, its applicability is an open issue. One may not willing to expend more effort into their design unless there is a strong reason behind the usage of fuzzy sets of higher order. Moreover, nothing prevents us from building fuzzy sets of higher order based on a family of terms that are not fuzzy sets only. One might consider a family of information granules such as sets over which a certain fuzzy set could be formed.

2.9.2. Type-2 Fuzzy Sets

Choice of membership functions or membership degrees may raise the issue that characterizing membership degrees, as single numeric values could be counter-intuitive given the nature of fuzzy sets themselves. An alternative can be sought by capturing the semantics of membership using intervals of possible membership grades rather than single numeric values. This is the concept of interval-valued fuzzy sets A (Figure 2.33). The lower A^- and upper A^+ bounds of the membership grades are used to capture the lack of uniqueness of numeric membership.

Type-2 fuzzy sets are a generalization of interval-valued fuzzy sets [29]. Instead of intervals of numeric values of membership degrees, memberships are fuzzy sets themselves. Consider a certain element x_j of the universe of discourse. The membership of x_j in A is captured by a fuzzy set formed over the unit interval. An example of type-2 fuzzy set is illustrated in Figure 2.34.

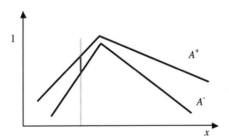

Figure 2.33: An interval-valued fuzzy set; the lower and upper bound of membership grades.

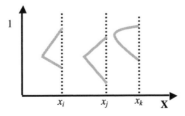

Figure 2.34: Type-2 fuzzy set; for each element of **X**, there is a corresponding fuzzy set of membership grades.

2.10. Conclusion

The chapter has summarized the fundamental notions and concepts of fuzzy set theory. The goal was to offer basic and key contents of interest for computational intelligence and intelligent systems theory and applications. Currently, a number of outstanding books and journals are available to help researchers, scientists, and engineers to master the fuzzy set theory and the contributions it brings to develop new approaches through hybridizations and new applications. The bibliography includes some of them. The remaining chapters of this book provide the readers with a clear picture of the current state of the art in the area.

References

[1] Cantor, G. (1883). *Grundlagen einer allgemeinen Mannigfaltigkeitslehre*, Teubner, Leipzig.
[2] Cantor, G. (1895). Beiträge zur Begründung der transfiniten Mengenlehre, *Math. Ann.*, **46**, pp. 481–512.
[3] Zadeh, L. (1965). Fuzzy sets, *Inf. Control*, **8**, pp. 338–353.
[4] Dubois, D. and Prade, H. (1997). The three semantics of fuzzy sets, *Fuzzy Sets Syst.*, **2**, pp. 141–150.
[5] Dubois, D. and Prade, H. (1998). An introduction to fuzzy sets, *Clin. Chim. Acta*, **70**, pp. 3–29.
[6] Zadeh, L. (1978). Fuzzy sets as a basis for a theory of possibility, *Fuzzy Sets Syst.*, **3**, pp. 3–28.
[7] Klir, G. and Yuan, B. (1995). *Fuzzy Sets and Fuzzy Logic: Theory and Applications*, Prentice Hall, Upper Saddle River, New Jersey, USA.
[8] Pedrycz, W. and Gomide, F. (2007). *Fuzzy Systems Engineering: Toward Human-Centric Computing*, Wiley Interscience, Hoboken, New Jersey, USA.
[9] Garmendia, L., Yager, R., Trillas, E. and Salvador, A. (2003). On t-norms based measures of specificity, *Fuzzy Sets Syst.*, **133**, pp. 237–248.
[10] Yager, R. (1983). Entropy and specificity in a mathematical theory of evidence, *Int. J. Gen. Syst.*, **9**, pp. 249–260.
[11] Klement *et al.*, (2000). *Triangular Norms*. Springer, Dordrecht, Netherlands.
[12] Hajek, P. (1998). *Mathematics of Fuzzy Logic*, Kluwer Academic Publishers, Dordrecht Norwell, New York, London.
[13] Klement, P. and Navarra, M. (1999). A survey on different triangular norm-based fuzzy logics. *Fuzzy Sets and Systems*, **101**, pp. 241–251.
[14] Dubois, D. and Prade, H. (1985). A review of fuzzy aggregation connectives, *Inf. Sci.*, **36**, pp. 85–121.
[15] Bouchon-Meunier, B. (1998). *Aggregation and Fusion of Imperfect Information*, Physica-Verlag, Heidelberg, Germany.
[16] Calvo, T., Kolesárová, A., Komorníková, M. and Mesiar, R. (2002). Aggregation operators: properties, classes and construction methods, in *Aggregation Operators: New Trends and Applications*, Physica-Verlag, Heidelberg, Germany.
[17] Dubois, D. and Prade, H. (2004). On the use of aggregation operations in information fusion, *Fuzzy Sets Syst.*, **142**, pp. 143–161.
[18] Beliakov et al., 2007.
[19] Dyckhoff, H. and Pedrycz, W. (1984). Generalized means as a models of compensative connectives, *Fuzzy Sets Syst.*, **142**, pp. 143–154.
[20] Yager, R. (1988). On ordered weighted averaging aggregation operations in multicriteria decision making, *IEEE Trans. Syst. Man Cybern.*, **18**, pp. 183–190.

[21] Yager, R. and Rybalov, A. (1996). Uninorm aggregation operators, *Fuzzy Sets Syst.*, **80**, pp. 111–120.

[22] Zadeh, L. (1971). Similarity relations and fuzzy orderings, *Inf. Sci.*, **3**, pp. 177–200.

[23] Zadeh, L. (1975a,b). The concept of linguistic variables ad its application to approximate reasoning I, II III, *Inf. Sci.*, **8**(9), pp. 199–251, 301–357, 43–80.

[24] Zadeh, L. (1999). From computing with numbers to computing with words: from manipulation of measurements to manipulation of perceptions, *IEEE Trans. Circuits Syst.*, **45**, pp. 105–119.

[25] Pedrycz, W., Skowron, A. and Kreinovich, V. (2008). *Handbook of Granular Computing*, John Wiley & Sons, Chichester, West Sussex, England.

[26] Lin, T. (2004). Granular computing: rough sets perspectives, *IEEE Connect.*, **2**, pp. 10–13.

[27] Zadeh, L. (1999). Fuzzy logic = computing with words, in Zadeh, L. and Kacprzyk, J. (eds.), *Computing with Words in Information and Intelligent Systems*, Physica-Verlag, Heidelberg, Germany, pp. 3–23.

[28] Oliveria, J. (1993). On optimal fuzzy systems with I/O interfaces, *Proc. of the Second IEEE Int. Conf. on Fuzzy Systems*, San Francisco, California, USA, pp. 34–40.

[29] Mendel, J. (2007). Type-2 fuzzy sets and systems: an overview, *IEEE Comput. Intell. Mag.*, **2**, pp. 20–29.

Chapter 3

Granular Computing

Andrzej Bargiela*,‡ *and Witold Pedrycz*†,§

**The University of Nottingham, Nottingham, UK*
†*University of Alberta, Edmonton, Canada*
‡*andrzej.bargiela@nottingham.ac.uk*
§*wpedrycz@ualberta.ca*

Research into human-centered information processing, as evidenced through the development of fuzzy sets and fuzzy logic, has brought additional insight into the transformative nature of the aggregation of inaccurate and/or fuzzy information in terms of the semantic content of data aggregates. This insight has led to the suggestion of the development of the granular computing (GrC) paradigm some 15 years ago and takes as a point of departure an empirical validation of the aggregated data in order to achieve the closest possible correspondence of the semantics of data aggregates and the entities in the problem domain. Indeed, it can be observed that information abstraction combined with empirical validation of abstractions has been deployed as a methodological tool in various scientific disciplines. This chapter is focused on exploring the foundations of GrC and casting it as a structured combination of algorithmic and non-algorithmic information processing that mimics human, intelligent synthesis of knowledge from imprecise and/or fuzzy information.

3.1. Introduction

Granular computing (GrC) is frequently defined in an informal way as a general computation theory for effectively using granules such as classes, clusters, subsets, groups, and intervals to build an efficient computational model for complex applications with which to process large volumes of information presented as either raw data or aggregated problem domain knowledge. Though the term GrC is relatively recent, the basic notions and principles of granular computing have appeared under different names in many related fields, such as information hiding in programming, granularity in artificial intelligence, divide and conquer in theoretical computer science, interval computing, cluster analysis, fuzzy and rough set theories, neutrosophic computing, quotient space theory, belief functions, machine learning, databases, and many others. In the past few years, we have witnessed a renewed and fast-growing interest in GrC. Granular computing has begun to play important roles in bioinformatics, e-business, security, machine learning, data mining, high-performance computing, and wireless mobile computing in terms of efficiency, effectiveness, robustness and structured representation of uncertainty.

With the vigorous research interest in the GrC paradigm [3–10, 17, 20, 21, 25–28, 33, 36–44], it is natural to see that there are voices calling for clarification of the distinctiveness of GrC from the underpinning constituent disciplines and from other computational paradigms proposed for large-scale/complex information possessing. Recent contributions by Yao [36–39] attempt to bring together various insights into GrC from a broad spectrum of disciplines and cast the GrC framework as structured thinking at the philosophical level and structured problem solving at the practical level.

In this chapter, we elaborate on our earlier proposal [11] and look at the roots of granular computing in the light of the original insight of Zadeh [40] stating, "fuzzy information granulation in an intuitive form underlies *human problem solving*." We suggest that *human problem solving* has strong foundations in axiomatic set theory and theory of computability and that it underlies some recent research results linking intelligence to physical computation [1, 2]. In fact, re-examining human information processing in this light brings granular computing from a domain of computation and philosophy to one of physics and set theory.

The set theoretical perspective on GrC adopted in this chapter offers also a good basis for the evaluation of other human-centered computing paradigms such as the generalized constraint-based computation recently communicated by Zadeh [44].

3.2. Set Theoretical Interpretation of Granulation

The commonly accepted definition of granulation introduced in [17, 21], and [37] is:

Definition 1. *Information granulation is a grouping of elements based on their indistinguishability, similarity, proximity or functionality.*

This definition serves well the purpose of constructive generation of granules but does little to differentiate granulation from clustering. More importantly however, *Definition 1* implies that the nature of information granules is fully captured by their interpretation as subsets of the original dataset within the intuitive set theory of Cantor [13]. Unfortunately, an inevitable consequence of this is that the inconsistencies (paradoxes) associated with intuitive set theory, such as "cardinality of set of all sets" (Cantor) or "definition of a set that is not a member of itself" (Russel), are imported into the domain of information granulation.

In order to provide a more robust definition of information granulation, we follow the approach adopted in the development of axiomatic set theory. The key realization there was that the commonly accepted intuition, that one can form any set one wants, should be questioned. Accepting the departure point of intuitive set theory, we can say that, normally, sets are not members of themselves, i.e., normally, ~(y in y). But the axioms of intuitive set theory do not exclude the existence of "abnormal" sets, which are members of themselves. So, if we consider a set of all "normal" sets: $x = \{y|{\sim}(y\ in\ y)\}$, we can axiomatically guarantee the existence of set x:

$$\exists x \forall y (y \in x \Leftrightarrow \omega(y \in y)).$$

If we then substitute x for y, we arrive at a contradiction:

$$\exists x \forall x (x \in x \Leftrightarrow \omega(x \in x)).$$

So, the unrestricted comprehension axiom of the intuitive set theory leads to contradictions and cannot therefore serve as a foundation of set theory.

3.2.1. *Zermelo–Fraenkel Axiomatization*

An early attempt at overcoming the above contradiction was an axiomatic scheme developed by Ernst Zermelo and Abraham Fraenkel [45]. Their idea was to restrict the comprehension axiom schema by adopting only those instances of it that are necessary for the reconstruction of common mathematics. In other words, the standard approach, of using a formula $F(y)$ to collect the set y having the property F, leads to the generation of an object that is not a set (otherwise we arrive at a contradiction). So, looking at the problem the other way, they have concluded that the contradiction constitutes a de facto proof that there are other semantical entities in addition to sets.

The important observation that we can make here is that the semantical transformation of sets through the process of applying some set-forming formula applies also to the process of information granulation and, consequently, information granules should be considered semantically distinct from the granulated entities. We therefore arrive at a modified definition of information granulation as follows:

Definition 2. *Information granulation is a semantically meaningful grouping of elements based on their indistinguishability, similarity, proximity, or functionality.*

Continuing with the Zermelo–Fraenkel approach, we must legalize some collections of sets that are not sets. Let $F(y, z_1, z_2, \ldots, z_n)$ be a formula in the language of set theory (where $z_1, z_2, \ldots, z_n$ are optional parameters). We can say that for any values of parameters $z_1, z_2, \ldots, z_n$, the formula F defines a "class" A

$$A = \{y \mid F(y, z_1, z_2, \ldots, z_n)\}$$

which consists of all y's possessing the property F. Different values of $z_1, z_2, \ldots, z_n$ give rise to different classes. Consequently the axiomatization of set theory involves the formulation of axiom schemas that represent possible instances of axioms for different classes.

The following is a full set of axioms of the Zermelo–Fraenkel set theory:

Z1, Extensionality:

$$\forall x \forall y [\forall z (z \in x \equiv z \in y) \Rightarrow x = y]$$

Asserts that if sets x and y have the same members, the sets are identical.

Z2, Null Set:

$$\exists x \sim \exists y (y \in x)$$

Asserts that there is a unique empty set.

Z3, Pair Set:

$$\forall x \forall y \exists z \forall w (w \in z \equiv w = x \vee w = y)$$

Asserts that for any sets x and y, there exists a pair set of x and y, i.e., a set that has only x and y as members.

Z4, Unions:

$$\forall x \exists y \forall z (z \in y \equiv \exists w (w \in x \wedge z \in w)$$

Asserts that for any set x, there is a set y containing every set that is a member of some member of x.

Z5, Power Set:

$$\forall x \exists y \forall z (z \in y \equiv \exists w (w \in z \Rightarrow w \in x)$$

Asserts that for any set x, there is a set y which contains as members all those sets whose members are also elements of x, i.e., y contains all of the subsets of x.

Z6, Infinite Set:

$$\exists x [\emptyset \in x \wedge \forall y (y \in x \Rightarrow \bigcup \{y, \{y\}\} \in x)]$$

Asserts that there is a set x which contains $\emptyset$ as a member and which is such that, whenever y is a member of x, then $y \bigcup \{y\}$ is a member of x.

Z7, Regularity:

$$\forall x[x \neq \emptyset \Rightarrow \exists y(y \in x \wedge \forall z(z \in x \Rightarrow\, \sim (z \in y)))]$$

Asserts that every set is "well-founded", i.e., it rules out the existence of circular chains of sets as well as infinitely descending chains of sets. A member y of a set x with this property is called a "minimal" element.

Z8, Replacement Schema:

$$\forall x \exists y F(x, y) \Rightarrow \forall u \exists v \forall r(r \in v = \exists s(s \in u \wedge F_{x,v}[s, r]))$$

Asserts that given a formula $F(x, y)$ and $F_{x,y}[s, r]$ as a result of substituting s and r for x and y, every instance of the above axiom schema is an axiom. In other words, given a functional formula F and a set u, we can form a new set v by collecting all of the sets to which the members of u are uniquely related by F. It is important to note that elements of v need not be elements of u.

Z9, Separation Schema:

$$\forall u \exists v \forall r(r \in v \equiv r \in u \wedge F_x[r])$$

Asserts that there exists a set v which has, as members, precisely the members of u that satisfy the formula F. Again, every instance of the above axiom schema is an axiom.

Unfortunately, the presence of the two axiom schemas, Z6 and Z7, implies infinite axiomatization of the Zermelo–Fraenkel (ZF) set theory. While it is fully acknowledged that the ZF set theory, and its many variants, has advanced our understanding of cardinal and ordinal numbers and has led to the proof of the property of "well-ordering" of sets (with the help of an additional "Axiom of Choice"; ZFC), the theory seems unduly complex for the purpose of a set theoretical interpretation of information granules.

3.2.2. *Von Neumann–Bernays–Goedel Axiomatization*

A different approach to the axiomatization of set theory designed to yield the same results as ZF but with a finite number of axioms (i.e., without the reliance on axiom schemas) was proposed by von Neumann in 1920 and subsequently refined by Bernays in 1937 and Goedel in 1940 [15]. The defining aspect of von Neumann–Bernays–Goedel set theory (NBG) is the introduction of the concept of "proper class" among its objects. NBG and ZFC are very closely related and in fact NBG is a conservative extension of ZFC.

In NBG, proper classes are differentiated from sets by the fact that they do not belong to other classes. Thus, in NBG, we have

$$x \Leftrightarrow \exists y(x \in y)$$

which can be phrased as follows: x is a set if it belongs to either a set or a class.

The basic observation that can be made about NBG is that it is essentially a two-sorted theory; it involves sets (denoted here by lower-case letters) and classes (denoted by upper-case letters). Consequently, the above statement about membership assumes one of the following forms:

$$x \in y \quad \text{or} \quad x \in Y$$

and statements about equality are in the form

$$x = y \quad \text{or} \quad X \in Y$$

Using this notation, the axioms of NBG are as follows:

N1, Class Extensionality:

$$\forall x[x \in A \leftrightarrow x \in B) \Rightarrow A = B]$$

Asserts that classes with the same elements are the same.

N2, Set Extensionality:

$$\forall x[x \in a \leftrightarrow x \in b) \Rightarrow a = b]$$

Asserts that sets with the same elements are the same.

N3, Pairing:

$$\forall x \forall y \exists z \forall w(w \in z \equiv w = x \vee w = y))$$

Asserts that for any set x and y, there exists a set $\{x, y\}$ that has exactly two elements x and y. It is worth noting that this axiom allows the definition of ordered pairs and taken together with the Class Comprehension axiom, it allows implementation of relations on sets as classes.

N4, Union:

$$\forall x \exists y \forall z(z \in y \equiv \exists w(w \in x \wedge z \in w))$$

Asserts that for any set x there exists a set which contains exactly the elements of elements of x.

N5, Power Set:

$$\forall x \exists y \forall z [z \in y \equiv \forall w (w \in z \Rightarrow w \in x)$$

Asserts that for any set x, there is a set which contains exactly the subsets of x.

N6, Infinite Set:

$$\exists x \left[\emptyset \in x \wedge \forall y (y \in x \Rightarrow \bigcup \{y, \{y\}\} \in x) \right]$$

Asserts that there is a set x which contains an empty set as an element and contains $y \bigcup \{y\}$ for each of its elements y.

N7, Regularity:

$$\forall x [x \neq \emptyset \Rightarrow \exists y (y \in x \wedge \forall z (z \in x \Rightarrow \sim (z \in y)))]$$

Asserts that each nonempty set is disjoined from one of its elements.

N8, Limitation of size:

$$\sim x \Leftrightarrow |x| = |V|$$

Asserts that if the cardinality of x equals the cardinality of the set theoretical universe V, x is not a set but a proper class. This axiom can be shown to be equivalent to the axioms of Regularity, Replacement, and Separation in NBG. Thus the classes that are proper in NBG are, in a very clear sense, big, while sets are small.

It should be appreciated that the latter has a very profound implication on computation, which processes proper classes. This is because the classes built over countable sets can be uncountable and, as such, do not satisfy the constraints of the formalism of the Universal Turing Machine.

N9, Class Comprehension schema:

Unlike in the ZF axiomatization, this schema consists of a finite set of axioms (thus giving finite axiomatization of NBG).

Axiom of Sets: For any set x, there is a class X such that $x = X$

Axiom of Complement: For any class X, the complement $V - X = \{x | x \notin X\}$

Axiom of Intersection: For any classes X and Y, the intersection $X \cap Y = \{x | x \in X \wedge x \in Y\}$ is a class.

Axiom of Products: For any classes X and Y, the class $X \times Y = \{(x, y) | x \in X \wedge y \in Y\}$ is a class. This axiom actually provides far more than is needed for representing relations on classes. What is actually needed is just that $V \times Y$ is a class.

Axiom of Converses: For any class X, the class $Conv1(X) = \{(y, x) \mid (x, y) \in X\}$ and the class $Conv2(X) = \{(y, (x, z)) \mid (x, (y, z)) \in X\}$ exist.

Axiom of Association: For any class X, the class $Assoc1(X) = \{((x, y), z) \mid (x, (y, z)) \in X\}$ and the class $Assoc2(X) = \{(w, (x, (y, z))) \mid (w, ((x, y, z))) \in X\}$ exist.

Axiom of Ranges: For any class X, the class $Rng(X) = \{y \mid (\exists x(x, y) \in X\}$ exists.

Axiom of Membership: The class $[\in] = \{(x, y) \mid x \in y\}$ exists.

Axiom of Diagonal: The class $[=] = \{(x, y) \mid x \in y\}$ exists. This axiom can be used to build a relation asserting the equality of any two of its arguments and consequently used to handle repeated variables.

With the above finite axiomatization, the NBG theory can be adopted as a set theoretical basis for granular computing. Such a formal framework prompts a powerful insight into the essence of granulation, namely that **the granulation process transforms the semantics of the granulated entities,** mirroring the semantical distinction between sets and classes.

The semantics of granules is derived from the domain that has, in general, higher cardinality than the cardinality of the granulated sets. Although, at first, it might be a bit surprising to see that such a semantical transformation is an essential part of information granulation, in fact we can point to a common framework of many scientific disciplines which have evolved by abstracting from details inherent to the underpinning scientific discipline and developing a vocabulary of terms (proper classes) that have been verified by reference to real life (ultimately to the laws of physics). An example of the granulation of detailed information into semantically meaningful granules might be the consideration of cells and organisms in biology rather than the consideration of molecules, atoms, or sub-atomic particles when studying the physiology of living organisms.

The operation on classes in NBG is entirely consistent with the operation on sets in the intuitive set theory. The principle of abstraction implies that classes can be formed out of any statement of the predicate calculus with the membership relation. Notions of equality, pairing, and such are thus matters of definitions (a specific abstraction of a formula) and not of axioms. In NBG, a set represents a class if every element of the set is an element of the class. Consequently, there are classes that do not have representations.

We therefore suggest that the advantage of adopting NBG as a set theoretical basis for granular computing is that it provides a framework within which one can discuss a hierarchy of different granulations without running the risk of inconsistency. For instance, one can denote a "large category" as a category of granules whose collection of granules and collection of morphisms can be represented by a class. A "small category" can be denoted as a category of granules contained in sets. Thus, we can speak of "category of all small categories" (which is a "large category") without the risk of inconsistency.

A similar framework for a set theoretical representation of granulation is offered by the theory of types published by Russell in 1937 [29]. The theory assumes a linear hierarchy of types: with type 0 consisting of objects of undecided type and, for each natural number n, type $n+1$ objects are sets of type n objects. The conclusions that can be drawn from this framework with respect to the nature of granulation are exactly the same as those drawn from the NBG.

3.2.3. *Mereology*

An alternative framework for the formalization of granular computing, that of mereology, has been proposed by other researchers. The roots of mereology can be traced to the work of Edmund Husserl (1901) [16] and to the subsequent work of the Polish mathematician Stanislaw Lesniewski in the late 1920s [18, 19]. Much of this work was motivated by the same concerns about the intuitive set theory that have spurred the development of axiomatic set theories (ZF, NBG, and others) [15, 45].

Mereology replaces talk about "sets" with talk about "sums" of objects, objects being no more than the various things that make up wholes. However, such a simple replacement results in an "intuitive mereology" that is analogous to "intuitive set theory." Such "intuitive mereology" suffers from paradoxes analogous to Russel's paradox (we can ask: If there is an object whose parts are all the objects that are not parts of themselves; is it a part of itself?). So, one has to conclude that the mere introduction of the mereological concept of "partness" and "wholeness" is not sufficient and that mereology requires axiomatic formulation.

Axiomatic formulation of mereology has been proposed as a first-order theory whose universe of discourse consists of *wholes* and their respective *parts*, collectively called objects [31, 34]. A mereological system requires at least one primitive relation, e.g. dyadic Parthood, *x is a part of y*, written as *Pxy*. Parthood is nearly always assumed to partially order the universe. An immediately defined predicate is *x is a proper part of y*, written as *PPxy*, which holds if *Pxy* is true and *Pyx* is false. An object lacking proper parts is an *atom*. The mereological universe consists of all objects we wish to consider and all of their proper parts. Two other predicates commonly defined in mereology are Overlap and Underlap. These are defined as follows:

- *Oxy* is an overlap of *x* and *y* if there exists an object *z* such that *Pzx* and *Pzy* both hold.
- *Uxy* is an underlap of *x* and *y* if there exists an object *z* such that *x* and *y* are both parts of *z* (*Pxz* and *Pyz* hold).

With the above predicates, axiomatic mereology defines the following axioms:

M1, Parthood is Reflexive:
Asserts that an object is part of itself.

M2, Parthood is Antisymmetric:
Asserts that if Pxy and Pyx both hold, then x and y are the same object.

M3, Parthood is Transitive:
Asserts that if Pxy and Pyz hold, then Pxz holds.

M4, Weak Supplementation:
Asserts that if $PPxy$ holds, there exists a z such that Pzy holds but Ozx does not.

M5, Strong Supplementation:
Asserts that if Pyx does not hold, there exists a z such that Pzy holds but Ozx does not.

M5a, Atomistic Supplementation:
Asserts that if Pxy does not hold, then there exists an atom z such that Pzx holds but Ozy does not.

> **Top:** Asserts that there exists a "universal object", designated W, such that PxW holds for any x.
> **Bottom:** Asserts that there exists an atomic "null object", designated N, such that PNx holds for any x.

M6, Sum:
Asserts that if Uxy holds, there exists a z, called the "sum of x and y," such that the parts of z are just those objects which are parts of either x or y.

M7, Product:
Asserts that if Oxy holds, there exists a z, called the "product of x and y," such that the parts of z are just those objects which are parts of both x and y.

M8, Unrestricted Fusion:
Let f be a first-order formula having one free variable. Then the fusion of all objects satisfying f exists.

M9, Atomicity:
Asserts that all objects are either atoms or fusions of atoms.

It is clear that if "parthood" in mereology is taken as corresponding to "subset" in set theory, there is some analogy between the above axioms of *classical extensional mereology* and those of standard Zermelo–Fraenkel set theory. However, there are some philosophical and common sense objections to some of the above axioms, e.g., transitivity of parthood (M3). Also the set of above axioms is not minimal since it is possible to derive Weak Supplementation axiom (M4) from Strong Supplementation axiom (M5).

Axiom M6 implies that if the universe is finite or if *Top* is assumed, then the universe is closed under sum. Universal closure of product and of supplementation relative to W requires *Bottom*. W and *N* are evidently the mereological equivalents of the universal and the null sets. Because sum and product are binary operations, M6 and M7 admit the sum and product of only a finite number of objects. The *fusion* axiom, M8, enables taking the sum of infinitely many objects. The same holds for products. If M8 holds, then W exists for infinite universes. Hence *Top* needs to be assumed only if the universe is infinite and M8 does not hold. It is somewhat strange that while the *Top* axiom (postulating W) is not controversial, the *Bottom* axiom (postulating *N*) is. Lesniewski rejected the *Bottom* axiom and most mereological systems follow his example. Hence, while the universe is closed under sum, the product of objects that do not overlap is typically undefined. Such defined mereology is equivalent to Boolean algebra lacking a 0. Postulating *N* generates a mereology in which all possible products are definable but it also transforms extensional mereology into a Boolean algebra without a null element [34].

The full mathematical analysis of the theories of parthood is beyond the intended scope of this paper and the reader is referred to the recent publication by Pontow and Shubert [46] in which the authors prove, by set theoretical means, that there exists a model of general extensional mereology where arbitrary summation of attributes is not possible. However, it is clear from the axiomatization above that the question about the existence of a universal entity containing all other entities and the question about the existence of an empty entity as part of all existing entities are answered very differently by set theory and mereology. In set theory, the existence of a universal entity is contradictory and the existence of an empty set is mandatory while in mereology the existence of a universal set is stipulated by the respective fusion axioms and the existence of an empty entity is denied. Moreover, it is worth noting that in mereology there is no straightforward analogue to the set theoretical is-element-of relation [46].

So, taking into account the above, we suggest the following answer to the underlying questions of this section: Why granulation is necessary? Why is the set theoretical representation of granulation appropriate?

– The **concept of granulation is necessary** to denote the semantic transformation of granulated entities in a way that is analogous to semantic transformation of sets into classes in axiomatic set theory;

– Granulation interpreted in the context of axiomatic set theory is **very different from clustering**, since it deals with semantical transformation of data and does not limit itself to a mere grouping of similar entities;

– The set theoretical interpretation of granulation enables a **consistent** representation of a hierarchy of information granules.

3.3. Abstraction and Computation

Having established an argument for semantical dimension to granulation, one may ask, how is the meaning (semantics) instilled into real-life information granules? Is the meaning instilled through an algorithmic processing of constituent entities or is it a feature that is independent of algorithmic processing?

The answers to these questions are hinted at by von Neumann's *limitation of size principle*, mentioned in the previous section, and are more fully informed by Turing's theoretical model of computation. In his original paper [35], Turing has defined computation as an automatic version of doing what people do when they manipulate numbers and symbols on paper. He proposed a conceptual model which included: (a) an arbitrarily long tape from which one could read as many symbols as needed (from a countable set); (b) a means to read and write those symbols; (c) a countable set of states storing information about the completed processing of symbols; and (d) a countable set of rules that govern what should be done for various combinations of input and system states. A physical instantiation of computation, envisaged by Turing, was a human operator (called computer) who was compelled to obey the rules (a)–(d) above. There are several important implications of Turing's definition of computation. First, the model implies that computation explores only a subset of capabilities of human information processing. Second, the constraint that the input and output are strictly symbolic (with symbols drawn from a countable set) implies that the computer does not interact directly with the environment. These are critical limitations meaning that Turing's computer on its own is unable (by definition) to respond to external, physical stimuli. *Consequently, it is not just wrong but essentially meaningless to speculate on the ability of Turing machines to perform human-like intelligent interaction with the real world.*

To phrase it in mathematical terms, the general form of computation, formalized as a universal Turing machine (UTM), is defined as a mapping of sets that have at most cardinality N_0 (infinite, countable) onto sets with cardinality N_0. The practical instances of information processing, such as clustering of data, typically involve a finite number of elements in both the input and output sets and therefore represent a more manageable mapping of a finite set with cardinality max_1 onto another finite set with cardinality max_2. The hierarchy of computable clustering can be therefore represented as in Figure 3.1.

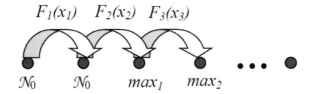

Figure 3.1: Cardinality of sets in a hierarchy of clusterings implemented on UTM.

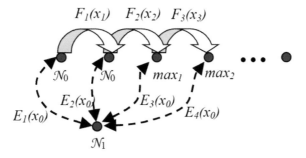

Figure 3.2: Mapping of abstractions from the real-world domain (cardinality N_1) onto the sets of clusters.

The functions $F_1(x_1) \rightarrow x_2$, $F_2(x_2) \rightarrow x_3$, $F_3(x_3) \rightarrow x_4$ represent mappings of:

– infinite (countable) input set onto infinite (countable) output set;
– infinite (countable) input set onto finite output set; and
– finite input set onto finite output set, respectively.

The functional mappings, deployed in the process of clustering, reflect the criteria of similarity, proximity, or indistinguishability of elements in the input set and, on this basis, grouping them together into a separate entity to be placed in the output set. In other words, the functional mappings generate data abstractions on the basis of pre-defined criteria and consequently represent UTM computation. However, we need to understand how these criteria are selected and how they are decided to be appropriate in any specific circumstance. Clearly, there are many ways of defining similarity, proximity, or indistinguishability. Some of these definitions are likely to have good real-world interpretation, while others may be difficult to interpret or indeed may lead to physically meaningless results.

We suggest that the process of instilling the real-world interpretation into data structures generated by functional mappings $F_1(x_1) \rightarrow x_2$, $F_2(x_2) \rightarrow x_3$, $F_3(x_3) \rightarrow x_4$, involves reference to the real world, as illustrated in Figure 3.2. This is represented as execution of "experimentation" functions $E_*(x_0)$. These functions map the real-world domain x_0, which has cardinality N_1 (infinite, continuum), onto sets x_1, x_2, x_3, x_4, respectively.

At this point, it is important to underline that the experimentation functions $E_1(x_0) \to x_1$, $E_2(x_0) \to x_2$, $E_3(x_0) \to x_3$, $E_4(x_0) \to x_4$ are not computational, in the UTM sense, because their domains have cardinality N_1. So, the process of defining the criteria for data clustering, and implicitly instilling the meaning into information granules, relies on the laws of physics and not on the mathematical model of computation. Furthermore, the results of experimentation do not depend on whether the experimenter understands or is even aware of the laws of physics. It is precisely because of this that we consider the experimentation functions as providing objective evidence.

3.4. Experimentation as a Physical Computation

Recent research [30] has demonstrated that analogue computation, in the form of recurrent analogue neural networks (RANN), can exceed the abilities of a UTM if the weights in such neural networks are allowed to take continuous rather than discrete weights. While this result is significant in itself, it relies on assumptions about the continuity of parameters that are difficult to verify. So, although the brain looks remarkably like a RANN, drawing any conclusions about the hyper-computational abilities of the brain, purely on the grounds of structural similarities, leads to the same questions about the validity of the assumptions about continuity of weights. Of course, this is not to say that these assumptions are not valid; they may well be valid, but we just highlight that this has not yet been demonstrated in a conclusive way.

A pragmatic approach to bridging the gap between the theoretical model of hyper-computation, as offered by RANN, and the human, intelligent information processing (which, by definition, is hyper-computational) has been proposed by Bains [1, 2]. Her suggestion was to reverse the original question about the hyper-computational ability of systems and to ask: *if the behavior of physical systems cannot be replicated using Turing machines, how can they be replicated?* The answer to this question is surprisingly simple: *we can use the inherent computational ability of physical phenomena in conjunction with the numerical information processing ability of UTM.* In other words, the readiness to refine numerical computations in the light of objective evidence coming from a real-life experiment instills the ability to overcome the limitations of the Turing machine. We have advocated this approach in our earlier work [6] and have argued that the hyper-computational power of granular computing is equivalent to "keeping an open mind" in intelligent, human information processing.

In what follows, we describe the model of physical computation, as proposed in [1], and cast it in the framework of granular computing.

3.4.1. *A Model of Physical Computation*

We define a system under consideration as an identifiable collection of connected elements. A system is said to be *embodied* if it occupies a definable volume and has a collective contiguous boundary. In particular, a UTM with its collection of input/output data, states and, collection of rules, implementing some information processing algorithm, can be considered to be a system G whose physical instantiations may refer to specific I/O, processing, and storage devices as well as specific energy states. The matter, space, and energy outside the boundaries of the embodied system are collectively called the *physical environment* and will be denoted here by P.

A *sensor* is any part of the system that can be changed by physical influences from the environment. Any forces, fields, energy, matter, etc. that may be impinging on the system are collectively called the *sensor input* ($i \in X$), even where no explicitly defined sensors exist.

An *actuator* is any part of the system that can change the environment. Physical changes to the embodied system that manifest themselves externally (e.g., emission of energy, change of position, etc.) are collectively called the *actuator output* ($h \in Y$) of G. A coupled pair of sensor input i_t and actuator output h_t represents an instance of experimentation at time t and is denoted here as E_t.

Since the system G, considered in this study, is a computational system (modeled by UTM) and since the objective of the evolution of this system is to mimic human intelligent information processing, we will define G_t as the *computational intelligence function* performed by the embodied system G. Function G_t maps the input to the output at specific time instances t resolved with arbitrarily small accuracy $\delta t > 0$, so as not to preclude the possibility of a continuous physical time. We can thus formally define the computational intelligence function as:

$$G_t(i_t) \rightarrow h_{t+\delta t}.$$

In the proposed physical model of computation, we stipulate that G_t causes only an immediate output in response to an immediate input. This stipulation does not prevent one from implementing some plan over time but it implies that a controller that would be necessary to implement such a plan is part of the intelligence function. The adaptation of G_t in response to evolving input i_t can be described by the *computational learning function*, $L_G : L_G(G_t, i_t) \rightarrow G_{t+\delta t}$.

Considering now the impact of the system behavior on the environment, we can define the *environment reaction function* mapping system output h(environment input) to the environment output i (system input):

$$P_t(h_t) \rightarrow i_{t+\delta t}$$

The adaptation of the environment P over time can be described by the *environment learning function*, $L_P : L_P(P_t, h_t) \rightarrow P_{t+\delta t}$.

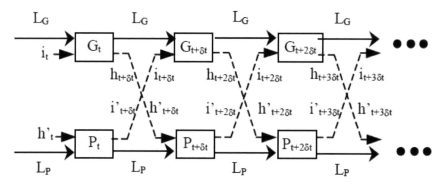

Figure 3.3:   Evolution of a system in an experiment with physical interaction.

3.4.2. *Physical Interaction between P and G*

The interaction between the system G and its physical environment P may be considered to fall into one of two classes: *real interaction* and *virtual interaction*. Real interaction is a purely physical process in which the output from the environment P is, in its entirety, forwarded as an input to the system G and, conversely, the output from G is fully utilized as input to P.

Referring to the notation in Figure 3.3, real interaction is one in which $h_t = h'_t$ and $i_t = i'_t$ for all time instances t. Unfortunately, this type of interaction does not accept the limitations of the UTM, namely the processing of only a pre-defined set of symbols rather than a full spectrum of responses from the environment. Consequently, this type of interaction places too high demands on the information processing capabilities of G and, in practical terms, is limited to the interaction of physical objects as governed by the laws of physics. In other words, the intelligence function and its implementation are one and the same.

3.4.3. *Virtual Interaction*

An alternative mode of interaction is *virtual interaction*, which is mediated by the symbolic representation of information. Here we use the term *symbol* as it is defined in the context of UTM: a letter or sign taken from a finite alphabet to allow distinguishability.

We define V_t as the *virtual computational intelligence function*, analogous to G_t in terms of information processing, and V'_t as the *complementary computational intelligence function*, analogous to G_t in terms of communication with the physical environment. With the above definitions, we can lift some major constraints of physical interactions, with important consequences. The complementary function V'_t can implement an interface to the environment, filtering real-life information input from the environment and facilitating transfer of actuator output, while the

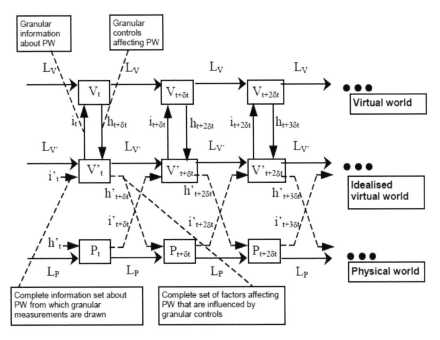

Figure 3.4: Evolution of a system in an experiment with virtual interaction.

virtual intelligence function V_t can implement UTM processing of the filtered information. This means that i_t does not need to be equal to i'_t and h_t does not need to be equal to h'_t. In other words, inputs and outputs may be considered selectively rather than in their totality. The implication is that many physically distinguishable states may have the same symbolic representation at the virtual computational intelligence function level. The relationship between the two components of computational intelligence is illustrated in Figure 3.4.

It should be pointed out that, typically, we think of the complementary function V'_t as some mechanical or electronic device (utilizing the laws of physics in its interaction with the environment) but a broader interpretation that includes human perception, as discussed by Zadeh in [40], is entirely consistent with the above model. In this broader context, the UTM implementing the virtual computational intelligence function can be referred to as *computing with perceptions* or *computing with words* (see Figure 3.5).

Another important implication of the virtual interaction model is that V and P need not have any kind of conserved relationship. This is because only the range/ modality of subsets of i'_t and h'_t attach to V and these subsets are defined by the choice of sensor/actuator modalities. So, we can focus on the choice of modalities, within the complementary computational intelligence function, as a mechanism through which one can exercise the assignment of semantics to both inputs and

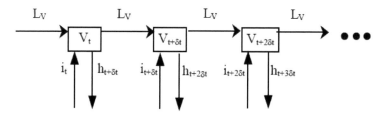

Figure 3.5:　The paradigm of computing with perceptions within the framework of virtual interaction.

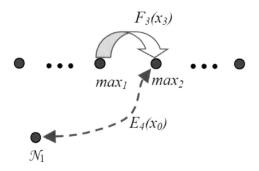

Figure 3.6:　An instance of granular computing involving two essential components: algorithmic clustering and empirical evaluation of granules.

outputs of the virtual intelligence function. To put it informally, the complementary function is a facility for defining a "language" we chose to communicate with the real world.

Of course, to make the optimal choice (one that allows undistorted perception and interaction with the physical environment), it would be necessary to have a complete knowledge of the physical environment. So, in its very nature the process of defining the semantics of inputs and outputs of the virtual intelligence function is iterative and involves evolution of our understanding of the physical environment.

3.5. Granular Computation

An important conclusion from the discussion above is that the discovery of semantics of information abstraction, sometimes referred to as structured thinking, or a philosophical dimension of granular computing, can be reduced to physical experimentation. This is a very welcome development as it gives a good basis for the formalization of the granular computing paradigm.

We argue here that granular computing should be defined as a **structured combination** of algorithmic abstraction of data and non-algorithmic, empirical verification of the semantics of these abstractions. This definition is general in that it neither prescribes the mechanism of algorithmic abstraction nor elaborates on the techniques of experimental verification. Instead, it highlights the essence of combining computational and non-computational information processing. Such a definition has several advantages:

- it emphasizes the complementarity of the two constituent functional mappings;
- it justifies the hyper-computational nature of GrC;
- it places physics alongside set theory as the theoretical foundations of GrC;
- it helps to avoid confusion between GrC and purely algorithmic data processing while taking full advantage of the advances in algorithmic data processing.

3.6. Design of Information Granules

Building information granules constitutes a central item on the agenda of granular computing with far-reaching implications on its applications. We present a way of moving from data to numeric representatives, information granules and their linguistic summarization. The organization of the overall scheme and the relationships among the resulting constructs are displayed in Figure 3.7.

Clustering as a design prerequisite of information granules

Along with a truly remarkable diversity of detailed algorithms and optimization mechanisms of clustering, the paradigm itself delivers a viable prerequisite for the formation of information granules (associated with the ideas and terminology of fuzzy clustering, rough clustering, and others) and applies to both numeric data and information granules. Information granules built through clustering are predominantly data-driven, viz. clusters (either in the form of fuzzy sets, sets, or rough sets) are a manifestation of a structure encountered (discovered) in the data.

Numeric prototypes are formed by invoking clustering algorithms, which yield a partition matrix and a collection of the prototypes. Clustering realizes a certain process of abstraction producing a small number of prototypes based on a large number of numeric data. Interestingly, clustering can also be completed in the

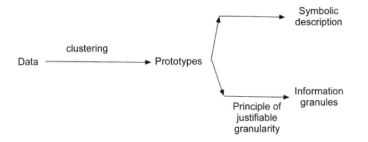

Figure 3.7: From data to information granules and linguistic summarization.

feature space. In this situation, the algorithm returns a small collection of abstracted features (groups of features) that might be referred to as meta-features.

Two ways of generalization of numeric prototypes treated as key descriptors of data and manageable chunks of knowledge are considered: (i) symbolic and (ii) granular. In the symbolic generalization, one ignores the numeric values of the prototypes and regards them as sequences of integer indexes (labels). Along this line developed are concepts of (symbolic) stability and (symbolic) resemblance of data structures. The second generalization motivates the construction of information granules (*granular* prototypes), which arise as a direct quest for delivering a more comprehensive representation of the data than the one delivered through numeric entities. This entails that information granules (including their associated level of abstraction) have to be prudently formed to achieve the required quality of the granular model.

As a consequence, performance evaluation embraces the following sound alternatives: (i) evaluation of the representation capabilities of numeric prototypes, (ii) evaluation of the representation capabilities of granular prototypes, and (iii) evaluation of the quality of the granular model.

Evaluation of the representation capabilities of numeric prototypes

In the first situation, the representation capabilities of numeric prototypes are assessed with the aid of a so-called granulation–degranulation scheme yielding a certain reconstruction error. The essence of the scheme can be schematically portrayed as follows:

$$x \to \text{internal representation} \to \text{reconstruction.}$$

The formation of the internal representation is referred to as granulation (encoding), whereas the process of degranulation (decoding) can be sought as an inverse mechanism to the encoding scheme. In terms of detailed formulas, one encounters the following flow of computing:

- Encoding leading to the degrees of activation of information granules by input x, say $A_1(x), A_2(x), \ldots, A_c(x)$ with

$$A_i(x) = \frac{1}{\sum_{j=1}^{c} \left(\frac{\|x - v_i\|}{\|x - v_i\|} \right)^{2/(m-1)}}$$

In case the prototypes are developed with the use of the Fuzzy C-Means (FCM) clustering algorithm, the parameter $m (> 1)$ stands for the fuzzification coefficient and $\| \cdot \|$ denotes the Euclidean distance.

– Degranulation (decoding) producing a reconstruction of x via the following expression:

$$\hat{x} = \frac{\sum\limits_{i=1}^{c} A_i^m(x)v_i}{\sum\limits_{i=1}^{c} A_i^m(x)v}$$

It is worth stressing that the above-stated formulas are a consequence of the underlying optimization problems. For any collection of numeric data, the reconstruction error is the sum of squared errors (distances) of the original data and their reconstructed versions.

The principle of justifiable granularity

The principle of justifiable granularity guides the construction of an information granule based on the available experimental evidence [50, 51]. In a nutshell, the resulting information granule delivers a summarization of data (viz. the available experimental evidence). The underlying rationale behind the principle is to deliver a concise and abstract characterization of the data such that (i) the produced granule is *justified* in light of the available experimental data and (ii) the granule comes with a well-defined *semantics*, meaning that it can be easily interpreted and become distinguishable from the others.

Formally speaking, these two intuitively appealing criteria are expressed by the criterion of coverage and the criterion of specificity. Coverage states how much data are positioned behind the constructed information granule. Put differently, coverage quantifies the extent to which the information granule is supported by the available experimental evidence. Specificity, on the other hand, is concerned with the semantics of the information granule, stressing the semantics (meaning) of the granule.

One-dimensional case

The definition of coverage and specificity requires formalization and this depends on the formal nature of the information granule to be formed. As an illustration, consider an interval form of the information granule A. In the case of intervals built on the basis of one-dimensional numeric data (evidence) $x_1, x_2, \ldots, x_N$, the coverage measure is associated with a count of the number of data embraced by A, namely

$$\text{cov}(A) = \frac{1}{N} card\{x_k | x_k \in A\}$$

card (.) denotes the cardinality of A, viz. the number (count) of elements x_k belonging to A. In essence, coverage has a visible probabilistic flavor. The specificity of A, $\text{sp}(A)$ is regarded as a decreasing function g of the size (length) of the information granule. If the granule is composed of a single element, sp(A) attains the highest value and returns 1. If A is included in some other information granule B, then $sp(A) > sp(B)$. In a limit case, if A is an entire space, $sp(A)$ returns zero. For an interval-valued information granule $A = [a, b]$, a simple implementation of specificity with g being a linearly decreasing function comes as

$$sp(A) = g(length(A)) = 1\frac{|b - a|}{range}$$

where *range* stands for an entire space over which intervals are defined.

If we consider a fuzzy set as a formal setting for information granules, the definitions of coverage and specificity are reformulated to take into account the nature of membership functions admitting a notion of partial membership. Here we invoke the fundamental representation theorem stating that any fuzzy set can be represented as a family of its α-cuts, namely

$$A(x) = \sup_{\alpha \in [0,1]} [\min(\alpha, A_\alpha(x))]$$

where

$$A_\alpha(x) = \{x | A(x) \geq \alpha\}$$

The supremum (sup) operation is taken over all values of the threshold α. Recall that by virtue of the representation theorem, any fuzzy set is represented as a collection of sets. Having this in mind and considering coverage as a point of departure for constructs of sets (intervals), we have the following relationships:

– Coverage

$$\text{cov}(A) = \int_X^\sqcup A(x)dx / N$$

where X is a space over which A is defined; moreover, one assumes that A can be integrated. The discrete version of the coverage expression comes in the form of the sum of membership degrees. If each data point is associated with some weight, the calculations of the coverage involve these values:

$$\text{cov}(A) = \int_X^\sqcup w(x)A(x)dx / \int_X^\sqcup w(x)dx$$

– Specificity

$$sp(A) = \int_0^1 sp(A_\alpha)d\alpha$$

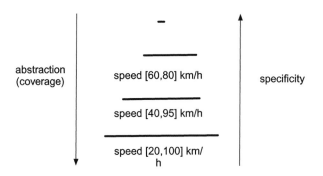

Figure 3.8: Relationships between the abstraction (coverage) and specificity of information granules of speed: emergence of a hierarchy of interval information granules of varying specificity.

The criteria of coverage and specificity are in an obvious relationship (Figure 3.8). We are interested in forecasting the speed: the more specific the statement about the prediction of speed is, the lower the likelihood of its satisfaction (coverage).

Let us introduce the following product of the criteria:

$$V = \text{cov}(A)sp(A).$$

It is apparent that the coverage and specificity are in conflict; the increase in coverage is associated with the drop in the specificity. Thus the desired solution is the one where the value of V attains its maximum.

The design of the information granule is accomplished by maximizing the above product of coverage and specificity. Formally speaking, consider that an information granule is described by a vector of parameters p, $V(p)$. The principle of justifiable granularity gives an information granule that maximizes V, $p_{\text{opt}} = \arg_p V(p)$.

To maximize the index V by adjusting the parameters of the information granule, two different strategies are encountered:

(i) A two-phase development is considered. First, a numeric representative (mean, median, mode, etc.) is determined first. It can be regarded as an initial representation of the data. Next, the parameters of the information granule are optimized by maximizing V. For instance, in the case of an interval, one has two bounds (a and b) to be determined. These two parameters are determined separately, viz. a and b are formed by maximizing $V(a)$ and $V(b)$. The data used in the maximization of $V(b)$ involve data larger than the numeric representative. Likewise, $V(a)$ is optimized on the basis of data lower than this representative.

(ii) a single-phase procedure in which all parameters of the information granule are determined at the same time.

Multi-dimensional case

The results of clustering coming in the form of numeric prototypes $v_1, v_2, \ldots, v_c$ can be further augmented by forming information granules, giving rise to so-called *granular* prototypes. This can be regarded as the result of the immediate usage of the principle of justifiable granularity and its algorithmic underpinning as elaborated earlier. Around the numeric prototype v_i, one spans an information granule V_i, $V_i = (v_i, \rho_i)$, whose optimal size is obtained as the result of the maximization of the well-known criterion

$$\rho_{i,opt} = \arg\max_{\rho i} [\text{cov}(V_i) sp(V_i)]$$

where

$$\text{cov}(V_i) = \tfrac{1}{N} card\{x_k | \, |x_k - v_i| \le n\rho_i\}$$

$$\text{cov}(V_i) = 1 - \rho_i$$

assuming that we are concerned with normalized data. In the case of the FCM method, the data come with their membership grades (entries of the partition matrix). The coverage criterion is modified to reflect this. Let us introduce the following notation:

$$\Omega_i = \{x_k | \, \|x_k - v_i\| \le n\rho_i\}$$

Then the coverage is expressed in the form

$$\text{cov}(V_i) = \frac{1}{N} \sum_{x_k \in \Omega_i} u_i$$

Representation aspects of granular prototypes

It is worth noting that given a collection of granular prototypes, one can conveniently assess their abilities to represent the original data (experimental evidence). The reconstruction problem, as outlined before for numeric data, can be formulated as follows: given x_k, complete its granulation and degranulation using the granular prototypes $V_i, i = 1, 2, \ldots, c$. The detailed computing generalizes the reconstruction process completed for the numeric prototypes and for given x yields a granular result $\hat{X} = (\hat{x}, \hat{\rho})$ where

$$\hat{v} = \frac{\sum_{i=1}^{c} A_i^m(x) v_i}{\sum_{i=1}^{c} A_i^m(x)} \qquad \hat{\rho} = \frac{\sum_{i=1}^{c} A_i^m(x) \rho_i}{\sum_{i=1}^{c} A_i^m(x)}$$

The quality of reconstruction uses the coverage criterion formed with the aid of the Boolean predicate

$$T(x_k) = \begin{cases} 1 & \text{if } \|\hat{v}_i - x_k\| \leq \hat{\rho} \\ 0, & \text{otherwise} \end{cases}$$

It is worth noting that in addition to the global measure of quality of granular prototypes, one can associate with them their individual quality (taken as the product of the coverage and specificity computed in the formation of the corresponding information granule).

The principle of justifiable granularity highlights an important facet of elevation of the type of information granularity: the result of capturing a number of pieces of numeric experimental evidence comes as a single abstract entity—information granule. As various numeric data can be thought of as information granules of type 0, the result becomes a single information granule of type 1. This is a general phenomenon of elevation of the type of information granularity. The increased level of abstraction is a direct consequence of the diversity present in the originally available granules. This *elevation* effect is of general nature and can be emphasized by stating that when dealing with experimental evidence composed of information granules of type n, the result becomes a single information granule of type $(n+1)$. Some generalizations and their augmentations are reported in [53, 56]

As a way of constructing information granules, the principle of justifiable granularity exhibits a significant level of generality in two important ways. First, given the underlying requirements of coverage and specificity, different formalisms of information granules can be engaged. Second, experimental evidence could be expressed as information granules articulated in different formalisms, and on this basis, a certain information granule is formed.

It is worth stressing that there is a striking difference between clustering and the principle of justifiable granularity. First, clustering leads to the formation of at least two information granules (clusters), whereas the principle of justifiable granularity produces a single information granule. Second, when positioning clustering and the principle vis-à-vis each other, the principle of justifiable granularity can be sought as a follow-up step facilitating an augmentation of the numeric representative of the cluster (e.g., a prototype) and yielding granular prototypes where the facet of information granularity is retained.

Granular probes of spatiotemporal data

When coping with spatiotemporal data (say, time series of temperature recorded over in a given geographic region), a concept of spatiotemporal probes arises as an efficient vehicle to describe the data, capture their local nature, and articulate their local characteristics as well as elaborate on their abilities as modeling artifacts (building blocks). The experimental evidence is expressed as a collection of data $z_k = z(x_k, y_k, t_k)$ with the corresponding arguments describing the location (x, y), time (t), and the value of the temporal data z_k.

Here, an information granule is positioned in a three-dimensional space:

(i) space of spatiotemporal variable z;
(ii) spatial position defined by the positions (x, y);
(iii) temporal domain described by time coordinate.

The information granule to be constructed is spanned over some position of the space of values z_0, spatial location (x_0, y_0), and temporal location t_0. With regard to the spatial location and the temporal location, we introduce some predefined level of specificity, which imposes a level of detail considered in advance. The coverage and specificity formed over the special and temporal domains are defined in the form

$$\text{cov}(A) = card\{z(x_k, y_k, t_k)|\; \|z(x_k, y_k, t_k) - z_0\| < n\rho\},$$

$$sp(A) = \max\left(0, 1 - \frac{|z - z_0|}{L_z}\right),$$

$$sp_x = \max\left(0, 1 - \frac{|x - x_0|}{L_x}\right),$$

$$sp_y = \max\left(0, 1 - \frac{|y - y_0|}{L_y}\right),$$

$$sp_t = \max\left(0, 1 - \frac{|t - t_0|}{L_t}\right),$$

where the above specificity measures are monotonically decreasing functions (linear functions in the case shown above). There are some cutoff ranges $(L_x, L_y...)$, which help impose a certain level of detail used in the construction of the information granule. Information granule A in the space of the spatiotemporal variable is carried out as before by maximizing the product of coverage of the data and the specificity, $\text{cov}(A)sp(A)$; however, in this situation, one considers the specificity that is associated with two other facets of the problem. In essence, A is produced by maximizing the product $\text{cov}(A)sp(A)sp_x, sp_y sp_t$.

3.6.1. Granular Models

The concept

The paradigm shift implied by the engagement of information granules becomes manifested in several tangible ways including (i) a stronger dependence on data when building structure-free, user-oriented, and versatile models spanned over selected representatives of experimental data, (ii) emergence of models at various varying levels of abstraction (generality) being delivered by the specificity/generality of information granules, and (iii) building a collection of individual local models and supporting their efficient aggregation.

Here, several main conceptually and algorithmically far-reaching avenues are emphasized. Notably, some of them have been studied to some extent in the past and several open up new directions worth investigating and pursuing. In what follows, we elaborate on them in more detail pointing out the relationships among them [52].

data → numeric models. This is a traditionally explored path that has been present in system modeling for decades. The original numeric data are used to build the model. There are a number of models, both linear and nonlinear, exploiting various design technologies, estimation techniques, and learning mechanisms associated with evaluation criteria where accuracy and interpretability are commonly exploited, with the Occam razor principle assuming a central role. The precision of the model is an advantage; however, the realization of the model is impacted by the dimensionality of the data (making the realization of some models not feasible); questions of memorization and a lack of generalization abilities are also central to the design practices.

data → numeric prototypes. This path is associated with the concise representation of data by means of a small number of representatives (prototypes). The tasks falling within this scope are preliminary to data analytics problems. Various clustering algorithms constitute generic development vehicles using which the prototypes are built as a direct product of the grouping method.

data → numeric prototypes → symbolic prototypes. This alternative branches off to symbolic prototypes where, on purpose, we ignore the numeric details of the prototypes with the intent to deliver a qualitative view of the information granules. Along this line, concepts such as the symbolic (qualitative) stability and qualitative resemblance of structure in data are established.

data → numeric prototypes → granular prototypes. This path augments the previous one by bringing the next phase in which the numeric prototypes are enriched by their granular counterparts. The granular prototypes are built in such a way that they deliver a comprehensive description of the data. The principle of justifiable granularity helps quantify the quality of the granules as well as deliver a global view of the granular characterization of the data.

data → numeric prototypes → symbolic prototypes → qualitative modeling. The alternative envisioned here builds upon the one where symbolic prototypes are formed and subsequently used in the formation of qualitative models, viz. the models capturing qualitative dependencies among input and output variables. This coincides with the well-known subarea of AI known as qualitative modeling, see [47] with a number of applications reported in [48, 49, 54, 55].

data → numeric prototypes → granular prototypes → granular models. This path constitutes a direct extension of the previous one when granular prototypes are sought as a collection of high-level abstract data based on which a model is being constructed. By virtue of the granular data, we refer to such models as granular models.

Construction of granular models

By granular model, we mean a model whose result is inherently an information granule as opposed to numeric results produced by a numeric model. In terms of this naming, neural networks are (nonlinear) numeric models. In contrast, granular neural networks produce outputs that are information granules (say, intervals).

There are two fundamental ways of constructing granular models:

(i) Stepwise development. One starts with a numeric model developed with the use of the existing methodology and algorithms and then elevates the numeric parameters of the models to their granular counterparts following the way outlined above. This design process dwells upon the existing models and, in this way, one takes full advantage of the existing modeling practices. By the same token, one can envision that the granular model delivers a substantial augmentation of the existing models. In this sense, we can talk about granular neural networks, granular fuzzy rule-based models. In essence, the design is concerned with the transformation $a \xrightarrow{\epsilon} A = G(a)$ applied to the individual parameters, where G is a certain formalism of information granulation. It is worth noticing that in the overall process, there are two performance indexes optimized: in the numeric model, one usually considers the root mean squared error (*RMSE*), while in the granular augmentation of the model, one invokes another performance index that takes into consideration the product of the coverage and specificity.

(ii) A single-step design. One proceeds with the development of the granular model from scratch by designing granular parameters of the model. This process uses only a single performance index that is of interest to evaluate the quality of the granular result.

One starts with a numeric (type-0) model $M(x; a)$ developed on the basis of input–output data $D = (x_k, target_k)$. Then one elevates it to type-1 by optimizing a level of information granularity allocated to the numeric parameters a, thus making them granular.

The way of transforming (elevating) a numeric entity a to an information granule A is expressed formally as follows: $A = G(a)$. Here, G stands for a formal setting of information granules (say, intervals, fuzzy sets, etc.) and ε denotes a level of information granularity.

One can envision two among a number of ways of elevating a certain numeric parameter a into its granular counterpart.

If A is an interval, its bounds are determined as

$$A = [\min(a(1-\varepsilon), a(1+\varepsilon)), \max((a(1-\varepsilon), a(1-\varepsilon)))], \varepsilon \in [0, 1],$$

Another option comes in the form

$$A = [\min(a/(1+\varepsilon), a(1+\varepsilon)), \max((a/(1+\varepsilon), a(1+\varepsilon)))], \varepsilon \geq 0.$$

If A is realized as a fuzzy set, one can regard the bounds of its support determined in the ways outlined above.

Obviously, the higher the value of ε, the broader the result and higher the likelihood of satisfying the coverage requirement. Higher values of ε yield lower specificity of the results. Following the principle of justifiable granularity, we maximize the product of coverage and specificity by choosing a value of ε.

The performance of the granular model can be studied by analyzing the values of coverage and specificity for various values of the level of information granularity ε. Some plots of such relationships are presented in Figure 3.9. In general, as noted earlier, increasing values of ε result in higher coverage and lower values of specificity.

By analyzing the pace of changes in the coverage versus the changes in the specificity, one can select a preferred value of ε as such beyond which the coverage does not increase in a substantial way yet the specificity deteriorates significantly. One can refer to Figure 3.9, where both curves (a) and (b) help identify suitable values of ε. One can develop a global descriptor of the quality of the granular model by computing the area under curve; the larger the area is, the better the overall quality

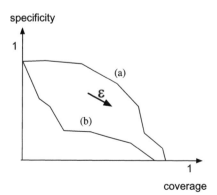

Figure 3.9: Characteristics of the granular models presented in the coverage-specificity coordinates.

of the model (quantified over all levels of information granularity) is. For instance, in Figure 3.5, the granular model (a) exhibits better performance than (b).

The level of information granularity allocated to all parameters of the model is the same. Different levels of information granularity can be assigned to individual parameters; an allocation of these levels could be optimized in such a way that the values of the performance index V become maximized, whereas a balance of information granularity is retained. In a formal way, we consider the following optimization task:

$$\underset{\varepsilon}{\text{Min}}\, V,$$

subject to the constraints

$$\sum_{i=1}^{P} \varepsilon_i = P\varepsilon\varepsilon_i \in [0, 1]$$

or

$$\sum_{i=1}^{P} \varepsilon_i = P\varepsilon\varepsilon_i \geq 0,$$

where the vector of levels of information granularity is expressed as $\varepsilon = [\varepsilon_1 \varepsilon_2 \ldots \varepsilon_P]$ and P stands for the number of parameters of the model. By virtue of the nature of this optimization problem, the use of evolutionary methods could be a viable option.

3.7. An Example of Granular Computation

We illustrate here an application of the granular computation, cast in the formalism of set theory, to a practical problem of analyzing traffic queues. A three-way intersection is represented in Figure 3.10. The three lane-occupancy detectors (inductive loops), labeled here as "east," "west," and "south," provide counts of vehicles passing over them. The counts are then integrated to yield a measure of traffic queues on the corresponding approaches to the junction. A representative sample of the resulting three-dimensional time series of traffic queues is illustrated in Figure 3.11.

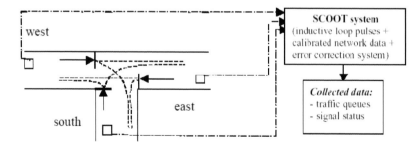

Figure 3.10:   A three-way intersection with measured traffic queues.

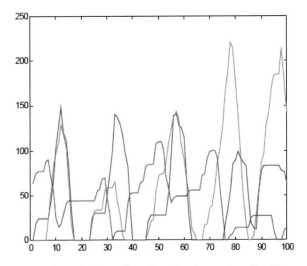

Figure 3.11: A subset of 100 readings from the time series of traffic queues data.

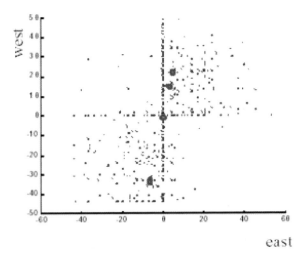

Figure 3.12: FCM prototypes as a subset of the original measurements of traffic queues.

It is quite clear that, on its own, data depicted in Figure 3.11 reflect primarily the signaling stages of the junction. This view is reinforced if we plot the traffic queues on a two-dimensional plane and apply some clustering technique (such as FCM) to identify prototypes that are the best (in terms of the given optimality criterion) representation of data. The prototypes, denoted as small circles in Figure 3.12, indicate that the typical operation of the junction involves simultaneously increasing and simultaneously decreasing queues on the "east" and "west" junctions. This of course corresponds to "red" and "green" signaling stages. It is worth emphasizing

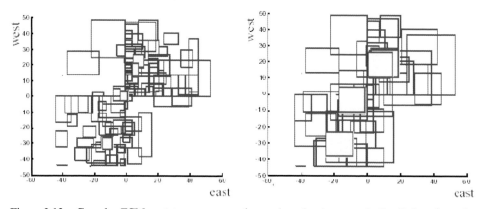

Figure 3.13: Granular FCM prototypes representing a class that is semantically distinct from the original point data.

here that the above prototypes can be considered a simple subset of the original numerical data since the nature of the prototypes is entirely consistent with that of the original data.

Unfortunately, within this framework, the interpretation of the prototype indicating "zero" queue in both "east" and "west" directions is not very informative. In order to uncover the meaning of this prototype, we resort to a granulated view of data. Figure 3.13 represents traffic queue data that have been granulated based on the maximization of information density measure discussed in [12]. The semantics of the original readings is now changed from point representation of queues into interval (hyperbox) representation of queues. In terms of set theory, we are dealing here with a class of hyperboxes, which is semantically distinct from point data.

Applying FCM clustering to granular data results in granular prototypes denoted in Figure 3.13 as rectangles with bold boundaries overlaid on the granulated data. In order to ascertain that the granulation does not distort the essential features of the data, different granulation parameters have been investigated and a representative sample of two granulations is depicted in Figure 3.13. The three FCM prototypes lying in the areas of simultaneous increase and decrease in traffic queues have identical interpretations as the corresponding prototypes in Figure 3.12. However, the central prototype highlights a physical property of traffic that was not captured by the numerical prototype.

Figure 3.14 illustrates the richer interpretation of the central prototype. It is clear that the traffic queues on the western approach are increasing, while the traffic queues on the eastern approach are decreasing. This is caused by the "right turning" traffic being blocked by the oncoming traffic from the eastern junction. It is worth noting that the prototype is unambiguous about the absence of a symmetrical situation where an increase in traffic queues on the eastern junction would occur simultaneously with the decrease in the queues on the western junction. The fact

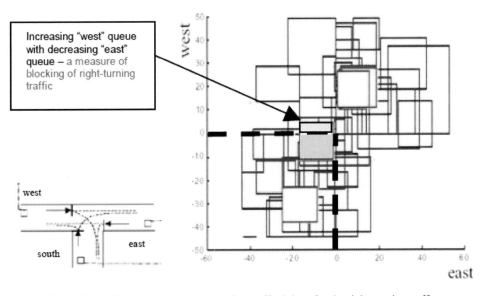

Figure 3.14: Granular prototype capturing traffic delays for the right-turning traffic.

that this is a three-way junction with no right turn for the traffic from the eastern junction has been captured purely from the granular interpretation of data. Note that the same cannot be said about the numerical data illustrated in Figure 3.12.

As we have argued in this chapter, the essential component of granular computing is the experimental validation of the semantics of the information granules. We have conducted a planned experiment in which we placed counting devices on the entrance to the "south" link. The proportion of the vehicles entering the "south" junction (during the green stage of the "east–west" junction) to the count of vehicles on the stop line on the "west" approach represents a measure of the right turning traffic. The ratio of these numerical counts was 0.1428. Similar measurements derived from two different granulations depicted in Figure 3.13 were 0.1437 and 0.1498. We conclude therefore that the granulated data captured the essential characteristics of the right turning traffic and that, in this particular application, the granulation parameters do not affect the result to a significant degree (which is clearly a desirable property).

A more extensive experimentation could involve the verification of the granular measurement of the right-turning traffic for drivers that have different driving styles in terms of acceleration and gap acceptance. Although we do not make any specific claim in this respect, it is possible that the granulation of traffic queue data would need to be parameterized with the dynamic driver behavior data. Such data could be derived by differentiating the traffic queues (measurement of the speed of change of queues) and granulating the resulting six-dimensional data.

References

[1] S. Bains, Intelligence as physical computation, *AISB J.*, **1**(3), 225–240 (2003).

[2] S. Bains, Physical computation and embodied artificial intelligence, PhD thesis, The Open University (2005).

[3] A. Bargiela and W. Pedrycz, *Granular Computing: An Introduction*, Kluwer Academic (2002).

[4] A. Bargiela and W. Pedrycz, From numbers to information granules: a study of unsupervised learning and feature analysis, in H. Bunke, A. Kandel (eds.), *Hybrid Methods in Pattern Recognition*, World Scientific (2002).

[5] A. Bargiela and W. Pedrycz, Recursive information granulation: aggregation and interpretation issues, *IEEE Trans. Syst. Man Cybern. SMC-B*, **33**(1), 96–112 (2003).

[6] A. Bargiela, Hypercomputational characteristics of granular computing, in *1st Warsaw Int. Seminar on Intelligent Systems - WISIS 2004*, Invited Lectures, Warsaw (2004).

[7] A. Bargiela, W. Pedrycz, and M. Tanaka, An inclusion/exclusion fuzzy hyperbox classifier, *Int. J. Knowledge-Based Intell. Eng. Syst.*, **8**(2), 91–98 (2004).

[8] A. Bargiela, W. Pedrycz, and Hirota K., Granular prototyping in fuzzy clustering, *IEEE Trans. Fuzzy Syst.*, **12**(5), 697–709 (2004).

[9] A. Bargiela and W. Pedrycz, A model of granular data: a design problem with the Tchebyschev FCM, *Soft Comput.*, **9**(3), 155–163 (2005).

[10] A. Bargiela and W. Pedrycz, Granular mappings, *IEEE Trans. Syst. Man Cybern. SMC-A*, **35**(2), 288–301 (2005).

[11] A. Bargiela and W. Pedrycz, The roots of granular computing, *Proc. IEEE Granular Computing Conf.*, Atlanta, 741–744 (2006).

[12] A. Bargiela, I. Kosonen, M. Pursula, and E. Peytchev, Granular analysis of traffic data for turning movements estimation, *Int. J. Enterp. Inf. Syst.*, **2**(2), 13–27 (2006).

[13] G. Cantor, Über einen Satz aus der Theorie der stetigen Mannigfaltigkeiten, *Göttinger Nachr.*, 127–135 (1879).

[14] D. Dubois, H. Prade, and R. Yager (eds.), *Fuzzy Information Engineering*, Wiley, New York (1997).

[15] K. Goedel, *The Consistency of the Axiom of Choice and of the Generalized Continuum Hypothesis with the Axioms of Set Theory*. Princeton University Press, Princeton, NJ (1940).

[16] E. Husserl, Logische Untersuchungen. Phänomenologie und Theorie der Erkenntnis, in *Logical Investigations* (1970).

[17] M. Inuiguchi, S. Hirano, and S. Tsumoto (eds.), *Rough Set Theory and Granular Computing*, Springer, Berlin (2003).

[18] S. Lesniewski, Uber Funktionen, deren Felder Gruppen mit Rucksicht auf diese Funktionen sind, *Fundamenta Mathematicae XIII*, 319–332 (1929).

[19] S. Lesniewski, Grundzuge eines neuen Systems der Grundlagen der Mathematik, *Fundamenta Mathematicae XIV*, 1–81 (1929).

[20] T. Y. Lin, Granular computing on binary relations, in L. Polkowski and A. Skowron (eds.), *Rough Sets in Knowledge Discovery: Methodology and Applications*, Physica-Verlag, Heidelberg, 286–318 (1998).

[21] T. Y. Lin, Y. Y. Yao, and L. A. Zadeh (eds.), *Data mining, Rough Sets and Granular Computing*, Physica-Verlag (2002).

[22] M. Matsuyama, *How to Summarize and Analyze Small Data Sets*, Kawaboku Publishers, Tokyo (1937).

[23] Z. Pawlak, *Rough Sets: Theoretical Aspects of Reasoning About Data*, Kluwer Academic, Dordrecht (1991).

[24] Z. Pawlak, Granularity of knowledge, indiscernibility and rough sets, *Proc. IEEE Conf. Fuzzy Syst.*, 106–110 (1998).

[25] W. Pedrycz, *Fuzzy Control and Fuzzy Systems*, Wiley, New York (1989).

[26] W. Pedrycz and F. Gomide, *An Introduction to Fuzzy Sets*, Cambridge, MIT Press, Cambridge, MA (1998).

[27] W. Pedrycz, M. H. Smith, and A. Bargiela, Granular clustering: a granular signature of data, *Proc. 19th Int. (IEEE) Conf. NAFIPS'2000*, Atlanta, 69–73 (2000).

[28] W. Pedrycz, A. Bargiela, Granular clustering: a granular signature of data, *IEEE Trans. Syst. Man Cybern.*, **32**(2), 212–224 (2002).

[29] B. Russel, New foundations for mathematical logic, *Am. Math. Mon.*, **2** (1937).

[30] H. Siegelmann, *Neural Networks and Analogue Computation: Beyond the Turing Limit*, Birkhäuser, Boston, MA (1999).

[31] P. Simons, *Parts: A Study in Ontology*, Oxford Univ. Press (1987).

[32] A. Skowron, Toward intelligent systems: calculi of information granules, *Bull. Int. Rough Set Soc.*, **5**, 9–30 (2001).

[33] A. Skowron and J. Stepaniuk, Information granules: towards foundations of granular computing, *Int.J. Intell. Syst.*, **16**, 57–85 (2001).

[34] A. Tarski, Foundations of the geometry of solids, in *Logic, Semantics, Metamathematics: Papers 1923–38*, Hackett, 1984 (1956).

[35] A. Turing, On computable numbers, with an application to the entscheidungsproblem, *Proc. London Math. Soc.*, **42**, 230–265 (1936).

[36] Y. Y. Yao and J. T. Yao, Granular computing as a basis for consistent classification problems, *Proceedings PAKDD'02 Workshop on Foundations of Data Mining*, 101–106 (2002).

[37] Y. Y. Yao, Granular computing, *Proc. 4th Chinese National Conference on Rough Sets and Soft Computing*, **31**, 1–5 (2004).

[38] Y. Y. Yao, A partition model of granular computing, *LNCS Trans. Rough Sets*, **1**, 232–253 (2004).

[39] Y. Y. Yao, Perspectives on granular computing, *Proc. IEEE Conf. on Granular Computing*, **1**, 85–90 (2005).

[40] L. A. Zadeh, Toward a theory of fuzzy information granulation and its centrality in human reasoning and fuzzy logic, *Fuzzy Sets Syst.*, **90**, 111–127 (1997).

[41] L. A. Zadeh, Fuzzy sets and information granularity, in N. Gupta, R. Ragade, R. Yager (eds.), *Advances in Fuzzy Set Theory and Applications*, North-Holland (1979).

[42] L. A. Zadeh, Fuzzy sets, *Inform Control*, **8**, 338–353 (1965).

[43] L. A. Zadeh, From computing with numbers to computing with words: from manipulation of measurements to manipulation of perceptions, *Int.J. Appl. Math Comput. Sci.*, **12**(3), 307–324 (2002).

[44] L. A. Zadeh, Granular computing: the concept of generalized constraint-based computation, Private Communication.

[45] E. Zermelo, Untersuchungen ueber die Grundlagen der Mengenlehre, *Math. Annalen*, **65**, 261–281 (1908).

[46] C. Pontow, R. Schubert, A mathematical analysis of parthood, *Data Knowl. Eng.*, **59**(1), 107–138 (2006).

[47] K. Forbus, Qualitative process theory, *Artif. Intell.*, **24**, 85–168 (1984).

[48] F. Guerrin, Qualitative reasoning about an ecological process: interpretation in hydroecology, *Ecol. Model.*, **59**, 165–201 (1991).

[49] W. Haider, J. Hu, J. Slay, B. P. Turnbull, and Y. Xie, Generating realistic intrusion detection system dataset based on fuzzy qualitative modeling, *J. Network Comput. Appl.*, **87**, 185–192 (2017).

[50] W. Pedrycz and W. Homenda, Building the fundamentals of granular computing: a principle of justifiable granularity, *Appl. Soft Comput.*, **13**, 4209–4218 (2013).

[51] W. Pedrycz, *Granular Computing*, CRC Press, Boca Raton, FL (2013).

[52] W. Pedrycz, Granular computing for data analytics: a manifesto of human-centric computing, *IEEE/CAA J. Autom. Sin.*, **5**, 1025–1034 (2018).

[53] D. Wang, W. Pedrycz, and Z. Li, Granular data aggregation: an adaptive principle of justifiable granularity approach, *IEEE Trans. Cybern.*, **49**, 417–426 (2019).

[54] Y. H. Wong, A. B. Rad, and Y. K. Wong, Qualitative modeling and control of dynamic systems, *Eng. Appl. Artif. Intell.*, **10**(5), 429–439 (1997).

[55] J. Žabkar, M. Možina, I. Bratko, and J. Demšar, Learning qualitative models from numerical data, *Artif. Intell.*, **175**(9–10), 1604–1619 (2011).

[56] Z. Zhongjie and H. Jian, Stabilizing the information granules formed by the principle of justifiable granularity, *Inf. Sci.*, **503**, 183–199 (2019).

Chapter 4

Evolving Fuzzy and Neuro-Fuzzy Systems: Fundamentals, Stability, Explainability, Useability, and Applications

Edwin Lughofer

Department of Knowledge-Based Mathematical Systems,
Johannes Kepler University Linz, Altenbergerstrasse 69, A-4040 Linz,
edwin.lughofer@jku.at

This chapter provides an all-round picture of the development and advances in the fields of *evolving fuzzy systems* (EFS) and *evolving neuro-fuzzy systems* (ENFS) which have been made during the last 20 years since their first-time appearance around the year 2000. Their basic difference to the conventional (neuro-)fuzzy systems is that they can be learned, from data, on-the-fly during (fast) online processes in an incremental and mostly single-pass manner. Therefore, they stand for emerging topic in the field of soft computing and artificial intelligence for addressing modeling problems in the quickly increasing complexity of online data streaming applications and Big Data challenges, implying a shift from batch off-line model design phases (as conducted since the 1980s) to online (active) model teaching and adaptation. The focus will be on the definition of various model architectures used in the context of EFS and ENFS, on providing an overview of the basic learning concepts and learning steps in E(N)FS with a wide scope of references to E(N)FS approaches published so far (fundamentals), and on discussing advanced aspects towards an improved stability, reliability, and useability (usually must-to-haves to guarantee robustness and user-friendliness) as well as towards an educated explainability and interpretability of the models and their outputs (usually a nice-to-have to find reasons for predictions and to offer insights into the systems' nature). The chapter will be concluded with a list of real-world applications where various E(N)FS approaches have been successfully applied with satisfactory accuracy, robustness, and speed.

4.1. Introduction: Motivation

Due to the increasing complexity and permanent growth of data acquisition sites, in today's industrial systems there is an increasing demand for fast modeling algorithms from online data streams [1]. Such algorithms are ensuring that models can be quickly adapted to the actual system situation and thus provide reliable outputs any time during online real-world processes. There, changing operating conditions, environmental influences, and new unexplored system states may trigger a quite dynamic behavior, causing previously trained models to become inefficient or even inaccurate [2]. In this sense, conventional static models, which are trained once in an off-line stage and are not able to adapt dynamically to the actual system states, are not an adequate alternative method for coping with these demands (severe downtrends in accuracy have been examined in previous publications). A list of potential real-world application examples relying on online dynamic aspects, and thus demanding flexible modeling techniques, can be found in Tables 4.1 and 4.2.

Another challenge which has recently become a very hot topic within the machine learning community, and is given specific attention in the European framework program Horizon 2020 and in the upcoming Horizon Europe 2021–2027 program, is the processing and mining of so-called Big Data [3], usually stemming from very large data bases VLDBs [4]. The use of Big Data takes place in many areas such as meteorology and geotechnical engineering [5], magnetic resonance imaging, credit scoring [6], connectomics [7], complex physics simulations, and biological and environmental research [8]. This data is so big (often requesting a size of several exabytes) that it cannot be handled in a one-shot experience [9], as it can exceed the virtual memory of today's conventional computers. Thus, standard batch modeling techniques are not applicable.

In order to tackle the aforementioned requirements, the field of evolving intelligent systems (EISs) [10] or, in a wider machine learning sense, the field of learning in non-stationary environments (LNSEs) [2] enjoyed increasing attention during the last years. This even led to the emergence of a journal in 2010, named *Evolving Systems*, published by Springer (Heidelberg)[1], with 396 peer-reviewed papers published so far and a current impact factor of 2.070 (in the year 2020). Both fields support learning topologies which operate in a single-pass manner and are able to update models and surrogate statistics on-the-fly and on demand. The single-pass nature and incrementality of the updates assure online and, in most cases, even real-time learning and model training capabilities. While EISs focus mainly on adaptive evolving models within the field of soft computing, LNSEs go a step further and also join incremental machine learning and data mining techniques, originally stemming from the area of, "incremental heuristic search" [11]. The update in these approaches concerns both parameter adaptation and structural changes, depending on the degree of change required. The structural changes are usually enforced by evolution and pruning components, and are finally responsible for the term *evolving* in EISs. In this context, *evolving* should not be confused with *evolutionary* (as has sometimes happened in the past, unfortunately). Evolutionary approaches are usually applied in

---

[1] http://www.springer.com/physics/complexity/journal/12530

the context of complex optimization problems and learn parameters and structures based on genetic operators, but they do this by using all the data in an iterative optimization procedure rather than integrating new knowledge permanently on-the-fly.

Apart from dynamic adaptation requirements in industrial predictive maintenance systems [12] as well as control [13] and production environments, another important aspect of evolving models is that they provide the opportunity for making self-learning computer systems and machines. In fact, evolving models are permanently updating their knowledge and understanding of diverse complex relationships and dependencies in real-world application scenarios by integrating new system behaviors and environmental influences (which are manifested in the captured data). This is typically achieved in a fully autonomous fashion [14], and their learning follows a life-long learning context and thus is never really terminated, but lasts as long as new information arrives. In this context, they are also able to properly address the principles of continual learning and task-based incremental learning [15] in specific data stream environments, where new data chunks characterize new tasks (typically with some relation to older tasks): based on their occurrence in the streams, evolving mechanisms may autonomously evolve new model components and structures and thus expand knowledge of the models on-the-fly to account for the new tasks. Due to these aspects, they can be seen as a valuable contribution within the field of computational intelligence [16] and even in the field of artificial intelligence (AI) [17].

There are several possibilities for using an adequate model architecture within the context of an evolving system. This strongly depends on the learning problem at hand, in particular, whether it is supervised or unsupervised. In the case of the latter, techniques from the field of clustering, usually termed as *dynamic clustering* [18] are a prominent choice. In the case of supervised classification and regression models, the architectures should support decision boundaries or approximation surfaces with an arbitrary nonlinearity degree. Moreover, the choice may depend on past experience with some machine learning and data mining tools; for instance, it is well-known that SVMs are usually among the top 10 performers for many classification tasks [19]; thus, they are a reasonable choice to be used in an online classification setting as well (in the form of incremental SVMs [20, 21]). Soft computing models such as neural networks [22], fuzzy systems [23] or genetic programming [24], and any hybrid concepts of these (e.g., neuro-fuzzy systems [25]) are all known to be universal approximators [26] and thus are able to resolve non-linearities implicitly contained in the systems' behavior. Neural networks usually suffer from their black box nature, i.e., not allowing operators and users any insight into the models extracted from the streams, although approaches for more explanation of model outputs arose during recent years; however, these are basically operating on an output level rather than on an internal model component level, the latter opening up further process insights for experts (new knowledge gaining). Genetic programming is a more promising choice in this direction; however, it may suffer from expanding unnecessarily complex formulas with many nested functional terms (termed as the bloating effect [27]), which are again hard to interpret.

Fuzzy systems are specific mathematical models which build upon the concept of fuzzy logic, first introduced in 1965 by Lotfi A. Zadeh [28]. They are a very useful option to offer interpretability on a structural model component level, as they contain rules that are linguistically readable. This mimics human thinking about relationships and structural dependencies present in a system. This will become clearer in the subsequent section when mathematically defining possible architecture variants within the field of fuzzy systems. Furthermore, the reader may refer to Chapter 1 of this book, where basic concepts of fuzzy sets and systems are introduced and described in detail.

Fuzzy systems have been widely used in the context of data stream mining and evolving systems during the last two decades (starting around the year 2000). They are termed as *evolving fuzzy systems* (EFS) [29], and in combination with concepts from the field of neuronal networks they are termed as *evolving neuro-fuzzy systems* (ENFS) [30]. They wed the concept of robust incremental learning of purely data-driven models (in order to obtain the highest possible precision for prediction on new samples) with aspects of interpretability and explainability of learned model components (typically, in the form of linguistically readable rules) [31, 32]. This opens up new research horizons in the context of on-the-fly feedback integration of human knowledge into the models [33]. This in turn, may enrich evolving models with other more subjective and cognitive viewpoints and interpretation aspects than those contained in pure objective data, turning them into a hybrid AI concept [34].

The upper plot in Figure 4.1 shows the development of the number of publications in the field of evolving (neuro-)fuzzy systems over the time frame of nearly 30 years, significantly starting at around 2000 and with a further significant increase during the "golden early emerging years" (2006–2014), followed by saturation during the last 5–6 years. By the end of 2020, there were 1652 in total. On the other hand, regarding the citation trends shown in the lower plot, an explosion can be seen from 2012 to 2019, where the number of citations approximately tripled, from 1,000 to 3,000 per year. This underlines the growing importance of evolving (neuro-)fuzzy systems during the recent decades in research and industry—which goes hand-in-hand with the importance of evolving systems in general, as described above. In sum, a remarkable number of 24,547 references have been made to papers in the field of evolving (neuro-)fuzzy systems.

4.2. Architectures for EFS

The first five subsections are dedicated to architectures for regression problems, for which evolving fuzzy systems (EFS) have been used preliminarily, including the

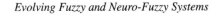

Total Publications

1.652 Analyze

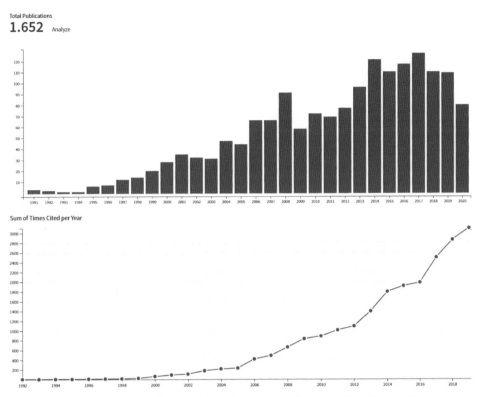

Sum of Times Cited per Year

Figure 4.1:   Upper plot: the development of publications in the field of evolving (neuro-)fuzzy systems over the last 30 years; lower plot: the development in terms of citations, 24,547 in total.

extensions to neuro-fuzzy systems. Then, various variants of fuzzy classification model structures are discussed, having been introduced for representing decision boundaries in various forms in evolving fuzzy classifiers (EFC), ranging from the classical single-model architecture to multi-model variants and deep rule-based architectures.

4.2.1. *Mamdani*

Mamdani fuzzy systems [35] are the most common choice for coding expert knowledge/experience into a rule-based IF-THEN form; examples in several application scenarios can be found in [36, 37] or [38, 39].

In general, assuming p input variables (features), the definition of the ith rule in a single-output Mamdani fuzzy system is as follows:

$$\text{Rule}_i \quad \text{IF } (x_1 \text{ IS } \mu_{i1}) \text{ AND} \dots \text{AND } (x_p \text{ IS } \mu_{ip}) \text{ THEN } l_i(\vec{x}) \text{ IS } \Phi_i$$

with Φ_i the consequent fuzzy set in the fuzzy partition of the output variable used in the consequent $l_i(\vec{x})$ of the ith rule, and $\mu_{i1}, \dots, \mu_{ip}$ are the fuzzy sets appearing in the rule antecedents. The *rule firing degree* (also called *rule activation level*) for a concrete input vector $\vec{x} = (x_1, \ldots, x_p)$ is then defined by

$$\mu_i(\vec{x}) = \underset{j=1}{\overset{p}{\mathsf{T}}} \mu_{ij}(x_j), \tag{4.1}$$

with T being a specific conjunction operator, denoted as *t*-norm [40]—most frequently, minimum or product is used, i.e.,

$$\mu_i(\vec{x}) = \underset{j=1}{\overset{p}{\min}}(\mu_{ij}(x_j)) \quad \mu_i(\vec{x}) = \prod_{j=1}^{p}(\mu_{ij}(x_j)) \tag{4.2}$$

with $\mu_{ij}(x_j)$ being the membership degree of x_j to the jth fuzzy set in the ith rule.

It may happen that $\Phi_i = \Phi_j$ for some $i \neq j$. Hence, a t-conorm [40] is applied which combines the rule firing levels of those rules having the same consequents to one output set. The most common choice for the t-conorm is the maximum operator. In this case, the consequent fuzzy set is cut at the alpha-level:

$$\alpha_i = \max_{j_i=1,\ldots,C_i}(\mu_{j_i}(\vec{x})) \tag{4.3}$$

with C_i being the number of rules whose consequent fuzzy set is the same as that for Rule i, and j_i the indices of these rules. This is done for the whole fuzzy rule base and the various α-cut output sets are joined to one fuzzy area employing the *supremum operator*. An example of such a fuzzy output area for a fuzzy output partition containing four fuzzy sets $A1$, $A2$, $A3$, and $A4$ is shown in Figure 4.2.

In order to obtain a crisp output value, a defuzzification method is applied, the most commonly used being the mean of maximum (MOM) over the whole area, the center of gravity (COG) or the bisector [41] which is the vertical line that will divide the whole area into two sub-regions of equal areas. For concrete formulas of the defuzzification operators, please refer to [42, 43]. MOM and COG are examples shown in Figure 4.2.

Due to the defuzzification process, it is quite intuitive that the inference in Mamdani fuzzy systems loses some accuracy, as an output fuzzy number is reduced to a crisp number. Therefore, they have been hardly been applied within the context of online modeling and data stream mining, where the main purpose is to obtain an accurate evolving fuzzy model in the context of *precise evolving fuzzy modeling*—an exception can be found in [44] termed as the SOFMLS approach and in [45] using a switching architecture with Takagi–Sugeno type consequents, see below.

4.2.2. *Takagi–Sugeno*

Takagi–Sugeno (TS) fuzzy systems [46] are the most common architectural choice in evolving fuzzy systems approaches [30]. This has several reasons. First of all, they enjoy a large attraction in many fields of real-world applications and systems

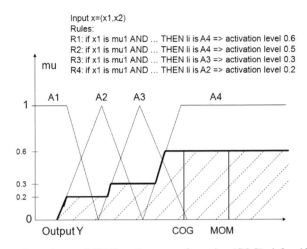

Figure 4.2: Mean of maximum (MOM) and center of gravity (COG) defuzzification for a rule consequent partition (fuzzy partition in output variable Y) in a Mamdani fuzzy system; the shaded area indicates the joint consequents (fuzzy sets) in the active rules (applying supremum operator); the cutoff points (alpha cuts) are according to maximal membership degrees obtained from the rule antecedent parts of the active rules.

engineering [23], ranging from process control [13, 47, 48], system identification [49–51], through condition monitoring [52, 53] and chemometric calibration tasks [54, 55], to predictive and preventive maintenance [12, 56]. Thus, their robustness and applicability in the standard batch modeling case has been practically verified for several decades. Second, they are known to be universal approximators [57], i.e., they are able to model any implicitly contained non-linearity with a sufficient degree of accuracy, while their interpretable capabilities are still intact or may even offer advantages: while the antecedent parts remain linguistic, the consequent parts can be interpreted either in a more physical sense (see [58]) or as local functional tendencies [32], see also Section 4.5.2. Finally, parts of their architecture (the consequents) can be updated exactly by recursive procedures, as will be described in Section 4.3.1, achieving *true optimal incremental solutions*.

4.2.2.1. *Takagi–Sugeno standard*

A single rule in a (single output) standard TS fuzzy system is of the form

$$\text{Rule}_i\text{: IF } (x_1 \text{ IS } \mu_{i1}) \text{ AND } \ldots \text{ AND } (x_p \text{ IS } \mu_{ip}) \tag{4.4}$$

$$\text{THEN } l_i(\vec{x}) = w_{i0} + w_{i1}x_1 + w_{i2}x_2 + \ldots + w_{ip}x_p, \tag{4.5}$$

where $\vec{x} = (x_1, \ldots, x_p)$ is the p-dimensional input vector and μ_{ij} the fuzzy set describing the j-th antecedent of the rule. Typically, these fuzzy sets are associated with a linguistic label. As in the case of Mamdani fuzzy systems, the AND connective is modeled in terms of a t-norm, i.e., a generalized logical conjunction [40].

The output of a TS system consisting of C rules is realized by a linear combination of the outputs produced by the individual rules (through the l_i's) ($\rightarrow$ fuzzy inference), where the contribution of each rule is indicated by its normalized degree of activation Ψ_i and thus,

$$\hat{f}(\vec{x}) = \hat{y} = \sum_{i=1}^{C} \Psi_i(\vec{x}) \cdot l_i(\vec{x}) \quad \text{with} \quad \Psi_i(\vec{x}) = \frac{\mu_i(\vec{x})}{\sum_{j=1}^{C} \mu_j(\vec{x})}, \quad (4.6)$$

with $\mu_i(\vec{x})$ as in Eq. (4.1).

The most convenient choice for fuzzy sets in EFS and fuzzy system design in general are Gaussian functions, which lead to so-called *fuzzy basis function networks* [59]. Multivariate kernels based on the axis-parallel normal distribution are achieved for representing the rules' antecedent parts

$$\mu_i(\vec{x}) = \prod_{i=1}^{p} exp\left(-\frac{1}{2} \frac{(x_i - c_i)^2}{\sigma_i^2} \right). \quad (4.7)$$

In this sense, the linear hyper-planes l_i are connected with multivariate Gaussians to form an overall smooth function. Then, the output form in Eq. (4.6) has some synergies with Gaussian mixture models (GMMs) [60, 61], often used for clustering and pattern recognition tasks [62, 63]. The difference is that the l_i's are hyper-planes instead of singleton weights and do not reflect the degree of density of the corresponding rules (as in the case of GMMs through *mixing proportions*), but the linear trend of the approximation/regression surface in the corresponding local parts.

4.2.2.2. *Takagi–Sugeno generalized*

Recently, the generalized form of Takagi–Sugeno fuzzy systems has been offered to the evolving fuzzy systems community, launching its origin in [64] and [65], later explored and further developed in [66] and in [67]. The basic principle is that it employs multidimensional normal (Gaussian) distributions in arbitrary positions for representing single rules. Thus, it overcomes the deficiency of not being able to model local correlations between input and output variables appropriately, as is the case for standard rules using the classical t-norm operators [40]—these may induce inexact approximations of real local trends [68].

An example for visualizing this problematic nature is provided in Figure 4.3: in the left image, axis-parallel rules (represented by ellipsoids) are used for modeling the partial tendencies of the regression curves which are not following the input axis direction, but are rotated to some degree; obviously, the volumes of the rules are artificially blown up and the rules do not represent the real characteristics of

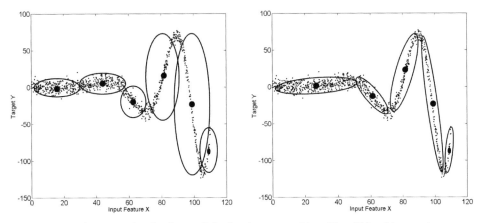

Figure 4.3: Left: conventional axis-parallel rules (represented by ellipsoids) achieve an inaccurate representation of the local trends (correlations) of a nonlinear approximation problem (defined by noisy data samples); right: generalized rules (by rotation) achieve a much more accurate and compact representation (5 rules instead of 6 actually needed).

the local tendencies well leading to *information loss*. In the right image, non-axis-parallel rules using general multivariate Gaussians are applied for a more accurate representation (rotated ellipsoids).

The generalized fuzzy rules have been defined in [64] as

$$\text{Rule}_i: \text{IF } \vec{x} \text{ IS (about) } \mu_i \text{ THEN } l_i(\vec{x}) = w_{i0} + w_{i1}x_1 + w_{i2}x_2 + \ldots + w_{ip}x_p, \tag{4.8}$$

where μ_i denotes a high-dimensional kernel function, which in accordance with the basis function network spirit is given by the generalized multivariate Gaussian distribution

$$\mu_i(\vec{x}) = exp\left(-\frac{1}{2}(\vec{x} - \vec{c}_i)^T \Sigma_i^{-1}(\vec{x} - \vec{c}_i) \right) \tag{4.9}$$

with $\vec{c}_i$ being the center and Σ_i^{-1} the inverse covariance matrix of the ith rule, allowing any possible rotation and spread of the rule.

In order to maintain (input/output) interpretability of the evolved TS fuzzy models for users/operators (see also Section 4.5.2), the authors in [67] foresee a projection concept to form fuzzy sets and classical rule antecedents. Interpretability relies on the angle between the principal component directions and the feature axes, which has the effect that long spread rules are more effectively projected than when using the inner contour spreads (through axis-parallel cutting points). The spread σ_i of the projected fuzzy set is set according to

$$\sigma_i = \max_{j=1,\ldots p}\left(\frac{r}{\sqrt{\lambda_j}} cos(\phi(\vec{e}_i, \vec{a}_j)) \right), \tag{4.10}$$

with r being the range of influence of one rule, usually set to 1, representing the (inner) characteristic contour/spread of the rule (as mentioned above). The center of the fuzzy set in the ith dimension is set to be equal to the ith coordinate of the rule center. $\phi(\vec{e}_i, \vec{a}_j)$ denotes the angle between the principal component direction represented by the eigenvector $\vec{a}_j$ and the ith axis vector $\vec{e}_i$; λ_j denotes the eigenvalue of the jth principal component.

4.2.2.3. Takagi–Sugeno extended

An extended version of Takagi–Sugeno fuzzy systems in the context of evolving systems has been applied in [69]. There, instead of a hyper-plane $l_i = w_{i0} + w_{i1}x_1 + w_{i2}x_2 + \ldots + w_{ip}x_p$ the consequent function for the ith rule is defined as the LS_SVM model according to [70]

$$l_i(\vec{x}) = \sum_{k=1}^{N} \alpha_{ik} K(\vec{x}, \vec{x}_k) + \beta_i, \tag{4.11}$$

with $K(.,.)$ being a kernel function fulfilling the Mercer criterion [71] for characterizing a symmetric positive semi-definite kernel [72], N the number of training samples, and α and β the consequent parameters (support vectors and intercept) to learn. The advantage of these consequents is that they are supposed to provide more accuracy, as a support vector regression modeling [70] is applied to each local region. Hence, non-linearities within local regions may be better resolved. On the other hand, the consequents are more difficult to interpret. SVM modeling for consequents has also been conducted in [73] in an incremental manner, but there, by using classical TS consequent functions (yielding a linear SVM modeling without kernels).

Another extended version of Takagi–Sugeno fuzzy systems was proposed in [74], where the rule consequents were defined through a nonlinear mapping Φ, realized by wavelet-type functions (typically modeled through the use of the Mexican hat function [75]). Therefore, each rule consequent represents a specific area of the output space in the wavelet domain, which makes the fuzzy system compactly applicable to time series data with (many) lagged inputs (different resolutions). This has been achieved in combination with an interval output vector to form a variant of a type-2 (TS) fuzzy system, see the subsequent section.

4.2.3. *Type-2 Fuzzy Systems*

Type-2 fuzzy systems were invented by Lotfi Zadeh in 1975 [76] for the purpose of modeling the uncertainty in the membership functions of the usual (type-1) fuzzy sets. The distinguishing feature of a type-2 fuzzy set $\tilde{\mu}_{ij}$ versus its type-1 counterpart

μ_{ij} is that the membership function values of $\tilde{\mu}_{ij}$ are blurred; i.e., they are no longer a single number in [0, 1], but instead a continuous range of values between 0 and 1, say $[a, b] \subseteq [0, 1]$. One can either assign the same weighting or assign a variable weighting to membership function values in $[a, b]$. When the former is done, the resulting type-2 fuzzy set is called an interval type-2 fuzzy set. When the latter is done, the resulting type-2 fuzzy set is called a general type-2 fuzzy set [77].

The ith rule of an interval-based type-2 fuzzy system is defined in the following way [78, 79]:

$$\text{Rule}_i: \text{IF } x_1 \text{ IS } \tilde{\mu}_{i1} \text{ AND} \ldots \text{AND } x_p \text{ IS } \tilde{\mu}_{ip} \text{ THEN } l_i(\vec{x}) = \tilde{f}_i$$

with $\tilde{f}_i$ being a general type-2 uncertainty function.

In the case of a Takagi–Sugeno-based consequent scheme (e.g., used in [80], the first approach of an evolving type-2 fuzzy system), the consequent function becomes

$$l_i(\vec{x}) = \tilde{w}_{i0} + \tilde{w}_{i1}x_1 + \tilde{w}_{i2}x_2 + \ldots + \tilde{w}_{ip}x_p \tag{4.12}$$

with $\tilde{w}_{ij}$ being an interval set (instead of a crisp continuous value), i.e.,

$$\tilde{w}_{ij} = [c_{ij} - s_{ij}, c_{ij} + s_{ij}]. \tag{4.13}$$

In the case of a Mamdani-based consequent scheme (e.g., used in [81], a recent evolving approach), the consequent function becomes: $l_i = \tilde{\Phi}_i$, with $\tilde{\Phi}_i$ a type-2 fuzzy set.

An enhanced approach for eliciting the final output is applied, so-called Karnik–Mendel iterative procedure [82] where a type of reduction is performed before the defuzzification process. In this procedure, the consequent values $\bar{l}_i = c_{i0} - s_{i0} + (c_{i1} - s_{i1})x_1 + (c_{i2} - s_{i2})x_2 + \ldots + (c_{ip} - s_{ip})x_p$ and $\underline{l}_i = c_{i0} + s_{i0} + (c_{i1} + s_{i1})x_1 + (c_{i2} + s_{i2})x_2 + \ldots + (c_{ip} + s_{ip})x_p$ are sorted in ascending order denoted as $\bar{y}_i$ and $\underline{y}_i$ for all $i = 1, \ldots, C$. Accordingly, the membership values, $\bar{\Psi}_i(\vec{x})$ and $\underline{\Psi}_i(\vec{x})$, are sorted in ascending order denoted as $\bar{\psi}_i(\vec{x})$ and $\underline{\psi}_i(\vec{x})$. Then, the outputs $\bar{y}$ and $\underline{y}$ are computed by

$$\bar{y} = \frac{\sum_{i=1}^{L} \bar{\psi}_i(\vec{x})\bar{y}_i + \sum_{i=L+1}^{C} \underline{\psi}_i(\vec{x})\bar{y}_i}{\sum_{i=1}^{L} \bar{\psi}_i(\vec{x}) + \sum_{i=L+1}^{C} \underline{\psi}_i(\vec{x})}, \qquad \underline{y} = \frac{\sum_{i=1}^{R} \underline{\psi}_i(\vec{x})\underline{y}_i + \sum_{i=R+1}^{C} \bar{\psi}_i(\vec{x})\underline{y}_i}{\sum_{i=1}^{R} \underline{\psi}_i(\vec{x}) + \sum_{i=R+1}^{C} \bar{\psi}_i(\vec{x})},$$

$$\tag{4.14}$$

with L and R being positive numbers, often $L = \frac{C}{2}$ and $R = \frac{C}{2}$. Taking the average of $\bar{y}$ and $\underline{y}$ yields the final output value y.

4.2.4. *Interval-Based Fuzzy Systems with Mixed Outputs*

A specific variant of an evolving fuzzy system architecture was proposed in [83] where the input fuzzy sets represent crisp intervals (thus, a specific realization of the trapezoidal function and also termed as *granules* [84]) and where the consequents of the fuzzy system contain a combination of interval output and hyper-plane output. The regression coefficients themselves are interval values. Hence, a rule is defined as

$$\text{Rule}_i: \text{IF } l_1^i \leq x_1 \leq L_1^i \text{ AND } \dots \text{ AND } l_1^p \leq x_p \leq L_1^p$$

$$\text{THEN } l_i(\vec{x}) = \tilde{f}_i \text{ AND } u_1^i \leq y \leq U_1^i, \tag{4.15}$$

with $l_i(\vec{x})$ as defined in Eq. (4.12) and an additional consequent term (that output y lies in an interval) to be able to make an advanced output interpretation. Especially, this directly yields an uncertainty value possibly contained in model predictions, without requiring the derivation and design of explicit error bars, etc. Furthermore, for experts, intervals may be more easy to understand than hyper-planes when gaining insights into the dependencies/relations the system contains [83].

In a modified form obtained by substituting the input intervals with conventional type-1 fuzzy sets and an additional consequent functional with a reduced argument-list, this type of evolving fuzzy system has recently been successfully applied in [85] to properly address missing values in data streams, see also Section 4.6.2.

4.2.5. *Neuro-Fuzzy Systems*

A neuro-fuzzy system is typically understood as a specific form of layered (neural) models, where, in one or several layers, components from the research field of fuzzy sets and systems are integrated [25]—e.g., fuzzy-set based activation functions. Typically, an evolving neuro-fuzzy system comprises the layers as shown in Figure 4.4: a fuzzification layer (Layer 1), a rule activation (= membership degree

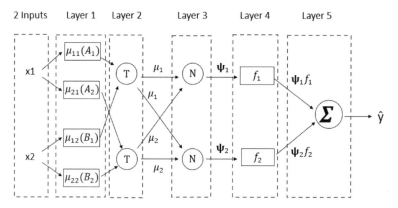

Figure 4.4:   Typical layered structure of an evolving neuro-fuzzy system (ENFS) with two inputs and two rules/neurons.

calculation) layer (Layer 2), a normalization layer (Layer 3), a functional consequent layer (Layer 4), and a weighted summation (= output) layer (Layer 5).

In functional form, by using forward propagation of layers, the output inference of an evolving neuro-fuzzy system containing C rules/neurons is defined as

$$\hat{y}(\vec{x}) = \hat{y} = \sum_{i=1}^{C} \Psi_i(\vec{x}) \cdot f_i(\vec{x}), \tag{4.16}$$

with the normalization layer

$$\Psi_i(\vec{x}) = \frac{\mu_i(\vec{x})}{\sum_{j=1}^{C} \mu_j(\vec{x})}, \tag{4.17}$$

and the rule activation layer in standard (axis-parallel) form

$$\mu_i(\vec{x}) = \mathsf{T}_{j=1}^{p} \mu_{ij}(x_j), \tag{4.18}$$

with p, the number of input variables (or regressors as transformed input variables). $\mu_i \in [0, 1]$ denotes an aggregated rule/neuron membership degree over fuzzy set activation levels $\mu_{ij} \in [0, 1]$, $j = 1, \ldots, p$ (performed in the fuzzification layer), with the aggregation T typically performed by using a t-norm [40], but in recent works also with some extended norms; see, e.g., [86, 87]—basically, for the purpose of gaining more flexibility (and thus interpretability) of rule antecedent parts, see also Section 4.5.2.

The final realization of evolving neuro-fuzzy systems is achieved through the definition of the functionals $f_1, \ldots, f_C$, also termed as rule consequent functions (appearing in the functional consequent layer). In most of the current E(N)FS approaches [30] [88], consequents of the Takagi–Sugeno–Kang type [89] are employed, which are generally defined through polynomials of order m (here for the ith rule)

$$f_i(\vec{w}_i, \vec{x}) = w_{i0} + \sum_{m1=1}^{m} \sum_{j_1 \leq j_2 \leq \ldots \leq j_{m1} \in \{1,\ldots,p\}} w_{i, j_1 \ldots j_{m1}} x_{j_1} \ldots x_{j_{m1}}, \tag{4.19}$$

where P denotes the number of input variables (comprising the dimensionality of the data set and the learning problem) and $x_1, \ldots, x_p$ the input variables. In the special case of Sugeno fuzzy systems [90], m is set to 0 and thus $f_i(\vec{w}_i, \vec{x}) = w_{i0}$, whereas in the special case of Takagi–Sugeno fuzzy systems [46], m becomes 1 and thus f_i a hyper-plane defined by: $f_i(\vec{w}_i, \vec{x}) = w_{i0} + w_{i1} * x_1 + \ldots + w_{ip} * x_p$. The latter, in combination with evolving fuzzy models, resulted in the classical *eTS* models, as originally proposed in [91] and used by many other E(N)FS approaches [30] [88].

Extensions of the basic layered neuro-fuzzy architecture shown in Figure 4.4 concern the following:

- The addition of one or more hidden layers for achieving a higher degree of model nonlinearity and an advanced interpretation of the knowledge contained in the input features/measurements—e.g., a recurrent layer could be integrated in order to represent connective weights between different time lags of one or more variables [92] or to perform local rule feedback [93], or to achieve an auto-associative structure with cross-links between the rule antecedents [94]; please refer to [25] for several possibilities of additional (advanced) layers.
- The integration of feature weights into the construction of the fuzzy neurons; this yields a feature weighting aspect in order to address the curse of dimensionality in a soft manner, as well as a better readability of the rules, as features with low weights assigned during the stream learning process can be seen as unimportant and thus out-masked when showing the fuzzy neurons/rules to experts, see also Section 4.4.2 for details. A recent architecture addressing this issue has been published in [86].
- More complex construction of the fuzzy neurons through advanced norms operating on the activation functions (fuzzy sets). The typical connection strategy of fuzzy set activation levels is realized through the usage of classical t-norms [40], leading to pure AND-connections among rule antecedent parts. Advanced concepts allowing a mixture of ANDs and ORs with a kind of intensity activation level of both have been realized for neuro-fuzzy systems in [86, 87] through the construction of uni- and uninull-neurons based on the usage of uni-norms and related concepts [95]. An evolving neuro-fuzzy system approach with the integration of uninull-neurons has been recently published in [96].
- More complex fuzzy-set based activation functions are added in order to yield transformation of the data to a compressed localized time and/or frequency space, such as the usage of wavelets as proposed in [97].
- Integrating recurrency in the layers in order to be able to model the dependencies of the various lags among several and within single features; this is especially important for time-series based modeling and forecasting purposes. A first attempt this direction has been made in [98], where the concept of long-short term memory (LSTM) networks has been employed to span the recurrent layer and where type-2 fuzzy sets are used in the neurons as activation functions.

A new type of evolving neuro-fuzzy architecture has been proposed by Silva *et al.* in [99] termed as neo-fuzzy neuron networks, and applied in the evolving context. It relies on the idea of using a set of TS fuzzy rules for each input dimension independently and then connecting these with a conventional sum for obtaining the final model output. In this sense, the curse of dimensionality is cleverly addressed by subspace decomposition into univariate model viewpoints. The domain of each input i is thereby granulated into m, complimentary membership functions, where m can be autonomously evolved from data.

In all of these architectures, a common denominator is the usage of linear output weights (also termed as consequent parameters), which are linear parameters $\vec{w}_i, i = 1, \ldots, C$ and should be incrementally updated in a single-pass manner to best follow the local output trends over stream samples in the approximation/regression/forecasting problem. Section 4.3.1 provides an overview of variants for achieving this in a robust manner.

4.2.6. *Cloud-Based Fuzzy Models*

In [100], a completely new form of fuzzy rule-based systems has been proposed that is based on the concept of *data clouds*. Data clouds are characterized by a set of previous data samples with common properties (closeness in terms of the input–output mapping). This allows for a more loose characterization of samples belonging to the same cloud than traditional fuzzy rules are able to offer. All of these (see above) are mainly characterized through the definition of concrete membership functions, whose realization induces the final shape of the rules: for instance, when using Gaussian membership functions, rules of ellipsoidal shape are induced. Thus, these assume that the local data distributions also (nearly) follow similar shapes, at least to some extent. This means that local distribution assumptions are implicitly made when defining the membership functions or the generalized rule appearance. Data clouds can circumvent this issue as they do not assume any local data distributions in advance. Figure 4.5 demonstrates a comparison between membership functions and clouds for a simple two-dimensional example.

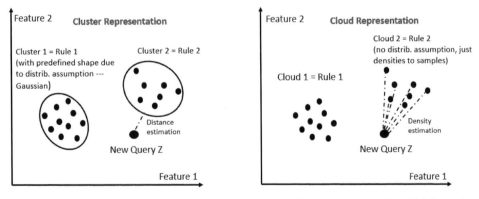

Figure 4.5: Left: clusters representing operation modes defined in conventional ellipsoidal shapes (as in the previous approaches above); right: clouds are just loose representations of sample densities—a new sample Z is then considered to belong to the nearest cloud according to its density [100].

Based on the clouds, the authors in [100] define a fuzzy rule for a single output model as follows:

$$\text{Rule}_i : \text{IF } \vec{x} \text{ IS like } \Xi_i \text{ THEN } l_i(\vec{x}) = w_{i0} + w_{i1}x_1 + w_{i2}x_2 + \ldots + w_{ip}x_p$$

$$(4.20)$$

In the case of a multi-output model, a whole matrix of consequent parameters is multiplied with $\vec{x}$ to form a set of consequent functions L_i. The fuzziness in this architecture is preserved in the sense that a particular data sample can belong to all clouds with a different degree (realized by the 'IS like' statement). This degree of fulfillment of the rule premise is determined by a local density γ_i, which can be calculated and updated in a single-pass manner based on the definition of a Cauchy-type function, see [100] for details. The latter just measures the local density, but does not assume any local data distribution. The overall output over all cloud-based rules is achieved by weighted averaging in the same manner as for classical TS fuzzy systems, see Section 4.2.2.

A cloud-based fuzzy rule base system can be represented by a layered architecture as visualized in Figure 4.4, where the first two layers are substituted by a single layer, which calculates the local density γ_i for a new sample to each data cloud (instead of a rule fulfillment degree based on fuzzy sets). Normalization, consequent, and output layers (Layers 3 to 5) are the same according to the weighted averaging of hyper-plane consequents given in Eq. (4.20), realized through Eq. (4.16) by substituting $\mu_i(\vec{x})$ with $\gamma_i(\vec{x})$ in the normalization Eq. (4.17).

This architecture is also used in a fuzzy classification variant termed as TEDAClass, see [101], and embedded in the ALMMo approach to learning multi-model event systems [102].

4.2.7. *Fuzzy Classifiers*

Fuzzy classifiers have enjoyed wide attraction for various applications for more than two decades, see, e.g. [103–106]. Their particular strength is their ability to model decision boundaries with an arbitrary nonlinearity degree while maintaining interpretability in the sense "which rules on the feature set imply which output class labels." In a winner-takes-all concept, the decision boundary proceeds between rule pairs having different majority class labels. As rules are usually nonlinear contours in the high-dimensional space, the nonlinearity of the decision boundary is induced—enjoying arbitrary complexity due to a possible arbitrary number of rules.

Due to their wide attraction for conventional off-line classification purposes, they have also been x used in the context of data stream classification. This led to the emergence of so-called *evolving fuzzy classifier* (EFC) approaches as a particular sub-field of evolving (neuro-) fuzzy systems, see [96, 107–111], which inherit some functionality in terms of incremental, single-pass updates of rules and parameters (see the subsequent section). In the subsequent subsections, the particular fuzzy classifier architectures used and partially even newly developed for EFCs are described.

4.2.7.1. *Classical and Extended Single-Model*

The rule in a classical fuzzy classification model architecture with singleton consequent labels as a widely studied architecture in the fuzzy system community [103, 112, 113] is defined by

$$\text{Rule}_i : \text{IF } x_1 \text{ IS } \mu_{i1} \text{ AND} \ldots \text{AND } x_p \text{ IS } \mu_{ip} \text{ THEN } l_i = L_i, \quad (4.21)$$

where L_i is the crisp output class label from the set $\{1, \ldots, K\}$ with K, the number of classes for the ith rule. This architecture precludes the use of confidence labels in the single classes per rule. In the case of clean classification rules, when each single rule contains/covers training samples from a single class this architecture provides an adequate resolution of the class distributions. However, in real-world problems, classes usually overlap significantly and therefore often rules containing samples from more than one class are extracted.

Thus, an extended fuzzy classification model that includes the confidence levels $conf_{i1,\ldots,K}$ of the ith rule in the single classes has been applied in an evolving, adaptive learning context, see, e.g., the first approaches in [107, 109, 114]

$$\text{Rule}_i : \text{IF } x_1 \text{ IS } \mu_{i1} \text{ AND} \ldots \text{AND } x_p \text{ IS } \mu_{ip}$$

$$\text{THEN } l_i = [conf_{i1}, conf_{i2}, \ldots, conf_{iK}] \quad (4.22)$$

Thus, a local region represented by a rule in the form of Eq. (4.22) can better model class overlaps in the corresponding part of the feature space: for instance, three classes overlap with the support of 200, 100, and 50 samples in one single fuzzy rule; then, the confidence in Class #1 would be intuitively 0.57 according to its relative frequency (200/350), in Class #2 it would be 0.29 (100/350), and in Class #3 it would be 0.14 (50/350). A more enhanced treatment of class confidence levels will be provided in Section 4.4.4 when describing options for representing reliability in class responses.

In a winner-takes-all context (the most common choice in fuzzy classifiers [103]), the final classifier output L will be obtained by

$$L = l_{i^*} \quad l_{i^*} = \text{argmax}_{1 \leq k \leq K} \; conf_{i^*k} \quad i^* = \text{argmax}_{1 \leq i \leq C} \; \mu_i(\vec{x}) \quad (4.23)$$

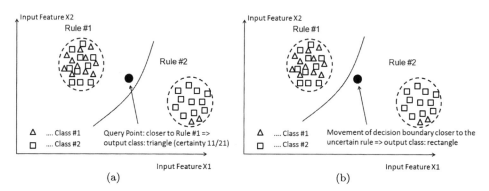

Figure 4.6: (a): Classification according to the winner-takes-all concept using Eq. (4.23); (b): the decision boundary moves towards the more unpurified rule due to the *gravitation concept* applied in Eq. (4.24).

In a more enhanced (weighted) classification scheme such as that used for evolving fuzzy classifiers (EFC) in [115], the *degree of purity* is respected as well and integrated into the calculation of the final classification response L:

$$L = \text{argmax}_{k=m,m*} \left(conf_k = \frac{\mu_1(\vec{x})h*_{1,k} + \mu_2(\vec{x})h*_{2,k}}{\mu_1(\vec{x}) + \mu_2(\vec{x})} \right) \quad (4.24)$$

with

$$h*_{1,k} = \frac{h_{1,k}}{h_{1,m} + h_{1,m*}} \quad h*_{2,k} = \frac{h_{2,k}}{h_{2,m} + h_{2,m*}}, \quad (4.25)$$

with $\mu_1(\vec{x})$ being the membership degree of the nearest rule (with a majority class m), and $\mu_2(\vec{x})$ the membership degree of the second nearest rule with a different majority class $m* \neq m$; $h_{i,k}$ denotes the class frequency of class k in rule i. This difference is important as two nearby lying rules with the same majority class label do not induce a decision boundary in between them.

Figure 4.6 shows an example of decision boundaries induced by Eq. (4.23) (left image) and by (4.24) (right image). Obviously, a more purified rule (i.e., having less overlap in classes; right side) is favored over that with significant overlap (left side); as the decision boundary moves away, more samples are classified to the majority class in the purified rule, which is intended to obtain a clearer, less uncertain decision boundary.

4.2.7.2. Multi-model one-versus-rest

The first variant of multi-model architecture is based on the well-known *one-versus-rest* classification scheme from the field of machine learning [62], and has been introduced in the fuzzy systems community, especially the evolving fuzzy systems community in [107]. It diminishes the problematic of having complex nonlinear multi-decision boundaries in case of multi-class classification problems, which is the case for single-model architecture as all classes are coded into one model. This is achieved by representing K binary classifiers for the K different classes, each one for the purpose of discriminating one single class from the others ($\rightarrow$ one-versus-rest). Thus, during the training cycle (batch or incremental), for the kth classifier all feature vectors resp. samples belonging to the kth class are assigned a label of 1, and all other samples belonging to other classes are assigned a label of 0.

The nice thing is that a (single model) classification model $D(f) = C$ resp. any regression model $D(f) = R$ (such as Takagi–Sugeno variants discussed above) can be applied for one sub-model in the ensemble. Interestingly, in [107] it has been shown that, using Takagi–Sugeno architecture for the binary classifiers by regressing on $\{0, 1\}$, the masking problem occurring in the *linear regression by indicator matrix* approach [116] can be avoided.

At the classification stage for a new query point $\vec{x}$, a model which is producing the maximal model response is used as the basis for the final classification label output L, i.e.,

$$
\begin{aligned}
L &= \text{argmax}_{m=1,\dots,K} \hat{f}_m(\vec{x}) && \text{in the case when } D(f) = R \\
L &= \text{argmax}_{m=1,\dots,K} conf_m(\vec{x}) && \text{in the case when } D(f) = C
\end{aligned}
\tag{4.26}
$$

A rule-based one-versus-rest classification scheme was proposed within the context of a MIMO (Multiple Input Multiple Output) fuzzy system and applied in an evolving classification context [117]. There, a rule is defined by

$$
\text{IF } \vec{x} \text{ IS (about) } \mu_i \text{ THEN } l_i = \vec{x}\Omega_i,
\tag{4.27}
$$

where

$$
\Omega_i =
\begin{bmatrix}
w_{i0}^1 & w_{i0}^2 & \cdots & w_{i0}^K \\
w_{i1}^1 & w_{i1}^2 & \cdots & w_{i1}^K \\
\vdots & \vdots & \vdots & \vdots \\
w_{ip}^1 & w_{ip}^2 & \cdots & w_{ip}^K
\end{bmatrix}
$$

and μ_i as in Eq. (4.9). Thus, a complete hyper-plane for each class per rule is defined. This offers the flexibility to regress on different classes within single rules and thus to resolve class overlaps in a single region by multiple regression surfaces [117].

4.2.7.3. *Multi-model all-pairs*

The multi-model *all-pairs* (*also termed as all-versus-all*) classifier architecture, originally introduced in the machine learning community [118, 119], and first introduced in (evolving) fuzzy classifiers design in [110], overcomes the often occurring imbalanced learning problems induced by the one-versus-rest classification scheme in the case of *multi-class (polychotomous)* problems. On the other hand, it is well-known that imbalanced problems cause severe down-trends in classification accuracy [120]. Thus, it is beneficial to avoid imbalanced problems while still trying to enforce the decision boundaries are easy are as possible to learn. This is achieved by the all-pairs architecture, as for each class pair (k, l) an own classifier is trained, decomposing the whole learning problem into binary, less complex sub-problems.

Formally, this can be expressed by a classifier $\mathbb{C}_{k,l}$, which is induced by a training procedure $\mathbb{T}_{k,l}$ when using (only) the class samples belonging to classes k and l

$$\mathbb{C}_{k,l} \longleftarrow \mathbb{T}_{k,l}(X_{k,l}) \quad X_{k,l} = \{\vec{x} | L(\vec{x}) = k \vee L(\vec{x}) = l\}, \tag{4.28}$$

with $L(\vec{x})$ being the class label associated with feature vector $\vec{x}$. This means that $\mathbb{C}_{k,l}$ is a classifier for separating samples belonging to class k from those belonging to class l.

When classifying a new sample $\vec{x}$, each classifier outputs a confidence level $conf_{k,l}$, which denotes the degree of preference of class k over class l for this sample. This degree lies in $[0, 1]$ where 0 means no preference, i.e., a crisp vote for class l; and 1 means full preference, i.e., a crisp vote for class k. This is conducted for each pair of classes and stored into a *preference relation matrix R*:

$$R = \begin{bmatrix} 0 & conf_{1,2} & conf_{1,3} & \cdots & conf_{1,K} \\ conf_{2,1} & 0 & conf_{2,3} & \cdots & conf_{2,K} \\ \vdots & \vdots & \vdots & \vdots & \vdots \\ conf_{K,1} & conf_{K,2} & conf_{K,3} & \cdots & 0 \end{bmatrix} \tag{4.29}$$

The preference relation matrix in Eq. (4.29) opens another interpretation dimension on the output level: considerations may go into partial uncertainty reasoning or preference relational structure in a fuzzy sense [121]. In the most convenient way, the final class response is often obtained by the following:

$$L = \text{argmax}_{k=1,\ldots,K}(score_k) = \text{argmax}_{k=1,\ldots,K}\left(\sum_{K \geq i \geq 1} conf_{k,i}\right), \tag{4.30}$$

i.e., the class with the highest score (=highest preference degree summed over all classes) is returned by the classifier.

In [119, 122], it was shown that pair-wise classification is not only more accurate than one-versus-rest technique, but also more efficient regarding computation times, see also [110], which is an important characteristic for fast stream learning problems. The reason for this is basically that binary classification problems contain significantly lower numbers of samples, as each sub-problem uses only a small subset of samples.

4.2.7.4. *Neuro-fuzzy systems as classifiers*

A further note goes to the usage of neuro-fuzzy systems as classifiers [123] as has recently been successfully applied in an evolving context in [96]. For binary classification problems, adoption of the architecture is not needed at all, as then a regression on {0, 1}-values is typically established. For multi-class classification problems, the architecture visualized in Figure 4.4 expands to a multi-output model, where each output represents one class. Thus, the value of this output (in 0, 1) directly contains the certainty that a new query point falls into this particular class. Applying a softmax operator (as is commonly used in neural classifiers [62]) on the certainty vector delivers the final output class. Learning can then be again conducted using a one-versus-rest classification technique as described in Section 4.2.7.2, through a loss function on each class versus the rest separately, see [96].

4.2.7.5. *Deep rule-based classifiers (DRB)*

The authors in [111] proposed a deep (fuzzy) rule-based architecture for solving classification problems with a high accuracy (due to multiple layers), but at the same time offering interpretability of the implicit neurons (as realized through cloud-based rules). The principal architecture is visualized in Figure 4.7.

The essential core component is that in the third layer, it contains massively parallel ensembles of IF-THEN rules, which are presented in the following form:

$$\text{Rule}_i : \text{IF } \vec{x} \sim P_{i,1} \ OR \ \vec{x} \sim P_{i,2} \ OR \ \ldots \ OR \ \vec{x} \sim P_{i,iN} \ \text{THEN } l_i = \text{Class } c_i, \tag{4.31}$$

where $\sim$ denotes similarity, which can be a fuzzy degree of satisfaction, a density-based value (as in the cloud-based fuzzy systems), or a typicality [124]. $P_{i,j}$ denotes

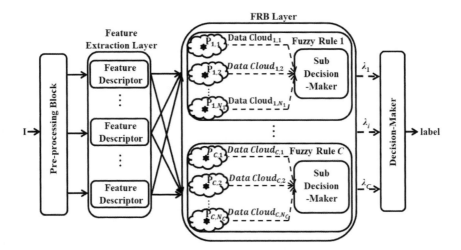

Figure 4.7: Architecture of a deep rule-based classifier [111].

the jth prototype of the ith class (having i_N prototypes in sum), usually estimated through (weighted) average of samples belonging to one prototype. It is thus remarkable that the rule appearance in Eq. (4.31) uses OR-connections to describe a single-class through possibilities of prototypes (learned from the data). Such a realization is not possible in all of the aforementioned architectures relying on classical t-norm concepts for connecting the rule antecedents. The final decision-making for new query samples is achieved through advanced decision-making mechanisms through confidence scores (apart from the "winner-takes-all" principle). The latter are elicited by a Gaussian kernel function through the membership degree of a new sample to each prototype in a single rule and by taking the maximal value, see [111] for details.

4.2.7.6. *Model ensembles*

A single model may indeed have its charm regarding a fast update/learning performance, but may suffer in predictive performance in case of higher noise levels and dimensionality in the data. This is because in the case of noisy data samples, single regression fits, especially when they are of non-linear type, often may provide unstable solutions. That is, the regression fits tend to over-fit due to fitting more the noise than the real underlying functional approximation trends [125], increasing the variance error much more than reducing the bias error—please refer to a detailed discussion of this problematic issue in [116]. Ensembles of models can typically increase the robustness in performance in such cases, as is known from the (classical) batch machine learning community [126] [127]. Furthermore, ensembles are potential candidates to properly deal with drifting data distributions in a natural way (especially by evolving new ensemble members upon drift alarms, etc. [128]). Thus, combining the idea of ensembling with E(N)FS, leading to a kind of online ensemble of E(N)FS with both increased robustness and flexibility, has recently emerged as an important topic in the evolving fuzzy systems community, see, e.g., [129–131].

An ensemble of fuzzy systems can be defined by $F_1 \cup F_2 \cup \ldots \cup F_m$, where each F stands for one so-called *ensemble member* or *base learner*, and whose output is generally defined as the following:

$$\hat{F} = Agg_{i=1}^{m} w_i \hat{F}_i, \tag{4.32}$$

with $\hat{F}_i$ being the predicted output from ensemble member F_i, w_i its weight (impact in the final prediction) and Agg a specific aggregation operator, whose choice depends on the ensembling concept used: e.g., in the case of bagging it is a simply average over all members' outputs [132] (thus, $w_i = 1/m$), or in the case of boosting it is a specific weighted aggregation function [133], see also Section 4.3.5.

Each ensemble member thereby denotes a single fuzzy system with any architecture as discussed above.

4.3. Fundamentals of Learning Algorithms

Data streams are one of the fundamental reasons for the necessity of applying evolving, adaptive models in general and evolving fuzzy systems in particular. This is simply because streams are theoretically an infinite sequence of samples, which cannot be processed at once within a batch process, not even in modern computers with high virtual memory capacities. Data streams may not necessarily be online based on permanent recordings, measurements, or sample gatherings, but can also arise due to a block- or sample-wise loading of batch data sites, e.g., in case of *very large data bases (VLDB)*[2] or in case of *big data* problems [134]; in this context, they are also often referred as *pseudo-streams*. In particular, a data stream (or pseudo-stream) is characterized by the following properties [1]:

- The data samples or data blocks are continuously arriving online over time. The frequency depends on the frequency of the measurement recording process.
- The data samples are arriving in a specific order, over which the system has no control.
- Data streams are usually not bounded in size; i.e., a data stream is alive as long as some interfaces, devices, or components at the system are switched on and are collecting data.
- Once a data sample/block is processed, it is usually discarded immediately, afterwards.

Changes in the process such as new operation modes, system states, varying environmental influences, etc. are usually implicitly also affecting the data stream in such a way that, for instance, *drifts* or *shifts* may arise (see Section 4.4.1), or new regions in the feature/system variable space are explored (knowledge expansion).

Formally, a stream can be defined as an infinite sequence of samples $(\vec{x}_1, \vec{y}_1)$, $(\vec{x}_2, \vec{y}_2), (\vec{x}_3, \vec{y}_3), \ldots$, where $\vec{x}$ denotes the vector containing all input features (variables) and $\vec{y}$, the output variables that should be predicted. In the case of unsupervised learning problems, $\vec{y}$ disappears—note, however, that in the context of fuzzy systems, only supervised regression and classification problems are studied. Often $y = \vec{y}$, i.e., single output systems, are encouraged especially as it is often possible to decast a MIMO (multiple input multiple output problem) system into single independent MISO (multiple input single output problem) systems (e.g., when the outputs are independent).

---

[2]http://en.wikipedia.org/wiki/Very_large_database

Handling streams for modeling tasks in an appropriate way requires the usage of *incremental learning* algorithms, which are deduced from the concept of incremental heuristic search [11]. These algorithms possess the property to build and learn models in a step-wise manner rather than with a whole data set at once. From a formal mathematical point of view, an incremental model update I of the former model f_N (estimated from the N initial samples) is defined by the following:

$$f_{N+m} = I(f_N, (\vec{x}_{N+1,\dots,N+m}, \vec{y}_{N+1,\dots,N+m})). \qquad (4.33)$$

So, the incremental model update is done by just taking the new m samples and the old model, but not using any prior data. Here, the whole model may also include some additional statistical help measures, which needs to be updated synchronously to the "real" model. If $m = 1$, we speak about *incremental learning in sample mode* or *sample-wise incremental learning*, otherwise about *incremental learning in chunk mode* or *chunk-wise incremental learning*. If the output vector starts to be missing in the data stream samples, but a supervised model has already been trained before, which is then updated with the stream samples either in unsupervised manner or by using its own predictions, then we speaks about *semi-supervised* (online) learning [135].

Two update modes in the incremental learning process are distinguished:

(1) Update of the model parameters: in this case, a fixed number of parameters $\Phi_N = \{\phi_1, \dots, \phi_l\}_N$ of the original model f_N is updated by the incremental learning process, and the outcome is a new parameter setting Φ_{N+m} with the same number of parameters, i.e., $|\Phi_{N+m}| = |\Phi_N|$. Here, we also speak about a *model adaptation* resp. a *model refinement* with new data.

(2) Update of the whole model structure: this case leads to the evolving learning concept, as the number of parameters may change and also the number of structural components may change automatically (e.g., rules are added or pruned in case of fuzzy systems) according to the characteristics of the new data samples $\vec{x}_{N+1,\dots,N+m}$. This means that usually (but not necessarily) $|\Phi_{N+m}| \neq |\Phi_N|$ and $C_{N+m} \neq C_N$ with C being the number of structural components. The update of the whole model structure may also include an update of the input structure, i.e., input variables/features may be exchanged during the incremental learning process—see also Section 4.4.2.

An important aspect in incremental learning algorithms is the so-called *plasticity–stability dilemma* [136], which describes the problem of finding an appropriate tradeoff between flexible model updates and structural convergence. This strongly depends on the nature of the stream: in some cases a more intense update is required than in others (drifting versus life-long concepts in the stream, see also Section 4.4.1). If an algorithm converges to an optimal solution or at least to the same solution as the hypothetical batch solution (obtained by using all data up to a certain sample at once), it is called a *recursive algorithm*.

An *initial batch mode training step* with the first amount of training samples is, whenever possible, usually preferable over *incremental learning from scratch*, i.e., building up the model sample-per-sample from the beginning. This is because within a batch mode phase, it is possible to carry out validation procedures (such as cross-validation [137] or bootstrapping [138]) in connection with search techniques for finding an optimal set of parameters for the learning algorithm to achieve a good generalization quality (nearly every E(N)FS approach has such learning parameters to tune). The obtained parameters are usually reliable start parameters for the incremental learning algorithm to evolve the model further. When performing incremental learning from scratch, the parameters have to be set to some blind default values, which may not necessarily be appropriate for the given data stream mining problem.

In a pure online learning setting, however, incremental learning from scratch is indispensable. Then, often the start default parameters of the learning engines need to be parameterized. Thus, it is essential that the algorithms require as less as possible parameters (see Section 4.3.6), or alternatively embed algorithms for adaptive changes of the learning parameters.

4.3.1. *Recursive Learning of Linear Parameters*

For learning the linear consequent (output weight) parameters $\vec{w}$, which are present in most of the fuzzy system architectures discussed in the previous section, the currently available EFS techniques typically rely on the optimization of the least squares error criterion, which is defined as the squared deviation between observed outputs $y(1), \ldots, y(N)$ and predicted model outputs $\hat{y}(1), \ldots, \hat{y}(N)$

$$\min_{\vec{w}} J = \|y - \hat{y}\|_{L_2} = \sum_{k=1}^{N} (y(k) - \hat{y}(k))^2. \tag{4.34}$$

As $\hat{y}(k)$ is typically elicited by a linearly weighted sum of rule/neuron activation levels (see Eq. (4.16)) with weights $\vec{w}$, this problem can be written as a classical linear least squares problem with a weighted regression matrix containing the global regressors $\vec{r}(k)$ and rule/neuron activation levels (in the last layer) as weights. Its exact definition depends on the chosen consequent functions (see the previous section): e.g., in the case of TS fuzzy models with hyper-planes, the regressor in the kth sample (denoting the kth row in the regression matrix) is given by the following:

$$\vec{r}(k) = \left[\Psi_1(\vec{x}(k)) \ x_1(k)\Psi_1(\vec{x}(k)) \ \ldots \ x_p(k)\Psi_1(\vec{x}(k)) \ \ldots \right.$$
$$\left. \Psi_C(\vec{x}(k)) \ x_1(k)\Psi_C(\vec{x}(k)) \ \ldots x_p(k)\Psi_C(\vec{x}(k)) \right] \tag{4.35}$$

with C being the current number of rules. In the case of higher order polynomials, the polynomial terms are also integrated in Eq. (4.35). For this problem, no matter how the regressors are constructed, it is well-known that a recursive solution exists that converges to the optimal one within each incremental learning step—see [139] and also [29] (Chapter 2) for its detailed derivation in the context of evolving TS fuzzy systems.

However, the problem with this *global learning* approach is that it does not offer any flexibility regarding rule evolution and pruning, as these cause a change in the size of the regressors and thus a dynamic change in the dimensionality of the recursive learning problem, which leads to a disturbance of the parameters in the other rules and to a loss of optimality. Therefore, the authors in [107] emphasize the usage of a *local learning* approach that learns and updates the consequent parameters for each rule separately. Adding or deleting a new rule, therefore, does not affect the convergence of the parameters of all other rules; thus, optimality in the least squares sense is preserved. The local learning approach leads to a weighted least squares formulation, which for the ith rule is given by the following:

$$\min_{\vec{w}_i} J_i = \sum_{k=1}^{N} \lambda^{N-k} \Psi_i(\vec{x}(k)) \left(y(k) - f_i(\vec{w}_i, \vec{x}(k)) \right)^2 . \qquad (4.36)$$

$y(k)$ denotes the observed (measured) target value in sample k and $f_i(\vec{w}_i, \vec{x}(k))$ the estimated target value through the consequent function f_i of the ith rule, which contains the linear consequent/output weight parameters $\vec{w}_i = [w_{i0}, w_{i1}, \ldots, w_{ip}]$ (with p being the number of parameters according to the length of the regressor vector). The symbol C denotes the number of rules. N is the number of samples (seen so far), and λ an optional forgetting factor in $[0, 1]$, which leads to an exponential decrease of weights over past samples. The weights $\Psi_i(\vec{x})$ denote the rule/neuron membership degree/activation level of a sample $\vec{x}$ to the ith rule and guarantee a (locally) stable inference for new query samples [29]. The weights are essential, as samples lying far away from an existing rule/neuron will receive lower weights in the estimation of the consequent parameters than those lying closer to it, which assures reliable local optimization and convergence—see [29], Chapter 2 for a detailed discussion.

This local LS error functional Eq. (4.36) turned out to be more or less the common denominator in current E(N)FS approaches [30]. The problem can be seen as a classical weighted least squares problem, where the weighting matrix is a diagonal matrix containing the basis function values Ψ_i for each input sample. Again, an exact recursive formulation can be derived (see [29], Chapter 2), which is termed as *recursive fuzzily weighted least squares* (RFWLS). As RFWLS is so fundamental and is used in most of the EFS approaches [30], we explicitly deploy the update formulas (from the kth to the $k + 1$st sample)

$$\vec{w}_i(k+1) = \vec{w}_i(k) + \gamma(k)(y(k+1) - \vec{r}^T(k+1)\vec{w}_i(k)), \tag{4.37}$$

$$\gamma(k) = \frac{P_i(k)\vec{r}(k+1)}{\dfrac{\lambda}{\Psi_i(\vec{x}(k+1))} + \vec{r}^T(k+1)P_i(k)\vec{r}(k+1)}, \tag{4.38}$$

$$P_i(k+1) = \frac{1}{\lambda}(I - \gamma(k)\vec{r}^T(k+1))P_i(k), \tag{4.39}$$

with $P_i(k) = (R_i(k)^T Q_i(k) R_i(k))^{-1}$ being the inverse weighted Hessian matrix and $\vec{r}(k+1)$ the regressor vector in the new, $k+1$st sample (its construction depends on the consequent function, see above). The (normalized) membership degree of a new sample to the ith rule $\Psi_i(\vec{x}(k+1))$ is integrated as fuzzy weight in the denominator in Eq. (4.38), and assures local convergence, as only consequent parameters of the most active rules are significantly updated and parameters of rules lying far away from the current sample (and thus yielding a low membership value) remain nearly unaffected (which is desired), see [29], Chapter 2 for a detailed analysis. Please note that convergence to global optimality in each single sample update is guaranteed as Eq. (4.36) is a convex, parabolic function, and Eq. (4.37) denotes a Gauss–Newton step, which converges within one iteration in the case of parabolas [139].

This assurance of convergence to optimality is guaranteed as long as there is no structural change in the rules' antecedents. However, due to rule center movements or resettings in the incremental learning phase (see Section 4.3.4), this is usually not the case. Therefore, a kind of sub-optimality is caused whose deviation degree to the real optimality could have been bounded for some EFS approaches such as FLEXFIS [140], PANFIS [141], or SOFMLS [44], and several extensions of and also some alternative approaches to RFWLS have been proposed, see Section 4.3.1.1.

Whenever a new rule is evolved by a rule evolution criterion (see also below), the parameters and the inverse weighted Hessian matrix (required for an exact update) have to be initialized. In [139], it is emphasized to set $\vec{w}$ to 0 and P_i to αI with α big enough. However, this is for the purpose of a global modeling approach starting with a faded out regression surface over the whole input space. In local learning, the other rules defining other parts of the feature space remain untouched. Thus, setting the hyper-plane of the new rule that may appear somewhere in between the other rules to 0 would lead to an undesired muting of one local region and to discontinuities in the online predictions [142]. Thus, it is more beneficial to inherit the parameter vector and the inverse weighted Hessian matrix from the most nearby lying rule [142].

4.3.1.1. *Improving the robustness of recursive linear consequent parameters learning*

Several extensions to the conventional RFWLS estimator were proposed in the literature during recent years, especially in order to address the sub-optimality problematic, to dampen the effect of outliers on the update of the parameters, to decrease the curse of dimensionality in the case of large regressor vectors, and also to address noise in the input and not only in the output as is the case for RFWLS due to the optimization of perpendicular distances between predicted and observed target values.

These extensions of RFWLS are as follows:

- In PANFIS [141], an additional constant α is inserted, conferring a noteworthy effect to foster the asymptotic convergence of the system error and weight vector being adapted, which acts like a binary function. In other words, the constant α is in charge to regulate the current belief of the weight vectors $\vec{w}_i$ and depends on the approximation and estimation errors. It is 1 whenever the approximation error is bigger than the system error, and is 0 otherwise. Thus, adaptation takes place in the first case and not in the second case (which may have advantages in terms of flexibility and computation time). A similar concept is used in the improved version of SOFNN, see [143].

- Generalized version of RFWLS (termed as FWGRLS) as used in GENEFIS [66]: this exploits the generalized RLS as derived in [144] and adopts it to the local learning context in order to gain its benefits as discussed above. The basic difference to RFWLS is that it adds a weight decay regularization term to the least squares problem formulation in order to punish more complex models. In a final simplification step, it ends up with similar formulas as in Eq. (4.37) to Eq. (4.39), but with the difference to subtract the term $\alpha P_i(k + 1)\nabla\phi(\vec{w}_i(k))$ in Eq. (4.37), with α a regularization parameter and ϕ the weight decay function: one of the most popular ones in the literature is the quadratic function defined as $\phi(\vec{w}_i(k)) = \frac{1}{2}\|\vec{w}_i(k)\|^2$; thus $\nabla\phi = \vec{w}_i(k)$).

- Modified recursive least squares algorithm as proposed in [44] to train both parameters and structures of the model with the support of linearization and Lyapunov functions [145]. It is remarkable that in this approach, the evolution or pruning of rules does not harm the convergence of the parameters, as these change only the dimension of the inverse Hessian and the weight matrices. Based on this approach, the bound on the identification error could be made even smaller in [146] with the usage of an own designed dead-zone recursive least square algorithm.

- Extended weighted recursive least squares (EWRLS), which also takes into account whenever two rules are merged and then performs different formulas to assure optimality in the least squares sense despite structural changes due to the merging process [147].

- Multi-innovation RFWLS as suggested in [148]: this variant integrates both, past error estimators (also termed as *innovation vectors*) and membership values on some recent past samples, into one single parameter update cycle. This is achieved through an expansion of RFWLS from the vectorized formulation to the matrix case. This achieves a compensation of structural changes and thus of sub-optimal solutions over an innovation length v (the size of the innovation vector). This finally results in optimality of the parameters with respect to the past v samples.

- Recursive correntropy was suggested in [149] and [150] for recursive updates within a global learning approach, and adopted to the local learning case in [148]: this variant integrates an exponential error term in the objective function formulation according to the discrete variant of the correntropy between predicted and measured output values, i.e., $\Phi(\vec{x}_k) = e^{-\frac{|y(k)-f_i(\vec{w}_i,\vec{x})(k)|}{2\phi^2}}$ serving as outlier fading factor; this gives larger errors lower weights during optimization, as the aim is to maximize the corr-entropy function [151].

- Recursive weighted total least squares (RWTLS) as introduced in [148]: it is an extension of the LS objective function formulation by integrating the sample reconstruction error in the local LS functional to properly account for both, noise in the inputs and output(s) (whereas RFWLS only respects noise in the output(s)). The mathematical derivation leads to a solution space formed by the weighted mean of input regressors (with weights given by the rule membership values) and the smallest eigenvalue of a weighted and mean-centered regression matrix in the total least squares sense (containing all regressor values plus the target value y). It can be recursively updated through the usage of generalized inverse iteration [152], where the (important) noise covariance matrix is autonomously and incrementally estimated from data through a recursive polynomial Kalman smoother with a particular state transition matrix.

Another possibility to achieve a better local optimality of the consequent parameters is presented in [153], which allows iterative re-optimization cycles on a batch of the most recent data samples. This is done in conjunction with an iterative optimization of nonlinear parameters (which reflect any possible structural changes); thus, sub-optimality can be completely avoided. On the other hand, it requires re-learning phases and thus does not meet the spirit of a real recursive, single-pass algorithm, as is the case for all extensions discussed above.

A final note goes to the possibility to apply RFWLS and all its related algorithms (i.) to binary fuzzy classifiers by performing a regression on $\{0, 1\}$, and (ii.) to multi-class classifiers based on one-versus-rest classification scheme (see Section 4.2.7.2) by conducting an indicator-based recursive learning per class separately, see [107].

4.3.2. *Recursive Learning of Nonlinear Parameters*

Nonlinear parameters occur in every model architecture as defined throughout Section 4.2.2, mainly in the fuzzy sets included in the rules' antecedent parts—except

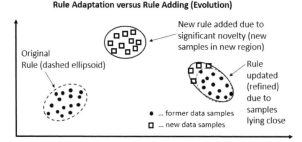

Figure 4.8: Example of rule update (left-hand side) versus rule evolution (right-hand side) based on new incoming data samples (rectangular markers).

for the extended version of TS fuzzy systems (Section 4.2.2.3), where they also appear in the consequents. Often, the parameters in the fuzzy sets define their centers c and characteristic spreads σ, but the parameters may appear in a different form— for instance, in the case of sigmoid functions they define the slope and the point of gradient change. Thus, we generally refer to a set of nonlinear parameters as Φ.

The incremental update of nonlinear parameters is necessary in order to adjust and move the fuzzy sets and rules composed of the sets to the actual distribution of the data in order to achieve well-placed positions. An example is provided in Figure 4.8 where the initial data cloud (circles) in the left upper part changes slightly the position due to new data samples (rectangles). Leaving the original rule (marked with a dashed ellipsoid as induced by multivariate Gaussians) untouched would cause a misplacement of the rule. Thus, it is beneficial to adjust the rule center and its spread according to the new samples (solid ellipsoid). This figure also shows the case when new stream samples appear which are far away from any existing rules (rectangles in the middle right part). Such samples should induce the evolution of a new rule in order to compactly represent this new knowledge contained in the new cloud (which will be handled in the subsequent section)—the update of older rules would induce inaccurately blown up rules, containing a (useless) mixture of local data representations.

One possibility to update the nonlinear parameters in EFS is again, similar to the consequent parameters, by applying a numerical incremental optimization procedure. Relying on the least squares optimization problem as in the case of recursive linear parameter updates, its formulation in dependence of the nonlinear parameters Φ becomes

$$\min_{\Phi; \vec{w}} J(\Phi, \vec{w}) = \sum_{k=1}^{N} \|(y_k - \hat{y}(\Phi, \vec{w}))\|_{L_2}. \qquad (4.40)$$

In the case of TS fuzzy systems, for instance, $\hat{y}(\Phi) = \sum_{i=1}^{C} l_i(\vec{x}) \Psi_i(\Phi(\vec{x}))$. Then, the linear consequent parameter $\vec{w}$ needs to be synchronously optimized to the non-linear parameters (thus, in optional braces) in order to guarantee an optimal solution. This can be done either in an alternating nested procedure, i.e., perform an optimization step for nonlinear parameters first, see below, and then optimize the linear ones, e.g., by Eq. (4.37), or within one joint update formula, e.g., when using one Jacobian matrix on all parameters).

Equation (4.40) is still a free optimization problem; thus, any numerical, gradient-based, or Hessian-based technique for which a stable incremental algorithm can be developed is a good choice: this is the case for the steepest descent, Gauss–Newton method, and Levenberg–Marquardt. Interestingly, a common parameter update formula can be deduced for all three variants [154]

$$\Phi(k+1) = \Phi(k) + \mu(k)P(k)^{-1}\psi(\vec{x}(k), \Phi)e(\vec{x}(k), \Phi), \qquad (4.41)$$

where $\psi(\vec{x}(k), \Phi) = \frac{\partial y}{\partial \Phi}(\vec{x}(k))$ is the partial derivative of the current model y after each nonlinear parameter is evaluated at the current input sample $\vec{x}(k)$, $e(\vec{x}(k), \Phi)$ is the residual in the kth sample: $e(\vec{x}(k), \Phi) = y_k - \hat{y}_k$, and $\mu(k)P(k)^{-1}$ is the learning gain with $P(k)$ an approximation of the Hessian matrix, which is realized in different ways:

- For the steepest descent algorithm, $P(k) = I$; thus, the update depends only on first order derivative vectors; furthermore, $\mu(k) = \frac{\mu}{\|\vec{r}(k)\|^2}$ with $\vec{r}(k)$ the current regression vector.
- For the Gauss–Newton algorithm,, $\mu(k) = 1 - \lambda$ and $P(k) = (1 - \lambda)H(k)$ with $H(k)$ the Hessian matrix, which can be approximated by $Jac^T(k)Jac(k)$ with Jac the Jacobian matrix (including the derivatives w.r.t. all parameters in all rules for all samples up to the kth) resp. by $Jac^T(k)diag(\Psi_i(\vec{x}(k)))Jac(k)$ in the case of the weighted version for local learning (see also Section 4.3.1)—note that the Jacobian matrix reduces to the regression matrix R in the case of linear parameters, as the derivatives are the original input variables. Additionally to updating the parameters according to Eq. (4.41), the update of the matrix P is required, which is given by the following:

$$P(k) = \lambda P(k-1) + (1 - \lambda)\psi(\vec{x}(k), \Phi)\psi(\vec{x}(k), \Phi)^T. \qquad (4.42)$$

- For the Levenberg–Marquardt algorithm, $P(k) = (1 - \lambda)H(k) + \alpha I$ with $H(k)$ as in the case of Gauss–Newton and again $\mu(k) = 1 - \lambda$. The update of the matrix P is done by the following:

$$P(k) = \lambda P(k-1) + (1 - \lambda)\left(\psi(\vec{x}(k), \Phi)\psi(\vec{x}(k), \Phi)^T + \alpha I\right). \qquad (4.43)$$

Using matrix inversion lemma [155] and some reformulation operations to avoid matrix inversion in each step ($P(k)^{-1}$ is required in Eq. (4.41)) leads to the well-known recursive Gauss–Newton approach, which is, e.g., used in [69] for recursively updating the kernel widths in the consequents and also for fine-tuning the regularization parameter. It also results in the recursive least squares approach in the case of linear parameters (formulas for the local learning variant in Eq. (4.37)). In the case of recursive Levenberg–Marquardt (RLM) algorithm, a more complex reformulation option is requested to approximate the update formulas for $P(k)^{-1}$ directly (without an intermediate inversion step). This leads to the recursive equations as successfully used in the EFP method by Wang and Vrbanek [156] for updating centers and spreads in Gaussian fuzzy sets (multivariate Gaussian rules).

4.3.3. *Learning of Consequents in EFC*

The most common choice in EFC design for consequent learning is simply to use the class majority voting for each rule separately. This can be achieved by incrementally counting the number of samples falling into each class k and rule i, h_{ik}, (the rule that is the nearest one in the current data stream process). The class with majority count $k* = argmax_{k=1}^{K} h_{ik}$ is the consequent class of the corresponding (ith) rule in the case of the classical single-model architecture Eq. (4.21). The confidences in each class per rule can be obtained by the relative frequencies among all classes $conf_{ik} = \frac{h_{ik}}{\sum_{k=1}^{K} h_{ik}}$ in the case of extended architecture in Eq. (4.22). For all-pairs classifiers, the same strategy can be applied within each single binary classifier. For the one-versus-rest architecture, RFWLS and all of its robust extensions can be applied to each class separately with the usage of an indicator-based RFWLS scheme [96]. An enhanced confidence calculation scheme will be handled under the scope of *reliability* in Section 4.4.4.

4.3.4. *Evolving Mechanisms*

A fundamental issue in *evolving systems*, which differs from *adaptive systems*, is that they possess the capability to change their structure during online, incremental learning cycles—adaptive systems are only able to update their parameters as described in the two preliminary subsections, which typically induce only a movement and/or a reshaping of model components. The evolving technology, however, addresses the dynamic expansion and contraction of the model structure and thus the knowledge contained in the model—which typically induces the addition or deletion of whole model components. Therefore, most of the EFS approaches foresee the following fundamental concepts (or at least a significant subset of them):

- *Rule evolution*: It addresses the problem of when and how to evolve new rules on-the-fly and on demand → knowledge expansion.
- *Rule pruning*: It addresses the problem of when and how to prune rules in the rule base on-the-fly and on demand → knowledge contraction.

- *Rule merging*: It addresses the problem to merge two or more rules together once they become overlapping and thus contain redundant information → model simplification.
- *Rule splitting*: It addresses the problem of when and how to split rules (into two) that contain an inhomogeneous data representation and thus contribute inaccurately to the model output → knowledge refinement.

The first issue guarantees the inclusion of new systems states, operation modes, process characteristics in the models to enrich their knowledge and expand them to so far unexplored regions in the feature space. The second issue guarantees that a rule base cannot grow forever and become extremely large; hence, it is responsible for smart computation times and compactness of the rule base, which may be beneficial for interpretability reasons, see Section 4.5.2. In addition, it is a helpful engine for preventing model over-fitting. The third issue takes care to avoid unnecessary complexity due to redundant information contained in two or more rules, which can happen because of data cloud/cluster fusion effects. The fourth issue avoids inaccurate, blown-up rules due to data cloud/cluster delamination effects, often happening because of a permanent adaptation of rules during gradually drifting states. Figure 4.9 visualizes the induction of the four cases due to the characteristics

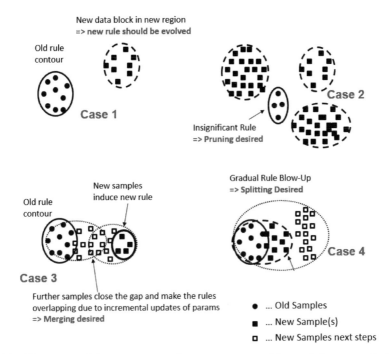

Figure 4.9: Four cases of data stream sample appearances requiring evolving concepts: from rule evolution (Case 1) via rule pruning (Case 2) and merging (Case 3) to rule splitting (Case 4).

of new incoming data samples (rectangular markers): old rules are shown by ellipsoidal solid lines and updated and new ones by dashed and dotted lines.

The current state-of-the-art in EFS is that these concepts are handled in many different ways in different approaches, see [30] for a recent larger collection of published approaches. Due to space limitations of this book chapter, it is not possible to describe all the various options for rule evolution, pruning, merging, and splitting anchored in the various EFS approaches. Therefore, in the following subsections, we outline the most important directions which enjoy some common understanding and usage in various approaches.

4.3.4.1. *Rule evolution*

One concept that is widely used for autonomous rule evolution is the *incremental, evolving clustering* technique (see [157] for a survey of methods), which searches for an optimal grouping of the data into several clusters, ideally following the natural distribution of data clouds, in an incremental and evolving manner (i.e., new clusters are automatically added on demand from stream samples). In particular, the aim is that similar samples should contribute to the (formation of the) same cluster while different samples should fall into different clusters [158].

In the case of using prototype-based clustering techniques emphasizing clusters with *convex shapes* (e.g., ellipsoids), each evolved cluster can be directly associated with a rule representing a compact local region in the feature space. Due to projection onto the axes, the fuzzy sets composing the rule antecedents can be obtained— see [67] for various projection possibilities. Similar considerations can be made when performing clustering in the principal component space, as proposed in [159].

In the case when clusters with arbitrary shapes are evolved from the stream, also termed as *data clouds* as proposed and used in evolving cloud-based models [100] (see Section 4.2.6), the centers of the clouds can be associated with the centers of the rules and the ranges of influence of the rules are estimated by empirical density estimators, which are also directly used as rule membership degrees, thus termed as empirical membership functions [160]. Such empirical functions have been successfully embedded in the autonomous learning multimodel systems approach (ALMMo) [102], where the concepts of eccentricity and typicality are used to form clouds in arbitrary shapes [124]; it is remarkable that these two concepts do not need any learning parameters and thus can be used in a full plug-and-play manner from each other.

In order to check new samples for cluster compatibility versus incompatibility (based on which it can be decided whether a new cluster = rule needs to be evolved or not), the compatibility concepts applied in the various approaches differ from each other:

- Some are using distance-oriented criteria (e.g., DENFIS [161], FLEXFIS [140], eFuMo [162, 163], ePFM [164], or InFuR [165]), where the distance of new incoming samples to existing clusters/rules is checked and decided whether sufficient novelty is present, and if so, a new rule is evolved.
- Some are using density-based criteria (e.g., eT [91] and its extension eTS+ [166] with several successors as summarized in [14], or the approach in [167]), which are mostly relying on potential concepts to estimate whether new samples fall into a newly arising dense region where no cluster/rule has been defined so far, thus showing a higher density than prototypes already generated. Similar concepts are adopted in cloud-based approaches [101, 102], where it is additionally checked whether a new data cloud possibly overlap, with existing clouds, and if so, the already available prototype (or focal point) is replaced by the new sample. Different inner norms can be used when recursively calculating the density [168], which induces different types of distance measures in the Cauchy-type density calculation.
- Some others are using statistical-oriented criteria (e.g., ENFM [169], GS-EFS [67] or SAFIS [170] and its extensions [171, 172], PANFIS [141], GENEFIS [66]), especially to check for the significance of the present rules as well as prediction intervals and tolerance regions surrounding the rules, or to check the goodness of fit tests based on statistical criteria (e.g., F-statistics) for candidate splits. The leaves are replaced with a new subtree, inducing an expansion of the hierarchical fuzzy model (as in, e.g., in [173] or in the incremental LOLIMOT (Local Linear Model Tree) approach proposed in [174]).
- Some are also using fuzzy-set-theoretic concepts such as coverage subject to ϵ-completeness (e.g., SOFNN [143, 175] or SCFNN [176]).
- Some are relying on Yager's participatory learning concept [177], comparing the arousal index and a specific compatibility measure with thresholds—as performed in ePL [178, 179] and eMG [64].
- Granular evolving methods, IBeM [83], FBeM [65, 180], and eGNN [181, 182], consider a maximum expansion region (a hyper-rectangle) around information granules. Granules and expansion regions are time varying and may contract and enlarge independently for different attributes based on the data stream, the frequency of activation of granules and rules, and on the size of the rule base.

The compatibility concept directly affects the rule evolution criterion, often being a threshold (e.g., a maximal allowed distance) or a statistical control limit (e.g., a prediction interval or tolerance region), which decides whether a new rule should be evolved or not. Distance-based criteria may be more prone to outliers than density-based and statistical-based ones; on the other hand, the latter ones are usually more lazy until new rules are evolved (e.g., a significant new dense area is required such that a new rule is evolved there). All of the aforementioned rule evolution criteria have the appealing characteristic that they are unsupervised; thus, no current values of the target variables are de facto required. This makes them directly applicable to systems with significant latency and time lags for target recordings [183].

For supervised learning without any latency, evolution criteria can be also based on the (accumulated) error between the measured and estimated outputs together. The error may thus indicate a high bias of the model to generalize well to new data; hence, its flexibility (degree of nonlinearity) needs to be increased by evolving new rules. This is taken into account, e.g., in the following methods: GD-FNN [184], SAFIS [170], SCFNN [176], AHLTNM [185], eFuMo [163], and others. It has the advantage that the actual model performance is checked to realize whether the model can (still) generalize to the new data or not; this may even be the case when extrapolation on new samples is already high, depending on the extrapolation behavior of the model (often influenced by its degree of nonlinearity), an issue which is not respected by any unsupervised criterion. An example of this aspect is visualized in Figure 4.10, where rectangular new samples fall into the extrapolation region of the rules, but do not induce a high error (as they are close to the model surface shown as solid line); on the other hand, circular new samples also falling into the extrapolation region are far away from the model surface, thus inducing a high error → evolution required (the evolved model shown as dotted line).

It may also be recommended to consider multiple criteria and different conditions for cluster/rule evolution. This is, for instance, performed by NEUROFast [186] or eFuMo [163]. In eFuMo, the concept of delay of evolving mechanisms

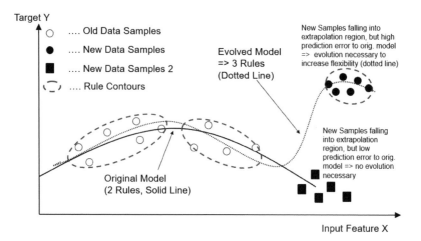

Figure 4.10:   Rule evolution due to high model error on new samples (circular filled dots) → evolved model in dotted line; rectangular new samples do not require an expansion of the original model (solid line), as the model error on them is low.

is introduced, which is an interval in which evolving mechanisms are not enabled. Only adaptation of centers and model parameters is conducted during such time intervals. The delay of evolving mechanisms takes place after a change in the structure of the system performed by any evolving mechanism. The model should have a certain period to adapt to the new structure.

Whenever a new rule $C + 1$ is evolved, usually its center is set to the current data sample $\vec{c}_{C+1} = \vec{x}$ and its initial spread is typically in such a way that minimal coverage with neighboring rules is achieved, also often to assure ϵ-completeness (the concrete formula is typically approach-dependent). The consequent parameters $\vec{w}_{C+1}$ are either set to those ones of the nearest rule (as originally suggested in [91]) or to a vector of zeros, according to the considerations regarding good parameter convergence made in [29] (Chapter 2). The inverse Hessian matrix of the new rule P_{C+1} is set to αI, with α a big value and I the identity matrix, again according to the considerations regarding good parameter convergence made in [29] (Chapter 2).

Fundamental and quite common to many incremental clustering approaches is the update of the centers $\vec{c}$ defining the cluster prototype given by

$$\vec{c}(N + 1) = \frac{N\vec{c}(N) + \vec{x}(N + 1)}{N + 1} \tag{4.44}$$

and the update of the inverse covariance matrix Σ^{-1} defining the shape of ellipsoidal clusters (applicable in the case when Gaussian functions are applied for rule representation), given by the following:

$$\Sigma^{-1}(N + 1) = \frac{\Sigma^{-1}(N)}{1 - \alpha} - \frac{\alpha}{1 - \alpha} \frac{(\Sigma^{-1}(N)(\vec{x} - \vec{c}))(\Sigma^{-1}(N)(\vec{x} - \vec{c}))^T}{1 + \alpha((\vec{x} - \vec{c})^T \Sigma^{-1}(N)(\vec{x} - \vec{c}))}, \tag{4.45}$$

with $\alpha = \frac{1}{N+1}$ and N the number of samples seen so far. Usually, various clusters/rules are updated, each representing an own covariance matrix Σ_i^{-1}; thus, the symbol $N = k_i$ then represents the number of samples "seen by the corresponding cluster so far," i.e., falling into the corresponding cluster so far (denoted as the *support of the cluster (rule)*). Note that these updates are adiabatic in the sense that they deliver the same solution as the batch off-line estimations.

4.3.4.2. *Rule pruning*

Mechanisms for pruning rules are convenient to delete old or inactive ones, which are no longer valid. These mechanisms are of utmost importance to assure a fast computation speed in model updates—with the ultimate aim to meet real-time demands; that is, the model update is finished with a new sample before the next one arrives. Furthermore, for explanation and interpretability aspects (see Section 4.5), it is beneficial to achieve compact rule bases and networks.

In general, it may happen that a rule is created in a part of the input–output space where there are just a few representative samples, which seems to indicate a new knowledge that should be covered by the model (due to the evolution of a new rule, see above). This may be originally (at the time of creation) justified by errors in measurements or due to a change of the system behavior. Later, however, this change may not be confirmed, such that the rule remains insignificant (compared to other rules—see the second case in Figure 4.9) and/or remains untouched for a longer time (also termed as *idle rule*).

The mechanisms to remove rules are mainly based on the following principles:

- The age of the rule as proposed in the xTS approach [187] which is defined as the ratio between the accumulated time of past samples falling into the rule and the current time—rules are removed according to the ratio between the support set and the overall number of samples and their age.
- The size of the support set of the cluster, also termed as *rule utility* as proposed in eTS+ approach [166], and which is elicited by the ratio between the number of cluster activations and the time the rule was evolved and added to the model. A similar concept was used in the ALMMo approach [102].
- The contribution of the rule to the output error—as performed in SAFIS [170], GAP-RBF [188], and GD-FNN [184].
- The combination of the age and the total number of activations—as performed in IBeM [83], FBeM [65], and eGNN [181, 182].

Successful concepts were further proposed : (i) in SOFNN [175], which is based on the sensitivity of the model output error according to the change of local model parameters (inspired by optimal brain surgeon concepts [189]); (ii) in PANFIS [141], where rules are removed when they are inconsequential in terms of contributing to past outputs and possible future estimations; (iii) in eFuMo [163] as an extension of the age concepts in eTS+ [166] based on the rate between the support set and the age of the cluster; (iv) in the granular approach proposed in [190] as the concept of the half-life of a rule (or granule).

4.3.4.3. *Rule merging*

Most of the E(N)FS approaches that are applying an adaptation of the rule contours, e.g., by recursive adaptation of the nonlinear antecedent parameters, are equipped with a merging strategy for rules. Whenever rules move together due to the nature of data stream samples falling in between these, they may become inevitably overlapping, see the third case in Figure 4.9 for an example: new samples marked by filled rectangles seem to open up a new region in the feature space (knowledge expansion), desiring the evolution of a new rule; however, later, when new samples (marked by non-filled rectangles) appear in between the two rules, they induce a movement of the two rules together, finally becoming overlapping and/or representing one homogeneous data cloud. This is also termed as the (sequential, stream-based) data cluster fusion effect.

Various criteria have been suggested to identify such occurrences and to eliminate them. In [191], a generic concept has been defined for recognizing such over-lapping situations based on fuzzy set and rule level. It is applicable for most of the conventional EFS techniques relying on a geometric-based criterion employing a rule inclusion metric, applicable independently of the evolving learning engine. This has been expanded in [67] to the case of generalized, adjacent rules in the feature space, where it is checked whether the same trends in the rule antecedents as well as consequents appear, thus indicating a kind of joint homogeneity between the rules. This in turn avoids information and accuracy loss of the model. Generic rule merging formulas have been established in [67, 191]

$$\vec{c}^{new} = \frac{\vec{c}^l k_l + \vec{c}^k k_k}{k_l + k_k}$$

$$\Sigma_{new}^{-1} = \frac{k_l \Sigma_l^{-1} + k_k \Sigma_k^{-1} + \frac{k_l k_k}{k_l + k_k} diag\left(\frac{1}{((\vec{c}^{new} - \vec{c}^i)^T (\vec{c}^{new} - \vec{c}^i))}\right) . * I}{k_l + k_k} \quad (4.46)$$

$$k_{new} = k_l + k_k.$$

with indices k and l denoting the two rules to be merged, $\vec{c}_{new}$ the new (merged) center, Σ_{new}^{-1} its inverse covariance matrix. $(\vec{c}^{new} - \vec{c}^i)$ is a row vector with $i = argmin_{k,l}(k_k, k_l)$, i.e., the index of the less supported rule (with support k_i), and *diag* the vector of diagonal entries; the division in the numerator $(1/...)$ (the rank-1 modification term for increasing robustness of the update) is done component-wise for each element of the matrix $(\vec{c}^{new} - \vec{c}^i)^T (\vec{c}^{new} - \vec{c}^i)$.

eFuMo [163] expands the concepts in [67] by also taking into account the prediction of the local models, where three conditions for merging are defined: angle condition, correlation condition, and distance ratio condition. An instantaneous similarity measure is introduced in FBeM [65] for multidimensional trapezoidal fuzzy sets, say A^{i_1} and A^{i_2}, as

$$S(A^{i_1}, A^{i_2})$$
$$= 1 - \frac{1}{4n} \Sigma_{j=1}^n \left(|l_j^{i_1} - l_j^{i_2}| + |\lambda_j^{i_1} - \lambda_j^{i_2}| + |\Lambda_j^{i_1} - \Lambda_j^{i_2}| + |L_j^{i_1} - L_j^{i_2}| \right), \quad (4.47)$$

where $A^i = (l^i, \lambda^i, \Lambda^i, L^i)$ is an n-dimensional trapezoid. Such a measure is more discriminative than, for example, the distance between centers of neighbouring clusters, and its calculation is fast. In ENFM [169], two clusters are merged when the membership of the first cluster to the second cluster center is greater than a predefined threshold, and vice-versa. In SOFNN [175] and extensions [143, 192], clusters are merged when they exhibit the same centers; in the extensions of SOFNN [143, 192] similarity is calculated on fuzzy set level based on the Jaccard index and when this is higher than a threshold, two fuzzy sets are merged: once fuzzy sets for all premise parts in two (or more) rules fall together (as being merged), these rules can be directly replaced by a single rule. Further various similarity measures for fuzzy sets and rules can be found in [193, 194], most of which can be adopted to the online single-pass case in the context of E(N)FS, as they are pretty fast to calculate and do not need historic data samples.

Furthermore, merging of clusters does not only provide a less redundant (over-lapping) representation of the local data distributions, but also keeps E(N)FS, in general, more compact and thus more interpretable and faster to adapt. Especially, the distinguishability and simplicity concepts as two important interpretability criteria (see Section 4.5.2) are addressed and often preserved by homogeneous rule merging.

4.3.4.4. *Rule splitting*

Rule splitting becomes evident whenever rules become blown up and/or their (local) errors increase significantly over time, which can happen either

(1) due to cluster delamination effects, where at the beginning, it seems that only one cluster (rule) is required to properly represent a local data distribution, but later two heterogeneous clouds crystallize out to appear in the local region;
(2) due to (permanent) gradually drifting patterns whose intensity is not strong enough to induce the evolution of a new cluster (rule);
(3) due to inappropriately set (too pessimistic) cluster evolution thresholds, such that too many local clouds are formed to one joint cluster (rule)—often such a threshold (usually, apparent in all ENFS methods) is difficult to set in advance for a new stream modeling problem.

The first two occurrences are visualized in Figure 4.11. Several techniques for splitting rules properly in an incremental single-pass context have been proposed. Basically, they use the concepts of local rule errors and volumes of rules as criteria to decide when to best perform a split.

In NeuroFAST [186], clusters are split according to their mean square error (MSE). The algorithm calculates the error in each P step and splits the rule and the local model with the greatest error. The mechanism of splitting in eFuMo [163] is based on the relative estimation error, which is accumulated in a certain time interval. The error is calculated for each sample that falls in one of the existing clusters. The initialization of the resulting clusters is based on the eigenvectors of

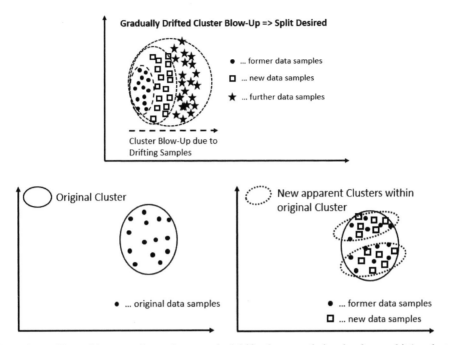

Figure 4.11: Upper: blown-up cluster due to gradual drifts always updating the cluster a bit (no cluster evolution is triggered); lower: showing a cluster delamination effect due to samples originally appearing as one cluster (left), but when new samples fall into this cluster, two heterogeneous data clouds turn out (right).

the cluster covariance matrix, as in [195] and in [196] where non-linear system identification by evolving Gustafson–Kessel fuzzy clustering and supervised local model network learning for a drug absorption spectra process is presented.

An efficient (fast) incremental rule splitting procedure in the context of generalized evolving fuzzy systems is presented in [197], especially for the purpose of splitting blown-up rules with high local estimation errors over the past iterations and extraordinary high volumes compared to other rules (measured in terms of statistical process control strategies [1]). In this sense, it can autonomously compensate for those drifts, which cannot be automatically detected (e.g., slowly gradual ones), see Section 4.4.1. The splitting is conducted along the first principal component of the covariance matrix (the longest direction span of a rule ellipsoid in the multi-dimensional space), by dividing a rule i to be split into two equal halves:

$$\vec{c}_i(split1) = \vec{c}_i + a_i \frac{\sqrt{\lambda_i}}{2} \quad \vec{c}_i(split2) = \vec{c}_i - a_i \frac{\sqrt{\lambda_i}}{2} \tag{4.48}$$

with $\vec{c}_i(split1)$ and $\vec{c}_i(split2)$ being the centers of the two split rules; λ_i corresponds to the largest eigenvalue of the covariance matrix of rule i, i.e., $\lambda_i = \max(\Lambda)$ and a_i to the corresponding eigenvector, both of which can be obtained through classical eigendecomposition of the covariance matrix Σ_i. The latter is obtained for the two split rules as follows:

$$\Sigma_i(split1) = \Sigma_i(split2) = A\Lambda^* A^T, \quad \Lambda_{jj}^* = \begin{cases} \Lambda_{jj} & j \neq 1 \\ \dfrac{\Lambda_{jj}}{4} & j = 1 \end{cases} \tag{4.49}$$

where Λ_{11} is assumed to be the entry for the largest eigenvalue and A, a matrix containing eigenvectors of the original covariance Σ_i (stored in columns).

The error criterion by calculating an adaptive threshold, which is based on the number of rules compared to an upper allowed maximal number of rules (e.g., parameterized by a user), is also used in AHLTNM [185]. This approach has the appealing aspect that an undesired rule explosion, which would make an evolved rule base totally uninterpretable, can be avoided. The split in [185] operates on halving hyper-boxes, which geometrically represent rules embedding trapezoidal fuzzy sets.

4.3.5. *Evolving Model Ensembles*

During the last 2–3 years, a few approaches have emerged which are not dealing with the update and evolution of a single ENFS model, but with a whole ensemble of ENFS models—see Section 4.2.7.6 for motivation to build up model ensembles (diversity, robustness in terms of low and noisy samples, etc.). The approaches basically differ in three aspects: (i) how and with which samples the single-base learners are evolved in order to assure diversity among them; (ii) when and how ensemble members are evolved and pruned; and (iii) how the members are aggregated to produce the final prediction/classification output, i.e., the definition of the aggregation operator Agg in Eq. (4.32) and the learning of its included (weight) parameters.

A variant to address model ensembling is through the concept of bagging [132], where sample bootstraps, also termed as *bags*, are generated from the whole data set by drawing with replications. The probability that a sample appears at least one time in a bootstrap is 0.632, but it can appear 0 or multiple times according to the probabilities achieved through a binomial distribution. It is well-known from the literature that generating models from various bags (also termed as *ensemble members*) increases sample significance and robustness against higher noise levels when the members are combined to an overall output—so, it can be also expected for (neuro-)fuzzy systems, while being learned on various bags extracted from the data stream.

The approach in [198] (termed as OB-EFS) proposes an online bagging variant of evolving fuzzy systems for regression problems, using generalized smart EFS as base members [67] and where the bags are simulated through a statistically funded online sampling based on the Poisson distribution, which exactly simulates the off-line drawing procedure with replications. It embeds an autonomous pruning of ensemble members in a soft manner by down-weighing the prediction of members with extraordinary high accumulated error trends in a weighted averaging scheme. In this sense, it automatically emphasizes those members better fitting the current data situation in the stream. Furthermore, it integrates an automatic evolution of members in the case of explicitly detecting drifts based on the Hoeffding-inequality [199] on accumulated past performance indicators.

An online bagging approach for stream classification problems has been recently proposed in [200], which uses the eClass0 [201] and the ALMMo-0 [160] (which is based on 0-order AnYa-type fuzzy classifiers [100], see also Section 4.2.6) approaches as base members, and dynamically extracts a subset of members based on various diversity statistics measures in order to form various ensembles, which are then combined to an overall output by an advanced combination module. The dynamically changing ensemble members make this approach greatly flexible to address the arising drifts (see also Section 4.4.1).

Another ensemble approach for stream classification problems has been previously proposed in [130], which is based on an online boosting concept, as (single-model) evolving fuzzy classifier are trained based on different subset of features, thus acting as evolving weak classifiers (as typically also carried out in boosting concepts [202]). Their predictions are amalgamated through weights of the base members which are increased or decreased according to their classification correctness on recent stream samples: this mimics the weights as assigned in the classical (off-line) ada-boost approach [133]. The base members are evolved based on the parsimonious evolving fuzzy classifiers (pClass) concept proposed in [117], which employs one-versus-rest classification (see Section 4.2.7.2) in combination with TS fuzzy models for establishing the $\{0, 1\}$-regression models based on indicator entries. Similarly to OB-EFS, it employs the Hoeffding inequality to decide when to evolve a new member.

A remarkable online (trained) boosting variant for regression problems has been introduced in [129], which employs the interval-based granular architecture [65] as discussed in Section 4.2.4 for the base members and which learns weights of the base members used in advanced weighted aggregation operators [203] from the data. Thus, it can be seen as a trained combiner of ensemble members [204], which typically may outperform fixed combiners, because they can adapt to the data in a supervised context (to best explain the real target values). Another key issue of this approach is that it is able to optimize meta-parameters (steering rule evolution and merging) by a multi-objective evolutionary approach [205], which integrates four objectives based on statistical measures and model complexity. A variant/extension of this technique is proposed in [206] with the usage of empirical data analysis for forming evolving data clouds as base learners which are represented in a cloud-based fuzzy system.

Finally, another variant for creating model ensembles on-the-fly is the concept of sequential ensembling as proposed in [131]. This introduces a completely different point of view on a data stream by not permanently updating an ensemble of existing models, but by generating a new fuzzy system on each new incoming data chunk. The combination of the fuzzy systems over chunks is then called *sequential ensemble*, which in fact is an ensemble of fuzzy systems rather than of evolving fuzzy systems. This is because each fuzzy system is trained from scratch with a classical batch training approach. The basic key idea, thereby, is how to combine the predictions of the members for new data chunks in order to flexibly react onto drifts. This is achieved through five different concepts respecting changes in the input data distributions as well as target concepts. A central key feature is that it can spontaneously react onto cyclic drifts by autonomously reactivating older members (trained on previous chunks).

4.3.6. *EFS Approaches and Learning Steps*

As can be noted from Figure 4.1, the total number of publications in the field of evolving neuro-fuzzy systems is 1,652 (status at the end of year 2020). After a rough checking and counting, it turned out that in these publications, approximately 500–600 different EFS approaches containing different structural and parameter learning algorithms have been published so far (with the most significant explosion during the last 10 years). Hence, it is simply impossible to provide a full list of all approaches with a description of their basic characteristics and properties within this chapter. We, thus, refer to the recent survey in [30], which discusses several methods in more detail, with respect to their parametrization efforts and which types of rule evolution and antecedent learning concepts they address. We also refer to a previous version of this chapter published in [88], where 32 "core approaches" are listed in tables along four pages and their basic properties compared against each other. These core approaches were basically those ones that performed early pioneering works in E(N)FS during the 2000s up to 2013, i.e., during times where the community was much smaller (about 25–30 key persons).

Furthermore, a lot of approaches (more than 100 in total) are self-evidently referenced in this chapter during the summarization of the core learning concepts in E(N)FS as demonstrated in the previous (sub)sections and also further below—in this context, several pioneering works are addressed that propose essentially novel learning concepts beyond state-of-the-art at the time of their publication appearance. Moreover, when coming to the useability and past applications of E(N)FS in

Section 4.6, we provide a larger list of E(N)FS approaches in Tables 4.1 and 4.2 along with the indication of in which real-world scenarios they have been applied successfully applied.

In order to provide readers of this chapter a principal touch on how an evolving approach looks like and operates incrementally, typically in single-pass mode, on incoming samples, we demonstrate a pseudo-code skeleton in Algorithm 4.1. This shows, more or less, a common denominator regarding basic learning steps on a

---

Algorithm 4.1. Basic Learning Steps in an E(N)FS Approach

Input: Current model EFS with C rules.

(1) Load new data sample $\vec{x}$.
(2) Pre-process data sample (normalization, transformation to reduced space, feature selection, ...).
(3) **If** rule-base in EFS is empty ($C = 0$),

   (a) Initialize the first rule, typically with its center to the data sample $\vec{c}_{C+1} = \vec{x}$ and its spread σ_{C+1} or Σ_{C+1} to a minimal coverage value; return.

(4) **Else**, perform the following steps (5-9):
(5) Check if rule evolution criteria are fulfilled

   (a) If yes, evolve a new rule (Section 4.3.4.1) and perform Step (3)(a); set $C = C + 1$; return.
   (b) If no, proceed with the next step.

(6) Update antecedent parts of (some or all) rules (Sections 4.3.4 or 4.3.2).
(7) Check if the rule pruning and/or merging criteria of updated rules are fulfilled

   (a) If yes, prune the rule or merge the corresponding rule(s) to one rule (Sections 4.3.4.2 and 4.3.4.3); set $C = C - 1$.
   (b) If no, proceed with the next step.

(8) Check if the rule splitting criteria of the updated rules are fulfilled

   (a) If yes, split the corresponding rul(e) into two rules (Section 4.3.4.4); overwrite the rule with one split rule and append the other split rule as the $C + 1$st rule, set $C = C + 1$.

(9) In the case of neuro-fuzzy approaches: construct neurons for the updated rules using internal norms.
(10) Update consequent parameters (of some or all) rules (Sections 4.3.3 for classification and 4.3.1 for regression)

Output: Updated model EFS.

---

single sample as used in E(N)FS approaches based on single models. One comment refers to the update of antecedents and consequents (Steps 6 and 10); some approaches may only update those of *some* rules (e.g., the rule corresponding to the winning cluster), others may always update those of *all* rules. The former may have some advantages regarding preventing the *unlearning effect* in parts where actual samples do not fall [29], and the latter typically achieves significance and thus reliability in the rule parameters faster (as more samples are used for updating).

A further comment goes to Step 2, which, depending on the approach, may contain several techniques for pre-processing a new sample. For instance, several methods support a transformation and/or feature selection step (see Section 4.4.2) in order to reduce curse of dimensionality in the case of multi-dimensional large-scale streams (Big Data); this, in turn, decreases the effect of over-fitting and improves robustness of the model updates. Methods which are not scale-invariant (such as methods based on Euclidean distances in the cluster space) require a normalization of the stream sample in order to avoid the (undesired) domination of features with larger ranges and/or higher medians than other features [207], which typically leads to the formation of wrongly placed rules. Please note that all the methods for updating the consequent parameters described in Sections 4.3.1 and 4.3.1.1 are *scale-invariant* (so, the demand for normalization solely depends on the criteria used for updating the antecedent space).

Furthermore, Steps 8 (pruning and/or merging) and 9 (splitting) may appear in a different order or may not be even used in an EFS approach at all—leaving only the evolution step in Step 5, which, however, is necessary to make an incremental learning approach actually evolving; without this step, the approach would be simply adaptive (updating only the parameters without evolving its structure), as being apparent in several adaptive methods [49], already proposed during the 1990s, e.g., within the scope of adaptive control [208].

4.4. Stability and Reliability

Two important issues when learning from data streams are (i) the assurance of stability during the incremental learning process and (ii) the investigation of the reliability of model outputs in terms of predictions, forecasts, quantifications, classification statements, etc. These usually lead to an enhanced *robustness* of the evolved models. Stability is usually guaranteed by all properly designed E(N)FS approaches, as long as the data streams from which the models are learnt appear in a quite "smooth, expected" fashion. However, specific occasions such as *drifts* and *shifts* [209] or high noise levels may appear in these, which require a specific handling within the learning engine of the EFS approaches in order to assure model stability by avoiding catastrophic forgetting and/or diverging parameters and structures.

Another problem is dedicated to high-dimensional streams, usually stemming from large-scale time-series [210] embedded in the data, and mostly causing a *curse of dimensionality* effect, which leads to over-fitting and thus to a decrease of their parameter stability and finally to significant downtrends in model accuracy. A few EFS approaches have embedded an online dimensionality reduction procedure so far in order to diminish this effect, see the discussion in Section 4.4.2.

Although high noise levels can be automatically handled by all the consequent learning techniques described in Section 4.3.1 as well as by the antecedent learning engines discussed in Sections 4.3.2 and 4.3.4, reliability aspects in terms of calculating certainty in model outputs by respecting the noise and data uncertainty can be an additional valuable issue in order to understand model outputs better and to perform an adequate handling of them by experts/operators. Drift handling is included in several basic EFS methods in a straightforward manner, that is, by using forgetting factors in consequent learning, as described in Section 4.3.1.

This section is dedicated to a summary of developments in stability, reliability, and robustness of EFS achieved so far, which can be also generically used in combination with most of the EFS approaches published so far.

4.4.1. *Drift Handling in Streams*

In data-stream mining environments, *concept drift* means that the statistical properties of either the input or target variables change over time in unforeseen ways. In particular, drifts either denote changes in the underlying data distribution (input space drift) or in the underlying relationship between model inputs and targets (target concept drift)—see [209, 211] for recent surveys on drifting concepts. Figure 4.12 demonstrates two input space drifts in (a) and two target concept drifts in (b). In Figure 4.12 (a), in the left-most case indicates a drift in the mean of the distribution of the circular class, which leads to significant class overlap, the right case shows

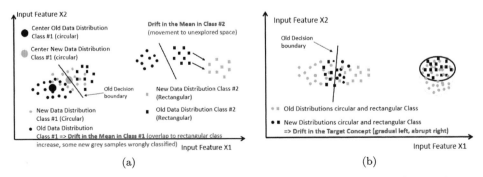

(a) (b)

Figure 4.12: Two drift concepts: (a) typical drifts in the input space (increasing class overlaps or moving to unexplored space); (b) typical drifts in the target concept (left: gradual, around the decision boundary, right: abrupt, class overlaid by other classes).

the same but moving into an unexplored region. In Figure 4.12(b), the left case shows a gradual case where samples get more overlapping around the decision boundary, the right case shows an abrupt case where samples from a new class fall into the same region as samples from an older class. From a practical point of view, such drifts can happen because the system behavior and environmental conditions change dynamically during the online learning process, which makes the relations and concepts contained in the old data samples obsolete. They are frequent occurrences in non-stationary environments [2] nowadays and thus desire a specific treatment.

Such drifting situations are contrary to new operation modes or system states that should be integrated into the models with the same weight as the older ones in order to extend the models (knowledge expansion, see Section 4.3.4), but keeping the relations in states seen before untouched (being still valid and thus necessary for future predictions). Drifts, however, usually mean that the older learned relations (as structural parts of a model) are not valid any longer, which should be thus incrementally out-weighed and forgotten over time [209]. This is especially necessary when class overlaps increase, as shown in three out of four cases in Figure 4.12.

A smooth forgetting concept for consequent learning employing the idea of exponential forgetting [208] is used in most of the current EFS approaches [30, 88]. The strategy in all of these is to integrate a forgetting factor $\lambda \in 0, 1$ for strengthening the influence of newer samples in the Kalman gain γ —see Eq. (4.38). Figure 4.13 shows the weight impact of samples obtained for different forgetting factor values.

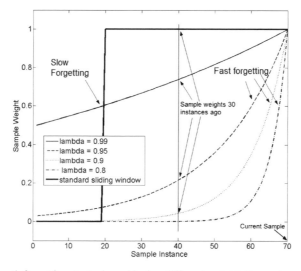

Figure 4.13:   Smooth forgetting strategies achieving different weights for past samples; compared to a sliding window with fixed width inducing a complete forgetting of older samples.

This is also compared to a standard sliding window technique, which weights all samples up to a certain point of time in the past equally, but forget all others before completely → non-smooth forgetting that may induce catastrophic forgetting [212]. The effect of this forgetting factor integration is that changes of the target concept in regression problems can be tracked properly; i.e., a movement and shaping of the current regression surface towards the new output behavior is enforced, see [213].

Regarding drift handling in the antecedent part in order to address changes in the (local) data distributions of the input space—as exemplarily shown in the upper plot of Figure 4.11—some techniques may be used, such as a reactivation of rule centers and spreads from a converged situation by an increase of the learning gain on new incoming samples. This was first conducted for EFS in the pioneering work in [213] in combination with the two approaches eTS [91] and FLEXFIS [140], based on the concept of *rule ages* (being able to measure the intensity of drifts according to changes in the second derivative). It has the effect that rules are helped out from their stuck, converged positions to cover the new data cloud appearances of the drifted situation well, while forgetting samples from the older clouds (occurring before the drift took place). In eFuMo [163], the forgetting in antecedent learning is integrated as the degree of the weighted movement of the rule centers $\vec{c}$ towards a new data sample $\vec{x}_{N+1}$

$$\vec{c}_i(N+1) = \vec{c}_i(N) + \Delta\vec{c}_i(N+1)$$

$$\text{with} \quad \Delta\vec{c}_i(N+1) = \frac{\mu_i(\vec{x}_{N+1})^\eta(\vec{x}_{N+1} - \vec{c}_i(N))}{s_i(N+1)} \tag{4.50}$$

with $s_i(N+1) = \lambda s_i(N) + \mu_i(\vec{x}_{N+1})^\eta$ being the sum of the past memberships $\mu_i(\vec{x}_j), j = 1, \ldots, N$, η the fuzziness degree also used as a parameter in fuzzy C-means, and λ the forgetting factor. Forgetting is also integrated in the inverse covariance matrix and determinant update defining the shape of the clusters.

Handling of *local drifts*, which are drifts that may appear with different intensities in different parts of the feature space (thus affecting different rules with varying intensity), is considered in [214]. The idea of this approach is that different forgetting factors are used for different rules instead of a global factor. This steers the local level of flexibility of the model. Local forgetting factors are adapted according to the local drift intensity (elicited by a modified variant of the Page–Hinkley test [215]), and the contribution of the rules in previous model errors. Such dynamic adaptation of the forgetting factor, according to the current drift intensity, has the appealing effect that during non-drift phases the conventional life-long adaptation of the fuzzy model takes place. This, in turn, increases sample significance and thus stability of the learned parameters and structure during non-drift phases— a permanent forgetting during these may end up with decreased performance, as could be verified in [214].

The distinction between target concept drifts and input space drifts could be achieved in [216] by using a semi-supervised and a fully unsupervised drift indicator. It, thus, can operate on scarcely labeled (selected by online active learning methods, see Section 4.6.1), and also fully unlabeled samples. It uses evolving fuzzy classifiers in the extended single-model architecture form with EFC-SM as the learning engine, which embeds generalized rules [217].

Another form of drift is the so-called *cyclic drift*, where changes in the (input/target) data distribution may happen at a certain point of time, but, later, older distributions are revisited. ENFS approaches to deal with such drift cases were addressed in [74, 218] using type-2 recurrent neuro-fuzzy systems, termed as eT2RFNN. The idea is to prevent re-learning of older local distributions from scratch and thus to increase the early significance of the rules. Furthermore, EFS ensemble techniques as discussed in Section 4.3.5 automatically embed mechanisms to address cyclic drifts early and properly, by activating and/or over-weighing those members (previously learned) in the calculation of final predictions that best meet the data distribution in the current data chunks.

Whenever a drift cannot be explicitly detected or it implicitly triggers the evolution of a new rule/neuron, a posteriori *drift compensation* [197] is a promising option in order to (back-)improve the accuracy of the rules. This can be achieved through incremental rule splitting techniques as discussed in Section 4.3.4.4. Furthermore, such rule splitting concepts are typically parameter-free, which abandons the usage and tuning of a forgetting factor, thus decreasing parametrization effort.

4.4.2. On-line Curse of Dimensionality Reduction

High dimensionality of the data stream mining and modeling problem becomes apparent whenever a larger variety of features and/or system variables are recorded, e.g., in multi-sensor networks [219], which characterize the dependencies and interrelations contained in the system/problem to be modeled. For models, including localized granular components as is the case of evolving neuro-fuzzy systems, it is well-known that *curse of dimensionality* is very severe in the case when a high number of variables are used as model inputs [23] [84]. This is basically because in high-dimensional spaces, someone cannot speak about locality any longer (on which these types of models rely), as all samples are moving to the edges of the joint feature space—see [116] (Chapter 1) for a detailed analysis of this problem.

Therefore, the reduction of the dimensionality of the learning problem is highly desired. In a data stream sense, to ensure an appropriate reaction onto the system dynamics, the feature reduction should be conducted online and be open for *anytime changes*. One possibility is to track the importance levels of features over time and to cut out those ones that are unnecessary—as has been used in connection with EFS for regression problems in [66, 166] and for classification problems in a first attempt in [109]. In [166], the contribution of the features in the consequents of the rules is measured in terms of their gradients in the hyper-planes; those features whose contribution over all rules is negligible can be discarded. This has been extended in [66] by also integrating the contribution of the features in the antecedent space (regarding their significance in the rules premise parts). A further approach has been suggested in [220], where an online global crisp feature selection was extended to a local variant, where for each rule a separate feature (importance) list was incrementally updated. This was useful to achieve more flexibility due to local feature selection characteristics, as features may become important differently in different parts of the feature space.

However, features that are unimportant at an earlier point of time may become important at a later stage (*feature reactivation*). This means that crisply cutting out some features with the usage of online feature selection and ranking approaches such as [221, 222] can fail to represent the recent feature dynamics appropriately. Without a re-training cycle, which, however, slows down the process and causes additional sliding window parameters, this would lead to discontinuities in the learning process, as parameters and rule structures have been learned on different feature spaces before.

An approach that addresses input structure changes incrementally on-the-fly is presented in [223] for classification problems using classical single model and one-versus-rest based multi-model architectures, see Section 4.2.7.2 (in connection with FLEXFIS-Class learning engine). It operates on a global basis; hence; features are either seen as important or unimportant for the whole model. The basic idea is that feature weights $\lambda_1, \ldots, \lambda_p \in 0, 1$ for the p features included in the learning problem are calculated based on a stable separability criterion [224] (deduced from Fisher's separability criterion [225] as used in (incremental) discriminant analysis [226, 227]):

$$J = trace(S_w^{-1} S_b) \tag{4.51}$$

with S_w the within scatter matrix modeled by the sum of the covariance matrices for each class, and S_b the between scatter matrix modeled by the sum of the degree of mean shift between classes. The criterion in Eq. (4.51) is applied (i) dimension-wise to see the impact of each feature separately—note that in this case, it reduces to a ratio of two variances—and (ii) for the remaining $p - 1$ feature subspace in order to gain the quality of separation when excluding each feature. The latter approach is termed as LOFO (leave-one-feature-out) approach and has also been successfully applied in an evolving neuro-fuzzy approach for extracting (interpretable) rules in the context of heart sounds identification [228]. The former has been successfully used recently in an evolving neuro-fuzzy systems approach termed as ENFS-Uni0 [96], for rule length reduction and thus for increasing the readability of rules.

In both cases, p criteria $J_1, \ldots, J_p$ according to Eq. (4.51) are obtained. For normalization purposes to 0, 1, finally the feature weights are defined by the following:

$$\lambda_j = 1 - \frac{J_j - \min_{j=1,\ldots,p}(J_j)}{\max_{j=1,\ldots,p}(J_j) - \min_{j=1,\ldots,p}(J_j)}. \tag{4.52}$$

To be applicable in online learning environments, updating the weights in incremental mode is achieved by updating the within-scatter and between-scatter matrices using the recursive covariance matrix formula [226]. This achieves a smooth change of feature weights = feature importance levels over time with new incoming samples. Hence, this approach is also denoted as *smooth and soft online dimension reduction*—the term *softness* comes from the decreased weights instead of a crisp deletion. Down-weighed features then play a marginal role during the learning process, e.g., the rule evolution criterion relies more on the highly weighted features. This, in turn, reduces curse of dimensionality effects during adapting the models.

The feature weights concept has been also employed in the context of data stream regression problems in [67], there with the usage of generalized rules as defined in Section 4.2.2.2. The features weights are calculated by a combination of future-based expected statistical contributions of the features in all rules and their influences in the rules' hyper-planes (measured in terms of gradients). A re-scaled Mahalanobis distance measure was developed to integrate weights in the rule evolution condition in a consistent and monotonic fashion, that is, lower weights, in fact, always induce lower distances. Figure 4.14 visualizes the effect of the unimportance of Feature #2

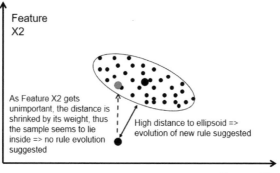

Figure 4.14: No rule evolution suggested although sample lies outside the tolerance region of a rule, whenever Feature X2 becomes unimportant; thus, the distance of a new sample to the ellipsoid shrank by the re-scaled Mahalanobis distance [67].

on the rule evolution criterion respecting the re-scaled Mahalanobis distance of a sample to a rule ellipsoid (as shaped out in the case when using multivariate Gaussians).

Another possibility for achieving a smooth input structure change was proposed in [229] for regression problems with the usage of partial least squares (PLS). PLS performs a transformation of the input space into latent variables (LVs) by maximizing the covariance structure between inputs and the target [230]. The coordinate axes are turned into a position (achieving latent variables as weighted linear combination of the original ones) that allows to better explain the complexity of the modeling problem. Typically, a lower number of LVs is needed to achieve an accurate regression. Scores on the lower number of LVs (projected samples) can then be directly used as inputs in the evolving fuzzy models. LVs are updated incrementally with new incoming samples based on the concept of Krylov sequences in combination with Gram–Schmidt orthogonalization, see [229]. The LVs internally update the importance of the features in the loadings. Previous works in [142, 159, 231] and [232] also perform an incremental update of the LV space for evolving models, but using unsupervised principal component analysis (PCA) [233].

4.4.3. *Convergence Analysis and Assurance*

Another important criterion when applying EFS is some sort of convergence of the parameters included in the fuzzy systems over time to optimality in the objective function sense—this accounts for the stability aspect in the stability–plasticity dilemma [234], which is important in the life-long learning context. When using the recursive (fuzzily weighted) least squares approach, as being done by many of the current techniques, convergence to optimality is guaranteed as long as there is no structural change [139], i.e., no neurons or rules are evolved and/or moved. FLEXFIS [140] takes care of this issue and can achieve sub-optimality in the LS sense subject to a constant due to a decreasing learning gain in the cluster partitions.

Another and an even more direct way to guarantee stability is to show convergence of the model error itself, mostly to provide an upper bound on the (development of the) model error over time. This could be accomplished (i) in the PANFIS approach [141] by the usage of an extended recursive LS method, which integrates a binary multiplication factor in the inverse Hessian matrix update that is set to 1 when the approximation error is bigger than the system error, and (ii) in SOFMLS [44] by applying a modified least squares algorithm to train both parameters and structures with the support of linearization and Lyapunov functions [145]. It is remarkable that in this approach, the evolution or pruning of rules does not harm the convergence of the parameters, as these only change the dimension of the inverse Hessian and the weight matrices. Based on, SOFMLS approach, the bound on the identification error could be made even smaller in [146] with the usage of an own designed dead-zone recursive least square algorithm. SEIT2-FNN [80] employs a heuristic-based approach by resetting the inverse Hessian matrix to $q * I$ with I the identity matrix after several update iterations of the consequent parameters. This resetting operation keeps the inverse Hessian matrix bounded and helps to avoid divergence of parameters.

In [180], an evolving controller approach was designed based on neuro-fuzzy model architecture, and by proving a stability theorem using bounded inputs from linear matrix inequalities and parallel distributed computing concepts. This guarantees robust parameter solutions becoming convergent over time and omitting severe disturbances in control actions. Advanced convergence considerations have also been made in [235], where the stability of AnYa type EFS [100] has been proven through the Lyapunov theory, which shows that the average identification error converges to a small neighborhood of zero. An extension of this approach has been proposed in [236] through the maximization of the cross-correntropy for avoiding convergence problems due to the learning size in the gradient-based learning and to approach steady-state convergence performance even in the case of non-Gaussian noise.

For consequent parameter learning, a better convergence can also be achieved by using the recursively (weighted) multi-innovation least squares approach as discussed in Section 4.3.1.1; the degree of convergence and thus robustness of the solution depends on the innovation length, which, on the other hand, slows down the update process. A good tradeoff value is 10 as shown in [148] for various data sets. Further improvements for robust consequent learning with some convergence thematic are extensively discussed throughout Section 4.3.1.1, specifically addressing a proper handling of various noise and drift aspects in real-world data streams. Finally, it should be stressed that convergence of a real (global) optimal joint antecedent–consequent parameters solution can be only assured when performing re-optimization steps from time to time on both the linear consequents and nonlinear antecedent parameters (based on recent past samples). This has been achieved successfully recently in [153].

4.4.4. *Reliability and Uncertainty*

Reliability deals with the *expected quality of model predictions* in terms of classification statements, quantification outputs or forecasted values in time series as a prerequisite to explainability, see subsequent section. Reliability points to the trustworthiness of the predictions of current query points which may be basically influenced by two factors:

- The quality of the training data resp. data stream samples seen so far

- The nature and localization of the current query point for which a prediction should be obtained

The trustworthiness/certainty of the predictions may support/influence the users/operators during a final decision finding—for instance, a query assigned to a class may cause a different user's reaction when the trustworthiness about this decision is low, compared to when it is high.

The first factor basically concerns the noise level in measurement data. Noise can thereby occur in various forms, such as white noise, Gaussian noise or chaotic noise [237], and affecting input variables, targets or both. Noise may also cover aspects in the direction of uncertainties in users' annotations in classification problems: a user with lower experience level may cause more inconsistencies in the class labels, causing overlapping classes, finally increasing conflict cases (see below); similar occasions may happen in the case when several users annotate samples on the same systems, but have different opinions in borderline cases.

The second factor concerns the position of the current query point with respect to the definition space of the model. A model can show a perfect trend with little uncertainty within the training samples range, but a new query point may appear far away from all training samples seen so far. This yields a severe degree of extrapolation when conducting the model inference process and furthermore a low reliability in making a prediction for the query. In a classification context, a query point may also fall close in a highly overlapped region or close to the decision boundary between two classes. The first problem is denoted as *ignorance*, the second as *conflict* [115, 121]. A visualization of these two occasions is shown in Figure 4.15 (a) (for conflict) and (b) (for ignorance). The conflict case is due to a sample falling between two classes and the ignorance case due to a query point falling outside

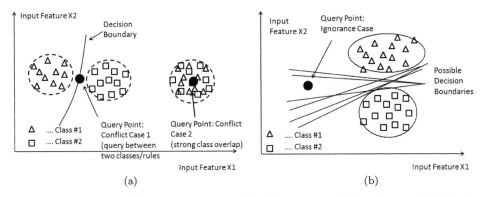

(a) (b)

Figure 4.15: (a): two conflict cases: query point falls in between two distinct classes and within the overlap region of two classes; (b) ignorance case as query point lies significantly away from the training samples, thus increasing the *variability of the version space* [121]; in both figures, rules modeling the two separate classes are shown by an ellipsoid, the decision boundaries indicated by solid lines.

the range of training samples, whose classes are indeed linearly separable, but by several possible decision boundaries (also termed as the *variability of the version space* [121]).

4.4.4.1. *Addressing uncertainty for classification problems*

In the classification context, conflict and ignorance can be reflected and represented by the means of fuzzy classifiers in a quite natural way [238]. These concepts have been tackled in the field of evolving fuzzy classifiers (EFC), see [110], where multiple binary classifiers are trained in an all-pairs context for obtaining simpler decision boundaries in multi-class classification problems (see Section 4.2.7.3). On a single rule level, the confidence in a prediction can be obtained by the confidence in the different classes coded into the consequents of the rules having the form of Eq. (4.22). This provides a perfect conflict level (close to $0.5 \rightarrow$ high conflict, close to $1 \rightarrow$ low conflict) in case of overlapping classes within a single rule. If a query point $\vec{x}$ falls between rules with different majority classes (different maximal confidence levels), then the extended weighted classification scheme in Eq. (4.24) is requested to represent a conflict level properly. If the confidence in the final output class L, $conf_L$, is close to 0.5, conflict is high; when it is close to 1, conflict is low. In case of all-pairs architecture, Eq. (4.24) can be used to represent conflict levels in each of the internal binary classifiers. Furthermore, an overall conflict level on the final classifier output is obtained by [110] the following:

$$conflict_{\deg} = \frac{score_k}{score_k + score_l} \qquad (4.53)$$

with k and l being the classes with the two highest scores.

The ignorance criterion can be resolved in a quite natural way, represented by a degree of extrapolation, and thus by

$$Ign_{\deg} = 1 - \max_{i=1}^{C} \mu_i(\vec{x}), \qquad (4.54)$$

with C being the number of rules currently contained in the evolved fuzzy classifier. In fact, the degree of extrapolation is a good indicator of the degree of ignorance, but not necessarily sufficient, see [115] for an extended analysis and further concepts. However, integrating the ignorance levels into the preference relation scheme of all-pairs evolving fuzzy classifiers according to Eq. (4.29) for obtaining the final classification statement, helped to boost the accuracies of the classifier significantly [110]. This is because the classifiers that show a strongly extrapolated situation in the current query are down-weighted towards 0, thus masked out, in the scoring process. This led to an out-performance of incremental machine learning classifiers

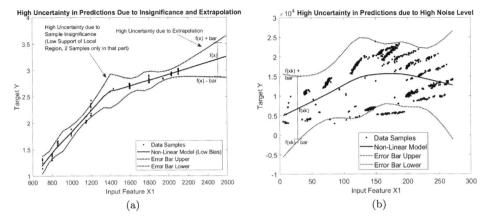

Figure 4.16: (a): High uncertainty due to extrapolation (right part) and sample insignificance (middle part, only two samples support local region); (b): high uncertainty due to high noise level over the whole definition range.

from MOA framework[3] [239] on several large-scale problems. The overall ignorance level of an all-pairs classifier is the minimal ignorance degree calculated by Eq. (4.54) over all binary classifiers.

4.4.4.2. *Addressing Uncertainty for Regression Problems*

In the regression context, the estimation of parameters through RWFLS and modifications (see Section 4.3.1) can usually deal with high noise levels in order to find a non-overfitting trend of the approximation surface. This is especially the case through advanced strategies (total least squares, recursive correntropy, etc.) as discussed in Section 4.3.1.1 and also in a recent paper dealing with this topic in detail in [148]. However, RFWLS and extensions are not able to represent uncertainty levels of the model predictions. These can be modeled by so-called error bars or confidence intervals [240]. Figure 4.16 shows the uncertainty of approximation functions (shown in solid lines obtained by regression on the dotted data samples) as modeled by error bars (shown as dashed lines surrounding the solid lines); left for a case with increasing extrapolation on the right-hand side (error bars open up and and thus uncertainty in predictions becomes higher), right for a case with high noise level contained in the data (leading to wide error bars and thus to a high uncertainty).

The pioneering approach for achieving *uncertainty in evolving fuzzy modeling* for regression problems was proposed in [54]. The approach is deduced from

---

[3]http://moa.cms.waikato.ac.nz/

statistical noise and quantile estimation theory [241]. The idea is to find a lower and an upper fuzzy function for representing a confidence interval, i.e.,

$$\underline{f}(x_k) \leq f(x_k) \leq \overline{f}(x_k) \quad \forall k \in \{1, \ldots, N\}, \tag{4.55}$$

with N being the number of data samples seen so far. The main requirement is to define the band to be as narrow as possible while containing a certain percentage of the data. Its solution is based on the calculation of the expected covariance of the residual between the model output and new data in local regions as modeled by a linear hyper-plane. The following formulas for the local error bars (in the j-th rule) were obtained in [54] after several mathematical derivations,

$$\overline{\underline{f}}_j(x_k) = \Psi_j(x_k) l_j(x_k) \pm t_{\alpha, \Sigma(N)-\mathrm{deg}} \hat{\sigma} \sqrt{(x_k \Psi_j(x_k))^T P_j (\Psi_j(x_k) x_k)}, \tag{4.56}$$

where $t_{\alpha, \Sigma(N)-\mathrm{deg}}$ stands for the percentile of the t-distribution for a $100(1-2\alpha)$ percentage confidence interval (default $\alpha = 0.025$) with $\Sigma(N) - deg$ degrees of freedom, and P_j denotes the inverse Hessian matrix. deg denotes the degrees of freedom in a local model, and $\Sigma(N)$ the sum of membership degrees over the past samples. The symbol $\hat{\sigma}$ is the variance of model errors and the first term denotes the prediction of the jth local rule. The error bars for all local rules are averaged with normalized rule membership weights Ψ (similarly as in the conventional fuzzy systems inference process, see Section 4.2.2.1) to form an overall error bar additionally to the output prediction provided by the fuzzy system. The term after $\pm$ provides the output uncertainty for the current query sample x_k.

Another approach to address uncertainty in model outputs is proposed in [65, 83], where fuzzy rule consequents are represented by two terms, a linguistic one—containing a fuzzy set (typically of trapezoidal nature)—and a functional one—as in the case of TS fuzzy systems. The linguistic term offers a direct fuzzy output, which, according to the widths of the learned fuzzy sets, may reflect more or less uncertainty in the active rules (i.e., those rules which have non-zero or at least ϵ membership degree). A granular prediction is given by the convex hull of those sets which belong to active rules. The width of the convex hull can be interpreted as confidence interval and provided as final model output uncertainty.

4.4.4.3. *Parameter uncertainty*

Apart from model uncertainty, *parameter uncertainty* can be an important aspect when deciding whether the model is stable and robust. Especially in the cases of insufficient or poorly distributed data, parameter uncertainty typically increases. Parameter uncertainty in EFS has been handled in [242, 243] in terms of the use of the Fisher information matrix [244], with the help of some key measures extracted from it. In [242], parameter uncertainty is used for guiding the design of experiments process in an online incremental manner, see also Section 4.6.1.3. In [243], it is used for guiding online active sample selection, see also Section 4.6.1.

4.5. Explainability and Interpretability

This section is dedicated to two topics of growing importance during recent years in the machine learning and soft computing community, namely *explainability* and *interpretability*. While explainability offers an expert or a user a kind of model-based insight and an associated reasoning why certain predictions have been made by the model, interpretability goes a step further and tries to offer understandable aspects about the evolved model, such as embedded partial relations between features that may offer new insights and further knowledge about the (constitutions of the) process for experts/users.

Fuzzy systems indeed offer an architecture that is per se interpretable and explainable (as also discussed in the introduction); however, when being trained from data, they may become at least a (dark) gray box model or even nearly non-interpretable [51]. The situation is even worse when performing evolving concepts (as discussed through Section 4.3) for incrementally updating the fuzzy systems from streams, because these—apart from some pruning and merging concepts—basically try to model the data distributions and implicitly contained relations/dependencies as accurately as possible. This is also termed as *precise modeling* in literature [245] . The focus on precise modeling was the main one during the last two decades in the EFS community. However, several developments and concepts arose during the latest years that addressed interpretability and explainability of EFS. These will be described in the following subsections.

4.5.1. *Explainability*

Explainability of artificial intelligence (AI) has become a huge topic during the past years [246], especially in the field of machine learning and deep learning models [247], which is also reflected in new important objectives of the European community research programme "Horizon Europe" (aiming to last until 2027). This is because AI models primarily fully operate as black boxes when being trained from data; thus, human experts do not know where the predictions come from, why they have been made, etc. However, for users it is often important that predictions are well understood in order to be able to accept the models decisions, but also to be able to gain new insights into the process and relations. The explanation of model decisions may also become an essential aspect to stimulate human feedback, especially when reasons are provided for the decisions [248] and features most influencing the decisions are highlighted [249]. Then, when the model seems to be wrong from human users' first glance, by looking at the explained reason and induced features, they may be persuaded to change their opinion or they may be confirmed in their first intuition. In the latter case, they can directly associate the rule leading to the reason shown and thus may change or even discard it. This in turn means that the model is enriched with knowledge provided by the human users and thus can benefit from it—becoming more accurate, more precise in certain regimes and parts of the system.

In evolving neuro-fuzzy systems, explainability is already automatically granted to some extent, especially due to the granular rule-based structure (see Section 4.2) and whenever the input features have an interpretable meaning for the experts. For instance, a reason for a certain decision could be explained by showing the most active rules (in readable IF-THEN form) during the inference and production of a decision. However, due to the primary focus on precise modeling aspects, the explainability may be diminished. The authors in [250] provided several aspects in order to improve the explainability of evolving fuzzy classifiers (in single model architecture as presented in Section 4.2.7.1). It contains the following concepts:

- The *reason for model decisions* in linguistic form: the most active fuzzy rule(s) for current query instances is (are) prepared in transparent form and shown to the humans as reason.
- The *certainty of model decisions* in relation to the final output and possible alternative suggestions. This indicates the degree of ambiguity, i.e., the "clearness" of a model output.
- The *feature importance levels* for the current model decision: (i) to reduce the length of the rules (=reasons) to show only the most essential premises and thus to increase their readability; (ii) to get a better feeling about which features and corresponding conditions in the rules' antecedents strongly influenced the decision.
- The *coverage degree* of the current instance to be predicted/classified: this is another form of certainty, which tells the human how novel the content in the current sample is. In the case of high novelty content (equivalent to a low coverage), the human may pay additional attention to provide his feedback, which may be in some cases even highly recommended (e.g., to encourage her/him to define new fault types, new classes or new operation modes).

In [250], the final reasoning why a certain decision has been made is based on geometric considerations—an example in a two-dimensional classification problem for doing so is indicated in Figure 4.17. There, the rules have ellipsoidal contours that result from multi-dimensional Gaussian kernels for achieving arbitrarily rotated positions (generalized rules as defined in Section 4.2.2.2). The fuzzy sets shown along the axes (HIGH, MEDIUM, LOW) can be obtained by projection of the higher-dimensional rule contours onto the single axes, see, e.g., [67].

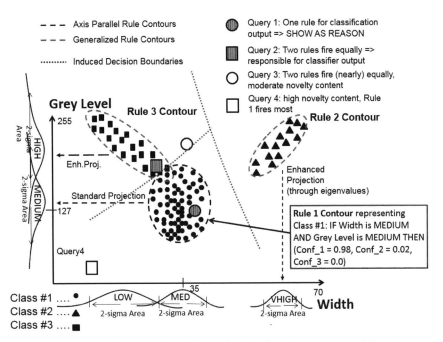

Figure 4.17: A geometric interpretation of fuzzy classification rules as extracted from data samples containing three classes (their contours shown as dotted ellipsoids).

Also shown in Fig. 4.17 are four query point cases whose classification interpretation can be seen as follows:

- *Query 1 (circle, shaded)*: In the case of this sample, only one rule (Rule 1) fires significantly, and it is, therefore, sufficient to show this rule to the human (operator/user) (in IF-THEN form) as a reason for the final model output. In our example, Rule 1 reads as the following:

Rule 1: IF Width is MEDIUM AND Grey Level is MEDIUM, THEN Class #1 with ($conf_1 = 0.98$, $conf_2 = 0.02$, $conf_3 = 0.0$).

Thus, the reason why Class #1 has been returned is that the width of the object is MEDIUM (around 35 units) and its (average) gray level is MEDIUM (i.e., somewhere around 127 when assuming a range of 0, 255).

- *Query 2 (rectangular, shaded)*: Rule 3 fires most actively, but also Rule 1 fires significantly, so the induced linguistic IF-THEN forms of both are to be shown to the human, as the classification response will depend mainly on the weighted scoring of these two rules.
- *Query 3 (circle, non-shaded)*: this query point lies in between Rules 1, 2, and 3, but it is significantly closer to Rules 1 and 3; thus, their induced linguistic

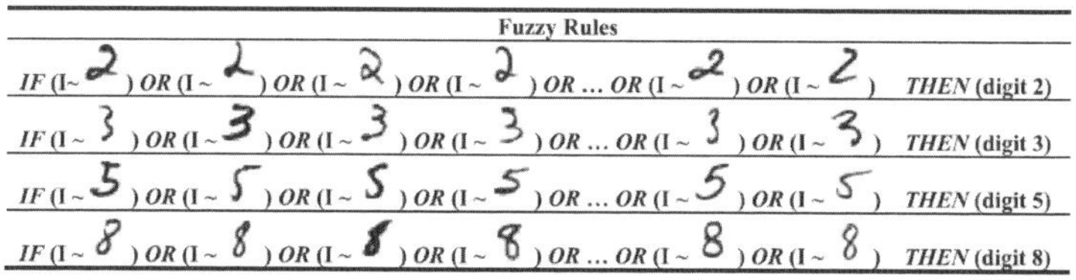

Fuzzy Rules
IF (I~ *2*) OR (I~ *2*) OR (I~ *2*) OR (I~ *2*) OR ... OR (I~ *2*) OR (I~ *2*) THEN (digit 2)
IF (I~ *3*) OR (I~ *3*) OR (I~ *3*) OR (I~ *3*) OR ... OR (I~ *3*) OR (I~ *3*) THEN (digit 3)
IF (I~ *5*) OR (I~ *5*) OR (I~ *5*) OR (I~ *5*) OR ... OR (I~ *5*) OR (I~ *5*) THEN (digit 5)
IF (I~ *8*) OR (I~ *8*) OR (I~ *8*) OR (I~ *8*) OR ... OR (I~ *8*) OR (I~ *8*) THEN (digit 8)

Figure 4.18: Explainable AnYa fuzzy rules extracted from the hand-written digits data base MNIST, as also used in DRB classifiers [111].

IF-THEN forms are to be shown to the human; the novelty content of this query is moderate.

- *Query 4 (rectangular, non-shaded)*: this query point indicates high novelty content, as it lies far away from all extracted rules; since Rule 1 is by far the closest, its induced linguistic IF-THEN form will be shown to the human. This type of uncertainty is not covered by the weighted output scoring, as it remains on the "safe" side of the decision boundary, shown as a dotted line. Thus, this uncertainty is separately handled by the concept of *coverage*.

In [250], these explanation concepts for evolving fuzzy classifier decisions were successfully integrated within an annotation GUI. They significantly helped the operators to achieve a more consistent and homogeneous labeling of images (showing the surface of micro-fluidic chips) into ten different fault classes, and this over a longer time frame, than when not using any explanations.

Another form of advanced explanation capability has been offered by the approach proposed in [111] under the scope of deep rule-based classifiers, which internally use massively parallel fuzzy rule bases. Therein, each rule is formed by a connection of ORs between antecedents to represent a certain class; the single antecedents are realized through the representation of prototypes for the consequent class. An example for the application scenario of hand-digit recognition in images (based on the MNIST data base) is provided in Figure 4.18. It can be realized that, for instance, for the digit number 2 various prototypical hand-written images are the representatives for this class (as connected by an OR in the respective rule)—in this case, they have been extracted autonomously from the data base based on an evolving density-based approach for clouds as demonstrated in [100]. The prototypes can then be directly associated with the centers of the clouds (incrementally updated from the data stream). For a new sample image, when its output class is 2 from the DRB classifier, a direct explanation of the reason for this output can be provided by simply showing the prototype with the highest (cloud-based) activation level(s), i.e., those that are, thus, the most similar to the new sample image. In this sense, a "similarity-based" output explanation on image sample level (with a for users understandable context) can be achieved.

4.5.2. *Interpretability*

Improved transparency and interpretability of the evolved models may be useful in several real-world applications where the operators and experts intend to gain a deeper understanding of the interrelations and dependencies in the system. This may enrich their knowledge and enable them to interpret the characteristics of the system on a deeper level. Concrete examples are decision support systems or classification systems, where the description of classes by certain linguistic dependencies among features may provide answers to important questions (e.g., for providing the health state (= one class) of a patient [251]) and support the experts/user in taking appropriate actions. Another example is the substitution of expensive hardware with *soft sensors*, referred to as *eSensors* in an evolving context; [252, 253]: the model has to be linguistically or physically understandable, reliable, and plausible to an expert, before it can be substituted with the hardware. In other cases, it is beneficial to provide further insights into the control behavior [51, 254].

Interpretability, apart from pure complexity reduction, has been addressed little in the evolving systems community so far. A position paper published in *Information Sciences* journal [32] summarizes the achievements in EFS, provides avenues for new concepts as well as concrete formulas and algorithms and points out open issues as important future challenges. The basic common understanding is that complexity reduction as a key prerequisite for compact and, therefore, transparent models is handled in most of the EFS approaches (under the pruning and merging aspect discussed in Sections 4.3.4.2 and 4.3.4.3), whereas other important criteria (known to be important from conventional batch off-line design of fuzzy systems [245, 255]), have been loosely handled in EFS so far. These criteria include the following:

- Type of construction of rules/neurons
- Distinguishability and simplicity
- Consistency
- Coverage and completeness
- Feature importance levels
- Rule importance Levels
- Interpretation of consequents
- Knowledge expansion

Rule construction is basically achieved through the usage of specific norms for combining the fuzzy sets in the rule antecedent parts. Thereby, the realization of the connections between the rule antecedent parts is essential in order to represent a rule properly (modeling the data distribution best with the highest possible interpretability, etc.). For instance, in Rule 1 in the previous subsection, the realization is achieved through a classical AND-connection, which is typically realized by a t-norm [40]. Almost all of the EFS approaches published so far use a t-norm to produce a canonical conjunctive normal form of rules (only AND-connections between singleton antecedents).

An exception is a recent published approach in [96], termed as ENFS-Uni0, where uni-nullneurons are constructed based on n-uninorms [256]. Depending on the value of the neutral element in the n-uninorms (which can be learned from the data), more an AND or more an OR is represented in the corresponding rule antecedent connections to a certain degree. These neurons can be, thus, transferred to linguistically readable rules achieved through partial AND/OR-connections, allowing an extended interpretation aspect—e.g., a classification rule's core part can be an ellipsoid (achieved by AND) with some wider spread along a certain feature (as connected by an OR to some degree)—see also [86] for a detailed explanation. Another exception is the deep rule-based evolving classifier approach proposed in [111], which internally processes a massively parallel rule base, where each rule is of 0-order AnYa-type form [100] (see also Section 4.2.6), connecting the antecedent part of the internal rules (measured in terms of similarity degrees to prototypes) with OR-connections. This yields a good flexibility to represent single classes by various exemplar realizations contained in the data (see also previous section).

Distinguishability and *simplicity* are handled under the scope of complexity reduction, where the difference between these two lies in the occurrence of the degree of overlap of rules and fuzzy sets: redundant rules and fuzzy sets are highly over-lapping and therefore indistinguishable and thus should be merged, whereas obsolete rules or close rules showing similar approximation/classification trends belong to an unnecessary complexity which can be simplified (due to pruning). Merging and pruning are embedded in most of the E(N)FS approaches published so far, see Section 4.3.4.3, hence this interpretability criterion is a well covered one. Figure 4.19 visualizes an example of a fuzzy partition extracted in the context of house price estimation [257] when conducting native precise modeling (a) and when conducting some simplification steps according to merging and pruning during the model update (b). Only in the upper case, it is possible to assign linguistic labels to the fuzzy sets and hence to achieve interpretation quality.

Consistency addresses the problem of assuring that no contradictory rules, i.e., rules that possess similar antecedents but dissimilar consequents are present in the system. This can be achieved by merging redundant rules, i.e., those one which are similar in their antecedents, with the usage of the participatory learning concept (introduced by Yager [177]). An appropriate merging of the linear parameter vectors $\vec{w}$ is given by [191] the following:

$$\vec{w}_{new} = \vec{w}_{R_1} + \alpha \cdot Cons(R_1, R_2) \cdot (\vec{w}_{R_2} - \vec{w}_{R_1}), \qquad (4.57)$$

where $\alpha = k_{R_2}/(k_{R_1} + k_{R_2})$ represents the *basic learning rate* with k_{R_1} the support of the more supported rule R_1 and $Cons(R_1, R_2)$ the *compatibility measure* between

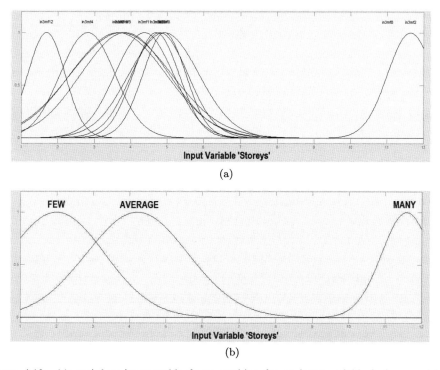

Figure 4.19: (a): weird un-interpretable fuzzy partition for an input variable in house pricing; (b) the same partition achieved when conducting merging, pruning options of rules and sets during the incremental learning phase $\rightarrow$ assignments of linguistic labels possible

the two rules within the participatory learning context. The latter is measured by a consistency degree between the antecedents and consequents of the two rules. It relies on the exponential proportion between rule antecedent similarity degree (overlap) and rule consequent similarity degree.

Coverage and *completeness* refers to the problem of a well-defined coverage of the input space by the rule-base. Formally, ϵ-completeness requires that for each new incoming data sample there exists at least one rule to which this sample has a membership degree of at least ϵ. For instance, SOFNN [143] and SAFIS [170] take care of this issue by evolving new rules when this situation is not met (any longer). Other techniques such as [258] always generate new rules in order to guarantee a minimal coverage of ϵ over the input space. An alternative and more profound option for data stream regression problems is offered as well in [32], which propose to integrate a punishment term for ϵ-completeness into the least squares optimization problem. Incremental optimization techniques based on gradients of the extended optimization function may be applied in order to approach but not necessarily fully assure ϵ-completeness. On the other hand, the joint optimization guarantees a reasonable tradeoff between model accuracy and model coverage of the feature space.

Feature importance levels are an outcome of the online dimensionality reduction concept discussed in Section 4.4.2. With their usage, it is possible to obtain an interpretation of the input structure level of which features are more important and which ones are less important. Furthermore, they may also lead to a reduction of the rule lengths, thus increasing rule transparency and readability, as features with weights smaller than ϵ have a very low impact on the final model output and therefore can be eliminated from the rule antecedent and consequent parts when showing the rule base to experts/operators.

Rule importance levels could serve as essential interpretation component as they tend to show the importance of each rule in the rule base. Furthermore, rule weights may be used for a smooth rule reduction during learning procedures, as rules with low weights can be seen as unimportant and may be pruned or even re-activated at a later stage in an online learning process (*soft rule pruning mechanism*).. This strategy may be beneficial when starting with an expert-based system, where originally all rules are fully interpretable (as designed by experts/users); however, some may turn out to be superfluous over time for the modeling problem at hand. Furthermore, rule weights can be used to handle inconsistent rules in a rule base (see, e.g., [259, 260], thus serving as another possibility to tackle the problem of consistency (see above). The usage of rule weights and their updates during incremental learning phases, was, to our best knowledge, not studied so far in the evolving fuzzy community.

Interpretation of consequents is assured by nature in case of classifiers with consequent class labels plus confidence levels; in the case of TS fuzzy systems, it is assured as soon as local learning of rule consequents is used [29, 107] (Chapter 2) and [32] (as done by most of the E(N)FS approaches [30]), please also refer to Section 4.3.1: then, a snuggling of the partial linear trends along the real approximation surface is guaranteed, thus providing information on which parts of the feature space the model will react and in which way and intensity (gradients of features). Such trends can be nicely used for an intrinsic influence analysis of input variables onto the output (in a global or local manner) and thus also contributes to some sort of explainability as discussed in the previous subsection.

Knowledge expansion refers to the automatic integration of new knowledge arising during the online process on demand and on-the-fly, also in order to expand the interpretation range of the models. It is handled by all conventional EFS approaches through rule evolution and/or splitting, see Sections 4.3.4.1 and 4.3.4.4.

4.5.2.1. *Visual interpretability over time*

Visual interpretability over time refers to an interesting add-on to *linguistic interpretability* (as discussed above), namely to the representation of a model and its changes in a visual form. In the context of evolving modeling from streams, such

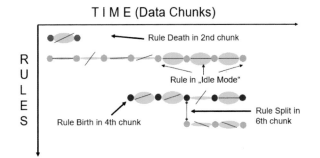

Figure 4.20: An example of a rule chain system as occurred for a specific data stream: each rule is arranged in a separate row, its progress over time shown horizontally; each circular marker denotes a data chunk. Note that in the second chunk one rule dies (is pruned), whereas in the fourth chunk a new rule is evolved and in the sixth chunk a big rule (the third one) is split into two; the second rule remains in more or less idle mode during the last three chunks (as not being changed at all).

a technique could be especially useful if models evolve quickly, since monitoring a visual representation might then be easier than following a frequently changing linguistic description. Under this scope, alternative interpretability criteria may then become interesting to discover which are more dedicated to the timely development of the evolving fuzzy model—for instance, a trajectory of rule centers showing their movement over time, or trace paths showing birth, growth, pruning, and merging of rules. The first attempts in this direction have been conducted in [261], employing the concept of *rule chains*. These have been significantly extended in [262] by setting up a visualization framework with a grown-up user frontend (GUI), integrating various similarity, coverage, and overlap measures as well as specific techniques for an appropriate catchy representation of high-dimensional rule antecedents and consequents. Internally, it uses the FLEXFIS approach [140] as an incremental learning engine for evolving a fuzzy rule base.

An example of a typical rule chain system is provided in Figure 4.20. The size of the ellipsoids indicates the similarity of the rules' antecedent parts between two consecutive time instances (marked as "circles"), the rotation degree of the small lines indicates the similarity of the rules' consequent parts in terms of their angle between two consecutive time instances: a high angle indicates a larger change between two time instances, and thus the rule has been intensively updated during the last chunk. This may provide the human with an idea about the dynamics of the system. Also, when several rules die out or are born within a few chunks, the human may gain some insight into the system dynamics and this may stimulate her/him to react properly. Furthermore, rules that fluctuate highly, changing their antecedents and consequents much in a back-and-forth manner, may be taken with care and even removed by a human.

4.6. Implementation Issues, Useability, and Applications

In order to increase the useability of evolving (neuro-)fuzzy systems, several issues are discussed in this section, ranging from the reduction of sample annotation and measurement efforts through active learning and a proper online design of experiments, a proper handling of missing data to the decrease of computational resources as well as to online evaluation measures for supervising modeling performance. At the end of this section, a list of real-world applications making use of evolving (neuro-)fuzzy systems will be discussed.

4.6.1. *Reducing Sample Annotation and Measurement Efforts*

Most of the aforementioned ENFS methods require supervised samples in order to guide the incremental and evolving learning mechanisms into the right direction, and to maintain their predictive performance. This is especially true for the recursive update of consequent parameters and input/output product-space clustering. Alternatively, predictions may be used by the update mechanisms to reinforce the model. However, erroneous and imprecise predictions may spread, sum up over time, and deteriorate model performance [2].

The problem in today's industrial systems with increasing complexity is that target values may be costly or even impossible to obtain and measure. For instance, in decision support and classification systems, ground truth labels of samples (from a training set, historic data base) have to be gathered by experts or operators to establish reliable and accurate classifiers, which typically require time-intensive annotation and labeling cycles [250, 263]. Within a data stream mining process, this problem becomes even more apparent as experts have to provide a ground truth feedback quickly to meet real-time demands.

Therefore, it is important to decrease the number of samples for model update using sample selection techniques: annotation feedbacks or measurements for only those samples are required, which are expected to maintain or increase accuracy. This task can be addressed by *active learning* [264], a technique where the learner has control over which samples are used to update the models [265]. However, conventional active learning approaches operate fully in batch mode by iterating multiple times over a data base, which makes them inapplicable for (faster) stream processing demands [266, 267].

4.6.1.1. *Single-pass active learning for classification problems*

To select the most appropriate samples from data streams, *single-pass active learning* (SP-AL) also termed as *online active learning* for evolving fuzzy classifiers has been proposed in [115], in combination with classical single model architecture (see Section 4.2.7.1) and with multi-model architecture employing the all-pairs concept (see Section 4.2.7.3). It relies on the concepts of *conflict* and *ignorance* [121]. The former addresses the degree of uncertainty in the classifier decision in terms of the class overlapping degree considering the local region where a sample falls within and in terms of the closeness of the sample to the decision boundary. The latter addresses the degree of novelty in the sample, see also Section 4.4.4.

A variant of SP-AL is provided in [268, 269], where a *meta-cognitive* evolving scheme that relies on *what-to-learn*, *when-to-learn*, and *how-to-learn* concepts is proposed. The what-to-learn aspect is handled by a sample deletion strategy, i.e., a sample is not used for model updates when the knowledge in the sample is similar to that of the model. Meta-cognitive learning has been further extended in [270] to regression problems (with the use of a fuzzy neural network architecture) and in [271] with the integration of a budget-based selection strategy. Such a budget-based learning was demonstrated to be of great practical usability, as it explicitly constrains sample selection to a maximal allowed percentage.

An overview and detailed comparison of several online active learning methods in combination with EFS, also in combination with other machine learning model architectures, can be found in the survey [272].

4.6.1.2. *Single-pass active learning for regression problems*

In the case of regression problems, permanent measurements of the targets can also be costly, e.g., in chemical or manufacturing systems that require manual checking of product quality. Therefore, online active learning for regression has been proposed in [243] for evolving generalized fuzzy systems (see Section 4.2.2.2), which relies on: (i) the novelty content of a sample (ignorance) with respect to the expected extrapolation behavior of the model; (ii) the predicted output uncertainty measured in terms of local error bars (see Section 4.4.4); and (iii) the reduction of parameter uncertainty measured by the change in the E-optimality of the Fisher information matrix [244]. In this sense, it can be seen as an uncertainty-based sampling technique, where the most uncertain samples for current model predictions are selected in order to "sharpen" or even expand the model's approximation surface. An immediate glance of an uncertainty-based sampling can be achieved when inspecting Figure 4.16 (a): samples lying in the left most region of the input (x-axis) can be safely predicted and thus would not be selected, will incoming samples lying in the right most region desire much more the concrete target values, as their prediction is unsafe due to extrapolation (no training samples occurring there before).

This approach has been extended in [270] with meta-cognitive learning concepts (inspired from human cognitions) and with some recurrency aspects for interval-type fuzzy systems (see Section 4.2.4).

4.6.1.3. On-line design of experiments (DoE)

In an extended way of thinking about the sample gathering process, it is not only a matter of deciding whether targets should be measured/labeled for available samples, but also which samples in the input space should be gathered at all. A central questions therein is should the model expand its knowledge or increase significance of its parameters? If so, *where* in the input space should the model best expand its knowledge or increase significance of its parameters? To answer these questions, techniques from the field of design of experiments (DoE) [273, 274] are required. These typically rely on several criteria in order to check in which regions of the feature space the model produces its highest errors, is most uncertain about its predictions (e.g., due to sample insignificance) or most sensitive in its outputs (e.g., due to high, changing gradients). In this context, a pioneering single-pass online method for E(N)FS has been proposed in [242]. It relies on a combination of pseudo Monte-Carlo sampling algorithm (PM-CSA) [275] and maximin optimization criterion based on uniformly generated samples which are satisfying a membership degree criterion for the worst local model (worst in terms of the normalized sum of the squared error on past samples). Currently, to our best knowledge, this is still the only method available for E(N)FS.

4.6.2. *Handling of Missing Data and Imbalanced Problems*

When streams are measured in online systems, single data samples to be processed and used for model updates may be incomplete; that is, they do not carry the full information as one or more input values are simply missing. Such incompleteness of the data, also known as *missing data*, may arise due to incomplete observations, data transfer problems, malfunction of sensors or devices, incomplete information obtained from experts or on public surveys, among others [276]. The likelihood that missing data appear in samples increases with the dimensionality of the learning problem. Consider a multi-sensor networks collecting measurements from 1000 channels, then it is not so unrealistic that at least 1 channel (=0.1%) is not well-measured permanently. However, discarding the whole 1000-dimensional samples and simply not using it for updates when 99.9% of the data is still available is a high waste.

Therefore, data imputation and estimation methods have been suggested in literature, see [277] for a survey on classification problems. These perform an imputation of missing values based on maximum likelihood and parameter estimations or based on the dependencies between input variables, but are basically dedicated to batch off-line learning problem settings. In combination with evolving (fuzzy) systems, a pioneering approach has been recently proposed in [85]. It exploits the interpretable open structure of an extended fuzzy granular system, where the consequent is composed by a Mamdani part (fuzzy set) and a Takagi–Sugeno part (functional consequent; a similar concept as defined in the interval-based granular systems, see Section 4.2.4), but with an additional reduced functional consequent part, where the input with the missing value is excluded. The approach uses the midpoint of the input membership functions related to the most active rule for missing values imputation. Currently, to our best knowledge, this is still the only method available for E(N)FS.

Imbalanced classification problems are characterized by a high imbalance of the number of samples belonging to different classes. Typically, when the ratio between the majority and the minority class exceeds ten, someone speaks about an imbalanced problem [120]. Such problems typically lead to an overwhelming number of classes with a lower number of samples by classes with a higher number. In the extreme case, classes with a lower number of samples are completely out-masked in the classifiers, and thus never returned as model outputs [116] (hence, no classification accuracy achieved on them at all).

Evolving (neuro-)fuzzy systems approaches to handle such unpleasant effects have been, to our best knowledge, not addressed so far (and are thus still an open problem). An exception goes to the approach in [217], which integrates new classes on the fly into the fuzzy classifiers in a single-pass manner and, thereby, uses the all-pairs architecture as defined in Section 4.2.7.3. Due to the all-pairs structure, it is possible that a new class (formed by only a couple of samples) becomes "significant" (and thus "returnable") in the classifier much earlier than in a global (single) model. This is because smaller classifiers are trained between all class pairs (wherein the new class may become a "winner" during prediction much easier) and their outputs amalgamated within a balanced relational concept.

4.6.3. *On Improving Computational Demands*

When dealing with online data stream processing problems, usually computational demands required for updating the fuzzy systems are essential criteria whether to install and use the component, or not. It can be a kick-off criterion, especially in real-time systems, where the update is expected to terminate in real-time, i.e., before the next sample is loaded, the update cycle should be finished. In addition, the model predictions should be in-line with the real-time demands, but these are known to be very fast in the case of a (neuro-)fuzzy inference scheme (significantly below milliseconds) [23, 42, 207]. An extensive evaluation and especially a comparison of computational demands for a large variety of EFS approaches over a large variety of learning problems with different number of classes, different dimensionality, etc., is unrealistic. A loose attempt in this direction has been made by Komijani et al. in [69], where they classify various EFS approaches in terms of computation speed into three categories: *low, medium, and high.*

Interestingly, the update of consequent/output parameters is more or less following the complexity of $O(Cp^2)$ with p the dimensionality of the feature/regressor space and C the number of rules, when local learning is used, and following the complexity of $O((Cp)^2)$, when global learning is applied. The quadratic terms p^2 resp. $(Cp)^2$ are due to the multiplication of the inverse Hessian with the actual regressor vector in Eq. (4.38), and because their sizes are $(p+1) \times (p+1)$ and $p+1$ in case of local learning (storing the consequent parameters of one rule) resp. $(C(p+1)) \times (C(p+1))$ and $C(p+1)$ in case of global learning (storing the consequent parameters of all rules). This computational complexity of $O(Cp^2)$ also holds for all extensions of RFWLS, as discussed in Section 4.3.1.1, with the exception of multi-innovation RLS, which requires $O(Cvp^2)$ complexity, with v the innovation length. Regarding antecedent learning, rule evolution, splitting, and pruning, most of the EFS approaches proposed in literature try to be restricted to have at most cubic complexity in terms of the number of rules plus the number of inputs. This may guarantee some sort of smooth termination in an online process, but it is not a necessary prerequisite and has to be inspected for the particular learning problem at hand.

However, some general remarks on the improvement of computational demands can be given: first of all, the reduction of *unnecessary complexity* such as merging of redundant overlapping rules and pruning of obsolete rules (as discussed in Section 4.3.4) is always beneficial for speeding up the learning process. This also ensures that fuzzy systems are not growing forever and, thus, restricted in their expansion and virtual memory requests. In this sense, a newly designed E(N)FS method should be always equipped with merging and pruning techniques. Second, some fast version of incremental optimization techniques could be adopted to fuzzy systems estimation; for instance, there exists a fast RLS algorithm for recursively estimating linear parameters in nearly linear time ($O(Nlog(N))$), but with the costs of some stability and convergence, see [278] or [279]. Another possibility for decreasing the computation time for learning is the application of single-pass online active learning for exquisitely selecting only a subset of samples, based on which the model will be updated, please also refer to Section 4.6.1.

4.6.4. *Evaluation Measures*

Evaluation measures may serve as indicators about the actual state of the evolved fuzzy systems, pointing to its accuracy and trustworthiness in predictions. In a data streaming context, the temporal behavior of such measures plays an essential role in order to track the model development over time resp. to realize down-trends in accuracy at an early stage (e.g., caused by drifts), and to react appropriately (e.g., conducting a re-modeling phase, changes at the system setup, etc.). Furthermore, the evaluation measures are indispensable during the development phase of EFS approaches. In literature dealing with incremental and data-stream problems [280], three variants of measuring the (progress of) model performance are suggested:

- Interleaved-test-and-then-train.
- Periodic hold out test.
- Fully-train-and-then-test.

Interleaved-test-and-then-train, also termed as *accumulated one-step ahead error/accuracy*, is based on the idea of measuring model performance in one-step ahead cycles, i.e., based on one newly loaded sample only. In particular, the following steps are carried out:

(1) Load a new sample (the Nth).
(2) Predict its target $\hat{y}$ using the current evolved fuzzy systems.
(3) Compare the prediction $\hat{y}$ with the true target value y and update the performance measure pm:

$$pm(y, \hat{y})(N) \leftarrow upd(pm(y, \hat{y})(N-1)) \qquad (4.58)$$

(4) Update the evolved fuzzy system (arbitrary approach).
(5) Erase sample and goto Step 1.

This is a rather optimistic approach, assuming that the target response is immediately available for each new sample after its prediction. Often, it may be delayed [183, 281], postponing the update of the model performance to a later stage. Furthermore, in the case of single sample updates its prediction horizon is minimal, making it difficult to really provide a clear distinction between training and test data, and hence weakening their independence. In this sense, this variant is sometimes too optimistic, under-estimating the true model error. On the other hand, all training samples are also used for testing; thus, it is quite practicable for small streams. In the case of delayed target measurements, the sample-wise interleaved-test-and-then-train scenario can also be extended to a chunk-wise variant, with the chunk-size depending on the duration of the expected delay [131]. Then, all samples from each chunk are predicted ($\rightarrow$ more pessimistic multi-step ahead prediction), and, once their target values are available, the model is updated. This has been handled, e.g., in [131] with sequential ensemble methods.

The periodic holdout procedure can "look ahead" to collect a batch of examples from the stream for use as test examples. In particular, it uses each odd data block for learning and updating the model and each even data block for eliciting the model performance on this latest block; thereby, the data block sizes may be different for training and testing, and may vary in dependence of the actual stream characteristics. In this sense, a lower number of samples is used for model updating/tuning than in the case of *interleaved-test-and-then-train* procedure. In experimental test designs, where the streams are finite, it is thus more practicable for longer streams. On the other hand, this method would be preferable in scenarios with concept drift, as it would measure a model's ability to adapt to the *latest trends* in the data—whereas in *interleaved-test-and-then-train* procedure all the data seen so far is reflected in the current accuracy/error, becoming less flexible over time. Forgetting may be integrated into Eq. (4.58), but this requires an additional tuning parameter (e.g., a window size in case of sliding windows). The following steps are carried out in a periodic holdout process:

(1) Load a new data block $X_N = \vec{x}_{N*m+1}, \ldots, \vec{x}_{N*m+m}$ containing m samples.
(2) If N is odd:

  (a) Predict the target values $\hat{y}_1, \ldots, \hat{y}_m$ using the current evolved fuzzy systems.
  (b) Compare the predictions $\hat{y}_{N*m+1}, \ldots, \hat{y}_{N*m+m}$ with the true target values $y_{N*m+1}, \ldots, y_{N*m+m}$, and calculate the performance measure (one or more of Eq. (4.59) to Eq. (4.64)) using $\vec{y}$ and $\hat{\vec{y}}$.
  (c) Erase block and go to Step 1.

(3) Else (N is even):

  (a) Update the evolved fuzzy system (arbitrary approach) with all samples in the buffer using the real target values.
  (b) Erase block and go to Step 1.

Last but not least, an alternative to the online evaluation procedure is to evolve the model an a certain training set and then evaluate it on an independent test set, termed as *fully-train-and-then-test*. This procedure is most heavily used in many applications of EFS, especially in nonlinear system identification and forecasting problems, as summarized in Tables 4.1 and 4.2. It extends the prediction horizon of *interleaved-test-and-then-train* procedure with the size of the test set, but only does this on one occasion (at the end of learning). Therefore, it is not useable in drift cases or severe changes during online incremental learning processes and should be only used during development and experimental phases.

Regarding appropriate model performance measures, the most convenient choice in classification problems is the number of correctly classified samples (accuracy). In the time instance, N (processing the Nth sample), the update of the performance measure as in Eq. (4.58) is then conducted by

$$Acc(N) = \frac{Acc(N-1) * (N-1) + I(\hat{y}, y)}{N} \tag{4.59}$$

with $Acc(0) = 0$ and I the indicator function, i.e., $I(a, b) = 1$ whenever $a == b$, otherwise $I(a, b) = 0$, $\hat{y}$ the predicted class label and y the real one. It can be used in the same manner for eliciting the accuracy on whole data blocks as in the periodic hold out case.

Another important measure is the so-called *confusion matrix* [282], which is defined as

$$C = \begin{bmatrix} N_{11} & N_{12} & \cdots & N_{1K} \\ N_{21} & N_{22} & \cdots & N_{2K} \\ \vdots & \vdots & \vdots & \vdots \\ N_{K1} & N_{K2} & \cdots & N_{KK} \end{bmatrix} \qquad (4.60)$$

with K the current number of classes, where the diagonal elements denote the number of class j samples that have been correctly classified as class j samples and the element N_{ij} denotes the number of class i samples which are wrongly classified to class j. These can be simply updated by counting. Several well-known measures for performance evaluation in classification problems can then be extracted from the confusion matrix, such as different variants of (balanced) accuracies (e.g., the standard accuracy is simply the trace of the confusion matrix divided by all its elements), the false alarm and miss-detection rates in the case of binary problems, or several kappa statistics.

The confusion matrix assumes fully labeled samples or at least scarcely labeled samples according to active learning based selections. In some cases, data streams are appearing in fully unsupervised manner. In such cases, an unsupervised calculation of the classifier accuracy can be conducted with concepts as discussed in [283] (for the off-line case) and in [216] for the online single-pass case. The basic idea is based on the assumption that the uncertainty estimates of the two most likely classes correspond to a bimodal density distribution. Such uncertainty estimates are available for evolving fuzzy classifiers according to the rule-coded and/or calculated confidence degrees based on reliability concepts, see Section 4.4.4. The bimodal density distributions can be assumed to be two separate Gaussians, especially in the case of binary classification tasks, as the confidence in the output class is one minus the confidence in the other class, and vice versa. A typical example is visualized in Figure 4.21, where the misclassification rate (=1-accuracy) is the area under the overlap region (normalized to the whole area covered by both Gaussians). Thus, the more these distributions overlap, the more inaccurate the classifier is assumed to be. The histograms forming the distributions can be simply updating for streams by counting the samples falling into each bin.

Furthermore, often someone may not only be interested in how strong the samples are mis-classified, but also how certain they are classified (either correctly or

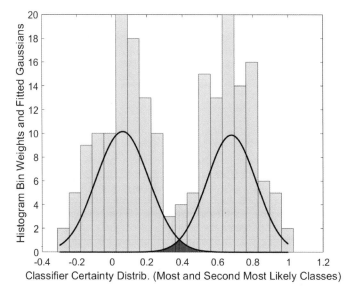

Figure 4.21:   Classifier output certainty distribution estimated from the discrete stream sampling case in histogram form, the solid black lines denote the fitted Gaussian mixture model, the vertical black line marker the cutting point and the red shaded area the expected misclassification intensity.

wrongly). For instance, a high classification accuracy with a lot of certain classifier outputs may have a higher value than with a lot of uncertain outputs. Furthermore, a high uncertainty degree in the statements points to a high degree of conflict (compare with Eq. (4.24) and Figure 4.6), i.e., a lot of samples falling into class overlap regions. Therefore, a measure telling the average certainty degree over samples classified so far is of great interest—a widely used measure is provided in [284]

$$Cert\_deg(N) = \frac{1}{N} \sum_{i=1}^{N} \left(1 - \frac{1}{K} \sum_{k=1}^{K} |conf_k(i) - y_k(i)| \right), \qquad (4.61)$$

with N being the number of samples seen so far, and K the number of classes; $y_k(i) = 1$ if k is the class the current sample i belongs to, and $y_k(i) = 0$ otherwise, and $conf_k(i)$ the certainty level in class k when classifying sample i, which can be calculated by Eq. (4.24), for instance.

In the case of regression problems, the most common choices are the root mean squared error (RMSE), the mean absolute error (MAE), or the average percentual deviation (APE). Their updates are achieved by the following:

$$RMSE(N) = \sqrt{\frac{1}{N} * \left((N-1) * (RMSE(N-1)^2) + (y - \hat{y})^2 \right)}, \qquad (4.62)$$

$$MAE(N) = \frac{1}{N} * \left((N-1) * MAE(N-1) + |y - \hat{y}| \right), \qquad (4.63)$$

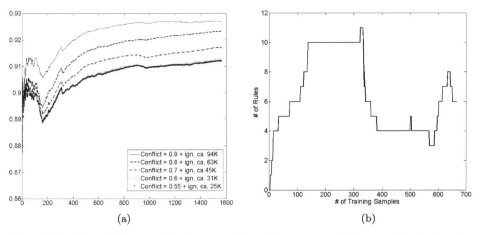

Figure 4.22: (a): typical accumulated accuracy increasing over time in the case of active learning variants (reducing the number of samples used for updating while still maintaining a high accuracy); (b): typical evolution of the number of rules over time.

$$APE(N) = \frac{1}{N} * \left((N - 1) * APE(N - 1) + \frac{|y - \hat{y}|}{range(y)} \right) \tag{4.64}$$

with y being the observed value and $\hat{y}$ the predicted value of the current sample. Their batch calculation for even blocks in a periodic hold out test is following the standard procedure and thus can be realized from Wikipedia. Instead of calculating the concrete error values, often the observed versus predicted curves over time and their correlation plots are shown. This gives an even better impression under which circumstances and at which points of time the model behaves in which way. A systematic error shift can be also realized.

Apart from accuracy criteria, other measures rely on the complexity of the models. In most EFS application cases (refer to Tables 4.1 and 4.2), the development of the number of rules over time is plotted as a two-dimensional function. Sometimes, the number of fuzzy sets are also reported as additional criteria that depend on the rule lengths. These mostly depend on the dimensionality of the learning problem. In the case of embedded feature selection, there may be a big drop in the number of fuzzy sets once some features are discarded resp. out-weighted (compare with Section 4.4.2). Figure 4.22 shows a typical accumulated accuracy curve over time in the left image (using an all-pairs EFC including active learning option with different amount of samples selected for updating), and a typical development of the number of rules in the right one: at the start, rules are evolved and accumulated, later some rules turned out to be superfluous, and, hence, are back-pruned and merged. This guarantees an anytime flexibility. The accumulated accuracy trend lines as shown in Figure 4.22 (a) are elicited by using Eq. (4.59) on each new incoming sample (for which the real class is available) and storing all the updated accuracies in a vector.

4.6.5. Real-World Applications of EFS: An Overview

Due to space restrictions, a complete description of application scenarios in which EFS have been successfully implemented and used so far is simply impossible. Thus, we restrict ourselves to a compact summary within Tables 4.1 and 4.2 showing application types and classes and indicating which EFS approaches have been used

Table 4.1: Application classes in which EFS approaches have been successfully applied (Part 1).

Application Type/Class (alphabetically)	EFS approaches (+ refs)	Comment
Active learning / human–machine interaction	FLEXFIS-Class [250], EFC-SM and EFC-AP [115], FLEXFIS-PLS [285], GS-EFS [243], meta-cognitive methods McIT2FIS [269] and RIVMcSFNN [270]	Reducing the annotation effort and measurement costs in industrial processes
Adaptive online control	Evolving PID and MRC controllers RECCo [286], eFuMo [162, 163], rGK [287], self-evolving NFC [288], adaptive controller in [289], robust evolving controller [180], evolving cloud-based controller [254], parsimonious controller [290], myoelectric-based control [291]	Design of fuzzy controllers which can be updated and evolved on-the-fly
Chemometric modeling and process control	FLEXFIS++ [55, 142]; the approach in [54]	The application of EFS onto processes in chemical industry (high-dim. NIR spectra)
EEG signals classification and processing	eTS [292], epSNNr [293], MSAFIS [294]	Time-series modeling with the inclusion of time delays
Evolving smart sensors (eSensors)	eTS+ [252] (gas industry), eTS+ [253, 295] (chemical process industry), PANFIS [141] (NOx emissions)	Evolving predictive and forecasting models in order to substitute cost-intensive hardware sensors
Forecasting and prediction (general)	AHLTNM [185] (daily temp.), eT2FIS [81] (traffic flow), eFPT [296] (Statlog from UCI), eFT [173] and eMG [64] (short-term electricity load), FLEXFIS+ [257] and GENEFIS [66] (house prices), incremental LoLiMoT [174] (max. cyl. pressure), rGK [287] (sales prediction), ePFM [164], the approach in [297], EFS-SLAT [298] and others	Various successful implementations of EFS for forecasting and prediction
Financial domains	eT2FIS [81], evolving granular systems [83, 299], ePL [300], PANFIS [141], SOFNN [301], ALMMo [102], IT2-GSETSK [258]	Time-series modeling with the inclusion of time delays
Health-care and bioinformatics applications	EFuNN [302], evolving granular systems [181] (Parkinson monitoring), TEDAClass [101], DRB classifier [111] (hand-written digits), MSAFIS [294] (EEG signals), ALMMo [303] (heart sounds)	Various classification problems in the health-care domain

Table 4.2: Application classes in which EFS approaches have been successfully applied (Part 2).

Application Type/Class (alphabetically)	EFS approaches (+ refs)	Comment
Identification of dynamic benchmark problems	DENFIS [161], eT2FIS [81], eTS+ [166], GS-EFS [67], SAFIS [171], SEIT2FNN [80], SOFNN [301], IRSFNN [304]	Mackey–Glass, Box–Jenkins, chaotic time series prediction, etc.
On-line design of experiments	SUHICLUST combined with EFS [242]	Actively steering sample gathering in the input space
On-line fault detection and condition monitoring	eMG for classification [179], FLEXFIS++ [305], rGK [287], evolving cloud-based classifier [201], pEnsemble+ [306], evolving cloud-based model [307], EFuNN [308]	EFS applied as SysID models for extracting residuals and classifying faults
On-line monitoring	eTS+ [252] (gas industry)	Supervision of system behaviors
Predictive maintenance, prognostics and process optimization	IPLS-GEFS [229, 309], EBeTS [310]	Multi-stage prediction of arising problems, RUL estimations and suggestions for proper reaction
Robotics	eTS+ [311], evolving granular models [312]	Self-localization, autonomous navigation
Time-series modeling and forecasting	DENFIS [313], ENFM [169], eTS-LS-SVM [69] (sun spot), ENFS-OL [314], Ensemble of evolving data clouds [206]	Local modeling of multiple time-series versus instance-based learning
User behavior identification and analysis	eClass and eTS [315, 316], eTS+ [317], FPA [318], approach in [319], RSEFNN [320]	Analysis of the user's behaviors in multi-agent systems, on computers, indoor environments, car driving, etc.
Video processing	eTS, eTS+ [187, 321]	Real-time object identification, obstacles tracking and novelty detection
Visual quality control and online surface inspection	EFC-SM and EFC-AP [217, 322], pClass [117]	Image classification tasks based on feature vectors
Web mining	eClass0 [323], eT2Class (evolving type-2) [324]	High-speed mining in web articles

in the circumstance of which application type. In all of these cases, E(N)FS helped to increase automatization capability, improving performance of the models and finally increasing the useability of the whole systems; in some cases, no models have been (could be) applied before at all due to a too complex or even impossible physical description of the whole process.

4.7. Open Issues and Future Directions

Even though, based on all the facets discussed throughout the first six section in this chapter, the reader may get a good impression about the methodological richness and the range of applicability of current state-of-the-art evolving neuro-fuzzy systems approaches, there are still some open problems that have not been handled with sufficient care and necessary detail so far; in particular:

- **Profound robustness in learning and convergence assurance:** as indicated in Section 4.3.1.1, a lot of approaches have been suggested for improving the robustness of consequent parameters learning; in fact, several bounds exist on the achievable model/system error, but an assurance of convergence to the real optimal solution in an incremental, single-pass manner is still not fully granted; it is only achievable through re-iterative optimization jointly with the antecedent space, which, however, does not meet the single-pass spirit and may significantly slow down the learning process. Furthermore, hardly any approaches exist to guarantee stability or provide bounds on the sub-optimality of the antecedent space (and the nonlinear parameters contained therein, typically rule/neuron centers and spreads). Recursive optimization of nonlinear parameters have been indeed discussed in Section 4.3.2, but are still in their infancy and loosely used so far—most of the ENFS approaches employ incremental, evolving clustering techniques that are typically operating in a more heuristic manner for learning the antecedent parameters and structures.
- **Evolving model ensembles:** in the batch learning community there exists a wide range of ensemble techniques for the purpose of improving the robustness of single models (especially in the case of high noise with unknown distribution), which can be basically grouped into independent ensemble learning, sequential ensemble learning, and simultaneous ensemble learning—see also Chapter 16 of this book for demonstrating ensemble learning paradigms and a statistical analysis of the bias–variance–covariance error decomposition problematic therein. A few evolving ensemble approaches (around five in total) emerged during the last two years in order to take advantage of the higher robustness of ensembles also in the case stream modeling purposes, which are discussed in Section 4.3.5; several important ensembling concepts, known to be successful in the batch learning case (e.g., negative correlation learning), have not been handled so far for the evolving

case. In addition, it is still an open challenge when to best evolve new and to prune older ensemble members.

- **Uncertainty in model outputs:** in fact, uncertainty in the inputs are naturally handled by ENFS due to the learning and autonomous evolution of fuzzy sets and rules (describing uncertainty through their levels of granulation and ranges of influence, see Section 4.2); however, uncertainty in the outputs for regression problems have been more or less just loosely addressed by two concepts: interval-based modeling as described in Section 4.2.4 and error bars as described in Section 4.4.4.2. More statistically funded concepts such as probability estimates (for the predictions) as achieved by Gaussian process models or support vector machines (when applying Gaussian kernels) or whole output likelihood distributions as achieved by particle filtering techniques have not been studied so far.

- **Drifts versus anomalies:** Section 4.4.1 provides several concepts proposed during the last years for handling drifts in streams adequately by outweighing older samples, adding new rules, splitting rules, etc. However, a distinction between drifts, i.e., regular dynamic changes due to process dynamics and non-stationary environments that should be integrated into the models, and anomalies indicating possible arising problems, which should not be integrated into the models has not been actually studied so far. It may be a precarious issue because it typically depends on the type of anomalies and drifts how different and in which pattern(s) they appear (as changes) in data samples; hence, a generic concept for this distinction would be a highly challenging issue.

- **Explainability and interpretability of ENFS:** almost all of the ENFS approaches developed so far rely on precise modeling aspects; that is, they intend to achieve highest possible accuracy for predicting new data samples with a best possible number of structural components (rules and neurons). Little has been investigated so far into the direction of at least maintaining or even improving interpretability and explainability of model components and outputs (which are in principle offered by ENFS due to their IF-THEN rule-based structure, as discussed in Section 4.2). Some first concepts are available as demonstrated in Section 4.5, but they are more present on a discussion- and position-oriented basis rather than being implemented to and tested with concrete ENFS algorithms (with a few exceptions as noted there).

- **Active learning and online design of experiments with ENFS:** single-pass active learning in combination with ENFS for reducing target labeling/measurement efforts was investigated in several approaches for both, classification and regression problems in literature as demonstrated in Section 4.6.1; some challenges regarding budget-based selection and especially structural-based (rather than sampling-based) selection are still open. Furthermore, complete online guidance on the measurement setup (in the form of online DoE) in order to select parts of the input space to measure next has been studied so far only in [242].

- **Applications of ENFS in the context of continual learning:** Due to their evolving and incremental learning properties, ENFS would be able to properly address the principles of continual learning and task-based incremental learning [15] in specific data stream environments, where new data chunks characterize new tasks (typically with some relation to older tasks); applications in this directions together with some methodological expansions for improving their performance on new tasks properly have not been carried out so far.
- **Applications of ENFS in predictive maintenance and prescriptive analytics:** two hot fields of applications with strong and wide objectives in the Horizon 2020 and the new Horizon Europe 2021–2027 framework programmes and where system dynamics aspects often may play a major role [12], but where ENFS have been hardly applied so far, see Table 4.2 for three approaches in total.

Acknowledgments

The author acknowledges the support by the "LCM—K2 Center for Symbiotic Mechatronics" within the framework of the Austrian COMET-K2 program and the Austrian Science Fund (FWF): contract number P32272-N38, acronym IL–EFS.

References

[1] J. Gama, *Knowledge Discovery from Data Streams* (Chapman & Hall/CRC, Boca Raton, Florida, 2010).

[2] M. Sayed-Mouchaweh and E. Lughofer, *Learning in Non-Stationary Environments: Methods and Applications* (Springer, New York, 2012).

[3] J. Dean, *Big Data, Data Mining, and Machine Learning: Value Creation for Business Leaders and Practitioners* (John Wiley and Sons, Hoboken, New Jersey, 2012).

[4] G. Blokdyk, *Very large database: A Complete Guide* (CreateSpace Independent Publishing Platform, 2018).

[5] W. Zhang, *MARS Applications in Geotechnical Engineering Systems: Multi-Dimension with Big Data* (Science Press, Beijing, 2019).

[6] W. Härdle, H.-S. Lu and X. Shen, *Handbook of Big Data Analytics* (Springer Verlag, Cham, Switzerland, 2018).

[7] M. Xia and Y. He, Functional connectomics from a 'big data' perspective, *NeuroImage*, **160**, 152–167 (2017).

[8] O. Reichmann, M. Jones and M. Schildhauer, Challenges and opportunities of open data in ecology, *Science*, **331**(6018), 703–705 (2011).

[9] X. Wu, X. Zhu, G. Wu and W. Ding, Data mining with big data, *IEEE Trans. Knowl. Data Eng.*, **26**(1), 97–107 (2014).

[10] P. Angelov, D. Filev and N. Kasabov, *Evolving Intelligent Systems—Methodology and Applications* (John Wiley & Sons, New York, 2010).

[11] S. Koenig, M. Likhachev, Y. Liu and D. Furcy, Incremental heuristic search in artificial intelligence, *Artif. Intell. Mag.*, **25**(2), 99–112 (2004).

[12] E. Lughofer and M. Sayed-Mouchaweh, *Predictive Maintenance in Dynamic Systems: Advanced Methods, Decision Support Tools and Real-World Applications* (Springer, New York, 2019).

[13] G. Karer and I. Skrjanc, *Predictive Approaches to Control of Complex Systems* (Springer Verlag, Berlin, Heidelberg, 2013).

[14] P. Angelov, *Autonomous Learning Systems: From Data Streams to Knowledge in Real-Time* (John Wiley & Sons, New York, 2012).

[15] M. Delange, R. Aljundi, M. Masana, S. Parisot, X. Jia, A. Leonardis, G. Slabaugh and T. Tuytelaars, A continual learning survey: defying forgetting in classification tasks, *IEEE Trans. Pattern Anal. Mach. Intell.*, doi: 10.1109/TPAMI.2021.3057446 (2021).

[16] P. Angelov and N. Kasabov, Evolving computational intelligence systems. In *Proceedings of the 1st International Workshop on Genetic Fuzzy Systems*, Granada, Spain, pp. 76–82, (2005).

[17] A. Joshi, *Machine Learning and Artificial Intelligence* (Springer Nature, Switzerland, 2020).

[18] O. Nasraoui and C.-E. B. N'Cir, *Clustering Methods for Big Data Analytics: Techniques, Toolboxes and Applications (Unsupervised and Semi-Supervised Learning)* (Springer Verlag, Cham, Switzerland, 2019).

[19] X. Wu, V. Kumar, J. Quinlan, J. Gosh, Q. Yang, H. Motoda, G. MacLachlan, A. Ng, B. Liu, P. Yu, Z.-H. Zhou, M. Steinbach, D. Hand and D. Steinberg, Top 10 algorithms in data mining, *Knowl. Inf. Syst.*, **14**(1), 1–37 (2006).

[20] Z. Liang and Y. Li, Incremental support vector machine learning in the primal and applications, *Neurocomputing*, **72**(10–12), 2249–2258 (2009).

[21] P. Laskov, C. Gehl, S. Krüger and K. Müller, Incremental support vector learning: analysis, implementation and applications, *J. Mach. Learn. Res.*, **7**, 1909–1936 (2006).

[22] S. Haykin, *Neural Networks: A Comprehensive Foundation,* 2nd edn. (Prentice Hall Inc., Upper Saddle River, New Jersey, 1999).

[23] W. Pedrycz and F. Gomide, *Fuzzy Systems Engineering: Toward Human-Centric Computing* (John Wiley & Sons, Hoboken, New Jersey, 2007).

[24] M. Affenzeller, S. Winkler, S. Wagner and A. Beham, *Genetic Algorithms and Genetic Programming: Modern Concepts and Practical Applications* (Chapman & Hall, Boca Raton, Florida, 2009).

[25] P. de Campos Souza, Fuzzy neural networks and neuro-fuzzy networks: a review the main techniques and applications used in the literature, *Appl. Soft Comput.*, **92**, 106275 (2020).

[26] V. Balas, J. Fodor and A. Varkonyi-Koczy, *Soft Computing based Modeling in Intelligent Systems* (Springer, Berlin, Heidelberg, 2009).

[27] L. Trujillo, E. Naredo and Y. Martinez, Preliminary study of bloat in genetic programming with behavior-based search. In M. Emmerich, et al. (eds.), *EVOLVE — A Bridge between Probability, Set Oriented Numerics, and Evolutionary Computation IV* (Advances in Intelligent Systems and Computing), vol. 227, Springer, Berlin Heidelberg, Germany, pp. 293–304 (2013).

[28] L. Zadeh, Fuzzy sets, *Inf. Control*, **8**(3), 338–353 (1965).

[29] E. Lughofer, *Evolving Fuzzy Systems: Methodologies, Advanced Concepts and Applications* (Springer, Berlin Heidelberg, 2011).

[30] I. Skrjanc, J. Iglesias, A. Sanchis, E. Lughofer and F. Gomide, Evolving fuzzy and neuro-fuzzy approaches in clustering, regression, identification, and classification: a survey, *Inf. Sci.*, **490**, 344–368 (2019).

[31] P. Angelov and X. Gu, *Empirical Approach to Machine Learning* (Springer Nature, Switzerland, 2019).

[32] E. Lughofer, On-line assurance of interpretability criteria in evolving fuzzy systems: achievements, new concepts and open issues, *Inf. Sci.*, **251**, 22–46 (2013).

[33] E. Lughofer, Model explanation and interpretation concepts for stimulating advanced human-machine interaction with 'expert-in-the-loop'. In J. Zhou and F. Chen (eds.), *Human and Machine Learning: Visible, Explainable, Trustworthy and Transparent*, Springer, New York, pp. 177–221 (2018).

[34] S. Bhattacharyya, V. Snasel, D. Gupta and A. Khanna, *Hybrid Computational Intelligence: Challenges and Applications (Hybrid Computational Intelligence for Pattern Analysis and Understanding)* (Academic Press, London, 2020).

[35] E. Mamdani, Application of fuzzy logic to approximate reasoning using linguistic systems, *Fuzzy Sets Syst.*, **26**(12), 1182–1191 (1977).

[36] K. Kumar, S. Deep, S. Suthar, M. Dastidar and T. Sreekrishnan, Application of fuzzy inference system (FIS) coupled with Mamdani's method in modelling and optimization of process parameters for biotreatment of real textile wastewater, *Desalin. Water Treat.*, **57**(21), 9690–9697 (2016).

[37] E. Pourjavad and A. Shahin, The application of Mamdani fuzzy inference system in evaluating green supply chain management performance, *Int. J. Fuzzy Syst.*, **20**, 901–912 (2018).

[38] A. Geramian, M. Mehregan, N. Mokhtarzadeh and M. Hemmati, Fuzzy inference system application for failure analyzing in automobile industry, *Int. J. Qual. Reliab. Manage.*, **34**(9), 1493–1507 (2017).

[39] A. Reveiz and C. Len, Operational risk management using a fuzzy logic inference system, *J. Financ. Transform.*, **30**, 141–153 (2010).

[40] E. Klement, R. Mesiar and E. Pap, *Triangular Norms* (Kluwer Academic Publishers, Dordrecht Norwell New York London, 2000).

[41] W. Leekwijck and E. Kerre, Defuzzification: criteria and classification, *Fuzzy Sets Syst.*, **108**(2), 159–178 (1999).

[42] A. Piegat, *Fuzzy Modeling and Control* (Physica Verlag, Springer Verlag Company, Heidelberg, New York, 2001).

[43] H. Nguyen, M. Sugeno, R. Tong and R. Yager, *Theoretical Aspects of Fuzzy Control* (John Wiley & Sons, New York, 1995).

[44] J. Rubio, SOFMLS: online self-organizing fuzzy modified least square network, *IEEE Trans. Fuzzy Syst.*, **17**(6), 1296–1309 (2009).

[45] W. Ho, W. Tung and C. Quek, An evolving Mamdani–Takagi–Sugeno based neural-fuzzy inference system with improved interpretability—accuracy. In *Proceedings of the WCCI 2010 IEEE World Congress of Computational Intelligence*, Barcelona, pp. 682–689 (2010).

[46] T. Takagi and M. Sugeno, Fuzzy identification of systems and its applications to modeling and control, *IEEE Trans. Syst. Man Cybern.*, **15**(1), 116–132 (1985).

[47] R. Babuska, *Fuzzy Modeling for Control* (Kluwer Academic Publishers, Norwell, Massachusetts, 1998).

[48] A. Banzaouia and A. Hajjaji, *Advanced Takagi–Sugeno Fuzzy Systems: Delay and Saturation* (Springer, Cham Heidelberg, 2016).

[49] R. Qi, G. Tao and B. Jiang, *Fuzzy System Identification and Adaptive Control* (Springer Nature, Switzerland, 2019).

[50] J. Abonyi, *Fuzzy Model Identification for Control* (Birkhäuser, Boston, USA, 2003).

[51] O. Nelles, *Nonlinear System Identification* (Springer, Berlin, 2001).

[52] Q. Ren, S. Achiche, K. Jemielniak and P. Bigras, An enhanced adaptive neural fuzzy tool condition monitoring for turning process. In *Proceedings of the International IEEE Conference on Fuzzy Systems (FUZZ-IEEE) 2016*, Vancouver, Canada (2016).

[53] F. Serdio, E. Lughofer, A.-C. Zavoianu, K. Pichler, M. Pichler, T. Buchegger and H. Efendic, Improved fault detection employing hybrid memetic fuzzy modeling and adaptive filters, *Appl. Soft Comput.*, **51**, 60–82 (2017).

[54] I. Skrjanc, Confidence interval of fuzzy models: an example using a waste-water treatment plant, *Chemom. Intell. Lab. Syst.*, **96**, 182–187 (2009).

[55] R. Nikzad-Langerodi, E. Lughofer, C. Cernuda, T. Reischer, W. Kantner, M. Pawliczek and M. Brandstetter, Calibration model maintenance in melamine resin production: integrating drift detection, smart sample selection and model adaptation, *Anal. Chim. Acta*, **1013**, 1–12 (featured article) (2018).

[56] B. Thumati, M. Feinstein and J. Sarangapani, A model-based fault detection and prognostics scheme for takagisugeno fuzzy systems, *IEEE Trans. Fuzzy Syst.*, **22**(4), 736–748, (2014).

[57] Y.-Q. Zhang, Constructive granular systems with universal approximation and fast knowledge discovery, *IEEE Trans. Fuzzy Syst.*, **13**(1), 48–57 (2005).

[58] L. Herrera., H. Pomares, I. Rojas, O. Valenzuela and A. Prieto, TaSe, a taylor series-based fuzzy system model that combines interpretability and accuracy, *Fuzzy Sets Syst.*, **153**(3), 403–427 (2005).

[59] L. Wang and J. Mendel, Fuzzy basis functions, universal approximation and orthogonal least-squares learning, *IEEE Trans. Neural Networks.* **3**(5), 807–814 (1992).

[60] N. E. Day, Estimating the components of a mixture of normal distributions, *Biometrika*, **56**(463–474) (1969).

[61] H. Sun and S. Wang, Measuring the component overlapping in the Gaussian mixture model, *Data Min. Knowl. Discovery*, **23**, 479–502 (2011).

[62] C. Bishop, *Pattern Recognition and Machine Learning* (Springer, New York, 2007).

[63] R. Duda, P. Hart and D. Stork, *Pattern Classification,* 2nd edn. (Wiley-Interscience (John Wiley & Sons), Southern Gate, Chichester, West Sussex, England, 2000).

[64] A. Lemos, W. Caminhas and F. Gomide, Multivariable Gaussian evolving fuzzy modeling system, *IEEE Trans. Fuzzy Syst.*, **19**(1), 91–104 (2011).

[65] D. Leite, R. Ballini, P. Costa and F. Gomide, Evolving fuzzy granular modeling from nonstationary fuzzy data streams, *Evolving Syst.*, **3**(2), 65–79 (2012).

[66] M. Pratama, S. Anavatti and E. Lughofer, GENEFIS: towards an effective localist network, *IEEE Trans. Fuzzy Syst.*, **22**(3), 547–562 (2014).

[67] E. Lughofer, C. Cernuda, S. Kindermann and M. Pratama, Generalized smart evolving fuzzy systems, *Evolving Syst.*, **6**(4), 269–292 (2015).

[68] J. Abonyi, R. Babuska and F. Szeifert, Modified Gath-Geva fuzzy clustering for identification of Takagi–Sugeno fuzzy models, *IEEE Trans. Syst. Man Cybern. Part B: Cybern.*, **32**(5), 612–621 (2002).

[69] M. Komijani, C. Lucas, B. Araabi and A. Kalhor, Introducing evolving Takagi–Sugeno method based on local least squares support vector machine models, *Evolving Syst.*, **3**(2), 81–93 (2012).

[70] A. Smola and B. Schölkopf, A tutorial on support vector regression, *Stat. Comput.*, **14**, 199–222 (2004).

[71] J. Mercer, Functions of positive and negative type and their connection with the theory of integral equations, *Philos. Trans. R. Soc. London, Ser. A*, **209**, 441–458 (1909).

[72] A. Zaanen, *Linear Analysis* (North Holland Publishing Co., 1960).

[73] W. Cheng and C. Juang, An incremental support vector machine-trained TS-type fuzzy system for online classification problems, *Fuzzy Sets Syst.*, **163**(1), 24–44 (2011).

[74] M. Pratama, J. Lu, E. Lughofer, G. Zhang and M. Er, Incremental learning of concept drift using evolving type-2 recurrent fuzzy neural network, *IEEE Trans. Fuzzy Syst.*, **25**(5), 1175–1192 (2017).

[75] R. Abiyev and O. Kaynak, Fuzzy wavelet neural networks for identification and control of dynamic plants—a novel structure and a comparative study, *IEEE Trans. Ind. Electron.*, **55**(8), 3133–3140 (2008).

[76] L. Zadeh, The concept of a linguistic variable and its application to approximate reasoning, *Inf. Sci.*, **8**(3), 199–249 (1975).

[77] J. Mendel and R. John, Type-2 fuzzy sets made simple, *IEEE Trans. Fuzzy Syst.*, **10**(2), 117–127 (2002).

[78] Q. Liang and J. Mendel, Interval type-2 fuzzy logic systems: theory and design, *IEEE Trans. Fuzzy Syst.*, **8**(5), 535–550 (2000).

[79] J. Mendel, *Uncertain Rule-Based Fuzzy Logic Systems: Introduction and New Directions* (Prentice Hall, Upper Saddle River, 2001).

[80] C. Juang and Y. Tsao, A self-evolving interval type-2 fuzzy neural network with on-line structure and parameter learning, *IEEE Trans. Fuzzy Syst.*, **16**(6), 1411–1424 (2008).

[81] S. Tung, C. Quek and C. Guan, eT2FIS: an evolving type-2 neural fuzzy inference system, *Inf. Sci.*, **220**, 124–148 (2013).

[82] N. Karnik and J. Mendel, Centroid of a type-2 fuzzy set, *Inf. Sci.*, **132**(1–4), 195–220 (2001).

[83] D. Leite, P. Costa and F. Gomide, Interval approach for evolving granular system modeling. In M. Sayed-Mouchaweh and E. Lughofer (eds.), *Learning in Non-Stationary Environments: Methods and Applications*, Springer, New York, pp. 271–300 (2012).

[84] W. Pedrycz, A. Skowron and V. Kreinovich, *Handbook of Granular Computing* (John Wiley & Sons, Chichester, West Sussex, England, 2008).

[85] C. Garcia, D. Leite and I. Skrjanc, Incremental missing-data imputation for evolving fuzzy granular prediction, *IEEE Trans. Fuzzy Syst.*, **28**(10), 2348–2361 (2020).

[86] P. de Campos Souza and E. Lughofer, An advanced interpretable fuzzy neural network model based on uni-nullneuron constructed from n-uninorms, *Fuzzy Sets Syst.*, on-line and in press (https://doi.org/10.1016/j.fss.2020.11.019) (2021).

[87] P. de Campos Souza, Pruning fuzzy neural networks based on unineuron for problems of classification of patterns, *J. Intell. Fuzzy Syst.*, **35**(1), 2597–2605 (2018).

[88] E. Lughofer, Evolving fuzzy systems—fundamentals, reliability, interpretability and useability. In P. Angelov (ed.), *Handbook of Computational Intelligence*, World Scientific, New York, pp. 67–135 (2016).

[89] M. Sugeno and G. Kang, Structure identification of fuzzy model, *Fuzzy Sets Syst.*, **26**, 15–33 (1988).

[90] M. Sugeno, *Industrial Applications of Fuzzy Control* (Elsevier Science, Amsterdam, 1985).

[91] P. Angelov and D. Filev, An approach to online identification of Takagi–Sugeno fuzzy models, *IEEE Trans. Syst. Man Cybern. Part B: Cybern.*, **34**(1), 484–498 (2004).

[92] E.-H. Kim, S.-K. Oh and W. Pedrycz, Reinforced hybrid interval fuzzy neural networks architecture: design and analysis, *Neurocomputing*, **303**, 20–36 (2018).

[93] C. Juang, Y.-Y. Lin and C.-C. Tu, A recurrent self-evolving fuzzy neural network with local feedbacks and its application to dynamic system processing, *Fuzzy Sets Syst.*, **161**(19), 2552–2568 (2010).

[94] Y. Bodyanskiy and O. Vynokurova, Fast medical diagnostics using autoassociative neuro-fuzzy memory, *Int. J. Comput.*, **16**(1), 34–40 (2017).

[95] T. Calvo, B. D. Baets and J. Fodor, The functional equations of frank and alsina for uninorms and nullnorms, *Fuzzy Sets Syst.*, **120**, 385–394 (2001).

[96] P. de Campos Souza and E. Lughofer, An evolving neuro-fuzzy system based on uni-nullneurons with advanced interpretability capabilities, *Neurocomputing*, **451**, 231–251 (2021).

[97] Y. Bodyanskiy and O. Vynokurova, Hybrid adaptive wavelet-neuro-fuzzy system for chaotic time series identification, *Inf. Sci.*, **220**, 170–179 (2013).

[98] W. Yuan and L. Chao, Online evolving interval type-2 intuitionistic fuzzy LSTM-neural networks for regression problems, *IEEE Access*, **7**, 35544 (2019).

[99] A. M. Silva, W. Caminhas, A. Lemos and F. Gomide, A fast learning algorithm for evolving neo-fuzzy neuron, *Appl. Soft Comput.*, **14B**, 194–209 (2014).

[100] P. Angelov and R. Yager, A new type of simplified fuzzy rule-based system, *Int. J. Gen. Syst.*, **41**(2), 163–185 (2012).

[101] D. Kangin, P. Angelov and J. Iglesias, Autonomously evolving classifier TEDAClass, *Inf. Sci.*, **366**, 1–11 (2016).

[102] P. Angelov, X. Gu and J. Principe, Autonomous learning multimodel systems from data streams, *IEEE Trans. Fuzzy Syst.*, **26**(4), 2213–2224 (2018).

[103] L. Kuncheva, *Fuzzy Classifier Design* (Physica-Verlag, Heidelberg, 2000).

[104] Y. Y. T. Nakashima, G. Schaefer and H. Ishibuchi, A weighted fuzzy classifier and its application to image processing tasks, *Fuzzy Sets Syst.*, **158**(3), 284–294 (2006).

[105] F. Rehm, F. Klawonn and R. Kruse, Visualization of fuzzy classifiers, *Int. J. Uncertainty Fuzziness Knowledge-Based Syst.*, **15**(5), 615–624 (2007).

[106] C.-F. Juang and P.-H. Wang, An interval type-2 neural fuzzy classifier learned through soft margin minimization and its human posture classification application, *IEEE Trans. Fuzzy Syst.*, **23**(5), 1474–1487 (2015).

[107] P. Angelov, E. Lughofer and X. Zhou, Evolving fuzzy classifiers using different model architectures, *Fuzzy Sets Syst.*, **159**(23), 3160–3182 (2008).

[108] P. Angelov and X. Zhou, Evolving fuzzy-rule-based classifiers from data streams, *IEEE Trans. Fuzzy Syst.*, **16**(6), 1462–1475 (2008).

[109] A. Bouchachia and R. Mittermeir, Towards incremental fuzzy classifiers, *Soft Comput.*, **11**(2), 193–207 (2006).

[110] E. Lughofer and O. Buchtala, Reliable all-pairs evolving fuzzy classifiers, *IEEE Trans. Fuzzy Syst.*, **21**(4), 625–641 (2013).

[111] P. Angelov and X. Gu, Deep rule-based classifier with human-level performance and characteristics, *Inf. Sci.*, **463–464**, 196–213 (2018).

[112] D. Nauck and R. Kruse, NEFCLASS-X: a soft computing tool to build readable fuzzy classifiers, *BT Technol. J.*, **16**(3), 180–190 (1998).

[113] H. Ishibuchi and T. Nakashima, Effect of rule weights in fuzzy rule-based classification systems, *IEEE Trans. Fuzzy Syst.*, **9**(4), 506–515 (2001).

[114] A. Bouchachia, Incremental induction of classification fuzzy rules. In *IEEE Workshop on Evolving and Self-Developing Intelligent Systems (ESDIS) 2009*, Nashville, USA, pp. 32–39 (2009).

[115] E. Lughofer, Single-pass active learning with conflict and ignorance, *Evolving Syst.*, **3**(4), 251–271 (2012).

[116] T. Hastie, R. Tibshirani and J. Friedman, *The Elements of Statistical Learning: Data Mining, Inference and Prediction*, 2nd edn. (Springer, New York Berlin Heidelberg, 2009).

[117] M. Pratama, S. Anavatti, M. Er and E. Lughofer, pClass: an effective classifier for streaming examples, *IEEE Trans. Fuzzy Syst.*, **23**(2), 369–386 (2015).

[118] E. Allwein, R. Schapire and Y. Singer, Reducing multiclass to binary: a unifying approach for margin classifiers, *J. Mach. Learn. Res.*, **1**, 113–141 (2001).

[119] J. Fürnkranz, Round robin classification, *J. Mach. Learn. Res.*, **2**, 721–747 (2002).

[120] H. He and E. Garcia, Learning from imbalanced data, *IEEE Trans. Knowl. Data Eng.* **21**(9), 1263–1284 (2009).

[121] E. Hüllermeier and K. Brinker, Learning valued preference structures for solving classification problems, *Fuzzy Sets Syst.*, **159**(18), 2337–2352 (2008).

[122] J. Fürnkranz, Round robin rule learning. In *Proceedings of the International Conference on Machine Learning (ICML 2011)*, Williamstown, MA, pp. 146–153 (2001).

[123] D. Nauck and R. Kruse, A neuro-fuzzy method to learn fuzzy classification rules from data, *Fuzzy Sets Syst.*, **89**(3), 277–288 (1997).

[124] P. Angelov, X. Gu and J. Principe, A generalized methodology for data analysis, *IEEE Trans. Cybern.*, **48**(10), 2981–2993 (2018).

[125] C. Schaffer, Overfitting avoidance as bias, *Mach. Learn.,* **10**(2), 153–178 (1993).

[126] Z. Zhou, *Ensemble Methods: Foundations and Algorithms* (Chapman & Hall/CRC Data Mining and Knowledge Discovery Series, Boca Raton, Florida, 2012).

[127] P. Brazdil, C. Giraud-Carrier, C. Soares and R. Vilalta, *Metalearning* (Springer, Berlin Heidelberg, 2009).

[128] P. Sidhu and M. Bathia, An online ensembles approach for handling concept drift in data streams: diversified online ensembles detection, *Int. J. Mach. Learn. Cybern.,* **6**(6), 883–909 (2015).

[129] D. Leite and I. Skrjanc, Ensemble of evolving optimal granular experts, OWA aggregation, and time series prediction, *Inf. Sci.,* **504**, 95–112 (2019).

[130] M. Pratama, W. Pedrycz and E. Lughofer, Evolving ensemble fuzzy classifier, *IEEE Trans. Fuzzy Syst.,* **26**(5), 2552–2567 (2018).

[131] E. Lughofer and M. Pratama, Online sequential ensembling of fuzzy systems. In *Proceedings of the IEEE Evolving and Adaptive Intelligent Systems Conference (EAIS) 2020,* Bari, Italy (2020).

[132] L. Breiman, Bagging predictors, *Mach. Learn.,* **24**(2), 123–140 (1996).

[133] M. Collins, R. Schapire and Y. Singer, Logistic regression, AdaBoost and Bregman distances, *Mach. Learn.,* **48**(1–3), 253–285 (2002).

[134] T. White, *Hadoop: The Definitive Guide* (O'Reilly Media, 2012).

[135] O. Chapelle, B. Schoelkopf and A. Zien, *Semi-Supervised Learning* (MIT Press, Cambridge, MA, 2006).

[136] W. Abraham and A. Robins, Memory retention the synaptic stability versus plasticity dilemma, *Trends Neurosci.,* **28**(2), 73–78 (2005).

[137] M. Stone, Cross-validatory choice and assessment of statistical predictions, *J. R. Stat. Soc.,* **36**(1), 111–147 (1974).

[138] B. Efron and R. Tibshirani, *An Introduction to the Bootstrap* (Chapman and Hall/CRC, 1993).

[139] L. Ljung, *System Identification: Theory for the User* (Prentice Hall PTR, Prentice Hall Inc., Upper Saddle River, New Jersey, 1999).

[140] E. Lughofer, FLEXFIS: a robust incremental learning approach for evolving TS fuzzy models, *IEEE Trans. Fuzzy Syst.,* **16**(6), 1393–1410 (2008).

[141] M. Pratama, S. Anavatti, P. Angelov and E. Lughofer, PANFIS: a novel incremental learning machine, *IEEE Trans. Neural Networks Learn. Syst.,* **25**(1), 55–68 (2014).

[142] C. Cernuda, E. Lughofer, L. Suppan, T. Röder, R. Schmuck, P. Hintenaus, W. Märzinger and J. Kasberger, Evolving chemometric models for predicting dynamic process parameters in viscose production, *Anal. Chim. Acta,* **725**, 22–38 (2012).

[143] G. Leng, X.-J. Zeng and J. Keane, An improved approach of self-organising fuzzy neural network based on similarity measures, *Evolving Syst.,* **3**(1), 19–30 (2012).

[144] Y. Xu, K. Wong and C. Leung, Generalized recursive least square to the training of neural network, *IEEE Trans. Neural Networks,* **17**(1) (2006).

[145] J. L. Salle and S. Lefschetz, *Stability by Lyapunov's Direct Method: With Applications* (Academic Press, New York, 1961).

[146] J. Rubio, Stability analysis for an online evolving neuro-fuzzy recurrent network. In P. Angelov, D. Filev and N. Kasabov (eds.), *Evolving Intelligent Systems: Methodology and Applications,* John Wiley & Sons, New York, pp. 173–200 (2010).

[147] D. Ge and X. Zeng, Learning evolving T-S fuzzy systems with both local and global accuracy— a local online optimization approach, *Appl. Soft Comput.,* **68**, 795–810 (2018).

[148] E. Lughofer, Improving the robustness of recursive consequent parameters learning in evolving neuro-fuzzy systems, *Inf. Sci.,* **545**, 555–574 (2021).

[149] R. Bao, H. Rong, P. Angelov, B. Chen and P. Wong, Correntropy-based evolving fuzzy neural system, *IEEE Trans. Fuzzy Syst.,* **26**(3), 1324–1338 (2018).

[150] H. Rong, Z.-X. Yang and P. Wong, Robust and noise-insensitive recursive maximum correntropy-based evolving fuzzy system, *IEEE Trans. Fuzzy Syst.*, **28**(9), 2277–2284 (2019).

[151] B. Chen, X. Liu, H. Zhao and J. C. Principe, Maximum correntropy Kalman filter, *Automatica*, **76**, 70–77 (2017).

[152] G. Golub and C. V. Loan, *Matrix Computations,* 3rd edn. (John Hopkins University Press, Baltimore, Maryland, 1996).

[153] X. Gu and P. Angelov, Self-boosting first-order autonomous learning neuro-fuzzy systems, *Appl. Soft Comput.*, **77**, 118–134 (2019).

[154] L. Ngia and J. Sjöberg, Efficient training of neural nets for nonlinear adaptive filtering using a recursive Levenberg-Marquardt algorithm, *IEEE Trans. Signal Process.*, **48**(7), 1915–1926 (2000).

[155] J. Sherman and W. Morrison, Adjustment of an inverse matrix corresponding to changes in the elements of a given column or a given row of the original matrix, *Ann. Math. Stat.*, **20**, 621 (1949).

[156] W. Wang and J. Vrbanek, An evolving fuzzy predictor for industrial applications, *IEEE Trans. Fuzzy Syst.*, **16**(6), 1439–1449 (2008).

[157] A. Bouchachia, Evolving clustering: an asset for evolving systems, *IEEE SMC Newsl.*, **36** (2011).

[158] G. Gan, C. Ma and J. Wu, *Data Clustering: Theory, Algorithms, and Applications (ASA-SIAM Series on Statistics and Applied Probability)* (Society for Industrial & Applied Mathematics, USA, 2007).

[159] G. Klancar and I. Skrjanc, Evolving principal component clustering with a low runtime complexity for LRF data mapping, *Appl. Soft Comput.*, **35**, 349–358 (2015).

[160] P. Angelov and X. Gu, Autonomous learning multi-model classifier of 0 order (almmo-0). In *Proceedings of the Evolving and Intelligent Systems (EAIS) Conference 2017*, Ljubljana, Slovenia, IEEE Press (2017).

[161] N. K. Kasabov and Q. Song, DENFIS: dynamic evolving neural-fuzzy inference system and its application for time-series prediction, *IEEE Trans. Fuzzy Syst.*, **10**(2), 144–154 (2002).

[162] A. Zdsar, D. Dovzan and I. Skrjanc, Self-tuning of 2 DOF control based on evolving fuzzy model, *Appl. Soft Comput.*, **19**, 403–418 (2014).

[163] D. Dovzan, V. Logar and I. Skrjanc, Implementation of an evolving fuzzy model (eFuMo) in a monitoring system for a waste-water treatment process, *IEEE Trans. Fuzzy Syst.*, **23**(5), 1761–1776 (2015).

[164] L. Maciel, R. Ballini and F. Gomide, Evolving possibilistic fuzzy modeling for realized volatility forecasting with jumps, *IEEE Trans. Fuzzy Syst.*, **25**(2), 302–314 (2017).

[165] S. Blazic and I. Skrjanc, Incremental fuzzy c-regression clustering from streaming data for local-model-network identification, *IEEE Trans. Fuzzy Syst.*, **28**(4), 758–767 (2020).

[166] P. Angelov, Evolving Takagi–Sugeno fuzzy systems from streaming data, eTS+. In P. Angelov, D. Filev and N. Kasabov (eds.), *Evolving Intelligent Systems: Methodology and Applications*, John Wiley & Sons, New York, pp. 21–50 (2010).

[167] A. Almaksour and E. Anquetil, Improving premise structure in evolving Takagi–Sugeno neuro-fuzzy classifiers, *Evolving Syst.*, **2**, 25–33 (2011).

[168] I. Skrjanc, S. Blazic, E. Lughofer and D. Dovzan, Inner matrix norms in evolving cauchy possibilistic clustering for classification and regression from data streams, *Inf. Sci.*, **478**, 540–563 (2019).

[169] H. Soleimani, K. Lucas and B. Araabi, Recursive gathgeva clustering as a basis for evolving neuro-fuzzy modeling, *Evolving Syst.*, **1**(1), 59–71 (2010).

[170] H.-J. Rong, N. Sundararajan, G.-B. Huang and P. Saratchandran, Sequential adaptive fuzzy inference system (SAFIS) for nonlinear system identification and prediction, *Fuzzy Sets Syst.*, **157**(9), 1260–1275 (2006).

[171] H.-J. Rong, Sequential adaptive fuzzy inference system for function approximation problems. In M. Sayed-Mouchaweh and E. Lughofer (eds.), *Learning in Non-Stationary Environments: Methods and Applications*, Springer, New York (2012).

[172] H.-J. Rong, N. Sundararajan, G.-B. Huang and G.-S. Zhao, Extended sequential adaptive fuzzy inference system for classification problems, *Evolving Syst.*, 2(2), 71–82 (2011).

[173] A. Lemos, W. Caminhas and F. Gomide, Fuzzy evolving linear regression trees, *Evolving Syst.*, 2(1), 1–14 (2011).

[174] C. Hametner and S. Jakubek, Local model network identification for online engine modelling, *Inf. Sci.*, 220, 210–225 (2013).

[175] G. Leng, T. McGinnity and G. Prasad, An approach for on-line extraction of fuzzy rules using a self-organising fuzzy neural network, *Fuzzy Sets Syst.*, 150(2), 211–243 (2005).

[176] F.-J. Lin, C.-H. Lin and P.-H. Shen, Self-constructing fuzzy neural network speed controller for permanent-magnet synchronous motor drive, *IEEE Trans. Fuzzy Syst.*, 9(5), 751–759 (2001).

[177] R. R. Yager, A model of participatory learning, *IEEE Trans. Syst. Man Cybern.*, 20(5), 1229–1234 (1990).

[178] E. Lima, M. Hell, R. Ballini and F. Gomide, Evolving fuzzy modeling using participatory learning. In P. Angelov, D. Filev and N. Kasabov (eds.), *Evolving Intelligent Systems: Methodology and Applications*, John Wiley & Sons, New York, pp. 67–86 (2010).

[179] A. Lemos, W. Caminhas and F. Gomide, Adaptive fault detection and diagnosis using an evolving fuzzy classifier, *Inf. Sci.*, 220, 64–85 (2013).

[180] D. Leite, R. Palhares, C. S. Campos and F. Gomide, Evolving granular fuzzy model-based control of nonlinear dynamic systems, *IEEE Trans. Fuzzy Syst.*, 23(4), 923–938 (2015).

[181] D. Leite, P. Costa and F. Gomide, Evolving granular neural networks from fuzzy data streams, *Neural Networks*, 38, 1–16 (2013).

[182] D. Leite, M. Santana, A. Borges and F. Gomide, Fuzzy granular neural network for incremental modeling of nonlinear chaotic systems. In *Proceedings of the IEEE International Conference on Fuzzy Systems (FUZZ-IEEE) 2016*, pp. 64–71 (2016).

[183] G. Marrs, M. Black and R. Hickey, The use of time stamps in handling latency and concept drift in online learning, *Evolving Syst.*, 3(2), 203–220 (2012).

[184] S. Wu, M. Er and Y. Gao, A fast approach for automatic generation of fuzzy rules by generalized dynamic fuzzy neural networks, *IEEE Trans. Fuzzy Syst.*, 9(4), 578–594 (2001).

[185] A. Kalhor, B. Araabi and C. Lucas, An online predictor model as adaptive habitually linear and transiently nonlinear model, *Evolving Syst.*, 1(1), 29–41 (2010).

[186] S. Tzafestas and K. Zikidis, NeuroFAST: on-line neuro-fuzzy art-based structure and parameter learning TSK model, *IEEE Trans. Syst. Man Cybern. Part B*, 31(5), 797–802 (2001).

[187] P. Angelov, P. Sadeghi-Tehran and R. Ramezani, An approach to automatic real-time novelty detection, object identification, and tracking in video streams based on recursive density estimation and evolving Takagi–Sugeno fuzzy systems, *Int. J. Intell. Syst.*, 26(3), 189–205 (2011).

[188] G. Huang, P. Saratchandran and N. Sundararajan, A generalized growing and pruning RBF (GGAP-RBF) neural network for function approximation, *IEEE Trans. Neural Networks*, 16(1), 57–67 (2005).

[189] B. Hassibi and D. Stork, Second-order derivatives for network pruning: optimal brain surgeon. In S. Hanson, J. Cowan and C. Giles (eds.), *Advances in Neural Information Processing*, vol. 5, Morgan Kaufman, Los Altos, CA, pp. 164–171 (1993).

[190] D. Leite, P. Costa and F. Gomide, Granular approach for evolving system modeling. In *Proceedings of the International Conference on Information Processing and Management of Uncertainty in Knowledge-Based Systems*, Lecture Notes in Artificial Intelligence, pp. 340–349 (2010).

[191] E. Lughofer, J.-L. Bouchot and A. Shaker, On-line elimination of local redundancies in evolving fuzzy systems, *Evolving Syst.*, **2**(3), 165–187 (2011).

[192] G. Leng, A hybrid learning algorithm with a similarity-based pruning strategy for self-adaptive neuro-fuzzy systems, *Appl. Soft Comput.*, **9**(4), 1354–1366 (2009).

[193] C. Mencar, G. Castellano and A. Fanelli, Distinguishability quantification of fuzzy sets, *Inf. Sci.*, **177**, 130–149 (2007).

[194] V. V. Cross and T. A. Sudkamp, *Similarity and Compatibility in Fuzzy Set Theory: Assessment and Applications* (Springer, Physica, Heidelberg New York, 2010).

[195] B. Hartmann, O. Banfer, O. Nelles, A. Sodja, L. Teslic and I. Skrjanc, Supervised hierarchical clustering in fuzzy model identification, *IEEE Trans. Fuzzy Syst.*, **19**(6), 1163–1176 (2011).

[196] L. Teslic, B. Hartmann, O. Nelles and I. Skrjanc, Nonlinear system identification by Gustafson–Kessel fuzzy clustering and supervised local model network learning for the drug absorption spectra process, *IEEE Trans. Neural Networks*, **22**(12), 1941–1951 (2011).

[197] E. Lughofer, M. Pratama and I. Skrjanc, Incremental rule splitting in generalized evolving fuzzy systems for autonomous drift compensation, *IEEE Trans. Fuzzy Syst.*, **26**(4), 1854–1865 (2018).

[198] E. Lughofer, M. Pratama and I. Skrjanc, Online bagging of evolving fuzzy systems, *Inf. Sci.*, **570**, 16–33 (2021).

[199] W. Hoeffding, Probability inequalities for sums of bounded random variables, *J. Am. Stat. Assoc.*, **58**(301), 13–30 (1963).

[200] J. Iglesias, M. Sesmero, E. Lopez, A. Ledezma and A. Sanchis, A novel evolving ensemble approach based on bootstrapping and dynamic selection of diverse learners. In *Proceedings of the Evolving and Adaptive Intelligent Systems Conference (EAIS) 2020*, Bari, Italy (2020).

[201] B. Costa, P. Angelov and L. Guedes, Fully unsupervised fault detection and identification based on recursive density estimation and self-evolving cloud-based classifier, *Neurocomputing*, **150A**, 289–303 (2015).

[202] M. Islam, X. Yao, S. Nirjon, M. Islam and K. Murase, Bagging and boosting negatively correlated neural networks, *IEEE Trans. Syst. Man Cybern. Part B: Cybern.*, **38**(3), 771–784 (2008).

[203] R. Yager, On ordered weighted averaging aggregation operators in multicriteria decision making, *IEEE Trans. Syst. Man Cybern.*, **18**, 183–190 (1988).

[204] L. Kuncheva, *Combining Pattern Classifiers: Methods and Algorithms* (Wiley-Interscience (John Wiley & Sons), Southern Gate, Chichester, West Sussex, England, 2004).

[205] C. C. Coello and G. Lamont, *Applications of Multi-Objective Evolutionary Algorithms* (World Scientific, Singapore, 2004).

[206] E. Soares, P. Costa, B. Costa and D. Leite, Ensemble of evolving data clouds and fuzzy models for weather time series prediction, *Appl. Soft Comput.*, **64**, 445–453 (2018).

[207] R. Kruse, J. Gebhardt and R. Palm, *Fuzzy Systems in Computer Science* (Verlag Vieweg, Wiesbaden, 1994).

[208] K. Aström and B. Wittenmark, *Adaptive Control*, 2nd edn. (Addison-Wesley Longman Publishing Co., Inc., Boston, MA, USA, 1994).

[209] I. Khamassi, M. Sayed-Mouchaweh, M. Hammami and K. Ghedira, Discussion and review on evolving data streams and concept drift adapting, *Evolving Syst.*, **9**(1), 1–23 (2017).

[210] G. Box, G. Jenkins and G. Reinsel, *Time Series Analysis, Forecasting and Control* (Prentice Hall, Englewood Cliffs, New Jersey, 1994).

[211] J. Gama, I. Zliobaite, A. Bifet, M. Pechenizkiy and A. Bouchachia, A survey on concept drift adaptation, *ACM Comput. Surv.*, **46**(4), 44 (2014).

[212] O.-M. Moe-Helgesen and H. Stranden. Catastrophic forgetting in neural networks. Technical report, Norwegian University of Science and Technology, Trondheim, Norway (2005).

[213] E. Lughofer and P. Angelov, Handling drifts and shifts in on-line data streams with evolving fuzzy systems, *Appl. Soft Comput.*, **11**(2), 2057–2068 (2011).

[214] A. Shaker and E. Lughofer, Self-adaptive and local strategies for a smooth treatment of drifts in data streams, *Evolving Syst.*, **5**(4), 239–257 (2014).

[215] H. Mouss, D. Mouss, N. Mouss and L. Sefouhi, Test of Page-Hinkley, an approach for fault detection in an agro-alimentary production system. In *Proceedings of the Asian Control Conference*, vol. 2, pp. 815–818 (2004).

[216] E. Lughofer, E. Weigl, W. Heidl, C. Eitzinger and T. Radauer, Recognizing input space and target concept drifts with scarcely labelled and unlabelled instances, *Inf. Sci.*, **355–356**, 127–151 (2016).

[217] E. Lughofer, E. Weigl, W. Heidl, C. Eitzinger and T. Radauer, Integrating new classes on the fly in evolving fuzzy classifier designs and its application in visual inspection, *Appl. Soft Comput.*, **35**, 558–582 (2015).

[218] M. Pratama, J. Lu, E. Lughofer, G. Zhang and S. Anavatti, Scaffolding type-2 classifier for incremental learning under concept drifts, *Neurocomputing*, **191**, 304–329 (2016).

[219] C.-Y. Chong and S. Kumar, Sensor networks: evolution, opportunities and challenges, *Proc. IEEE*, **91**(8), 1247–1256 (2003).

[220] S. Alizadeh, A. Kalhor, H. Jamalabadi, B. Araabi and M. Ahmadabadi, Online local input selection through evolving heterogeneous fuzzy inference system, *IEEE Trans. Fuzzy Syst.*, **24**(6), 1364–1377 (2016).

[221] V. Bolon-Canedo, N. Sanchez-Marono and A. Alonso-Betanzos, *Feature Selection for High-Dimensional Data Artificial Intelligence: Foundations, Theory, and Algorithms* (Springer, Heidelberg Berlin, 2016).

[222] U. Stanczyk and L. Jain, *Feature Selection for Data and Pattern Recognition* (Springer, Heidelberg, New York, London, 2016).

[223] E. Lughofer, On-line incremental feature weighting in evolving fuzzy classifiers, *Fuzzy Sets Syst.*, **163**(1), 1–23 (2011).

[224] J. Dy and C. Brodley, Feature selection for unsupervised learning, *J. Mach. Learn. Res.*, **5**, 845–889 (2004).

[225] Y. Xu, J.-Y. Yang and Z. Jin, A novel method for fisher discriminant analysis, *Pattern Recognit.*, **37**(2), 381–384 (2004).

[226] M. Hisada, S. Ozawa, K. Zhang and N. Kasabov, Incremental linear discriminant analysis for evolving feature spaces in multitask pattern recognition problems, *Evolving Syst.*, **1**(1), 17–27 (2010).

[227] S. Pang, S. Ozawa and N. Kasabov, Incremental linear discriminant analysis for classification of data streams, *IEEE Trans. Syst. Men Cybern. Part B: Cybern.*, **35**(5), 905–914 (2005).

[228] P. de Campos Souza and E. Lughofer, Identification of heart sounds with an interpretable evolving fuzzy neural network, *Sensors*, **20**(6477) (2020).

[229] E. Lughofer, A.-C. Zavoianu, R. Pollak, M. Pratama, P. Meyer-Heye, H. Zörrer, C. Eitzinger, J. Haim and T. Radauer, Self-adaptive evolving forecast models with incremental PLS space updating for on-line prediction of micro-fluidic chip quality, *Eng. Appl. Artif. Intell.*, **68**, 131–151 (2018).

[230] M. Haenlein and A. Kaplan, A beginner's guide to partial least squares (PLS) analysis, *Understanding Stat.*, **3**(4), 283–297 (2004).

[231] N. Kasabov, D. Zhang and P. Pang, Incremental learning in autonomous systems: evolving connectionist systems for on-line image and speech recognition. In *Proceedings of IEEE Workshop on Advanced Robotics and its Social Impacts, 2005*, Hsinchu, Taiwan, pp. 120–125 (2005).

[232] D. P. Filev and F. Tseng, Novelty detection based machine health prognostics. In *Proc. of the 2006 International Symposium on Evolving Fuzzy Systems*, Lake District, UK, pp. 193–199 (2006).

[233] I. Jolliffe, *Principal Component Analysis* (Springer Verlag, Berlin Heidelberg New York, 2002).

[234] F. Hamker, RBF learning in a non-stationary environment: the stability-plasticity dilemma. In R. Howlett and L. Jain (eds.), *Radial Basis Function Networks 1: Recent Developments in Theory and Applications*, Physica-Verlag, Heidelberg, New York, pp. 219–251 (2001).

[235] H.-J. Rong, P. Angelov, X. Gu and J.-M. Bai, Stability of evolving fuzzy systems based on data clouds, *IEEE Trans. Fuzzy Syst.,* **26**(5), 2774–2784 (2018).

[236] H.-J. Rong, Z.-X. Yang and P. Wong, Robust and noise-insensitive recursive maximum correntropy-based evolving fuzzy system, *IEEE Trans. Fuzzy Syst.,* **28**(9), 2277–2284 (2020).

[237] V. Stojanovic and N. Nedic, Identification of time-varying OE models in presence of non-Gaussian noise: application to pneumatic servo drives, *Int. J. Robust Nonlinear Control,* **26**(18), 3974–3995 (2016).

[238] J. Hühn and E. Hüllermeier, FR3: a fuzzy rule learner for inducing reliable classifiers, *IEEE Trans. Fuzzy Syst.,* **17**(1), 138–149 (2009).

[239] A. Bifet, G. Holmes, R. Kirkby and B. Pfahringer, MOA: massive online analysis, *J. Mach. Learn. Res.,* **11**, 1601–1604 (2010).

[240] M. Smithson, *Confidence Intervals* (SAGE University Paper (Series: Quantitative Applications in the Social Sciences), Thousand Oaks, California, 2003).

[241] K. Tschumitschew and F. Klawonn, Incremental statistical measures. In M. Sayed-Mouchaweh and E. Lughofer (eds.), *Learning in Non-Stationary Environments: Methods and Applications*, Springer, New York, pp. 21–55 (2012).

[242] I. Skrjanc, Evolving fuzzy-model-based design of experiments with supervised hierarchical clustering, *IEEE Trans. Fuzzy Syst.,* **23**(4), 861–871 (2015).

[243] E. Lughofer and M. Pratama, On-line active learning in data stream regression using uncertainty sampling based on evolving generalized fuzzy models, *IEEE Trans. Fuzzy Syst.,* **26**(1), 292–309 (2018).

[244] B. Frieden and R. Gatenby, *Exploratory Data Analysis Using Fisher Information* (Springer Verlag, New York, 2007).

[245] J. Casillas, O. Cordon, F. Herrera and L. Magdalena, *Interpretability Issues in Fuzzy Modeling* (Springer Verlag, Berlin Heidelberg, 2003).

[246] F. Dosilovic, M. Brcic and N. Hlupic, Explainable artificial intelligence: a survey. In *Proceedings of the 41st International Convention Proceedings, MIPRO 2018*, Opatija, Croatia, pp. 210–215 (2018).

[247] W. Samek and G. Montavon, *Explainable AI: Interpreting, Explaining and Visualizing Deep Learning* (Springer Nature, Switzerland, 2019).

[248] Z. Bosnić, J. Demšar, G. Keşpret, P. Rodrigues, J. Gama and I. Kononenko, Enhancing data stream predictions with reliability estimators and explanation, *Eng. Appl. Artif. Intell.,* **34**, 178–192 (2014).

[249] E. Strumbelj and I. Kononenko, Explaining prediction models and individual predictions with feature contributions, *Knowl. Inf. Syst.,* **41**(3), 647–665 (2014).

[250] E. Lughofer, R. Richter, U. Neissl, W. Heidl, C. Eitzinger and T. Radauer, Explaining classifier decisions linguistically for stimulating and improving operators labeling behavior, *Inf. Sci.,* **420**, 16–36 (2017).

[251] T. Wetter, Medical decision support systems. In Computer Science, *Medical Data Analysis*, Springer, Berlin/Heidelberg, pp. 458–466 (2006).

[252] J. Macias-Hernandez and P. Angelov, Applications of evolving intelligent systems to the oil and gas industry. In P. Angelov, D. Filev and N. Kasabov (eds.), *Evolving Intelligent Systems: Methodology and Applications*, John Wiley & Sons, New York, pp. 401–421 (2010).

[253] P. Angelov and A. Kordon, Evolving inferential sensors in the chemical process industry. In P. Angelov, D. Filev and N. Kasabov (eds.), *Evolving Intelligent Systems: Methodology and Applications*, John Wiley & Sons, New York, pp. 313–336 (2010).

[254] G. Andonovski, P. Angelov, S. Blazic and I. Skrjanc, A practical implementation of robust evolving cloud-based controller with normalized data space for heat-exchanger plant, *Appl. Soft Comput.*, **48**, 29–38 (2016).

[255] M. Gacto, R. Alcala and F. Herrera, Interpretability of linguistic fuzzy rule-based systems: an overview of interpretability measures, *Inf. Sci.*, **181**(20), 4340–4360 (2011).

[256] P. Akella, Structure of n-uninorms, *Fuzzy Sets Syst.*, **158**, 1631–1651 (2007).

[257] E. Lughofer, B. Trawinski, K. Trawinski, O. Kempa and T. Lasota, On employing fuzzy modeling algorithms for the valuation of residential premises, *Inf. Sci.*, **181**(23), 5123–5142 (2011).

[258] M. Ashrafi, D. Prasad and C. Quek, IT2-GSETSK: an evolving interval type-II TSK fuzzy neural system for online modeling of noisy data, *Neurocomputing*, **407**, 1–11 (2020).

[259] D. Nauck, Adaptive rule weights in neuro-fuzzy systems, *Neural Comput. Appl.*, **9**, 60–70 (2000).

[260] A. Riid and E. Rüstern, Adaptability, interpretability and rule weights in fuzzy rule-based systems, *Inf. Sci.*, **257**, 301–312 (2014).

[261] S. Henzgen, M. Strickert and E. Hüllermeier, Rule chains for visualizing evolving fuzzy rule-based systems. In *Advances in Intelligent Systems and Computing*, vol. 226, *Proceedings of the 8th International Conference on Computer Recognition Systems CORES 2013*, Springer, Cambridge, MA, pp. 279–288 (2013).

[262] S. Henzgen, M. Strickert and E. Hüllermeier, Visualization of evolving fuzzy rule-based systems, *Evolving Syst.*, **5**(3), 175–191 (2014).

[263] D. Cruz-Sandoval, J. Beltran and M. Garcia-Constantino, Semi-automated data labeling for activity recognition in pervasive healthcare, *Sensors*, **19**(14), 3035 (2019).

[264] B. Settles, *Active Learning* (Morgan & Claypool Publishers, 2012).

[265] D. Cohn, L. Atlas and R. Ladner, Improving generalization with active learning, *Mach. Learn.*, **15**(2), 201–221 (1994).

[266] N. Rubens, M. Elahi, M. Sugiyama and D. Kaplan, Active learning in recommender systems. In F. Ricci, L. Rokach and B. Shapira (eds.), *Recommender Systems Handbook,* 2nd edn., Springer Verlag, New York (2016).

[267] M. Sugiyama and S. Nakajima, Pool-based active learning in approximate linear regression, *Mach. Learn.*, **75**(3), 249–274 (2009).

[268] K. Subramanian, A. K. Das, S. Sundaram and S. Ramasamy, A meta-cognitive interval type-2 fuzzy inference system and its projection based learning algorithm, *Evolving Syst.*, **5**(4), 219–230 (2014).

[269] K. Subramanian, S. Suresh and N. Sundararajan, A metacognitive neuro-fuzzy inference system (MCFIS) for sequential classification problems, *IEEE Trans. Fuzzy Syst.*, **21**(6), 1080–1095 (2013).

[270] M. Pratama, E. Lughofer, M. Er, S. Anavatti and C. Lim, Data driven modelling based on recurrent interval-valued metacognitive scaffolding fuzzy neural network, *Neurocomputing*, **262**, 4–27 (2017).

[271] M. Pratama, S. Anavatti and J. Lu, Recurrent classifier based on an incremental meta-cognitive scaffolding algorithm, *IEEE Trans. Fuzzy Syst.*, **23**(6), 2048–2066 (2015).

[272] E. Lughofer, On-line active learning: a new paradigm to improve practical useability of data stream modeling methods, *Inf. Sci.*, **415–416**, 356–376 (2017).

[273] G. Franceschini and S. Macchietto, Model-based design of experiments for parameter precision: state of the art, *Chem. Eng. Sci.*, **63**(19), 4846–4872 (2008).

[274] S. García, A. Fernandez, J. Luengo and F. Herrera, Advanced nonparametric tests for multiple comparisons in the design of experiments in computational intelligence and data mining: experimental analysis of power, *Inf. Sci.*, **180**, 2044–2064 (2010).

[275] B. Hartmann, J. Moll, O. Nelles and C.-P. Fritzen, Hierarchical local model trees for design of experiments in the framework of ultrasonic structural health monitoring. In *Proceedings of the IEEE International Conference on Control Applications*, pp. 1163–1170 (2011).

[276] T. Pigott, A review of methods for missing data, *Educ. Res. Eval.*, **7**(4), 353–383 (2001).

[277] J. Luengo, S. García and F. Herrera, On the choice of the best imputation methods for missing values considering three groups of classification methods, *Knowl. Inf. Syst.*, **32**, 77–108 (2012).

[278] S. L. Gay, Dynamically regularized fast recursive least squares with application to echo cancellation. In *Proceedings of the IEEE International Conference on Acoustic, Speech and Signal Processing*, Atalanta, Georgia, pp. 957–960 (1996).

[279] R. Merched and A. Sayed, Fast RLS Laguerre adaptive filtering. In *Proceedings of the Allerton Conference on Communication, Control and Computing*, Allerton, IL, pp. 338–347 (1999).

[280] A. Bifet and R. Kirkby, Data stream mining—a practical approach. Technical report, Department of Computer Sciences, University of Waikato, Japan (2011).

[281] K. Subramanian, R. Savita and S. Suresh, A meta-cognitive interval type-2 fuzzy inference system classifier and its projection based learning algorithm. In *Proceedings of the IEEE EAIS 2013 Workshop (SSCI 2013 Conference)*, Singapore, pp. 48–55 (2013).

[282] V. Stehman, Selecting and interpreting measures of thematic classification accuracy, *Remote Sens. Environ.*, **62**(1), 77–89 (1997).

[283] P. Donmez, G. Lebanon and K. Balasubramanian, Unsupervised supervised learning I: estimating classification and regression errors without labels, *J. Mach. Learn. Res.*, **11**, 1323–1351 (2010).

[284] N. Amor, S. Benferhat and Z. Elouedi, Qualitative classification and evaluation in possibilistic decision trees. In *Proceedings of the FUZZ-IEEE Conference*, Budapest, Hungary, pp. 653–657 (2004).

[285] C. Cernuda, E. Lughofer, G. Mayr, T. Röder, P. Hintenaus, W. Märzinger and J. Kasberger, Incremental and decremental active learning for optimized self-adaptive calibration in viscose production, *Chemom. Intell. Lab. Syst.*, **138**, 14–29 (2014).

[286] P. Angelov and I. Skrjanc, Robust evolving cloud-based controller for a hydraulic plant. In *Proceedings of the 2013 IEEE Conference on Evolving and Adaptive Intelligent Systems (EAIS)*, Singapore, pp. 1–8 (2013).

[287] D. Dovzan, V. Logar and I. Skrjanc, Solving the sales prediction problem with fuzzy evolving methods. In *WCCI 2012 IEEE World Congress on Computational Intelligence*, Brisbane, Australia (2012).

[288] A. Cara, L. Herrera, H. Pomares and I. Rojas, New online self-evolving neuro fuzzy controller based on the TaSe-NF model, *Inf. Sci.*, **220**, 226–243 (2013).

[289] H.-J. Rong, S. Han and G.-S. Zhao, Adaptive fuzzy control of aircraft wing-rock motion, *Appl. Soft Comput.*, **14**, 181–193 (2014).

[290] M. Ferdaus, M. Pratama, S. G. Anavatti, M. A. Garratt and E. Lughofer, Pac: a novel self-adaptive neuro-fuzzy controller for micro aerial vehicles, *Inf. Sci.*, **512**, 481–505 (2020).

[291] R. Precup, T. Teban, A. Albu, A. Borlea, I. A. Zamfirache and E. M. Petriu, Evolving fuzzy models for prosthetic hand myoelectric-based control, *IEEE Trans. Instrum. Meas.*, **69**(7), 4625–4636 (2020).

[292] C. Xydeas, P. Angelov, S. Chiao and M. Reoulas, Advances in EEG signals classification via dependant HMM models and evolving fuzzy classifiers, *International Journal on Computers in Biology and Medicine, special issue on Intelligent Technologies for Bio-Informatics and Medicine*, **36**(10), 1064–1083 (2006).

[293] N. Nuntalid, K. Dhoble and N. Kasabov, EEG classification with BSA spike encoding algorithm and evolving probabilistic spiking neural network. In *Neural Information Processing, LNCS,* vol. 7062, Springer Verlag, Berlin Heidelberg, pp. 451–460 (2011).

[294] J. Rubio and A. Bouchachia, MSAFIS: an evolving fuzzy inference system, *Soft Comput.*, **21**, 2357–2366 (2015).

[295] P. Angelov and A. Kordon, Adaptive inferential sensors based on evolving fuzzy models: an industrial case study, *IEEE Trans. Syst. Man Cybern. Part B: Cybern.*, **40**(2), 529–539 (2010).

[296] A. Shaker, R. Senge and E. Hüllermeier, Evolving fuzzy patterns trees for binary classification on data streams, *Inf. Sci.*, **220**, 34–45 (2013).

[297] P. V. de Campos Souza, A. J. Guimaraes, V. S. Araujo, T. S. Rezende and V. J. S. Araujo, Incremental regularized data density-based clustering neural networks to aid in the construction of effort forecasting systems in software development, *Appl. Intell.*, **49**, 1–14 (2019).

[298] D. Ge and X.-J. Zeng, Learning data streams online—an evolving fuzzy system approach with self-learning/adaptive thresholds, *Inf. Sci.*, **507**, 172–184 (2020).

[299] D. Leite, F. Gomide, R. Ballini and P. Costa, Fuzzy granular evolving modeling for time series prediction. In *Proceedings of the IEEE International Conference on Fuzzy Systems*, pp. 2794–2801 (2011).

[300] L. Maciel, A. Lemos, F. Gomide and R. Ballini, Evolving fuzzy systems for pricing fixed income options, *Evolving Syst.*, **3**(1), 5–18 (2012).

[301] G. Prasad, G. Leng, T. McGuinnity and D. Coyle, Online identification of self-organizing fuzzy neural networks for modeling time-varying complex systems. In P. Angelov, D. Filev and N. Kasabov (eds.), *Evolving Intelligent Systems: Methodology and Applications*, John Wiley & Sons, New York, pp. 201–228 (2010).

[302] N. Kasabov, *Evolving Connectionist Systems: Methods and Applications in Bioinformatics, Brain Study and Intelligent Machines* (Springer Verlag, London, 2002).

[303] E. Soares, P. Angelov and X. Gu, Autonomous learning multiple-model zero-order classifier for heart sound classification, *Appl. Soft Comput.*, **94**, 106449 (2020).

[304] Y.-Y. Lin, J.-Y. Chang and C.-T. Lin, Identification and prediction of dynamic systems using an interactively recurrent self-evolving fuzzy neural network, *IEEE Trans. Neural Networks Learn. Syst.*, **24**(2), 310–321 (2012).

[305] E. Lughofer, C. Eitzinger and C. Guardiola, On-line quality control with flexible evolving fuzzy systems. In M. Sayed-Mouchaweh and E. Lughofer (eds.), *Learning in Non-Stationary Environments: Methods and Applications*, Springer, New York, pp. 375–406 (2012).

[306] M. Pratama, E. Dimla, T. Tjahjowidodo, W. Pedrycz and E. Lughofer, Online tool condition monitoring based on parsimonious ensemble+, *IEEE Trans. Cybern.*, **50**(2), 664–677 (2020).

[307] G. Andonovski, S. Blazic and I. Skrjanc, Evolving fuzzy model for fault detection and fault identification of dynamic processes. In E. Lughofer and M. Sayed-Mouchaweh (eds.), *Predictive Maintenance in Dynamic Systems*, Springer, New York, pp. 269–285 (2019).

[308] S. Silva, P. Costa, M. Santana and D. Leite, Evolving neuro-fuzzy network for real-time high impedance fault detection and classification, *Neural Comput. Appl.*, **32**, 7597–7610 (2020).

[309] E. Lughofer, A. Zavoianu, R. Pollak, M. Pratama, P. Meyer-Heye, H. Zörrer, C. Eitzinger and T. Radauer, Autonomous supervision and optimization of product quality in a multi-stage manufacturing process based on self-adaptive prediction models, *J. Process Control*, **76**, 27–45 (2019).

[310] M. Camargos, I. Bessa, M. DAngelo, L. Cosme and R. Palhares, Data-driven prognostics of rolling element bearings using a novel error based evolving Takagi–Sugeno fuzzy model, *Appl. Soft Comput.*, **96**, 106628 (2020).

[311] X. Zhou and P. Angelov, Autonomous visual self-localization in completely unknown environment using evolving fuzzy rule-based classifier. In *2007 IEEE International Conference on Computational Intelligence Application for Defense and Security*, Honolulu, Hawaii, USA, pp. 131–138 (2007).

[312] D. Leite and F. Gomide, Evolving linguistic fuzzy models from data streams. In *Combining Experimentation and Theory*, Springer, Berlin, Heidelberg, pp. 209–223 (2012).

[313] H. Widiputra, R. Pears and N. Kasabov, Dynamic learning of multiple time se ries in a nonstationary environment. In M. Sayed-Mouchaweh and E. Lughofer (eds.), *Learning in Non-Stationary Environments: Methods and Applications*, Springer, New York, pp. 303–348 (2012).

[314] O. Tyshchenko and A. Deineko, An evolving neuro-fuzzy system with online learning/self-learning, *Int. J. Mod. Comput. Sci.*, **2**, 1–7 (2015).

[315] J. Iglesias, P. Angelov, A. Ledezma and A. Sanchis, Creating evolving user behavior profiles automatically, *IEEE Trans. Knowl. Data Eng.*, **24**(5), 854–867 (2012).

[316] J. Iglesias, P. Angelov, A. Ledezma and A. Sanchis, Evolving classification of agent's behaviors: a general approach, *Evolving Syst.*, **1**(3), 161–172 (2010).

[317] J. Andreu and P. Angelov, Towards generic human activity recognition for ubiquitous applications, *J. Ambient Intell. Hum. Comput.*, **4**, 155–156 (2013).

[318] L. Wang, H.-B. Ji and Y. Jin, Fuzzy passive–aggressive classification: a robust and efficient algorithm for online classification problems, *Inf. Sci.*, **220**, 46–63 (2013).

[319] I. Skrjanc, G. Andonovski, A. Ledezma, O. Sipele, J. A. Iglesias and A. Sanchis, Evolving cloud-based system for the recognition of drivers' actions, *Expert Syst. Appl.*, **99**(1), 231–238 (2018).

[320] Y.-T. Liu, Y.-Y. Lin, S.-L. Wu, C.-H. Chuang and C.-T. Lin, Brain dynamics in predicting driving fatigue using a recurrent self-evolving fuzzy neural network, *IEEE Trans. Neural Networks Learn. Syst.*, **27**(2), 347–360 (2015).

[321] X. Zhou and P. Angelov, Real-time joint landmark recognition and classifier generation by an evolving fuzzy system. In *Proceedings of FUZZ-IEEE 2006*, Vancouver, Canada, pp. 1205–1212 (2006).

[322] E. Weigl, W. Heidl, E. Lughofer, C. Eitzinger and T. Radauer, On improving performance of surface inspection systems by on-line active learning and flexible classifier updates, *Mach. Vision Appl.*, **27**(1), 103–127 (2016).

[323] J. Iglesias, A. Tiemblo, A. Ledezma and A. Sanchis, Web news mining in an evolving framework, *Inf. Fusion*, **28**, 90–98 (2016).

[324] C. Zain, M. Pratama, E. Lughofer and S. Anavatti, Evolving type-2 web news mining, *Appl. Soft Comput.*, **54**, 200–220 (2017).

Appendix

Symbols

N	Number of training samples (seen so far)
p	Dimensionality of the learning problem = the number of input features/variables
$\vec{x}$	One (current) data sample, containing p input variables
$\vec{x}(k)$ or $\vec{x}_k$	The kth data sample in a sequence of samples
$\{x_1, \ldots, x_p\}$	Input variables/features
$y(k)$ or y	Measured output/target value for regression problems in the kth or current sample
$\hat{y}(k)$ or $\hat{y}$	Estimated output/target value in the kth or current sample
$\hat{y}_i(k)$ or $\hat{y}_i$	Estimated output/target value from the ith rule in the kth or current sample
m	Polynomial degree of the consequent function; or number of ensemble members
r, reg	Regressors
X or R	Regression matrix
R_i	The ith rule, neuron
C	Number of rules, neurons, clusters in the evolving model
$P_i(k)$	Inverse Hessian matrix of the ith rule
$Q_i(k)$	Weight matrix for the ith rule
$P(k)$	Hessian matrix
Jac	Jacobian matrix
Φ	Set of parameters (in an ENFS)
Φ_{lin}	Set of linear parameters (in an ENFS)
Φ_{nonlin}	Set of nonlinear parameters (in an ENFS)
$\vec{c}_i$	Center vector of the ith rule, cluster
$\vec{\sigma}_i$	Ranges of influence/widths vector of the ith rule, cluster
Σ_i	Covariance matrix of the ith rule
win	Indicates the index of the winning rule, cluster (nearest to sample $\vec{x}$)
$\{\mu_{i1}, \ldots, \mu_{ip}\}$	Antecedent fuzzy sets of the ith rule (for p inputs)
$\mu_i(\vec{x})$	Membership/Activation degree of the ith rule for the current sample $\vec{x}$
$\Psi_i(\vec{x})$	Normalized membership degree of the ith rule for the current sample $\vec{x}$
l_i	Consequent function, singleton (class label) in the ith rule
$\vec{w}_i = \{w_{i0}, \ldots, w_{ip}\}$	Linear weights in the consequent function of the ith rule
L_r	Real class label of a data sample in classification problems

L	Output class label for classification problems (from a fuzzy classifier)
L_i	Output class label of the ith rule (neuron)
K	Number of classes in classification problems
$conf_{ij}$	Confidence of the ith rule in the jth class
$conf_i$	Confidence of the ith rule to its output class label
$conf$	Overall confidence of the fuzzy classifier to its output class label
J	Objective functional (to be optimized)
$e(.,.)$	residual between first and second argument
λ	Forgetting factor
ϕ	Angle between two vectors; weight decay function
$\vec{a}$	Eigenvector
A	Matrix containing all eigenvectors
$\vec{e}$	Axis vector
γ_i	Local density of the ith rule
$P_{i,j}$	jth prototype of the ith class
F_i	ith ensemble member

Abbreviations

Abbreviation	Meaning
AHLTNM	Adaptive habitually linear and transiently nonlinear model
AI	Artificial intelligence
ALMMo	Autonomous learning multimodel systems
AnYa	Angelov and yager system
APE	Average percentual deviation
COG	Center of gravity
DENFIS	Dynamic evolving neural-fuzzy inference system
DoE	Design of experiments
DRB	Deep rule-based classifiers
EBeTS	Error-Based evolving Takagi–Sugeno fuzzy model
eClass	Evolving classifier
EFC	Evolving fuzzy classifiers
EFC-AP	Evolving fuzzy classifier with all-pairs architecture
EFC-MM	Evolving fuzzy classifier with multi-model architecture
EFC-SM	Evolving fuzzy classifier with single model architecture

Abbreviation	Meaning
EFP	Evolving fuzzy predictor
eFPT	Evolving fuzzy pattern trees
EFS	Evolving fuzzy systems
EFS-SLAT	Evolving fuzzy systems with self-learning/adaptive thresholds
eFT	Evolving fuzzy trees
eFuMO	Evolving fuzzy model
EFuNN	Evolving fuzzy neural network
eGNN	Evolving granular neural networks
EIS	Evolving intelligent systems
eMG	Evolving multivariate gaussian
ENFS	Evolving neuro-fuzzy systems
ENFS-OL	Evolving neuro-fuzzy system with online learning/self-learning
ENFS-Uni0	Evolving neuro-fuzzy systems based on uni-null neurons
EPFM	Evolving possibilistic fuzzy modeling
ePL	Evolving participatory learning
epSNNr	Evolving probabilistic spiking neural network
eTS	Evolving Takagi–Sugeno
eTS-LS-SVM	Evolving TS model based on least squares SVM
eT2Class	Evolving type-2 fuzzy classifier
eT2FIS	Evolving type-2 neural fuzzy inference system
eT2RFNN	Evolving type-2 recurrent fuzzy neural network
EWRLS	Extended weighted recursive least squares
FBeM	Fuzzy set based evolving modeling
FLEXFIS	Flexible fuzzy inference systems
FPA	Fuzzy passive-aggressive classification
FWGRLS	Fuzzily weighted generalized recursive least squares
GAP-RBF	Growing and pruning radial basis function
GD-FNN	Genetic dynamic fuzzy neural network
GENEFIS	Generic evolving neuro-fuzzy inference system
GMMs	Gaussian mixture models
GS-EFS	Generalized smart evolving fuzzy systems
IBeM	Interval-based evolving modeling
InFuR	Incremental fuzzy C-regression clustering
IPLS-GEFS	Incremental PLS with generalized evolving fuzzy systems
IRSFNN	Interactively recurrent self-evolving fuzzy neural network
IT2-GSETSK	Evolving interval type-II generic self-evolving TSK neural system

Abbreviation	Meaning
LNSE	Learning in non-stationary environments
LOFO	Leave-one-feature-out approach
LOLIMOT	Local linear model tree
LS	Least squares
LS_SVM	Least squares support vector machine
LV	Latent variable
MAE	Mean absolute error
McIT2FIS	Metacognitive neuro-fuzzy inference system
MIMO	Multiple input multiple output
MNIST	Hand-written digit data base
MOM	Mean of maximum
MSAFIS	Modified sequential adaptive fuzzy inference system
NeuroFAST	Neuro function activity structure and technology
NFC	Neuro-fuzzy controller
OB-EFS	Online bagging of evolving fuzzy systems
PANFIS	Parsimonious network based on fuzzy inference system
PCA	Principal component analysis
pClass	Parsimonious evolving fuzzy classifier
pEnsemble	Parsimonious ensemble fuzzy classifier
PID	Proportional-integral-derivative
PLS	Partial least squares
PM-CSA	Pseudo monte-carlo sampling algorithm
RECCo	Self-evolving Cloud-based controller
RFWLS	Recursive fuzzily weighted least squares
rGK	recursive gustafson–kessel
RSEFNN	Recurrent self-evolving fuzzy neural network
RIVMcSFNN	Recurrent interval-valued metacognitive scaffolding fuzzy neural network
RLM	Recursive levenberg-marquardt
RMSE	Root mean squared error
RUL	Remaining useful life
RWTLS	Recursive weighted total least squares
SAFIS	Sequential adaptive fuzzy inference system
SCFNN	Self-constructing fuzzy neural network
SEIT2-FNN	Self-evolving interval type-2 fuzzy neural network
SOFMLS	Online self-organizing fuzzy modified least-squares network

Abbreviation	Meaning
SOFNN	Self organizing fuzzy neural network
SP-AL	Single-pass active learning
SUHICLUST	Supervised hierarchical clustering
SVMs	Support vector machines
TEDA	Typically and eccentricity based data analytics
TEDAClass	Typically and eccentricity based data analytics classifier
TS	Takagi–Sugeno
TSK	Takagi–Sugeno–Kang
VLDB	Very large data base
WLS	Weighted least squares

Chapter 5

Incremental Fuzzy Machine Learning for Online Classification of Emotions in Games from EEG Data Streams

Daniel Leite*,†, Volnei Frigeri Jr.‡, and Rodrigo Medeiros‡

*Faculty of Engineering and Science, Adolfo Ibáñez University, Santiago, Chile
†daniel.furtado@uai.cl
‡{vjunior.frigeri, rodrigo.nmedeiros19}@gmail.com

Emotions have an important role in human–computer interaction and decision-making processes. The identification of the human emotional state has become a need for more realistic and interactive machines and computer systems. The greatest challenge is the availability of high-performance online learning algorithms that can effectively handle individual differences and nonstationarities from physiological data streams, i.e., algorithms that self-customize to a new user with no subject-specific calibration data. We describe an evolving Gaussian fuzzy classification (eGFC) approach, which is supported by an online semi-supervised learning algorithm to recognize emotion patterns from electroencephalogram (EEG) data streams. We present a method to extract and select features from bands of the Fourier spectra of EEG data. The data are provided by 28 individuals playing the games Train Sim World, Unravel, Slender: The Arrival, and Goat Simulator for 20 minutes each—a public dataset. According to the arousal–valence system, different emotions prevail in each game (boredom, calmness, horror, and joy). We analyze 14 electrodes/brain regions individually, and the effect of time window lengths, bands, and dimensionality reduction on the accuracy of eGFC. The eGFC model is user-independent and learns its structure and parameters from scratch. We conclude that both brain hemispheres may assist classification, especially electrodes on the frontal (Af3–Af4) area, followed by the occipital (O1–O2) and temporal (T7–T8) areas. We observed that patterns may be eventually found in any frequency band; however, the alpha (8–13 Hz), delta (1–4 Hz), and theta (4–8 Hz) bands, in this order, are more monotonically correlated with the emotion classes. eGFC has been shown to be effective for real-time learning from a large volume of EEG data. It reaches a 72.20% accuracy using a compact 6-rule structure on average, 10-second time windows, and a 1.8 ms/sample average processing time on a highly stochastic time-varying 4-class classification problem.

5.1. Introduction

Machine recognition of human emotions has been a topic of increasing scientific, clinical, and technological interest [1, 2]. Emotions can be communicated through (i) non-physiological data, such as facial expressions, gestures, body language, eye blink count, and voice tones; and (ii) physiological data by using the electroencephalogram (EEG), electromyogram (EMG), and electrocardiogram (ECG) [3, 4]. Computer vision and audition, physiological signals, and brain–computer interfaces (BCI) are typical approaches to emotion recognition. The implications of non-physiological and physiological data analysis spread across a variety of domains in which artificial intelligence has offered decision-making support; control of mechatronic systems, software, and virtual agents; and realism, efficiency, and interaction [1].

EEG feature extraction has been a primary research issue in the field since learning algorithms to determine classification models and class boundaries are applied over the resulting feature space. Any feature extraction and time windowing method; kernel machine; aggregation function; Fourier, wavelet, or alternative transforms; energy or entropy equations; and so on—combined or not—can be applied over raw multi-channel EEG data to obtain an *optimal* representation, i.e., a representation that further facilitates learning a classification hypothesis. As a consequence, finding such an optimal representation means *finding a needle in a haystack*. An additional issue concerns generalization across individuals. Highly discriminative features and robust classifiers depend on the characteristics of the experimental group, inter- and intra-subject variability, and the classification task itself. For example, different effective features can be found in recordings from different subjects. Each subject has its own set of premises and uncertainties. Although several feature extraction methods have been evaluated within intelligent systems and BCI studies, their performance remains, in general, unsatisfactory [5].

A total of 4,464 time-frequency and dynamical features are investigated in [6], based on the benchmark SEED and DEAP EEG datasets. A discussion on how controversial literature results have been in relation to more effective channels, features, frequency bands, and cross-subject recognition issues is presented. L^1-norm penalty-based feature elimination is performed to achieve a more compact feature set—being Hjorth parameters and bilateral temporal lobes considered appealing to analyze time-varying EEG data. Although high-frequency (beta and gamma) bands have occasionally been pointed out to be more effective to differentiate emotions, all bands may contribute to classification [6–8], especially because brain activity does not consider emotions isolated, but together with other cognitive processes. A survey on evolutionary methods to systematically explore EEG features is given in [9]. A comparison among empirical mode decomposition, Daubechies-4 wavelet, and entropy-based extraction methods is provided in [10]. Principal component analysis (PCA) and Fisher projection have also been used for feature extraction [11]. A drawback of many extraction methods based on a combination of features concerns the loss of domain information, namely, specific channels, brain regions, and frequency bands are unknown after combinations. Domain information may be important for the purpose of model interpretability and brain response understanding.

Classifiers of EEG data are typically based on support vector machines (SVMs) using different kernels, the k-nearest neighbor (kNN) algorithm, linear discriminant analysis (LDA), Naive Bayes (NB) algorithm, and the multi-layer perceptron (MLP) neural network; see [1, 12] for a summary. Deep learning has also been applied to affective computing from physiological data. A deep neural network is used in [13] to classify the states of relaxation, anxiety, excitement, and fun by means of skin conductance and blood volume pulse signals with similar performance to that of shallow methods. A deep belief network (DBN), i.e., a probabilistic generative model with deep architecture, to classify positive, neutral, and negative emotions is described in [11]. Selection of electrodes and frequency bands is performed through the weight distributions obtained from the trained DBN, being differential asymmetries between the left and right brain hemispheres relevant features. A dynamical-graph convolutional neural network (DG-CNN) [3], trained by error back-propagation, learns an adjacency matrix related to different EEG channels to outperform DBN, transductive SVM, transfer component analysis (TCA), and other methods on the SEED and DREAMER benchmark EEG datasets.

Fuzzy methods to deal with uncertainties in emotion identification, especially using facial images and speech data, have recently been proposed. A two-stage fuzzy fusion strategy combined with a deep CNN (TSFF-CNN) is presented in [14]. Facial expression images and speech modalities are aggregated for a final classification decision. The method manages the ambiguity and uncertainty of emotional state information. The TSFF-CNN has outperformed non-fuzzy deep learning methods. In [15], a fuzzy multi-class SVM method uses features from the biorthogonal wavelet transform applied over images of facial expressions to detect emotions, namely, happiness, sadness, surprisingness, angriness, disgustingness, and fearfulness. An adaptive neuro-fuzzy inference system (ANFIS) that combines facial expression and EEG features has been shown to be superior to single-source-based classifiers in [16]. In this case, a 3D fuzzy extraction method for content analysis and a 3D fuzzy tensor to extract emotional features from raw EEG data are used. Extracted features are fed to ANFIS, which, in turn, identifies the valence status stimulated by watching a movie clip [16].

A method called multi-scale inherent fuzzy entropy (I-FuzzyEn), which uses empirical mode decomposition and fuzzy membership functions, is proposed to evaluate the complexity of EEG data [17]. Complexity estimates are useful as a bio-signature of health conditions. FuzzyEn has been shown to be more robust than analogous non-fuzzy methods in the sense of root mean square deviation. The online weighted adaptation regularization for regression (OwARR) algorithm [18] aims to estimate driver drowsiness from EEG data. OwARR uses fuzzy sets to perform part of the regularization procedure. Some offline training steps are needed to select domains. The idea is to reduce subject-specific calibration based on the EEG data. An ensemble of models using swarm-optimized fuzzy integrals for motor imagery recognition and robotic arm control is addressed in [19]. The ensemble uses the Sugeno or Choquet fuzzy integral supported by particle swarm optimization (PSO) to represent variations between individuals. The ensemble identifies the user's mental representation of movements from EEG patterns. In [5], a multimodal fuzzy fusion BCI for motor imagery recognition, also using the Choquet and Sugeno integrals, is given. Fuzzy aggregation aims to compensate for posterior probabilities in classification due to different EEG frequencies and multiple classifiers. Despite the above studies, the literature on fuzzy methods applied to EEG data analysis and BCI systems is scarce in the global picture.

All offline classifier-design methods mentioned above indirectly assume that the data sources are governed by stationary distributions since the classifiers are expected to keep their training performance during online operation using a fixed structure and parameters. Nonetheless, EEG data streams very often change, gradually and abruptly, due to movement artifacts, electrode and channel configuration, noise, and environmental conditions. Individually, factors such as fatigue, inattention, and stress also affect pre-designed classifiers in an uncertain way. The non-stationary nature of physiological signals and BCI systems leads the accuracy of both user-dependent and user-independent classifiers to degrade—being the former more susceptible to performance degradation—unless the classifiers are updated on the fly to represent the changes.

The present study deals with online learning and real-time emotion classification from EEG data streams generated by individuals playing computer games. We briefly present a recently proposed evolving Gaussian fuzzy classification (eGFC) approach [20], which is supported by an incremental semi-supervised online learning algorithm. eGFC is an instance of evolving granular system [21, 22], which, in turn, is a general-purpose online learning framework, i.e., a family of algorithms and methods to autonomously construct classifiers, regressors, predictors, and controllers in which any aspect of a problem may assume a non-pointwise (e.g., interval, fuzzy, rough, statistical) uncertain characterization, including data, parameters, features, learning equations, and covering regions [23–25]. In particular, eGFC has been successfully applied in data centers [26] to real-time anomaly detection and in smart grids [20] for power quality disturbance classification.

We use the public EEG dataset by [27], which contains time-indexed samples obtained from individuals exposed to visual and auditory stimuli according to a protocol. Brain activity is recorded by the 14 channels of the *Emotiv EPOC+* EEG device. We pre-process raw data by means of time windowing and filtering procedures to remove artifacts and undesirable frequencies. We choose to extract and analyze ten features (the maximum and mean values) from the delta (1–4 Hz), theta (4–8 Hz), alpha (8–13 Hz), beta (13–30 Hz), and gamma (30–64 Hz) bands, per EEG channel—140 features in total. Then, a unique user-independent eGFC model is developed from scratch based on sequential data from 28 consecutive players. Notice that user-dependent classification models are generally more accurate, but less generalizable. We choose a more generalizable eGFC model, which is the realistic approach in a multi-user environment. After recognizing a predominant emotion according to the arousal–valence system, i.e., boredom, calmness, horror, or joy, which are related to specific computer games, feedback can be implemented in a real or virtual environment to promote a higher level of realism and interactivity. The feedback step is out of the scope of this study.

The contributions of this paper in relation to the literature of the area are as follows:

- A new, user-independent time-varying Gaussian fuzzy classifier, eGFC, supplied with an online incremental learning algorithm to deal with uncertainties and nonstationarities of physiological EEG data streams—in particular, data streams due to visual and auditory stimuli with a focus on emotion recognition in computer games;
- Distinguished eGFC characteristics in relation to the literature of the area include: (i) real-time operation using adaptive granularity and interpretable fuzzy rule-based structure; (ii) storing data samples and knowing the task and existing number of classes *a priori* are needless; (iii) the ability to incorporate new spatio-temporal patterns on the fly, without human intervention;
- An analysis of the effects of time window lengths, brain regions, frequency bands, and dimensionality reduction on the classification performance.

5.2. Brain–Computer Interface

A BCI consists of electrodes and other bio-sensors, high-performance hardware, and a computing framework for pattern recognition, prediction, and decision-making support. An EEG-based BCI allows reading, analyzing, differentiating, and interpreting physiological signals reflected in brain waves [28]. A user may interact with computers, mechatronics, and even with other humans, from thoughts, movements, and environmental perceptions—which activate specific parts of the brain. A communication path among the elements of interest is needed [29].

Typical EEG-BCI applications target solutions that promote human–machine interaction [30]. The applications are different based on (i) the device used (invasive/non-invasive, in relation to the human body), (ii) stimulus (exogenous/endogenous), (iii) data processing (synchronous/asynchronous), and (iv) objective (active, passive, reactive) [4]. Noninvasive approaches prevail. Despite the lower spatial resolution provided by a set of passive electrodes placed on the scalp, and interference manifested as noise and data distortions, brain implants are too risky [31]. Moreover, the electrodes work synchronously, and the analysis of endogenous stimuli predominates, i.e., stimuli dependent on cognitive response to sensory stimuli, e.g., visual, auditory. The present study considers this context.

5.2.1. *Evoked Potential and the 10–20 System*

The location of electrodes on the scalp follows the international 10–20 system in order to reproduce replicable setups. The position depends on the references: *nasion*, in the superior part of the nose; and *inion*, on the back of the skull [1, 28]. A letter identifies the lobe. F stands for frontal, T for temporal, P for parietal, and O for occipital. Even and odd numbers refer to positions on the right and left brain hemispheres, respectively. The 10–20 system is employed in many commercial EEG, and is widely used in scientific research. Figure 5.1 shows the ideal position of the electrodes; P3 and P4 are ground (zero volts) points. The 14 points in green are, particularly, measured by the *Emotiv EPOC+* EEG device. The five blank spots (and other additional spots) can also be considered. For example, the *Open BCI* EEG device considers all the 19 spots shown in the figure.

　　Evoked potential is an electrical potential recorded by the EEG after the presentation of a stimulus. In computer games, we consider auditory evoked potential (AEP), elicited through earphones; and visual evoked potentials (VEP), elicited by non-stationary patterns presented on a monitor.

5.2.2. *The Arousal–Valence System and Games*

The dimension approach, or the arousal–valence system [32], considers human emotions in a continuous form, along the circumference of a circle. On the left side of the valence dimension are negative emotions, denoted by N, e.g., "angry," "bored," and related adjectives, whereas on the right side are positive emotions, P, e.g., "happy," "calm," and related adjectives. The upper part of the arousal dimension characterizes excessive emotional arousal or behavioral expression, while the lower part designates apathy. We assign a number from 1 to 4 to the arousal–valence quadrants (see Figure 5.2), according to the 4-class classification problem we have. A coarser or more detailed classification problem can be formulated.

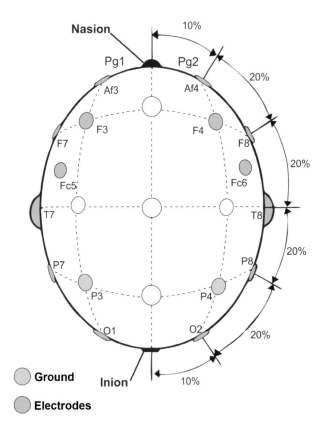

Figure 5.1:   The international 10–20 system to place electrodes on the scalp.

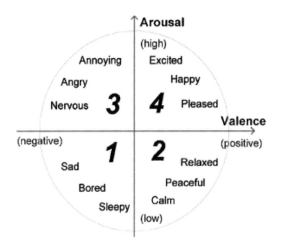

Figure 5.2:   The arousal-valence model of emotions.

Spectator and actor emotions while playing computer games are different in terms of strength [33]. While spectators are impressed with the game development, their emotions tend to be weaker and are categorized in the lower quadrants of the arousal–valence circle. On the contrary, as actors effectively change the outcome of the game, their mental activity is higher. Actors cognitively process images, build histories mentally, and evaluate characters and situations. At first, actor emotions are not prone to any quadrant. In emotion recognition, computer games have been widely used [4, 34], mainly because the brains of actors are subject to various kinds of emotions and cognitive processes.

5.3. eGFC: Evolving Gaussian Fuzzy Classifier

This section summarizes eGFC, a recently proposed semi-supervised evolving classifier [20]. Although eGFC handles partially labeled data, we assume that a label becomes available some time steps after the class estimate. Therefore, we perform a single supervised learning step using the corresponding input–output pair when the output is available. eGFC uses Gaussian membership functions to cover the data space with fuzzy granules. New data samples are associated with fuzzy rules and class labels. Granules are scattered in the data space to represent local information. eGFC global response comes from the aggregation of local models. A recursive algorithm constructs its rule base, and updates local models to deal with non-stationarities. eGFC addresses additional issues such as unlimited amounts of data, and scalability [21, 26].

A local fuzzy model is created if a sample is sufficiently different from the current knowledge. The learning algorithm expands, reduces, removes, and merges granules. Rules are reviewed according to inter-granular relations. eGFC provides nonlinear, non-stationary, and smooth discrimination boundaries among classes [20]. Before describing the eGFC structure and algorithm, the following section briefly summarizes some related online fuzzy classification methods.

5.3.1. *Some Related Online Learning Methods*

A previous fuzzy rule-based method for data stream classification, called eClass, is described in [35]—being eClass0 a model architecture that keeps class labels as rule consequent; and eClass1 a first order Takagi–Sugeno architecture. Incremental supervised algorithms are given to learn patterns from scratch. The structure of an eClass0 rule is related to that of eGFC [20] in the consequent sense, i.e., a class label is memorized. However, their learning procedures are completely different, primarily because eGFC learns from partially labeled data. While eClass0 uses focal points as rule antecedents, which are in fact an input data vector, eGFC uses Gaussian membership functions. eClass has shown encouraging results on intrusion detection, and on benchmark problems from the UCI Machine Learning Repository, such as Sonar, Credit Card, Ten-Digit, and Ionosphere. FLEXFIS-Class [36] is another example of a learning method to build models of eClass0 type on the fly. Similarly, its learning equations are fully distinct from those in [35]. New concepts, such as rule confidence and covariance matrix reset, are introduced in [36]. Parsimonious classifier, pClass [37], is a further example, which incorporates ideas such as online feature weighting and datum significance.

A dynamic incremental semi-supervised version of the fuzzy C-means clustering (DISSFCM) algorithm is given in [38]. The method handles streaming data chunks containing partially labeled instances. The total number of clusters is variable by applying a splitting procedure for lower-quality clusters. Incremental semi-supervision as a means to guide the clustering process is discussed. This issue is also addressed in [39], where a fraction of labeled instances is processed by the proposed online micro-cluster-based algorithm. Reliable micro-clusters are updated to represent concept drifts faster. A merging procedure for Gaussian evolving clustering (eGAUSS+) is presented in [40]. The criterion for merging is based on the sum of the volumes of two ellipsoidal clusters that enclose a minimal number of data instances, and the expected volume of the new cluster, which results from merging. Merging has a significant impact on any evolving classifier [22, 40].

A semi-supervised variety of evolving neuro-granular network (eGNN) for numerical data stream classification is given in [41]. The granular network evolves fuzzy hyper-boxes and utilizes null-norm–based neurons to classify data. The Rotation of the Twin Gaussians experiment—a synthetic concept drift—and the Arising of a New Class experiment—a concept shift—have shown the robustness of the granular neural network to non-stationarities. Deep learning methods for partially labeled data-stream classification have also been considered [42, 43]. Some potential problems arise naturally in deeper models since if a model is deep, training all parameters and layers to effectively represent concept changes tends to be a slower process, which requires a larger amount of data related to the new concept.

5.3.2. *Gaussian Functions and eGFC Rule Structure*

Learning in eGFC does not require initial rules. Rules are created and dynamically updated depending on the behavior of the system over time. When a data sample is available, a decision to either add a rule to the model structure or update the parameters of a rule is made. An eGFC rule, say R^i, is

$$\text{IF } \left((x_1 \text{ is } A_1^i) \text{ AND ... AND } (x_n \text{ is } A_n^i)\right), \text{ THEN } (y \text{ is } C^i)$$

in which x_j, $j = 1, \ldots, n$, are features, and y is a class. The data stream is denoted by $(\mathbf{x}, y)^h, h = 1, \ldots$. Moreover, A_j^i, $j = 1, \ldots, n; i = 1, \ldots, c$, are Gaussian membership functions built and updated incrementally; C^i is the class label of the i-th rule. Rules $R^i, i = 1, \ldots, c$, set up a zero-order Takagi–Sugeno rule base. The next sections give a semi-supervised way of constructing an eGFC model online, from scratch. The number of rules, c, is variable, which is a notable characteristic of the approach since guesses on how many data partitions exist are needless [21, 22]. In other words, eGFC rules are added, updated, merged, or removed on demand, i.e., the number of data partitions is automatically chosen by the learning algorithm based on the behavior of the data stream.

A normal Gaussian membership function, $A^i_j = G(\mu^i_j, \sigma^i_j)$, has height 1 [44]. It is characterized by the modal value μ^i_j and dispersion σ^i_j. Characteristics that make Gaussians appropriate include: easiness of learning as modal values and dispersions can be updated straightforwardly from a data stream; infinite support, i.e., since the data are priorly unknown, the support of Gaussians extends to the whole domain; and smooth class boundaries, produced by fuzzy granules obtained by the cylindrical extension and minimum T-norm aggregation of one-dimensional Gaussians [44].

5.3.3. *Adding Fuzzy Rules to the Evolving Classifier*

Rules are created and evolved as data are available. A new granule, γ^{c+1}, and rule, R^{c+1}, are created if none of the existing rules $\{R^1, \ldots, R^c\}$ are sufficiently activated by $\mathbf{x}^h$. Let $\rho^h \in 0, 1$ be an adaptive threshold. If

$$T\left(A^i_1(x^h_1), \ldots, A^i_n(x^h_n)\right) \leq \rho^h, \ \forall i, \ i = 1, \ldots, c, \tag{5.1}$$

in which T is any triangular norm, then the eGFC structure is expanded. The minimum (Gödel) T-norm is used. If ρ^h is set to 0, then eGFC is structurally stable. If ρ^h is equal to 1, eGFC creates a rule for each new sample, which is not practical. Structural and parametric adaptability are balanced for intermediate values (stability–plasticity tradeoff) [25]. ρ^h regulates how large granules can be. Different choices result in different granular perspectives of the same problem. Section 5.3.5 gives an incremental procedure to update ρ^h.

A new γ^{c+1} is initially represented by membership functions, $A^{c+1}_j \forall j$, with

$$\mu^{c+1}_j = x^h_j, \tag{5.2}$$

and

$$\sigma^{c+1}_j = 1/2\pi. \tag{5.3}$$

We call (5.3) the Stigler approach to standard Gaussian functions, or the *maximum approach* [24, 45]. The intuition is to start big, and let the dispersions gradually shrink when new samples activate the same granule. This strategy is appealing for a compact model structure.

In general, the class C^{c+1} of the rule R^{c+1} is initially undefined, i.e., the $(c+1)$-th rule remains unlabeled until a label is provided. If the corresponding output, y^h, associated with $\mathbf{x}^h$, becomes available, then

$$C^{c+1} = y^h. \tag{5.4}$$

Otherwise, the first labeled sample that arrives after the h-th time step, and activates the rule R^{c+1} according to (5.1), is used to define its class.

If a labeled sample activates a rule that is already labeled, but the sample label is different from that of the rule, then a new (partially overlapped) granule and a rule are created to represent new information. Partially overlapped Gaussian granules, tagged with different labels, tend to have their dispersions reduced over time by the parameter adaptation procedure described in Section 5.3.4. The modal values of the Gaussian granules may also drift, if convenient, to a more suitable decision boundary.

With this initial rule parameterization, preference is given to the design of granules balanced along its dimensions, rather than to granules with unbalanced geometry. eGFC realizes the principle of justifiable information granularity [46, 47], but allows the Gaussians to find more appropriate places and dispersions through updating mechanisms.

5.3.4. *Incremental parameter adaptation*

Updating the eGFC model consists in: contracting or expanding Gaussians $A_j^{i^*}$, $j = 1, \ldots, n$, of the most active granule, γ^{i^*}, considering labeled and unlabeled samples; moving granules toward regions of relatively dense population; and tagging rules when labeled data are available. Adaptation aims to develop more specific local models [24, 48] and provide better coverage to new data.

A rule R^i is a candidate to be updated if it is sufficiently activated by an unlabeled sample, $\mathbf{x}^h$, according to

$$min \left(A_1^i(x_1^h), \ldots, A_n^i(x_n^h) \right) > \rho^h. \tag{5.5}$$

Geometrically, $\mathbf{x}^h$ belongs to a region highly influenced by γ^i. Only the most active rule, R^{i^*}, is chosen for adaptation if two or more rules reach the ρ^h level for the unlabeled $\mathbf{x}^h$. For a labeled sample, i.e., for pairs $(\mathbf{x}, y)^h$, the class of the most active rule R^{i^*}, if defined, must match y^h. Otherwise, the second-most active rule among those that reached the ρ^h level is chosen for adaptation, and so on. If none of the rules are apt, then a new one is created (Section 5.3.3).

To include $\mathbf{x}^h$ in R^{i^*}, the learning algorithm updates the modal values and dispersions of the corresponding membership functions $A_j^{i^*}$, $j = 1, \ldots, n$, from

$$\mu_j^{i^*}(new) = \frac{(\varpi^{i^*} - 1)\mu_j^{i^*}(old) + x_j^h}{\varpi^{i^*}}, \qquad (5.6)$$

and

$$\sigma_j^{i^*}(new) = \left(\frac{(\varpi^{i^*} - 1)}{\varpi^{i^*}}\left(\sigma_j^{i^*}(old)\right)^2 + \frac{1}{\varpi^{i^*}}\left(x_j^h - \mu_j^{i^*}(old)\right)^2\right)^{1/2}, \qquad (5.7)$$

in which ϖ^{i^*} is the number of times the i^*-th rule was chosen to be updated. Notice that (5.6)–(5.7) are recursive and, therefore, do not require data storage. As σ^{i^*} defines a convex influence region around μ^{i^*}, very large and very small values may induce, respectively, a unique or too many granules per class. An approach is to keep $\sigma_j^{i^*}$ between a minimum value, $1/(4\pi)$, and the Stigler limit, $1/(2\pi)$ [24].

5.3.5. *Time-Varying Granularity*

Let the activation threshold, ρ^h, be time-varying, similar to [23]. The threshold assumes values in the unit interval according to the overall average dispersion

$$\sigma_{avg}^h = \frac{1}{cn}\sum_{i=1}^{c}\sum_{j=1}^{n}\sigma_j^{ih}, \qquad (5.8)$$

in which c and n are the number of rules and features so that

$$\rho(new) = \frac{\sigma_{avg}^h}{\sigma_{avg}^{h-1}}\rho(old). \qquad (5.9)$$

Given $\mathbf{x}^h$, rule activation levels are compared to ρ^h to decide between parametric and structural changes of the model. In general, eGFC starts learning from scratch and without knowledge of the data properties. Practice suggests $\rho^0 = 0.1$ as starting value. The threshold tends to converge to a proper value after some time steps if the classifier structure and parameters reach a level of maturity and stability. Non-stationarities guide ρ^h to values that better reflect the dynamic behavior of the current environment. A time-varying ρ^h avoids assumptions about how often the data stream changes.

5.3.6. *Merging Similar Rules*

Similarity between two granules with the same class label may be high enough to form a unique granule that inherits the information assigned to the merged granules.

Analysis of inter-granular relations requires a distance measure between Gaussian objects. Let

$$d(\gamma^{i_1}, \gamma^{i_2}) = \frac{1}{n} \left(\sum_{j=1}^{n} |\mu_j^{i_1} - \mu_j^{i_2}| + \sigma_j^{i_1} + \sigma_j^{i_2} - 2\sqrt{\sigma_j^{i_1} \sigma_j^{i_2}} \right) \tag{5.10}$$

be the distance between γ^{i_1} and γ^{i_2}. This measure considers Gaussians and the specificity of information, which is, in turn, inversely related to the Gaussians dispersions [49]. For example, if the dispersions, $\sigma_j^{i_1}$ and $\sigma_j^{i_2}$, differ from one another, rather than being equal, the distance between the underlying Gaussians is larger.

eGFC may merge the pair of granules that presents the smallest value of $d(.)$ for all pairs of granules. The underlying granules must be either unlabeled or tagged with the same class label. The merging decision is based on a threshold, Δ, or expert judgment regarding the suitability of combining granules to have a more compact model. For data within the unit hypercube, we use $\Delta = 0.1$ as the default, which means that the candidate granules should be quite similar and, in fact, carry quite similar information.

A new granule, say γ^i, which results from γ^{i_1} and γ^{i_2}, is built by Gaussians with modal values

$$\mu_j^i = \frac{\frac{\sigma_j^{i_1}}{\sigma_j^{i_2}} \mu_j^{i_1} + \frac{\sigma_j^{i_2}}{\sigma_j^{i_1}} \mu_j^{i_2}}{\frac{\sigma_j^{i_1}}{\sigma_j^{i_2}} + \frac{\sigma_j^{i_2}}{\sigma_j^{i_1}}}, \quad j = 1, \ldots, n, \tag{5.11}$$

and dispersion

$$\sigma_j^i = \sigma_j^{i_1} + \sigma_j^{i_2}, \quad j = 1, \ldots, n. \tag{5.12}$$

These relations take into consideration the uncertainty ratio of the original granules to define the appropriate location and size of the resulting granule. Merging granules minimizes redundancy [21, 22, 40, 50].

5.3.7. Removing Rules

A rule is removed from the eGFC model if it is inconsistent with the current environment. In other words, if a rule is not activated for a number of time steps, say h_r, then it is deleted from the rule base. However, if a class is rare or seasonal behaviors are envisioned, then it may be the case to set $h_r = \infty$, and keep the inactive rules. Additionally, in anomaly detection problems, unusual information granules may be more important than highly operative granules and therefore should not be removed. Removing granules and rules periodically helps keep the knowledge base updated in some applications.

Alternative local-model removing procedures can be mentioned. In [51], clusters are removed based on the size of their support sets. In [52], a rule is removed if it does not contribute to minimizing the estimation error. A combination of age and number of local activations are considered in [53]. The minimal distances allowed between cluster centers are suggested in [54].

5.3.8. *Semi-Supervised Learning from Data Streams*

The semi-supervised learning algorithm to construct and update an eGFC model along its lifespan is as follows.

---

eGFC: Online Semi-Supervised Learning

1: Initial number of rules, $c = 0$;

2: Initial hyper-parameters, $\rho^0 = \Delta = 0.1, h_r = 200$;

3: Read input data sample $\mathbf{x}^h, h = 1$;

4: Create granule γ^{c+1} (Eqs. (5.2)–(5.3)), unknown class C^{c+1};

5: **FOR** $h = 2, \ldots$ **DO**

6:　　Read $\mathbf{x}^h$;

7:　　Calculate rules' activation degree (Eq. (5.1));

8:　　Determine the most active rule R^{i^*};

9:　　Provide estimated class C^{i^*};

10:　　// Model adaptation

11:　　**IF** $T(A_1^i(x_1^h), \ldots, A_n^i(x_n^h)) \leq \rho^h \ \forall i, \ i = 1, \ldots, c$

12:　　　**IF** actual label y^h is available

13:　　　　Create labeled granule γ^{c+1} (Eqs. (5.2)–(5.4));

14:　　　**ELSE**

15:　　　　Create unlabeled granule γ^{c+1} (Eqs. (5.2)–(5.3));

16:　　　**END**

17:　　**ELSE**

18:　　　**IF** actual label y^h is available

19:　　　　Update the most active granule γ^{i^*} with $C^{i^*} = y^h$ (Eqs. (5.6)–(5.7));

20:　　　　Tag unlabeled active granules;

21:　　　**ELSE**

22:　　　　Update the most active γ^{i^*} (Eqs. (5.6)–(5.7));

23:　　　**END**

24:　　**END**

25:　　Update the ρ-level (Eqs. (5.8)–(5.9));

26:　　Delete inactive rules based on h_r;

27:　　Merge granules based on Δ (Eqs. (5.10)–(5.12));

28: **END**

5.4. Methodology

We address the problem of classifying emotions from EEG data streams. We describe a feature extraction method, evaluation measures, and experiments based on individual EEG channels and the multivariable BCI system.

5.4.1. *About the Dataset*

The incremental learning method and the eGFC classifier are evaluated from EEG data streams produced by individuals playing 4 computer games. A game motivates predominantly a particular emotion, according to the 4 quadrants of the arousal–valence system. The aim of the classifier is to assign a class of emotions to new samples. The classes are: bored (Class 1), calm (Class 2), angry (Class 3), and happy (Class 4). The raw data were provided by [27]. The data were produced by 28 individuals (experimental group), from 20 to 27 years old, male and female, including students and faculty members of the School of Technology of Firat University, Turkey. Individuals are healthy, with no disease history. Each individual played each game for 5 minutes (20 minutes in total) using the *Emotiv EPOC+* EEG device and earphones. The male–female (M-F) order of players is

F M M M F F M M M M M F M M M M M F F F F F M M M M M M

A single user-independent eGFC model is developed for the experimental group aiming at reducing individual uncertainty, and enhancing the reliability and generalizability of the system performance. Brain activity is recorded from 14 electrodes. The electrodes are placed on the scalp according to the 10–20 system, namely, at Af3, Af4, F3, F4, F7, F8, Fc5, Fc6, T7, T8, P7, P8, O1, and O2 (Figure 5.1). The sampling frequency is 128 Hz. Each individual produces 38,400 samples per game and 153,600 samples in total.

The experiments were conducted in a relatively dark and quiet room. A laptop with a 15.6 inch screen and a 16 GB graphics card was used to run the games. Maximum screen resolution and high-quality graphic rendering were chosen. The individuals were exposed to a 10-minute period of relaxation before the experiment. They repeatedly kept their eyes open and closed in 10-second intervals. None of the individuals had ever played the games before. The games were played in the same order, namely, Train Sim World, Unravel, Slender: The Arrival, and Goat Simulator. See Figure 5.3 for an illustration. According to a survey, the predominant classes of emotion for each game are, respectively, boredom (Class 1), calmness (Class 2), angriness/nervousness (Class 3), and happiness (Class 4). The classes do not portray a general opinion.

Figure 5.3: Examples of interfaces of the games Train Sim World, Unravel, Slender: The Arrival, and Goat Simulator, used to generate the EEG data streams.

5.4.2. *Feature Extraction and Experiments*

A fifth-order sinc filter is applied to the original raw EEG data to suppress the interference due to head, arms, and hands movement [27]. Subsequently, feature extraction is performed. We generate 10 features from each of the 14 EEG channels. They are the maximum and mean values of five bands of the Fourier spectrum. The bands are known as delta (1–4 Hz), theta (4–8 Hz), alpha (8–13 Hz), beta (13–30 Hz), and gamma (30–64 Hz). If 5-minute time windows over the original data are used to construct the frequency spectrum and extract a processed sample to be fed to eGFC, then each individual produces four samples—one sample per game, i.e., one sample per class or predominant emotion. Therefore, the 28 participants generate 112 processed samples. We also evaluated 1-minute, 30-second, and 10-second time windows, which yielded 560, 1120, and 3360 processed samples. Examples of spectra using 30-second time windows over data streams from frontal electrodes—Af3, Af4, F3, and F4—are illustrated in Figure 5.4. Notice that there is a higher level of energy in the delta, theta, and alpha bands, and that the maximum and mean values per band can be easily obtained to compose a 10-feature processed sample.

We performed two experiments. First, the data stream of individual electrodes is analyzed (univariate time-series analysis). 10-feature samples, $\mathbf{x}^h = x_1 \ldots x_{10}$, $h = 1, \ldots$, are fed to the eGFC model, which evolves from scratch as soon as the data samples arise. We perform the interleaved test-then-train approach, i.e., an eGFC estimate is given; then the true class $C = \{1, 2, 3, 4\}$ of $\mathbf{x}^h$ becomes available, and the pair $(\mathbf{x}, y)$ is used for a supervised learn the step.

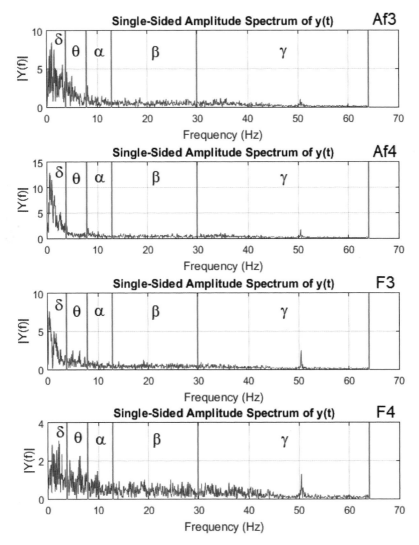

Figure 5.4: Examples of the spectra and bands obtained from the data streams generated by frontal EEG electrodes considering a time window of 30 seconds.

Classification accuracy, $Acc \in 0, 1$, is obtained recursively from

$$Acc(\text{new}) = \frac{h-1}{h} \, Acc(\text{old}) + \frac{1}{h} \, \tau, \tag{5.13}$$

in which $\tau = 1$ if the estimate is correct, i.e., $\hat{C}^h = C^h$; and $\tau = 0$, otherwise. A random (coin flipping) classifier has an expected Acc of 0.25 (25%) in the 4-class problem. Higher values indicate the level of learning from the data, which are quite noisy. From the investigation of individual electrodes, we expect to identify more discriminative areas of the brain.

A measure of model compactness is the average number of fuzzy granules over time,

$$c_{avg}(\text{new}) = \frac{h-1}{h} c_{avg}(\text{old}) + \frac{1}{h} c^h. \tag{5.14}$$

Second, we consider the global 140-feature problem (multivariate time-series analysis)—10 features are extracted from each electrode. Thus, $\mathbf{x}^h = x_1 \ldots x_{140}$, $h = 1, \ldots,$ are initially considered as inputs of the eGFC model. The classification model self-develops on the fly based on the interleaved test-then-train strategy. Dimension reduction is performed using the non-parametric Spearman's correlation-based score method by [49]. Essentially, a feature is better ranked if it is more correlated with a class, and less correlated with the rest of the features. The Leave n-Feature Out strategy, with $n = 5$, is used to gradually eliminate lower-ranked features.

5.5. Results and Discussions

5.5.1. *Individual Electrode Experiment*

We analyze EEG channels separately, as an attempt to uncover more promising regions of the brain to classify emotions in games. Default hyper-parameters are used to initialize eGFC. Input samples contain 10 entries. Table 5.1 shows the accuracy and compactness of eGFC models for different time window lengths.

We notice from Table 5.1 that the average accuracy for 5-minute windows, 21.1%, does not reflect that learning has in fact happened. This suggests that the filtering effect on extracting features from 5-minute windows suppresses crucial details to distinguish patterns related to emotions. Emotions tend to be sustained for shorter periods. Accuracies greater than 25% arise for smaller windows. The average eGFC accuracy for 1-minute windows, around 40.5%, is significant, especially due to the limitation of scanning the data from a single electrode (brain region) at a time. As window length reduces, accuracy increases when using a more compact fuzzy model structure. This is a result of the availability of a larger amount of processed samples (extracted from a smaller number of time windows), and the ability of the online learning algorithm to lead the structure and parameters of the eGFC models to a more stable setup after merging the Gaussian granules that approach each other. The difference between the average accuracy of the 30-second (44.0%) and 10-second (45.2%) time windows becomes small, which suggests saturation around 45–46%. Time windows smaller than 10 seconds tend to be needless.

Asymmetries between the accuracy of models evolved for the left and right brain hemispheres (direct pairs of electrodes) can be noticed. Although the right hemisphere is known to deal with emotional interpretation, and to be responsible

Table 5.1: eGFC classification results for individual electrodes.

5-minute time window

Left hemisphere			Right hemisphere		
Ch	Acc(%)	c_{avg}	Ch	Acc(%)	c_{avg}
Af3	18.8	24.8	Af4	19.6	22.9
F3	23.2	21.3	F4	20.5	21.2
F7	17.0	21.2	F8	25.0	19.1
Fc5	24.1	22.5	Fc6	20.5	19.0
T7	22.3	20.2	T8	24.1	21.2
P7	18.8	21.7	P8	18.8	21.7
O1	21.4	21.9	O2	21.4	21.9
Avg.	20.8	21.9	**Avg.**	21.4	21.0

1-minute time window

Left hemisphere			Right hemisphere		
Ch	Acc(%)	c_{avg}	Ch	Acc(%)	c_{avg}
Af3	43.4	17.3	Af4	41.6	13.1
F3	37.0	14.3	F4	39.6	15.5
F7	41.3	14.5	F8	31.6	10.3
Fc5	38.4	16.1	Fc6	41.8	18.6
T7	43.9	14.4	T8	50.4	15.9
P7	37.9	17.4	P8	33.8	15.7
O1	45.0	16.3	O2	40.5	16.6
Avg.	41.0	15.8	**Avg.**	39.9	15.1

30-second time window

Left hemisphere			Right hemisphere		
Ch	Acc(%)	c_{avg}	Ch	Acc(%)	c_{avg}
Af3	51.3	11.7	Af4	43.9	8.9
F3	40.5	10.3	F4	42.9	8.8
F7	44.2	10.3	F8	37.5	6.7
Fc5	41.3	10.8	Fc6	44.7	11.6
T7	40.4	10.2	T8	49.6	11.3
P7	46.3	9.4	P8	42.7	10.3
O1	45.9	10.1	O2	44.7	12.8
Avg.	44.3	10.4	**Avg.**	43.7	10.1

10-second time window

Left hemisphere			Right hemisphere		
Ch	Acc(%)	c_{avg}	Ch	Acc(%)	c_{avg}
Af3	52.6	6.3	Af4	44.0	5.5
F3	41.8	6.1	F4	43.8	5.9
F7	46.3	6.1	F8	40.2	4.8
Fc5	40.5	5.7	Fc6	46.8	6.8
T7	40.4	5.7	T8	51.5	6.2
P7	46.9	6.7	P8	45.2	6.5
O1	47.7	6.6	O2	45.2	7.0
Avg.	45.2	6.2	**Avg.**	45.2	6.1

for creativity and intuition; logical interpretation of situations—typical of the left hemisphere—is also present, as players seek reasons to justify decisions. Therefore, we notice the emergence of patterns in both hemispheres.

In general, with an emphasis on the 30-second and 10-second windows, the pair of electrodes Af3–Af4, in the frontal lobe, gives the best pattern recognition results, especially Af3, in the left hemisphere. The frontal lobe is the largest of the four major lobes of the brain. It is covered by the frontal cortex. The frontal cortex includes the premotor cortex and the primary motor cortex, which controls voluntary movements of specific body parts. Therefore, patterns that arise from the Af3–Af4 data streams may be strongly related to the brain commands to move hands and arms, which is indirectly related to the emotions of the players. A spectator, instead of a game actor, may have a classification model based solely on Af3–Af4 with diminished accuracy. The pair Af3–Af4 is closely followed by the pairs O1–O2 (occipital lobe) and T7–T8 (temporal lobe), which is somehow consistent with the results in [6–8]. The temporal lobe is useful for audition, language processing, declarative memory, and visual and emotional perception. The occipital lobe contains the primary visual cortex and areas of visual association. Neighbor electrodes, P7 and P8, also offer relevant information for classification.

According to [55],EEG asymmetry is related to approaching and withdrawal emotions, with approaching trends reflected in left-frontal activity and withdrawal trends reflected in relative right-frontal activity. The similar average accuracy between the brain hemispheres, reported in Table 5.1, portrays a mixture of approaching and withdrawal emotional patterns, typical of game playing. In [13], differential and rational asymmetries are considered to be input features of classifiers to assist recognition. Further discussions on asymmetries require more specific steady-state experiments and are therefore out of the scope of this study.

5.5.2. *Multivariate Experiment*

The multivariate 140-feature data stream is fed to eGFC. We take into account 10-second time windows over 20-minute recordings per individual—the best average set up secured in the previous experiment. Features are ranked based on Spearman's correlation score [49]. We use {channel, band, attribute} as notation to order the features from the most to the least important. Results are shown in Table 5.2. The bands are given in Greek letters for short. We observe from Table 5.2 a prevalence of alpha-band features in the first positions, followed by delta features and, then, Theta features. In other words, these bands are the most monotonically correlated to the games and their classes. To provide quantitative experimental evidence, we sum the monotonic correlations between a band and the classes of emotions (the sum of the 14 items that correspond to the 14 EEG channels). Figure 5.5 shows the

Table 5.2:   Ranking of features.

# Rank {channel, band, attribute}			
1:{F4,α,max}	2:{FC6,α,max}	3:{AF3,α,max}	4:{F7,α,max}
5:{O2,α,avg}	6:{T8,α,max}	7:{AF4,α,max}	8:{O2,δ,max}
9:{F3,θ,max}	10:{F3,δ,max}	11:{T8,δ,max}	12:{F3,δ,avg}
13:{T7,α,max}	14:{O2,α,max}	15:{P7,δ,avg}	16:{FC5,α,max}
17:{O2,θ,avg}	18:{P8,α,max}	19:{T7,δ,avg}	20:{T8,δ,avg}
21:{P7,α,max}	22:{T8,θ,max}	23:{F3,α,max}	24:{T8,θ,avg}
25:{F8,α,max}	26:{F3,θ,avg}	27:{FC6,α,avg}	28:{O1,α,max}
29:{T7,θ,avg}	30:{T7,δ,max}	31:{P7,δ,max}	32:{T8,α,avg}
33:{AF3,α,avg}	34:{AF3,θ,max}	35:{FC5,δ,max}	36:{F4,α,avg}
37:{AF3,θ,avg}	38:{AF4,α,avg}	39:{F7,θ,avg}	40:{F7,θ,max}
41:{O2,γ,max}	42:{AF4,δ,avg}	43:{AF4,θ,max}	44:{AF4,θ,avg}
45:{T7,β,max}	46:{F8,γ,avg}	47:{F3,α,avg}	48:{FC6,θ,avg}
49:{F8,β,avg}	50:{AF4,δ,max}	51:{P7,θ,avg}	52:{T7,θ,max}
53:{P8,δ,max}	54:{O2,α,avg}	55:{AF3,β,avg}	56:{AF3,β,max}
57:{F7,δ,avg}	58:{AF3,δ,avg}	59:{P8,δ,avg}	60:{FC6,δ,max}
61:{FC6,θ,max}	62:{F7,α,avg}	63:{F4,θ,max}	64:{FC5,β,avg}
65:{F4,β,avg}	66:{O1,γ,avg}	67:{FC5,γ,avg}	68:{F4,γ,max}
69:{F8,α,avg}	70:{O2,θ,max}	71:{F7,δ,max}	72:{T8,γ,avg}
73:{T7,γ,avg}	74:{P8,θ,max}	75:{T8,γ,max}	76:{FC5,θ,max}
77:{O2,β,avg}	78:{O1,α,avg}	79:{F3,β,avg}	80:{P8,β,max}
81:{T7,γ,max}	82:{F8,γ,max}	83:{FC5,θ,avg}	84:{P7,α,avg}
85:{O1,β,avg}	86:{P7,θ,max}	87:{O1,δ,avg}	88:{FC5,γ,max}
89:{T8,β,max}	90:{AF3,γ,max}	91:{FC6,δ,avg}	92:{F7,γ,avg}
93:{FC5,α,avg}	94:{O1,θ,avg}	95:{O1,θ,max}	96:{AF4,β,avg}
97:{FC5,δ,avg}	98:{F4,β,max}	99:{F4,δ,max}	100:{F8,β,max}
101:{O2,β,max}	102:{FC6,β,max}	103:{F7,γ,max}	104:{P8,β,avg}
105:{FC6,β,avg}	106:{F8,θ,avg}	107:{AF3,γ,avg}	108:{O1,β,max}
109:{F8,δ,avg}	110:{AF3,δ,max}	111:{P7,β,max}	112:{T7,α,avg}
113:{F4,θ,avg}	114:{P8,θ,avg}	115:{FC6,γ,max}	116:{F4,γ,avg}
117:{F7,β,max}	118:{FC6,γ,avg}	119:{P8,α,avg}	120:{F8,θ,max}
121:{F4,δ,avg}	122:{F3,γ,avg}	123:{F8,δ,max}	124:{T8,β,avg}
125:{AF4,β,max}	126:{P7,γ,avg}	127:{F3,γ,max}	128:{P8,γ,max}
129:{O1,γ,max}	130:{O1,δ,max}	131:{AF4,γ,max}	132:{O2,γ,avg}
133:{T7,β,avg}	134:{FC5,β,max}	135:{P7,γ,max}	136:{P7,β,avg}
137:{F7,β,avg}	138:{F3,β,max}	139:{AF4,γ,avg}	140:{P8,γ,avg}

result in dark yellow, and its decomposition per brain hemisphere. The global values are precisely 2.2779, 1.7478, 1.3759, 0.6639, and 0.6564 for the alpha, delta, theta, beta, and gamma bands, respectively.

Finally, we apply the strategy of leaving five features out at a time to evaluate single user-independent eGFC models. Each eGFC model delineates classification boundaries in a different multi-dimensional space. Table 5.3 shows the eGFC overall results for the multi-channel data streams. A quadcore laptop, i7-8550U, with 1.80 GHz, 8 GB RAM, and Windows 10 OS, is used.

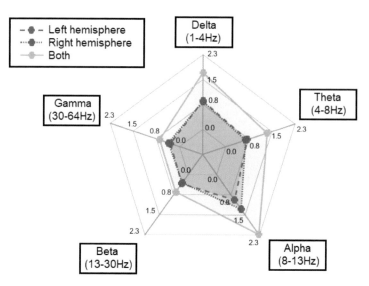

Figure 5.5: Spearman (monotonic) correlation between frequency bands and classes per brain hemisphere.

From Table 5.3, we testify that spatio-temporal patterns of brain activity are found in all bands of the Fourier spectrum, viz., delta, theta, alpha, beta, and gamma bands, as even lower ranked features positively affect the eGFC estimates. Features from any EEG channel may eventually assist in the classifier decision. The greatest eGFC accuracy, namely 72.20%, happens using all features extracted from the frequency spectrum. In this case, a stream of 3,360 samples is processed in 6.032 seconds (1.8 ms per sample, on average). As a sample is produced every 10 s (10-second time windows) and processed in 1.8 ms, we have shown that eGFC manages to operate in real time with much larger rule bases and Big data streams, such as streams generated by additional electrodes, and other physiological and non-physiological means, e.g., biosensors and facial images.

The average number of fuzzy rules, about 5.5, along the learning steps is similar for all the streams analyzed (see Table 5.3). An example of eGFC structural evolution (best case, 72.20%) is shown in Figure 5.6. Notice that the emphasis of the model and algorithm is to keep a high accuracy during online operation at the price of merging and deleting the rules occasionally. If a higher level of model memory is desired, i.e., a greater number of fuzzy rules is wanted, then the default eGFC hyper-parameters can be changed by turning off the rule removing threshold, $h_r = \infty$; and setting the merging parameter, Δ, to a lower value.

Figure 5.6 also shows that the effect of male–female shifts due to the consecutive use of the EEG device by different subjects of the experimental group does not necessarily imply a need for completely new granules and rules by the eGFC

Table 5.3:   eGFC classification results of online emotion recognition.

# Features	Acc (%)	c_{avg}	CPU Time (s)
140	72.20	5.52	6.032
135	71.10	5.70	5.800
130	71.46	5.68	5.642
125	71.25	5.75	5.624
120	70.89	5.79	5.401
115	70.92	5.68	5.193
110	70.68	5.73	4.883
105	70.68	5.71	4.676
100	70.24	5.78	4.366
95	70.12	5.69	4.290
90	69.91	5.66	3.983
85	66.31	5.53	3.673
80	65.09	5.45	3.534
75	65.48	5.26	3.348
70	64.08	5.26	2.950
65	63.42	5.37	2.775
60	62.56	5.33	2.684
55	60.95	5.33	2.437
50	60.57	5.57	2.253
45	60.39	5.53	2.135
40	54.13	5.14	1.841
35	52.29	5.28	1.591
30	52.52	5.54	1.511
25	50.95	5.61	1.380
20	51.42	5.58	1.093
15	49.28	5.57	0.923
10	48.63	5.58	0.739

model. Parametric adaptation of Gaussian granules is often enough to accommodate slightly different behavior. For example, the shifts from the sixth (female) to the seventh (male) players and from the seventh to the eighth (male) players did not require new rules. Nevertheless, if a higher level of memory is allowed, the rules for both genders can be maintained separately. Figure 5.7 illustrates the confusion matrix of the best eGFC model. We notice a relative balance of wrong estimates per class and confusion of estimates in all directions.

As Table 5.3 shows a snapshot of the eGFC performance in the last time step, $h = 3360$, in Figure 5.8 we provide the evolution of the accuracy index over time, i.e., from $h = 1$ to $h = 3360$, considering the eGFC model structure shown in Figure 5.6. The idea is to emphasize the online learning capability of the classifier. Notice that eGFC starts learning from scratch, with zero accuracy. After about 100 time steps, the estimation accuracy reaches a value of around 81.90%. The

F M M M F F M M M M M F M M M M F F F F F M M M M M M M
# of rules
Time step h
F: Female
M: Male
0
2
4
6
8
10
12
0
500
1000
1500
2000
2500
3000
3500

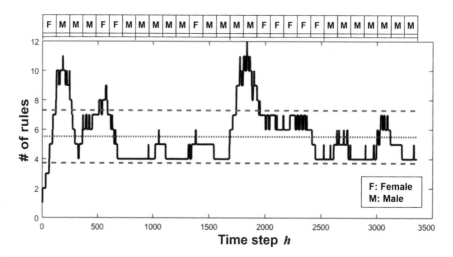

Figure 5.6: Structural evolution of the user-independent eGFC model from data streams of 28 players.

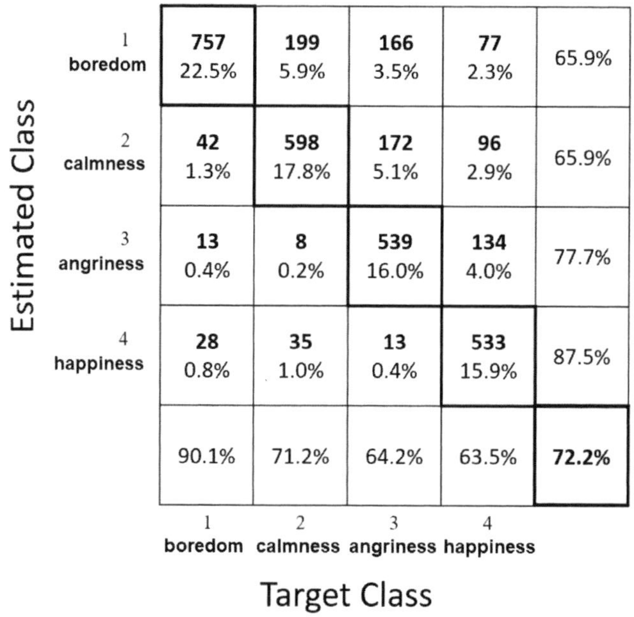

Estimated Class
1 boredom
757 22.5%
199 5.9%
166 3.5%
77 2.3%
65.9%
2 calmness
42 1.3%
598 17.8%
172 5.1%
96 2.9%
65.9%
3 angriness
13 0.4%
8 0.2%
539 16.0%
134 4.0%
77.7%
4 happiness
28 0.8%
35 1.0%
13 0.4%
533 15.9%
87.5%
90.1%
71.2%
64.2%
63.5%
72.2%
1 boredom
2 calmness
3 angriness
4 happiness
Target Class

Figure 5.7: Confusion matrix of the best eGFC model, $Acc = 72.20\%$.

information from multiple users is captured by updating the model parameters and often the model architecture. The mean accuracy along the time steps is kept around 75.08% ± 3.32% in spite of the nonstationary nature of the EEG data generated by multiple users playing games of different styles. Therefore, the eGFC model is user independent. User-dependent eGFC models are generally more accurate, such

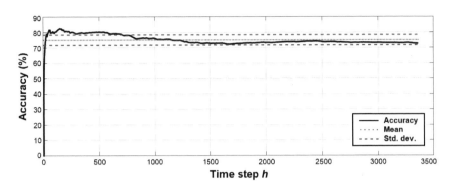

Figure 5.8:   Accuracy of the user-independent eGFC model over time.

as the 81.90%-accurate model developed for the first female user. In general, the empirical results—using EEG streams as the unique physiological source of data—and evolving fuzzy intelligence are encouraging for emotion pattern recognition.

5.6. Conclusion

We have evaluated an online incremental learning method that constructs and updates a fuzzy classifier from data streams. The classifier, called eGFC, is applied to real-time recognition of emotions in computer games.

A group of 28 people play Train Sim World, Unravel, Slender: The Arrival, and Goat Simulator (visual and auditory stimuli) for 20 minutes each, using an EEG device. An emotion prevails in each game, i.e., boredom, calmness, angriness, or happiness, which agrees with the arousal–valence system. A set of 140 features is extracted from the frequency spectrum produced by temporal data from 14 electrodes located in different brain regions. We analyzed the delta, theta, alpha, beta, and gamma bands, from 1 to 64 Hz. We examined the contribution of single electrodes to emotion recognition, and the effect of time window lengths and dimensionality reduction on the overall accuracy of the eGFC models.

We conclude that: (i) electrodes on both brain hemispheres assist the recognition of emotions expressed through a variety of spatio-temporal patterns; (ii) the frontal (Af3–Af4) area, followed by the occipital (O1–O2) and temporal (T7–T8) areas are, in this order, slightly more discerning than the others; (iii) although patterns may be found in any frequency band, the alpha (8–13 Hz) band, followed by the delta (1–4 Hz) and theta (4–8 Hz) bands, is more monotonically correlated with the emotion classes; (iv) the eGFC incremental learning method is able to process 140-feature samples using 1.8 ms per sample, on average. Thus, eGFC is suitable for real-time applications considering EEG and other sources of data simultaneously; (v) a greater number of features covering the entire spectrum and the use of 10-second time windows lead eGFC to its best performance, i.e., to 72.20% accuracy using

4 to 12 fuzzy granules and rules along the time steps. Such an eGFC model is general, i.e., it is user independent. We notice that a user-dependent eGFC model—based on the first female player—has been shown to be about 81.90% accurate, as expected due to a more restrictive experimental setting and model customization. Further studies on customized models for specific users are needed—as this capability of evolving granular methods is promising. In the future, wavelet transforms shall be evaluated with a focus on specific bands. A deep neural network, playing the role of feature extractor in high-dimension spaces, will be connected to eGFC for real-time emotion recognition. We also intend to evaluate an ensemble of customized evolving classifiers for benchmark EEG datasets.

Acknowledgement

This work received support from the Serrapilheira Institute (Serra 1812-26777) and from the National Council for Scientific and Technological Development (CNPq 308464/2020-6).

References

[1] M. Alarcao and M. J. Fonseca, Emotions recognition using EEG signals: a survey, *IEEE Trans. Affect. Comput.*, **10**(3), pp. 374–393 (2019).

[2] Y. Liu, O. Sourina and M. K. Nguyen, Real-time EEG-based emotion recognition and its applications, *Trans. Comput. Sci. XII (LNCS)*, **6670**, pp. 256–277 (2011).

[3] T. Song, W. Zheng, P. Song and Z. Cui, EEG emotion recognition using dynamical graph convolutional neural networks, *IEEE Trans. Affect. Comput.*, **11**(3), pp. 532–541 (2020).

[4] G. Vasiljevic and L. Miranda, Braincomputer interface games based on consumer-grade EEG devices: a systematic literature review, *Int. J. Hum.-Comput. Interact.*, **36**(2), pp. 105–142 (2020).

[5] L.-W. Ko, Y.-C. Lu, H. Bustince, Y.-C. Chang, Y. Chang, J. Ferandez, Y.-K. Wang, J. A. Sanz, G. P. Dimuro and C.-T. Lin, Multimodal fuzzy fusion for enhancing the motor-imagery-based brain computer interface, *IEEE Comput. Intell. Mag.*, **14**(1), p. 96106 (2019).

[6] X. Li, D. Song, P. Zhang, Y. Zhang, Y. Hou and B. Hu, Exploring EEG features in cross-subject emotion recognition, *Front. Neurosci.*, **12**, pp. 162–176 (2018), doi: 10.3389/fnins.2018.00162.

[7] M. Soleymani, M. Pantic and T. Pun, Multimodal emotion recognition in response to videos, *IEEE Trans. Affect. Comput.*, **3**(2), pp. 211–223 (2012).

[8] W.-L. Zheng, J.-Y. Zhu and B.-L. Lu, Identifying stable patterns over time for emotion recognition from EEG, *IEEE Trans. Affect. Comput.*, **10**(3), pp. 417–429 (2019).

[9] B. Nakisa, M. Rastgoo, D. Tjondronegoro and V. Chandran, Evolutionary computation algorithms for feature selection of EEG-based emotion recognition using mobile sensors, *Expert Syst. Appl.*, **93**(1), pp. 143–155 (2018).

[10] N. Zhuang, Y. Zeng, l. Tong, C. Zhang, H. Zhang and B. Yan, Emotion recognition from EEG signals using multidimensional information in EMD domain, *BioMed Res. Int.*, **2017**, pp. 1–9 (2017), doi:10.1155/2017/8317357.

[11] W.-L. Zheng and B.-L. Lu, Investigating critical frequency bands and channels for EEG-based emotion recognition with deep neural networks, *IEEE Trans. Auton. Ment. Dev.*, **7**(3), pp. 162–175 (2015).

[12] X. Gu, Z. Cao, A. Jolfaei, P. Xu, D. Wu, T.-P. Jung and C.-T. Lin, EEG-based brain-computer interfaces (BCIs): a survey of recent studies on signal sensing technologies and computational intelligence approaches and their applications, *arXiv:2001.11337*, p. 22 (2020).

[13] H. P. Martinez, Y. Bengio and G. N. Yannakakis, Learning deep physiological models of affect, *IEEE Comput. Intell. Mag.*, **8**(2), p. 2033 (2013).

[14] M. Wu, W. Su, L. Chen, W. Pedrycz and K. Hirota, Two-stage fuzzy fusion based-convolution neural network for dynamic emotion recognition, *IEEE Trans. Affect. Comput.*, pp. 1–1 (2020), doi:10.1109/TAFFC.2020.2966440.

[15] Y. Zhang, Z. Yang, H. Lu, X. Zhou, P. Phillips, Q. Liu and S. Wang, Facial emotion recognition based on biorthogonal wavelet entropy, fuzzy support vector machine, and stratified cross validation, *IEEE Access*, **4**, pp. 8375–8385 (2016).

[16] G. Lee, M. Kwon, S. Kavuri and M. Lee, Emotion recognition based on 3D fuzzy visual and EEG features in movie clips, *Neurocomputing*, **144**, pp. 560–568 (2014), doi: 10.1016/j.neucom.2014.04.008.

[17] Z. Cao and C.-T. Lin, Inherent fuzzy entropy for the improvement of EEG complexity evaluation, *IEEE Trans. Fuzzy Syst.*, **26**(2), p. 10321035 (2017).

[18] D. Wu, V. J. Lawhern, S. Gordon, B. J. Lance and C.-T. Lin, Driver drowsiness estimation from EEG signals using online weighted adaptation regularization for regression (OwARR), *IEEE Trans. Fuzzy Syst.*, **25**(6), p. 15221535 (2016a).

[19] S.-L. Wu, Y.-T. Liu, T.-Y. Hsieh, Y.-Y. Lin, C.-Y. Chen, C.-H. Chuang and C.-T. Lin, Fuzzy integral with particle swarm optimization for a motor-imagery-based brain-computer interface, *IEEE Trans. Fuzzy Syst.*, **25**(1), p. 2128 (2016b).

[20] D. Leite, L. Decker, M. Santana and P. Souza, EGFC: evolving Gaussian fuzzy classifier from never-ending semi-supervised data streams — with application to power quality disturbance detection and classification, in *IEEE World Congress Computational Intelligence (WCCI-FUZZ-IEEE)*, pp. 1–8 (2020).

[21] D. Leite, Evolving granular systems, Ph.D. thesis, School of Electrical and Computer Eng., University of Campinas (UNICAMP) (2012).

[22] I. Skrjanc, J. A. Iglesias, A. Sanchis, D. Leite, E. Lughofer and F. Gomide, Evolving fuzzy and neuro-fuzzy approaches in clustering, regression, identification, and classification: a survey. *Inf. Sci.*, **490**, pp. 344–368 (2019).

[23] C. Garcia, D. Leite and I. Skrjanc, Incremental missing-data imputation for evolving fuzzy granular prediction, *IEEE Trans. Fuzzy Syst.*, **28**(10), pp. 2348–2362 (2020).

[24] D. Leite, G. Andonovski, I. Skrjanc and F. Gomide, Optimal rule-based granular systems from data streams, *IEEE Trans. Fuzzy Syst.*, **28**(3), pp. 583–596 (2020).

[25] D. Leite, P. Costa and F. Gomide, Evolving granular neural networks from fuzzy data streams, *Neural Networks*, **38**, pp. 1–16 (2013).

[26] L. Decker, D. Leite, L. Giommi and D. Bonacorsi, Real-time anomaly detection in data centers for log-based predictive maintenance using an evolving fuzzy-rule-based approach, in *IEEE World Congress on Computational Intelligence (WCCI-FUZZ-IEEE)*, p. 8 (2020).

[27] T. B. Alakus, M. Gonenb and I. Turkogluc, Database for an emotion recognition system based on EEG signals and various computer games — GAMEEMO, *Biomed. Signal Process. Control*, **60**, p. 101951 (12p) (2020).

[28] L. Alonso and J. Gomez-Gil, Brain computer interfaces, a review, *Sensors*, **12**(2), pp. 1211–1279 (2012).

[29] M. Fatourechi, A. Bashashati, R. K. Ward and G. E. Birch, EMG and EOG artifacts in brain computer interface systems: a survey, *Clin. Neurophysiol.*, **118**(3), pp. 480–494 (2007).

[30] A. Ferreira, *et al.*, A survey of interactive systems based on brain-computer interfaces, *JIS*, **4**(1), pp. 3–13 (2013).

[31] C.-M. Kim, G.-H. Kang and E.-S. Kim, A study on the generation method of visual-auditory feedback for BCI rhythm game, *J. Korea Game Soc.*, **13**(6), pp. 15–26 (2013).

[32] J. Russell, A circumplex model of affect, *J. Pers. Soc. Psychol.*, **39**(6), pp. 1161–1178 (1980).

[33] J. Frome, Eight ways videogames generate emotion, *DiGRA Conf.*, pp. 831–835 (2007).

[34] L. Fedwa, M. Eid and A. Saddik, An overview of serious games, *Int. J. Comput. Game Technol.*, **2014**, p. 15 (2014).

[35] P. Angelov and X. Zhou, Evolving fuzzy-rule-based classifiers from data streams, *IEEE Trans. Fuzzy Syst.*, **16**(6), pp. 1462–1475 (2008).

[36] P. Angelov, E. Lughofer and X. Zhou, Evolving fuzzy classifiers using different model architectures, *Fuzzy Sets Syst.*, **159**(23), pp. 3160–3182 (2008).

[37] M. Pratama, S. Anavatti, M. Er and E. Lughofer, pClass: an effective classifier for streaming examples, *IEEE Trans. Fuzzy Syst.*, **23**(2), pp. 369–386 (2015).

[38] G. Casalino, G. Castellano and C. Mencar, Data stream classification by dynamic incremental semi-supervised fuzzy clustering, *Int. J. Artif. Intell. Tools*, **28**(8), p. 1960009 (26p) (2019).

[39] S. U. Din, J. Shao, J. Kumar, W. Ali, J. Liu and Y. Ye, Online reliable semi-supervised learning on evolving data streams, *Inf. Sci.*, **525**, pp. 153–171 (2020).

[40] I. Skrjanc, Cluster-volume-based merging approach for incrementally evolving fuzzy Gaussian clustering: eGAUSS+, *IEEE Trans. Fuzzy Syst.*, **28**(9), pp. 2222–2231 (2020).

[41] D. Leite, P. Costa and F. Gomide, Evolving granular neural network for semi-supervised data stream classification, in *International Joint Conference on Neural Networks (IJCNN)*, p. 8p (2010).

[42] Y. Li, Y. Wang, Q. Liu, C. Bi, X. Jiang and S. Sun, Incremental semi-supervised learning on streaming data, *Pattern Recognit.*, **88**, pp. 383–396 (2019).

[43] J. Read, F. Perez-Cruz and A. Bifet, Deep learning in partially-labeled data streams, in *30th Annual ACM Symposium on Applied Computing*, pp. 954–959 (2015).

[44] W. Pedrycz and F. Gomide, *Fuzzy Systems Engineering: Toward Human-Centric Computing*, 1st edn. Wiley: Hoboken, New Jersey (2007).

[45] S. M. Stigler, A modest proposal: a new standard for the normal, *Am. Stat.*, **36**(2), pp. 137–138 (1982).

[46] W. Pedrycz and W. Homenda, Building the fundamentals of granular computing: a principle of justifiable granularity, *Appl. Soft Comput.*, **13**(10), pp. 4209–4218 (2013).

[47] X. Wang, W. Pedrycz, A. Gacek and X. Liu, From numeric data to information granules: a design through clustering and the principle of justifiable granularity, *Knowl.-Based Syst.*, **101**, p. 100113 (2016).

[48] R. Yager, Measures of specificity over continuous spaces under similarity relations, *Fuzzy Sets Syst.*, **159**, pp. 2193–2210 (2008).

[49] E. Soares, P. Costa, B. Costa and D. Leite, Ensemble of evolving data clouds and fuzzy models for weather time series prediction, *Appl. Soft Comput.*, **64**, p. 445453 (2018).

[50] E. Lughofer, J.-L. Bouchot and A. Shaker, On-line elimination of local redundancies in evolving fuzzy systems, *Evolving Syst.*, **2**(3), pp. 165–187 (2011).

[51] P. Angelov, Evolving Takagi-Sugeno fuzzy systems from streaming data, eTS+, in P. Angelov, D. Filev and N. Kasabov (eds.), *Evolving Intelligent Systems: Methodology and Applications*. John Wiley & Sons, pp. 21–50 (2010).

[52] H. J. Rong, N. Sundararajan, G. B. Huang and P. Saratchandran, Sequential adaptive fuzzy inference system (SAFIS) for nonlinear system identification and prediction, *Fuzzy Sets Syst.*, **157**(9), pp. 1260–1275 (2006).

[53] N. Kasabov, Evolving fuzzy neural networks for supervised/unsupervised online knowledge-based learning, *IEEE Trans. Syst. Man Cybern. Part B: Cybern.*, **31**(6), pp. 902–918 (2001).

[54] B. H. Soleimani, C. Lucas and B. N. Araabi, Recursive Gath-Geva clustering as a basis for evolving neuro-fuzzy modeling, *Evolving Syst.*, **1**(1), pp. 59–71 (2010).

[55] R. J. Davidson, Anterior cerebral asymmetry and the nature of emotion, *Brain Cogn.*, **20**(1), p. 125151 (1992).

Chapter 6

Causal Inference in Medicine and in Health Policy: A Summary

Wenhao Zhang*, Ramin Ramezani[†], and Arash Naeim[‡]

Center for Smart Health, University of California, Los Angeles
*wenhaoz@g.ucla.edu
[†]raminr@ucla.edu
[‡]ANaeim@mednet.ucla.edu

A data science task can be deemed as making sense of the data or testing a hypothesis about it. The conclusions inferred from the data can greatly guide us in making informative decisions. Big Data have enabled us to carry out countless prediction tasks in conjunction with machine learning, such as to identify high-risk patients suffering from a certain disease and take preventable measures. However, healthcare practitioners are not content with mere predictions; they are also interested in the cause–effect relation between input features and clinical outcomes. Understanding such relations will help doctors to treat patients and reduce the risk effectively. Causality is typically identified by randomized controlled trials. Often, such trials are not feasible when scientists and researchers turn to observational studies and attempt to draw inferences. However, observational studies may also be affected by selection and/or confounding biases that can result in wrong causal conclusions. In this chapter, we will try to highlight some of the drawbacks that may arise in traditional machine learning and statistical approaches to analyzing the observational data, particularly in the healthcare data analytics domain. We will discuss causal inference and ways to discover the cause–effect from observational studies in the healthcare domain. Moreover, we will demonstrate the application of causal inference in tackling some common machine learning issues such as missing data and model transportability. Finally, we will discuss the possibility of integrating reinforcement learning with causality as a way to counter confounding bias.

6.1. What Is Causality and Why Does It Matter?

In this section, we introduce the concept of causality and discuss why causal reasoning is of paramount importance in analyzing data that arise in various domains such as healthcare and social sciences.

6.1.1. *What Is Causality?*

The truism "Correlation does not imply causation" is well known and generally acknowledged [2, 3]. The question is how to define "causality."

6.1.2. *David Hume's Definition*

The eighteenth-century philosopher David Hume defined causation in the language of the counterfactual: A is a cause of B, if:

(1) B is always observed to follow A, and
(2) If A had not been, B had never existed [4].

In the former case, A is a *sufficient causation* of B, and A is a *necessary causation* of B in the latter case [5]. When both conditions are satisfied, we can safely say that A causes B (*necessary-and-sufficient causation*). For example, sunrise causes a rooster' crow. This cause–effect relation cannot be described the other way around. If the rooster is sick, the sunrise still occurs. The rooster's crow is not a *necessary causation* of sunrise. Hence, the rooster's crow is an effect rather than the cause of sunrise.

6.1.3. *Causality in Medical Research*

In medical research, the logical description of causality is considered too rigorous and is occasionally not applicable. For example, smoking does not always lead to lung cancer. Causality in medical literature is often expressed in probabilistic terms [6, 49]. A type of chemotherapy treatment might increase the likelihood of survival of a patient diagnosed with cancer, but does not guarantee it. Therefore, we express our beliefs about the uncertainty of the real world in the language of probability.

One main reason for probabilistic thinking is that we can easily quantify our beliefs in numeric values and build probabilistic models to explain the cause, given our observation. In clinical diagnosis, doctors often seek the most plausible hypothesis (disease) that explains the evidence (symptom). Assume that a doctor observes a certain symptom S, and he or she has two explanations for this symptom, disease A or disease B. If this doctor can quantify his or her belief into conditional probabilities, i.e., *Prob*(*disease A* | *Symptom S*) and *Prob*(*disease B* | *Symptom S*) (the likelihood of disease A or B may occur, given that the symptom S is observed). Then, the doctor can choose the explanation that has a larger value of conditional probability.

6.1.4. *The Dilemma: Potential Outcome Framework*

When we study the causal effect of a new treatment, we are interested in how the disease responds when we "intervene" upon it. For example, a patient is likely to recover from cancer when receiving a new type of chemotherapy treatment.

To measure the causal effect on this particular patient, we shall compare the outcome of treatment to the outcome of no treatment. However, it is not possible to observe the two *potential outcomes* of the same patient at once, because this comparison is made using two parallel universes we imagine: (1) a universe where the patient is treated with the new chemotherapy and (2) the other where he or she is not treated. There is always one universe missing. This dilemma is known as the "fundamental problem of causal inference."

6.2. Why Causal Inference

A data science task can be deemed as making sense of the data or testing a hypothesis about it. The conclusions inferred from data can greatly guide us to make informative decisions. Big Data have enabled us to carry out countless prediction tasks in conjunction with machine learning. However, there exists a large gap between highly accurate predictions and decision making. For example, an interesting study [1] reports that there is a "surprisingly powerful correlation" ($\rho = 0.79$, $p < 0.0001$) between the chocolate consumption and the number of Nobel laureates in a country (Figure 6.1). The policy makers might hesitate to promote chocolate consumption as a way of obtaining more Nobel prizes. The developed Western countries where people eat more chocolate are more likely to have better education systems, and chocolate consumption has no direct impact on the number of Nobel laureates. As such, intervening on chocolate cannot possibly lead us to the desired outcome. In Section 6.3, we will explore more examples of the spurious correlations explained by confounders (in statistics, a confounder is a variable that impacts a dependent variable as well as an independent variable at the same time, causing a spurious correlation [67]) and how to use causal inference to gauge the real causal effect between variables under such circumstances.

In predictive tasks, understanding of causality, the mechanism through which an outcome is produced, will yield more descriptive models with better performance. In machine learning, for instance, one underlying assumption, generally, is that training and testing datasets have identical or at least comparable characteristics/distributions. This assumption is often violated in practice. For example, an activity recognition model built on a training cohort of highly active participants might perform poorly if it is applied over a cohort of bedridden elderly patients. In this example, the variables *age* and *mobility* are the causes that explain the difference between the two datasets. Therefore, understanding causality between various features and outcomes is an integral part of a robust and generalized machine learning model. Often, most statistical models rely upon pure correlations perform well under static conditions where the characteristics of the dataset are invariant. Once the context changes, such correlations may no longer exist. On the contrary, relying on the causal relations between variables can produce models less prone to change

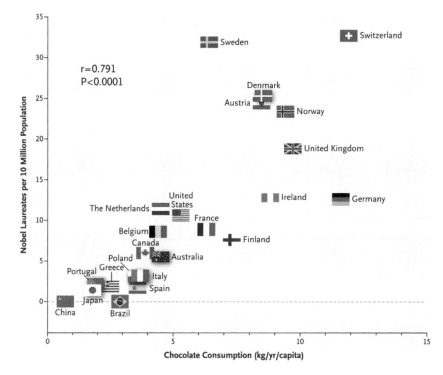

Figure 6.1: A spurious correlation between the chocolate consumption and the number of Nobel laureates by countries [1].

with context. In Section 4, we will discuss the external validity and transportability of machine learning models.

In many real-world data analytics, in addition to relying solely on statistical relations among data elements, it is essential for machine learning practitioners to ask questions surrounding "causal intervention" and "counterfactual reasoning," questions such as "What would Y be if I do X?" (causal intervention) or "Would the outcome change if I had acted differently?" (counterfactual). Suppose that one wants to find the effects of wine consumption on heart disease. We certainly live in a world in which we cannot run randomized controlled trials asking people to drink wine, say, 1 glass every night, and force them to comply with it for a decade to find the effect of wine on heart disease. In such scenarios, we normally resort to observational studies that may eventually highlight associations between wine consumption and reduced risk of heart disease. The simple reaction would be to intervene and to promote wine consumption. However, causal reasoning suggests that we think twice whether wine-reduced heart disease is a causal effect relation or the association is confounded by other factors, say, people who drink wine have more money and can buy better quality food, or have better quality of life in general. Counterfactual reasoning, on the other hand, often answers questions in retrospect, such as "Would the outcome change if I had acted differently?" Imagine a doctor who is treating a patient with kidney stones. The doctor is left with two choices, conventional treatment that includes open surgical procedures and a new treatment that only involves making a small puncture in the kidney. Each treatment may result in certain complications, raising the following questions: "Would the outcome be different if the other treatment had been given to this patient." The "if" statement is a counterfactual condition, a scenario that never happened. The doctor cannot go back in time and give a different treatment to the same patient under the exact same conditions. So, it behooves the doctor to think about counterfactual questions in advance. Counterfactual reasoning enables us to contemplate alternative options in decision-making to possibly avoid undesired outcomes. By understating causality, we will be able to answer questions related to intervention or counterfactuals, concepts we aim to cover in the following sections.

6.3. Randomized Controlled Trials

Due to the above-mentioned dilemma, a unit-level causal effect cannot be directly observed, as potential outcomes for an individual subject cannot be observed in a single universe. Randomized controlled trials (RCT) enable us to gauge the population-level causal effect by comparing the outcomes of two groups under different treatments, while other factors are kept identical. Then, the population-level causal effect can be expressed as *average causal effect* (ACE) in mathematical terms. For instance,

$$ACE = |Prob(Recovery|Treatment = Chemotherapy)$$

$$- Prob(Recovery|Treatment = Placebo)|$$

where ACE is also referred to as *average treatment effect* (ATE).

In a randomized controlled trial (RCT), treatment and placebo are assigned randomly to groups that have the same characteristics (e.g., demographic factors). The mechanism is to "disassociate variables of interest (e.g., treatment, outcome) from other factors that would otherwise affect them both" [5].

Another factor that might greatly bias our estimation of causal effect is the century-old problem of "finding confounders" [7–9]. A randomized controlled trial was first introduced by James Lind in 1747 to identify treatment for scurvy and then popularized by Ronald A. Fisher in the early 20th century. It is currently well acknowledged and considered the golden standard to identify the true causal effect without distortions introduced by confounding.

However, randomized controlled trials are not always feasible in clinical studies due to ethical or practical concerns. For example, in a smoking-cancer medical study, researchers have to conduct randomized controlled trials to investigate if in fact smoking leads to cancer. Utilizing such trials, researchers should randomly assign participants to an experiment group where people are required to smoke and a control group where smoking is not allowed. This study design will ensure that smoking behavior is the only variable that differs between the groups, and no other variables (i.e., confounders) will bias the results. On the contrary, an observational study where we merely follow and observe the outcomes of smokers and non-smokers will be highly susceptible to confounders and can reach misleading conclusions. Therefore, the better study design would be to choose RCTs; however, it is perceived as highly unethical to ask participants to smoke in a clinical trial.

Typically, randomized controlled trials are often designed and performed in a laboratory setting where researchers have full control over the experiment. In many real-world studies, data are collected from observations when researchers cannot intervene/randomize the independent variables. This highlights the need for a different toolkit to perform causal reasoning in such scenarios. In Section 6.3, we will discuss how to gauge the true causal effect from observational studies that might be contaminated with confounders.

6.4. Preliminaries: Structural Causal Models, Causal Graphs, and Intervention with Do-Calculus

In this section, we primarily introduce three fundamental components of causal reasoning: structural causal model (SCM), directed acyclic graphs (DAG), and intervention with do-calculus.

6.5. Structural Causal Model

The structural causal model (SCM), $\mathcal{M}$, was proposed by Pearl et al. [10, 11] to formally describe the interactions of variables in a system. A SCM is a 4-tuple $\mathcal{M} =< U, V, F, P(u) >$ where

(1) U is a set of background variables, exogenous, that are determined by factors outside the model.
(2) $V = \{V_1, \ldots, V_n\}$ is a set of endogenous variables that are determined by variables within the model.
(3) F is a set of functions $\{f_1, \ldots, f_n\}$ where each f_i is a mapping from $U_i \cup PA_i$ to V_i, where $U_i \subseteq U$ and PA_i (PA, is short for "parents") is a set of causes of V_i. In other words, f_i assigns a value to the corresponding $V_i \in V$, $v_i \leftarrow f_i(pa_iu_i)$, for $i = 1, \ldots, n$.
(4) $P(u)$ is a probability function defined over the domain of U.

Note that there are two sets of variables in a SCM, namely, exogenous variables, U, and endogenous variables, V. Exogenous variables are determined outside of the model and are not explained (or caused) by any variables inside our model.

Therefore, we generally assume a certain probability distribution $P(u)$ to describe the external factors. The values of endogenous variables, on the other hand, are assigned by both exogenous variables and endogenous variables. These causal mappings are captured by a set of non-parametric functions $F = \{f_1, \ldots, f_n\}$. f_i can be a linear or non-linear function to interpret all sorts of causal relations. The value assignments of endogenous variables are also referred to as the data generation process (DGP) where *nature* assigns the values of endogenous variables.

Let us consider a toy example: in a smoking-lung cancer study, we can observe and measure the treatment variable *smoking* (S) and the outcome variable *lung cancer* (L). Suppose these two factors are endogenous variables. There might be some unmeasured factors that interact with the existing endogenous variables, e.g., genotype (G). Then the SCM can be instantiated as,

$$U = \{G\}, \quad V = \{S, L\}, \quad F = \{f_S, f_L\}, \tag{6.1}$$

$$f_S : S \leftarrow f_S(G), \tag{6.2}$$

$$f_L : L \leftarrow f_L(S, G). \tag{6.3}$$

This SCM model describes that both *genotype* and *smoking* are direct causes of *lung cancer*. A certain genotype is responsible for nicotine dependence and hence explains the smoking behavior [50, 51]. However, no variable in this model explains the variable *genotype* and G is an exogenous variable.

6.6. Directed Acyclic Graph

Every SCM is associated with a directed acyclic graph (DAG). The vertices in the graph are the variables under study and the causal mechanisms and processes are edges in DAG. For instance, if variable X is the direct cause of variable Y, then there is a directed edge from X to Y in the graph. The previous SCM model can be visualized as follows:

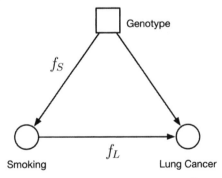

Figure 6.2: Graphical representation of an SCM model in Section 6.2.1. The square node denotes the exogenous variable, and the round nodes denote the endogenous variable. The directed edge represents the causal mechanism.

Note that the graphical representation encodes the causal relations in Eqs. (6.1)–(6.3) via a rather intuitive way. In the next section, we will show the strengths of the graphical representation when we need to study the independent relations among variables.

6.7. Intervention with Do-Calculus, do(·)

Do-calculus was developed by Pearl [12, 13] to gauge the effects of causal interventions. In the example of smoking-lung cancer, the likelihood of getting lung cancer in case of smoking can be expressed in this conditional probability, $Prob(L = 1|do(S = 1))$, which describes the causal effect identified in a randomized controlled trial. L and S are Bernoulli random variables which only take two values: 0 and 1. $L = 1$ denotes the fact of getting lung cancer, and $L = 0$ represents the observation of no lung cancer. $S = 1$ means the observation of smoking whereas $S = 0$ says that no smoking is observed. In other words, this post-intervention distribution represents the probability of getting lung cancer ($L = 1$) when we intervene upon the data generation process by deliberately forcing the participant to smoke, i.e., $do(S = 1)$. Post-intervention probability distribution refers to the probability terms that contain do-notation $do(\bullet)$. This post-intervention distribution is different from the conditional probability in an observational study: $Prob(L = 1 | S = 1)$, which only represents the likelihood of outcome ($L = 1$) when we observe that someone smokes. This conditional probability in observational study does not entail the true causal effect as it might be biased by confounders. We will discuss the confounding issue in the next section.

To recall, randomized controlled trials might be impractical or even unethical to conduct at times. For example, we cannot force participants to smoke in a randomized controlled experiment in order to find the cause–effect of an intervention ($do(S = 1)$). Do-calculus suggests us to raise the following question instead: Is it possible to estimate the post-intervention $Prob(L |do(S))$ from observational study? If we can express $Prob(L | do(S)$ in terms of the conditional probability $Prob(L|S)$ estimated in the observational study, then we can gauge the causal effect without performing randomized controlled trials.

6.7.1. Do-Calculus Algebra

Here we introduce the algebraic procedure of do-calculus that allows us to bridge the gap of probability estimation between observational study and randomized controlled trials. The goal of do-calculus is to reduce the post-intervention distribution that contains the $do(·)$ operator to a set of probability distributions of $do(·)$ free. The complete mathematical proof of do-calculus can be seen in [10, 14].

Rule 1. Prob(Y | do(X),Z,W)=Prob(Y | do(X),Z): If we observe that the variable W is irrelevant to Y (possibly conditional on the other variable Z), then the probability distribution of Y will not change.

Rule 2. Prob(Y | do(X),Z)=Prob(Y | X,Z): If Z is a set of variables blocking all backdoor paths from X to Y, then $Prob(Y | do(X)Z)$ is equivalent to $Prob(Y|XZ)$. Backdoor path will be explained shortly.

Rule 3. Prob(Y | do(X))=Prob(Y): We can remove do(X) from Prob(Y | do(X)) in any case where there are no causal paths from X to Y.

If it is not feasible to express the post-intervention distribution $Prob(L|do(S))$ in terms of do-notation-free conditional probabilities (e.g., $Prob(L|S)$) using the aforementioned rules, then randomized controlled trials are necessary to gauge the true causality.

6.7.2. *Backdoor Path and D-Separation*

In rule 2, the backdoor path refers to any path between cause and effect with an arrow pointing to cause in a directed acyclic graph (or a causal graph). For example, the backdoor path between smoking and lung cancer in Figure 6.2 is "smoking ← genotype → lung cancer." How do we know if a backdoor path is blocked or not?

Pearl, in his book [5], introduced the concept of d-separation that tells us how to block the backdoor path. Please refer to [15] for the complete mathematical proof.

(1) In a chain junction, A → B → C, conditioning on B prevents information about A from getting to C, or vice versa.
(2) In a fork or confounding junction, A ← B → C, conditioning on B prevents information about A from getting to C, or vice versa.
(3) In a collider, A → B ← C, exactly the opposite rules hold. The path between A and C is blocked when not conditioning on B. If we condition on B, then the path is unblocked. Bear in mind that if this path is blocked, A and C would be considered independent of each other.

In Figure 6.2, conditioning on genotype will block the backdoor path between smoking and lung cancer. Here, conditioning on genotype means that we only consider a specific genotype in our analysis. Blocking the backdoor between the cause and effect actually prevents the spurious correlation between them in an observational study. Please refer to the next section for more details on confounding bias.

6.8. What Is the Difference Between Prob($Y = y|X = x$) and Prob($Y = y|do(X = x)$)?

In [19], Pearl et al. explain the difference between the two distributions as follows, "*In notation, we distinguish between cases where a variable X takes a value x* *naturally and cases where we fix $X = x$ by denoting the latter $do(X = x)$. So $Prob(Y = y|X = x)$ is the probability that $Y = y$ conditional on finding $X = x$, while $Prob(Y = y|do(X = x))$ is the probability that $Y = y$ when we intervene to make $X = x$. In the distributional terminology, $Prob(Y = y|X = x)$ reflects the population distribution of Y among individuals whose X value is x. On the other hand, $Prob(Y = y|do(X = x))$ represents the population distribution of Y if everyone in the population had their X value fixed at x"*

This can be better understood with a thought experiment. Imagine that we study the association of barometer readings and weather conditions. We can express this association in terms of *Prob(Barometer|Weather)* or *Prob(Weather|Barometer)*. Notice that correlations can be defined in both directions. However, causal relations are generally unidirectional. *Prob(Weather = rainy|Barometer = low)* represents the probability of the weather being rainy when we see the barometer reading is low. *Prob(Weather = rainy|do(Barometer = low))* describes the likelihood of the weather being rainy after we manually set the barometer reading to low. Our common sense tells us that manually setting the barometer to low would not affect the weather conditions; hence, this post-intervention probability should be zero, whereas *Prob(Weather = rainy|Barometer = low)* might not be zero.

6.9. From Bayesian Networks to Structural Causal Models

Some readers may raise the question: "What is the connection between structural causal models and Bayesian networks, which also aims to interpret causality from the data using DAGs?". Firstly, the Bayesian network (also known as belief networks) was introduced by Pearl [52] in 1985 as his early attempt at causal inference. A classic example[1] of the Bayesian network is shown in Figure 6.3. The nodes in Bayesian networks represent the variables of interest, and the edges between linked variables denote their dependencies, and the strengths of such dependencies are quantified by conditional probabilities. The directed edges in this simple network (Figure 6.3) encode the following causal assumptions: (1) *Grass wet* is true if the *Sprinkler* is true or *Rain* is true. (2) *Rain* is the direct cause of *Sprinkler* as the latter is usually off on a rainy day to preserve the water usage. We can use this probabilistic model to reason the likelihood of a cause, given an effect is observed, e.g., the likelihood of a rainy day if we observe that the sprinkler is on is *Prob (Rain = True|Sprinkler = True) = 0.4* as shown by the conditional probability tables in Figure 6.3.

---

[1]The source of this example is at https://en.wikipedia.org/wiki/Bayesian_network.

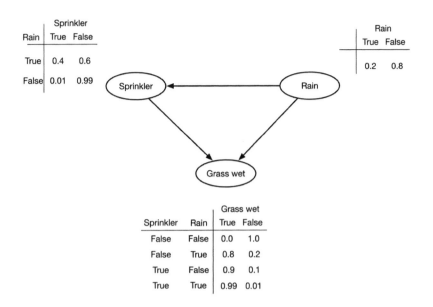

Rain	Sprinkler	
	True	False
True	0.4	0.6
False	0.01	0.99

Rain	
True	False
0.2	0.8

Sprinkler	Rain	Grass wet	
		True	False
False	False	0.0	1.0
False	True	0.8	0.2
True	False	0.9	0.1
True	True	0.99	0.01

Figure 6.3: A simple example of a Bayesian network with conditional probability tables.

However, "a Bayesian network is literally nothing more than a compact representation of a huge probability table. The arrows mean only that the probabilities of child nodes are related to the values of parent nodes by a certain formula (the conditional probability tables)" [5]. On the contrary, the arrows in the structural causal models describe the underlying data generation process between linked variables (i.e., cause and effect) using a function mapping instead of conditional probability tables. If we construct a SCM on the same example, the DAG remains unchanged, but the interpretations of the edges are different. For example, the edge of *Rain→ Sprinkler* indicates the function *Sprinkler ← f(Rain)*, which dictates how the effect (*Sprinkler*) would respond if we wiggle the cause (*Rain*). Note that Sprinkler is the effect and Rain is the cause, and the absence of the arrow *Sprinkler → Rain* in the DAG says that there is no such function, *Rain ← f(Sprinkler)*. Consider that we would like to answer an interventional question, "What is the likelihood of a rainy day if we manually turn on the sprinkler, *Prob(Rain = True|do(Sprinkler = True))*?" It is natural to choose SCMs for such questions: since we know that *Sprinkler* is not the direct cause of *Rain* according to the causal graph, **rule 3** of do-calculus algebra (Section 2.3.1) permits us to reduce *Prob do(Sprinkler = True))* to *Prob(Rain = True)*. That is, the status of *Sprinkler* has no impact on *Rain*. However, a Bayesian network is not equipped to answer such interventional and counterfactual questions. The conditional probability *Prob Rain = True) = 0.4* only says that an association between Sprinkler and Rain exists. Therefore, the ability to emulate interventions is one of the advantages of SCMs over Bayesian networks [5, 53].

However, the Bayesian network is an integral part of the development of causal inference frameworks as it is an early attempt to marry causality to graphical models. All the probabilistic properties (e.g., local Markov property) of Bayesian networks are also valid in SCMs [5, 15, 53]. Meanwhile, Bayesian networks also impact causal discovery research, which focuses on the identification of causal structures from data through computational algorithms [54].

6.10. Simpson Paradox and Confounding Variables

6.10.1. *Spurious Correlations Introduced by Confounder*

The famous phrase "correlation does not imply causation" suggests that the observed correlation between variables A and B does not automatically entail causation between A and B. Spurious correlations between two variables may be explained by a confounder. For example, considering the following case (Figure 6.4) where a spurious correlation between *yellow fingernails* and *lung cancer* is observed. One cannot simply claim that people who have yellow fingernails have higher risk of lung cancer as neither is the cause of the other. Confounding is a causal concept and cannot be expressed in terms of statistical correlation [16, 17].

Another interesting study [1] reported that there is a "surprisingly powerful correlation" ($rho = 0.79$, $p < 0.0001$) between chocolate consumption and the number of Nobel laureates in a country. It is hard to believe there is any direct causal relation between these two variables in this study. This correlation might be introduced again by a confounder (e.g., the advanced educational system in developed countries) that is not included in this study.

Pearl argues that [10]: "one cannot substantiate causal claims from association alone, even at the population level. Behind every causal conclusion there must lie some causal assumptions that is not testable in an observational study."

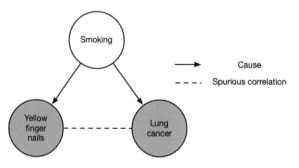

Figure 6.4: Smoking is a common cause and confounder for yellow fingernails and lung cancer. A spurious correlation may be observed between two groups who have yellow fingernails and lung cancer because of the third variable smoking.

Table 6.1: Kidney stone treatment. The fraction numbers indicate the number of success cases over the total size of the group. Treatment B is more effective than treatment A at the overall population level. But the trend is reversed in subpopulations.

	Treatment A	Treatment B
Small Stones $\left(\dfrac{357}{700} = 0.51\right)$	$\dfrac{81}{87} = 0.93$	$\dfrac{234}{270} = 0.87$
Large Stones $\left(\dfrac{343}{700} = 0.49\right)$	$\dfrac{192}{263} = 0.73$	$\dfrac{55}{80} = 0.69$
Overall	$\dfrac{273}{350} = 0.78$	$\dfrac{289}{350} = 0.83$

6.10.2. *Simpson Paradox Example: Kidney Stone*

Confounder (a causal concept) may not only introduce spurious correlations but also generate misleading results. Table 6.1 shows a real-life medical study [18] that compares the effectiveness of two treatments for kidney stones. Treatment A includes all open surgical procedures, while treatment B is percutaneous nephrolithotomy (which involves making only a small puncture(s) in the kidney). Both treatments are assigned to two groups with the same size (i.e., 350 patients). The fraction numbers indicate the number of success cases over the total size of the group.

If we consider the overall effectiveness of the two treatments, treatment A (success rate $= \frac{273}{350} = 0.78$) is inferior to treatment B (success rate $= \frac{289}{350} = 0.83$). At this moment, we may think that treatment B has a higher chance of cure. However, if we compare the treatments by the size of the kidney stones, we discover that treatment A is clearly better in both groups, patients with small stones and those with large stones. Why is the trend at the population level reversed when we analyze treatments in subpopulations?

If we inspect the table with more caution, we realize that treatments are assigned by severity, i.e., people with large stones are more likely to be treated with method A, while most of those with small stones are assigned with method B. Therefore, severity (the size of the stone) is a confounder that affects both the recovery and treatment as shown in Figure 6.5.

Ideally, we are interested in the pure causal relation of "treatment $X \rightarrow$ recovery" without any other unwanted effect from exogenous variables (e.g., the confounder *severity*). We de-confound the causal relation of "treatment $X \rightarrow$ recovery" by intervening in variable *Treatment* and forcing its value to be either A or B. By fixing the treatment, we can remove the effect coming from variable *Severity* to variable *Treatment*. Note that the causal edge of "Severity $\rightarrow$ Treatment" is absent in the mutilated graphical model shown in Figure 6.6. Since *Severity* does not affect

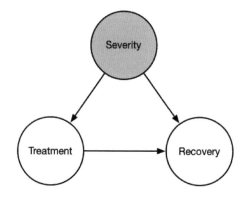

Figure 6.5:   Observational study that has a confounder, severity.

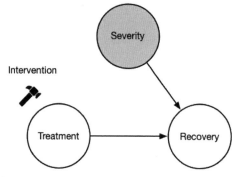

Figure 6.6: We simulate the intervention in the form of a mutilated graphical mode. The causal effect *Prob(Recovery|do(Treatment))* is equal to the conditional probability *Prob(Recovery| Treatment)* in this mutilated graphical model.

Treatment and *Recovery* at the same time after the intervention, it is no longer a confounder. Intuitively, we are interested in understanding, if we use treatment A on all patients, what will be the recovery rate, *Prob(Recovery|do(Treatment = A))*. Similarly, what is the recovery rate, *Prob(Recovery|do(Treatment = B))*, if we use treatment B only. If the former has larger values, then treatment A is more effective; otherwise, treatment B has a higher chance of cure. The notation $do(X = x)$ is a *do*-expression which fixes the value of $X = x$. Note that the probability *Prob(Recovery|do(Treatment))* marginalizes away the effect of severity by *Prob(Recovery|do(Treatment)) = Prob(Recovery|do(Treatment), Severity = treatmentA) + Prob(Recovery|do(Treatment), Severity = treatmentB)*. Essentially, we are computing the causal effects of "treatment$A \rightarrow$ recovery" and "treatment$B \rightarrow$ recovery":

$Prob(R = 1|do(T = A))$

$$= \sum_{s \in \{small, large\}} Prob(R = 1, \, S = s|do(T = A)) \; (law \; of \; total \; probability)$$

$$= \sum_{s \in \{small, large\}} Prob(R = 1|S = s, do(T = A))Prob(S = s|do(T = A))$$

$\times$ (definition of conditional probability

$$= \sum_{s \in \{small, large\}} Prob(R = 1|S = s, do(T = A))Prob(S = s)$$

$\times$ (rule #3 in $do - calculus$, see Section 2.3.1)

$$= \sum_{s \in \{small, large\}} Prob(R = 1|S = s, \, T = A)Prob(S = s)$$

$\times$ (rule #2 in $do - calculus$, see Section 2.3.1)

$$= Prob(R = 1|S = small, \, T = A)Prob(S = small)$$

$$+ Prob(R = 1|S = large, \, T = A)Prob(S = large)$$

$$= 0.93 \times 0.51 + 0.73 \times 0.49$$

$$= 0.832 \tag{3.1}$$

Similarly, we can compute

$Prob(R = 1|do(T = B))$

$$= \sum_{s \in \{small, large\}} Prob(R = 1, \, S = s|do(T = B)) \; (law \; of \; total \; probability)$$

$$= \sum_{s \in \{small, large\}} Prob(R = 1|S = s, do(T = B))Prob(S = s|do(T = B))$$

$\times$ (definition of conditional probability

$$= \sum_{s \in \{small, large\}} Prob(R = 1|S = s, do(T = B))Prob(S = s)$$

$\times$ (rule # 3 in *do-calculus*, see Section 2.3.1)

$$= \sum_{s \in \{small, large\}} Prob(R = 1|S = s, T = B)Prob(S = s)$$

$\times$ (rule # 2 in *do-calculus*, see Section 2.3.1)

$$= Prob(R = 1|S = small, T = B)Prob(S = small)$$

$$+ Prob(R = 1|S = large, T = B)Prob(S = large)$$

$$= 0.87 \times 0.51 + 0.69 \times 0.49$$

$$= 0.782 \tag{3.2}$$

Now we know the causal effects of $Prob(Recovery|do(Treatment = A)) = 0.832$ and $Prob(Recovery|do(Treatment = B)) = 0.782$. Treatment A is clearly more effective than treatment B. The results also align with our common sense that open surgery (treatment A) is expected to be more effective. A more informative interpretation of the results is that the difference of the two causal effects denotes the fraction of the population that would recover if everyone is assigned with treatment A compared to the other procedure. Recall that we have the opposite conclusion if we read the "effectiveness" at the population level in Table 6.1.

6.11. How to Estimate the Causal Effect Using Intervention?

The "interventionist" interpretation of causal effect is often described as the magnitude by which outcome Y is changed given a unit change in treatment T. For example, if we are interested in the effectiveness of a medication in the population, we would set up an experimental study as follows: (1) We administer the drug uniformly to the entire population, $do(T = 1)$, and compare the recovery rate $Prob(Y = 1|do(T = 1))$ to what we obtain under the opposite context $Prob(Y = 1|do(T = 0))$, where we keep everyone from using the drug in a parallel universe, $do(T = 0)$. Mathematically, we estimate the difference known as ACE (defined in Section 1.3),

$$ACE = Prob(Y = 1|do(T = 1)) - Prob(Y = 1|do(T = 0)) \tag{3.3}$$

"A more informal interpretation of ACE here is that it is simply the difference in the fraction of the population that would recover if everyone took the drug compared to when no one takes the drug" [19]. The question is how to estimate the intervention distribution with the do operator, $Prob(Y|do(T))$. We can utilize the following theorem to do so.

Theorem 1. The causal effect rule. Given a graph G in which a set of variables PA are designated as the parents of X, the causal effect of X on Y is given by

$$Prob(Y = y|do(X = x)) = \sum_z Prob(Y = y, |X = x, PA = z)Prob(PA = z)$$

$$\tag{3.4}$$

If we multiply and divide the right-hand side by the probability $Prob(X = x \mid PA = z)$, we get a more convenient form:

$$Prob(Y = y | do(x)) = \sum_z \frac{Prob(X = x, Y = y, PA = z)}{Prob(X = x, PA = z)} \qquad (3.5)$$

Now the computation of $Prob(Y|do(T))$ is reduced to the estimation of joint probability distributions $Prob(X, Y, PA)$ and $Prob(X, PA)$, which can be directly computed from the corresponding observational dataset. Please refer to [66] for details on probability distribution estimation.

6.12. External Validity and Transportability of Machine Learning Models

In the era of Big Data, we diligently and consistently collect heterogeneous data from various studies, for example, data collected from different experimentational conditions, underlying populations, locations, or even different sampling procedures. In short, the collected data are messy and rarely serve our inferential goal. Our data analysis should account for these factors. "The process of translating the results of a study from one setting to another is fundamental to science. In fact, scientific progress would grind to a halt were it not for the ability to generalize results from laboratory experiments to the real world" [5]. We initially need to take a better look at heterogeneous datasets.

6.13. How to Describe the Characteristics of Heterogeneous Datasets?

Big Data empowers us to conduct a wide spectrum of studies and to investigate the analytical results. We are normally inclined to incorporate or transfer such results to a new study. This naturally raises the question: Under what circumstances can we transfer the existing knowledge to new studies that are under different conditions? Before we come up with "licenses" of algorithms that permit such transfer, it is crucial to understand how the new dataset in the target study differs from the ones in existing studies.

Bareinboim [21] summarizes the differences in heterogeneous datasets over the four dimensions shown in Figure 6.7, which are certainly not enough to enumerate all possibilities in practice, but more dimensions can be added in future research.

In Figure 6.7,

d1) datasets may vary in the study population;
d2) datasets may vary in the study design. For instance, the study in Los Angeles is an experimental study under laboratory setting, while the study in New York is an observational study in the real world;

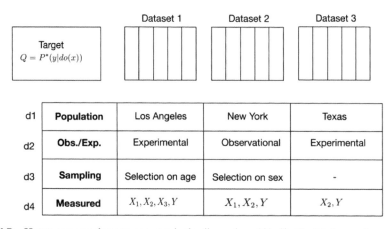

d1	**Population**	Los Angeles	New York	Texas
d2	**Obs./Exp.**	Experimental	Observational	Experimental
d3	**Sampling**	Selection on age	Selection on sex	-
d4	**Measured**	X_1, X_2, X_3, Y	X_1, X_2, Y	X_2, Y

Figure 6.7: Heterogeneous datasets can vary in the dimensions (d1, d2, d3, d4) shown above. Suppose we are interested in the causal effect $X \rightarrow Y$ in a study carried out in Texas and we have the same causal effect studied in Los Angeles and New York. This table exemplifies the potential differences between the datasets [20].

d3) datasets may vary in the collection process. For instance, dataset 1 may suffer from selection bias on variable age; for example, if the subjects recruited in study 1 are contacted only using landlines, the millennials are probably excluded in the study as they prefer mobile phones;

d4) Studies might also take measurements on different sets of variables.

6.14. Selection Bias

Selection bias is caused by preferential exclusion of data samples [22]. It is a major obstacle in validating statistical results, and it can hardly be detected in either experimental or observational studies.

6.14.1. *COVID-19 Example*

During the COVID-19 pandemic crisis, a statewide study reported that 21.2% of New York City residents have been infected with COVID-19 [23]. The study tested 3,000 New York residents statewide at grocery and big-box stores for antibodies that indicate whether someone has had the virus. Kozyrkov [24] argues that the study might be contaminated with selection bias. The hypothesis notes that the cohort in the study is largely skewed toward the group of people who are high-risk-takers and have had the virus. A large portion of the overall population may include people who are risk-averse and cautiously stay home; these people were excluded from the research samples. Therefore, the reported toll (i.e., 21.2%) is likely to be inflated. Here, we try to investigate a more generic approach to spot selection bias issues.

Causal inference requires us to make certain plausible assumptions when we analyze data. Datasets are not always complete; that is, it does not always tell the whole story. The results of the analyses (e.g., spurious correlation) from data alone can be often very misleading. You may recall the example of smokers who may develop lung cancer and have yellow fingernails. If we find this association (lung cancer and yellow fingernails) to be strong, we may come to the false conclusion that one causes the other.

Back to our COVID-19 story, what causal assumptions can we make in the antibody testing study? Consider Figure 6.8 in which each of the following assumptions represent an edge:

(1) We know that the antibody will be discovered if we do the related test.
(2) People who have had COVID-19 and survived would generate an antibody for that virus.
(3) Risk-taking people are more likely to go outdoors and participate in the testing study.
(4) In order to highlight the difference between the sample cohort and the overall population in the graph, Bareinboim [21, 22] proposed a hypothetical variable S (standing for "selection"). The variable bounded in the square in Figure 6.8 stands for the characteristics by which the two populations differ. You can also think of S as the inclusion/exclusion criteria. The variable S has incoming edges from the variables "risk taking" and "carried virus." This means that the sample cohort and overall population differ in these two aspects.

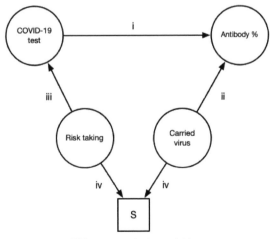

Difference producing variable

Figure 6.8: A graphical model that illustrates the selection bias scenario. The variable S (square shaped) is a difference-producing variable, which is a hypothetical variable that points to the characteristic by which the two populations differ.

Now we have encoded our assumptions into a transparent and straightforward diagram. You may wonder why we go through all the hassles to prepare this graphical diagram? What value does it add to our identification of selection bias or even the debiasing procedure?

Let us begin with the question of how it helps us to find the common pattern/principle of identifying selection bias?

Identify selection bias with a causal graph

First, a couple of quick tips for identifying selection bias: (1) find any collider variable on the backdoor path between the cause variable and the effect variable; (2) selection bias occurs when your data collection process is conditioning on these collider variables [22]. Note that these tips are only sufficient but not necessary conditions in finding selection bias. By conditioning we mean considering only some of the possibilities a variable can take and not all.

The backdoor path in tip (1) refers to any path between cause variable (COVID testing) and effect variable (antibody %) with an arrow pointing to cause variable ([5] , page 158). In our example, the only backdoor path is "COVID-19 test ← risk taking → S ← carried virus → antibody %." Spurious correlation will be removed if we block every backdoor path.

We observe that there are three basic components of the backdoor path: (1) a fork "COVID-19 test ← high risk → S"; (2) a collider "high risk → S ← carried"; (3) another fork "S ← carried virus → antibody %." Now we notice that this backdoor path is blocked if we do not condition on the variable S in the collider (recall d-separation). If we condition on the variable S (e.g., set S={high risk, have had virus}), the backdoor path will be opened up and spurious correlation is introduced in your antibody testing results.

Now we realize that if we condition on a collider on the backdoor path between cause → effect and open up the backdoor path, we will encounter the selection bias issue. With this conclusion, we can quickly identify whether our study has a selection bias issue given a causal graph. The procedures for this identification can also be automated when the graph is complex. So, we offload this judgement to algorithms and computers. Hopefully, you are convinced at this point that using a graphical model is a more generic and automated way of identifying selection bias.

Unbiased estimation with do-calculus

Now we are interested in the estimation of cause–effect between "COVID-19 test → Antibody %", $P(Antibody|do(test))$. In other words, the causal effect represents the likelihood of antibody discovery if we test everyone in the population. Our readers may wonder at this point if the do-calculus makes sense, but how would we compute and remove the do-operator? Recall the algebra of do-calculus introduced in Section 2.3.1. Let us compute $P(Antibody|do(test))$ as shown below:

$P(Antibody|do(test))$

$= P(Antibody|do(test), \{\})$ # Condition on nothing, an empty set.

$= P(Antibody|do(test), \{\}).$
The backdoor path in Fig. 6.8 is blocked naturally if we condition on nothing,
$\{\}$ According to rule b) of do-calculus, we can safely remove the *do* notation.

$= P(Antibody|test)$

$$= \sum_{\substack{i\in\{high,low\}\\j\in\{true,false\}}} P(Antibody, risk = i, virus = j|test) \text{ \# Law of total}$$

probability

$$= \sum_{\substack{i\in\{high,low\}\\j\in\{true,false\}}} P(Antibody|test, risk = i, virus = j)P(risk = i,$$

$$virus = j|test) \tag{4.1}$$

The last step of the equation shows the four probability terms measured in the study required to have an unbiased estimation. If we assume a closed world (risk={high, low}, virus={true, false}), it means that we need to measure every stratified group. Now we have seen that do-calculus can help us identify what pieces we need in order to recover the unbiased estimation.

6.15. Model Transportability with Data Fusion

Transferring the learned knowledge across different studies is crucial to scientific endeavors. Consider a new treatment that has shown effectiveness for a disease in an experimental/laboratory setting. We are interested in extrapolating the effectiveness of this treatment in a real-world setting. Assume that the characteristics of the cohort in the lab setting are different from the overall population in the real world, e.g., age, income, etc. Direct transfer of existing findings to a new setting will result in biased inference/estimation of the effectiveness of the drug. Certainly, we can recruit a new cohort that is representative of the overall population and examine whether the effectiveness of this treatment is consistent. However, if we could use the laboratory findings to infer our estimation goal in the real world, this would reduce the cost of repetitive data collection and model development. Let us consider a toy example of how causal reasoning could help with data fusion.

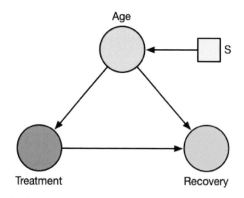

Figure 6.9:   A toy example shows how to transfer the existing inference in a lab setting to another population where the difference is the age, denoted by a hypothetical difference variable S (in yellow).

6.15.1. *A Toy Example of Data Fusion with Causal Reasoning*

Imagine that we developed a new treatment for a disease, and we estimated the effectiveness of the new drug for each age group in a randomized controlled experimental setting. Let $P(Recovery|do(Treatment), Age)$ denote the drug effect for each age group. We wish to generalize the lab results to a different population. Assume that the study cohort in lab setting and the target population are different and the differences are explained by a variable S as shown in Figure 6.9. Meanwhile, we assume that these causal effects of each specific age group are invariant across populations. We are interested in gauging the drug effect in the target population ($S = s^*$), and the query can be expressed as $P(Recovery = True|do(Treatment = True), S = s^*)$. Then the query can be solved as follows:

$$Query = P(Recovery|do(Treatment), S = s^*)$$

$$= \sum_{age} P(Recovery|do(Treatment), S = s^*, Age = age)$$

$$P(Age = age|do(Treatment), S = s^*)$$

$$= \sum_{age} P^*(Recovery|do(Treatment), Age = age)P^*(Age = age)$$

$$(4.2)$$

In the last step of the equation, $P^*(Recovery|do(Treatment), Age = age)$ is the effect we discovered through various experimental studies, and it is invariant across study cohorts. Hence, $P^*(Recovery|do(Treatment), Age = age) = P(Recovery|do(Treatment), Age = age)$. $P^*(Age = age)$ is the age distribution in the new population, and is a shorthand for $P(Age = age|S = s^*)$. We realize that to answer the query, we just need to compute the summation of the experimental findings weighted by the age distribution in the target population.

For example, we assume that we have discovered the effectiveness of the new treatment in different age groups through some experimental studies. The effectiveness is expressed as follows:

$$P(Recovery \mid do(Treatment), Age < 10) = 0.1$$
$$P(Recovery \mid do(Treatment), Age = 10 \sim 20) = 0.2$$
$$P(Recovery \mid do(Treatment), Age = 20 \sim 30) = 0.3$$
$$P(Recovery \mid do(Treatment), Age = 30 \sim 40) = 0.4$$
$$P(Recovery \mid do(Treatment), Age = 40 \sim 50) = 0.5$$

Meanwhile, the age distribution in our target population is as follows:

- group1 : Age $< 10 P^*(Age < 10) = 1/10$
- group2 : Age $= 10 \sim 20\ P^*(10 \leq Age < 20 = 2/10$
- group3 : Age $= 20 \sim 30\ P^*(20 \leq Age < 30) = 4/10$
- group4 : Age $= 30 \sim 40\ P^*(30 \leq Age < 40) = 2/10$
- group5 : Age $= 40 \sim 50\ P^*(40 \leq Age < 50) = 1/10$

According to equation (4.2), the effectiveness in the target population should be computed as

$$P(recovery \mid do(treatment), S = s^*)$$
$$= \sum_{age} P(recovery \mid do(treatment), age) P^*(age)$$
$$= 0.1 * \frac{1}{10} + 0.2 * \frac{2}{10} + 0.3 * \frac{4}{10} + 0.4 * \frac{2}{10} + 0.5 * \frac{1}{10} = 0.03 \quad (4.3)$$

6.16. Missing Data

Missing data occur when the collected values are incomplete for certain observed variables. Missingness might be introduced in a study for various reasons: for example, due to sensors that stop working because they run out of battery, data collection is done improperly by researchers, respondents refuse to answer some survey questions that may reveal their private information (e.g., income, disability) and many more reasons. The missing data issue is inevitable in many scenarios.

Typically, building machine learning predictors or statistical models with missing data may expose the consequent models to the following risks: (a) the partially observed data may bias the inference models, and the study outcomes may largely deviate from the true value; (b) the reduced sample size may lose the statistical power to provide any informative insights; (c) missing data, appearing as technical impediment, might also cause severe predictive performance degradation as most of the machine learning models assume datasets are complete when making inferences.

Extensive research endeavors have been dedicated to the problem of missing data. Listwise deletion or mean value substitutions are commonly used in dealing with this issue because of their simplicity. However, these naive methods fail to account for the relationships between the missing data and the observed data. Thus, the interpolations usually deviate from the real values by large. Rubin et al. introduce the concept of missing data mechanism which is widely adopted in the literature [27]. This mechanism classifies missing data into three categories:

- Missing completely at random (MCAR): The observed data are randomly drawn from the complete data. In other words, missingness is unrelated to other variables or itself. For example, in Figure 6.10, job performance rating is a partially observed variable, while variable IQ is complete without any missingness. The MCAR column shows that the missing ratings are independent of IQ values.

IQ	Job performance ratings			
	Complete	MCAR	MAR	MNAR
78	9	—	—	9
84	13	13	—	13
84	10	—	—	10
85	8	8	—	—
87	7	7	—	—
91	7	7	7	—
92	9	9	9	9
94	9	9	9	9
94	11	11	11	11
96	7	—	7	—
99	7	7	7	—
105	10	10	10	10
105	11	11	11	11
106	15	15	15	15
108	10	10	10	10
112	10	—	10	10
113	12	12	12	12
115	14	14	14	14
118	16	16	16	16
134	12	—	12	12

Figure 6.10: Example source [28]. Job performance rating is a partially observed variable, and variable IQ is a completely observed variable without any missingness. The second column shows the complete ratings. The 3rd/4th/5th columns show the observed ratings under MCAR/MAR/MNAR conditions, respectively.

- Missing at random (MAR): The missing values of the partially observed variable depend on other measured variables. The MAR column in Figure 6.9 shows that the missing ratings are associated with low IQs.
- Missing not at random (MNAR): MNAR includes scenarios when data are neither MCAR nor MNAR. For example, in Figure 6.10, the MNAR column shows that the missing ratings are associated with itself, i.e., low job performance ratings ($ratings < 9$) are missing.

Pearl et al. demonstrate that a theoretical performance guarantee (e.g., convergence and unbiasedness) exists for inference with data that are MCAR and MAR [29, 30]. In other words, we can still have bias-free estimations despite missing data. In Figure 6.10, assume that Y is the random variable that represents the job performance ratings. The expectations of job performance ratings under complete, MCAR, and MNAR columns are $\mathbb{E}^{Complete}[Y] = 10.35$, $\mathbb{E}^{MCAR}[Y] = 10.60$, and $\mathbb{E}^{MNAR}[Y] = 11.40$, respectively. It can be easily verified that the bias of $Bias_{MCAR} = |\mathbb{E}^{Complete}[Y] - \mathbb{E}^{MCAR}[Y]| = 0.25$ is less than $Bias_{MNAR} = |\mathbb{E}^{Complete}[Y] - \mathbb{E}^{MNAR}[Y]| = 1.05$. As the size of the dataset grows, $\mathbb{E}^{MCAR}[Y]$ will converge to the real expectation value $\mathbb{E}^{Complete}[Y]$, i.e., $Bias_{MCAR} =$. However, since the MNAR mechanism dictates that low ratings ($Y < 9$) are inherently missing from our observations, we cannot have a bias-free estimation, regardless of the sample size. We can notice that the observed data are governed by the missing mechanism. Therefore, the missing data issue is inherently a causal inference problem [30, 31].

Most statistical techniques proposed in the literature for handling missing data assume that data are MCAR or MAR [32–35]. For example, the expectation maximum likelihood algorithm is generally considered superior to other conventional methods (e.g., listwise or pairwise deletion) when the data are MCAR or MAR [28]. Moreover, it provides a theoretical guarantee (e.g., unbiasedness or convergence) [36] under MCAR or MAR assumptions. However, when it comes to MNAR, estimations with the conventional statistical techniques will be mostly biased. Mohan et al. report that we can achieve unbiased estimation in the MNAR scenario under certain constraints using causal methods [29–31].

6.17. Causal Perspective of Missing Data

In this section, we briefly explore and discuss the causal approaches proposed by Mohan and Pearl in dealing with missing data [29–31]. Firstly, we introduce the concept of causal graph representation for missing data—missing graph(s) (m-graph(s) for short). Then we introduce the definition of recoverability, a formal definition of unbiased estimation with missing data. Next, we discuss under what conditions we can achieve recoverability. At last, we identify the unsolved problems with data that are MNAR.

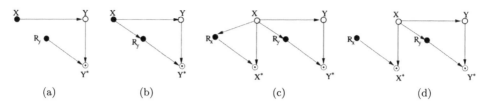

Figure 6.11: m-graphs for data that are (a) MCAR, (b) MAR, (c, d) MNAR; hollow and solid circles denote partially and fully observed variables, respectively [29].

6.17.1. *Preliminary on Missing Graphs*

Let $G(\mathbb{V}, E)$ be the causal graph (a DAG) where $\mathbb{V} = V \cup U \cup V^* \cup \mathbb{R}$. V denotes the set of observable nodes, which represent observed variables in our data. These observable nodes can be further grouped into fully observable nodes, V^{obs}, and partially observable nodes, V^{mis}. Hence, $V = V^{obs} \cup V^{mis}$. V^{obs} denotes the set of variables that have complete values, whereas V^{mis} denotes the set of variables that are missing at least one data record. Each partially observed variable $v_i \in V^{mis}$ has two auxiliary variables R_{v_i} and V_i^*, where V_i^* is a proxy variable that is actually observed, and R_{v_i} denotes the causal mechanism responsible for the missingness of V_i^*,

$$v_i^* = f(r_{v_i}, v_i) = \begin{cases} v_i, & \text{if } r_{v_i} = 0 \\ missing, & \text{if } r_{v_i} = 1 \end{cases} \tag{5.1}$$

In missing graphs, R_{v_i} can be deemed as a switch that dictates the missingness of its proxy variable, V_i^*. For example, in Figure 6.11(a), X is a fully observable node which has no auxiliary variables. The partially observable node Y is associated with Y^* and R_{Y_i}. Y^* is the proxy variable that we actually observe on Y, and R_y masks the values of Y by its underlying missingness mechanism (e.g., MCAR, MAR, MNAR). E is the set of edges in m-graphs, and U is the set of unobserved variables (latent variables). The toy example in Figure 6.11 is not involved with any latent variable.

We can cast the classification of missingness mechanisms (e.g., MCAR, MAR, MNAR) onto m-graphs as depicted in Figure 6.11.

- Figure 6.11(a) shows the MCAR case where $R_y \perp\!\!\!\perp X^2$. The on–off status of R_y is solely determined by coin-toss. Bear in mind that the absence of an edge between two vertices in a causal graph is a strong constraint which indicates that there is no relation between them. The criterion to decide if an m-graph represents MCAR is $\mathbb{R} \perp\!\!\!\perp (V^{obs} \cup V^{mis} \cup U)$.

---

[2]This (conditional) independence is directly read off from causal graphs using the *d-separation* technique.

- Figure 6.11(b) shows the MAR case where $\mathbb{R}_y \perp\!\!\!\perp Y|X.R_y$ depends on the fully observed variable X. The criterion of deciding if a m-graph represents MAR is $\mathbb{R} \perp\!\!\!\perp (V^{mis} \cup U)|V^{obs}$.
- Figure 6.11(c,d) shows the MNAR cases where neither of the aforementioned criteria holds.

It is a clear advantage that we can directly read the missingness mechanism from the m-graphs using *d-separation*[3] without conducting any statistical test.

6.18. Recoverability

Before we can discuss under what conditions we can achieve bias-free estimation, we shall first introduce the definition of recoverability.

Definition 1. Recoverability [29]. Given an m-graph G, and a target query relation Q defined on the variables in V, Q is said to be recoverable in G if there exists an algorithm that produces a consistent estimate of Q for every dataset D such that P(D) is 1) compatible with G and 2) strictly positive over complete cases, i.e., $P(V^{obs}, V^{mis}, \mathbb{R} = 0) > 0$.

Corollary 1 [29]. A query relation Q is recoverable in G if and only if Q can be expressed in terms of the probability P(O) where $O = R, V^*V^{obs}$ is the set of observable variables in G.

6.18.1. *Recoverability When Data are MCAR*

Example 1. Taken from [29]. "Let X be the treatment and Y be the outcome as depicted in the m-graph in Figure 6.11(a). Let it be the case that we accidentally delete the values of Y for a handful of samples, hence $Y \in V_m$. Can we recover P(X,Y)?"

Yes, P(X,Y) under MCAR is recoverable. We know that $R_y \perp\!\!\!\perp (X, Y)$ holds in Figure 6.11(a). Thus, $P(X, Y) = P(X, Y \mid R_v) = P(X, Y|R_v = 0)$. When $R_v = 0$, we can safely replace Y with Y^* as $P(X, Y) = P(X, Y^*|R_v = 0)$. Note that $P(X, Y)$ has been expressed in terms of the probability $(P(X, Y^*|R_v = 0))$ that we can compute using observational data. Hence, we can recover P(X,Y) with no bias.

6.18.2. *Recoverability When Data are MAR*

Example 2. Taken from [29]. "Let X be the treatment and Y be the outcome as depicted in the m-graph in Figure 6.11(b). Let it be the case that some patients who

---

[3]Watch this video about d-separation: https://www.youtube.com/watch?v=yDs_q6jKHb0.

underwent treatment are not likely to report the outcome, hence $X \in R_v$. Can we recover P(X,Y)?"

Yes, P(X,Y) under MAR is recoverable. We know that $R_y \perp\!\!\!\perp Y|X$ holds in Figure 6.11(b). Thus, $P(X, Y) = P(Y \mid X)P(X) = P(Y \mid X, R_v)P(X) = P(Y|X, R_v = 0)P(X)$. When $R_v = 0$, we can safely replace Y with Y^* as $P(X, Y) = P(Y * |X, R_v = 0)P(X)$. Note that $P(X, Y)$ has been expressed in terms of the probability $(P(Y * |X, R_v = 0)P(X))$ that we can compute using observational data. Hence, we can recover P(X,Y) with no bias.

6.18.3. *Recoverability When Data are MNAR*

Example 3. Taken from [29]. "Figure 6.11(d) depicts a study where (i) some units who underwent treatment $(X = 1)$ did not report the outcome Y, and (ii) we accidentally deleted the values of treatment for a handful of cases. Thus we have missing values for both X and Y which renders the dataset MNAR. Can we recover $P(X, Y)$?"

Yes, $P(X, Y)$ in (d) is recoverable. We know that $X \perp\!\!\!\perp R_x$ and $(R_y \cup R_y) \perp\!\!\!\perp Y|X$ hold in Figure 6.11(d). Thus, $P(X, Y) = P(Y|X)P(X) = P(Y|X, R_y)P(X) = P(Y^*|X^*, R_y = 0, R_x = 0)P(X^*|R_x = 0)$. Note that $P(XY)$ has been expressed in terms of the probability $(P(Y^*|X^*, R_y = 0, R_x =)P(X^*|R_x = 0))$ that we can compute using observational data. Hence, we can recover $P(X, Y)$ with no bias.

In the original paper [29], $P(X, Y)$ is not recoverable in Figure 6.10(c). Mohan et al. provide a theorem (see Theorem 1 in [29]) which states the sufficient condition for recoverability.

6.19. Testability

In Figure 6.11(b), we assume that the missing mechanism R_y is the causal effect of X; hence the arrow pointing from X to R_y. The question naturally arises: "Is our assumption/model compatible with our data?" Mohan et al. propose an approach to testify the plausibility of missing graphs from the observed dataset [37].

6.19.1. *Testability of Conditional Independence (CI) in M-Graphs*

Definition 2 [37]. Let $X \cup Y \cup Z \subseteq V_o \cup V_m \cup R$ and $X \cap Y \cap Z \neq \emptyset$. $X \perp\!\!\!\perp Y|Z$ is testable if there exists a dataset D governed by a distribution $P(V_o, V^*, R)$ such that $X \perp\!\!\!\perp Y|Z$ is refuted in all underlying distributions $P(V_o, V_m, R)$ compatible with the distribution $P(V_o, V^*, R)$.

In other words, if the CIs can be expressed in terms of observable variables exclusively, then these CIs are deemed testable.

Theorem 2. Let $X, Y, Z \subset V_o \cup V_m \cup \mathbb{R}$ and $X \cap Y \cap Z = \emptyset$. The conditional independence statement $S : X \perp\!\!\!\perp Y | Z$ is directly testable if all the following conditions hold:

1. $Y \not\subseteq (R_{X_m} \cup R_{Z_m})$. In words, Y should contain at least one element that is not in $R_{X_m} \cup R_{Z_m}$.
2. $R_{X_m} \subseteq X \cup Y \cup Z$. In words, the missingness mechanisms of all partially observed variables in X are contained in $X \cup Y \cup Z$.
3. $R_{Z_m} \cup R_{Y_m} \subseteq Z \cup Y$. In words, the missingness mechanisms of all partially observed variables in Y and Z are contained in $Y \cup Z$.

6.19.2. *Testability of CIs Comprising Only Substantive Variables*

As for the CIs that only include substantive variables (e.g., Figure 6.11(b)), it is fairly easy to see that $X \perp\!\!\!\perp Y$ is testable when $X, Y \in V_o$.

6.20. Missing Data from the Causal Perspective

Given an incomplete dataset, our first step is to postulate a model based on causal assumptions of the underlying data generation process. Secondly, we need to determine whether the data reject the postulated model by identifiable testable implications of that model. The last step is to determine, from the postulated model, whether any method exists that produces consistent estimates of the queries of interest.

6.21. Augmented Machine Learning with Causal Inference

Despite the rising popularity of causal inference research, the route from machine learning to artificial general intelligence still remains uncharted. Strong artificial intelligence aims to generate artificial agents with the same level of intelligence as human beings. The capability of thinking causally is integral for achieving this goal [38]. In this section, we try to describe how to augment machine learning models with causal inference.

6.22. Reinforcement Learning with Causality

Smart agents not only passively observe the world but are also expected to actively interact with their surroundings and to shape the world. Let us consider a case study in recommender systems where we augment a reinforcement learning (RL) agent with causality.

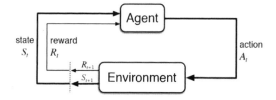

Figure 6.12:   A graphical illustration of the interaction between a reinforcement learning agent and its surrounding environment.

A reinforcement learning agent typically interacts with its surrounding environment as follows: choose the available **actions** from the observed **state** and collect the **reward** as the result of those actions. The goal of a reinforcement learning agent is to maximize the cumulative reward by choosing the optimal action in every interaction with the environment. Reinforcement learning (RL) has been widely adopted in recommender systems such as Amazon or eBay platforms in which items are being suggested to users based on learning their past purchases. Let us assume that these e-commerce recommender systems are implemented as reinforcement learning agents. Given a collection of recommended items, a reward is recorded when a purchase transaction is complete. To maximize the total revenue, the items presented on the recommendation page need to be thoughtfully chosen and placed. Meanwhile, the recommender system will learn the preference of the customers by observing their behaviors. In this scenario, the actions shown in Figure 6.12 are the items for the recommender systems, and the states are the customer preferences learned by the system. In the following section, we will introduce an instance of a reinforcement learning paradigm known as a multi-armed bandit. We will discuss issues that may arise in multi-armed bandit models such as the exploration and exploitation dilemma and the confounding issue. We finally describe how Thompson sampling and causal Thompson sampling could help resolve such shortcomings.

6.22.1. *Multi-Armed Bandit Model*

The multi-armed bandit model is inspired by imagining a gambler sitting in front of a row of slot machines, and deciding which machine to play with the goal of maximizing his/her total return. Let us say we have N slot machines. Each slot machine gives a positive reward with probability p, or a negative reward with probability $1 - p$. When a gambler just starts his game, he has no knowledge of those slot machines. As he plays a few hands, he would "learn" which slot machine is more rewarding (i.e., the reward distribution of these actions). For example, if there are five slot machines with the reward distribution of $0.1, 0.2, 0.3, 0.4, 0.5$, the gambler would always choose the last machine to play in order to have the maximum return.

Figure 6.13: A row of slot machines in Las Vegas.

However, the gambler does not have this reward information at the beginning of the game unless he or she pulls and tries each slot machine and estimates the reward.

Multi-armed bandit models have been widely adopted in the recommender systems. For example, an online video recommender system (e.g., YouTube) would pick a set of videos based on the user's watch history and expect high click-through-rate from the user side. In this scenario, the recommender system is the gambler and the videos are slot machines. The reward of each video is the user click.

6.22.2. *Exploration and Exploitation Dilemma*

Before we have the complete reward distribution of our actions, we would face the problem of which action to take based on our partial observation. If we take a greedy approach of always choosing the action with the maximum reward that we observed, this strategy might not be optimal. Let us understand it with the previous slot machine example where the true reward distribution is 0.1, 0.2, 0.3, 0.4, 0.5. Imagine that the gambler just sits in and only pulls a few arms; his reward estimation of these machines would be: 0.5, 0.0, 0.0, 0.0, 0.0. This information may convince him to choose the first arm to play even though the likelihood of reward for this machine is the lowest among all. The rest of the machines would never have the chance to be explored as their reward estimations are 0s. Therefore, we need to be careful not to get stuck in exploiting a specific action and forget to explore the unknowns. Over the years, there have been many proposals to handle this dilemma: (1) ϵ-greedy algorithm, (2) upper confidence bound algorithm, (3) Thompson sampling algorithm, and many other variants. We will get back to this dilemma shortly.

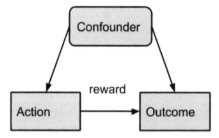

Figure 6.14:   A graphical illustration of confounding bias in reinforcement learning.

6.23. Confounding Issue in Reinforcement Learning

How to view reinforcement learning with the causal lens? Recall that all actions in reinforcement learning are associated with certain rewards. If we see the actions as treatments, we can view the reward as a causal effect of the outcome from each action taken.

In Section 6.3, we learned that confounders may bias the causal effect estimation given the scenarios depicted in Figure 6.14. The biased reward estimation would lead to a suboptimal policy. Therefore, it is essential to debias the reward estimation in the existence of confounders. Bareinboim et al. [39] propose a causal Thompson sampling technique, which draws its strength from "counterfactual reasoning." Specifically, the causal Thompson sampling algorithm enables reinforcement learning agents to compare the rewards resulting from the action that the agent is about to take and the alternative actions that are overlooked.

6.23.1. *Thompson Sampling*

In multi-armed bandit problems [40], the goal of maximizing the reward can be fulfilled in different ways. For instance, in our slot machine example, the gambler wants to estimate the true reward for each slot machine to make optimal choices and to maximize his profit in the end. One way is for the gambler to estimate and update the probability of winning at each machine based on his plays. The gambler would choose the slot machine with the maximum likelihood of winning in the next round.

In the Thompson sampling algorithm, however, maximizing the reward, unlike the greedy way, is done by balancing exploitation and exploration. The Thompson algorithm associates each machine with a beta probability distribution, which is essentially the distribution of success versus failure in slot machine events. In each turn, the algorithm will sample from associated beta distributions to generate the reward estimations and then choose to play the machine with the highest estimated reward. Beta distribution is parameterized by α and β in the following equation:

$$B(\alpha, \beta) = \frac{\Gamma(\alpha)\Gamma(\beta)}{\Gamma(\alpha + \beta)} \tag{6.1}$$

where Γ is the Gamma distribution. Let us inspect the property of beta distribution with the following examples and understand why it is a good candidate for the reward estimation in our slot machine example. In Figure 6.15(c), we can see that if we sample from the beta distribution when $\alpha = \beta = 5$, the estimated reward would most likely be around 0.5. When $\alpha = 5$ and $\beta = 2$, the peak moves toward the right and the sample values might be around 0.8 in most cases (see Figure 6.15(a)).

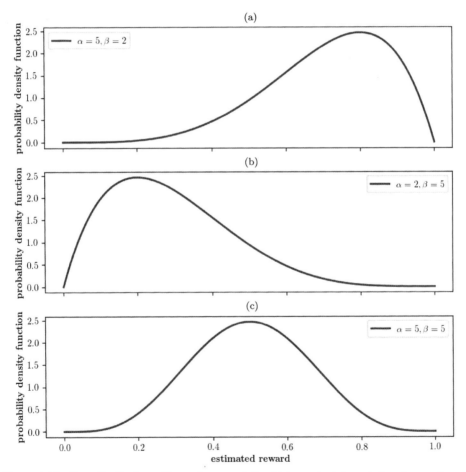

Figure 6.15: Beta distribution with varying α and β, which can be interpreted as the number of successes and failures in the Thompson sampling algorithm. Estimated reward likely to be around (a) 0.8, (b) 0.2, (c) 0.5.

If we treat α and β as the number of successes and failures, respectively, in our casino game, then the larger value of α in a beta distribution indicates a higher likelihood of payout, whereas the value of β in a beta distribution represents a lower likelihood of payout.

In the Thompson sampling algorithm, these beta distributions would be updated by maintaining the current number of successes (α) and failures (β). As we can see from Figure 6.15(b), we can still sample a large reward with a small likelihood. This gives the opportunity for the unrewarding machines to be chosen. Therefore, the Thompson sampling algorithm addresses the exploration and exploitation dilemma to a certain degree [40].

6.23.2. *Causal Thompson Sampling*

In [39], Bareinboim et al. argue that the reward estimation in typical reinforcement learning may be biased in the existence of unobserved confounders. Therefore, conventional Thompson sampling may choose those machines that are suboptimal and skip the real optimal choices. The authors proposed an augmented Thompson sampling with a counterfactual reasoning approach, which allows us to reason about a scenario that has not happened. Imagine that a gambler sits in front of two slot machines (M1 has a higher payout than M2). Say that the gambler is less confident in the reward estimation for the first machine than the second one. His natural predilection would be choosing the second slot machine (M2) as the gambler "believes" that the expected reward from the second machine is higher. Recall that unobserved confounders exist and may mislead the gambler into believing that the second machine is more rewarding, whereas the first machine is actually the optimal choice. Therefore, if the gambler can answer these two questions: "Given that I believe M2 is better, what would the payout be if I played M2?" (intuition), and "Given that I believe M2 is better, what would the payout be if I acted differently?" (counter-intuition). If the gambler can estimate the rewards of intuition and counter-intuition, he may rectify his misbelief in the existence of confounders and choose the optimal machine. Interested readers can refer to [39] for more details. Experimental results in [39] show that causal Thompson sampling solves the confounding issue with a toy example dataset. However, this work has not been validated on a realistic dataset. It is still not clear how to handle the confounding issue in practice. Therefore, this is still an open research question.

6.24. How to Discover the Causal Relations from Data?

In the previous sections, we have seen a number of examples where the causal diagrams are essential for the causal reasoning. For example, we use the causal graphs in Section 6.3 to demystify the confounding bias (e.g., the Simpson paradox).

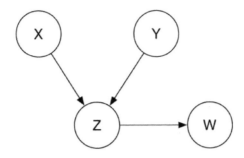

Figure 6.16:   A causal graph used for causal discovery illustration.

The causal graph in Figure 6.4 was constructed after careful inspection of the dataset with the help of domain experts. Some readers may wonder if the construction of these causal structures can be automated with minimum inputs and interventions from experts. In this section, we introduce the concept of causal discovery which identifies these causal relations from the observational dataset via some computational algorithms [55].

To recapitulate, a causal diagram encodes our assumptions about the causal story behind a dataset. These causal assumptions govern the data generation process. Therefore, the dataset should exhibit certain statistical properties that agree with the causal diagram. In particular, if we believe that a causal diagram G might have generated a dataset D, the variables that are independent of each other in G should also be tested as independent in dataset D. For example, the causal diagram in Figure 6.16 indicates that X and W are conditionally independent given Z as "$X \rightarrow Z \rightarrow W$" forms a chain structure (refer to the d-separation in Section 2.3.2). If a dataset is generated by the causal diagram in Figure 6.16, the data should suggest that X and W are independent conditional on Z, written as $X \perp\!\!\!\perp W|Z$. On the contrary, we can refute this causal diagram when the data suggest that the conditional independence (e.g., $X \perp\!\!\!\perp W|Z$) does not hold. Granted that the dataset D matches with every conditional independence relation suggested in the causal diagram G, we say that the causal model G is plausible for the dataset D. The task of causal discovery is to search through all the possible causal graphs and find the most plausible candidate.

The mainstream causal discovery methods can be categorized into two groups: constraint-based methods and score-based methods. Constraint-based approaches exploit the conditional independence test to search for the causal structure. Typical algorithms include PC algorithm [56] and FCI algorithm [57]. The PC algorithm (named after its authors, Peter and Clark) starts the search with a fully connected graph as shown in Figure 6.17(b). It repeatedly eliminates the edges between two variables if they are independent in the data, as shown

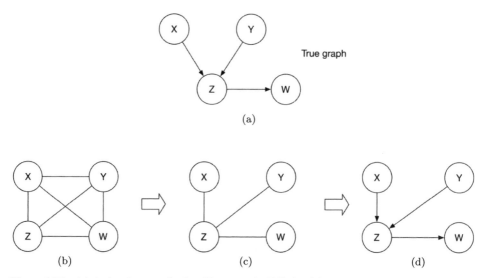

(a)

(b) (c) (d)

Figure 6.17: (a) A simple example that illustrates the PC algorithm. (a) The true causal structure. (b) The PC algorithm starts with a fully connected graph. (c) It removes the edges if the data suggest that the linked variables are independent, e.g., X and Y are independent. (d) It decides the causal directions using d-separation.

in Figure 6.17(c). For example, the statistical testing checks whether $Prob(X, Y) = Prob(X) \times Prob(Y)$ holds. If the equation is valid in the data, then we conclude that X and Y are independent. Finally, the PC algorithm decides the arrow directions using d-separations (Figure 6.17(d)). In particular, the algorithm finds the v-structure "$X \rightarrow Z \leftarrow Y$" when the data suggest that X and Y become dependent conditioning on Z. This procedure is performed in two steps: (1) verify that $Prob(X, Y) = Prob(X) \times Prob(Y)$; (2) verify that $Prob(X, Y \mid Z) \neq Prob(X \mid Z) \times Prob(Y \mid Z)$. The first step indicates that X and Y are initially independent if not conditioning on Z. The second step says that X and Y become dependent conditional on Z. Moreover, the PC algorithm identifies the chain structure "$X \rightarrow Z \rightarrow W$" when the data suggest that X and W are independent conditional on Z, that is, $Prob(X, W \mid Z) = Prob(X \mid Z) \times Prob(W \mid Z)$. The chain structure "$Y \rightarrow Z \rightarrow W$" is also identified in a similar way.

The score-based approach for causal discovery aims to optimize a predefined score function (e.g., Bayesian information criteria) that evaluates the fitness of a candidate causal graph against the given dataset. A common score-based method is the fast greedy equivalence search (FGES) [58]. This method starts the search with an empty graph and iteratively adds a directed edge in the existing structure if the fitness of the current graph is increased. This process continues till the fitness score is no longer improved. Next, the algorithm begins removing an edge if the deletion improves the score. The edge removal stops when the score cannot be improved further. Then the resulting graph is a plausible causal structure from the dataset [59].

However, causal structure learning with a high-dimensional dataset has been deemed challenging since the search space of directed acyclic graphs scales super-exponentially with the number of nodes. Generally, the search problem of identifying DAGs from data has been considered as NP-hard [60, 61]. This challenge greatly handicaps the wide usage of the aforementioned causal discovery methods. There exist ongoing efforts to make the search more efficient by relaxing certain assumptions [63], adopting parallelized computation methodology [64], and incorporating deep learning frameworks [65]. A detailed discussion on causal discovery is beyond the scope of this chapter. Those interested in learning more about causal discovery should refer to [58–65].

6.25. Conclusions

In this chapter, we explored the strengths of causal reasoning when facing problems such as confounding bias, model transportability, and learning from missing data. We present some examples to demonstrate that pure data-driven or correlation-based statistical analysis may generate misleading conclusions. We argued the need to consider causality in our models to support critical clinical decision-making. Machine learning has been widely employed in various healthcare applications with recently increased efforts on how to augment machine learning models with causality to improve interpretability [41, 42] and predictive fairness [45, 46] and to avoid bias [43, 44]. The model interpretability can be enhanced through the identification of the cause–effect relation between the model input and outcome. We can observe how the model outcome responds to the intervention upon inputs. For example, powerful machine learning models can be built for early detection of type 2 diabetes mellitus using a collection of features such as age, weight, HDL cholesterol, and triglycerides [47]. However, healthcare practitioners are not content with mere predictions—they are also interested in the variables upon which the intervention will help reduce the risk of the disease effectively. Understanding causality is crucial to answer such questions. We also showed how causality can address confounding bias and selection bias in data analyses. The literature shows that causal inference can be adopted in deep learning modeling to reduce selection bias in recommender systems [43, 44]. Model fairness aims to protect the benefit of people in the minority groups or historically disadvantageous groups from the discriminative decisions produced by AI. Causal inference can also ensure model fairness against such social discriminations [45]. In addition to the attempts and progress made in this field, there are many low-hanging fruits in combining causal inference with machine learning methods. We hope that this brief introduction to causal inference will inspire more readers who are interested in this research area.

References

[1] F. H. Messerli. Chocolate consumption, cognitive function, and Nobel laureates. *N. Engl. J. Med.*, **367**(16):1562–1564 (2012).

[2] D. E. Geer Jr. Correlation is not causation. *IEEE Secur. Privacy*, **9**(2):93–94 (2011).

[3] K. E. Havens. Correlation is not causation: a case study of fisheries, trophic state and acidity in Florida (USA) lakes. *Environ. Pollut.*, **106**(1):1–4 (1999).

[4] D. Hume. An enquiry concerning human understanding, in *Seven Masterpieces of Philosophy*, Routledge, pp. 191–284 (2016).

[5] J. Pearl and D. Mackenzie. Beyond adjustment: the conquest of mount intervention, in *The Book of Why: The New Science of Cause and Effect*, Basic Books, p. 234 (2018).

[6] A. Morabia. Epidemiological causality. *Hist. Philos. Life Sci.*, **27**(3–4):365–379 (2005).

[7] S. A. Julious and M. A. Mullee. Confounding and Simpson's paradox. *BMJ*, **309**(6967): 1480–1481 (1994).

[8] P. W. Holland and D. B. Rubin. On Lord's paradox, in H. Wainer and S. Messick (eds.), *Principals of Modern Psychological Measurement*, Hillsdale, NJ: Lawrence Earlbaum, pp. 3–25 (1983).

[9] S. Greenland and H. Morgenstern. Confounding in health research. *Annu. Rev. Public Health*, **22**(1):189–212 (2001).

[10] J. Pearl et al. Causal inference in statistics: an overview. *Stat. Surv.*, **3**:96–146 (2009).

[11] P. Hünermund and E. Bareinboim. Causal inference and data-fusion in econometrics. *arXiv preprint arXiv:1912.09104* (2019).

[12] J. Pearl. The do-calculus revisited. *arXiv preprint arXiv:1210.4852* (2012).

[13] R. R. Tucci. Introduction to Judea Pearl's do-calculus. *arXiv preprint arXiv:1305.5506* (2013).

[14] Y. Huang and M. Valtorta. Pearl's calculus of intervention is complete. *arXiv preprint arXiv:1206.6831* (2012).

[15] D. Geiger, T. Verma, and J. Pearl. Identifying independence in Bayesian networks. *Networks*, **20**(5):507–534 (1990).

[16] T. J. VanderWeele and I. Shpitser. On the definition of a confounder. *Ann. Stat.*, **41**(1):196–220 (2013).

[17] S. Greenland, J. M. Robins, and J. Pearl. Confounding and collapsibility in causal inference. *Stat. Sci.*, **14**(1):29–46 (1999).

[18] C. R. Charig, D. R. Webb, S. R. Payne, and J. E. Wickham. Comparison of treatment of renal calculi by open surgery, percutaneous nephrolithotomy, and extracorporeal shockwave lithotripsy. *Br. Med. J. (Clin. Res. Ed.)*, **292**(6524):879–882 (1986).

[19] J. Pearl, M. Glymour, and N. P. Jewell. The effects of interventions, in *Causal Inference in Statistics: A Primer*, John Wiley & Sons, pp. 53–55 (2016).

[20] E. Bareinboim. Causal data science. https://www.youtube.com/watch?v=dUsokjG4DHc (2019).

[21] E. Bareinboim and J. Pearl. Causal inference and the data-fusion problem. *Proc. Natl. Acad. Sci.*, **113**(27):7345–7352 (2016).

[22] E. Bareinboim and J. Pearl. Controlling selection bias in causal inference, in *Proceedings of the Fifteenth International Conference on Artificial Intelligence and Statistics*, pp. 100–108 (2012).

[23] J. Berke. A statewide antibody study estimates that 21% of New York City residents have had the coronavirus, Cuomo says (2020).

[24] C. Kozyrkov. Were 21% of New York City residents really infected with the novel coronavirus? (2020).

[25] W. Zhang, W. Bao, X.-Y. Liu, K. Yang, Q. Lin, H. Wen, and R. Ramezani. A causal perspective to unbiased conversion rate estimation on data missing not at random, *arXiv:1910.09337* (2019).

[26] A. B. Ryder, A. V. Wilkinson, M. K. McHugh, K. Saunders, S. Kachroo, A. D'Amelio, M. Bondy, and C. J. Etzel. The advantage of imputation of missing income data to evaluate the association between income and self-reported health status (SRH) in a Mexican American cohort study. *J. Immigr. Minor. Health*, **13**(6):1099–1109 (2011).

[27] D. B. Rubin. Inference and missing data. *Biometrika*, **63**(3):581–592 (1976).

[28] C. K. Enders. *Applied Missing Data Analysis*. Guilford Press (2010).

[29] K. Mohan, J. Pearl, and J. Tian. Graphical models for inference with missing data, in C. J. C. Burges, L. Bottou, M. Welling, Z. Ghahramani, and K. Q. Weinberger (eds.), *Advances in Neural Information Processing System*, pp. 1277–1285 (2013).

[30] J. Pearl and K. Mohan. Recoverability and testability of missing data: introduction and summary of results. Available at SSRN 2343873 (2013).

[31] K. Mohan and J. Pearl. Missing data from a causal perspective, in *Workshop on Advanced Methodologies for Bayesian Networks*, Springer, pp. 184–195 (2015).

[32] J. Yoon, J. Jordon, and M. Van der Schaar. Gain: missing data imputation using generative adversarial nets. *arXiv preprint arXiv:1806.02920* (2018).

[33] S. van Buuren and K. Groothuis-Oudshoorn. Mice: multivariate imputation by chained equations in *R. J. Stat. Software*, **45**:1–68 (2010).

[34] Y. Deng, C. Chang, M. S. Ido, and Q. Long. Multiple imputation for general missing data patterns in the presence of high-dimensional data. *Sci. Rep.*, **6**:21689 (2016).

[35] J. L. Schafer and J. W. Graham. Missing data: our view of the state of the art. *Psychol. Methods*, **7**(2):147 (2002).

[36] R. J. A. Little and D. B. Rubin. *Statistical Analysis with Missing Data*, vol. 793. John Wiley & Sons (2019).

[37] J. Pearl. On the testability of causal models with latent and instrumental variables, in *Proceedings of the Eleventh Conference on Uncertainty in Artificial Intelligence*, Morgan Kaufmann Publishers Inc., pp. 435–443 (1995).

[38] M. Ford. *Architects of Intelligence: The truth About AI from the People Building It*. Packt Publishing Ltd (2018).

[39] E. Bareinboim, A. Forney, and J. Pearl. Bandits with unobserved confounders: a causal approach, in *Advances in Neural Information Processing Systems*, pp. 1342–1350 (2015).

[40] D. Russo, B. Van Roy, A. Kazerouni, I. Osband, and Z. Wen. A tutorial on Thompson sampling. *arXiv preprint arXiv:1707.02038* (2017).

[41] J. Kim and J. Canny. Interpretable learning for self-driving cars by visualizing causal attention, in *Proceedings of the IEEE International Conference on Computer Vision*, pp. 2942–2950 (2017).

[42] R. Moraffah, M. Karami, R. Guo, A. Raglin, and H. Liu. Causal interpretability for machine learning-problems, methods and evaluation. *ACM SIGKDD Explor. Newsl.*, **22**(1):18–33 (2020).

[43] W. Zhang, W. Bao, X.-Y. Liu, K. Yang, Q. Lin, H. Wen, and R. Ramezani. Large-scale causal approaches to debiasing post-click conversion rate estimation with multi-task learning, in *Proceedings of the Web Conference 2020*, pp. 2775–2781 (2020).

[44] T. Schnabel, A. Swaminathan, A. Singh, N. Chandak, and T. Joachims. Recommendations as treatments: debiasing learning and evaluation, in *International Conference on Machine Learning*, pp. 1670–1679. PMLR (2016).

[45] M. J. Kusner, J. R. Loftus, C. Russell, and R. Silva. Counterfactual fairness. *arXiv preprint arXiv:1703.06856* (2017).

[46] J. R. Loftus, C. Russell, M. J. Kusner, and R. Silva. Causal reasoning for algorithmic fairness. *arXiv preprint arXiv:1805.05859* (2018).

[47] L. Kopitar, P. Kocbek, L. Cilar, A. Sheikh, and G. Stiglic. Early detection of type 2 diabetes mellitus using machine learning-based prediction models. *Sci. Rep.*, **10**(1):1–12 (2020).

[48] H. C. S. Thom. A note on the gamma distribution. *Monthly Weather Review*, **86**(4):117–122 (1958).

[49] M. Parascandola. Causes, risks, and probabilities: probabilistic concepts of causation in chronic disease epidemiology. *Preventive Med.*, **53**(4–5):232–234 (2011).

[50] Z. Verde et al. 'Smoking genes': a genetic association study. *PLoS One*, **6**(10):e26668 (2011).

[51] J. MacKillop et al. The role of genetics in nicotine dependence: mapping the pathways from genome to syndrome. *Curr. Cardiovasc. Risk Rep.*, **4**(6):446–453 (2010).

[52] J. Pearl. Bayesian networks: a model CF self-activated memory for evidential reasoning, in *Proceedings of the 7th Conference of the Cognitive Science Society*, University of California, Irvine, CA, USA (1985).

[53] J. Pearl. Bayesian networks, causal inference and knowledge discovery. *UCLA Cognitive Systems Laboratory, Technical Report* (2001).

[54] D. Heckerman, C. Meek, and G. Cooper. A Bayesian approach to causal discovery, in *Computation, Causation, and Discovery*, 141–166 (1999).

[55] C. Glymour, K. Zhang, and P. Spirtes. Review of causal discovery methods based on graphical models. *Front. Genet.*, **10**:524 (2019).

[56] P. Spirtes, C. Glymour, and R. Scheines. *Causation, Prediction, and Search*, 2nd edn. Cambridge, MA: MIT Press (2001).

[57] P. Spirtes et al. Constructing Bayesian network models of gene expression networks from microarray data. Carnegie Mellon University. Journal contribution. https://doi.org/10.1184/R1/6491291.v1 (2000).

[58] J. Ramsey et al. A million variables and more: the Fast Greedy Equivalence Search algorithm for learning high-dimensional graphical causal models, with an application to functional magnetic resonance images. *Int. J. Data Sci. Anal.*, **3**(2):121–129 (2017).

[59] D. M. Chickering. Optimal structure identification with greedy search. *J. Mach. Learn. Res.*, **3**:507–554 (2002).

[60] D. M. Chickering. Learning Bayesian networks is NP-complete, in *Learning from Data*. Springer, New York, NY, pp. 121–130 (1996).

[61] D. M. Chickering, D. Heckerman, and C. Meek. Large-sample learning of Bayesian networks is NP-hard. *J. Mach. Learn. Res.*, **5**:1287–1330 (2004).

[62] Z. Hao et al. Causal discovery on high dimensional data. *Appl. Intell.*, **42**(3):594–607 (2015).

[63] T. Claassen, J. Mooij, and T. Heskes. Learning sparse causal models is not NP-hard. *arXiv preprint arXiv:1309.6824* (2013).

[64] T. D. Le et al. A fast PC algorithm for high dimensional causal discovery with multi-core PCs. *IEEE/ACM Trans. Comput. Biol. Bioinf.*, **16**(5):1483–1495 (2016).

[65] I. Ng et al. A graph autoencoder approach to causal structure learning. *arXiv preprint arXiv:1911.07420* (2019).

[66] K. P. Murphy. *Machine Learning: A Probabilistic Perspective*. MIT Press, Cambridge, MA (2012).

[67] T. J. VanderWeele, and I. Shpitser. On the definition of a confounder. *Ann. Stat.*, **41**(1):196 (2013).

Part II

Supervised Learning

Chapter 7

Fuzzy Classifiers

Hamid Bouchachia

Department of Computing & Informatics
Faculty of Science and Technology, Bournemouth University, UK
abouchachia@bournemouth.ac.uk

The present chapter discusses fuzzy classification with a focus on rule-based classification systems (FRS). The chapter consists of two parts. The first part deals with type-1 fuzzy rule-based classification systems (FRCS). It introduces the steps of building such systems before overviewing their optimality quality in terms of performance, completeness, consistency, compactness, and transparency/interpretability. The second part discusses incremental and online FRCS providing insight into both online type-1 and type-2 FRCS both at the structural and functional levels.

7.1. Introduction

Over the recent years, fuzzy rule-based classification systems have emerged as a new class of attractive classifiers due to their transparency and interpretability characteristics. Motivated by such characteristics, fuzzy classifiers have been used in various applications such as smart homes [7, 9], image classification [52], medical applications [51], pattern recognition [54], etc.

Classification rules are simple, consisting of two parts: the premises (conditions) and consequents that correspond to class labels as shown in the following:

Rule 1 : If x_1 is small then Class 1

Rule 2 : If x_1 is large then Class 2

Rule 3 : If x_1 is medium and x_2 is very small then Class 1

Rule 4 : If x_2 is very large then Class 2

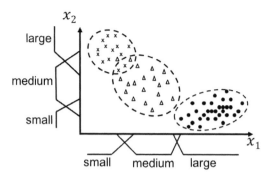

Figure 7.1:   Two-dimensional illustrative example of specifying the antecedent part of a fuzzy if–then rule.

where x_i corresponds to (the definition domain of) the input features (i.e., the dimensions of the input space). As an example, from Figure 7.1, one can derive the rule

If x_1 is large then Class 3.

Rules may be associated with degrees of confidence that explain how well the rule covers a particular input region.

Rule 5 : If x_2 is small then Class 1 **with confidence 0.8**.

Graphically, the rules partition the space into regions. Ideally, each region is covered by one rule as shown in Figure 7.1. each region is covered by one rule as shown in Figure 7.1.

Basically, there are two main approaches for designing fuzzy rule-based classifiers:

- **Human expertise:** The rules are explicitly proposed by the human expert. Usually, no tuning is required and the rules are used for predicting the classes of the input using certain inference steps (see Section 7.3).
- **Machine generated:** The standard way of building rule-based classifiers is to apply an automatic process that consists of certain steps: partitioning of the input space, finding the fuzzy sets of the rules' premises and associating class labels as consequents. To predict the label of an input, an inference process is applied. Usually additional steps are involved, especially for optimizing the rule base [20].

Usually, fuzzy classifiers come in the form of explicit if–then classification rules as was illustrated earlier. However, rules can also be encoded in neural networks, resulting in neuro-fuzzy architectures [31]. Moreover, different computational intelligence techniques have been used to develop fuzzy classifiers: evolutionary algorithms [20], rough sets [48], ant colony systems [23], immune systems [2], particle swarm optimization [43], petri nets [10], etc. These computational approaches are used for both the design and optimization of the classifier's rules.

7.2. Pattern Classification

The problem of pattern classification can be formally defined as follows: Let $T = \{(\mathbf{x}_i, y_i)_{i=1,...,N}\}$ be a set of training patterns. Each $\mathbf{x}_i = (x_{i1}, \ldots, x_{id}) \in X^1$ is a d-dimensional vector and $y_i \in Y = \{y_1, \ldots, y_C\}$, where Y denotes a discrete set of classes (i.e., labels). A classifier is inherently characterized by a decision function $f : X \rightarrow Y$ that is used to predict the class label y_i for each pattern $\mathbf{x}_i$. The decision function is learned from the training data patterns T drawn i.i.d at random according to an unknown distribution from the space $X \times Y$. An accurate classifier has a very small generalization error (i.e., it generalizes well to unseen patterns). In general, a loss (cost) is associated with errors, meaning that some misclassification errors are "worse" than others. Such a loss is expressed formally as a function $\ell(\mathbf{x}_i, y_i, f(\mathbf{x}_i))$ that can take different forms (e.g., 0-1, hinge, squared hinge, etc.) [18]. Ideally, the classifier (i.e., decision function) should minimize the expected error $E(f)$ (known as the empirical risk) $= (1/N) \sum_{i=1}^{N} \ell(\mathbf{x}_i, y_i, f(\mathbf{x}_i))$. Hence, the aim is to learn a function f among a set of all functions that minimize the error $E(f)$. The empirical risk may be regularized by putting additional constraints (terms) to restrain the function space, penalize the number of parameters and model complexity, and avoid overfitting (which occurs when the classifier does not generalize well on unseen data). The regularized risk is then $R(f) = E(f) + \lambda\Omega(f)$.

Classifiers can be either linear or nonlinear. A linear classifier (i.e., the decision function is linear and the classes are linearly separable) has the form: $y_i = g(\mathbf{w} \cdot \mathbf{x}_i) = g\left(\sum_{j=1}^{d} w_j x_{ij}\right)$, where $\mathbf{w}$ is a weight vector computed by learning from the training patterns. The function g outputs the class label. Clearly, the argument of decision function, $f = \sum_{j=1}^{d} w_j x_{ij}$, is a linear combination of the input and the weight vectors.

Linear classifiers are of two types, discriminative or generative. Discriminative linear classifiers try to minimize R (or its simplest version E) without necessarily caring about the way the (training) patterns are generated. Examples of discriminative linear classifiers are perceptron, support vector machines (SVM), logistic regression, and linear discriminant analysis (LDA).

Generative classifiers such as naive Bayes classifiers and hidden Markov models aim at learning a model of the joint probability $p(\mathbf{x}, y)$ over the data X and the label Y. They aim at inferring class-conditional densities $p(\mathbf{x}|y)$ and priors $p(y)$. The prediction decision is made by exploiting Bayes' rule to compute $p(y|\mathbf{x})$ and then by

---

[1] x_{ij} will be written as x_j (fuzzy variables) when not referring to a specific input vector $\mathbf{x}_i$.

selecting the label with the higher probability. The discriminative classifiers, on the other hand, aim at computing $p(y|\mathbf{x})$ directly from the pairs $(x_i, y_i)_{i=1\cdots N}$. Examples of generative linear classifiers are probabilistic linear discriminant analysis (LDA) and naive Bayes classifier.

Nonlinear classifiers (i.e., the decision function is not linear and can be quadratic, exponential, etc.). The straightforward formulation of nonlinear classifiers is the generalized linear classifier that tries to Nonlinearly map the input space onto another space $(X \subset \mathbb{R}^d \to Z \subset \mathbb{R}^K)$, where the patterns are separable. Thus, $\mathbf{x} \in \mathbb{R}^d \mapsto \mathbf{z} \in \mathbb{R}^K$, $z = f_1(\mathbf{x}), \ldots, f_K(\mathbf{x})^T$, where f_k is a nonlinear function (e.g., log-sigmoid, tan-sigmoid, etc.). For the ith sample $(\mathbf{x}_i)$, the decision function is then of the form: $y_i = g\left(\sum_{k=1}^K w_k f_k(\mathbf{x}_i)\right)$.

There are many nonlinear classification algorithms of different types, such as generalized linear classifiers, deep networks, multilayer perceptron, polynomial classifiers, radial basis function networks, etc., nonlinear SVM (kernels), k-nearest neighbor, rule-based classifiers (e.g., decision trees, fuzzy rule-based classifiers, different hybrid neuro-genetic-fuzzy classifiers), etc. [18].

Moreover, we can distinguish between two categories of classifiers: symbolic and sub-symbolic classifiers. The symbolic classifiers are those that learn the decision function in the form of rules:

$$\textbf{If } x_1 \text{ is } A \; \wedge \; x_2 \text{ is } B \; \wedge \; \cdots \; x_d \text{ is } Z \textbf{ then } \text{ class is } C. \tag{7.1}$$

Here, $\wedge$ is the logic operator "and" as one of the "t-norm" operators that can be used.

The advantage of this category of classifiers is the transparency and interpretability of their behavior. The sub-symbolic classifiers are those that do not operate on symbols and could be seen as a black box.

7.3. Fuzzy Rule-Based Classification Systems

Fuzzy rule-based systems represent knowledge in the form of fuzzy "IF-THEN" rules. These rules can be either encoded by human experts or extracted from raw data by an inductive learning process. Generically, a fuzzy rule has the form

$$R_r \equiv \text{ If } x_1 \text{ is } A_{r,1} \wedge \; \ldots \; \wedge x_d \text{ is } A_{r,d} \text{ then } y_r, \tag{7.2}$$

where $\{x_{i*}\}_{i=1\ldots d}$ are fuzzy linguistic input variables, $A_{r,i}$ are antecedent linguistic terms in the form of fuzzy sets that characterize the input space and y_r is the output. Each linguistic term (fuzzy set) is associated with a membership function that defines how each point in the input space formed by the input variables $(\{x_i\}_{i=1\ldots d})$ is mapped to a membership value (along with the linguistic variable) between 0 and 1. If the membership values are single values from [0,1], then the fuzzy sets are called *type-1 fuzzy sets* and the fuzzy rule/system is called a type-1 fuzzy rule/system.

The form of rule expressed by Eq. 7.2 can take different variations. The most well-known ones are the Mamdani type (known as *linguistic fuzzy rules*), Takagi–Sugeno type (known as *functional fuzzy rules*), and classification type. The former two have been introduced in the context of fuzzy control. Specifically, a linguistic fuzzy rule (*Mamdani type*) has the following structure:

$$\text{If } x_1 \text{ is } A_{r,1} \wedge \cdots \wedge x_d \text{ is } A_{r,d} \text{ then } y_1 \text{ is } B_{r,1} \wedge \cdots \wedge y_m \text{ is } B_{r,m}, \quad (7.3)$$

where x_i are fuzzy linguistic input variables, y_j are fuzzy linguistic output variables, and $A_{r,i}$ and $B_{r,j}$ are linguistic terms in the form of fuzzy sets that characterize x_i and y_j. Mamdani's model is known for its transparency since all of the rule's terms are linguistic terms.

Functional fuzzy rules differ from linguistic fuzzy rules at the consequent level. The consequent of a functional fuzzy rule is a combination of the inputs as shown in Eq. (7.4):

$$\text{If } x_1 \text{ is } A_{r,1} \wedge \cdots \wedge x_d \text{ is } A_{r,d} \text{ then } \begin{cases} y_{r,1} = f_{r,1}(\mathbf{x}) \\ \cdots \\ y_{r,m} = f_{r,m}(\mathbf{x}) \end{cases} \quad (7.4)$$

A rule consists of n input fuzzy variables $(x_1, x_2, \ldots, x_d)$ and m output variables $(y_1, y_2, \ldots, y_m)$ such that $y_{r,j} = f_{r,j}(\mathbf{x})$. The most popular form of f is the polynomial form: $y_{r,j} = f_{r,j}(\mathbf{x}) = b_{r,j}^1 x_1 + \cdots + b_{r,j}^d x_d + b_{r,j}^0$, where $b_{r,j}^i$'s denote the system's $m + 1$ output parameters. These parameters are usually determined using iterative optimization methods. Functional FRS are used to approximate nonlinear systems by a set of linear systems.

In this chapter, we focus on classification systems where a rule looks as follows:

$$\text{If } x_1 \text{ is } A_{r,1} \wedge \cdots \wedge x_d \text{ is } A_{r,d} \text{ then } y_r \text{ is } C_r \tau_r, \quad (7.5)$$

where C_r, τ_r indicate, respectively, the class label and the certainty factor associated with the rule r. A certainty factor represents the confidence degree of assigning the input, $\mathbf{x}_i = x_{i1}, \ldots, x_{id}{}'$, to a class C_r, i.e., how good the rule covers the space of a class C_r. For a rule r, it is expressed as follows [29]:

$$\tau_r = \frac{\sum_{\mathbf{x}_i \in C_r} \mu_{A_r}(\mathbf{x}_i)}{\sum_{i=1}^{N} \mu_{A_r}(\mathbf{x}_i)}, \quad (7.6)$$

where $\mu_{A_r}(\mathbf{x}_i)$ is obtained as follows:

$$\mu_{A_r}(\mathbf{x}_i) = \prod_{p=1}^{d} \mu_{A_{r,p}}(x_{ip}). \tag{7.7}$$

Equation (7.7) uses the product, but can also use any t-norm:

$$\mu_{A_r}(\mathbf{x}_i) = T(\mu_{A_{r,1}}(x_{i1}), \ldots, \mu_{A_{r,d}}(x_{id})).$$

Moreover, the rule in Eq. (7.5) could be generalized to multi-class consequents to account for class distribution and, in particular, overlap.

$$\text{If } x_1 \text{ is } A_{r,1} \wedge \cdots \wedge x_d \text{ is } A_{r,d} \text{ then } y_r \text{ is } C_1\tau_1, \ldots, C_K\tau_K. \tag{7.8}$$

This formulation was adopted in particular in [8], where τ_j's correspond to the proportion of patterns of each class in the region covered by the rule j.

Note also that the rule's form in Eq. (7.5) could be seen as a special case of the functional fuzzy rule model, in particular, the *zero-order model*, where the consequent is a singleton.

Furthermore, there exists another type of fuzzy classification system based on multidimensional fuzzy sets, where rules are expressed in the form [7]

$$R_r \equiv \text{If } \mathbf{x} \text{ is } K_i \text{ then } y_r \text{ is } C_j, \tag{7.9}$$

where K_i is a cluster and $\mathbf{x} = [x_1, \ldots, x_d]^t$. The rule means that if the sample $\mathbf{x}$ is CLOSE to K_i, then the label of $\mathbf{x}$ should be that of class C_j.

Classes in the consequent part of the rules can be determined following two options:

- The generation of the fuzzy sets (partitions) is done using supervised clustering. That is, each partition will be labeled and will emanate from one class. In this case, certainty factors associated with the rules will be needless [7–9].
- The generation of the fuzzy sets is done using clustering, so that partitions can contain patterns from different classes at the same time. In this case, a special process is required to determine the rule consequents. Following the procedure described in [27], the consequent is found:

$$y_r = \underset{j=1\cdots C}{\text{argmax}}\{v_j\}, \tag{7.10}$$

where v_j is given as

$$v_j = \sum_{\mathbf{x}_k \in C_r} \mu_r(\mathbf{x}_k) = \sum_{\mathbf{x}_k \in C_r} \left(\prod_{p=1}^{d} \mu_{A_{r,p}}(x_{kp}) \right). \tag{7.11}$$

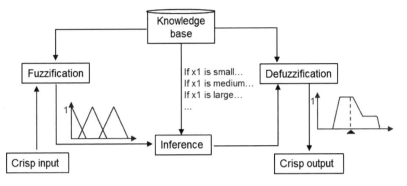

Figure 7.2: Structure of a fuzzy classifier.

Given a test pattern, $\mathbf{x}_k$, entering the system, the output of the fuzzy classifier with respect to this pattern is the winner class, w, referred in the consequent of the rule with the highest activation degree. The winning class is computed as follows:

$$y(\mathbf{x}_k) = \underset{j=1\cdots C}{\mathrm{argmax}}\{w_j(\mathbf{x}_k)\}, \qquad (7.12)$$

where w_j is given as

$$w_j(\mathbf{x}_k) = max\{\mu_r(\mathbf{x}_k) * \tau_r | y_r = j\}, \qquad (7.13)$$

where τ_r is expressed by Eq. (7.6). If there is more than one winner (taking the same maximum value w_j), then the pattern is considered unclassifiable/ambiguous.

As shown in Figure 7.2, a general fuzzy rule-based system consists mainly of four components: the knowledge base, the inference engine, the fuzzifier, and the defuzzifier, which are briefly described below. Note that fuzzy classifiers generally do not include the defuzzification step, since a fuzzy output is already indicative.

1. The knowledge base consists of a rule base that holds a collection of fuzzy IF–THEN rules and a database that includes the membership functions defining the fuzzy sets used by the fuzzy rule system.
2. The inference engine maps the input to the rules and computes an aggregated fuzzy output of the system according to an inference method. The common inference method is the Max-Min composition [40], where rules are first combined with the input before aggregating using some operator (Mamdani, Gödel, etc.) to produce a final output or rules are combined first before acting on the input vector. Typical inference in classification systems is rather simple as explained earlier. It consists of sequentially computing the following degrees:

   (a) Activation, i.e., the product/t-norm of the antecedent part; see Eq. (7.7).
   (b) Association, i.e., combine the confidence factors with the activation degree to determine association degree of the input with the classes; see Eq. (7.13).

   (c) Classification, i.e., choose the class with the highest association degree; see Eq. (7.12).

3. Fuzzification transforms the crisp input into fuzzy input, by matching the input to the linguistic values in the rules' antecedents. Such values are represented as membership functions (e.g., triangular, trapezoidal and Gaussian) and stored in the database. These functions specify a partitioning of the input and eventually the output space. The number of fuzzy partitions determines that of the rules. There are three types of partitioning: grid, tree, and scatter. The latter is the most common one, since it finds the regions covering the data using clustering. Different clustering algorithms have been used [57]. Known algorithms are Gustafson–Kessel and Gath–Geva [1], mountain [60], subtractive [3], fuzzy hierarchical clustering [55], fuzzy c-means [6] and mixture models [9], and leader-like algorithm [49].

4. The defuzzifier transforms the aggregated fuzzy output generated by the inference engine into a crisp output because very often a crisp output of the system is required for facilitating decision making. The known defuzzification methods are center of area, height-center of area, max criterion, first of maxima, and middle of maxima. However, the most popular method is center of area [44]. Recall that fuzzy classification systems do not involve necessarily defuzzification.

   Algorithm 7.1 illustrates the main steps for generating rules and predicting the label of the class of new input.

Algorithm 7.1 : Generic steps of a fuzzy classifier.

Generating:

1: Given a dataset, generate partitions (i.e., clusters, granules) using any type of partitioning (grid, tree, or scatter).
2: Transform the granules into fuzzy patches (fuzzy memberships) making sure that all of the input space is covered by the fuzzy patches (i.e., the fuzzy membership functions should overlap).
3: For each granule, generate a class label as consequent following Eqs. (7.10) and (7.11)
4: Compute the certainty factors of the rules (Eq. (7.6)) and produce the rules Premise–Consequent–CF and store them in a rule base.

Predicting:

1: Given an input, compute the firing degree with respect to each rule by applying Eq. (7.7).
2: Compute the winning class by applying Eqs. (7.12) and (7.13).

7.4. Quality Issues of Fuzzy Rule-Based Systems

In general, knowledge maintenance entails the activities of knowledge validation, optimization, and evolution. The validation process aims at checking the consistency of knowledge by repairing/removing contradictions. Optimization seeks the compactness of knowledge by alleviating all types of redundancy and rendering the knowledge base transparent. Finally, evolution of knowledge is about incremental learning of knowledge without jeopardizing the old knowledge, allowing a continuous and incremental update of the knowledge.

This section aims at discussing the optimization issues of rule-based systems. Optimization in this context deals primarily with the transparency of the rule base. Given the symbolic representation of rules, the goal is to describe the classifier with a small number of concise rules relying on transparent and interpretable fuzzy sets intelligible by human experts. Using data to automatically build the classifier is a process that does not always result in a transparent rule base [32]. Hence, there is a need to optimize the number and the structure of the rules while keeping the classifier accuracy as high as possible (more discussion on this tradeoff will follow below). Note that beyond classification, the Mamdani model is geared toward more interpretability; hence the name of linguistic fuzzy modeling. Takagi–Sugeno model is geared towards accuracy, hence the name precise fuzzy modeling or functional fuzzy model [21].

Overall, the quality of the rule base (knowledge) can be evaluated using various criteria: performance, comprehensibility, and completeness, which are explained in the following subsections.

7.4.1. *Performance*

A classifier, independently of its computational model, is judged on its performance. That is, how well does the classifier perform on unseen novel data? Measuring performance measure is about assessing the quality of decision-making. Accuracy is one of the mostly used measures. It quantifies the extent to which the system meets the human being decision. Thus, accuracy measures the ratio of correct decisions. Expressively, *Accuracy = Correct/Test*, where *correct* and *test* indicate respectively the number of patterns well classified (corresponding to true positives + true negatives decisions), while *Test* is the total number of patterns presented to the classifier. However, but accuracy as a sole measure for evaluating the performance of the classifier might be misleading in some situations like in the case of imbalanced classes. Obviously different measures can be used, like precision (positive predictive value), false positive rate (false alarm rate), true positive rate (sensitivity), and ROC curves [19]. It is, therefore, recommended to use multiple performance measures to objectively evaluate the classifier.

7.4.2. *Completeness*

Knowledge is complete if, for making a decision, all the needed knowledge elements are available. Following the architecture portrayed in Figure 7.2, the system should have all ingredients needed to classify a pattern. The other aspect of completeness is the coverage of the discourse representation space. That is, all input variables (dimensions) to be considered should be fully covered by the fuzzy sets using *the frame of cognition* FOC) [40], which stipulates that a fuzzy set (patch) along a dimension must satisfy: normality, typicality, full membership, convexity, and overlap.

7.4.3. *Consistency*

Consistency is a key issue in knowledge engineering and is considered one important part of the rule base comprehensibility assessment [17, 45, 59]. In the absence of consistency, the knowledge is without value and its use leads to contradictory decisions. Inconsistency results from conflicting knowledge elements. For instance, two rules are in conflict if they have identical antecedents but different consequents. In the case of fuzzy rule-based classification, there is no risk to have inconsistency, since each rule corresponds to a given region of the data space. Moreover, even if an overlap between antecedents of various rules exists, the output for a given data point is unambiguously computed using the confidence factors related to each rule in the knowledge base.

7.4.4. *Compactness*

Compactness is about the conciseness and the ease of understanding and reasoning about knowledge. Systems built on a symbolic ground, such as rule-based systems, are easy to understand and to track how and why they reach a particular decision. To reinforce this characteristic, the goal of system design is to reduce, as much as possible, the number of rules to make the system's behavior more transparent. Thus, a small number of rules and a small number of conditions in the antecedent of rules ensures high compactness of the system's rule base.

To reduce the complexity of the rule-base and consequently to get rid of redundancy and strengthen compactness, the optimization procedure can consist of a certain number of steps [8].

All these steps are based on similarity measures. There are a number of measures based on set-theoretic, proximity, interval, logic, linguistic approximation, and fuzzy-valued [58]. In the following, the optimization steps are described.

- Redundant partitions: they are discovered by computing the similarity of the fuzzy sets describing these partitions to the universe. A fuzzy set A_{ij}^r is removed if

$$Sim(A_{ij}^r, U) > \epsilon, \tag{7.14}$$

where $\epsilon \in (0, 1)$ and indicates a threshold (a required level of similarity), U indicates the universe that is defined as follows:

$$\forall x_k, \mu_U(x_{ki}) = 1.$$

Any pattern has a full membership in the universe of discourse.
- Merging of fuzzy partitions: two fuzzy partition are merged if their similarity exceeds a certain threshold:

$$Sim(A_{ij}^r, A_{ik}^r) > \tau, \tag{7.15}$$

where A_{ij}^r, A_{ik}^r are the jth and k^{th} partitions of the feature i in the rule r
- Removal of weakly firing rules: this consists of identifying rules whose output is always close to 0.

$$\mu_i^r < \beta \tag{7.16}$$

- Removal of redundant rules: there is redundancy if the similarity (e.g., overlap) between the antecedents of the rules is high, exceeding some threshold δ. The similarity of the antecedents of two rules r and p is given as

$$sim(A^r, A^p) = \min_{i=1,n}\{Sim(A_i^r, A_i^p)\}, \tag{7.17}$$

where the antecedents A^r and A^p are given by the set of fuzzy partitions representing the n features $A^r =< A_1^r, \ldots, A_n^r >$ and $A^r =< A_1^r, \ldots, A_n^r >$. That is, similar rules (i.e., having similar antecedents and same consequent) are merged. In doing so, if some rules have the same consequence, the antecedents of those rules can be connected. However, this may result in a conflict if the antecedents are not the same. One can, however, rely on the following rules of thumb:

— If, for some set of rules with the same consequent, a variable takes all forms (it belongs to all forms of fuzzy set, e.g., small, medium, large), then such a variable can be reduced from the antecedent of that set of rules. In other words, this set of rules is independent of the variable that takes all possible values. This variable the corresponds to "*don't care.*"
For instance, if we consider Table 7.1, rules 1, 3, and 4 are about class C_1 and the input variable x_2 takes all possible linguistic variables. The optimization will replace these rules with a generic rule as shown in Table 7.2.

Table 7.1: Rules of the rule base.

	x_1	x_2	x_3	x_4	*Class*
1	S	S	S	S	1
2	M	S	M	M	2
3	S	M	S	S	1
4	S	L	S	S	1
5	M	S	L	M	2

Table 7.2: Combining rules 1, 3, and 4.

	x_1	x_2	x_3	x_4	*Class*
1	S	S	S	S	1
3	S	M	S	S	1
4	S	L	S	S	1
1'	S	-	S	S	1

Table 7.3: Combining rules 2 and 5.

	x_1	x_2	x_3	x_4	*Class*
2	M	S	M	M	2
5	M	S	L	M	2
2'	M	S	(M ∨ L)	M	2

— If, for some set of rules with the same consequent, a variable takes a subset of all possible forms (e.g., small and medium), then the antecedents of such rules can be combined by or("ing") the values corresponding to that variable. For instance, if we consider Table 7.1, the rules 2 and 5 are about class C_2 such that the variable x_3 takes the linguistic values: medium and large, while the other variables take the same values. The two rules can be replaced with one generic rule as shown in Table 7.3.

7.4.5. *Feature selection*

To enhance the transparency and the compactness of the rules, it is important that the if-part of the rules does not involve many features. Low classification performance generally results from non-informative features. The very conventional way to get rid of these features is to apply feature selection methods. Basically, there exist three classes of feature selection methods [25]:

1. **Filters:** The idea is to filter out features that have small potential to predict the outputs. The selection is done as a pre-processing step ahead of the classification task. Filters are preprocessing techniques and refer to statistical selection methods such as principal components analysis, LDA, and single value decomposition. For instance, Tikk et al. [53] describe a feature ranking algorithm for fuzzy modelling aiming at higher transparency of the rule-based. Relying on interclass separability as in LDA and using the backward selection method, the features are sequentially selected. Vanhoucke et al. [56] used a number of measures that rely mutual information to design a highly transparent classifier and particularly to select the features deemed to be the most informative. Similar approach has been taken in [50] using a mutual information-based feature selection for optimizing a fuzzy rule based system. Lee et al. [33] applied fuzzy entropy (FE) in the context of fuzzy classification to achieve low complexity and high classification efficiency. First FE was used to partition the pattern space into non-overlapping regions. Then, it was applied to select relevant features using the standard forward selection or backward elimination.

2. **Wrappers:** Select features that optimize the accuracy of a chosen classifier. Wrappers largely depend on the classifier to judge how well feature subsets are at classifying the training samples. For instance, in [12], the authors use a fuzzy wrapper and a fuzzy C4.5 decision tree to identify discriminative features. Wrappers are not very popular in the area of fuzzy rule-based systems. But many references claimed their methods to be wrappers, while actually they are embedded.

3. **Embedded:** Embedded methods perform variable selection in the process of training and are usually specific to given learning machines. In [13] to design a fuzzy rule-based classifier while selecting the relevant features, multi-objective genetic algorithms are used. The aim is to optimize the precision of the classifier. Similar approach is suggested in [11], where the T-S model is considered. In the same vein, in [46], the selection of features is done while a fuzzy rule classifier is being optimized using the Choquet Integral. The embedded methods dominate the other two categories due to the natural process of optimization rule-based system to obtain high interpretable rules.

7.5. Unified View of Rule-Based Optimization

Different taxonomies related to interpretability of fuzzy systems in general have been suggested:

- Mencar et al. [14] proposed a taxonomy in terms of interpretability constraints to the following levels: the fuzzy sets, the universe of discourse, the fuzzy granules, the rules, the fuzzy models the learning algorithms.

- Zhou and Gan [61] proposed a taxonomy in terms of low-level interpretability and high-level interpretability. Low-level interpretability is associated with the fuzzy set level to capture the semantics, while high-level interpretability is associated with the rule level.
- Gacto et al. [21] proposed a taxonomy inspired from the second one and distinguished between complexity-based interpretability equivalent to the high-level interpretability and semantics-based interpretability equivalent to low-level interpretability associated with the previous taxonomy.

A straight way to deal with interpretability issues in a unified way, by considering both transparency and performance at the same time, is to use optimization methods. We can use either meta-heuristics (evolutionary methods) or special-purpose designed methods. In the following some studies are briefly reported on.

Ishibuchi et al. [26] propose a genetic algorithm for rule selection in classification problems, considering the following two objectives: to maximize the number of correctly classified training patterns and to minimize the number of selected rules. This improves the complexity of the model, thanks to the reduction in the number of rules and the use of don't-care conditions in the antecedent part of the rule. Ishibuchi et al. [27, 28] present a multi-objective evolutionary algorithm (MOEA) for classification problems with three objectives: maximizing the number of correctly classified patterns, minimizing the number of rules, and minimizing the number of antecedent conditions. Narukawa et al. [38] rely on NSGA-II to optimize the rule base by eliminating redundant rules using multi-objective optimization that aims at increasing the accuracy while minimizing the number of rules, and the premises.

Additional studies using evolutionary algorithms, in particular multi-objective evolutionary algorithms, can be found in a recent survey by Fazzoli et al. [20].

In comparison to previously mentioned studies, others have used special purpose optimization methods. For instance, Mikut et al. [37] used decision trees to generate rules before an optimization process is applied. This later consists of feature selection using an entropy-base method and applying iteratively a search-based formula that combines accuracy and transparency to find the best configuration of the rule base.

Nauck [39] introduced a formula that combines by product three components: complexity (expressed as the proportion of the number of classes to the total number of variables used in the rules), coverage, (the average extent to which the domain of each variable is covered by the actual partitions of the variable), and partition complexity (quantified for each variable as inversely proportional to the number of partitions associated with that variable).

Guillaume and Charnomordic [24] devised a distance-based formula to decide whether two partitions can be merged. The formula relies on the intra-distance (called internal distance) of a fuzzy set for a given variable and the inter-distance (called external distance) of fuzzy sets for a variable, similar to that used for computing clusters. Any pairs of fuzzy sets that minimize the combination of these two measures over the set of data points will be merged.

Valente de Oliveira et al. [15, 16] used backpropagation to optimize a performance index that consists of three constraining terms: accuracy, coverage, and distinguishability of fuzzy sets.

7.6. Incremental and Online Fuzzy Rule-Based Classification Systems

Traditional fuzzy classification systems are designed in batch (offline) mode, that is, by using the complete training data at once. Thus, offline development of fuzzy classification systems assumes that the process of rule induction is done in a one-shot experiment, such that the learning phase and the deployment phase are two sequential and independent stages. For stationary processes, this is sufficient, but if, for instance, the rule system's performance deteriorates due to a change of the data distribution or a change of the operating conditions, the system needs to be re-designed from scratch. Many offline approaches do simply perform "adaptive tuning," that is, they permanently re-estimate the parameters of the computed model. However, it is quite often necessary to adapt the structure of the rule-base. In general, for time-dependent and complex non-stationary processes, efficient techniques for updating the induced models are needed. Such techniques must be able to adapt the current model using only the new data. They have to be equipped with mechanisms to react to gradual changes or abrupt ones. The adaptation of the model (i.e., rules) should accommodate any information brought in by the new data and reconcile this with the existing rules.

Online development of fuzzy classification systems [9], on the other hand, enables both learning and deployment to happen concurrently. In this context, rule learning takes place over long periods of time, and is inherently open-ended [8]. The aim is to ensure that the system remains amenable to refinement as long as data continues to arrive. Moreover, online systems can also deal with both applications starving of data (e.g., experiments that are expensive and slow to produce data as in some chemical and biological applications) as well as applications that are data intensive [5, 7].

Generally, online systems face the challenge of accurately estimating the statistical characteristics of data in the future. In non-stationary environments, the challenge becomes even more important, since the FRS's behavior may need to change drastically over time due to concept drift [7, 22]. The aim of online learning is to ensure continuous adaptation. Ideally, only the learning model (e.g., only rules) and uses that model as basis in the future learning steps. As new data arrive, new rules may be created and existing ones may be modified allowing the system to evolve over time.

Online and incremental fuzzy rule systems have been recently introduced in a number of studies involving control [3], diagnostics [35], and pattern classification [4, 8, 34, 35, 49]. Type-1 fuzzy systems are currently quite established, since they do not only operate online, but also consider related advanced concepts such as concept drift and online feature selection.

For instance in [8], an integrated approach called FRCS was proposed. To accommodate incremental rule learning, appropriate mechanisms are applied at all steps: (1) *incremental supervised clustering* to generate the rule antecedents in a progressive manner; (2) *online and systematic* update of fuzzy partitions; and (3) *incremental feature selection* using an *incremental version* of the Fisher's interclass separability criterion to dynamically select features in an online manner.

In [7], a fuzzy rule-based system for online classification is proposed. Relying on fuzzy min–max neural networks, the paper explains how fuzzy rules can be continuously online generated to meet the requirements of non-stationary dynamic environments, where data arrives over long periods of time. The classifier is sensitive to drift. It is able to detect data drift [22] using different measures and react to it. An outline of the algorithm proposed is described in Algorithm 7.2. Actually IFCS consists of three steps:

a) Initial one-shot experiment training: Available data is used to obtain an initial model of the IFCS.
b) Training over time before saturation: Given a saturation training level, incoming data is used to further adjust the model.
c) Correction after training saturation: Beyond the saturation level, incoming data is used to observe the evolution of classification performance which allow to correct the classifier if necessary.

In [9] a growing type-2 fuzzy classifier (GT2FC) for online fuzzy rule learning from real-time data streams is presented. To accommodate dynamic change, GT2FC relies on a new semi-supervised online learning algorithm called 2G2M (Growing Gaussian Mixture Model). In particular, 2G2M is used to generate the type-2 fuzzy membership functions to build the type-2 fuzzy rules. GT2FC is designed to accommodate data online and to reconcile labeled and unlabeled data using self-learning. Moreover. GT2FC maintains low complexity of the rule base using online optimization and feature selection mechanisms. Type-2 fuzzy classification is very suitable for dealing with applications where input is prone to faults and noise. Thus, GT2FC offers the advantage of dealing with uncertainty in addition to self-adaptation in an online manner.

Algorithm 7.2 : Steps of the incremental fuzzy classification system (IFCS).

1: **if** Initial=true **then**
2:    $\mathcal{M} \leftarrow$ Train_Classifier($<$TrainingData, Labels$>$)
3:    $\mathcal{E} \leftarrow$ Test_Classifier($<$TestingData, Labels$>$,$\mathcal{M}$)
         // Just for the sake of observation
4: **end if**
5: i$\leftarrow$0
6: **while** true **do**
7:    i$\leftarrow$ i+1
8:    Read $<$Input, Label$>$
9:    **if** IsLabeled(Label)=true **then**
10:      **if** Saturation_Training(i)=false **then**
11:         $\mathcal{M} \leftarrow$ Train_Classifier($<$Input, Label$>$,$\mathcal{M}$)
12:         If Input falls in a hyperbox with Flabel, then Flabel $\leftarrow$ Label
13:      **else**
14:         Err $\leftarrow$ Test_Classifier($<$Input, Label$>$,$\mathcal{M}$)
15:         Cumulated_Err $\leftarrow$ Cumulated_Err+Err
16:         **if** Detect_Drift(Cumulated_Err)=true **then**
17:            $\mathcal{M} \leftarrow$ Reset(Cumulated_Err,$\mathcal{M}$)
18:         **else**
19:            $\mathcal{M} \leftarrow$ Update_Classifier($<$Input, Label$>$,$\mathcal{M}$)
20:            If Input falls in a hyperbox with Flabel, then Flabel $\leftarrow$ Label
21:         **end if**
22:      **end if**
23:   **else**
24:      Flabel$\leftarrow$ Predict_Label(Input,$\mathcal{M}$)
25:      $\mathcal{M} \leftarrow$ Update_Classifier($<$Input,Flabel$>$,$\mathcal{M}$)
26:   **end if**
27: **end while**

Before proceeding further with type-2 fuzzy systems, it is important to define type-2 fuzzy sets. In contrast to the membership function associated with a type-1 fuzzy set is that takes single values from [0,1], the membership of a type-2 set is uncertain (i.e., fuzzy) and takes interval (or a more general form) rather than a specific value. Specifically, at the operational level, type-2 fuzzy rule systems (T2 FRS) differ from type-2 fuzzy rule systems (T1 FRS) in the type of fuzzy sets and the operations applied on these sets. T2 fuzzy sets are equipped mainly with two newly introduced operators called the *meet,* ⊓ and join, ⊔ which correspond

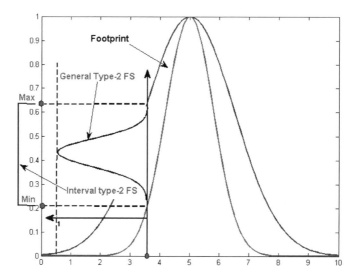

Figure 7.3: Type-2 fuzzy sets.

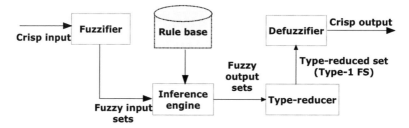

Figure 7.4: Type-2 fuzzy logic system.

to the fuzzy intersection and fuzzy union. As shown in Figure 7.4, T2 FRS at the structural level is similar to T1 FRS but contains an additional module, the *type-reducer*. In a classification type-2 fuzzy rule system, the fuzzy rules for a C-class pattern classification problem with d input variables can be formulated as

$$R_j \equiv \text{if } x_1 \text{ is } \tilde{A}_{j,1} \wedge \ldots \wedge x_d \text{ is } \tilde{A}_{j,d} \text{ then } C_i, \tag{7.18}$$

where $\mathbf{x} = x_1, \ldots, x_d{}^t$ such that each x_i is a an input variable and $\tilde{A}_{r,i}$ the corresponding fuzzy term in the form of type-2 fuzzy set. We may associate these fuzzy sets with linguistic labels to enhance interpretability. C_i is a consequent class, and $j = 1, \ldots, N$ is the number of fuzzy rules. The inference engine computes the output of type-2 fuzzy sets by combining the rules. Specifically, the meet operator is used to connect the type-2 fuzzy propositions in the antecedent. The degree of activation of the jth rule using the d input variables is computed as

$$\tilde{\beta}_j(\mathbf{x}) = \prod_{q=1}^{d} \mu_{\tilde{A}_{j,q}}(x_q), \ j = 1, \ldots, N. \tag{7.19}$$

The meet operation that replaces the fuzzy "and" in T1 FRS is given as follows:

$$\tilde{A} \sqcap \tilde{B} = \sum_{u \in J_\mathbf{x}} \sum_{w \in J_\mathbf{x}} f_\mathbf{x}(u) * g_\mathbf{x}(w)/(u \wedge w), \quad \mathbf{x} \in X. \tag{7.20}$$

If we use the interval Singleton T2 FRS, the meet is given for input $\mathbf{x} = \mathbf{x}'$ by the firing set, i.e.,

$$\tilde{\beta}_j(\mathbf{x}) = \underline{\beta}_j(\mathbf{x}), \overline{\beta}_j(\mathbf{x})$$

$$= \underline{\mu}_{A_{j,1}}(x_1) * \cdots * \underline{\mu}_{A_{j,d}}(x_d),$$

$$\times \overline{\mu}_{A_{j,1}}(x_1) * \cdots * \overline{\mu}_{A_{j,d}}(x_d). \tag{7.21}$$

In [9], the Gaussian membership function is adopted and it is given as follows:

$$\mu_A(x) = exp\left\{-\frac{(x-m)^2}{2\sigma^2}\right\} = \mathcal{N}(m, \sigma; x), \tag{7.22}$$

where m and σ are the mean and the standard deviation of the function, respectively. To generate the lower and upper membership functions, the authors used concentration and dilation hedges to generate the footprint of Gaussians with uncertain deviation as shown in Fig. 7.5. These are given as follows:

$$\overline{\mu}_{\tilde{A}}(x) = \mu_{DIL(A)}(x) = \mu_A(x)^{1/2} \tag{7.23}$$

$$\underline{\mu}_{\tilde{A}}(x) = \mu_{CON(A)}(x) = \mu_A(x)^2 \tag{7.24}$$

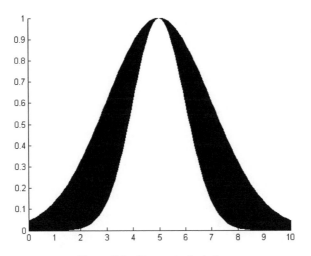

Figure 7.5: Uncertain deviation.

According to Eq. (7.22), we obtain the following expressions:

$$\overline{\mu}_{\tilde{A}}(x) = \mathcal{N}(m, \sqrt{2}\sigma; x) \tag{7.25}$$

$$\underline{\mu}_{\tilde{A}}(x) = \mathcal{N}\left(m, \frac{\sigma}{\sqrt{2}}; x\right) \tag{7.26}$$

Type-reducer is responsible for converting T2 FSs obtained as output of the inference engine into T1 FSs. Type-reduction for FRS (linguistic and functional models) was proposed by Karnik and Mendel [30, 36]. This will not be adopted in our case, since the rules' consequent represents the label of a class. Traditionally, in type-1 fuzzy classification systems, the output of the classifier is determined by the rule that has the highest degree of activation:

$$\text{Winner} = C_{j^*}, \quad j^* = \underset{1 \leq j \leq N}{\text{argmax}} \ \beta_j; \tag{7.27}$$

where β_j is the firing degree of the j rule. In type-2 fuzzy classification systems, we have an interval $\tilde{\beta}_j = \underline{\beta}_j, \overline{\beta}_j$ as defined in Eq. (7.23). Therefore, we compute the winning class by considering the center of the interval $\underline{\beta}_j(x), \overline{\beta}_j(x)$, that is

$$\text{Winner} = C_{j^*}, \text{ where} \tag{7.28}$$

$$j^* = \underset{1 \leq j \leq N}{\text{argmax}} \ \frac{1}{2}\left(\underline{\beta}_j(x) + \overline{\beta}_j(x)\right). \tag{7.29}$$

For the sake of illustration, an excerpt of rules generated is shown in Table 7.4.

Table 7.4: Fuzzy rules for $D2$.

Rule	Antecedent	C
1	x_1 IN N(−17.60, [0.968,1.93]) ∧(x_2 IN N(−2.31, [1.42,2.85]) ∨ (x_2 IN N(−9.45, [2.04, 4.08]))	2
2	(x_1 IN N(−5.27, [2.62, 5.24]) ∨ x_1 IN N(−13.10, [1.44,2.89])) ∧ x_2 IN N(1.61, [1.01,2.02])	2
3	x_1 IN N(−13.10, [1.44,2.89]) ∧ (x_2 IN N(1.61, [1.01,2.02]) ∨ x_2 IN N(−15.12, [0.98,1.96]))	2
4	x_1 IN N(5.47, [1.28,2.56]) ∧ (x_2 IN N(7.78, [1.19,2.39]) ∨ x_2 IN N(−6.10, [0.97,1.94]))	1
5	(x_1 IN N(−5.27, [2.62, 5.24]) ∨ x_1 IN N(5.470, [1.28,2.56]) ∨ x_1 IN N(9.79, [1.89, 3.78]) ∧ x_2 IN N(−5.30, [1.91,3.83])	1
6	x_1 IN N(2.69, [0.93,1.87]) ∧ x_2 IN N(−9.45, [2.04, 4.08])	1
7	(x_1 IN N(0.28, [0.97,1.93]) ∨ x_1 IN N(−17.60, [0.96,1.93])) ∧ x_2 IN N(−2.31, [1.42,2.85])	2

7.7. Conclusion

This chapter briefly presents fuzzy rule-based classifiers. The working cycle for both type-1 and type-2 fuzzy classification systems has been described. Because the primary requirement of such systems is interpretability, quality issues have been lengthily discussed including various approaches with some illustrative studies. Toward the end, the chapter also introduces incremental and online learning of fuzzy classifiers.

Fuzzy classifiers and rule-based classifiers in general are suited for human interpretability. Complex applications and automatic generation of clusters could produce classifiers with complex rule base. Therefore, the role of engineering transparency in such rule-based systems is crucial. It is worth nothing that transparency has recently become a major topic in machine learning, and it looks like the fuzzy community is ahead by many years.

While type-1 fuzzy classifiers have been extensively studied in the past in different contexts, type-2 fuzzy classifiers have not gained much popularity like their predecessors. It is expected that this category of fuzzy classifiers will continue to be studied in the future, especially with regard to transparency, interpretability, and online generation [41, 42, 47] and deployment.

References

[1] J. Abonyi, R. Babuska and F. Szeifert. Modified Gath-Geva fuzzy clustering for identification of Takagi-Sugeno fuzzy models. *IEEE Trans. Syst. Man Cybern. Part B: Cybern.*, **32**(5):612–621 (2002).

[2] B. Alatas and E. Akin. Mining fuzzy classification rules using an artificial immune system with boosting. In *Lecture Notes in Computer Science*, vol. 3631, pp. 283–293 (2005).

[3] P. Angelov. An approach for fuzzy rule-base adaptation using on-line clustering. *Int. J. Approximate Reasoning*, **35**(3):275–289 (2004).

[4] P. Angelov, E. Lughofer and X. Zhou. Evolving fuzzy classifiers using different model architectures. *Fuzzy Sets Syst.*, **159**:3160–3182 (2008).

[5] O. Arandjelovic and R. Cipolla. Incremental learning of temporally coherent Gaussian mixture models. In *Proceedings of the 16th British Machine Vision Conference*, pp. 759–768 (2005).

[6] A. Bouchachia. Incremental rule learning using incremental clustering. In *Proc. of the 10th conf. on Information Processing and Management of Uncertainty in Knowledge-Based Systems*, vol. 3, pp. 2085–2092 (2004).

[7] A. Bouchachia. Fuzzy classification in dynamic environments. *Soft Comput.*, **15**(5):1009–1022 (2011).

[8] A. Bouchachia and R. Mittermeir. Towards incremental fuzzy classifiers. *Soft Comput.*, **11**(2):193–207 (2007).

[9] A. Bouchachia and C. Vanaret. GT2FC: an online growing interval type-2 self-learning fuzzy classifier. *IEEE Trans. Fuzzy Syst.*, **22**(4):999–1018 (2014).

[10] X. Chen, D. Jin and Z. Li. Fuzzy petri nets for rule-based pattern classification. In *Communications, Circuits and Systems and West Sino Expositions, IEEE 2002 International Conference on*, vol. 2, pp. 1218–1222 (2002).

[11] Y.-C. Chen, N. R. Pal and I-F Chung. An integrated mechanism for feature selection and fuzzy rule extraction for classification. *IEEE Trans. Fuzzy Syst.*, **20**(4):683–698 (2012).

[12] M. Cintra and H. Camargo. Feature subset selection for fuzzy classification methods. In *Information Processing and Management of Uncertainty in Knowledge-Based Systems. Theory and Methods*, vol. 80 of *Communications in Computer and Information Science*, pp. 318–327, Springer (2010).

[13] O. Cordon, M. del Jesus, F. Herrera, L. Magdalena and P. Villar. A multiobjective genetic learning process for joint feature selection and granularity and context learning in fuzzy rule-based classification systems. In *Interpretability Issues in Fuzzy Modeling*, pp. 79–99, Springer-Verlag (2003).

[14] C. Corrado Mencar and A. Fanelli. Interpretability constraints for fuzzy information granulation. *Inf. Sci.*, **178**(24):4585–4618 (2008).

[15] J. de Oliveira. Semantic constraints for membership function optimization. *IEEE Trans. Syst. Man Cybern. Part A: Syst. Humans*, **29**(1):128–138 (1999).

[16] J. de Oliveira. Towards neuro-linguistic modeling: constraints for optimization of membership functions. *Fuzzy Sets Syst.*, **106**:357380 (1999).

[17] D. Dubois, H. Prade and L. Ughetto. Checking the coherence and redundancy of fuzzy knowledge bases. *IEEE Trans. Fuzzy Syst.*, **5**(3):398–417 (1997).

[18] P. Duda, E. Hart and D. Stork. *Pattern Classification*. New York, Wiley (2001).

[19] T. Fawcett. An introduction to ROC analysis. *Pattern Recogn. Lett.*, **27**(8):861–874 (2006).

[20] M. Fazzolari, R. Alcalá, Y. Nojima, H. Ishibuchi and F. Herrera. A review of the application of multiobjective evolutionary fuzzy systems: current status and further directions. *IEEE Trans. Fuzzy Syst.*, **21**(1):45–65 (2013).

[21] M. Gacto, R. Alcalá and F. Herrera. Interpretability of linguistic fuzzy rule-based systems: an overview of interpretability measures. *Inf. Sci.*, **181**(20):4340–4360 (2011).

[22] J. Gama, I. Zliobaite, A. Bifet, M. Pechenizkiy and A. Bouchachia. A survey on concept drift adaptation. *ACM Comput. Surv.*, **46**(4):1–44 (2013).

[23] M. Ganji and M. Abadeh. A fuzzy classification system based on ant colony optimization for diabetes disease diagnosis. *Expert Syst. Appl.*, **38**(12):14650–14659 (2011).

[24] S. Guillaume and B. Charnomordic. A new method for inducing a set of interpretable fuzzy partitions and fuzzy inference systems from data. In *Interpretability Issues in Fuzzy Modeling*, pp. 148–175, Springer-Verlag (2003).

[25] I. Guyon and A. Elisseeff. An introduction to variable and feature selection. *J. Mach. Learn. Res.*, **3**:1157–1182 (2003).

[26] H. Ishibuchi, T. Murata and I. Türkşen. Single-objective and two-objective genetic algorithms for selecting linguistic rules for pattern classification problems. *Fuzzy Sets Syst.*, **89**(2):135–150 (1997).

[27] H. Ishibuchi and Y. Nojima. Analysis of interpretability-accuracy tradeoff of fuzzy systems by multiobjective fuzzy genetics-based machine learning. *Int. J. Approx. Reasoning*, **44**(1):4–31 (2007).

[28] H. Ishibuchi and T. Yamamoto. Fuzzy rule selection by multi-objective genetic local search algorithms and rule evaluation measures in data mining. *Fuzzy Sets Syst.*, **141**(1):59–88 (2004).

[29] H. Ishibuchi and T. Yamamoto. Rule weight specification in fuzzy rule-based classification systems. *IEEE Trans. Fuzzy Syst.*, **13**(4):428–435 (2005).

[30] N. Karnik and J. Mendel. Operations on type-2 fuzzy sets. *Fuzzy Sets Syst.*, **122**(2):327–348 (2001).

[31] N. Kasabov. *Foundations of Neural Networks, Fuzzy Systems and Knowledge Engineering*, MIT Press (1996).

[32] L. Kuncheva. How good are fuzzy if-then classifiers? *IEEE Trans. Syst. Man Cybern. Part B: Cybern.*, **30**(4):501–509 (2000).

[33] H.-M. Lee, C-M. Chen, J.-M. Chen and Y.-L. Jou. An efficient fuzzy classifier with feature selection based on fuzzy entropy. *IEEE Trans. Syst. Man Cybern.*, **31**:426–432 (2001).

[34] D. Leite, L. Decker, M. Santana and P. Souza. EGFC: evolving Gaussian fuzzy classifier from never-ending semi-supervised data streams with application to power quality disturbance detection and classification. In *2020 IEEE International Conference on Fuzzy Systems (FUZZ-IEEE)*, pp. 1–9 (2020).

[35] E. Lughofer. *Evolving Fuzzy Systems—Methodologies, Advanced Concepts and Applications* (Studies in Fuzziness and Soft Computing), Springer (2011).

[36] J. M. Mendel. On KM algorithms for solving type-2 fuzzy set problems. *IEEE Trans. Fuzzy Syst.*, **21**(3):426–446 (2013).

[37] R. Mikut, J. Jäkel and L. Gröll. Interpretability issues in data-based learning of fuzzy systems. *Fuzzy Sets Syst.*, **150**(2):179–197 (2005).

[38] K. Narukawa, Y. Nojima and H. Ishibuchi. Modification of evolutionary multiobjective optimization algorithms for multiobjective design of fuzzy rule-based classification systems. In *The 14th IEEE International Conference on Fuzzy Systems*, pp. 809–814 (2005).

[39] D. Nauck. Measuring interpretability in rule-based classification systems. In *The 12th IEEE International Conference on Fuzzy Systems*, vol. 1, pp. 196–201 (2003).

[40] W. Pedrycz and F. Gomide. *Introduction to Fuzzy sets: Analysis and Design*, MIT Press (1998).

[41] M. Pratama, J. Lu, E. Lughofer, G. Zhang and S. Anavatti. Scaffolding type-2 classifier for incremental learning under concept drifts. *Neurocomputing*, **191**:304–329 (2016).

[42] M. Pratama, J. Lu and G. Zhang. Evolving type-2 fuzzy classifier. *IEEE Trans. Fuzzy Syst.*, **24**(3):574–589 (2016).

[43] C. Rani and S. N. Deepa. Design of optimal fuzzy classifier system using particle swarm optimization. In *Innovative Computing Technologies (ICICT), 2010 International Conference on*, pp. 1–6 (2010).

[44] J. Saade and H. Diab. Defuzzification techniques for fuzzy controllers. *IEEE Trans. Syst. Man Cybern. Part B: Cybern.*, **30**(1):223–229 (2000).

[45] H. Scarpelli, W. Pedrycz and F. Gomide. Quantification of inconsistencies in fuzzy knowledge bases. In *The 2nd European Congress on Intelligent Techniques and Soft Computing*, pp. 1456–1461 (1994).

[46] E. Schmitt, V. Bombardier and L. Wendling. Improving fuzzy rule classifier by extracting suitable features from capacities with respect to the choquet integral. *IEEE Trans. Syst. Man Cybern. Part B: Cybern.*, **38**(5):1195–1206 (2008).

[47] H. Shahparast and E. G. Mansoori. Developing an online general type-2 fuzzy classifier using evolving type-1 rules. *Int. J. Approximate Reasoning*, **113**:336–353 (2019).

[48] Q. Shen and A. Chouchoulas. A rough-fuzzy approach for generating classification rules. *Pattern Recognit.*, **35**(11):2425–2438 (2002).

[49] E. Soares, P. Angelov, B. Costa and M. Castro. Actively semi-supervised deep rule-based classifier applied to adverse driving scenarios. In *2019 International Joint Conference on Neural Networks (IJCNN)*, pp. 1–8 (2019).

[50] L. Snchez, M. R. Surez, J. R. Villar and I. Couso. Mutual information-based feature selection and partition design in fuzzy rule-based classifiers from vague data. *Int. J. Approximate Reasoning*, **49**(3):607–622 (2008).

[51] W. Tan, C. Foo and T. Chua. Type-2 fuzzy system for ECG arrhythmic classification. In *FUZZ-IEEE*, pp. 1–6 (2007).

[52] S. R. Thiruvenkadam, S. Arcot and Y. Chen. A PDE based method for fuzzy classification of medical images. In *The 2006 IEEE International Conference on Image Processing*, pp. 1805–1808 (2006).

[53] D. Tikk, T. Gedeon and K. Wong. A feature ranking algorithm for fuzzy modelling problems. In *Interpretability Issues in Fuzzy Modeling*, pp. 176–192, Springer-Verlag (2003).

[54] R. Toscano and P. Lyonnet. Diagnosis of the industrial systems by fuzzy classification. *ISA Trans.*, **42**(2):327–335 (2003).

[55] G. Tsekouras, H. Sarimveis, E. Kavakli and G. Bafas. A hierarchical fuzzy-clustering approach to fuzzy modeling. *Fuzzy Sets Syst.*, **150**(2):245–266 (2005).

[56] V. Vanhoucke and R. Silipo. Interpretability in multidimensional classification. In *Interpretability Issues in Fuzzy Modeling*, pp. 193–217, Springer-Verlag (2003).

[57] H. Vernieuwe, B. De Baets and N. Verhoest. Comparison of clustering algorithms in the identification of Takagi-Sugeno models: a hydrological case study. *Fuzzy Sets Syst.*, **157**(21):2876–2896 (2006).

[58] D. Wu and J. Mendel. A vector similarity measure for linguistic approximation: interval type-2 and type-1 fuzzy sets. *Inf. Sci.*, **178**(2):381–402 (2008).

[59] R. Yager and H. Larsen. On discovering partial inconsistencies in validating uncertain knowledge bases by reflecting on the input. *IEEE Trans. Syst. Man Cybern. Part B: Cybern.*, **21**(4):790–801 (1991).

[60] R. R. Yager and D. P. Filev. Approximate clustering via the mountain method. *IEEE Trans. Syst. Man Cybern.*, **24**(8):1279–1284 (1994).

[61] S. Zhou and J. Gan. Low-level interpretability and high-level interpretability: a unified view of data-driven interpretable fuzzy system modelling. *Fuzzy Sets Syst.*, **159**(23):3091–3131 (2008).

Chapter 8

Kernel Models and Support Vector Machines

Denis Kolev*, Mikhail Suvorov*, and Dmitry Kangin†

*Faculty of Computational Mathematics and Cybernetics
Moscow State University, 119991, Moscow, Russia
†Faculty of Informatics and Control Systems
Bauman Moscow State Technical University, 105005, Moscow, Russia
{dkolev,msuvorov}@msdk-research.com
dkangin@gmail.com

8.1. Introduction

Nowadays, the amount of information produced by different sources is steadily growing. For this reason, statistical data analysis and pattern recognition algorithms have become increasingly pervasive and highly demanded [1, 2]. The most studied and widely applied approaches are based on parametrically linear models. They combine learning and evaluation simplicity with a well-grounded theoretical basis. On the other hand, linear methods impose strong restrictions on the data structure model, significantly reducing performance in some cases. Nonlinear methods provide more flexible models, but they usually suffer from very complex, time-demanding learning procedures and possible overfitting.

In this chapter, we discuss a framework for the parametrically linear methods that determine nonlinear models: namely, kernel methods. These methods preserve the theoretical basis of linear models, while providing more flexibility at the same time. This framework extends the existing machine learning methods.

Support vector machines (SVMs) play a significant role in the scope of linear and kernel methods. For several reasons, SVMs are one of the most popular approaches for regression and classification. The given approach is theoretically well-grounded and studied, which provides the capability for adequate adaptation of the method. It is known that SVMs are universal approximators in some specific conditions. Also, due to model sparseness (described in due course), methods are widely used for the processing of streaming/large data. SVM classifiers have been rated as one of the best-performing types of machine learning algorithms [3]. A number of problem-specific techniques are based on "SVM-driven" ideas. In this chapter, we discuss the SVM and its extensions, focusing on their relationship with kernel methods.

The rest of the chapter is structured as follows. In the second section, we discuss the theoretical basis of kernel methods and offer illustrative examples. In the third section, we list the main kernel machines and explain their principles. The fourth section focuses on the SVM and its extensions.

8.2. Basic Concepts and Theory

Here, we present a brief overview of the basic concepts and theorems about kernels and kernel models. We will use the following notation hereafter, unless stated otherwise.

$X \subset \mathbb{R}^n$—set of objects/vectors, Universum.

n—dimensionality of the object space.

$Y \subset \mathbb{R}^m$—set of responses.

m—dimensionality of responses.

$X_N = \{(x_1, y_1), \ldots, (x_N, y_N)\}$—sample, where

$x_i \in X$—sample object/vector, $i = 1, \ldots, N$,

$y_i \in Y$—response to x_i, $i = 1, \ldots, N$.

$\mathcal{H}$—Hilbert space of functions or reproducing kernel Hilbert space.

$K(x, t)$—kernel function defined on $X \times X$.

8.2.1. Regression and Classification Problems

In many real-world problems, the classical approach of building a mathematical model of the relationship between inputs and outputs turns out to be unsound. Complicated dependencies, inputs of complex structures, and noise are all the reasons that hinder mathematical modeling. In fact, developing a strict mathematical model is often infeasible or related to strong performance and application constraints, which may limit model scalability. The alternative consists of information models that allow for the restoration of rather complex input–output relationships, as well as dealing with noise and outliers. In this chapter, we focus on regression and classification problems [1] and the use of kernel approaches to solve them.

The inputs and outputs of real-world problems have diverse and complicated structures. However, in many cases, they can be quantified. Hereafter we will consider sets of data objects as subsets of $\mathbb{R}^n$. Furthermore, we state the problem of recognition as follows:

Consider a subset $X \subseteq \mathbb{R}^n$. We refer to its elements as *objects*. The coordinates x_i of object $x \in X$ are called *features* and are marked by a Roman index i. Each object x is associated with a vector $y \in Y \subseteq \mathbb{R}^m$, which is regarded as a characteristic of objects in X. We assume that there exists a law f that governs the correspondence between objects and their characteristics. So, f can be regarded as a map $X \to Y$ and

$$y = f(x), \quad x \in X, \ y \in Y$$

We have only some assumptions about this law/mapping and a *training set*. The concept of a training set is critical in recognition theory because it is the main source of obtaining f or, at least, its approximation $\hat{f}$. Usually, we assume that the mapping of $\hat{f}$ belongs to a certain family of maps $F \subseteq X^Y$. Then, the training set is used to choose one mapping from this family. More formally, a *training set* refers to a set X_N of pairs $(x_i y_i)$:

$$X_N = \{(x_i, y_i) | y_i = f(x_i), i = 1, \ldots, N\}.$$

On this basis, the learning algorithm can be regarded as a mapping μ, so that

$$\hat{f} = \mu(X_N), \quad \hat{f} \in F$$

When Y is a finite set such that $Y = \{L_1, \ldots, L_R\}$, the problem is known as a classification problem. All elements L_r in Y are called *labels*.

When $Y \subseteq \mathbb{R}$ and Y contains an innumerable number of elements, the problem is known as a regression problem.

8.2.2. *Support Vector Machines: Classification Problem and Dividing Hyperplanes*

To illustrate the recognition problem discussed above, we will give a simple example of a classification problem inspired by Vapnik and Chervonenkis [4, 5]. Let $X = \mathbb{R}^2$ and $Y = \{-1, 1\}$. Then, objects can be regarded as two-dimensional points represented by either red squares ($y = -1$) or green circles ($y = 1$). Following Vapnik and Chervonenkis, we initially consider a simple case of a linearly separable training set, as presented in Figure 8.1. Given that the points of a training set of different classes are linearly divisible, the goal is to find a hyperplane H that will divide X into two parts: H_+ and H_-. A hyperplane is determined by its normal

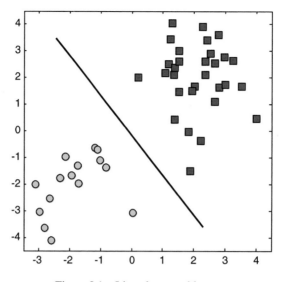

Figure 8.1: Linearly separable case.

vector w and an intercept ρ. A vector x belongs to the hyperplane if and only if

$$\langle w, x \rangle - \rho = 0.$$

The hyperplane can be chosen in different ways. Vapnik and Chervonenkis proposed a procedure for selecting some optimal hyperplane. They formalized optimality using the notation of a separating band, which is the space between two hyperplanes parallel to H that contain no points of the training set X_N. They showed that the size of this band equals (for proof, refer to Section 8.4.1)

$$\frac{2}{\|w\|}$$

Then, they stated the problem of quadratic programming as follows:

$$\|w\|^2 \to \min_{w}$$

w.r.t

$$y_i(\langle w, x_i \rangle - \rho) \geq 1,$$

$$i = 1, \ldots, N$$

This can be generalized for the case of a linearly nonseparable training set by introducing so-called *slack* variables $\xi_i \geq 0$, which allow violating the constraint

$$y_i(\langle w, x_i \rangle - \rho) \geq 1 - \xi_i.$$

So, the final version of the problem becomes

$$\|w\|^2 + C \sum_{i=1}^{N} \xi_i \to \min_{w, \xi}$$

w.r.t

$$y_i \left(\langle w, x_i \rangle - \rho \right) \geq 1 - \xi_i$$

$$\xi_i \geq 0,$$

$$i = 1, \ldots, N.$$

Formally speaking, in the case of a linearly nonseparable sample, the set of optimization problem constraints defines an empty set. The introduction of slack variables prevents such a situation, allowing misclassifications which are penalized by the functional under optimization.

8.2.3. *SVM Solver: Toward Nonlinearity and Polynomial Kernel*

In this section, we do not investigate the main properties of the problem solution; we instead focus on the techniques that introduce nonlinearity into the model, describing briefly the background theory and the most vital theorems.

Consider the solution to an optimization problem stated by a two-class SVM classifier. Earlier, we drew attention to a convex quadratic programming problem that has a single solution. Usually, the SVM model is investigated from the standpoint of the dual optimization problem [6], which is formulated as follows:

$$-\frac{1}{2} \alpha Q \alpha^T + \sum_{i=1}^{N} \alpha_i \to \max_{\alpha}$$

$w.r.t$

$$0 \leq \alpha_i \leq C, \quad \forall i = 1, \ldots, N$$

$$\sum_{i=1}^{N} \alpha_i y_i = 0.$$

Here, the N-dimensional vector $\alpha \in \mathbb{R}^N$ represents the vector of Lagrange multipliers corresponding to each constraint in the primal problem. The matrix $Q \in \mathbb{R}^{N \times N}$ is a matrix of "class-corresponding" inner products with elements

$$Q_{ij} = \langle x_i, x_j \rangle y_i y_j.$$

According to the differential Karush–Kuhn–Tucker conditions of the primal problem (which will be described in due course), the normal vector of the resulting hyperplane can be expressed as

$$w = \sum_{i=1}^{N} y_i \alpha_i x_i$$

Therefore, the class label of the arbitrary vector x can be evaluated as

$$y(x) = \text{sign} \left(\sum_{i=1}^{N} \alpha_i y_i \langle x_i, x \rangle - \rho \right).$$

Evidently, the optimization problem depends on the values of the Lagrange multipliers and the inner products between the vectors from the learning set and classified vector. This information is sufficient for performing classification.

The SVM classification model discussed here is linear, which means that it performs adequately only when the classes in the learning set (and in the Universum) are linearly separable. However, this limitation can be overcome. In particular, many specially developed techniques can be applied, including feature engineering, mixture of experts, and others. There is a special approach for the SVM model (as well as a wide range of other machine learning methods), which retains the overall model structure as it is in the linear case, but allows the fitting of nonlinear separation surfaces. This approach is referred to as "mapping to linearization space" or just the "kernel trick" [7].

Further to the dual optimization problem and final discrimination function, we note that the optimization problem depends on pairwise inner products in the learning set. The final classification rule also depends only on the inner products between vectors in the learning set and classified vector. It leads the way to the described approach. The idea is to replace the standard inner product with some two-argument nonlinear function [8], so that

$$\langle x, t \rangle \rightarrow K(x, t),$$

$$Q_{ij} = K(x_i, x_j) y_i y_j,$$

$$y(x) = \text{sign} \left(\sum_{i=1}^{N} \alpha_i y_i K(x_i, x) - \rho \right).$$

A simple example can be provided. Suppose that the replacement is

$$\langle x, t \rangle \rightarrow (\langle x, t \rangle + 1)^2.$$

Then, the decision rule is one of a second-order polynomial type, i.e.,

$$y(x) = \text{sign} \left(\sum_{i=1}^{N} \alpha_i y_i \langle x, x_i \rangle^2 + 2 \sum_{i=1}^{N} \alpha_i y_i \langle x, x_i \rangle + \sum_{i=1}^{N} \alpha_i y_i - \rho \right)$$

However, two important questions should be answered to ensure the proper use of such an approach:

1) What function $K(x, t)$ can be used to replace the inner product?
2) What is the set of possible discrimination surfaces that can be fitted using a given $K(x, t)$?

8.2.4. *Kernel Function Discussion*

The kernel trick can be defined in different ways. Consider a function Φ that maps the data from the initial space $\mathbb{R}^n$ to some Hilbert space $\mathcal{H}$, $\Phi \colon \mathbb{R}^n \to \mathcal{H}$. The inner product in the space H is denoted by $\langle \cdot, \cdot \rangle_{\mathcal{H}}$. In the general case, the space $\mathcal{H}$ can be infinite-dimensional.

A classification model is learned in the space $\mathcal{H}$ using mapped data as a learning set,

$$\Phi(X_N) = \{\Phi(x_1), \ldots, \Phi(x_N)\}.$$

It is supposed that for all $x, t \in \mathbb{R}^n$, the inner product for the mapped vectors is evaluated as

$$\langle \Phi(x), \Phi(t) \rangle_{\mathcal{H}} = K(x, t),$$

where $K(x, t)$ is a symmetric two-argument function, in general nonlinear, and defined for vectors in $\mathbb{R}^n$. $\Phi(x)$ can be regarded as a new feature map, which means that the kernel trick is similar to feature engineering.

Therefore, the final classification model can be expressed as

$$y(x) = \operatorname{sign}\left(\sum_{i=1}^{N} \alpha_i y_i \langle \phi(x_i), \phi(x) \rangle_{\mathcal{H}} - \rho\right) = \operatorname{sign}\left(\sum_{i=1}^{N} \alpha_i y_i K(x_i, x) - \rho\right).$$

The kernel trick assists in building a linear classification model in a different space, resulting in a generally nonlinear classification model in the initial data space. For this reason, the function $K(x, t)$ must be an inner product of $\Phi(x)$ and $\Phi(t)$ in some Hilbert space for all $x, t \in \mathbb{R}^n$. Such functions are usually referred to as "kernels" (this is not a strict definition) and there are many examples of such functions:

- Linear kernel $K(x, t) = \langle x, t \rangle$,
- Polynomial kernel $K(x, t) = \langle x, t \rangle^d$ or $K(x, t) = (\langle x, t \rangle + \beta)^d$,
- Exponential kernel $K(x, t) = \exp\left(-\frac{\|x - t\|^2}{2\sigma^2}\right)$,
- Student-type RBF kernel $K(x, t) = (\beta + \gamma \|x - t\|^2)^{-\alpha}$, $\beta > 0, \gamma > 0, \alpha > 0$.

Discussing the wideness of the set of discriminative functions that can be learned using a given kernel function, it is essential to point out that the classification rule is based on a linear combination of kernel functions with one fixed input argument. Therefore, the set of functions that can be obtained is limited by the linear spectrum of the kernel:

$$\text{span}(K) = \left\{ f : \mathbb{R}^n \to \mathbb{R} \,|\, \exists x_1, \ldots, x_N \in \mathbb{R}^n : f(x) = \sum_{i=1}^{N} \alpha_i K(x, x_i) \right\}.$$

We further investigate the underlying theory of the kernel trick in detail, including the criteria for a function to be a kernel and the importance of the spectrum of kernels. We conclude Section 8.2 with the representer theorem, showing the significance of kernel theory for machine learning.

8.2.5. Kernel Definition via Matrix

The above mentioned discussion leads us to the following definition of a kernel function.

Definition 8.1. ([9]): A function $K : X \times X \to R$ is known as a positive definite kernel if for any finite subset $X_N = \{x_1, \ldots, x_N\} \subset X$ the corresponding matrix $K(X_N, X_N)$:

$$K(X_N X_N) = \begin{bmatrix} K(x_1, x_1) & \cdots & K(x_1, x_N) \\ \vdots & \ddots & \vdots \\ K(x_N, x_1) & \cdots & K(x_N, x_N) \end{bmatrix},$$

is symmetric, i.e., $K(X_N, X_N) = K(X_N, X_N)^T$, and non-negative definite.

The latter we understand as for any $t \in \mathbb{R}^N$

$$\langle K(X_N, X_N)t, t \rangle \geq 0.$$

It follows directly from the definition that

$$\forall x, t \in X,$$

$$K(x, t) \geq 0,$$

$$K(x, t) = K(t, x).$$

It should be pointed out that this fact provides an important link to the kernel SVM. This is because a non-negative matrix $K(X_N, X_N)$ ensures the concavity of the dual problem, which is essential for optimization.

8.2.6. *Reproducing Kernel (RKHS) via Linear Operator*

Up to this point, we introduced the definition of a positive definite kernel. Now we consider one of the most important entities in the theory of reproducing kernels: reproducing kernel Hilbert space (RKHS) [10].

Let X be a non-empty subset of $\mathbb{R}^n$. Then, let $\mathcal{H}$ be a Hilbert space of functions over X:

$$f : X \rightarrow \mathbb{R}.$$

Definition 8.2. *A function* $: X \times X \rightarrow \mathbb{R}$ *is known as a reproducing kernel of* $\mathcal{H}$ *if and only if*

1. $\forall x \in X K(\cdot, x) \in \mathcal{H}$,
2. $\forall f \in \mathcal{H} \langle f, K(\cdot, x) \rangle_{\mathcal{H}} = f(x)$.

The function $K(\cdot, x)$ is called a reproducing kernel for point x. Here, $\langle \cdot, \cdot \rangle_{\mathcal{H}}$ is some voluntarily chosen function the satisfies the definition of an inner product. From the definition, it follows that the reproducing kernel is a symmetric function:

$$K(x, t) = \langle K(\cdot, t), K(\cdot, x) \rangle_{\mathcal{H}}$$

$$= \{\text{property of the real} - \text{valued inner product}\} = \langle K(\cdot, x), K(\cdot, t) \rangle_{\mathcal{H}}$$

$$= K(t, x).$$

The reproducing property may be defined in a different way. Consider a functional $L_x : \mathcal{H} \rightarrow \mathbb{R}$ such that

$$\forall f \in \mathcal{H} \, L_x f = f(x).$$

The "evaluation functional" L_x can be defined for any $x \in X$. It is easy to show that L_x is a linear functional. Using this notation, we introduce another definition of RKHS.

Definition 8.3. *A Hilbert space of functions* $\mathcal{H}$ *is an RKHS if and only if* $\forall x \in X$ *and the evaluation functional* L_x *is bounded. That is to say:*

$$\forall x \in X \exists C_x : \forall f \in \mathcal{H} : |L_x f| \leq C_x \|f\|_{\mathcal{H}} = C_x \sqrt{\langle f, f \rangle_{\mathcal{H}}}.$$

This means that if the two functions f and g are close in terms of the RKHS norm, they will be close at every point. This can be expressed as follows:

$$|f(x) - g(x)| = |L_x(f - g)| \leq C_x \|f - g\|_{\mathcal{H}}.$$

Now, we can state a theorem that links the two definitions.

Theorem 8.1. *A Hilbert space* $\mathcal{H}$ *is an RKHS* $\Leftrightarrow$ *it has a reproducing kernel.*

According to the Riesz–Frechet theorem, for every bounded linear functional $A : \mathcal{H} \to \mathbb{R}$ there exists an element $\theta \in \mathcal{H} : \forall f \in \mathcal{H}, Af = \langle f, \theta \rangle_{\mathcal{H}}$. In our case, $A \equiv L_x$. Therefore, one side of the theorem ($\Rightarrow$) is a specific case of the Riesz–Frechet theorem. The other side ($\Leftarrow$) can be proved using the Cauchy–Schwartz inequality.

8.2.7. *Moore–Aronszajn Correspondence Theorem*

The problem of selecting reproducing kernels must also be addressed. The Moore–Aronszajn theorem builds a correspondence between positive definite kernels and RKHS.

Theorem 8.2 (Moore–Aronszajn [10]): *Suppose $K : X \times X \to \mathbb{R}$ is a positive definite kernel $\Rightarrow \exists!$ Hilbert space $\mathcal{H}$ of functions over X, where K is a reproducing kernel.*

Therefore, for each positive definite kernel, there is a unique corresponding RKHS.

8.2.8. *Mercer's Theorem*

We further investigate the properties of positive definite kernels in the RKHS. For this purpose, we introduce a strictly positive Borel measure μ on X. We define $L_{\mu}^2(X)$ as a linear space of functions which can be expressed as follows:

$$f \in L_{\mu}^2(X) : \int_X |f(x)|^2 d\mu(x) < \infty.$$

A symmetric positive definite kernel $K : X \times X \to \mathbb{R}$, which is square-integrable,

$$\int_X \int_X K^2(x, t) d\mu(x) d\mu(t) < \infty,$$

induces [11] a linear operator $L_K : L_{\mu}^2(X) \to L_{\mu}^2(X)$, which is defined by

$$L_K f(x) = \int_X K(x, t) f(t) d\mu(t).$$

It possesses a countable system of eigenfunctions $\{\phi_k\}_{k=1}^{\infty}$ forming an orthonormal basis of $L_{\mu}^2(X)$ with corresponding eigenvalues $\{\lambda_k\}_{k=1}^{\infty}$.

Theorem 8.3 (**Mercer [12]**): *Let $X \subset \mathbb{R}^n$ be closed and μ be a strictly positive Borel measure on X. This means that this measure of every non-empty subset in X is positive, and K is a square-integrable continuous function on $X \times X$, being a positive definite kernel. Then*

$$K(x, t) = \sum_{k=1}^{\infty} \lambda_k \phi_k(x) \phi_k(t)$$

This series converges absolutely for each pair $(x, t) \in X \times X$ and uniformly on each compact subset of X.

This theorem enables the building of a map $\Phi : X \to \ell^2$, where ℓ^2 is a Hilbert space of square summable sequences, so that

$$\Phi(x)_k = \sqrt{\lambda_k} \phi_k(x).$$

It follows that kernel K can be regarded as a scalar product in ℓ^2:

$$K(x, t) = \langle \phi(x), \phi(t) \rangle_{\ell^2} = \sum_{k=1}^{\infty} (\Phi(x)_k \Phi(t)_k) = \sum_{k=1}^{\infty} \lambda_k \phi_k(x) \phi_k(t).$$

As kernel K is supposed to be continuous, the feature map Φ is also continuous. Returning to the SVM example, Mercer's theorem explains the correctness of using positive definite kernels. Any square-integrable positive definite kernel can be considered an inner product between the maps of two vectors in some Hilbert space (namely ℓ^2) replacing the inner product in the initial space $\mathbb{R}^n$. $\Phi(x)$ can be regarded as a feature map to the transformed feature space,

$$\Phi : X \to \ell^2.$$

Thus, the SVM builds a linear classifier in the ℓ^2 space.

8.2.9. *Polynomial Kernel Example*

To illustrate the theoretical points raised so far, we return to the example of a polynomial kernel. This will build a link between the RKHS reproducing kernel, the positive definite kernel, and the kernel trick.

Consider the problem of fitting a linear regression in a two-dimensional space. For the training set $X_N = \{(x_1, y_1), \ldots, (x_N, y_N)\}, x_i \in \mathbb{R}^2, y_i \in \mathbb{R}$, the goal is to restore parameter w so that $\forall i = 1, \ldots, N$ the output value of the parametric function $f(x_i, w)$ is close to y_i. The word "close" can be understood as a (sub)optimal solution of any regular empirical error measure, such as the least-squares or SVM-type measure. For the current example, we assume that least-squares optimization is used as a learning procedure, i.e.,

$$\sum_{i=1}^{N} (f(x_i, w) - y_i)^2 \to \min_{w}.$$

We consider function $f(x, w)$ to be linear:

$$f(x, w) = \langle x, w \rangle = \sum_{i=1}^{2} x_i w_i, \; w \in \mathbb{R}^2.$$

Suppose that the kernel trick is performed, meaning that the regression is transformed into a second-order polynomial as follows:

$$\langle x, t \rangle_{\mathbb{R}^2} \to K(x, t) = \langle x, t \rangle_{\mathbb{R}^2}{}^2 = \langle \phi(x), \phi(t) \rangle_{\mathcal{H}}.$$

Then, the feature map $\Phi(x)$ is defined as

$$\Phi : x = \begin{bmatrix} x_1 \\ x_2 \end{bmatrix} \to \begin{bmatrix} x_1^2 \\ x_2^2 \\ \sqrt{2}x_1x_2 \end{bmatrix} \in \mathbb{R}^3.$$

Thus, $\mathcal{H}$ may be understood as $\mathbb{R}^3$. The inner product in this space is evaluated as

$$\langle x, t \rangle_{\mathbb{R}^2}{}^2 = \langle \phi((x), \phi((t)) \rangle_{R^3} = x_1^2 t_1^2 + x_2^2 t_2^2 + 2x_1 x_2 t_1 t_2.$$

In this case, the parameter $w \in \mathbb{R}^3$ is growing in dimensionality. However, the function model still depends linearly on w, which usually simplifies the learning procedure. The model function is

$$f(x, w) = \sum_{i=1}^{3} w_i \Phi(x)_i = w_1 x_1^2 + w_2 x_2^2 + w_3 \sqrt{2}x_1 x_2,$$

where $\Phi(x)_i$ denotes the i-th coordinate in the transformed feature map.

If we consider $f(x, w)$ as a function member of the Hilbert space of second-order polynomials over $\mathbb{R}^2$, $P^2(\mathbb{R}^2)$, then every function in $P^2(\mathbb{R}^2)$ can be specified by its three coefficients, i.e.,

$$g(u) = au_1^2 + bu_2^2 + cu_1u_2 \longleftrightarrow \begin{bmatrix} a \\ b \\ c/\sqrt{2} \end{bmatrix}.$$

Here, $\longleftrightarrow$ denotes some schematic correspondence of the polynomial to vectors from $\mathbb{R}^3$. We denote the inner product in $P^2(\mathbb{R}^2)$ as a sum of pairwise multiplications of the corresponding coefficients,

$$\langle g_1, g_2 \rangle_{P^2(\mathbb{R}^2)} = a_1 a_2 + b_1 b_2 + \frac{c_1 c_2}{2}$$

where $g_i(u) = a_i u_1^2 + b_i u_2^2 + c_i u_1 u_2 \in P^2(\mathbb{R}^2)$.

One can see that the polynomial

$$K(u, x) = x_1^2 u_1^2 + x_2^2 u_2^2 + 2 x_1 x_2 u_1 u_2 \leftrightarrow \begin{bmatrix} x_1^2 \\ x_2^2 \\ \sqrt{2} x_1 x_2 \end{bmatrix},$$

$$K(\cdot, x) \in P^2(\mathbb{R}^2) \forall x \in \mathbb{R}^2,$$

is a reproducing kernel of $P^2(\mathbb{R}^2)$. Indeed,

$$\forall g \in P^2(\mathbb{R}^2) \quad \langle g, K(\cdot, x) \rangle_{P^2(\mathbb{R}^2)} = a x_1^2 + b x_2^2 + \frac{2 x_1 x_2 c}{2} = g(x).$$

Therefore, mapping $\Phi : \mathbb{R}^2 \to \mathbb{R}^3$ is equivalent to mapping $\Psi : \mathbb{R}^2 \to P^2(\mathbb{R}^2)$, where

$$\Psi(x) = K(\cdot, x).$$

The inner product between the data mapped by Ψ is evaluated as $\langle \psi(x), \psi(t) \rangle_{P^2(\mathbb{R}^2)}$. Mapping Ψ is equivalent to mapping Φ as

$$K(x, t) = \langle \phi(x), \quad \phi(t) \rangle_{\mathbb{R}^3} = \langle \psi(x), \quad \psi(t) \rangle_{P^2(\mathbb{R}^2)} \forall x, \quad t \in \mathbb{R}^2$$

Therefore, the regression learning procedure is reduced to a search for the polynomial

$$\pi \in P^2(\mathbb{R}^2), \quad \pi \leftrightarrow \begin{bmatrix} \pi_1 \\ \pi_2 \\ \pi_3/\sqrt{2} \end{bmatrix},$$

so that $\forall i = 1, \ldots, N \langle \pi, \psi(x_i) \rangle_{P^2(\mathbb{R}^2)} = \pi_1 x_1^2 + \pi_2 x_2^2 + \pi_3 x_1 x_2$ is close to y_i. However, because π is defined by three coefficients, the function model is linear with respect to its parameters. The final optimization ("learning") procedure is

$$\sum_{i=1}^{N} (\pi_1 x_{i1}^2 + \pi_2 x_{i2}^2 + \pi_3 x_{i1} x_{i2} - y_i)^2 \to \min_{\pi}$$

where x_{ii} corresponds to the i-th entry of the i-th learning sample.

It is possible to generalize the result provided here. Every kernel trick is equivalent to defining a new type of feature map, where K is a reproducing kernel of the linearization space. However, the fitted parameters are not always included in the RKHS inner product in a linear way, which may cause problems during optimization. For instance, if we map the data onto the space of all continuous functions, the learning procedure becomes equivalent to the variational optimization over all continuous functions. However, we will further show that this problem can be overcome in most cases and that it is possible to leave the model linear with respect to the optimized parameters.

8.2.10. *RKHS Approximation*

The next question we address is an arbitrary dividing surface using kernel K. Consider an RKHS $\mathcal{H}$, a Hilbert space of real-valued functions over $X \subseteq R^n$, where K is a reproducing kernel. If X is a compact subset, we can form the space of kernel sections as

$$K(X) = \overline{\text{span}}\{K_t, t \in X\},$$

which is a closure of a linear span of functions $K_t(\cdot) = K(\cdot, t)$. It is clear that $K(X) \subseteq \mathcal{H}$. However, if we aim to build an arbitrary function (specifying some dividing surface), we must call for the opposite embedding $\mathcal{H} \subseteq K(X)$. In other words, for any positive number ε and any function $f \in \mathcal{H}$, there should exist a function $g \in K(X)$ such that function f is well approximated by g. That is to say,

$$\|f - g\|_{\mathcal{H}} \leq \varepsilon$$

Returning to the RKHS, it can be shown that $K(X)$ is dense in $\mathcal{H}$. This means that any function from the RKHS can be approximated at any given precision ε by a linear combination of reproducing kernels. Formally speaking [13],

$$\forall \varepsilon > 0, \ \forall f \in \mathcal{H} \ \exists N > 0, \ x_1, \ldots, x_N \in X, \ \alpha_1 \ldots, \alpha_N \in \mathbb{R}:$$

$$\left\| f - \sum_{i=1}^{N} \alpha_i K(\cdot, x_i) \right\|_{\mathcal{H}} \leq \varepsilon.$$

Thus, if we return to the SVM model, we can claim that the wideness of possible decision function forms is limited by the RKHS of the selected kernel.

In practice, most kernels are parametric functions. Thus, it is reasonable to analyze how the corresponding RKHS depends on kernel parameters. Consider a family of parameterized positive definite kernel functions

$$K = \{K(\cdot, \cdot | \theta) : X \times X \to \mathbb{R} | \theta \in \Theta\}$$

where Θ is a set of acceptable values for θ. As an example of such a family, we can take a Gaussian kernel with different variance values. A natural question that arises is whether the corresponding RKHS depends on kernel parameters. In general, the answer is yes, but this is not true in all cases. For instance, a Gaussian kernel with different variances corresponds to the RKHS of all continuous real-valued functions, which is independent of variance parameters. At the same time, polynomial kernels with different degrees correspond to different RKHS (spaces of polynomials with different degrees).

8.2.11. *Examples of Universal Kernels*

Using the notation from the previous subsection, we introduce a property known as the *universality* of the kernel [13].

Definition 8.4. A positive definite kernel $K : X \times X \to \mathbb{R}$, $X \subseteq \mathbb{R}^n$ is called universal if it is a reproducing kernel of RKHS $\mathbb{R}(X)$, which is the space of all continuous real-valued functions defined on X.

Using the previous result, we can state that any continuous real-valued function $f \in \mathbb{R}(X)$ can be approximated with any given precision by a function $g \in K(X)$.

Therefore, the issue that must be addressed is the question of which kernels possess this property of universality. A number of universality criteria exist, but in this work, we present just a few examples of universal kernels and some sufficient conditions for universality.

Definition 8.5. A kernel $K : X \times X \to \mathbb{R}$ is strictly positive definite if it is a positive definite kernel and for any finite subset $X_N = \{x_1, \ldots, x_N\} \subset X$, the corresponding matrix $K(X_N, X_N)$,

$$K(X_N, X_N) = \begin{bmatrix} K(x_1, x_1) & \cdots & K(x_1, x_N) \\ \vdots & \ddots & \vdots \\ K(x_N, x_1) & \cdots & K(x_N, x_N) \end{bmatrix},$$

is strictly positive definite.

Theorem 8.2. *If a positive definite kernel is strictly positive definite, it is a universal kernel.*

The following positive definite kernels are examples of universal kernels:

- Exponential kernel $K(x, t) = \exp\left(-\frac{\|x-t\|^2}{2\sigma^2}\right)$,

- Survival kernel $K(x, t) = \prod_{i=1}^{n} \min(x_i, t_i)$,

- $K(x, t) = (\beta + \gamma \|x - t\|^2)^{-\alpha}$, $\beta > 0$, $\gamma > 0$, $\alpha > 0$.

8.2.12. *Why Span? Representer Theorem*

In this section, we present a very strong and very general result that is essential for kernel learning and which extends the possibility of applying the kernel trick to diverse machine learning models.

Theorem 8.5 (Representer theorem [14]): *Let X be a non-empty set and suppose that K is a positive definite kernel over X and a reproducing kernel of RKHS $\mathcal{H}$ of functions over X. Let us consider a training sample $X_N = \{(x_1, y_1), \ldots, (x_N, y_N)\}, i = 1, \ldots, N, x_i \in X, y_i \in \mathbb{R}$, a strictly monotonically increasing function $g : 0, +\infty) \to \mathbb{R}$. Then, for any arbitrary empirical risk function $E : (X \times \mathbb{R}^2)^N \to \mathbb{R}$, if f^* is a solution of the optimization problem*

$$E((x_1, y_1, f(x_1)), \ldots, (x_N, y_N, f(x_N))) + g(\|f\|) \to \min_{f \in \mathcal{H}},$$

then f^* has the structure

$$f^*(\cdot) = \sum_{i=1}^{N} \alpha_i K(\cdot, x_i).$$

The summand $g(\|f\|)$ in the functional under optimization corresponds to the regularization term that is usually added for noise-stability purposes.

The theorem is significant because it presents a parametrically linear model of a generally nonlinear function, which is an optimal solution for a very wide range of machine learning problems.

However, the theorem does not present the exact kernel form. It just states that such a reproducing kernel exists. Therefore, the theorem simplifies but does not remove the "model selection" problem.

8.3. Kernel Models and Applications

In this part of the chapter, we discuss kernel models, their properties, and their application to regression, density estimation, dimensionality reduction, filtering, and clustering. Kernels provide an elegant approach for incorporating nonlinearity into linear models, dramatically broadening the area of application for SVMs, linear regression, PCA, k-means, and other model families.

8.3.1. *Kernel Density Estimation*

One of the common problems in data mining is that of probability density estimation. It aims to restore an unknown probability distribution function based on some given data points that are supposed to be generated from the target distribution.

Formally, let $X_N = \{x_1, \ldots, x_N\}$ be an i.i.d. sample in $\mathbb{R}^n$ drawn from some unknown distribution $p(x)$. The aim is to build an estimate distribution $\hat{p}(x)$. In general, $\hat{p}(x)$ should be a consistent estimate at every point.

Such problems appear as sub-tasks in many different practical applications, including classification, clustering, and others. Kernel models are widely used for the estimation of probability density functions (pdf).

Kernel density estimation is closely related to the histogram density estimation approach, also referred to as the histogram method. For one-dimensional data, the estimator is calculated as

$$\hat{p}_h(x) = \frac{1}{N} \frac{\sum_{i=1}^{N} I\left[x - \frac{h}{2} < x_i < x + \frac{h}{2}\right]}{h}$$

where h is the bandwidth parameter (or window size) and I denotes the identification operator, i.e.,

$$Ic = \begin{cases} 1, & \text{if } c \text{ is true,} \\ 0, & \text{if } c \text{ is false.} \end{cases}$$

The estimate is sensitive to the bandwidth parameter as it may cause over-fitting or under-fitting. Examples of estimates for different bandwidths are shown in Figure 8.2. The original pdf is a solid red line, while its estimates are blue dashed lines. A bandwidth that is too small ($h = 0.1$) results in a very rough approximation, whereas a bandwidth that is too large ($h = 2$) leads to over-smoothing. A bandwidth of $h = 0.56$ seems to be a compromise between overly small and overly large windows.

However, in the case of small learning datasets, the histogram approach leads to unacceptable solutions. For this reason, the histogram function is often replaced by a non-negative symmetric smooth function $K(x)$, normalized at 1, i.e.,

$$\int K(x)dx = 1.$$

Then, the estimate becomes

$$\hat{p}_h(x) = \frac{1}{N} \frac{\sum_{i=1}^{N} K\left(\frac{x-x_i}{h}\right)}{h} = \frac{1}{N} \sum_{i=1}^{N} K_h(x-x_i),$$

where $K_h(x) = \frac{1}{h} K\left(\frac{x}{h}\right)$ is usually referred to as a scaled kernel. This approach is known as the Parzen–Rosenblatt method. Notice that histogram estimation is a special case of the Parzen–Rosenblatt method [15, 16].

Such a modification results in a smooth function. An example that illustrates the difference between regular histogram windows and Gaussian kernel estimation is shown in Figure 8.3.

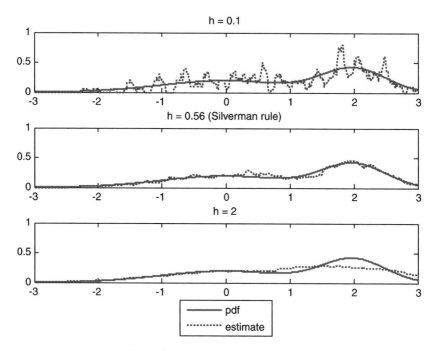

Figure 8.2:   Kernel density estimation.

As Figure 8.2 shows, density estimation relies on effective bandwidth parameter selection. Several approaches exist [17–21], but practically for one-dimensional data all of them are based on the result that the window size decreases as $O(N^{-\frac{1}{5}})$. The optimal bandwidth for a kernel K estimating one-dimensional density p can be determined by minimizing the asymptotic mean integrated squared error (AMISE):

$$h^* = \frac{R(K)^{\frac{1}{5}}}{s(K)^{\frac{2}{5}} R\left(\frac{\partial^2 p}{\partial x^2}\right)^{\frac{1}{5}} N^{\frac{1}{5}}}$$

where

$$R(f) = \int f^2(x)dx,$$

$$s(f) = \int x^2 f(x)dx.$$

However, such an estimate cannot be applied directly because it requires prior knowledge about the estimated distribution (in particular, the density $p(x)$). For some distributions, this bandwidth estimate is known. For Gaussian distributions,

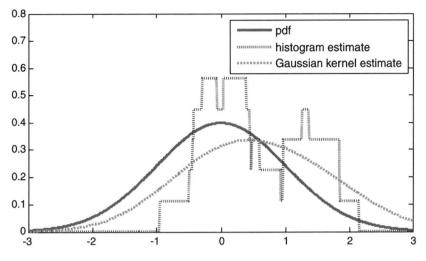

Figure 8.3: Kernel density estimation from 10 points; $h = 09$.

the following value, known as Silverman's rule of thumb [7], is commonly used:

$$h^* = \left(\frac{4\hat{\sigma}^5}{3N}\right)^{\frac{1}{5}}.$$

It can be obtained from the asymptotic formula by direct substitution of the parametric variance with its estimate $\hat{\sigma}^2$.

8.3.2. *The Nadaraya–Watson Kernel Regression*

In 1964, Nadaraya [22] and Watson [23] proposed a method for kernel regression based on a non-parametric regression technique. Having a sample of pairs $\{(x_i, y_i)\}_{i=1}^N$, we look forward to finding the most expected value of y for any value of x. Assuming that pairs $(x_i y_i)$ come from some distribution f on $X \times Y$, where $x_i \in X$, $y_i \in Y \subseteq \mathbb{R}$, the regression problem is formulated in terms of finding the conditional expectation $\bar{y}$:

$$\bar{y} = \mathbb{E}(y|x) = \int yf(y|x)dy = \frac{\int yf(x, y)dy}{f(x)}.$$

Kernel density estimation helps us to estimate the joint distribution $f(xy)$ of two random variables (that can be, in fact, multivariate variables) x and y. This can be expressed as follows:

$$\hat{f}(x, y) = \frac{1}{Nh_x h_y} \sum_{i=1}^N K\left(\frac{x - x_i}{h_x}\right) K\left(\frac{y - y_i}{h_y}\right).$$

Kernel density estimation also assists in estimating the marginal distribution $f(x)$ as follows:

$$\hat{f}(x) = \frac{1}{Nh_x} \sum_{i=1}^{N} K\left(\frac{x - x_i}{h_x}\right)$$

In the preceding equation, h_x and h_y are the corresponding bandwidths of the kernels. In turn, these estimators are used to calculate the conditional expectation

$$\bar{y} = \frac{\int y \hat{f}(x, y) dy}{\hat{f}(x)} = \frac{\sum_{i=1}^{N} K\left(\frac{x-x_i}{h_x}\right) y_i}{\sum_{i=1}^{N} K\left(\frac{x-x_i}{h_x}\right)}$$

assuming that $\int y K\left(\frac{y-y_i}{h_y}\right) dy = h_y y_i$.

Bandwidth selection addresses the same approaches that were discussed in the previous section.

Figure 8.4 illustrates the dependence of the Nadaraya–Watson estimator on the bandwidth parameter h_x. Again, an overly large bandwidth leads to over-smoothing, while an overly small bandwidth makes estimates excessively sensitive to outliers.

Regarding kernel regression, it is important to draw attention to a similar approach known as locally weighted regression (LWR) [24]. LWR also exploits kernels but in a different way, namely weighting examples by a kernel function K.

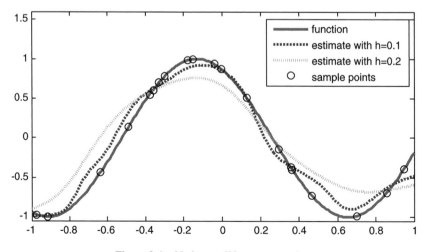

Figure 8.4: Nadaraya–Watson regression.

Linear regression weights w then become a function of data, i.e.,

$$w(x) = \underset{w}{\operatorname{argmin}} \sum_{i=1}^{N} K(x, x_i)(\langle w, x_i \rangle - y_i)^2$$

and

$$y(x) = \langle w(x), x \rangle.$$

The linear regression function $\langle w(x), x \rangle$ may be replaced with an arbitrary $f(x, w)$, resulting in more complex models. It has been shown that for uniformly (or regularly) distributed data, LWR is equivalent to kernel regression, while for non-uniform (irregular) data, LWR outperforms kernel regression [24–26].

8.3.3. *Kernel PCA*

Another example of kernel methods is a kernel extension of principal component analysis (PCA). PCA is a feature aggregation technique that aims to find a projection to an optimal linear subspace that happens to be a span of eigenvectors of the data matrix. Let

$$X_N = (x_1, \ldots, x_N) \in \mathbb{R}^{n \times N}, x_i \in \mathbb{R}^n, i \in \{1, \ldots, N\}$$

be a data matrix. PCA finds its decomposition on two matrices of lower rank

$$X_N \approx GW.$$

Columns of G represent an orthonormal basis of a linear L-dimensional subspace. In this subspace, $W = (w_1, \ldots, w_N) \in \mathbb{R}^{L \times N}$, where w_i is a representation of vector x_i. Subspace and orthogonal projection are chosen so that

$$\|X_N - GW\|^2 \to \underset{G,W}{\min},$$

which minimizes the reconstruction error. Alternatively, it can be seen as a variance maximization problem so that the projection explains (or keeps) as much variance of the original sample as possible [1].

Initially linear, the PCA approach can be extended easily to nonlinear cases [27]. The solution of PCA is based (e.g., [1]) on eigenvalue decomposition of the second moment (or covariance) matrix $C = X_N X_N^T = \sum_{i=1}^{N} x_i x_i^T$, which finds eigenvectors g and eigenvalues λ,

$$Cg = X_N X_N^T g = \lambda g.$$

The projection to an L-dimensional subspace of an arbitrary vector x is defined as:

$$proj(x) = G^T x.$$

For any kernel K, there exists a nonlinear map Φ, and we can rewrite the covariance matrix as

$$C_\Phi = \sum_{i=1}^{N} \Phi(x_i)\Phi(x_i)^T$$

to find its eigenvalue decomposition. This gives us the first L eigenvectors $g_1, \ldots, g_L$ so that

$$C_\Phi g_l = \lambda_l g_l.$$

Based on the definition of C_Φ, its eigenvectors are linear combinations of $\Phi(x_i)$, i.e.,

$$g_l = \sum_{i=1}^{N} \alpha_{il}\Phi(x_i).$$

Vectors α_l can be calculated by eigenvalue decomposition of the pairwise inner product matrix $K = K[X_N, X_N]$, $K_{ij} = K(x_i, x_j)$, namely

$$K\alpha_l = \lambda_l \alpha_l.$$

By normalizing eigenvectors so that $\langle g_l, g_l \rangle_{\mathcal{H}} = 1$, we obtain a rule for finding the nonlinear projection of any data vector x on each basis vector as

$$\langle g_l, \Phi(x) \rangle_{\mathcal{H}} = \sum_{i=1}^{N} \alpha_{il}\langle \Phi(x_i), \Phi(x) \rangle_{\mathcal{H}} = \sum_{i=1}^{N} \alpha_{il} K(x_i, x).$$

which yields the l-th coordinate of the vector x in the subspace of projection. It is worth noting that we do not have to know an implicit form of the map Φ, just the corresponding kernel K, which is used to calculate inner products.

The expression for C_Φ is tricky because, in the general case the RKHS corresponding to the mapping Φ is infinite-dimensional. Thus, the transpose operator is incorrect. Hence, C_Φ can be understood as a linear operator as follows:

$$C_\Phi z = \sum_{i=1}^{N} \Phi(x_i)\langle \Phi(x_i), z \rangle_{\mathcal{H}}, \forall z \in \mathcal{H}.$$

Kernel PCA enables the nonlinear dependences to be identified inside data. This property is illustrated in Figure 8.5. In the original feature space, two-dimensional data points form three concentric circles that are not linearly separated. Introducing

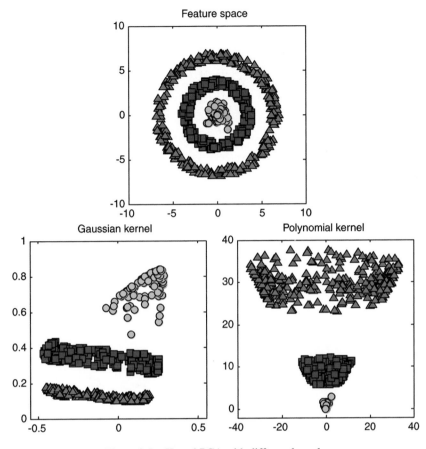

Figure 8.5: Kernel PCA with different kernels.

Gaussian or polynomial kernels into PCA allows a linearly separable dataset to be obtained.

8.3.4. *Kernel Linear Discriminant Analysis*

Linear discriminant analysis (LDA) focuses on a classification problem. Namely, for a given learning set

$$X_N = \{(x_1, y_1), \ldots, (x_N, y_N)\},$$

$x_i \in \mathbb{R}^n$, $y_i \in Y$, where $Y = \{L_1, \ldots, L_R\}$ is a set of class labels, the aim is to restore the labeling function $f : \mathbb{R}^n \to Y$.

The approach followed in LDA involves finding the normal vector w of the "optimal" (in terms of the given quality function) dividing plane in the data space. The projection of the data on the resulting vector gives a good separation of classes.

For two-class classification problems (i.e., $R = 2$), the optimal vector is determined as a solution of the following problem:

$$\frac{w^T S_B w}{w^T S_W w} \to \max_{w \in \mathbb{R}^n},$$

where

$$S_B = (\mu_1 - \mu_2)(\mu_1 - \mu_2)^T \in \mathbb{R}^{n \times n}$$

is the between-class covariance matrix;

$$S_W = \sum_{r=1}^{2} \sum_{i \, : \, y_i = L_r} (\mu_r - x_i)(\mu_r - x_i)^T \in \mathbb{R}^{n \times n}$$

is the within-class covariance matrix; and μ_r is the arithmetic mean of sample vectors of the class L_r such that

$$\mu_r = \frac{1}{N_r} \sum_{i \, : \, y_i = L_r} x_i,$$

where N_r is the number of samples in class L_r.

It can be shown that the resulting vector

$$w \propto S_W^{-1}(\mu_1 - \mu_2).$$

Similar to the previous examples, a kernel trick can be applied to the given model [28]. Suppose there is a mapping between the initial data space and some Hilbert space $\Phi : \mathbb{R}^n \to \mathcal{H}$, where

$$\langle \Phi(x), \Phi((t) \rangle_{\mathcal{H}} = K(x, t).$$

In this Hilbert space, the sample vector class means are calculated as

$$\mu_r^{\Phi} = \frac{1}{N_r} \sum_{i \, : \, y_i = L_r} \Phi(x_i).$$

Therefore, an inner product of the mean with the map of any arbitrary vector $x \in \mathbb{R}^n$ is

$$\langle \Phi(x), \mu_r^{\Phi} \rangle_{\mathcal{H}} = \frac{1}{N_r} \sum_{i \, : \, y_i = L_r} \langle \Phi(x), \Phi(x_i) \rangle_{\mathcal{H}} = \frac{1}{N_r} \sum_{i \, : \, y_i = L_r} K(x, x_i).$$

It is more complex to define the covariance matrix in the mapped feature space because it defines a linear operator in $\mathcal{H}$. However, we can determine the linear operator by its value over the vectors from the span of Φ. For example, the Hilbert space within-class covariance matrix is defined as

$$S_W^\Phi = \sum_{r=1}^{2} \sum_{i\,:\,y_i=L_r} \left[\left(\Phi\left(x_i\right) - \mu_r^\Phi\right) \left(\Phi\left(x_i\right) - \mu_r^\Phi\right)^T \right].$$

Suppose

$$w^\Phi = \sum_{i=1}^{N} \alpha_i \Phi(x_i),$$

then

$$S_W^\Phi w^\Phi = \sum_{r=1}^{2} \sum_{j\,:\,y_j=L_r} \langle \Phi(x_j) - \mu_r^\Phi, w^\Phi \rangle_{\mathcal{H}} \left[\Phi\left(x_j\right) - \mu_r^\Phi \right].$$

The coefficient $\langle \Phi(x_j) - \mu_r^\Phi, w^\Phi \rangle_{\mathcal{H}}$ can be computed easily using the properties of the inner product, which is shown as follows:

$$\langle \Phi(x_j) - \mu_r^\Phi, w^\Phi \rangle_{\mathcal{H}} = \sum_{i=1}^{N} \alpha_i \left[K\left(x_j, x_i\right) - \langle \Phi(x_j), \mu_r^\Phi \rangle_{\mathcal{H}} \right].$$

The result is a weighted sum of elements of $\mathcal{H}$. Similarly, a second-order function $\langle w^\Phi, S_W^\Phi W^\Phi \rangle_{\mathcal{H}}$ can be calculated. The optimal values of α_i, $i = 1, \ldots, N$, are still to be defined. Therefore, the resulting kernel LDA optimization problem is to find the maximum

$$\frac{\langle w^\Phi, S_B^\Phi W^\Phi \rangle_{\mathcal{H}}}{\langle w^\Phi, S_W^\Phi W^\Phi \rangle_{\mathcal{H}}} \to \max_{\alpha_i \in \mathbb{R}, i=1,\ldots,N},$$

$$w.r.t$$

$$w^\Phi = \sum_{i=1}^{N} \alpha_i \Phi(x_i).$$

The optimal solution of the stated kernel LDA problem is

$$\alpha \propto Q^{-1}\left(M_1 - M_2\right),$$

where

$$M_r \in \mathbb{R}^N, \ (M_r)_i = \frac{1}{N_r} \sum_{j\,:\,y_j=L_r} K\left(x_j, x_i\right),$$

$$Q = \sum_{r=1}^{2} K_r(I - E_{N_r}) K_r^T,$$

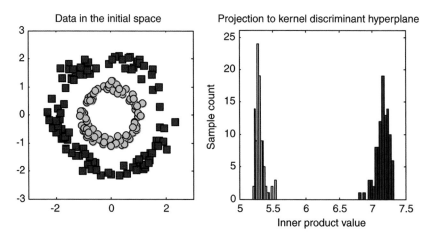

Figure 8.6: Kernel LDA projection example. Distribution of data in the initial space (left) and the result of the projection to the optimal vector in the RKHS (right).

and $E_{N_r} \in \mathbb{R}^{N_r \times N_r}$ is a matrix with elements equal to $\frac{1}{N_r}$,
$K_r \in \mathbb{R}^{N \times N_r}$, $(K_r)_{ij} = K(x_i, x_j^r)$, x_j^r—j-th vector in the r-th class.
As noted previously, a projection of the data on the optimal vector leads to the optimal separation. In terms of kernel LDA, the projection of the $\Phi(x)$ on the vector w^Φ is defined by the inner product as follows:

$$\langle w^\Phi, \Phi(x) \rangle_{\mathcal{H}} = \sum_{i=1}^{N} \alpha_i K(x, x_i).$$

Separating the property of the kernel LDA method is illustrated in Figure 8.6.

8.3.5. Kernelization of an Arbitrary Linear Model

Any linear model can be "kernelized" by replacing the inner products $\langle x, t \rangle$ with the kernel values $K(x, t)$. Here, we illustrate the idea using the example of the ridge regression model. Recall the classical ridge regression with the target function

$$\sum_{i=1}^{N} (y_i - \langle w, x_i \rangle)^2 + \lambda \|w\|^2 \to \min_{w}.$$

Here, the pairs (x_i, y_i) belong to the training sample X_N. This optimization problem can be solved analytically. With the help of linear algebra, we get

$$w = \left(\sum_{i=1}^{N} x_i x_i^T + \lambda I \right)^{-1} \left(\sum_{i=1}^{N} y_i x_i \right).$$

Now, with an appropriate kernel, we perform the mapping $x_i \to \Phi(x_i)$. Therefore,

$$\sum_{i=1}^{N} (y_i - \langle w, \Phi(x_i)\rangle_{\mathcal{H}})^2 + \lambda \|w\|^2 \to \min_{w \in \mathcal{H}}.$$

Assuming that $w = \sum_{i=1}^{N} \alpha_i \Phi(x_i)$, we can reformulate the optimization problem as

$$\sum_{i=1}^{N} \left(y_i - \sum_{j=1}^{N} \alpha_j \langle \Phi(x_j), \Phi(x_i)\rangle_{\mathcal{H}} \right)^2 + \lambda \alpha^T K(X_N, X_N)\alpha \to \min_{\alpha \in \mathbb{R}^N}.$$

Here, we denote the matrix of pairwise inner products of the training sample as $K(X_N, X_N)$,

$$[K(X_N, X_N)]_{ij} = K(x_i, x_j).$$

Then, the optimal solution of the stated problem is given by

$$\alpha = (K(X_N, X_N) + \lambda I)^{-1} \bar{y}.$$

This result can be interpreted as a special case of the representer theorem application.

Again, to calculate the y value for an arbitrary x, the exact form of the mapping Φ is not needed; we only have to know the corresponding kernel function.

$$y = \langle w, \Phi(x)\rangle = \alpha^T K(X_N, x) = \sum_{i=1}^{N} \alpha_i K(x_i, x).$$

The vector $K(X_N, x)$ consists of the inner products of the training sample objects and the point of evaluation.

Figure 8.7 shows an example of kernel ridge regression for the following model:

$$y = \frac{\sin \pi x}{\pi x} + \varepsilon,$$

where $\varepsilon \sim N(0, s^2)$ is normally distributed noise with zero mean and variance s^2 imposed on the signal.

Kernel ridge regression depends significantly on the selection of the kernel and its parameters. In the case of a Gaussian kernel [2, 4], overly large values of spread σ^2 lead to an over-smoothed solution, while an overly small σ^2 results in over-fitting. These effects are shown in Figure 8.8.

The same is the case with the regression parameter λ. The growth of this parameter will lead to smoothing and any decreases will produce a very sensitive model, as shown in Figure 8.9. To tune the parameters of the kernel ridge regression, a cross-validation technique may be applied [29].

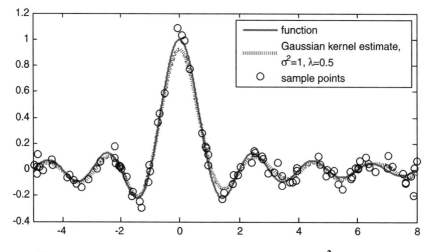

Figure 8.7:   Kernel ridge regression with a Gaussian kernel, $\sigma^2 = 1$, $\lambda = 0.5$.

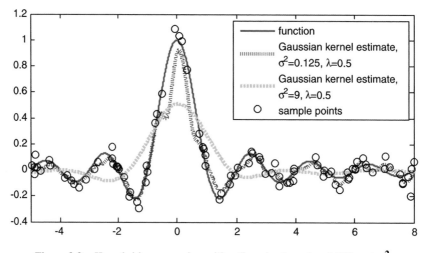

Figure 8.8:   Kernel ridge regression with a Gaussian kernel and different σ^2.

8.3.6. *Adaptive Kernel Filtering*

The proposed kernel models are applicable to adaptive filter design [30]. Adaptive kernel filtering admits online learning of the filters that are nonlinear. The learning procedure is computationally cheap because the optimization is convex.

Consider a system that takes as input streaming data vectors $x_i \in \mathbb{R}^n$, which are drawn independently from some unknown probability distribution, and produces output $f(x_i)$, aiming to predict a corresponding outcome y_i. One possible representation of such a system is shown in Figure 8.10.

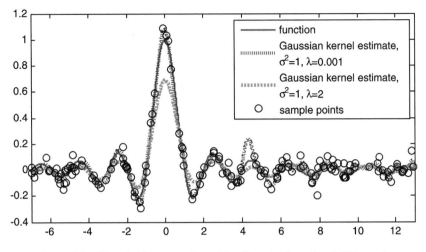

Figure 8.9: Kernel ridge regression with a Gaussian kernel and different λ.

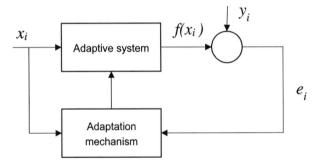

Figure 8.10: Adaptive system.

Therefore, the learning procedure is performed in an online way. In the case of a linear model, the output can be represented as an inner product:

$$f(x_i) = \langle x_i, w \rangle.$$

Learning can be performed using any online fitting procedure, such as stochastic gradient descent [30], recursive least squares [30], and others. However, such an approach limits the resulting filter output to a linear combination of the data vector components (i.e., linear function).

This limitation can be overcome using the kernel trick. Hereafter we use the least-squares functional, which is defined as follows:

$$R(X_N, f) = \sum_{i=1}^{N} (f(x_i) - y_i)^2.$$

Consider the stochastic gradient descent as a learning algorithm. Suppose that the target function is an inner product in the Hilbert space $\mathcal{H}$:

$$f(x) = \langle \Phi(x), w \rangle_{\mathcal{H}},$$

where $\Phi : \mathbb{R}^n \to \mathcal{H}$ is a map from the data space to the Hilbert space. Similar to the previous examples, we assume that

$$\forall x, t \in \mathbb{R}^n \langle \Phi(x), \Phi(t) \rangle_{\mathcal{H}} = K(x, t).$$

At each new learning pair (x_i, y_i), the parameter vector w_{i-1} is updated according to the gradient of $(\langle \Phi(x_i), w_{i-1} \rangle_{\mathcal{H}} - y_i)^2$:

$$w_i = w_{i-1} - v\left(\langle \Phi(x_i), w_{i-1} \rangle_{\mathcal{H}} - y_i\right) \Phi(x_i) = w_{i-1} + \alpha_i \Phi(x_i).$$

Here, v is a gradient descent step. Therefore, the resulting function f can be expressed as

$$f(x) = \sum_{i=1}^{N} \alpha_i K(x, x_i).$$

The overall algorithm is presented in Table 8.1.

The selection of the parameter v usually influences convergence and, more specifically, convergence speed. The required condition for convergence is

$$v < \frac{N}{\varsigma_{max}} \implies$$

$$\implies v < \frac{N}{\sum_{i=1}^{N} K(x_i, x_i)} = \frac{N}{tr\left(K(X_N, X_N)\right)} < \frac{N}{\varsigma_{max}}.$$

Here, ς_{max} is the maximal eigenvalue of the matrix $K(\mathbf{X}_N \mathbf{X}_N) \in R^{N \times N}$ of the samples' Hilbert space inner products, i.e.,

$$[K(X_N, X_N)]_{ij} = K\left(x_i, x_j\right).$$

Table 8.1: Adaptive kernel filtering algorithm

Kernel Least Mean Squares Algorithm

Input: $X_N = \{(x_1, y1), \ldots, (x_N, y_N)\}, x_i \in \mathbb{R}^n, y_i \in \mathbb{R}$
Output: $\alpha_1, \ldots, \alpha_N$
1. $w_0 = 0 \in \mathcal{H}$ — zero vector in the Hilbert space
2. for $\alpha_1, \ldots, \alpha_N$
    2.1. $e_i = (\langle \Phi(x_i), w_{i-1} \rangle_{\mathcal{H}} - y_i) = (\sum_{j=1}^{N} \alpha_j K(x_i, x_j))$
    2.2. $\alpha_i = -v e_i$

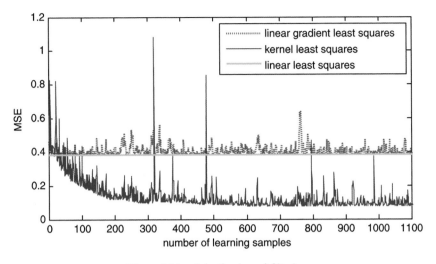

Figure 8.11: Adaptive kernel filtering.

An example of the performance of kernel least mean squares (LMS) is presented in Figure 8.11. The system's input was generated from the uniform distribution over unit a 10-dimensional cube. The output was stated as the sine of the squared norm of the corresponding input vector, which can be expressed as follows:

$$x_i \in \mathbb{R}^{10}, \; y_i = \sin\left(\|x_i\|^2\right).$$

The thin blue lines and dotted red lines represent the mean squared error (MSE) over the test set, depending on the number of learning samples used by an adaptive filter for kernel LMS and linear stochastic LMS correspondingly. The thick green line represents the MSE for the linear least-squares algorithm, which is a theoretical minimum for the linear model. The kernel model takes longer to converge but significantly outperforms the linear model in terms of MSE.

One of the most significant drawbacks of the system is the increasing order of the filter by each new accumulated learning data sample, which can be solved using a number of approaches limiting the order of the filter [32].

Kernel methods are widely applied in adaptive filtering. There exist techniques for regularized regression fitting, kernel extended least-squares algorithms, and many other kernel data mining models.

8.3.7. *Spectral Clustering*

Spectral clustering [33–36] is a clustering technique based on an analysis of the similarity matrix spectrum of the data. It is now regarded as one of the most popular clustering methods because it can be implemented straightforwardly and efficiently solved using standard linear algebra methods, and it also outperforms many other clustering approaches in different domains [36, 37]. Originally, the idea came from weighted graph analysis, but it can be shown that it has a connection to kernel methods.

The starting point of spectral clustering is building a similarity $N \times N$ matrix S of dataset $\{x_1, \ldots, x_N\}$, where $s_{ij} > 0$ is the similarity between x_i and x_j. These relationships can be represented in the form of the similarity graph $G = (V, E)$, where the vertex $v_i \in V$ corresponds to x_i and the edge $e_{ij} \in E$ is weighted by s_{ij}. This graph can be fully connected (i.e., all $s_{ij} > 0$) or each vertex can be connected to the k-nearest neighbors only (i.e., all other edges have $s_{ij} = 0$), resulting in a sparse matrix [36]. The problem of clustering then can be reformulated in terms of graph partitioning. Furthermore, the edges of the partition between different groups are expected to have low weights.

Following graph theory, we denote the degree of a vertex v_i as

$$d_i = \sum_{m=1}^{N} s_{ij}.$$

The degree matrix D is a diagonal matrix with $d_1, \ldots, d_N$ on the diagonal.

Spectral clustering algorithms are based on eigenvalue decomposition of the graph Laplacian matrix. This can be calculated in several ways:

1) The unnormalized graph Laplacian matrix [38, 39] is defined as

$$L = D - S.$$

2) The symmetric normalized graph Laplacian matrix [40] is defined as

$$L = D^{-\frac{1}{2}} (D - S) D^{-\frac{1}{2}} = I - D^{-\frac{1}{2}} S D^{-\frac{1}{2}}.$$

3) The random walk normalized graph Laplacian matrix [40] is defined as

$$L = D^{-1} (D - S) = I - D^{-1} S.$$

4) In [35], the authors define the graph Laplacian matrix as

$$L = D^{-\frac{1}{2}} S D^{-\frac{1}{2}},$$

which has the same eigenvectors as the symmetric normalized graph Laplacian matrix and eigenvalues λ_i, corresponding to $1 - \lambda_i$ of the latter.

After calculating the graph Laplacian matrix of the data to be clustered, eigenvalue decomposition is performed. Ordinary decomposition may be replaced with a generalized eigenvalue decomposition, as in the spectral clustering procedure described by Shi and Malik [41]. Eigenvectors, which are vector columns corresponding to the k-smallest eigenvalues, form matrix $V^{N \times k}$ containing new descriptions of the original objects as vector rows.

Finally, these vector rows are clustered. For instance, this is undertaken using the simple k-means algorithm. Ng, Jordan, and Weiss [35] suggest normalizing vector rows to have norm 1.

Spectral clustering can easily be implemented and solved using standard linear algebra methods. Despite the lack of theoretical proof, experiments show that spectral clustering algorithms can be applied to clusters with arbitrary shapes [36]. Intuitively, it follows that spectral clustering explores the spectrum of the similarity matrix. Thus, an appropriate similarity metric will lead to a reasonably good result.

Two examples of spectral clustering performance on datasets with complicated structures are given in Figure 8.12.

At the end of this section, we show that spectral clustering is related to the kernel k-means,

$$\sum_{j=1}^{k} \sum_{x \in \pi_j} w(x) \left\| \Phi(x) - \mu_j \right\|^2 \rightarrow \min_{\pi_j, \mu_j},$$

where $\pi = \left\{ \pi_j \right\}_{j=1}^{k}$ is a partitioning of data into clusters π_j. For a fixed partition, cluster centers are calculated similarly to standard k-means,

$$\mu_j = \arg \min_{\mu} \sum_{x \in \pi_j} w(x) \left\| \Phi(x) - \mu \right\|^2$$

and $x \in X_N$. The function $w(x)$ assigns some nonnegative weight to each object x. Mapping Φ is determined by some kernel function K. Note that there is no need to compute this mapping because $\|\cdot\|$ depends only on the inner products computed by K.

Normalized spectral clustering, which is closely connected to the normalized graph cut problem, can be expressed as a matrix trace minimization problem [34]

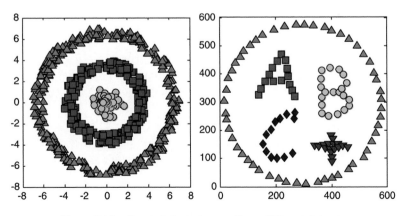

Figure 8.12: Spectral clustering results on different datasets.

as follows:

$$\text{trace} \left(V^T L V \right) \rightarrow \max_{V \in \mathbb{R}^{N \times K}, V^T V = 1},$$

where $L = D^{-\frac{1}{2}} S D^{-\frac{1}{2}}$.

Denoting the diagonal matrix formed by weights $w(x_i), i = 1, \ldots, N$ as W, the weighted kernel k-means optimization problem takes the form

$$\text{trace} \left(V^T W^{\frac{1}{2}} K (X_N, X_N) W^{\frac{1}{2}} V \right) \rightarrow \max_{V \in \mathbb{R}^{N \times K}, V^T V = 1},$$

which is close to that in normalized spectral clustering.

8.3.8. Gaussian Processes and Regression and Classification methods

A Gaussian process (GP) is a generalization of the Gaussian probability distribution [66]. The main difference is that a probability distribution describes random variables, which are scalars or vectors, while a stochastic process describes the properties of functions. In this section, we will not introduce GPs in a mathematically correct way; this would take a lot of space and is not strictly related to the chapter's topic. Instead, we will describe the main properties of this model, show its relation to kernel methods, and detail its application to regression and classification tasks.

Definition 8.6. A Gaussian process (GP) is a collection of random variables, any finite number of which have a joint Gaussian distribution.

GP defines a probability distribution on a set of functions $F = \{f : X \rightarrow \mathbb{R}\}$, where X is the parameter space of the functions in F. This distribution is defined by its mean and covariance functions as follows:

$$\mathbb{E} f(x) = m(x),$$
$$k \left(x, x' \right) = \mathbb{E} \left(f(x) - m(x) \right)^T \left(f(x') - m(x') \right).$$

In this case, we write that for each $x \in X$, the value of $f(x)$ is distributed as

$$f(x) \sim GP(m(x), k(x, x)) = N(m(x), k(x, x)).$$

Here, $N(\mu, \sigma^2)$ represents a Gaussian distribution with mean μ and variance σ^2. Following the definition of GP, we consider a distribution of the values of the function f on a set $X_N = (x_1, \ldots, x_N)$, denoted by

$$f_N = (f(x_1), \ldots, f(x_i), \ldots, f(x_N)),$$

which is a real vector-valued random variable. Therefore, following the definition

$$f_N \sim N\left(M\left(X_N\right), K\left(X_N, X_N\right)\right),$$

where $M(X_N) \in \mathbb{R}^N$, $K(X_N, X_N) \in \mathbb{R}^{N \times N}$ are multi-dimensional applications of functions $m(x)$, $k\left(x, x'\right)$ to dataset X_N correspondingly. As $K(X_N, X_N)$ is a covariance matrix and is, therefore, positive-definite for any finite set X_N, $k\left(x, x'\right)$ is a positive definite kernel.

It is important to stress that the random variable here is not $x \in X$. In fact, it is the function f. Furthermore, the distribution over f is constructed by defining the distribution over the values of the function for each finite set of arguments.

Based on the properties stated above, we consider the application of the model for regression and classification problems.

A **regression** problem for the case of GP is formalized as a computation of the parameters of the conditional distribution. Suppose we have a defined pair $m(x)$ and $k\left(x, x'\right)$, as well as a sample of pairs $D = \{(x_i, y_i)\}_{i=1}^{N}$. Now we would like to assess the distribution of $f(x^*)$ for a given x^*. For this, we consider the conditional distribution $p(f^* | f_N = y_N, x^*)$, i.e., its mean and covariance, as follows:

$$\mathbb{E}(f^* | f_N = y_N, x^*) = m\left(x^*\right) + K\left(x^*, X_N\right) K\left(X_N, X_N\right)^{-1}\left(y_N - M\left(X_N\right)\right),$$

$$\mathbb{D}(f^* | f_N = y_N, x^*) = k\left(x^*, x^*\right) - K\left(x^*, X_N\right) K\left(X_N, X_N\right)^{-1} K\left(x^*, X_N\right)^T.$$

Here, f^* is a shorter notation for the $f(x^*)$ random variable. One can see that the form of the expected value matches the result obtained in Section 8.3.5 and the form defined by the representer theorem (see Theorem 5). Indeed, assuming $m(x) \equiv 0$ and by defining

$$\alpha = K\left(X_N, X_N\right)^{-1} y_N,$$

we obtain the following expected value:

$$\mathbb{E}(f^* | f_N = y_N, x^*) = \sum_{i=1}^{N} \alpha_i k\left(x_i, x^*\right).$$

The difference between the results presented in Section 8.3.5 and those shown here is caused by the regularization term introduced before. It is possible to obtain the same result by assuming that

$$\forall i \in 1, \ldots, N \; y_i = f(x_i) + \varepsilon_i,$$

$$f(x) \sim GP\left(m(x), k(x, x)\right),$$

$$\varepsilon_i \sim N\left(0, \sigma^2\right).$$

The above-mentioned assumption, $m(x) \equiv 0$, is a common choice for the mean function. Additionally, it does not limit model flexibility if we are using universal kernels. At the same time, it is possible to introduce further flexibility into the model in a different way, namely, by assuming that $m(x)$ is a parametric function $m(x, \beta)$. In this case, the parameters β can be adjusted using the maximum likelihood method for a given sample D.

A **classification** problem for GP has a less straightforward formulation. In this section, we consider a two-class classification problem with a probabilistic formulation. For a linear classifier, the standard approach to define class probability is

$$p(y = +1|x) = \frac{1}{1 + e^{-\langle x, w \rangle}} = \sigma(\langle x, w \rangle).$$

For nonlinear cases, it is possible to replace $\langle x, w \rangle$ with a nonlinear function $f(x)$, so that the positive class probability would be expressed as $\sigma(f(x))$. Next, the behavior of $f(x)$ is modeled using GP, which is adjusted using data sample D. Here, $f(x)$ plays the role of a "hidden variable" in that we do not observe the values of the function itself and we are not particularly interested in its exact values; instead, we are observing the class labels that depend on the function.

For model derivation, we can reuse notations from the "regression" subsection with the main difference that $y_N \in \{+1, -1\}^N$. The predictive distribution of the values of this function for a specific input x^* can be expressed as

$$p(f^*|D, x^*) = \int p(f^*|X_N, f_N, x^*) p\left(f_N \mid X_N, y_N\right) df_N.$$

It is possible to obtain the class-prediction probability as

$$p(y^* = +1|D, x^*) = \int p(y^* = +1 \mid f^*) p(f^* \mid D, x^*) df^*$$

$$= \int \sigma(f^*) p(f^* \mid D, x^*) df^*.$$

The probability distribution $p(f_N | X_N, y_N)$ is non-Gaussian, and direct computation of $p(f^* | D, x^*)$ is impossible. However, several approaches have been proposed [?] involving different types of probabilistic approximation, including Laplace approximation or expectation propagation. In this section, we consider Laplace approximation in detail.

Laplace's method uses a Gaussian approximation $q(f_N | X_N, y_N)$ of the non-Gaussian distribution $p(f_N | X_N, y_N)$, so that the derivation of $p(f^* | D, x^*)$ becomes tractable. It performs a second-order Taylor expansion of $\log(p(f_N | X_N, y_N))$ around its maximum, defining a Gaussian distribution as follows:

$$q(f_N \mid X_N, y_N) = \mathcal{N}(\hat{f}_N, A^{-1}),$$

$$\hat{f}_N = argmax_{f_N}(\log(p(f_N \mid X_N, y_N))),$$

$$A = -\nabla\nabla \log(p(f_N \mid X_N, y_N))\big|_{f_N = \hat{f}_N}.$$

The process of finding the values of $\hat{f}_N$, A^{-1} can be interpreted as the model training process. It is possible to obtain these values using Newton's method.

After performing the approximation, it is possible to derive the mean $\mathbb{E}_q(f^* \mid D, x^*)$ and variance $\mathbb{D}_q(f^* \mid D, x^*)$. This is because the convolution of Gaussian distributions can be expressed analytically.

The integral defining $p(y^* = +1 \mid D, x^*)$ is still intractable and evaluated approximately. However, if the problem does not require computation of the probability of a class and requires only classification to be performed, it is possible to use the following rule:

$$p(y^* = +1 \mid D, x^*) > \frac{1}{2} \iff \mathbb{E}_q(f^* \mid D, x^*) > 0.$$

It is important to note that $\mathbb{E}_q(f^* \mid D, x^*)$ is expressed in the form of linear combinations of kernels, which is related to the representer theorem.

8.4. Support Vector Machines

Support vector machines (SVMs) are among the most pervasive techniques for solving data mining problems, including classification, regression, anomaly detection, and metric learning. Initially invented as a linear classification problem solver in the mid-1960s by Soviet scientists Vapnik and Chervonenkis [5], the SVM was further developed into a framework of statistical methods with common optimization approaches. The SVM plays a significant role in the scope of kernel machines due to the "sparsity" of the method, which is because the size of the learning set is the main limitation for such types of algorithms. The next part of this chapter covers the following: we first describe the SVM classifier [4] in more detail and specify its relation to kernel machines, after which we introduce several types of SVM for binary classification, regression, and multiclass classification; finally, we highlight some approaches for anomaly detection, incremental SVM learning, and metric fitting.

8.4.1. *Support Vector Classifier*

As noted in the first chapter, the main idea behind an SVM is to build a maximal margin classifier. Suppose that we have a labeled sample $X_N =$

$\{(x_1, y_1), \ldots, (x_N, y_N)\}$, $x_i \in \mathcal{R}^n$, $y_i \in \{1, -1\}$, and we need to solve a two-class classification problem. Assume that linear classification is considered, which means that the algorithm's decision rule can be expressed as

$$f(x) = \text{sign}(\langle w, x \rangle - \rho),$$

where $w \in \mathbb{R}^n$ and $\rho \in \mathbb{R}$. Therefore, the problem can be conceptualized as one involving finding w and ρ, or defining a hyperplane that separates the objects of different classes. It is also supposed that the sample set is linearly separable, which means that

$$\exists w \in \mathbb{R}^n, \exists \rho \in \mathbb{R} : \sum_{i=1}^{N} \mathrm{I}\left[(\langle w, x_i \rangle - \rho)y_i \le 0\right] = 0.$$

That is to say, all the objects are classified correctly. The margin function is defined as follows:

$$M(x_i, y_i) = (\langle w, x_i \rangle - \rho)y_i \begin{cases} \le 0, & \text{if } f(x_i) \ne y_i, \\ > 0, & \text{if } f(x_i) = y_i. \end{cases}$$

It is important to note that there may be infinitely many ways to define the hyperplane, as illustrated in Figure 8.13. In this figure, the two possible separation lines for two-dimensional classification problems are shown.

Vapnik *et al.* [42] suggested a "maximum margin" approach wherein the hyperplane is placed as far away as possible from the closest objects of both classes. So, a linear two-class SVM finds a "hyper-band" between two classes with maximal width.

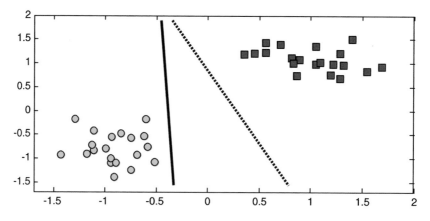

Figure 8.13: Different ways to define a hyperplane for the dataset.

Consider the maximal bandwidth problem in more detail. The distance between a given point $x_0 \in \mathbb{R}^n$ and a plane $P(w, \rho)$, as defined by

$$\langle x, w \rangle - \rho = 0,$$

can be calculated as follows:

$$d(P(w, \rho), x_0) = \frac{|\langle x_0, w \rangle - \rho|}{\|w\|}.$$

To find the best separating bandwidth, we maximize the distance from the closest data point in the learning set while considering class separation constraints. Therefore, the optimization problem for SVMs is stated as

$$\max_{w, \rho} \min_{x_i \in X_N} \frac{|\langle x_i, w \rangle - \rho|}{\|w\|},$$

$$w.r.t$$

$$y_i(\langle x_i, w \rangle - \rho) > 0, \quad \forall (x_i, y_i) \in X_N.$$

Note that for all $\alpha > 0$, the terms αw and $\alpha \rho$ define the same separating hyperplane. Therefore, we can strengthen the problem's constraints:

$$\forall (x_i, y_i) \in X_N \ (\langle w, x_i \rangle - \rho) y_i \geq 1,$$

which is to say that for the objects closest to the hyperplane, the inequality turns into equality. It is possible to show that there should be at least two closest objects (with the same distance) from both classes. Suppose $P(w^*, \rho^*) \equiv P^*$ is optimal. Let the closest vector from the class "-1" be denoted as x_{-1}, and let the one from the class "$+1$" be specified as x_{+1}. Without loss of generality, let us suppose that

$$d(P(w^*, \rho^*), x_{+1}) < d(P(w^*, \rho^*), x_{-1}).$$

Let $\varepsilon = d(P^*, x_{-1}) - d(P^*, x_{+1})$, and consider the following plane:

$$P\left(w^*, \left(\rho^* - \frac{\varepsilon}{2}\right)\right) = P_\varepsilon^*.$$

This hyperplane fits the learning set constraints (all the vectors are correctly classified), but the distance of each "-1" class sample is reduced by $\frac{\varepsilon}{2}$, and the distance of each "$+1$" class sample is enlarged by $\frac{\varepsilon}{2}$ compared to P^*. It is obvious that the object that is the closest to the hyperplane P_ε^* is still x_{+1}, but

$$d(P^*, x_{+1}) < d(P^*, x_{+1}) + \frac{\varepsilon}{2} = d(P_\varepsilon^*, x_{+1})$$

contradicts the "maximum distance" statement. Thus, the objects from classes "$+1$" and "-1" that are closest to the hyperplane are equidistant from it.

Therefore, the separation bandwidth can be expressed as follows:

$$h = \left\langle x_1 - x_{-1}, \frac{w}{\|w\|} \right\rangle = \frac{(\langle x_1, w \rangle - \rho) - (\langle x_{-1}, w \rangle - \rho)}{\|w\|} = \frac{2}{\|w\|}.$$

This value is to be maximized, which is to say that

$$\frac{2}{\|w\|} \to \max_{w}.$$

The formulation is easily converted into the standard SVM optimization problem as follows:

$$\frac{1}{2}\|w\|^2 \to \min_{w,\rho}$$

w.r.t.

$$y_i(\langle w, x_i \rangle - \rho) \geq 1, i = 1, \ldots, N.$$

However, it does not allow solving the classification problem for linearly non-separable classes. From a mathematical perspective, it comes from the point that the set defined by constraints $y_i(\langle w, x_i \rangle - \rho) \geq 1$ may be empty. To overcome this issue, the so-called "slack variables" ξ_i are introduced.

$$\frac{1}{2}\|w\|^2 + C\sum_{i=1}^{N} \xi_i \to \min_{w,\rho,xi}$$

w.r.t.

$$y_i(\langle w, x_i \rangle - \rho) \geq 1 - \xi_i,$$
$$\xi_i \geq 0, \; i = 1, \ldots, N.$$

In this case, the set of constraints defines an open set (because $\forall w, \rho$ there exist slack variables ξ_i that are large enough for the constraints to be met). The problem is defined as one of quadratic programming optimization. Usually, it is solved in its dual formulation. If we write down the Lagrangian and derive the Karush–Kuhn–Tucker (KKT) conditions, we yield the dual optimization problem as follows:

$$-\frac{1}{2}\alpha Q \alpha^T + \sum_{i=1}^{N} \alpha_i \to \max_{\alpha}$$

w.r.t.

$$\begin{cases} 0 \leq \alpha_i \leq C \, \forall i = 1, \ldots, N, \\ \sum_{i=1}^{N} \alpha_i y_i = 0, \end{cases}$$

where $\alpha \in \mathbb{R}^N$ is a vector of Lagrangian multipliers, $Q_{ij} = y_i y_j \langle x_i, x_j \rangle$. KKT conditions play an essential role in solving optimization problems and explaining the properties of the approach. We focus on the two main consequences of KKT conditions for the SVM.

The first KKT condition leads to an explicit representation of vector w,

$$w = \sum_{i=1}^{N} y_i \alpha_i x_i,$$

which can be interpreted as a special case of the representer theorem with the Lagrangian regarded as a regularized loss function. One of the key properties of the SVM is that most α_i will be reduced to zero. Only a relatively small subset of samples has corresponding non-zero alpha entries. Such samples are called *support vectors*.

A large number of zero entries in α can be explained by the second consequence of KKT conditions. It can be shown that vectors in the learning set can be split into three categories

$$\begin{cases} M(x_i, \ y_i) > 1, & \alpha_i = 0, & \xi_i = 0 : C - \text{group}, \\ M(x_i, \ y_i) = 1, & 0 < \alpha_i < C, & \xi_i = 0 : M - \text{group}, \\ M(x_i, \ y_i) < 1, & \alpha_i = C, & \xi_i > 0 : E - \text{group}, \end{cases}$$

where $M(x_i, \ y_i) = (\langle w, x_i \rangle - \rho) y_i$. C-group (*correct*) defines a subset of vectors from X_N lying beyond the boundaries of the separation band and, thus, that are well separated. The M-(*margin*) and E-(*error*) groups are the subsets of the vectors lying on the border and within the separation band, respectively. These groups are related to less separable vectors (E-group can contain misclassified vectors).

Therefore, all the vectors that lie beyond the boundaries of the separation band (C-group) have zero alpha entries. Considering that the algorithm aims to minimize the sum of ξ_i, the number of vectors in the M- and E-groups should be relatively small. Otherwise, this could be a sign of a poorly fitted classifier.

Another explanation for the sparsity of the SVM can be referred to as the "geometrical" explanation. Constraints of the primal optimization problem define a set, limited by a hyper-polyline (maybe, hyper-polygon) in the space of w. Each vector x_i in the sample determines a linear function in the space of w

$$f_i(w, \rho) = y_i \langle x_i, w \rangle - y_i \rho - 1,$$

defining a half-space, $f_i(w, \rho) \geq 0$, but not each linear functions is involved in forming the broken hyperplane, which represents a border of the set

$$\{w, \rho \mid f_i(w, \rho) \geq 0 \forall i = 1, \ldots, N\}.$$

An example with a sample set of five vectors is illustrated in Figure 8.14.

It is assumed that each hyperplane defines a half-space above it. Only three lines of five construct the border polyline.

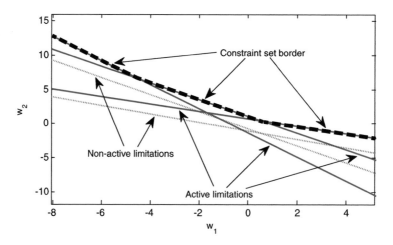

Figure 8.14: Active and non-active constraints.

8.4.2. *Examples of the Kernel Trick*

Let us now consider an application of kernels to an SVM more carefully. The so-called "kernel trick" [43] is a powerful tool that introduces nonlinearity into a model, allowing the separation of data that cannot be separated linearly.

In a linear SVM, we have

$$\frac{1}{2}\|w\|^2 + C\sum_{i=1}^{N}\xi_i \to \min_{w,\xi,\rho}$$

w.r.t.

$$y_i(\langle w, x_i\rangle - \rho) \geq 1 - \xi_i,$$
$$\xi_i \geq 0, \quad i = 1, \dots, N.$$

Slack variables ξ_i make the problem consistent even for linearly nonseparable cases, but it is still possible for a linear hyperplane to have poor discriminative ability, with classes being separated by a nonlinear surface. We may hope that with a map $\Phi : X \to \mathcal{H}$, the problem will become linearly separable in the RKHS $\mathcal{H}$. The idea of choosing RKHS is that the target function and conditions in the SVM depend only on inner products. This means that they can be calculated in $\mathcal{H}$ using the corresponding kernel function K without evaluating map Φ,

$$K(x, t) = \langle \Phi(x), \Phi(t)\rangle_{\mathcal{H}}.$$

In other words, we are trying to find such a feature space $\mathcal{H}$ with a corresponding reproducing kernel K so that the dividing function f in the input space can be represented as a linear combination:

$$f(x) = \sum_{i=1}^{N}\hat{\alpha}_i K(x, x_i).$$

The dual form of the linear SVM provides an elegant solution for determining linear coefficients $\hat{a}_i$. Actually, from KKT conditions, we have

$$w = \sum_{i=1}^{N} \alpha_i y_i x_i.$$

The image of w to the Hilbert space can be written as

$$w_{\mathcal{H}} = \sum_{i=1}^{N} \alpha_i y_i \Phi(x_i).$$

Then inner product $\langle w, x \rangle$, which determines a linear separating plane in the initial space, is replaced by a nonlinear separating surface determined by the following function:

$$f(x) = \langle w_{\mathcal{H}}, \Phi(x) \rangle_{\mathcal{H}} = \sum_{i=1}^{N} \alpha_i y_i \langle \Phi(x), \Phi(x_i) \rangle_{\mathcal{H}} = \sum_{i=1}^{N} \alpha_i y_i K(x, x_i).$$

Then, the following quadratic program is to be solved instead of the initial one:

$$\sum_{i=1}^{N} \alpha_i - \frac{1}{2} \sum_{i,j=1}^{N} \alpha_i \alpha_j y_i y_j K(x_i x_j) \to \max_{\alpha}$$

w.r.t.

$$0 \le \alpha_i \le C,$$

$$\sum_{i=1}^{N} \alpha_i y_i = 0.$$

The computational effectiveness of a kernel SVM arises from a relatively small number of non-zero α_i, which correspond to support vectors. It dramatically reduces the number of kernel function calculations that are required.

Example of a polynomial kernel SVM. Here, we illustrate the technique of a kernel SVM using two examples. The first one, shown in Figure 8.15, illustrates the ability of the polynomial kernel

$$K(x, t) = (\langle x, t \rangle + 1)^2$$

to restore a quadratic discriminant line. True class labels of the data are marked with a different color and shape, and the quadratic discriminant line of the kernel SVM is given in red. The filled points are support vectors.

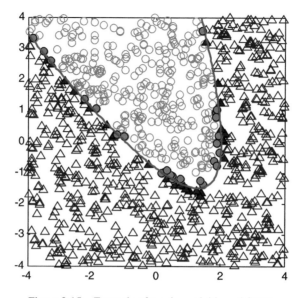

Figure 8.15:   Example of a polynomial kernel SVM.

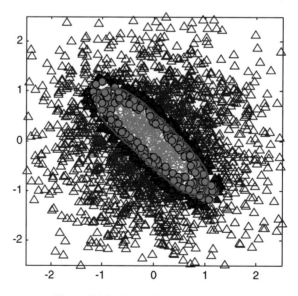

Figure 8.16:   Example of an RBF SVM.

The second example, shown in Figure 8.16, illustrates the performance of a radial basis function (RBF) SVM on data originating from the mixture of Gaussians. Once again, the true class labels of the data are marked with a different color and shape, while the discriminant line of RBF SVM is shown in red. Again, filled points represent support vectors.

8.4.3. *ν-SVM and C-SVM*

As mentioned before, we can state the optimization problem to find an optimal margin of the form

$$\frac{1}{2} \|w\|^2 \to \min_{w,\rho},$$
$$y_i(\langle w, x_i \rangle - \rho) \geq 1, i = 1, \ldots, N.$$

This statement, however, does not allow data to be misclassified, but the dataset is not guaranteed to be exactly divisible in the proposed model.

For this purpose, we relax the constraints to allow data to be misclassified. To do this, we introduce slack variables, making a penalty for misclassification, as follows:

$$\frac{1}{2} \|w\|^2 + C \sum_{i=1}^{N} \xi_i \to \min_{w,\rho,\xi}$$

w.r.t

$$y_i(\langle w, x_i \rangle - \rho) \geq 1 - \xi_i,$$
$$\xi_i \geq 0, \quad i = 1, \ldots, N.$$

where C is a parameter that controls the value of the misclassification penalty. The constraints imposed on each dataset element are often referred to as *soft margin constraints*, in contrast to *hard margin constraints*.

In turn, we can write the Lagrangian of the problem as follows:

$$L(w, \rho, \xi, \alpha, \beta) = \frac{1}{2} \|w\|^2 + C \sum_{i=1}^{N} \xi_i -$$

$$- \sum_{i=1}^{N} \alpha_i (y_i(\langle w, x_i \rangle - \rho) - 1 + \xi_i) - \sum_{i=1}^{N} \beta_i \xi_i,$$

where α_i and β_i are Largangian multipliers with a corresponding set of KKT conditions:

$$\alpha_i(y_i(\langle w, x_i \rangle - \rho) - 1 + \xi_i) = 0,$$
$$\beta_i \xi_i = 0,$$
$$y_i(\langle w, x_i \rangle - \rho) - 1 + \xi_i \geq 0,$$
$$\alpha_i \geq 0, \ \beta_i \geq 0, \ \xi_i \geq 0.$$

Differentiating the Lagrangian, we obtain

$$\frac{\partial L(w, \rho, \xi, \alpha, \beta)}{\partial w} = 0 \Rightarrow w = \sum_{i=1}^{N} \alpha_i y_i x_i,$$

$$\frac{\partial L(w, \rho, \xi, \alpha, \beta)}{\partial \rho} = 0 \Rightarrow \sum_{i=1}^{N} \alpha_i y_i = 0,$$

$$\frac{\partial L(w, \rho, \xi, \alpha, \beta)}{\partial \xi_i} = 0 \Rightarrow C - \beta_i = \alpha_i,$$

and then switch to the dual problem as follows:

$$\tilde{L}(\alpha) = \sum_{i=1}^{N} \alpha_i - \frac{1}{2} \sum_{i=1}^{N} \sum_{j=1}^{N} \alpha_i \alpha_j y_i y_j \langle x_j y_j \rangle \to \max_{\alpha}$$

w.r.t.

$$0 \leq \alpha_i \leq C, \ i = 1, \ldots, N$$

$$\sum_{i=1}^{N} \alpha_i y_i = 0.$$

This approach is referred to as C-SVM [44]. The dual representation gives rise to an alternative technique that can be addressed using misclassification, ν-SVM [45]. For this approach, the primal problem is stated as follows:

$$\frac{1}{2} \|w\|^2 - \nu\gamma + \frac{1}{N} \sum_{i=1}^{N} \xi_i \to \min_{w, \rho, \gamma}$$

w.r.t.

$$y_i(\langle w, x_i \rangle - \rho) \geq \gamma - \xi_i,$$
$$\xi_i \geq 0, \quad i = 1, \ldots, N.$$

Additionally, the dual problem is the following:

$$\tilde{L}(\alpha) = -\frac{1}{2} \sum_{i=1}^{N} \sum_{j=1}^{N} \alpha_i \alpha_j y_i y_j \langle x_i, x_j \rangle \to \max_{\alpha}$$

w.r.t.

$$0 \leq \alpha_i \leq \frac{1}{N}, i = 1, \ldots, N,$$

$$\sum_{i=1}^{N} \alpha_i y_i = 0, \ \sum_{i=1}^{N} \alpha_i \geq \nu.$$

Here, the parameter ν gives a lower bound for the fraction of support vectors, as well as an upper bound for the fraction of margin errors in the case of $\gamma > 0$. Actually, the first statement can be justified by noting that the maximum contribution to the last KKT inequality of each of the vectors is $\frac{1}{N}$. For this reason, the overall count of support vectors cannot be lower than νN. The last statement can be proved using the KKT conditions of the primal problem [45]. It is possible to prove that the formulation of the task is equivalent to C-SVM with $C = \frac{1}{N\gamma}$, if $\gamma > 0$.

8.4.4. ε-SVR and ν-SVR

SVMs are not restricted only to classification problems; they can also address regression problems. This family of methods is referred to as support vector regression (SVR).

Given a learning set $X_N = \{(x_1, y_1), \ldots, (x_N, y_N)\}$, $y_i \in \mathbb{R}$, we aim to find a regression function $\hat{f}(x)$ that approximates an unknown target function $f : X \to \mathbb{R}$. This target function has the following form:

$$\hat{f}(x) = \langle w, x \rangle - \rho.$$

We state the problem as a minimization of the regularized error function

$$E_1\left(\hat{f}, w\right) = \frac{1}{2} \sum_{i=1}^{N} E\{\hat{f}(x_i) - y_i\} + \frac{\lambda \|w\|^2}{2}, \quad \lambda \geq 0.$$

Here, we do not use a standard error function

$$E\{\hat{f}(x_i) - y_i\} = (\hat{f}(x_i) - y_i)^2,$$

as we aim to obtain a sparse solution. Instead, we use

$$E\{\hat{f}(x_i) - y_i\} = \begin{cases} \left|\hat{f}(x_i) - y_i\right| - \varepsilon, & \text{if } \left|\hat{f}(x_i) - y_i\right| > \varepsilon, \\ 0, & \text{else.} \end{cases}$$

Again, the statement is augmented by slack variables, which penalize the exit from

$$\left|\hat{f}(x_i) - y_i\right| < \varepsilon.$$

Introducing slack variables, we convert the problem into the form

$$E(\xi^1, \xi^2, w) = C \sum_{i=1}^{N} \{\xi_i^1 + \xi_i^2\} + \frac{\|w\|^2}{2} \to \min_{\xi^1, \xi^2, w}$$

$$\hat{f}(x_i) - y_i \geq -\varepsilon - \xi_i^1, \quad \xi_i^1 \geq 0 \; \forall i \in 1, \ldots, N.$$

$$\hat{f}(x_i) - y_i \leq \varepsilon + \xi_i^2, \quad \xi_i^2 \geq 0 \; \forall i \in 1, \ldots, N.$$

Here, $C = \frac{1}{2}\lambda^{-1}$.

As before, we introduce a Lagrangian to convert the problem into dual representation as follows:

$$L(w, \xi^1, \xi^2, \beta^1, \beta^2, \alpha^1, \alpha^2, \rho)$$

$$= C \sum_{i=1}^{N} \{\xi_i^1 + \xi_i^2\} + \frac{\|w\|^2}{2} - \sum_{i=1}^{N} \{\beta_i^1 \xi_i^1 + \beta_i^2 \xi_i^2\}$$

$$- \sum_{i=1}^{N} \alpha_i^1 \left\{\varepsilon + \xi_i^1 + \hat{f}(x_i) - y_i\right\} - \sum_{i=1}^{N} \alpha_i^2 \left\{\varepsilon + \xi_i^2 - \hat{f}(x_i) + y_i\right\}.$$

Differentiating, we obtain

$$\frac{\partial L}{\partial w} = 0 \Rightarrow w = \sum_{i=1}^{N} x_i (\alpha_i^1 - \alpha_i^2),$$

$$\frac{\partial L}{\partial \xi_i^1} = 0 \Rightarrow C = \alpha_i^1 + \beta_i^1,$$

$$\frac{\partial L}{\partial \xi_i^2} = 0 \Rightarrow C = \alpha_i^2 + \beta_i^2,$$

$$\frac{\partial L}{\partial \rho} = 0 \Rightarrow \sum_{i=1}^{N} (\alpha_i^1 - \alpha_i^2) = 0.$$

Finally, using the KKT conditions, we can obtain the final expression of the dual problem:

$$\tilde{L}(\alpha^1, \alpha^2) = -\frac{1}{2} \sum_{i=1}^{N} \sum_{j=1}^{N} (\alpha_i^1 - \alpha_i^2)(\alpha_j^1 - \alpha_j^2)\langle x_i, x_j \rangle$$

$$- \varepsilon \sum_{i=1}^{N} (\alpha_i^1 + \alpha_i^2) + \sum_{i=1}^{N} (\alpha_i^1 - \alpha_i^2) y_i \rightarrow \max_{\alpha^1, \alpha^2}$$

$$\alpha_i^1 \geq 0, \alpha_i^1 \leq C, \alpha_i^2 \geq 0, \alpha_i^2 \leq C.$$

It should also be mentioned that because the Lagrangian is dependent on x_i in the form of scalar products, one can apply a standard kernel trick.

The described approach is referred to as ε-SVR [46].

Similar to the ν-SVM, we can define the ν-SVR method [45]. The primal problem is formulated as follows:

$$E(\xi^1, \xi^2, w, \varepsilon) = \frac{C}{N} \sum_{i=1}^{N} \{\xi_i^1 + \xi_i^2\} + C\varepsilon\nu + \frac{\|w\|^2}{2} \rightarrow \min_{\xi^1, \xi^2, w, \varepsilon}$$

$$\hat{f}(x_i) - y_i \geq -\varepsilon - \xi_i^1, \; \xi_i^1 \geq 0 \forall i \in 1, \dots, N,$$

$$\hat{f}(x_i) - y_i \leq \varepsilon + \xi_i^2, \; \xi_i^2 \geq 0 \forall i \in 1, \dots, N,$$

$$\varepsilon \geq 0.$$

The dual problem, in this case, is written as

$$L(a^1, a^2) = -\frac{1}{2} \sum_{i=1}^{N} \sum_{j=1}^{N} (a_i^1 - a_i^2)(a_j^1 - a_j^2)\langle x_i, x_j \rangle \rightarrow \max_{a^1, a^2},$$

$$0 \leq a_i^1 \leq \frac{C}{N}, \; 0 \leq a_i^2 \leq \frac{C}{N},$$

$$\sum_{i=1}^{N} (a_i^1 - a_i^2) = \sum_{i=1}^{N} (a_i^1 + a_i^2) \leq \nu C.$$

ε-SVR regression for the function $y = x^2$ is shown in Figures 8.17, 8.18, and 8.19. We compare the models for different counts of learning points. The support vectors are marked by black boxes around learning points. The Gaussian radial basis kernel is chosen for this example. The predictive performance improves as the number of points increases. Here, we can see that sparsity of the solution is exposed again. In Figure 8.19, we have 30 learning points, only 18 of which are support vectors.

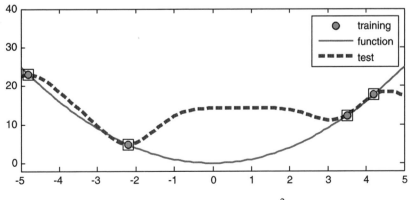

Figure 8.17: ε-SVR regression of the function $y = x^2$; four learning points.

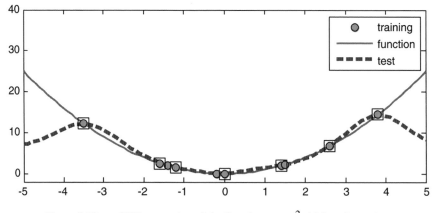

Figure 8.18: ε-SVR regression of the function $y = x^2$; 10 learning points.

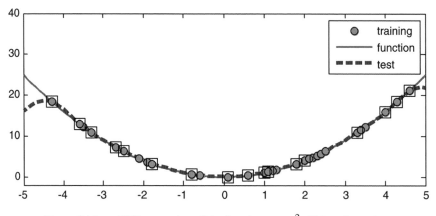

Figure 8.19: ε-SVR regression of the function $y = x^2$; 30 learning points.

8.4.5. *Multiclass SVM*

A multiclass SVM classifier is assumed to assign labels to the input objects, where the set of labels is finite and can consist of two (or, generally, more) elements. Formally, the classifier is trained over a sample set

$$X_N = \{(x_1, y_1), \ldots, (x_N, y_N)\}, \ x_i \in \mathbb{R}^n, \ y_i \in \{L_1, \ldots, L_R\}, \ R \geq 2.$$

The SVM classification model was initially adapted for two-class problems, and there is no common approach for solving multiclass classification problems.

We present three main approaches for multiclass SVM adaptation.

- One-versus-all approach. For each of the R classes, a two-class SVM classifier is trained to separate the given class from the other classes. If we denote the model separating r-th class as

$$y_r(x) = \text{sign}(f_r(x)) = \text{sign}\left(\sum_{i=1}^{N} y_i^r \alpha_i^r K(x, x_i) + \rho_r\right),$$

$$y_i^r = \begin{cases} 1, & \text{if } y_i = L_r, \\ -1, & \text{otherwise}, \end{cases}$$

the classification of the input vector x is performed using a winner-takes-all strategy:

$$y(x) = L_{r^*}, \quad r^* = \arg\max_{r=1,\dots,R} [f_r(x)].$$

The proposed method requires training R classifiers. However, this architecture suffers from the so-called "imbalanced learning problem." This arises when the training set for one of the classes has significantly fewer samples than all the rest in sum.

- One-versus-one strategy. For each unordered pair of classes $(L_r, L_{r'})$, a two-class SVM classifier is trained, which separates objects in class L_r from objects in class $L_{r'}$, disregarding the other classes. Let us denote such pairwise classifiers as follows:

$$y_{rr'}(x), \quad y_{rr'} : \mathbb{R}^n \to \{L_r, L_{r'}\}.$$

To classify a new incoming object x, the following procedure is performed. First, we need to calculate how many times each class occurs as a winner in pair classification:

$$n_r(x) = |\{L_{r'} \mid y_{rr'}(x) = L_r\}|.$$

Then, a class with maximal "pairwise wins" is selected:

$$y(x) = L_{r^*}, \quad r^* = \text{argmax}_{r=1,\dots,R} [n_r(x)].$$

This approach requires $\frac{R(R-1)}{2}$ classifiers to be trained, which is computationally complex for large values of R. This architecture can be exceptionally useful to tackle the imbalanced learning problem, where the samples count from all the classes but one has a clear majority over this class. To address this, a weighted voting procedure can be applied with some pre-defined preference matrix with confidence weights for different pairs of classifiers [47]. A comparison of different strategies is given in [48].

- Directed acyclic graph (DAG) classification [49]. This approach is similar to the one-versus-one strategy because a classifier should be fitted for each pair of classes. However, the final decision of the input label is produced not by

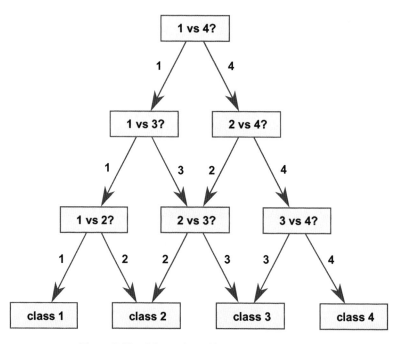

Figure 8.20: Directed acyclic graph classification.

applying all $\frac{R(R-1)}{2}$ classifiers, but just $R-1$. For classification, a decision tree is produced so that each class corresponds to a single leaf. Each node of the graph is linked to some of the $\frac{R(R-1)}{2}$ classifiers, where each outgoing edge is linked to the corresponding classifier's result. One of the nodes is selected as a root, and starting from the root, the classification process descends to one of the leaves. An example of DAG for four classes is given in Figure 8.20.

The main advantage of DAG is its learning simplicity compared to the one-versus-one strategy. However, the classification results are usually not stable because only a subpart of the classifiers is engaged in decision-making.

8.4.6. *One-Class SVM*

A special case of classification problems is one-class classification. This classification problem aims to distinguish between "normal" data and outliers. Such problems emerge when a training set consists only of one-class examples and under the assumption of other classes existing. One class may be well structured and described, while the other may be unstructured and unclear. This problem can be viewed as a type of probability distribution estimation or as a form of anomaly detection.

Schölkopf *et al.* [50] showed that an SVM-based approach is applicable to this class of problems. The idea of a one-class SVM is to map the data onto the feature space corresponding to an appropriate kernel and to separate them from the origin with maximum margin. The quadratic program implementing this approach is given as follows:

$$\frac{1}{2}\|w\|^2 + \frac{1}{\nu N}\sum_{i=1}^{N}\xi_i - \rho \to \min_{w,\xi,\rho},$$

w.r.t.

$$\langle w, \Phi(x_i)\rangle \geq \rho - \xi_i,$$

$$\xi_i \geq 0, \ i = 1, \ldots, N.$$

The decision function

$$f(x) = \text{sign}(\langle w, \Phi(x)\rangle - \rho)$$

describes the desired class (i.e., probability distribution or membership function, normal state opposite to anomalies), which is positive for most examples in the training set.

To transfer to the dual form of the problem, we express the weights via KKT conditions:

$$w = \sum_{i=1}^{N}\alpha_i \Phi(x_i),$$

$$0 \leq \alpha_i \leq \frac{1}{\nu N}, \quad \sum_{i=1}^{N}\alpha_i = 1.$$

In turn, the decision function can be rewritten as

$$f(x) = \text{sign}\left(\sum_{i=1}^{N}\alpha_i K(x, x_i) - \rho\right).$$

Those objects with $\alpha_i > 0$ are support vectors. It can be proven that for any x_i with $0 < \alpha_i < \frac{1}{\nu N}$, it holds that $\langle w, \Phi(x_i)\rangle = \rho$ at the optimum and

$$\rho = \langle w, \Phi(x_i)\rangle = \sum_{j=1}^{N}\alpha_j K(x_i, x_j).$$

Finally, the dual problem is given as

$$\frac{1}{2} \sum_{i,j=1}^{N} \alpha_i \alpha_j K\left(x_i, x_j\right) \rightarrow \min_{\alpha}.$$

w.r.t.

$$0 \leq \alpha_i \leq \frac{1}{\nu N}, \quad \sum_{i=1}^{N} \alpha_i = 1.$$

The parameter ν is of special interest as it possesses the following theoretically proven ν-property. If the solution to a one-class SVM problem satisfies $\rho \neq 0$, then

(1) ν is an upper bound on the fraction of outliers in the learning set (vectors x_i for which $\alpha_i = \frac{1}{\nu N}$);
(2) ν is a lower bound on the fraction of SVs in the learning set (vectors x_i for which $\alpha_i > 0$);
(3) If, additionally, data are generated independently from the distribution, which does not contain discrete components, and the kernel is analytic and non-constant, then with probability 1, asymptotically ν equals both the fraction of SVs and the fraction of outliers.

Figure 8.21 shows the contour lines provided by a one-class SVM learned on a set of two-dimensional points from a Gaussian mixture

$$p(x) = 0.5\, p(x \mid \mu_1, \Sigma_1) + 0.5\, p(x \mid \mu_2, \Sigma_2),$$

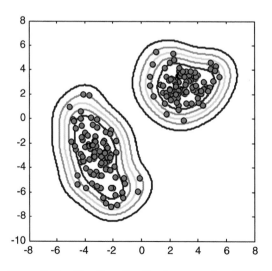

Figure 8.21: Density estimation by a one-class SVM.

where $\mu_1 = (3, 3)^T$, Σ_1 is an identity matrix, $\mu_2 = (-3, -3)^T$, and

$$\Sigma_2 = \begin{pmatrix} 1 & -0.5 \\ -0.5 & 2 \end{pmatrix}.$$

8.4.7. *Incremental SVM Learning*

Most SVM-type models admit incremental learning [51]. This means that the model can be fitted sample-per-sample or in batch mode, but the model requires the storage of all the previous learning sets. However, such algorithms could be useful in cases where the learning data are not provided at one moment but are split into batches that arrive sequentially (e.g., in streaming data analysis).

In this part, we state the algorithm for incremental SVM learning (i.e., adding one more sample to the learning set for the SVM classifier). Suppose that we have a two-class C-SVM classifier defined by its parameters (w, ρ), and estimated for the kernel $K(x, t)$ over the learning sample X_N.

Assume that we need to add the new sample (x_{N+1}, y_{N+1}) to the dataset. Therefore, we need to assign a corresponding value α_{N+1} and to update all previous values α_i, $i = 1, \ldots, N$ and ρ. These parameters should be changed so that KKT conditions are met, which is a necessary and sufficient condition for optimality.

Before discussing the algorithm itself, we should refer once again to the KKT conditions for the two-class SVM, defining three groups of samples from X_N and the constraints to be met.

(1) Margin group (M-group, $M \subset X_N$) — Subset of vectors x_m at the border of the dividing band; the corresponding KKT condition for x_m is

$$M(x_m) = \sum_{i=1}^{N} \alpha_i y_m y_i K(x_i, x_m) + \rho y_m = 1 \iff \alpha_m \in (0, C).$$

(2) Correct group (C-group, $C \subset X_N$) — Subset of vectors x_c correctly classified by the model,

$$M(x_c) = \sum_{i=1}^{N} \alpha_i y_c y_i K(x_i, x_c) + \rho y_c > 1 \iff \alpha_c = 0.$$

(3) Error-group (E-group, $E \subset X_N$) — Subset of vectors lying within the dividing band or even misclassified,

$$x_e : M(x_e) = \sum_{i=1}^{N} \alpha_i y_e y_i K(x_i, x_e) + \rho y_e < 1 \iff \alpha_e = C.$$

A further KKT condition that should be considered is

$$\sum_{i=1}^{N} \alpha_i y_i = 0.$$

Here, we should mention that KKT conditions are necessary and sufficient for a point to be a solution to the dual optimization problem.

Initially, we assign $\alpha_{N+1} = 0$, leaving the rest of the values $\alpha \in \mathbb{R}^N$ and $\rho \in \mathbb{R}$ unchanged. If margin $M(x_{N+1}) > 1$ (see C-group), then all KKT conditions are met and, therefore, learning is finished.

If margin $M(x_{N+1}) \leq 1$, then KKT conditions are violated. In this case, we increase α_{N+1} so that the following hold:

(i) Margins of all points from M-group stay equal to 1,

$$\forall x_m \in M \ M(x_m) = 1;$$

(ii) $\sum_{i=1}^{N} \alpha_i y_i + \alpha_{N+1} y_{N+1} = 0$;

(iii) Margins of all points from C-group stay above 1,

$$\forall x_c \in C \ M(x_c) > 1;$$

(iv) Margins of all points from E-group stay below 1,

$$\forall x_e \in E \ M(x_e) < 1.$$

Therefore, during the change of all the parameters (α, ρ), only α_{N+1} violates the KKT conditions.

We denote the i-th vector from the C-, E-, and M-groups x_i^c, x_i^e, x_i^m with labels y_i^c, y_i^e, y_i^m, respectively.

Consider the first two limitations. Assume that at the previous iteration, we have the model α_{old}, ρ_{old}. Suppose that $\alpha_{old}^m \in \mathbb{R}^{|M|}$ is a sub-vector of α_{old} related to the vectors from M-group. Once again, as the new learning data x_{N+1} arrive, we have to update all previous parameters of the classifier and calculate α_{N+1} iteratively. First, we assign $\alpha_{N+1} = 0$, which can violate KKT conditions (as mentioned before). Therefore, we must change the α values. First, we fix the values of α for C-group to 0 and for E-group to C. Hence, we change only α^m values. If we increase α_{N+1} by $\Delta \alpha_{N+1} > 0$, we can calculate the corresponding $\Delta \alpha^m$, $\Delta \rho$ while holding i and ii.

$$F^m \begin{bmatrix} \alpha_{old}^m + \Delta \alpha^m \\ \rho + \Delta \rho \end{bmatrix} + k_{N+1}^m (\alpha_{N+1} + \Delta \alpha_{N+1}) = 1,$$

where

$$F^m = \begin{bmatrix} (y^m)^T & 0 \\ Q^{mm} & y^m \end{bmatrix} \in \mathbb{R}^{|M|+1 \times |M|+1},$$

$$y^m = \left[y_1^m, \ldots, y_i^m, \ldots, y_{|M|}^m \right]^T,$$

$$k_{N+1}^m \in \mathbb{R}^{|M|+1}, \ k_{N+1}^m = \begin{bmatrix} y_{N+1} \\ y_{N+1} y_1^m \langle x_1^m \ x_{N+1} \rangle \\ \cdots \\ y_{N+1} y_i^m \langle x_i^m, \ x_{N+1} \rangle \\ \cdots \\ y_{N+1} y_{|M|}^m \langle x_{|M|}^m, \ x_{N+1} \rangle \end{bmatrix},$$

$$Q_{ij}^{mm} = y_i^m y_j^m \langle x_i, \ x_j^m \rangle, \quad i, j = 1, \ldots, |M|$$

Q^{mm} is a matrix of inner products of the objects in the M-group. Therefore, considering that conditions i and ii are met for α_{old}, ρ_{old} and α_{N+1}, it is possible to derive the following:

$$\begin{bmatrix} \Delta \alpha^m \\ \Delta \rho \end{bmatrix} = -(F^m)^{-1} k_{N+1}^m \Delta \alpha_{N+1}.$$

However, considering conditions i–iv, we can claim that $\Delta \alpha_{N+1}$ is bounded, and we increase it until one of the following conditions is met:

(1) For one of the data vectors in the C-group, the value of $M(x_i^c)$ reaches 1. Then this data vector is moved to the M-group with the corresponding α_i^c set to 0, α_{N+1} is increased by the corresponding $\Delta \alpha_{N+1}$, and the procedure continues with the new structure of the data subsets.

(2) For one of the data vectors in the E-group, the value of $M(x_i^e)$ reaches 1. Then this data vector is moved to the M-group with the corresponding α_i^e set to 0, α_{N+1} is increased by the corresponding $\Delta \alpha_{N+1}$, and the procedure continues with the new structure of the data subsets.

(3) For one of the data vectors in the M-group, the value of α_i^m reaches $\alpha_i^m = C$. Then this data vector is moved to the E-group with the corresponding α_i^m set to C, α_{N+1} is increased by the corresponding $\Delta \alpha_{N+1}$, and the procedure continues with the new structure of the data subsets.

(4) For one of the data vectors in the M-group, the value of α_i^m is set to 0. Then this data vector is moved to the C-group with the corresponding α_i^m set to 0, α_{N+1} is increased by the corresponding $\Delta \alpha_{N+1}$, and the procedure continues with the new structure of the data subsets.

(5) $\alpha_{N+1} = C$. Then the new data vector is moved to the E-group, and the algorithm terminates.

(6) $M(x_{N+1}) = 1$. Then the new data vector is moved to the M-group with the current value of α_{N+1} and the algorithm terminates.

If conditions 1–4 are met, then the structure of the E, C, and M groups should be re-arranged. This means that the vector α^m should be increased by $\Delta\alpha^m$ and augmented/reduced by the corresponding α of the migrating vector. Matrix F^m should be recalculated. α_{N+1} is increased by $\Delta\alpha_{N+1}$. Then, a new iteration of the described procedure is performed taking into account the new structures of the sets C, E, and M. Iterations are repeated until KKT conditions are met, which is equivalent to conditions 5 and 6.

For each condition from 1 to 4, an effective computational technique exists that allows the inverse inner product matrix $(F^m)^{-1}$ for the M-group to be calculated iteratively using the Woodbury formula. However, it is usually the case that the M-group is relatively small.

8.4.8. *Deep Learning with SVM*

Due to the structure of the SVM and the explicit minimization of classifier complexity, the SVM has an attractive property of high generalization capability compared to many other machine learning methods. At the same time, it largely depends on the input features, which can be noisy, very complex (e.g., having spatial correlations), or dangerously large (due to the curse of dimensionality). Although the kernel trick can be regarded as a feature extraction method, it is a natural intention to couple the generalization power of the SVM with some powerful feature selection or extraction techniques.

Artificial neural networks (ANNs) are one of the most popular machine learning methods that can be successfully applied to a large number of classification and regression tasks. The very structure of ANNs allows dividing them into two logical parts: feature extractor and decision rule. For example, in a neural network such as AlexNet [62], convolutional layers extract features out of pixel intensities (i.e., serve as a feature extractor), while the top fully connected layers do the decision making (i.e., act as a decision rule). This interpretation of the ANN architecture makes it easy to come to the idea of replacing the top decision-making layers with another classifier. Indeed, many researchers substitute the head of a trained network with an SVM classifier and train it while keeping the network features fixed [64, 65]. Alternatively, unsupervised ANN models such as autoencoders can be used to generate features for the SVM classifier.

The approach is attractive and helps decrease error and increase accuracy for many classification problems. One may notice, however, that in this case, feature extraction is separated from classifier optimization, which is the opposite of the original ANN architecture wherein the features are learned to minimize the error function explicitly.

In [63], the authors demonstrated the feasibility of adding an SVM head to an ANN feature extractor in such a way as to train the features with regard to the SVM target directly. Let us denote the outputs of the last feature extraction layer as x_n, $n = 1, \ldots, N$, where n is an input image index. Then, the SVM optimization takes the form

$$\min_{w} w^T w + C \sum_{n=1}^{N} \max(1 - w^T x_n y_n, 0)$$

for the hinge loss or

$$\min_{w} w^T w + C \sum_{n=1}^{N} \max(1 - w^T x_n y_n, 0)^2$$

for the squared hinge loss. The latter variant is differentiable and penalizes errors more strongly.

Now, to facilitate the standard backpropagation algorithm, we need to ensure that the SVM loss function is differentiable with respect to the features of the last layer. Fortunately, this can be done easily. If we denote the loss function as $L(w)$, then

$$\frac{\partial L(w)}{\partial x_n} = -C y_n w \times \mathrm{I}\left[w^T x_n y_n < 1\right]$$

in the case of hinge loss and

$$\frac{\partial L(w)}{\partial x_n} = -2C y_n w \times \max(1 - w^T x_n y_n, 0)$$

in the case of squared hinge loss.

At this point, feature extraction is incorporated directly into the SVM objective, and the features are learned to minimize SVM loss. This leads to better performance on tasks such as facial expression recognition, MNIST, and CIFAR-10.

Some recent works have also shown connections between kernel learning and ANNs. This includes studies such as [61], which show the equivalence of ANNs of infinite width to Gaussian processes. Following these results, it is clear that kernel methods have provided important insights into the generalization capacities of ANNs, particularly by studying their training in functional spaces rather than finite-dimensional vector spaces.

8.4.9. *Metric Learning*

At a first glance, the problem of metric learning seems to be unrelated to the issue of SVM applications. However, the SVM approach can be fruitful for learning a metric.

The problem of metric learning involves finding a metric that pulls objects of the same class closer and pushes objects from different classes as far away as possible from one another. It is common to find this metric in a family of Mahalanobis metrics parameterized by a positive semidefinite matrix $M \in R^{n \times n}$,

$$\rho_M(x, t) = (x - t)^T M (x - t), \ M = M^T, \ M \geq 0.$$

Although the Mahalanobis metric has a probabilistic origin (i.e., in that it is used to measure the distance between two random vectors), it can be seen as a Euclidean distance in a linearly transformed space. In other words, for any Mahalanobis metric ρ_M, there exists a linear map specified by matrix $L \in R^{k \times n}$ so that

$$\rho_M(x, t) = (x - t)^T M (x - t) = (x - t)^T L^T L(x - t) = \|L(x - t)\|^2 .$$

Starting from this point, most metric learning methods seek to find the best (under some conditions) linear map L.

It may be desired that in the new space for each object, its distance to all neighbors of the same class is smaller than its distance to any neighbors of different classes. This leads to the following constraints on the Mahalanobis metric ρ_M:

$$\min_{\substack{x_j \in \mathcal{N}(x_i) \\ y_j \neq y_i}} \rho_M(x_i, x_j) \geq \min_{\substack{x_j \in \mathcal{N}(x_i) \\ y_j = y_i}} \rho_M(x_i, x_j) + 1, \ \forall (x_i, y_i) \in X,$$

where $\mathcal{N}(x_i)$ is the neighborhood of x_i determined by Euclidean distance.

Finding the Mahalanobis metric with the smallest possible Frobenius norm results in an MLSVM model [52].

$$\frac{\lambda}{2} \|M\|_F^2 + \frac{1}{N} \sum_{i=1}^N \xi_i \to \min_{M \geq 0, \xi \geq 0}$$

w.r.t.

$$\min_{\substack{x_j \in \mathcal{N}(x_i) \\ y_j \neq y_i}} \rho_M(x_i, x_j) \geq \max_{\substack{x_j \in \mathcal{N}(x_i) \\ y_j = y_i}} \rho_M(x_i, x_j) + 1 - \xi_i.$$

$$\xi_i \geq 0.$$

Note that ρ_M depends linearly on the matrix M. This leads to the quadratic programming problem linking MLSVM to the SVM approach. Slack variables ξ_i are introduced, as in an SVM, to obtain the soft margin constraints. This optimization problem can be solved using a modified Pegasos method [52] without transforming it into a dual form.

Other approaches for metric learning involve finding a linear transformation L such that the transformed target space neighborhood $\mathcal{N}(x_i)$ consists of objects of the same class as x_i only. Objects x_j in this neighborhood are called target neighbors and denoted as

$$j \rightsquigarrow i$$

Notice that this motivation leads to better performance of the kNN algorithm in the transformed space. In the original space, some objects of different classes may be closer (in terms of Euclidean distance) to x_i than target neighbors. These objects are impostors x_k and are defined as follows:

$$\|L(x_i - x_k)\|^2 \leq \|L(x_i - x_j)\|^2 + 1, \ j \rightsquigarrow i, \ y_i \neq y_k.$$

The loss function in this LMNN model [53] differs from the one in the MLSVM. It is represented as a sum of two terms, one pulling target neighbors closer together and the other pushing impostors apart. Denoting this loss function as

$$y_{ij} = \begin{cases} 1, \ y_i = y_j, \\ 0, \ y_i \neq y_j, \end{cases}$$

we obtain the following optimization problem:

$$(1 - \mu) \sum_{j \rightsquigarrow i} \|L(x_i - x_j)\|^2 +$$

$$+ \mu \sum_{i, j \rightsquigarrow i} \sum_k (1 - y_{ik}) \left[1 + \|L(x_i - x_j)\|^2 - \|L(x_i - x_k)\|^2 \right]_+$$

$$\rightarrow \min_L .$$

This optimization problem can be converted into an SVM-like form as follows:

$$(1 - \mu) \sum_{j \rightsquigarrow i} \|L(x_i - x_j)\|^2 + \mu \sum_{i, j \rightsquigarrow i} \sum_k (1 - y_{ik}) \xi_{ijk} \rightarrow \min_{L, \xi}$$

w.r.t.

$$\|L(x_i - x_k)\|^2 - \|L(x_i - x_j)\|^2 \geq 1 - \xi_{ijk}, \ \forall i, \ j \rightsquigarrow i, \ k : y_i \neq y_k$$

$$\xi_{nkl} \geq 0, \ M = L^T L \geq 0.$$

Notice that all functions in both models depend on the input objects only through inner products. This allows the kernel trick and nonlinearity to be incorporated into metric learning.

8.4.10. *Structured SVM*

Here, we expand the classification problem, relaxing the restrictions for the labels set in the way described in [43]. As usual, we consider a sample set $X \subseteq \mathbb{R}^n$ and associate each of its elements with some labels from a finite set Y. In the algorithms we referred to before, it is assumed that label $y \in Y \subseteq \mathbb{R}$, but here, we abandon this constraint and allow labels to be any arbitrary objects (e.g., strings or graphs), which are often referred to as "structured." As before, we define a map $f : X \to Y$ and a training set

$$X_N = \{(x_1, y_1), \ldots, (x_N, y_N)\},$$

and we are trying to learn a map $\hat{f} : X \to Y$ to give an approximation of f.

To tackle a problem with such complex structured labels, we also define a discriminant function

$$F(x, y \mid w) : X \times Y \to \mathbb{R},$$

where w is a vector of parameters. This function yields the maximum for the most "suitable" pairs of x and y, and so it should represent the map $\hat{f}$ in the form

$$\hat{f}(x \mid w) = \underset{y \in Y}{\operatorname{argmax}} \, F(x, y \mid w).$$

To use common optimization schemes, we restrict the function $F(x, y \mid w)$ to depend linearly on the parameters

$$F(x, y \mid w) = \langle w, \Psi(x, y) \rangle.$$

Here, Ψ is a function, dependent on the data samples, referred to as the "joint feature map," $\Psi : X \times Y \to \mathbb{R}^K$, $w \in \mathbb{R}^K$. If, for example, $Y = \{1, \ldots, R\} \subset N$ and

$$\Psi(x, y) = \{[y = 1] x, \, [y = 2] x, \ldots, [y = R] x\} \in \mathbb{R}^{R \times n},$$

then the method performs as a multiclass SVM.

The maximization problem can be reformulated [54] as a maximum margin problem:

$$\frac{1}{2} \|w\|^2 \to \underset{w}{\min}$$

with respect to constraints defining that the maximum is reached only on the given labeling $\hat{f}$. These constraints can be written for all x_i, $y_i = f(x_i)$ as follows:

Importantly, these constraints ensure that we have an exact labeling. Although they are nonlinear, they can be replaced with $N(|Y| - 1)$ linear constraints as follows:

$$\forall (x_i, y_i) \in X_N, \qquad \forall y \in \backslash y_i$$

$$\langle w, \Delta(x_i, y) \rangle > 0,$$

where $\Delta(x_i, y) = (\Psi(x_i, y_i) - \Psi(x_i, y))$.

As in an ordinary SVM, w can be rescaled so that it satisfies the following conditions:

$$\forall x_i, y_i, \ y \in Y \backslash y_i, \ \langle w, \Delta(x_i, y) \rangle \geq 1.$$

To allow classifier errors on the dataset, slack variables ξ_i are introduced:

$$\frac{1}{2} \|w\|^2 + \frac{C}{N} \sum_{i=1}^{N} \xi_i \to \min_{w, \xi}$$

w.r.t.

$$\forall x_i, y_i, \ y \in Y \backslash y_i, \ \ \langle w, \Delta(x, y) \rangle \geq 1 - \xi_i,$$

$$\xi_i \geq 0, \quad 1 \leq i \leq N.$$

The dual version of the problem can be derived by introducing Lagrangian multipliers:

$$L(w, \xi, \alpha, \beta) = \frac{1}{2} \|w\|^2 + \frac{C}{N} \sum_{i=1}^{N} \xi_i$$

$$- \sum_{i=1}^{N} \beta_i \xi_i - \sum_{i=1}^{N} \sum_{y \in Y \backslash y_i} \alpha_{iy} \{\langle w, \Delta(x, y) \rangle \geq 1 - \xi_i\},$$

$$\frac{\partial L}{\partial w} = w - \sum_{i=1}^{N} \sum_{y \in Y \backslash y_i} \alpha_{iy} \Delta(x_i, y) = 0,$$

$$\frac{\partial L}{\partial \xi_i} = \frac{C}{N} - \beta_i - \sum_{y \in Y \backslash y_i} \alpha_{iy} = 0.$$

The kernel trick can be applied as usual, and the dual program should be written as follows:

$$\sum_{i=1, y\in Y\backslash y_i}^{N} \alpha_{iy} - \frac{1}{2} \sum_{i=1,\; y\in Y\backslash y_i}^{N} \sum_{j=1,\; y'\in Y\backslash y_j}^{N} \alpha_{iy}\alpha_{jy'}\, K(\Delta(x_i, y), \Delta(x_j, y')) \to \max_{\alpha},$$

$$\alpha_{iy} \geq 0, \quad \sum_{i, y\in Y\backslash y_i} \alpha_{iy} \leq \frac{C}{N} \; \forall i = 1 \ldots N$$

Several alternative formulations of the problem exist, which differ in terms of the way slack variables are defined, but they are not ideologically different. These alternatives can be found in [43].

The critical problem with the described method arises from the large number of constraints, which leads to the exponential complexity of the optimization algorithm based on the "dimensionality" of the space Y. To avoid this problem, the cutting plane relaxation technique is used, which provides polynomial complexity but considers only some of the constraints, giving the most severe restrictions. This means for the constraints to be violated by a value that does not exceed some pre-specified value ε, the optimization is provided within a loop, while the constraint list is complemented until all the constraints are violated not more than on ε.

It is possible to use the structured SVM approach to solve various tasks once a correct feature-specific joint feature map Ψ is chosen, taking contributions from both input and output. Given some problem-specific function Ψ, the structured SVM can be used for image segmentation [55] and object detection problems [56], protein alignment structure identification [57], and other applications.

For the case of natural grammar analysis, we have a grammar that incorporates grammar rules G_i. String parsing can be viewed as a process of grammar rule application. The hierarchy of rule applications is organized into a tree. The function Ψ then represents the histogram of grammar rules application event frequency [58]. Then, the structure $y \in Y$, which is found by optimization of the function $F(x, y\,|\,w)$, represents a parse tree prediction.

Let us consider in more detail the problem of image segmentation as a structured SVM application. For each of the pixels in an image I, we should assign an integer value $Y = \{1 \ldots K\}$, which is referred to as a segment label. Let us define a graph (V, E) with a set of vertices V, each corresponding to one pixel of the image I, and a set of edges E, giving a neighborhood relation. The assignment of the segment labels can be done within the conditional random field (CRF) framework [58]. The energy, or cost, functional is considered, which assigns the fine on each element label and on joint assignment of the labels to the neighbors.

Alternatively, it can be interpreted as a graph labeling problem for the graph (V, E), expressed as follows:

$$E_w(Y) = \sum_{v_i \in V} U_i(v_i, y_i) + \sum_{(v_i, v_j) \in E} D_{ij}(v_i, v_j, y_i, y_j) \rightarrow \min_y.$$

Optimization problems of this kind are usually solved using algorithms such as graph-cuts or α-expansion [59, 60].

Here U is referred to as unary potential and D denotes pairwise potential. However, there remains the problem of defining these potentials. Then, imagine that we have a learning set of the images of the same size with the corresponding "ground truth" segmentations, namely:

$$\{(I_1, Y_1), (I_2, Y_2), (I_3, Y_3), \ldots (I_N, Y_N)\}, \; I_i \in \mathbb{R}^{n \times m}, \; Y_i \in \{1 \ldots K\}^{n \times m}.$$

A structured SVM enables us to define this as an optimization problem, which is aimed at finding a functional that enables the images to be segmented as closely as possible to the "ground truth."

For each of the pixels p_{ik} in the image I_k, we associate some feature vector $x_{ik} \in \mathbb{R}^l$, where l is the dimensionality of the feature vector. Here, x_{ik} can be either a SIFT descriptor or simply a color value (e.g., RGB), or any other feature.

First, let us define the unary potential for the image I_k as follows:

$$U_i^k(v_i, y_i) = \langle w_{y_i}, x_{ik} \rangle, \quad w_{y_i} \in \mathbb{R}^l.$$

It is worth mentioning here that the graph is the same for all images since they have the same size Let us also define the following:

$$\psi_i^k(y_i) = (I(y_i = 1)x_{ik}^T, \ldots, I(y_i = K)x_{ik}^T)^T.$$

It follows that if we denote $w^U = (w_1, w_2, \ldots w_K)^T$, then

$$U_i^k(v_i, y_i) = \langle w^U, \psi_i^k, (y_i) \rangle = \langle w_{y_i}, x_{ik} \rangle.$$

Second, define the pairwise potential as $D_{ij}^k(v_i, v_j, y_i, y_j) = w_{y_i, y_j} \in \mathbb{R}$.

Let us also define

$$\psi_{ij}(y_i, y_j) = (I(y_i = 1, y_j = 1), \ldots, I(y_i = p, y_j = r), \ldots,$$
$$I(y_i = K, y_j = K)).$$

In addition, suppose

$$w^V = (w_{ij})_{(i,j) \in \{1 \ldots K\}^2}.$$

Then

$$D_{ij}^k(v_i, v_j, y_i, y_j) = \langle w^V, \psi_{ij}(y_i, y_j) \rangle = w_{y_i, y_j}.$$

We can represent an optimized energy function for the image I_k in the following way:

$$E_w^k(Y) = \sum_{v_i \in V} U_i^k(v_i, y_i) + \sum_{(v_i, v_j) \in E} D_{ij}(v_i, v_j, y_i, y_j)$$

$$= \sum_{v_i \in V} \langle w^U, \psi_i^k(y_i) \rangle + \sum_{(v_i, v_j) \in E} \langle w^V, \psi_{ij}(y_i y_j) \rangle.$$

Therefore, $E_w^k(Y)$ is a linear function of $w \equiv (w^U w^V)$. If we define

$$\Psi(I_k, Y) = (\Psi^D(I_k, Y), \Psi^V(Y)) = \left(\sum_{v_i \in V} \psi_i^k(y_i), \sum_{(v_i, v_j) \in E} \psi_{ij}(y_i, y_j) \right),$$

then

$$E_w^k(Y) = \langle w, \psi(I_k, Y) \rangle.$$

We can state a structured SVM problem for the weights w, with $-\Psi(I_k, Y)$ as a joint feature map. One should pay attention to ensure that for each constraint, the evaluation of the maximum operator is equivalent to the optimization problem for the energy function $E_w^k(Y)$, which can be difficult.

8.5. Conclusion

Kernel methods serve as powerful and theoretically proven tools for a broad range of machine learning problems.

The problems we address in this chapter are those of classification, clustering, and regression. While the first two problems are aimed at finding a discriminant function to divide a dataset into groups, the latter seeks to estimate a function that governs the relationships between variables. The key question is how accurately these functions can be approximated using information contained in the training set.

Here, we rely on the assumption that such functions can be taken from a reproducing kernel Hilbert space with a corresponding kernel and evaluated on the given training set. Some of the kernels, known as universal kernels, can accurately approximate any function. Mercer's theorem shows kernels as inner products in RKHS. All of these developments pave the way for the technique of the "kernel trick," which enables a linear model's inner products to be substituted with kernel function values. The representer theorem presents a parametrically linear model of generally nonlinear functions, which is an optimal solution for a wide range of machine learning problems.

Nowadays, the use of kernel techniques in machine learning is pervasive. In fact, any linear model built on inner products can be kernelized, as in kernel filtering and kernel linear discriminant analysis, neither of which is "linear" at all. We have highlighted the use of kernels in the Nadaraya–Watson regression and density estimation problems. To reveal nonlinear dependencies in data, kernels can also be introduced into principal component analysis. Kernelizing of k-means leads to spectral clustering, which links kernel methods with graph theory.

Kernels provide an extension for the widely used and deservedly praised support vector machine (SVM) approach. For linear kernels, the SVM searches for the best discriminant hyperplane that divides two classes with the largest possible margin between them. Replacing the inner products in an SVM model with appropriate kernel values results in an implicit mapping of input vectors to RKHS, where they can be linearly separated (with a successful kernel choice). In the input space, this results in a nonlinear dividing surface.

The SVM itself has many interesting extensions. Its model allows control over the misclassification rate, which is implicit in C-SVM and explicit in ν-SVM, where the parameter ν gives an upper bound for the fraction of margin errors. An SVM can be extended to multiclass problems with one-versus-one or one-versus-all approaches. It can also be modified to solve regression tasks resulting in ε-SVR and ν-SVR or to estimate densities resulting in a one-class SVM. Following the tendency toward online learning methods, SVM models can be incrementally updated. The SVM's idea of maximizing the margin between classes is also applicable in adjacent areas, including metric learning. Finally, the idea of supervised learning can be expanded to composite, structured objects, including graphs, as well as regularly used real-valued labels, and this is supported by structured SVM models.

References

[1] C. M. Bishop (2006). *Pattern Recognition and Machine Learning* (Information Science and Statistics). Springer-Verlag New York, Inc., Secaucus, NJ, USA.

[2] T. Hastie, R. Tibshirani, and J. Friedman (2003). *The Elements of Statistical Learning: Data Mining, Inference, and Prediction*. Springer-Verlag New York.

[3] X. Wu, V. Kumar, J. R. Quinlan, J. Ghosh, Q. Yang, H. Motoda, G. McLachlan, A. Ng, B. Liu, P. Yu, Z.-H. Zhou, M. Steinbach, D. Hand, and D. Steinberg (2008). Top 10 algorithms in data mining. *Knowl. Inf. Syst.*, **14**, pp. 1–37.

[4] V. N. Vapnik (1995). *The Nature of Statistical Learning Theory*. Springer-Verlag New York, Inc., New York, NY, USA.

[5] V. Vapnik and A. Chervonenkis (1964). A note on one-class of perceptrons. *Autom. Remote Control*, **25**, pp. 112–120.

[6] S. Boyd and L. Vandenberghe. (2004). Convex Optimization. Cambridge University Press, New York, NY, USA.

[7] B. W. Silverman (1986). *Density Estimation for Statistics and Data Analysis*. Chapman & Hall, London.

[8] B. Schölkopf, C. J. C. Burges, and A. J. Smola (eds.) (1999). *Advances in Kernel Methods: Support Vector Learning*. MIT Press, Cambridge, MA, USA.

[9] M. Cuturi (2010). Positive definite kernels in machine learning. *arXiv:0911.5367v2* [stat.ML].

[10] N. Aronszajn (1950). Theory of reproducing kernels. *Trans. Am. Math. Soc.*, **68**(3), pp. 337–404.

[11] H. Q. Minh, P. Niyogi, and Y. Yao (2006). Mercer's theorem, feature maps, and smoothing. *COLT*, pp. 154–168.

[12] J. Mercer (1909). Functions of positive and negative type, and their connection with the theory of integral equations. *Philos. Trans. R. Soc. London*, **209**, pp. 415–446.

[13] C. A. Micchelli, Y. Xu, and H. Zhang (2006). Universal kernels. *J. Mach. Learn. Res.*, **6**, pp. 2651–2667.

[14] B. Schölkopf, R. Herbrich, and A. J. Smola (2001). A generalized representer theorem. *Computational Learning Theory.* Lecture Notes in Computer Science, pp. 416–426.

[15] M. Rosenblatt (1956). Remarks on some nonparametric estimates of a density function. *Ann. Math. Stat.*, **27**(3), pp. 832–837.

[16] E. Parzen (1962). On estimation of a probability density function and mode. *Ann. Math. Stat.*, **33**(3), pp. 1065–1076.

[17] B. U. Park and J. S. Marron (1990). Comparison of data-driven bandwidth selectors. *J. Am. Stat. Assoc.*, **85**(409), pp. 66–72.

[18] B. U. Park and B. A. Turlach (1992). Practical performance of several data driven bandwidth selectors (with discussion). *Comput. Stat.*, **7**, pp. 251–270.

[19] S. J. Sheather (1992). The performance of six popular bandwidth selection methods on some real datasets (with discussion). *Comput. Stat.*, **7**, pp. 225–281.

[20] S. J. Sheather and M. C. Jones (1991). A reliable data-based bandwidth-selection method for kernel density estimation. *J. R. Stat. Soc.*, **53B**, pp. 683–690.

[21] M. C. Jones, J. S. Marron and S. J. Sheather (1996). A brief survey of bandwidth selection for density estimation. *J. Am. Stat. Assoc.*, **91**(433), pp. 401–407.

[22] E. A. Nadaraya (1964). On estimating regression. *Theory Probab. Appl.*, **9**(1), pp. 141–142.

[23] G. S. Watson (1964). Smooth regression analysis. *Sankhya*, **26**(15), pp. 175–184.

[24] C. G. Atkeson, A. W. Moore, and S. Schaal (1997). Locally weighted learning. *Artif. Intell. Rev.*, **11**, pp. 11–73.

[25] H.-G. Müller (1987). Weighted local regression and kernel methods for nonparametric curve fitting. *J. Am. Stat. Assoc.*, **82**(397), pp. 231–238.

[26] M. C. Jones, S. J. Davies, and B. U. Park (1994). Versions of kernel-type regression estimators. *J. Am. Stat. Assoc.*, **89**(427), pp. 825–832.

[27] B. Schölkopf, A. J. Smola, and K.-R. Müller (1999). Kernel principal component analysis, in *Advances in Kernel Methods: Support Vector Learning*, B. Schölkopf, C. J. C. Burges, and A. J. Smola (eds.), MIT Press, Cambridge, MA, pp. 327–352.

[28] S. Mika, G. Ratsch, J. Weston, B. Scholkopf, and K. Muller (1999). Fisher discriminant analysis with kernels, in *Neural Networks for Signal Processing IX*, Y.-H. Hu, J. Larsen, E. Wilson, and S. Douglas (eds.), IEEE Press, Piscataway, NJ, pp. 41–48.

[29] P. Exterkate, P. J. F. Groenen, C. Heij, and D. van Dijk (2013). Nonlinear forecasting with many predictors using kernel ridge regression. CREATES Research Papers 2013-16, School of Economics and Management, University of Aarhus.

[30] M. H. Hayes (1996). *Statistical Digital Signal Processing and Modeling*, 1st ed. John Wiley & Sons, Inc., New York, NY, USA.

[31] L. Bottou (1998). Online algorithms and stochastic approximations, in *Online Learning and Neural Networks*, D. Saad (ed.), Cambridge University Press, Cambridge, UK.

[32] W. Liu, J. C. Príncipe, and S. Haykin (2010). Appendix B: approximate linear dependency and system stability, in *Kernel Adaptive Filtering: A Comprehensive Introduction*, J. C. Principe, W. Liu, and S. Haykin (eds.), John Wiley & Sons, Inc., Hoboken, NJ, USA.

[33] U. Luxburg (2007). A tutorial on spectral clustering. *Stat. Comput.*, **17**(4), pp. 395–416.

[34] I. S. Dhillon, Y. Guan, and B. Kulis (2004). Kernel k-means: spectral clustering and normalized cuts, in *Proceedings of the 10th ACM SIGKDD International Conference on Knowledge Discovery and Data Mining (KDD '04)*, pp. 551–556.

[35] A. Y. Ng, M. I. Jordan, and Y. Weiss (2001). On spectral clustering: analysis and an algorithm. *Adv. Neural Inf. Process. Syst.,* **14**, pp. 849–856.

[36] U. von Luxburg (2007). A tutorial on spectral clustering. *Stat. Comput.,* **17**(4), pp. 395–416.

[37] S. Balakrishnan, M. Xu, A. Krishnamurthy, and A. Singh (2011). Noise thresholds for spectral clustering. *NIPS,* pp. 954–962.

[38] B. Mohar (1991). The Laplacian spectrum of graphs, in *Graph Theory, Combinatorics, and Applications,* Y. Alavi, G. Chartrand, O. R. Oellermann, and A. J. Schwenk (eds.), vol. 2, Wiley, pp. 871–898.

[39] B. Mohar (1997). Some applications of Laplace eigenvalues of graphs, in *Graph Symmetry: Algebraic Methods and Applications,* G. Hahn and G. Sabidussi (eds.), NATO ASI Series, Springer Netherlands, pp. 225–275.

[40] F. Chung (1997). Spectral graph theory. *Washington: Conference Board of the Mathematical Sciences.*

[41] J. Shi and J. Malik (2000). Normalized cuts and image segmentation. *IEEE Trans. Pattern Anal. Mach. Intell.,* **22**(8), pp. 888–905.

[42] B. E. Boser, I. M. Guyon, and V. N. Vapnik (1992). A training algorithm for optimal margin classifiers, in *Proceedings of the 5th Annual Workshop on Computational Learning Theory (COLT'92),* pp. 144–152.

[43] M. Aizerman, E. Braverman, and L. Rozonoer (1964). Theoretical foundations of the potential function method in pattern recognition learning. *Autom. Remote Control,* **25**, pp. 821–837.

[44] C. Cortes and V. Vapnik (1995). Support-vector networks. *Mach. Learn.,* **20**, pp. 273–297.

[45] B. Schölkopf, A. Smola, R. C. Williamson, and P. L. Bartlett (2000). New support vector algorithms. *Neural Comput.,* **12**, pp. 1207–1245.

[46] H. Drucker, C. J. C. Burges, L. Kaufman, A. J. Smola, and V. N. Vapnik (1997). Support vector regression machines, in Proceedings of the 9th International Conference on Neural Information Processing Systems *(NIPS'96),* pp. 155–161.

[47] E. Hüllermeier and K. Brinker (2008). Learning valued preference structures for solving classification problems. *Fuzzy Sets Syst.,* pp. 2337–2352.

[48] E. Lughofer and O. Buchtala (2013). Reliable all-pairs evolving fuzzy classifiers. *IEEE Trans. Fuzzy Syst.,* **21**(4), pp. 625–641.

[49] J. C. Platt, N. Cristianini, and J. Shawe-Taylor (2000). Large margin DAGs for multiclass classification, in *Proceedings of Neural Information Processing Systems, NIPS'99,* pp. 547–553.

[50] B. Scholkopf, J. Platt, J. Shawe-Taylor, A. Smola, and R. Williamson (2001). Estimating the support of a high-dimensional distribution. *Neural Comput.,* **13**(7), pp. 1443–1472.

[51] G. Cauwenberghs and T. Poggio (2001). Incremental and decremental support vector machine learning, in Proceedings of the 13th International Conference on Neural Information Processing Systems *(NIPS'00),* pp. 388–394.

[52] N. Nguyen and Y. Guo (2008). Metric learning: a support vector approach, in *Proceedings of the European conference on Machine Learning and Knowledge Discovery in Databases,* Springer-Verlag Berlin Heidelberg, pp. 125–136.

[53] K. Q. Weinberger and L. K. Saul (2009). Distance metric learning for large margin nearest neighbor classification. *J. Mach. Learn. Res.,* **10**, pp. 207–244.

[54] I. Tsochantaridis, T. Joachims, T. Hofmann, and Y. Altun (2005). Large margin methods for structured and interdependent output variables. *J. Mach. Learn. Res.,* pp. 1453–1484.

[55] A. Lucchi, Y. Li, K. Smith, P. Fua (2012). Structured image segmentation using kernelized features. *Comput. Vision: ECCV,* pp. 400–413.

[56] I. Tsochantaridis, T. Hofmann, T. Joachims, and Y. Altun (2004). Support vector machine learning for interdependent and structured output spaces, in *21th International Conference on Machine Learning (ICML),* ACM, Banff, Alberta, Canada, p. 104.

[57] T. Joachims, T. Hofmann, Y. Yue, and C.-N. Yu (2009). Predicting structured objects with support vector machines. Research Highlight, *Commun. ACM*, **52**(11), pp. 97–104.

[58] M. B. Blaschko and C. H. Lampert (2008). Learning to localize objects with structured output regression. *Comput. Vision: ECCV*, pp. 2–15.

[59] Y. Boykov, O. Veksler, and R. Zabih (2001). Fast approximate energy minimization via graph cuts. *IEEE Trans. Pattern Anal. Mach. Intell.*, **23**(11), pp. 1222–1239.

[60] Y. Boykov and V. Kolmogorov (2004). An experimental comparison of min-cut/max-flow algorithms for energy minimization in vision. *IEEE Trans. Pattern Anal. Mach. Intell.*, **26**(9), pp. 1124–1137.

[61] J. Lee, Y. Bahri, R. Novak, S. S. Schoenholz, J. Pennington, and J. Sohl-Dickstein (2018). Deep neural networks as Gaussian processes, in *International Conference on Learning Representations, arXiv:1711.00165*.

[62] A. Krizhevsky, I. Sutskever and G. E. Hinton (2012). ImageNet classification with deep convolutional neural networks, in Proceedings of the 25th International Conference on Neural Information Processing Systems *(NIPS'12)*, pp. 1097–1105.

[63] Y. Tang (2015). Deep learning using linear support vector machines. *arXiv:1306.0239*.

[64] F. J. Huang and Y. LeCun (2006). Large-scale learning with SVM and convolutional for generic object categorization, in *IEEE Computer Society Conference on Computer Vision and Pattern Recognition (CVPR'06)*, pp. 284–291.

[65] S. A. Wagner (2016). SAR ATR by a combination of convolutional neural network and support vector machines. *IEEE Trans. Aerosp. Electron. Syst.*, **52**(6), pp. 2861–2872.

[66] C. E. Rasmussen and C. K. I. Williams (2005). *Gaussian Processes for Machine Learning*. MIT Press.

[67] M. Gönen and E. Alpaydın (2011). Multiple kernel learning algorithms. *J. Mach. Learn. Res.*, **12**, pp. 2211–2268.

[68] S. Qiu and T. Lane (2009). A framework for multiple kernel support vector regression and its applications to siRNA efficacy prediction. *IEEE/ACM Trans. Comput. Biol. Bioinf.*, **6**(2), pp. 190–199.

[69] F. R. Bach, G. R. G. Lanckriet, and M. I. Jordan (2004). Multiple kernel learning, conic duality, and the SMO algorithm, in *Proceedings of the 21st International Conference on Machine Learning*, Banff, Canada.

[70] R. E. Schapire (2013). Explaining adaboost, in *Empirical Inference*. Springer, pp. 37–52.

https://doi.org/10.1142/9789811247323_0009

Chapter 9

Evolving Connectionist Systems for Adaptive Learning and Knowledge Discovery: From Neuro-Fuzzy to Spiking, Neurogenetic, and Quantum Inspired: A Review of Principles and Applications

*Nikola Kirilov Kasabov**

Auckland University of Technology, Auckland, New Zealand
**nkasabov@aut.ac.nz*

This chapter follows the development of a class of neural networks called evolving connectionist systems (ECOS). ECOS combine the adaptive/evolving learning ability of neural networks and the approximate reasoning and linguistically meaningful explanation features of symbolic representation, such as fuzzy rules. This chapter includes hybrid expert systems, evolving neuro-fuzzy systems, evolving spiking neural networks, neurogenetic systems, and quantum-inspired systems, all discussed from the point of few of their adaptability and model interpretability. The chapter covers both methods and their numerous applications for data modeling, predictive systems, data mining, and pattern recognition across the application areas of engineering, medicine and health, neuroinformatics, bioinformatics, adaptive robotics, etc.

9.1. Early Neuro-Fuzzy Hybrid Systems

The human brain uniquely combines low-level neuronal learning in the neurons and the connections between them and higher-level abstraction leading to knowledge discovery. This is the ultimate inspiration for the development of the evolving connectionist systems described in this chapter.

---

*https://academics.aut.ac.nz/nkasabov; University of Ulster, https://pure.ulster.ac.uk/en/persons/nik-kasabov; University of Auckland, https://unidirectory.auckland.ac.nz/profile/nkas001

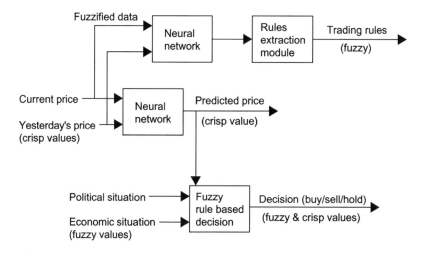

Figure 9.1:   A hybrid NN-fuzzy rule-based expert system for financial decision support [5].

In the past 50 years or so, several seminal works in the areas of neural networks [1, 2] and fuzzy systems [3, 4] opened a new field of information science— the creation of new types of hybrid systems that combine the learning ability of neural networks at a lower level of information processing, and the reasoning and explanation ability of fuzzy rule-based systems at the higher level. An exemplar system is shown in Figure 9.1, where, at a lower level, a neural network (NN) module predicts the level of a stock index and, at a higher level, a fuzzy reasoning module combines the predicted values with some macroeconomics:

Variables, using the following types of fuzzy rules [5].

IF <the predicted by the, NN module stock is high>

AND <the economic situation is good>

THEN <buy stock>   (9.1)

These fuzzy expert systems continued the development of the hybrid NN-rule-based expert systems that used crisp propositional and fuzzy rules [6–8].

The integration of neural networks and fuzzy systems into expert systems attracted many researchers to join this theme. The low-level integration of fuzzy rules into a single neuron model and larger neural network structures, tightly coupling learning and fuzzy reasoning rules into connectionists structures, was initiated by Professor Takeshi Yamakawa and other Japanese scientists, and promoted at a series of IIZUKA conferences in Japan [3, 9]. Many models of fuzzy neural networks were developed based on these principles [5, 10–15].

9.2. Evolving Connectionist Systems

9.2.1. *Principles of Evolving Connectionist Systems*

The evolving neuro-fuzzy systems developed these ideas further, where instead of training a fixed connectionist structure, the structure and its functionality were evolving from incoming data, often in an online, one-pass learning mode. This is the case with the evolving connectionist systems, Evolving Connectionist Systems (ECOS) [12–14, 16–18].

ECOS are modular connectionist-based systems that evolve their structure and functionality in a continuous, self-organized, online, adaptive, interactive way from incoming information [12]. They can process both data and knowledge in a supervised and/or an unsupervised way. ECOS learn local models from data through clustering of the data and associating a local output function for each cluster represented in a connectionist structure. They can incrementally learn single data items or chunks of data and also incrementally change their input features [17, 19]. Elements of ECOS have been proposed as part of the classical NN models, such as SOM, RBF, FuzzyARTMap, Growing neural gas, neuro-fuzzy systems, and RAN (for a review see [17]). Other ECOS models, along with their applications, have been reported in [20, 21].

The principle of ECOS is based on *local learning*—neurons are allocated as centers of data clusters and the system creates local models in these clusters. Fuzzy clustering, as a means to create local knowledge-based systems, was stimulated by the pioneering work of Bezdek, Yager, and Filev [22, 23].

To summarize, the following are the main principles of ECOS as stated by Kasabov [12]:

1. Fast learning from a large amount of data, e.g., using "one-pass" training, starting with little prior knowledge;
2. Adaptation in a real-time and an online mode where new data is accommodated as it comes based on local learning;
3. "Open," evolving structure, where new input variables (relevant to the task), new outputs (e.g., classes), new connections and neurons are added/evolved "on the fly";
4. Both data learning and knowledge representation are facilitated in a comprehensive and flexible way, e.g., supervised learning, unsupervised learning, evolving clustering, "sleep" learning, forgetting/pruning, and fuzzy rule insertion and extraction;
5. Active interaction with other ECOSs and with the environment in a multi-modal fashion;

6. Representing both space and time in their different scales, e.g., clusters of data, short- and long-term memory, age of data, forgetting, etc.;
7. A system's self-evaluation in terms of behavior, global error and success, and related knowledge representation.

In 1998, Walter Freeman, who attended the ICONIP conference, commented on the proposed ECOS concepts: "Through the 'chemicals' and let the system grow."

The development of ECOS as a trend in neural networks and computational intelligence that started in 1998 [12], continued as many improved or new computational *methods* that use the ECOS principles have been developed along with many *applications*.

9.2.2. Neuro-Fuzzy ECOS: EFuNN and DENFIS

Here, we will briefly illustrate the concepts of ECOS on two implementations: EFuNN [16] and DENFIS [18]. Examples of EFuNN and DENFIS are shown in Figures 9.2 and 9.3, respectively. In ECOS, clusters of data are created based on similarity between data samples either in the input space (this is the case in some of the ECOS models, e.g., the dynamic neuro-fuzzy inference system DENFIS), or in both the input and output space (this is the case, e.g., in the EFuNN models). Samples (examples) that have a distance to an existing node (cluster center, rule node) less than a certain threshold are allocated to the same cluster. Samples that do not fit into existing clusters form new clusters. Cluster centers are continuously adjusted

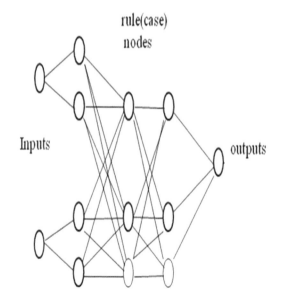

Figure 9.2:   An example of EFuNN model.
Source: Kasabov [16].

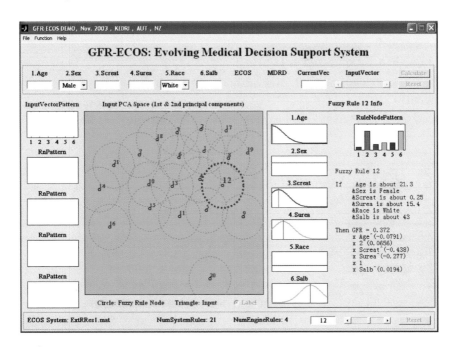

Figure 9.3: An example of DENFIS model.
Source: Marshall et al. [17] and Kasabov [24, 25].

according to new data samples, and new clusters are created incrementally. ECOS learn from data and automatically create or update a local fuzzy model/function, e.g.,

$$IF <data\ is\ in\ a\ fuzzy\ cluster\ Ci> THEN\ <the\ model\ is\ Fi>, \qquad (9.2)$$

where Fi can be a fuzzy value, a logistic or linear regression function (Figure 9.3) or a NN model [17, 18].

A special development of ECOS is *transductive reasoning and personalized modeling*. Instead of building a set of local models (e.g., prototypes) to cover the whole problem space, and then use these models to classify/predict any new input vector, in transductive modelling for every new input vector a new model is created based on selected nearest neighbor vectors from the available data. Such ECOS models are NFI and TWNFI [26]. In TWNFI for every new input vector, the neighborhood of closet data vectors is optimized using both the distance between the new vector and the neighboring ones and the weighted importance of the input variables, so that the error of the model is minimized in the neighborhood area [27].

9.2.3. *Methods that Use Some ECOS Principles*

Among other methods that use or have been inspired by the ECOS principles are:

— Evolving self-organized maps (ESOM) [28];

— Evolving clustering methods (ECM and ECMC) [18];
— Incremental feature learning in ECOS [29];
— Online ECOS optimization [30, 31];
— Evolving Takagi–Sugeno fuzzy model based on switching to neighboring models [32];
— Clustering and co-evolution to construct neural network ensembles [33].

Among other methods that use or have been inspired by the ECOS principles, these are (publications are available from www.ieeexplore.ieee.org; Google Scholar; Scopus):

— Online ECOS optimization, developed by Zeke Chan et al;
— Assessment of EFuNN accuracy for pattern recognition using data with different statistical distributions, developed by Ronei Marcos de Moraes et al;
— Recursive clustering based on a Gustafson–Kessel algorithm, by D. Dovžan and I. Škrjanc;
— Using a map-based encoding to evolve plastic neural networks, by P. Tonelli and J Mouret.
— Evolving Takagi–Sugeno fuzzy model based on switching to neighbouring models, by A. Kalhor, B. N. Araabi, and C. Lucas;
— A soft computing based approach for modelling of chaotic time series, by J. Vajpai and J. B. Arun;
— Uni-norm based evolving neural networks and approximation capabilities, by F. Bordignon and F. Gomide;
— Machine learning within an unbalanced distributed environment research notes, by H. J. Prueller;
— FLEXFIS: a robust incremental learning approach for evolving Takagi–Sugeno fuzzy models, by E. D. Lughofer;
— Evolving fuzzy classifiers using different model architectures, by P. Angelov, E. Lughofer, and X. Zhou [15];
— RSPOP: Rough set–based pseudo outer-product fuzzy rule identification algorithm, by K. K. Ang and C. Quek;
— SOFMLS: online self-organizing fuzzy modified least-squares network, by J. de Jesús Rubio;
— Finding features for real-time premature ventricular contraction detection using a fuzzy neural network system, by J. S. Lim;
— Evolving fuzzy rule-based classifiers, by P. Angelov, X. Zhou, and F. Klawonn;
— A novel generic Hebbian ordering-based fuzzy rule base reduction approach to Mamdani neuro-fuzzy system, by F. Liu, C. Quek, and G. S. Ng;

— Implementation of fuzzy cognitive maps based on fuzzy neural network and application in prediction of time series, by H. Song, C. Miao, W. Roel, and Z. Shen;

— Development of an adaptive neuro-fuzzy classifier using linguistic hedges, by B. Cetisli;

— A meta-cognitive sequential learning algorithm for neuro-fuzzy inference system, by K. Subramanian and S. Suresh;

— Meta-cognitive RBF network and its projection based learning algorithm for classification problems, by G. S. Babu and S. Suresh;

— SaFIN: A self-adaptive fuzzy inference network, by S. W. Tung, C. Quek, and C. Guan;

— A sequential learning algorithm for meta-cognitive neuro-fuzzy inference system for classification problems, by S. Suresh and K. Subramanian;

— Architecture for development of adaptive online prediction models, by P. Kadlec and B. Gabrys;

— Clustering and co-evolution to construct neural network ensembles, by F. L. Minku and T. B. Ludermir;

— Algorithms for real-time clustering and generation of rules from data, by D. Filev and P. Angelov;

— SAKM: Self-adaptive kernel machine: A kernel-based algorithm for online clustering, by H. Amadou Boubacar, S. Lecoeuche, and S. Maouche.

— A BCM theory of meta-plasticity for online self-reorganizing fuzzy-associative learning, by J. Tan and C. Quek;

— Evolutionary strategies and genetic algorithms for dynamic parameter optimization of evolving fuzzy neural networks, by F. L. Minku and T. B. Ludemir;

— Incremental leaning and model selection for radial basis function network through sleep learning, by K. Yamauchi and J. Hayami;

— Interval-based evolving modeling, by D. F. Leite, P. Costa, and F. Gomide;

— Evolving granular classification neural networks, by D. F. Leite, P. Costa, and F. Gomide;

— Stability analysis for an online evolving neuro-fuzzy recurrent network, by J. de Jesus Rubio;

— A TSK fuzzy inference algorithm for online identification, by K. Kim, E. J. Whang, C. W. Park, E. Kim, and M. Park;

— Design of experiments in neuro-fuzzy systems, by C. Zanchettin, L. L. Minku and T. B. Ludermir;

— EFuNNs ensembles construction using a clustering method and a coevolutionary genetic algorithm, by F. L. Minku and T. B. Ludermir;

— eT2FIS: An evolving type-2 neural fuzzy inference system, by S. W. Tung, C. Quek, and C. Guan;

— Designing radial basis function networks for classification using differential evolution, by B. O'Hora, J. Perera, and A. Brabazon;

— A meta-cognitive neuro-fuzzy inference system (McFIS) for sequential classification problems, by K. Subramanian, S. Sundaram, and N. Sundararajan;

— An evolving fuzzy neural network based on the mapping of similarities, by J. A. M. Hernández and F. G. Castaeda;

— Incremental learning by heterogeneous bagging ensemble, by Q. L. Zhao, Y. H. Jiang, and M. Xu;

— Fuzzy associative conjuncted maps network, by H. Goh, J. H. Lim, and C. Quek;

— EFuNN ensembles construction using CONE with multi-objective GA, by F. L. Minku and T. B. Ludermir;

— A framework for designing a fuzzy rule-based classifier, by J. Guzaitis, A. Verikas, and A. Gelzinis;

— Pruning with replacement and automatic distance metric detection in limited general regression neural networks, by K. Yamauchi, 2009;

— Optimal incremental learning under covariate shift, by K. Yamauchi;

— Online ensemble learning in the presence of concept drift, by L. L. Minku, 2011 (www.theses.bham.ac.uk);

— Design of linguistically interpretable fuzzy rule-based classifiers, by H. Ishibuchi, Y. Kaisho, and Y. Nojima;

— A compensatory neurofuzzy system with online constructing and parameter learning, by M. F. Han, C. T. Lin, and J. Y. Chang;

— Incremental learning and model selection under virtual concept drifting environments, by K. Yamauchi;

— Active learning in nonstationary environments, by R. Capo, K. B. Dyer, and R. Polikar;

— Real time knowledge acquisition based on unsupervised learning of evolving neural models, by G. Vachkov;

— Flexible neuro-fuzzy systems, by L. Rutkowski and K. Cpalka;

— A self-adaptive neural fuzzy network with group-based symbiotic evolution and its prediction applications, by C. J. Lin and Y. J. Xu;

— SOFMLS: online self-organizing fuzzy modified least-squares network, by J. de Jesús Rubio;

— A self-organizing fuzzy neural network based on a growing-and-pruning algorithm, by H. Han and J. Qiao;

— Online elimination of local redundancies in evolving fuzzy systems, by E. Lughofer, J. L. Bouchot, and A. Shaker;

— Backpropagation-Free Learning Method for Correlated Fuzzy Neural Networks, by A. Salimi-Badr and M. M. Ebadzadeh;

— A projection-based split-and merge clustering algorithm, by M. Cheng, T. Ma, and Y. Liu;

— Granular modelling, by M. Tayyab, B. Belaton, and M. Anbar;
— Permutation entropy to detect synchronisation, by Z. Shahriari and M. Small;
— Evolving connectionist systems: Characterisation, simplification, formalisation, explanation and optimisation (M.~J.Watts, 2004, PhD thesis; https://ourarhcive. otago.ac.nz).

to mention only a few of the ECOS further developed methods.

9.2.4. *ECOS-Based Applications*

Based on the ECOS concepts and methods, sustained engineering applications have been developed, some of them included in the list below and presented in [19] in detail:

— Discovery of diagnostic markers for early detection of bladder cancer, colorectal cancer and other types of cancer based on EFuNN (Pacific Edge Biotechnology Ltd, https://www.pacificedgedx.com) [21, 34];
— Medical diagnosis of renal function evaluation using DENFIS [24];
— Risk analysis and discovery of evolving economic clusters in Europe, by N. Kasabov, L. Erzegovesi, M. Fedrizzi, and A. Beber;
— Adaptive robot control system based on ECOS [35];
— Personalized modeling systems (www.knowledgeengineering.ai);
— Monthly electricity demand forecasting based on a weighted evolving fuzzy neural network approach, by P. C. Chang, C. Y. Fan, and J. J. Lin;
— Decision making for cognitive radio equipment, by W. Jouini, C. Moy, and J. Palicot;
— An incremental learning structure using granular computing and model fusion with application to materials processing, by G. Panoutsos and M. Mahfouf;
— Evolving fuzzy systems for data streams, by R. D. Baruah and P. Angelov;
— Handwritten digits classification, by G. S. Ng, S. Erdogan, D. Shi, and A. Wahab;
— Online time series prediction system with EFuNN-T, by X. Wang;
— Comparative analysis of the two fuzzy neural systems ANFIS and EFuNN for the classification of handwritten digits, by T. Murali, N. Sriskanthan, and G. S. Ng;
— Online identification of evolving Takagi–Sugeno–Kang fuzzy models for crane systems, by R. E. Precup, H. I. Filip, M. B. Rădac, E. M. Petriu, and S. Preitl;
— Modelling ozone levels in an arid region—a dynamically evolving soft computing approach, by S. M. Rahman, A. N. Khondaker, and R. A. Khan;
— A software agent framework to overcome malicious host threats and uncontrolled agent clones, by Sujitha, G. Annie, and T. Amudha;
— Comparing evaluation methods based on neural networks for a virtual reality simulator for medical training, by R. M. de Moraes and L. S. Machado;

— eFSM—A novel online neural-fuzzy semantic memory model, by W. L. Tung and C. Quek;

— Stock trading using RSPOP: A novel rough set-based neuro-fuzzy approach, by K. K. Ang and C. Quek;

— A stable online clustering fuzzy neural network for nonlinear system identification, by J. J. Rubio and J. Pacheco;

— Evolving granular neural networks from fuzzy data streams, by D. Leite, P. Costa, and F. Gomide;

— Neural networks for QoS network management, by R. del-Hoyo-Alonso and P. Fernández-de-Alarcón;

— Adaptive online co-ordination of ubiquitous computing devices with multiple objectives and constraints, by E. Tawil and H. Hagras;

— Advances in classification of EEG signals via evolving fuzzy classifiers and dependent multiple HMMs, by C. Xydeas, P. Angelov, S. Y. Chiao, and M. Reoullas;

— Online data-driven fuzzy clustering with applications to real-time robotic tracking, by P. X. Liu and M. Q. H. Meng;

— Evolving fuzzy systems for pricing fixed income options, by L. Maciel, A. Lemos, F. Gomide, and R. Ballini;

— Combustion engine modelling using an evolving local model network, by C. Hametner and S. Jakubek;

— Intelligent information systems for online analysis and modelling of biological data, by M. J. Middlemiss, (2001, PhD thesis, www.otago.ourarchive.ac.nz)

— Evolving neurocomputing systems for horticulture applications, by B. J. Woodford;

— Neuro-fuzzy system for post-dialysis urea rebound prediction, by A. T. Azar, A. H. Kandil, and K. M. Wahba;

— ARPOP: An appetitive reward-based pseudo-outer-product neural fuzzy inference system inspired from the operant conditioning of feeding behavior in Aplysia, by E. Y. Cheu, C. Quek, and S. K. Ng, 2012;

— Artificial ventilation modeling using neuro-fuzzy hybrid system, by F. Liu, G. S. Ng, C. Quek, and T. F. Loh;

— A data fusion method applied in an autonomous robot, by Y. Qingmei and S. Jianmin;

— Evolving fuzzy neural networks applied to odor recognition, by C. Zanchettin and T. B. Ludermir;

— A reduced rule-based localist network for data comprehension, by R. J. Oentaryo and M. Pasquier;

— Faster self-organizing fuzzy neural network training and a hyperparameter analysis for a brain–computer interface, by D. Coyle, G. Prasad and T. M. McGinnity;

— Adaptive anomaly detection with evolving connectionist systems, by Y. Liao, V. R. Vemuri, and A. Pasos;
— Creating evolving user behavior profiles automatically, by J. A. Iglesias, P. Angelov, and A. Ledezma;
— Autonomous visual self-localization in completely unknown environment using evolving fuzzy rule-based classifier, by X. Zhou and P. Angelov;
— Online training evaluation in virtual reality simulators using evolving fuzzy neural networks, by L. S. Machado and R. M. Moraes;
— Predictive functional control based on an adaptive fuzzy model of a hybrid semi-batch reactor, by D. Dovžan and I. Škrjanc;
— An online adaptive condition-based maintenance method for mechanical systems, by F. Wu, T. Wang, and J. Lee;
— Driving profile modeling and recognition based on soft computing approach, by A. Wahab, C. Quek, and C. K. Tan;
— Human action recognition using meta-cognitive neuro-fuzzy inference system, by K. Subramanian and S. Suresh;
— Hybrid neural systems for pattern recognition in artificial noses, by C. Zanchettin and T. B. Ludermir;
— A novel brain-inspired neural cognitive approach to SARS thermal image analysis, by C. Quek, W. Irawan, and G. S. Ng;
— Intrinsic and extrinsic implementation of a bio-inspired hardware system, by B. Glackin, L. P. Maguire, and T. M. McGinnity;
— Financial volatility trading using a self-organising neural-fuzzy semantic network and option straddle-based approach, by W. L. Tung and C. Quek;
— A Bluetooth routing protocol using evolving fuzzy neural networks, by C. J. Huang, W. K. Lai, S. Y. Hsiao, and H. Y. Liu;
— QoS provisioning by EFuNNs-based handoff planning in cellular MPLS networks, by B. S. Ghahfarokhi, and N. Movahhedinia;
— Hybrid active learning for reducing the annotation effort of operators in classification systems, by E. Lughofer;
— Classification of machine operations based on growing neural models and fuzzy decision, by G. Vachkov;
— Computational intelligence tools for next generation quality of service management, by R. del-Hoyo, B. Martín-del-Brío, and N. Medrano;
— Solving the sales prediction problem with fuzzy evolving methods, by D. Dovzan, V. Logar and I. Skrjanc;
— Predicting environmental extreme events in Algeria using DENFIS, by Heddam et al. [36];
— ICMPv6-based DoS and DDoS attacks detection using machine learning techniques, open challenges, and blockchain applicability, by M. Tayyab, B. Belaton, and M. Anbar;

— Prognostic of rolling elemn baring, by M. O. Camargos, R. M. Palhares, I. Bessa, and L. B. Cosme;
— Estimating dissolved gas and tail-water in water dams, by S. Heddam and O. Kisi;
— The implementation of univariable scheme-based air temperature for solar radiation prediction: New development of dynamic evolving neural-fuzzy inference system model, by O. Kisi, S. Heddam, and Z. M. Yaseend [37];
— Multiple time series prediction [38].

While the ECOS methods presented above use McCulloch and Pitts model of a neuron, the further developed evolving spiking neural network (eSNN) architectures use a spiking neuron model applying the same or similar ECOS principles and applications.

9.3. Evolving Spiking Neural Networks

9.3.1. *Main Principles, Methods, and Examples of eSNN*

A single biological neuron and the associated synapses is a complex information processing machine that involves short-term information processing, long-term information storage, and evolutionary information stored as genes in the nucleus of the neuron. A spiking neuron model assumes input information represented as trains of spikes over time. When sufficient input information is accumulated in the membrane of the neuron, the neuron's post-synaptic potential exceeds a threshold and the neuron emits a spike at its axon (Figure 9.4).

Some of the state-of-the-art models of a spiking neuron include early models by Hodgkin and Huxley [39]; more recent models by Maas, Gerstner, Kistler, Izhikevich, and others, e.g., Spike Response Models (SRM); Integrate-and-Fire Model (IFM) (Figure 9.4); Izhikevich models; adaptive IFM; probabilistic IFM (for details, see: [6, 7, 40–42]).

Based on the ECOS principles, an evolving spiking neural network architecture (eSNN) was proposed [19, 43]. It was initially designed as a visual pattern recognition system. The first eSNNs were based on the Thorpe's neural model [44],

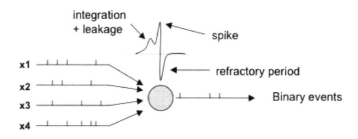

Figure 9.4: The structure of the LIFM.

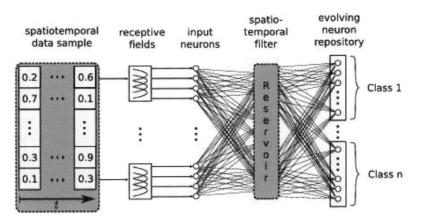

Figure 9.5:   A reservoir-based eSNN for spatio-temporal pattern classification.

in which the importance of early spikes (after the onset of a certain stimulus) is boosted, called rank–order coding and learning. Synaptic plasticity is employed by a fast-supervised one-pass learning algorithm. Different eSNN models were developed, including the following:

— Reservoir-based eSNN for spatio- and spectro-temporal pattern recognition shown in Figure 9.5 (following the main principles from Verstraeten et al. [45]);
— Dynamic eSNN (deSNN) [46] a model that uses both rank–order and time-based STDP learning [47] to account for spatio-temporal data;

and many more (for references, see [48]).

Extracting fuzzy rules from an eSNN would make the eSNN not only efficient learning models, but also knowledge-based models. A method was proposed in [49] and illustrated in Figures 9.6 and 9.7. Based on the connection weights (W) between the receptive field layer (L1), and the class output neuron layer (L2), the following fuzzy rules are extracted:

$$IF\ (input\ variable\ v\ is\ SMALL)\ THEN\ class\ C_i;$$

$$IF\ (v\ is\ LARGE)\ THEN\ class\ C_j. \tag{9.3}$$

In principle, eSNN use spike information representation, spiking neuron models, SNN learning and encoding rules, and the stricture is evolving to capture spatio-temporal relationship from data. The eSNN has been further developed as computational neurogenetic models as discussed below.

9.3.2. *Quantum-Inspired Optimization of eSNN*

eSNN have several parameters that need to be optimized for an optimal performance. Several successful methods have been proposed for this purpose, among them are

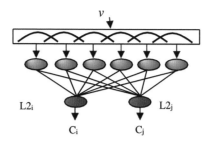

Figure 9.6: A simplified structure of an eSNN for 2-class classification showing only one input variable using 6 receptive fields to convert the input values into spike trains.

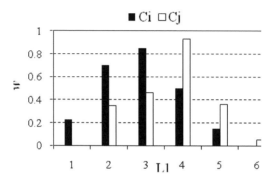

Figure 9.7: The connection weights of the connections to class C_i and C_j output neurons respectively are interpreted as fuzzy rules Eq. (9.3).

quantum-inspired evolutionary algorithm, QiEA [50]; and quantum-inspired particle swarm optimization method, QiPSO [51].

Quantum-inspired optimization methods use the principle of superposition of states to represent and optimize features (input variables) and parameters of the eSNN [19]. Features and parameters are represented as qubits that are in a superposition of 1 (selected), with a probability α, and 0 (not selected) with a probability β. When the model has to be calculated, the quantum bits "collapse" in 1 or 0.

9.3.3. *Some Applications Based on eSNN*

Numerous applications based on the different eSNN models have been reported, among them:

— Online data modelling with eSNN [52];
— Advanced spiking neural network technologies for neurorehabilitation [53];
— Object movement recognition (EU FP7 Marie Curie EvoSpike project 2011–2012, INI/ETH/UZH, https://cordis.europa.eu/project/id/272006);

— Multimodal audio and visual information processing [43];
— Ecological data modelling and prediction of the establishment of invasive species [54];
— Multi-model eSNN for the prediction of pollution in London areas [55];
— Integrated brain data analysis [56];
— Predictive modelling method and case study on personalized stroke occurrence prediction [57];
— Financial time series prediction [38];
— Other applications [48].

9.4. Computational Neuro-Genetic Models (CNGM) Based on eSNN

9.4.1. *Main Principles*

A neurogenetic model of a neuron is proposed in [19] and studied in [58]. It utilizes information about how some proteins and genes affect the spiking activities of a neuron such as *fast excitation, fast inhibition, slow excitation*, and *slow inhibition*. An important part of the model is a dynamic gene/protein regulatory network (GRN) model of the dynamic interactions between genes/proteins over time that affect the spiking activity of the neuron—Figure 9.8.

New types of neuro-genetic fuzzy rules can be extracted from such CNGM in the form of

$$IF <GRN \text{ is represented by a function } F> AND <input \text{ is } Small>$$

$$THEN <Class\ C>. \tag{9.4}$$

This type of eSNN is further developed into a comprehensive SNN framework called NeuCube for spatio-/spectro-temporal data modeling and analysis as presented in the next section.

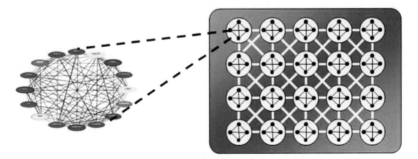

Figure 9.8: A schematic diagram of a CNGM framework, consisting of a GRN as part of an eSNN [58].

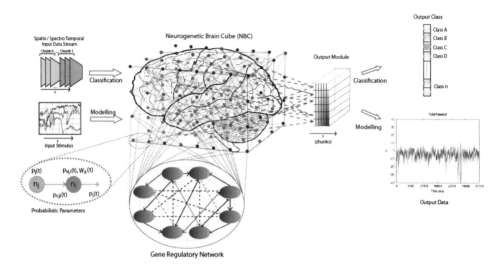

Figure 9.9: A block diagram of the NeuCube architecture (from [56]).

9.4.2. *The NeuCube Architecture*

The latest development of neurogenetic systems is NeuCube [56], initially designed for spatio-temporal brain data modeling, but then it was used for climate data modeling, stroke occurrence prediction, and other applications [59].

The NeuCube framework is depicted in Figure 9.9. It consists of the following functional parts (modules):

— Input information encoding module;
— 3D SNN reservoir module (SNNr);
— Output (e.g., classification) module;
— Gene regulatory network (GRN) module (Optional);
— Optimization module.

The input module transforms input data into trains of spikes. Spatio-temporal data (such as EEG, fMRI, climate) is entered into the main module—the 3D SNN cubes (SNNc). Input data is entered into *pre-designated spatially located* areas of the SNNc that correspond to the spatial location in the origin where data was collected (if there is such).

Learning in the SNN is performed in two stages:

— Unsupervised training, where spatio-temporal data is entered into relevant areas of the SNNc over time. Unsupervised learning is performed to modify the initially set connection weights. The SNNc will learn to activate same groups of spiking neurons when similar input stimuli are presented, also known as a *polychronization* effect [7].

— Supervised training of the spiking neurons in the output classification module, where the same data that was used for unsupervised training is now propagated again through the trained SNNc and the output neurons are trained to classify the spatio-temporal spiking pattern of the SNNc into pre-defined classes (or output spike sequences). As a special case, all neurons from the SNN are connected to every output neuron. Feedback connections from output neurons to neurons in the SNN can be created for reinforcement learning. Different SNN methods can be used to learn and classify spiking patterns from the SNNr, including the deSNN [60] and SPAN models [61].

The latter is suitable for generating spike trains in response to certain patterns of activity of the SNNc.

Memory in the NeuCube architecture is represented as a combination of the three types of memory described below, which are mutually interacting,

— Short-term memory, represented as changes of the PSP and temporary changes of synaptic efficacy;
— Long-term memory, represented as a stable establishment of synaptic efficacy— LTP and LTD;
— Genetic memory, represented as a genetic code.

In NeuCube, similar activation patterns (called "polychronous waves") can be generated in the SNNc with recurrent connections to represent short-term memory. When using STDP learning connection weights change to form LTP or LTD, which constitute long-term memory. Results of the use of the NeuCube suggest that the NeuCube architecture can be explored for learning long (spatio-)temporal patterns and to be used as associative memory. Once data is learned, the SNNc retains the connections as a long-term memory. Since the SNNc learns functional pathways of spiking activities represented as structural pathways of connections, when only a small initial part of input data is entered the SNNc will "synfire" and "chain-fire" *learned connection pathways* to reproduce *learned functional pathways*. Thus, a NeuCube can be used as an associative memory and as a predictive system.

9.4.3. *Applications of NeuCube*

Current applications of the NeuCube include (see [62, 63]):

• Brain data modeling and analysis, such as:

  – Modeling EEG, fMRI, DTI data;
  – Personalized brain data modeling [64];
  – Sleep data modeling;

- Predicting brain re-wiring through mindfulness [65];
- Emotion recognition [66];

- Audio/Visual signals

  - Speech, sound, and music recognition;
  - Video of moving object recognition

- Multisensory streaming data modelling

  - Prediction of events from temporal climate data (stroke) [67];
  - Hazardous environmental event prediction;
  - Predicting risk of earthquakes [62];
  - Predicting flooding in Malaysia by M Othman et al;
  - Predicting pollution in London area [55];
  - Predicting extreme weather from satellite images;
  - Predicting traffic flow [68];
  - Odor recognition [69].

The above applications are only few of the current projects.

9.4.4. *Neuromorphic Implementations*

The different types of eSNN and neurogenetic systems, especially the NeuCube architecture, are suitable to be implemented as a neuromorphic hardware system for embedded applications. For this purpose, both digital (e.g., [70]) and analogue (e.g., [71]) realizations can be used.

9.5. Conclusion

This chapter presents briefly the methods of ECOS. ECOS facilitate adaptive learning and knowledge discovery from complex data. ECOS integrating principles are derived from neural networks, fuzzy systems, evolutionary computation, quantum computing, and brain information processing. ECOS methods also include eSNN, deSNN, NeuCube, neurogenetic, and quantum inspired. ECOS applications are manifold, but perhaps most welcome in the environmental and health sciences, where the diagnostic phenomena are chaotic in nature and the data sets are massive and often incomplete. In the field of sustainability science, whether it is in analyzing issues related to sustainable resource utilization, countering global environmental issues, or the assurance of the continuity of life, (particularly human life) on earth, the speed of transformation is most rapid. Massive data sets with the characteristics just described need to be analyzed, virtually in real time, for prognoses to be made and solutions to the issues sought at a heightened level of urgency. In this sense, evolving connectionist systems for adaptive learning and knowledge discovery can make a great contribution to the methodologies of intelligent evolving systems.

Acknowledgment

The work on this chapter is supported by the Knowledge Engineering and Discovery Research Institute (KEDRI, http://www.kedri.aut.ac.nz). Some of the methods, techniques and applications are publicly available from https://www.kedri.aut.ac.nz; https://www.theneucom.com; https://www.kedri.aut.ac.nz/neucube/; https://neucube.io. I would like to acknowledge the work of many authors who developed methods and applications of ECOS referring to the presented here material. I have not been able to reference all or even a part of their work. Many of them have contributed greatly to the foundations of ECOS, e.g., S. Amari, T. Yamakawa, W. Freeman, J. Taylor, S. Grossberg, P. Angelov, D. Filev, J. Pratt, S. Ozawa, T. Ludemir, Z.G. Hou, C. Alippi, P. Pang, Lughofer, B. Gabrys, M. Watts, Dovzan and Skrjanc, F. Gomide, Ang and Quek, Rubio, Aznarte, Cetisli, Subramanian and Suresh, Babu and Suresh, Tung, Boubacar, Yamauchi, Hayashi, L. Goh, Ishibuchi, Hwang and Song, Capo, Vachkov, Rutkowski and Cpalka, Han and Qiao, Zanchettin, O'Hora, Hernandez and Castaeda, Guzaitis, and many more. I would like to acknowledge the editor of this volume Plamen Angelov for his incredible energy and efforts to put all these chapters together.

References

[1] Amari, S. (1967). A theory of adaptive pattern classifiers, *IEEE Trans. Electron. Comput.*, **16**, 299–307.

[2] Amari, S. (1990). Mathematical foundations of neurocomputing, *Proc. IEEE*, **78**, 1143–1163.

[3] Zadeh, L. A. (1965). Fuzzy sets, *Inf. Control*, **8**, 338–353.

[4] Zadeh, L. A. (1988). Fuzzy logic, *IEEE Comput.*, **21**, 83–93.

[5] Kasabov, N. (1996). *Foundations of Neural Networks, Fuzzy Systems and Knowledge Engineering*, Cambridge, Massachusetts, MIT Press, 550p.

[6] Hopfield, J. (1995). Pattern recognition computation using action potential timing for stimulus representation, *Nature*, **376**, 33–36.

[7] Izhikevich, E. M. (2004). Which model to use for cortical spiking neurons? *IEEE Trans. Neural. Networks*, **15**(5), 1063–1070.

[8] Kasabov, N. and Shishkov, S. (1993). A connectionist production system with partial match and its use for approximate reasoning, *Connect. Sci.*, **5**(3/4), 275–305.

[9] Yamakawa, T., Uchino, E., Miki, T. and Kusanagi, H. (1992). A neo fuzzy neuron and its application to system identification and prediction of the system behaviour. *Proc. of the 2nd International Conference on Fuzzy Logic & Neural Networks*, Iizuka, Japan, pp. 477–483.

[10] Furuhashi, T., Hasegawa, T., Horikawa S. and Uchikawa, Y. (1993). An adaptive fuzzy controller using fuzzy neural networks, *Proceedings of Fifth IFSA World Congress*, pp. 769–772.

[11] Lin and Lee, 1996.

[12] Kasabov, N. (1998). Evolving fuzzy neural networks: algorithms, applications and biological motivation. In: Yamakawa, T. and Matsumoto, G. (eds.) *Methodologies for the Conception, Design and Application of Soft Computing*, World Scientific, pp. 271–274.

[13] Kasabov, N., Kim, J. S., Watts, M. and Gray, A. (1997). FuNN/2: a fuzzy neural network architecture for adaptive learning and knowledge acquisition, *Inf. Sci.*, **101**(3–4), 155–175.

[14] Angelov, (2002).

[15] Angelov, P., Filev, D. P. and Kasabov, N. (eds.) (2010). *Evolving Intelligent Systems: Methodology and Applications*, IEEE Press and Wiley.

[16] Kasabov, N. (2001). Evolving fuzzy neural networks for on-line supervised/unsupervised, knowledge–based learning, *IEEE Trans. Syst. Man Cybern. Part B: Cybern.*, **31**(6), 902–918.

[17] Kasabov (2003). *Evolving Connectionist Systems*, Springer.

[18] Kasabov, N. and Song, Q. (2002). DENFIS: dynamic, evolving neural-fuzzy inference systems and its application for time-series prediction, *IEEE Trans. Fuzzy Syst.*, **10**, 144–154.

[19] Kasabov, N. (2007). *Evolving Connectionist Systems: The Knowledge Engineering Approach*, Springer (1st ed., 2003).

[20] Watts, M. (2009). A decade of Kasabov's evolving connectionist systems: a review, *IEEE Trans. Syst. Man Cybern. Part C: Appl. Rev.*, **39**(3), 253–269.

[21] Futschik, M. and Kasabov, N. (2002). Fuzzy clustering in gene expression data analysis, *Proc. of the World Congress of Computational Intelligence WCCI'2002*, Hawaii, IEEE Press.

[22] Bezdek, J. (ed.) (1987). *Analysis of Fuzzy Information*, vols. 1, 2, 3, CRC Press, Boca Raton, Florida.

[23] Yager, R. R. and Filev, D. (1994). Generation of fuzzy rules by mountain clustering, *J. Intell. Fuzzy Syst.*, **2**, 209–219.

[24] Marshall, M. R., et al. (2005). Evolving connectionist system versus algebraic formulae for prediction of renal function from serum creatinine, *Kidney Int.*, **6**, 1944–1954.

[25] Kasabov, N. (2002). *Evolving Connectionist Systems: Methods and Applications in Bioinformatics, Brain Study and Intelligent Machines*, Springer Verlag, London, New York, Heidelberg.

[26] Song, Q. and Kasabov, N. (2006). TWNFI: a transductive neuro-fuzzy inference system with weighted data normalisation for personalised modelling, *Neural Networks*, **19**(10), 1591–1596.

[27] Kasabov, N. and Hu, Y. (2010). Integrated optimisation method for personalised modelling and case study applications, *Int. J. Funct. Inf. Personal. Med.*, **3**(3), 236–256.

[28] Deng, D. and Kasabov, N. (2003). On-line pattern analysis by evolving self-organising maps, *Neurocomputing*, **51**, 87–103.

[29] Ozawa, S., Pang, S., and Kasabov, N. (2010). On-line feature extraction for evolving intelligent systems, in: P. Angelov, D. Filev, and N. Kasabov (eds.) *Evolving Intelligent Systems*, IEEE Press and Wiley, (7), 151–172.

[30] Minku, F. L. and Ludermir, T. B. (2005). Evolutionary strategies and genetic algorithms for dynamic parameter optimisation of evolving fuzzy neural networks. In: Proceedings of IEEE Congress on Evolutionary Computation (CEC), Edinburgh, September, vol. 3, pp. 1951–1958.

[31] Chan, Z. and Kasabov, N. (2004). Evolutionary computation for on-line and off-line parameter tuning of evolving fuzzy neural networks, *Int. J. of Computational Intelligence and Applications*, Imperial College Press, vol. 4, No. 3, 309–319.

[32] Angelov, P. and Filev, D. (2004). An approach to on-line identification of evolving Takagi–Sugeno models, *IEEE Trans. Syst. Man Cybern. Part B*, **34**(1), 484–498.

[33] Minku, F. L. and Ludermir, T. B. (2006). EFuNNs ensembles construction using a clustering method and a coevolutionary genetic algorithm. In: Proceedings of the IEEE Congress on Evolutionary Computation, Vancouver, July 16–21, IEEE Press, Washington, DC, pp. 5548–5555.

[34] Futschik, M., Jeffs, A., Pattison, S., Kasabov, N., Sullivan, M., Merrie, A. and Reeve, A. (2002). Gene expression profiling of metastatic and non-metastatic colorectal cancer cell-lines, *Genome Lett.*, **1**(1), 1–9.

[35] Huang, L., et al. (2008). Evolving connectionist system based role allocation for robotic soccer, *Int. J. Adv. Rob. Syst.*, **5**(1), 59–62.

[36] Heddam, S., Watts, M. J., Houichi, L., Djemili, L. and Sebbar, A. (2018). Evolving connectionist systems (ECoSs): a new approach for modelling daily reference evapotranspiration (ET0), *Environ. Monit. Assess.*, **190**, 216, https://doi.org/10.1007/s10661-018-6903-0.

[37] Kisi, O., Heddam, S. and Yaseen, Z. M. (2019). The implementation of univariable scheme-based air temperature for solar radiation prediction: new development of dynamic evolving neural-fuzzy inference system model, *Appl. Energy*, **241**, 184–195.

[38] Widiputra, H., Pears, R. and Kasabov, N. (2011). Multiple time-series prediction through multiple time-series relationships profiling and clustered recurring trends. In: Huang, J. Z., Cao, L. and Srivastava, J. (eds.) *Advances in Knowledge Discovery and Data Mining*. PAKDD 2011. Lecture Notes in Computer Science, vol. 6635, Springer, Berlin, Heidelberg, pp. 161–172.

[39] Hodgkin, A. L. and Huxley, A. F. (1952). A quantitative description of membrane current and its application to conduction and excitation in nerve, *J. Physiol.*, **117**, 500–544.

[40] Hebb, D. (1949). *The Organization of Behavior*, John Wiley and Sons, New York.

[41] Gerstner, W. (1995). Time structure of the activity of neural network models, *Phys. Rev.*, **51**, 738–758.

[42] Kasabov (2010). To spike or not to spike: A probabilistic spiking neural model, *Neural Networks*, **23**(1), 16–19.

[43] Wysoski, S., Benuskova, L. and Kasabov, N. (2010). Evolving spiking neural networks for audiovisual information processing, *Neural Networks*, **23**(7), 819–835.

[44] Thorpe, S., Delorme, A., et al. (2001). Spike-based strategies for rapid processing, *Neural Networks*, **14**(6–7), 715–725.

[45] Verstraeten, D., Schrauwen, B., D'Haene, M. and Stroobandt, D. (2007). An experimental unification of reservoir computing methods, *Neural Networks*, **20**(3), 391–403.

[46] Kasabov, N., et al. (2013a). Dynamic evolving spiking neural networks for on-line spatio- and spectro-temporal pattern recognition, *Neural Networks*, **41**, 188–201.

[47] Song, S., Miller, K., Abbott, L., et al. (2000). Competitive Hebbian learning through spike-timing-dependent synaptic plasticity, *Nat. Neurosci.*, **3**, 919–926.

[48] Schliebs, S. and Kasabov, N. (2013). Evolving spiking neural network: a survey, *Evol. Syst.*, **4**, 87–98.

[49] Soltic, S. and Kasabov, N. (2010). Knowledge extraction from evolving spiking neural networks with rank order population coding, *Int. J. Neural Syst.*, **20**(6), 437–445.

[50] Defoin-Platel, M., Schliebs, S. and Kasabov, N. (2009). Quantum-inspired evolutionary algorithm: a multi-model EDA, *IEEE Trans. Evol. Comput.*, **13**(6), 1218–1232.

[51] Nuzly, H., Kasabov, N. and Shamsuddin, S. (2010). Probabilistic evolving spiking neural network optimization using dynamic quantum inspired particle swarm optimization, *Proc. ICONIP 2010*, Part I, LNCS, vol. 6443.

[52] Lobo, J. L., Del Ser, J., Bifet, A. and Kasabov, N. (2020). Spiking neural networks and online learning: an overview and perspectives, *Neural Networks*, **121**, 88–100, https://www.sciencedirect.com/science/article/pii/S0893608019302655?via{\%}3Dihub.

[53] Chen, Y., Hu, J., Kasabov, N., Hou, Z. and Cheng, L. (2013). NeuCubeRehab: a pilot study for EEG classification in rehabilitation practice based on spiking neural networks, *Proc. ICONIP 2013*, Springer, Berlin, Heidelberg, vol. 8228, pp. 70–77.

[54] Schliebs, S., et al. (2009). Integrated feature and parameter optimization for evolving spiking neural networks: exploring heterogeneous probabilistic models, *Neural Networks*, **22**, 623–632.

[55] Maciag, P. S., Kasabov, N., Kryszkiewicz, M. and Bembenik, R. (2019). Air pollution prediction with clustering-based ensemble of evolving spiking neural networks and a case study on London area, *Environ. Modell. Software*, **118**, 262–280, https://www.sciencedirect.com/science/article/pii/S1364815218307448?dgcid=author.

[56] Kasabov, N. (2014). NeuCube: a spiking neural network architecture for mapping, learning and understanding of spatio-temporal brain data, *Neural Networks*, **52**, 62–76, http://dx.doi.org/10.1016/j.neunet.2014.01.006.

[57] Kasabov, N., Liang, L., Krishnamurthi, R., Feigin, V., Othman, M., Hou, Z. and Parmar, P. (2014). Evolving spiking neural networks for personalised modelling of spatio-temporal data and early prediction of events: a case study on stroke, *Neurocomputing*, **134**, 269–279.

[58] Benuskova, L. and Kasabov, N. (2007). *Computational Neuro-genetic Modelling*, Springer, New York.

[59] Kasabov et al. (2015). Evolving spatio-temporal data machines based on the NeuCube neuromorphic framework: Design methodology and selected applications, *Neural Networks*, **78**, 1–14 (2016). http://dx.doi.org/10.1016/j.neunet.2015.09.011.

[60] Kasabov et al. (2013b). Dynamic evolving spiking neural networks for on-line spatio- and spectro-temporal pattern recognition, *Neural Networks*, **41**, 188–201.

[61] Mohemmed, A., Schliebs, S., Matsuda, S. and Kasabov, N. (2013). Evolving spike pattern association neurons and neural networks, *Neurocomputing*, **107**, 3–10.

[62] Kasabov, N., Scott, N., Tu, E., Marks, S., Sengupta, N., Capecci, E., Othman, M., Doborjeh, M., Murli, N., Hartono, R., Espinosa-Ramos, J., Zhou, L., Alvi, F., Wang, G., Taylor, D., Feigin, V., Gulyaev, S., Mahmoudh, M., Hou, Z.-G. and Yang, J. (2016). Design methodology and selected applications of evolving spatio-temporal data machines in the NeuCube neuromorphic framework, *Neural Networks*, **78**, 1–14.

[63] Kasabov, N. (2018). *Time-Space, Spiking Neural Networks and Brain-Inspired Artificial Intelligence*, Springer.

[64] Doborjeh, M., Kasabov, N., Doborjeh, Z., Enayatollahi, R., Tu, E., Gandomi, A. H. (2019). Personalised modelling with spiking neural networks integrating temporal and static information, *Neural Networks*, **119**, 162–177.

[65] Doborjeh, Z., Doborjeh, M., Taylor, T., Kasabov, N., Wang, G. Y., Siegert, R. and Sumich, A. (2019). Spiking neural network modelling approach reveals how mindfulness training rewires the brain, *Sci. Rep.*, **9**, 6367, https://www.nature.com/articles/s41598-019-42863-x.

[66] Tan, C., Sarlija, M. and Kasabov, N. (2021). NeuroSense: short-term emotion recognition and understanding based on spiking neural network modelling of spatio-temporal EEG patterns, *Neurocomputing*, **434**, 137–148, https://authors.elsevier.com/sd/article/S0925-2312(20)32010-5.

[67] Kasabov, N., Liang, L., Krishnamurthi, R., Feigin, V., Othman, M., Hou, Z. and Parmar, P. (2014). Evolving spiking neural networks for personalised modelling of spatio-temporal data and early prediction of events: a case study on stroke, *Neurocomputing*, **134**, 269–279.

[68] Laña, I., Lobo, J. L., Capecci, E., Del Ser, J. and Kasabov, N. (2019). Adaptive long-term traffic state estimation with evolving spiking neural networks, *Transp. Res. Part C: Emerging Technol.*, **101**, 126–144, https://doi.org/10.1016/j.trc.2019.02.011.

[69] Vanarse, A., Espinosa-Ramos, J. I., Osseiran, A., Rassau, A. and Kasabov, N. (2020). Application of a brain-inspired spiking neural network architecture to odour data classification, *Sensors*, **20**, 2756.

[70] Furber, S. (2012). To build a brain, *IEEE Spectr.*, **49**(8), 39–41.

[71] Indiveri, G., Linares-Barranco, B., Hamilton, T., Van Schaik, A., Etienne-Cummings, R., Delbruck, T., Liu, S., Dudek, P., Hafliger, P., Renaud, S., et al. (2011). Neuromorphic silicon neuron circuits, *Front. Neurosci.*, **5**, 1–23.

[72] Doborjeh, Z., Kasabov, N., Doborjeh, M. and Sumich, A. (2018). Modelling peri-perceptual brain processes in a deep learning spiking neural network architecture, *Sci. Rep.*, **8**, 8912, doi:10.1038/s41598-018-27169-8; https://www.nature.com/articles/s41598-018-27169-8.

[73] Ibad, T., Kadir, S. J. A. and Ab Aziz, N. B. (2020). Evolving spiking neural network: a comprehensive survey of its variants and their results, *J. Theor. Appl. Inf. Technol.*, **98**(24), 4061–4081.

[74] Kasabov, N. (1994). Connectionist fuzzy production systems. In: Ralescu, A. L. (eds.) *Fuzzy Logic in Artificial Intelligence*. FLAI 1993. Lecture Notes in Computer Science (Lecture Notes in Artificial Intelligence), vol. 847, Springer, Berlin, Heidelberg, pp. 114–128.

[75] Kasabov, N. (1995). Hybrid connectionist fuzzy production systems: towards building comprehensive AI, *Intell. Autom. Soft Comput.*, **1**(4), 351–360.

[76] Kasabov, N. (1993). Hybrid connectionist production systems, *J. Syst. Eng.*, **3**(1), 15–21.

[77] Kasabov, N. (1991). Incorporating neural networks into production systems and a practical approach towards the realisation of fuzzy expert systems, *Comput. Sci. Inf.*, **21**(2), 26–34 (1991).

[78] Kasabov, N., Schliebs, R. and Kojima, H. (2011). Probabilistic computational neurogenetic framework: from modelling cognitive systems to Alzheimer's disease, *IEEE Trans. Auton. Ment. Dev.*, **3**(4), 300–311.

[79] Kasabov, N. (ed.) (2014). *Springer Handbook of Bio-/Neuroinformatics*, Springer.

[80] Kumarasinghe, K., Kasabov, N. and Taylor, D. (2021). Brain-inspired spiking neural networks for decoding and understanding muscle activity and kinematics from electroencephalography signals during hand movements, *Sci. Rep.*, **11**, 2486, https://doi.org/10.1038/s41598-021-81805-4.

[81] Kumarasinghe, K., Kasabov, N. and Taylor, D. (2020). Deep learning and deep knowledge representation in spiking neural networks for brain-computer interfaces, *Neural Networks*, **121**, 169–185, https://doi.org/10.1016/j.neunet.2019.08.029.

[82] Schliebs, R. (2005). Basal forebrain cholinergic dysfunction in Alzheimer's disease — interrelationship with β-amyloid, inflammation and neurotrophin signaling, *Neurochem. Res.*, **30**, 895–908.

https://doi.org/10.1142/9789811247323_0010

Chapter 10

Supervised Learning Using Spiking Neural Networks

Abeegithan Jeyasothy[*,¶], *Shirin Dora*[†,‖], *Suresh Sundaram*[‡,**]
and Narasimhan Sundararajan[§,††]

[*]*School of Computer Science and Engineering, Nanyang Technological University, Singapore*
[†]*Department of Computer Science, Loughborough University, United Kingdom*
[‡]*Department of Aerospace Engineering, Indian Institute of Science, Bangalore, India*
[§]*School of Electrical and Electronic Engineering,*
Nanyang Technological University (Retired Professor), Singapore
[¶]*abeegith1@e.ntu.edu.sg*
[‖]*s.dora@lboro.ac.uk*
[**]*vssuresh@iisc.ac.in*
[††]*ensundara@ntu.edu.sg*

Spiking neural networks (SNNs), termed as the third generation of neural networks, are inspired by the information processing mechanisms employed by biological neurons in the brain. Higher computational power and the energy-efficient nature of SNNs have led to the development of many learning algorithms to train SNNs for classification problems using a supervised learning paradigm. This chapter begins by providing a brief introduction to spiking neural networks along with a review of existing supervised learning algorithms for SNNs. It then highlights three recently developed learning algorithms by the authors that exploit the biological proximity of SNNs for training the SNNs. Performance evaluation of the proposed algorithms, along with a comparison with some other important existing learning algorithms for SNNs, is presented based on multiple problems from the UCI machine learning repository. The performance comparison highlights the better performance achieved by the recently developed learning algorithms. Finally, this chapter presents possible future directions of research in the area of SNNs.

10.1. Introduction

Advances in machine learning have often been driven by new findings in neuroscience. This is also true for spiking neural networks (SNN), which represent and process information using some mechanisms that are inspired by biological neurons. SNNs employ spiking neurons whose inputs and outputs are binary events in time called spikes. The binary nature of spikes renders them extremely energy-efficient compared to artificial neural networks (ANNs) whose inputs and outputs are real values. Furthermore, it has been shown that spiking neurons are computationally more powerful than sigmoidal neurons [1]. Implementation of SNNs in chips has resulted in an active and growing area of research referred to as neuromorphic computing. These aspects of SNNs have led to a surge in research on the development of learning methods for SNNs.

The discrete nature of spikes renders the response of spiking neurons non-differentiable. As a result, learning algorithms for ANNs cannot be directly used to train SNNs. Therefore, most of the current learning approaches for SNNs were developed by adapting existing learning algorithms for ANNs or building upon the learning mechanisms observed in biology. In this chapter, we focus on the recently developed supervised learning schemes for developing spiking neural networks to handle classification problems. We first provide a brief overview of currently existing learning algorithms for SNNs. We then highlight in detail three of our recently developed learning algorithms for SNNs that exploit the current understanding of various biological learning phenomena.

The three recent learning algorithms consist of two batch learning algorithms and one online learning algorithm. The two batch learning algorithms are: (i) two-stage margin maximization spiking neural network (TMM-SNN) and (ii) synaptic efficacy function-based leaky-integrate-and-fire neuron (SEFRON) and (iii) the online learning algorithm is online meta-neuron based learning algorithm (OMLA). These learning algorithms have been chosen as they are based on diverse biological phenomena. TMM-SNN and SEFRON employ local learning rules to update the synaptic weights in the network as is the case with biological learning mechanisms. TMM-SNN directly uses the potentials contributed by presynaptic neurons to update the weights while SEFRON employs a modified spike-time-dependent plasticity (STDP) [2] for learning. TMM-SNN employs constant weights whereas SEFRON uses a time-varying weights model. Unlike TMM-SNN and SEFRON, OMLA is inspired by the concept of tripartite synapses [3] in the brain, which allows OMLA to consider both local and global information in the network for learning. Similar to TMM-SNN, OMLA also uses a constant weight model.

The chapter begins by providing the necessary background for understanding and simulating SNNs in Section 10.2. Section 10.3 provides an overview of existing learning algorithms for SNNs. Section 10.4 describes the three different learning algorithms for classification using SNNs. Section 10.5 presents the results of performance evaluation of these learning algorithms for SNNs. Finally, Section 10.6 summarizes the chapter and provides important future directions for further research in this area.

10.2. Spiking Neural Networks

Spiking neural networks (SNNs) are used in many applications. However, we are limiting our presentation here to cover only the usage of SNNs in a supervised learning environment. In SNNs, an additional dimension, time, is included in the computations. The inputs and outputs for spiking neurons can be described using a binary vector, where the length of the vector is the input time interval, 1's in the vector represent the occurrence of a spike, and 0's in the vector represent the absence of the spike. The position of 1's in the vector indicates the time of the spike.

Figure 10.1 shows a generic architecture of a typical spiking neural network. The design of an SNN architecture is very similar to that of any other neural network. However, the main differences are the temporal input nature of a spiking neuron and the operation of a spiking neuron. In a nutshell, the fundamental functioning of any spiking neuron can be described as follows: For an input spike, either a positive or a negative postsynaptic potential is generated. Postsynaptic potentials from all the input spikes are accumulated in a spiking neuron. An output spike is generated when the accumulated potential crosses a threshold. After an output spike, the postsynaptic potential of a spiking neuron resets and the neuron starts accumulating postsynaptic potentials again after a refractory period.

Using SNNs for real-world dataset problems is not very straightforward, as most of the real-world datasets consist of analog values. Hence the datasets have to be encoded into spike patterns for use with SNNs. This chapter focuses on setting the context for using SNNs in a supervised learning environment for real-world datasets. Accordingly, this section is divided into four subsections. First, the different encoding mechanisms to convert real-valued inputs into spike patterns are presented. In the second subsection, the concept of a supervised learning environment for SNNs is defined and the mechanisms for decoding the SNN outputs to work with supervised learning algorithms are presented. In the next subsection, different types of spiking

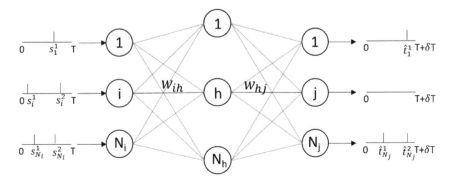

Figure 10.1: A generic architecture of a spiking neural network.

neuron models are presented. Finally, the different weight models used in a spiking neural network are highlighted.

10.2.1. *Encoding Methods*

For a real-valued input x where $x \in (0, 1)$, some encoding scheme is needed to convert these real-valued data into a spike pattern. Generally, there are two types of encoding schemes, viz., a rate encoding and a temporal encoding scheme. Both types of encoding, schemes differ significantly [4]. Frequency and time of spikes carry the information in rate encoding and temporal encoding respectively. In rate encoding, the spike vector for an input is generated by the frequency of the input. In temporal encoding, the spike vector is generated by a set of functions called receptive field neurons (RF neurons) that mimic the functioning of the biological sensory neurons.

10.2.1.1. *Rate encoding*

In rate encoding, the real value of the input is used as the frequency of occurrence of the spikes in the time interval T. The Poisson distribution is the popular choice for rate coding to generate spikes in random order. For example, if there are 300 time steps in the time interval T, for a real-valued input with 0.25, any random $75 (= 300 \times 0.25)$ time steps will have a spike and the remaining 225 time steps will not have any spikes. A generic rate encoding scheme is given by $R(\mathbf{x}) = \mathbf{s}$, where

$$\mathbf{s} = \{s^1, s^2, \ldots, s^f\}. \tag{10.1}$$

Here $f \in [0, T]$ is the total number of spikes generated for input x, where $f = T * x$.

Figure 10.2 shows the generation of a spike pattern for a real-valued input $x = 0.2$ using rate encoding. Ten time steps are used in the spike interval. Hence two $(f = 10 * 0.2)$ spikes are generated for an input $x = 0.2$. The timing of the two spikes is s^1 and s^2.

10.2.1.2. *Temporal encoding*

The basic principle of temporal encoding is that the real-valued input is mapped to a receptive field (RF) neuron (function) and the output of the RF neuron is used as the firing strength to determine the time of the spike. Based on the type and number of

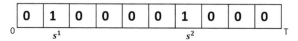

Figure 10.2:   Generating a spike pattern for real-valued input data $(x = 0.2)$ using the rate encoding scheme.

RF neurons used in the encoding scheme, temporal encoding can be categorized into three major groups, such as direct encoding, population encoding, and polynomial encoding.

Direct Encoding: In direct encoding, one RF neuron is used whereas in population encoding and polynomial encoding, multiple RF neurons are used in mapping a single real-valued input. Generally, a linear function is used for direct encoding. A general direct encoding equation is given by $\phi = x$, where ϕ is the firing strength and is used to compute the time of spike (s) as

$$s = T \cdot (1 - \phi) \tag{10.2}$$

Population Encoding: Population encoding is the most commonly employed encoding technique for evaluating spiking neural networks on problems with real-valued features [5]. The difference between population encoding and polynomial encoding is that in population encoding the same closed functions with evenly spaced centers are used as RF neurons, whereas in polynomial encoding, different functions (eg., Chebyshev polynomials) are used as RF neurons. The similarity between population encoding and polynomial encoding is that the input data are projected into a higher dimensional space $\mathbf{R}^q$ by the RF neurons (where q is the number of RF neurons used in the encoding scheme).

In population encoding, for a given input x, each RF neuron produces a firing strength ϕ_r, where r $(r \in \{1, q\})$ represents the rth RF neuron ($q = 1$ for direct encoding). The firing strength ϕ_r determines the presynaptic firing time s_r $\left(s_r = T.\left(1 - \phi_r\right)\right)$ for the rth RF neuron.

Generally, Gaussian functions are used as the receptive field neurons. However, other types of closed functions can also be used, e.g., squared cosine functions, etc. The center (μ_r) and width (σ_r) of the rth Gaussian receptive field used for encoding an input feature having the range $[I_{min}, I_{max}]$ are initialized as

$$\mu_r = I_{min} + \frac{(2r - 3)}{2} \frac{(I_{max} - I_{min})}{q - 2}, \qquad r \in \{1, \cdots, q\} \tag{10.3}$$

$$\sigma_r = \frac{1}{\gamma} \frac{(I_{max} - I_{min})}{q - 2}, \qquad r \in \{1, \cdots, q\}. \tag{10.4}$$

Based on the center and width of the receptive fields from Eqs. (10.3) and (10.4), respectively, the firing strength (ϕ_r) of the rth receptive field for x is given as

$$\phi_r = exp\left(-\frac{(x - \mu_r)^2}{2\sigma_r^2}\right). \tag{10.5}$$

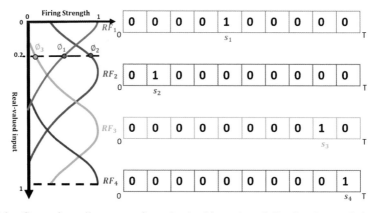

Figure 10.3:   Generating spike patterns for real-valued input ($x = 0.2$) using the population encoding scheme.

For firing strength (ϕ_r), spike time s_r is calculated using Eq. (10.2). A generic temporal encoding scheme is denoted by $P(\mathbf{x}) = \mathbf{s}$ where s is given by

$$\mathbf{s} = \{s_1, s_2, \ldots, s_q\} \tag{10.6}$$

where $\mathbf{s} \in [0, T]^q$. In direct encoding and population encoding, a higher RF neuron firing strength (ϕ_r closer to 1) corresponds to an early presynaptic firing (s_r closer to 0's) and a lower RF neuron firing strength (ϕ_r closer to 0) corresponds to a late presynaptic firing (s_r closer to T's).

Figure 10.3 shows the generation of a spike pattern for a real-valued input $x = 0.2$ using population encoding. Four RF neurons are used; hence the dimensions of the input are increased by 4 times. It can be observed that the 4th RF neuron has 0 firing strength and the 2nd RF neuron has the highest firing strength. Therefore, the spike times $s_4 = 10$ and $s_2 = 2$, respectively. Figures 10.2 and 10.3 illustrate the different encoding schemes. The same real-valued input $x = 0.2$ is used in all the encoding schemes. Ten time steps are used in the spike interval. The generated spike pattern is significantly different for each encoding scheme. In Figure 10.2, the spike occurs at two random time steps within the interval. The frequency of the spikes carries the information about the real-valued input. In Figure 10.3, the time of the spike is determined by the firing strengths of the RF neurons. In these two cases, the time of the spike carries the information of the given real-valued input.

10.2.2. *Overall Problem Definition:Some Preliminaries*

Converting a real-valued input to a spike pattern is a pre-processing step. After that, the supervised learning problem can be formulated for temporal inputs (spikes). We have unified the notations for spike times to avoid the differences in the notation of the different encoding mechanisms. We refer to Figure 10.1 for defining the notations in an SNN. For a spike input, we indicate the index of the attribute by a subscript and the order of the spike by a superscript e.g., s_i^k means the spike time of the kth spike of the ith input neuron. Here $i \in [0, N_i]$, where N_i is the total number of attributes and $k \in [0, f_i]$, where f_i is the total number of spikes for the ith input neuron.

For a temporal input **s** where $s \in [0, T]^{N_i}$, an SNN classifier $SNN(s)$ produces an output **y**,

$$\mathbf{y} = \{y_1, y_2, \ldots, y_{N_j}\}$$
$$y_j = \{\hat{t}_j^1, \hat{t}_j^2, \ldots, \hat{t}_j^{f_j}\}$$

(10.7)

Here N_j is the total number of output classes and y_j is the vector of postsynaptic firing time from the jth output classes and $y_j \in [0, T + \delta T]^{f_j}$. f_j is the total number of spikes for the jth output neuron, T is the presynaptic spike time interval limit, and δT represents an incremental smaller time after T to allow late postsynaptic spikes. $\hat{t}_j^k$ is the kth output spike of the jth output neuron.

We use s with layer index for spikes in the input and hidden layers. $\hat{t}$ is used only for spikes in the output layer. The same notations will be followed in the remaining sections. The weight w_{ih} means the weight between the ith neuron in the current layer and the hth neuron in the next layer.

In a supervised learning environment, the error signal is determined at the output layer. The error signal is then used in the supervised learning algorithm to update the weights. Different decoding schemes and coded class labels are used, depending on the encoding scheme used to convert the real-valued inputs.

10.2.2.1. *A typical classification problem*

A typical classification problem requires the SNN to predict a class label for a given input spike pattern. In an analog neural network, the predicted class label is determined by the output neuron that has a higher response value. Similar analogy is used in SNN to predict the class label. However, a decoding method has to be used to determine the output spiking neuron that has a higher response value for given input spikes.

Decoding methods are used to estimate the predicted class for a given input spike pattern based on the response of the output neurons in the network. Decoding methods for an input pattern are determined based on the encoding method used in the pre-processing step. We know that both encoding methods carry the input information in different formats—rate encoding carries the input information in the frequency of the spike and temporal encoding carries the input information in the time of the spikes. For inputs generated from the rate-encoding scheme and temporal-encoding scheme, a frequency-based decoding scheme and a time-based decoding scheme are used, respectively.

Rate-based decoding scheme   For inputs generated from a rate-encoding scheme, the frequency (or total count) of the input will be high for higher input values and low otherwise. Similarly, the response of the output neuron is determined by the frequency of the output spikes. Therefore, the output class label for an input spike pattern is determined by the output neuron that fires the most number of spikes and the class label $\hat{c}$ is predicted as

$$\hat{c} = \underset{j}{\operatorname{argmax}}(f_j) \tag{10.8}$$

Coded class labels are assigned to align with the decoding methods. For a rate decoding scheme, coded class labels may have higher frequency values for the desired class labels and lower frequency values for other class labels. For an input spike pattern belonging to the class c_k, a generic coded class label is determined by

$$\hat{f}_j = \begin{cases} F_d & \text{if } j = c_k \\ F_d - F_m & \text{otherwise} \end{cases} \tag{10.9}$$

Here, $\hat{f}_j$ is the coded class label for the jth output neuron, F_d is the desired frequency of the correct class label, and F_m is the margin frequency, which reduces the frequency of the spikes for undesired output classes.

Temporal decoding scheme   For inputs generated from a temporal encoding scheme, the spike time of the input is closer to $0s$ for a higher input value and closer to Ts otherwise. Hence the response of the output neuron is determined by the spiking times of the output spikes. The output class label for an input spike pattern is determined by the output neuron that fires first and the class label $\hat{c}$ is predicted as

$$\hat{c} = \underset{j}{\operatorname{argmin}} \left\{ \mathbf{y}^1 \right\}, \tag{10.10}$$

where $\mathbf{y}^1$ indicates the vector of the spike time of the 1st spike of all the output neurons.

For a temporal decoding scheme, coded class labels may have low spike time values for the desired class label and high spike time values for other class labels. For an input spike pattern belonging to the class c_k, a generic coded class label is determined by

$$\hat{y}_j = \begin{cases} \hat{t}_d & \text{if } j = c_k \\ \hat{t}_d + \hat{t}_m & \text{otherwise} \end{cases} \tag{10.11}$$

Here, $\hat{y}_j$ is the coded class label for the jth output neuron, $\hat{t}_d$ is the desired spike time of the correct class label, and $\hat{t}_m$ is the margin spike time, which delays the firing of the spikes for undesired output classes.

10.2.3. *Spiking Neuron Models*

In a biological neuron, information from one neuron is passed to another neuron in the form of an action potential. In SNNs, a spike is a simplified representation of an action potential in a biological neuron. Figure 10.4 shows the different phases of an action potential in a biological neuron. In the absence of any stimulus, the neuron is in the resting state, and the membrane potential of the neuron in this state is termed as the resting potential. In the presence of an external stimulus (input to the neuron), the neuron starts depolarizing, i.e., the membrane potential of the neuron starts growing. This phase is termed as the depolarization phase. The membrane potential rises sharply once the potential reaches a threshold value and an action potential is said to have occurred when the membrane potential reaches the peak value. After generating an action potential, the membrane potential of the neuron decays abruptly (repolarization phase) and undershoots the resting potential. This phase is termed as the refractory period. In this period, the neuron exhibits a subdued response to any external stimulus and its membrane potential slowly returns to the resting potential. It has been shown in the literature that the strength of the stimulus only determines the occurrence or non-occurrence of an action potential and not the amplitude of the action potential. In SNNs, a spiking neuron mimics the generation of an action

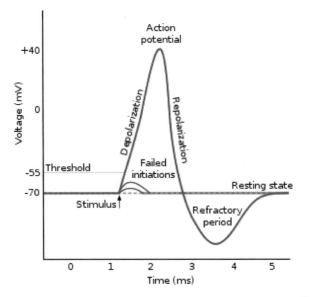

Figure 10.4: Different phases of an action potential (picture from https://en.wikipedia.org/wiki/Action_potential).

potential in a biological neuron. A spike in SNNs is a binary event in time and it represents the occurrence or non-occurrence of an action potential. A spiking neuron model reproduces the functional characteristics of generating an action potential in a biological neuron. The functioning of a biologically plausible spiking neuron is accurately described by the Hodgkin–Huxley model [6]. It reproduces all the stages of an action potential in a biological neuron. However, the high computational requirements of the Hodgkin–Huxley, etc. model render it unsuitable for implementing in a supervised learning environment. To overcome these issues, several mathematically tractable spiking neuron models e.g., the Izhikevich neuron model [7], the leaky integrate-and-fire model, the spike response model, etc., have been developed which reproduce the different aspects of the Hodgkin–Huxley model to varying degrees of accuracy.

Generally, the leaky integrate-and-fire (LIF) model [8, 9] and the spike response model (SRM) [10, 11] are the commonly used spiking neuron models in a supervised learning environment. In a supervised learning environment, some error signals should update the network parameters so that the desired outputs can be achieved. In the SNN context, the network parameters are associated with the postsynaptic potentials. In the LIF and SRM, the postsynaptic potentials can be broken down into two components consisting of a weight and a function so that the weight can be updated during the supervised learning phase.

10.2.3.1. *Leaky integrate-and-fire (LIF) model*

The leaky integrate-and-fire (LIF) neuron model is a highly simplified version of the Hodgkin–Huxley model. It reproduces the depolarization phase of an action potential, but the repolarization phase and refractory period are not implicitly reproduced by the LIF neuron model. The membrane potential of the neuron is explicitly reset after generating a spike to model the repolarization phase. The LIF neuron model employs an absolute refractory period, during which the membrane potential of the neuron is fixed at the resting potential.

The LIF neuron model employs an electrical circuit with a resistance (R) and a capacitance (C) to emulate the membrane potential of a neuron. The electrical circuit is shown in Figure 10.5. The current $I(t)$ in the figure represents the presynaptic input current at time t. The current causes the voltage to build up across the capacitor, which represents the membrane potential $(v(t))$ of a neuron. Once the voltage across the capacitor crosses a certain threshold value, the neuron generates a spike and the potential of the neuron is reset to the resting potential. This neuron model is termed as the leaky integrate-and-fire model because, in the absence of any presynaptic current, the voltage across the capacitor decays to zero due to the current induced by the capacitor in the RC circuit.

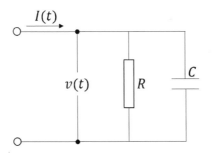

Figure 10.5: An RC circuit used to model a leaky integrate-and-fire neuron.

The dynamics of the RC circuit in Figure 10.5 is described as follows:

$$I(t) = \frac{v(t)}{R} + C\frac{dv}{dt} \tag{10.12}$$

The input current $I(t)$ has two components, viz. the current through the resistance R and the current that charges the capacitor C. Here, $\frac{v(t)}{R}$ is the component of current that goes through the resistance R and $C\frac{dv}{dt}$ is the component of current that charges the capacitor. From Eq. (10.12), the membrane potential of the neuron is given as

$$\tau_m\frac{dv}{dt} = RI(t) - v(t) \tag{10.13}$$

where τ_m is the time constant of the circuit. Let us assume that the simulation begins at $t = t_0$ and $v(t_0) = v_r$, where v_r is the resting potential. Based on this initial condition, the solution of Eq. (10.13) is given as

$$v(t) = v_r \exp\left(-\frac{(t-t_0)}{\tau_m}\right) + \frac{1}{C}\int_0^{t-t_0}\exp\left(-\frac{s}{\tau_m}\right)I(t-s)ds. \tag{10.14}$$

A generalization of the leaky integrate-and-fire neuron that does not allow any leakage of current at the capacitor is termed as an integrate-and-fire neuron.

10.2.3.2. *Spike Response Model (SRM)*

In comparison to the leaky integrate-and-fire neuron model, the spike response model (SRM) is capable of modeling an action potential more accurately as it implicitly models the refractory period. Assuming that the last spike by the postsynaptic neuron was generated at $\hat{t}$, the SRM describes the membrane potential $(v(t))$ at time t as

$$v(t) = \eta(t - \hat{t}) + \int_0^\infty \kappa(t - \hat{t}, s)I(t-s)ds \tag{10.15}$$

where the functions $\eta(.)$ and $\kappa(.)$ are termed as the kernel functions. The function $\eta(.)$ determines the shape of an action potential and models the refractory period of the spiking neuron. The function $\kappa(.)$ determines the response of the neuron to an input current $I(t)$. The function $\kappa(.)$ is used to model the differences between the effects of input current on the membrane potential of a neuron during and after the refractory period. During the refractory period, a given input current will result in a smaller change in the membrane potential of the neuron. After the refractory period, the same input current will produce a normal change in the membrane potential of the neuron. Besides the $\eta(.)$ and $\kappa(.)$ functions, the SRM employs a dynamic threshold function, represented by $\theta(t-\hat{t})$. The threshold of the neuron is maximum immediately after a spike and it slowly decays to the normal value.

By comparing Eqs. (10.14) and (10.15), it can be observed that the LIF model is a special case of the SRM model. A generic SRM equation of membrane potential $v(t)$ that is suitable for a supervised learning environment can be re-written as

$$v_h(t) = \overbrace{\sum_{i=1}^{N_i}\sum_{k=1}^{f_i} w_{ih}\ \epsilon(t - s_i^k)}^{\text{postsynaptic potentials}} + \overbrace{\sum_{k=1}^{f_h} v(t - s_h^k)}^{\text{refractory response}} + External\ inputs. \qquad (10.16)$$

Equation (10.16) can be directly used in a supervised learning environment. The postsynaptic potential term in Eq. (10.16) is similar to that of a LIF model. In Eq. (10.16), $v_h(t)$ is the accumulated membrane potential in the hth output neuron, and w_{ih} is the weight between the ith input neuron and the hth output neuron. w_{ih} is the weight between the ith input neuron and the hth output neuron. More details on different weight models are covered in the next subsection. $\epsilon(t)$ is the spike response function and $v(t)$ is the refractory response function. $\epsilon(t)$ and $v(t)$ are some kernels to model the shape of the spike response. $v(t)$ is a negative kernel and it takes the hth output neuron's spikes s_h^k as the inputs. $v(t)$ ensures that the accumulated potential $v_h(t)$ is reset and starts to accumulate postsynaptic potentials after every output spike s_h^k. External inputs are any additional inputs and they are generally not used in the learning framework.

The next output spike $s_h^{f_h+1}$ is produced as

$$s_h^{f_h+1} = \{t|v_h(t) = \theta_h\} \qquad (10.17)$$

here θ_h is the firing threshold for the hth output neuron.

10.2.4. *Synapse/Weight Models*

Input spike potentials (or spike responses) are amplified by either positive or negative factors to produce excitatory postsynaptic potentials or inhibitory postsynaptic potentials, respectively. The amplification factor is the weight of the connection. Weights are the learnable parameters in an SNN. Weight models can be categorized into three major groups, viz., constant weight models, dynamic weight models, and time-varying weight models. The main difference between constant weight models and the other two weight models is that the constant weight model does not have any temporal elements and the other two weight models do have some temporal elements. Additional temporal elements in the weight models improve the computational power of the spiking neuron. The difference between a dynamic weight model and a time-varying weight model is that the dynamic weight model is reactive to the input spike and changes the weight based on the frequency of the spike, whereas time-varying weight is a learnable time function for input spikes.

10.2.4.1. *Constant Weight Model*

A constant weight model imitates the long-term plasticity observed in biological neurons [12, 13]. Long-term plasticity is associated with the number of physical vesicle release sites in the presynaptic (input) side of a neural connection. Long-term plasticity is one of the possible biological mechanisms to explicitly determine the synaptic strength (weight). In long-term plasticity, the synaptic strength (weight) of a synapse (connection) stays nearly constant. This is the inspiration for constant weight models in spiking neural networks (or any artificial neural networks). Constant weight models are widely used in analog neural networks and in the early developments in SNNs.

10.2.4.2. *Dynamic Weight Model*

A dynamic weight model imitates the short-term plasticity observed in the biological neurons [14, 15]. Short-term plasticity controls quanta of vesicle release per impinging spike; the release process is a product of two factors: facilitation and depression. Facilitation and depression processes are coupled through their dependence calcium concentration, and their interplay dictates synaptic strength and dynamics in response to the variability of impinging spikes. Similar to this biological phenomenon, the dynamic weight models in SNNs regulate the weight of a connection based on the incoming spikes. Generally, dynamic weight models are suitable for the rate encoding scheme, where the input spikes have different frequencies. For the temporal encoding scheme, dynamic weight models act like constant weight models.

10.2.4.3. *Time-Varying Weight Models*

Time-varying weight models are inspired by the gamma-aminobutyric acid (GABA)-switch phenomenon observed in the biological synapse [16, 17]. This phenomenon is observed during the development of an infant's brain and during other physiological changes. During a GABA-switch, the synapse (connection) changes from excitatory (positive weight) to inhibitory (negative weight), or vice versa. Inspired by this phenomenon, a time-varying weight model allows both positive and negative weights in the same connection. Time-varying weight is a learnable function in time. This is one advantage of time-varying weights compared to constant or dynamic weights, as the other two weight models can have only positive or negative weight in one connection.

10.3. A Review of Learning Algorithms for SNNs

The most important part of a supervised learning environment is the learning algorithm used to train the SNN. Using the learning algorithms developed for analog neural networks in the realm of SNN is not very straightforward. Most of the learning algorithms for analog neural networks use the derivatives of the output activation functions (gradient-based learning algorithms). However, outputs in SNNs are binary events in time and the discontinuity in membrane potential makes it very challenging to determine the derivative of the output activation function. These challenges involved in adapting gradient-based learning algorithms opened up the exploration of directly adapting learning phenomena observed in biological neurons. This chapter is divided into three subsections. First, an overview of gradient-based learning algorithms for SNNs is presented. Second, an overview of biologically-inspired learning algorithms for SNNs is presented. Finally, an overview of other algorithms being used in SNNs is presented.

10.3.1. *Gradient-Based Learning Algorithms*

There have been many attempts to adapt gradient-based learning algorithms to train SNN classifiers [5, 18]. However, gradient-based learning algorithms in SNNs are severely limited by the discontinuous nature of the spiking activity. Initially in SpikeProp [5], the gradient-based learning algorithm was adapted for temporal encoded inputs. In SpikeProp, the discontinuity in membrane potential during the firing of an output spike is approximated with a linear function around the firing time. This approximation permitted one to determine the derivative of the output activation function. However, the non-firing of an output neuron (silent neuron or dead neuron) was a challenge for this approach. Several improvements have been proposed to improve the performance of SpikeProp [19, 20]. The initial SpikeProp worked with the temporal encoding scheme with a single spike. Later, it was also extended to work with multiple spike inputs [21]. The above-mentioned methods have been developed for shallow network architectures. In [22], temporal encoded inputs are transformed into an exponential term to work with deep architectures. Generally, rate coding is one of the widely used encoding methods for deep architectures [23].

10.3.2. *Biologically Inspired Learning Algorithms*

The functionality of a spiking neuron is inspired by the functionality of a biological neuron. This allowed researchers to adapt the phenomena observed in the brain to develop algorithms to train SNNs. Spike-time-dependent plasticity (STDP) [2] is the most common biological phenomenon adapted for SNN. Other than the STDP rule, a meta-neuron learning rule inspired from the regulation of neural connection weight by astrocyte cells is also used in SNN.

10.3.2.1. *STDP-based learning algorithms*

Spike-time-dependent plasticity (STDP) is one of the common phenomena observed in the brain. In STDP, the change in weight is computed by the difference in the time of the presynaptic spike with respect to the postsynaptic spike. Figure 10.6 shows the standard STDP rule. In the STDP rule, if the time of the input spike is close to the time of the output spike, it may have a higher influence on the change in weight. The positive and negative influence on the change in weight is determined by the time of the input spike with respect to the output spike. If an input spike fires before the output spike, then the input spike will have a positive influence on the weight change; otherwise a negative weight change will occur. The weight change in the STDP rule can be described as

$$\Delta w(\delta s) = \begin{cases} +A_+ \cdot exp(-\delta s/\tau_+) & \text{if } \delta s \geq 0 \\ -A_- \cdot exp(\delta s/\tau_-) & \text{if } \delta s < 0 \end{cases} \tag{10.18}$$

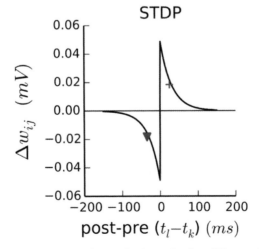

Figure 10.6: The standard STDP rule. The *x* axis shows the time difference between post- and pre-synaptic spikes. The end cross shows the strengthening of the connection (positive weight change) and the blue triangle shows the weakening of the connection (negative weight change) (Image from https://journals.plos.org/ploscompbiol/article?id=10.1371/journal.pcbi.1004566.)

where δs = Postsynaptic spike time − Presynaptic spike time and $\Delta w(\delta s)$ is the change in weight calculated for δs. (A_+, A_-) and (τ_+, τ_-) are the amplitude and time constant of the positive and negative learning window, respectively.

The STDP rule has laid the foundation for many SNN learning algorithms. In ReSuMe [24], the STDP and anti-STDP rules are used in a supervised learning environment. Improvements to the ReSuMe learning algorithm have been made by combining delay learning [25] and adding dynamic firing threshold [26]. In [27], the ReSuMe algorithm has been extended to a multilayer architecture. The STDP rule is also used in a normalized form [28] or with the Bienenstock–Cooper–Munro rule [29] to overcome the local learning nature.

10.3.2.2. Meta-neuron-based learning algorithm

Another biological phenomenon observed in our brain is the regulation of the synaptic connection by astrocyte cells. An astrocyte cell can have up to 100,000 connections with other cells, which allows them to access non-local information. This allows astrocyte cells to modulate the weights of each connection using nonlocal information. This phenomenon was adapted in a supervised learning algorithm as a meta-neuron-based learning algorithm. An additional neuron called a meta-neuron is used in the learning algorithm to mimic the functioning of the astrocyte cells. [30]

10.3.3. *Rank Order Learning*

Many learning algorithms for SNNs utilize the concept of rank order learning (ROL), [31] which is inspired by the fast processing times exhibited by neurons in the visual areas of the brain. The fast processing times indicate that very few spikes are required for the information to reach the brain from the retina. Based on this idea, rank order learning employs the order of first spikes generated by a group of presynaptic neurons.

To better understand ROL, consider an example with four presynaptic neurons and a single postsynaptic neuron as shown in Figure 10.7. Based on the temporal order of presynaptic spikes, the ranks of presynaptic neurons are estimated to be 3, 1, 2, and 0, respectively. Using these ranks, the weights of the connections between the four presynaptic neurons and the postsynaptic neuron are initialized as λ_3, λ_1, λ_2, and λ_0. Here, λ is the modulation factor and is always set to a value in the interval [0, 1].

Several variants of rank order learning have been proposed in the literature to improve its performance on real-world problems [32–39]. Rank order learning is used to develop an online learning algorithm for a four-layered SNN [32]. The network employs contrast-sensitive neuronal maps and orientation-selective neuronal maps in the second and third layers, respectively. The first layer in the network is used to present input spike patterns to the network and the last layer is

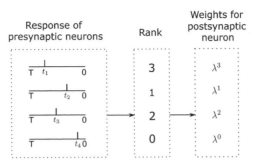

Figure 10.7: An illustrative example of rank order learning using the spikes generated by four presynaptic neurons and a single postsynaptic neuron.

used to determine the predicted class label. The number of neuronal maps in the last layer is not fixed a priori and is determined by the learning algorithm during training. The weights for neurons in the last layer are learnt in a supervised manner to maximize the classification performance. Later, the authors proposed a modified architecture with a single output neuron [34]. Wysoski *et al.* further extended this architecture to simultaneously handle both auditory and visual inputs [33]. The online learning algorithm mentioned above employs rank order learning, which utilizes only the first spike generated by each neuron for learning. The information in subsequent spikes is not used in learning. Kasabov *et al.* proposed a dynamic evolving SNN to exploit the information present in the spikes generated after the first spike [35]. Dynamic evolving SNN uses the first spike to initialize the weights, and subsequent spikes are used to fine-tune the initial weights.

10.3.4. *Other Learning Algorithms*

Many learning algorithms for SNNs use the postsynaptic potential of a neuron for learning as it continuously provides an accurate estimate of a spiking neuron's state at any given time. In [40], the authors developed a learning approach that utilizes the difference between the potential and the threshold for learning.

In [41], the authors overcame the discontinuous nature of spikes by convolving the input and output spike patterns with a mathematical function to convert them into continuous analog signals.

In the next section, we describe three learning algorithms, namely TMM-SNN, OMLA, and SEFRON.

10.4. Classification Using SNNs

10.4.1. *A Two-Stage Margin Maximization Spiking Neural Network*

In this section, we describe a learning algorithm for a three-layered SNN that maximizes the interspike interval between spikes generated by neurons that are associated with different classes. The network is trained in two stages and is, thus, referred to as a two-stage margin maximization spiking neural network (TMM-SNN). The first stage of the learning algorithm is termed as the structure learning stage and the second stage is termed as the output weights learning stage. During the structure learning stage, the learning algorithm evolves the number of neurons in the hidden layer of the network and updates the weights of connections between the input neurons and the hidden layer neurons. For updating weights in this stage, TMM-SNN uses the normalized membrane potential (NMP) learning rule, which relies only on the locally available information on a synapse. To estimate the change in the weight of a particular synapse, the NMP learning rule utilizes the current weight of the synapse and the proportion of unweighted postsynaptic membrane potential that is contributed by the presynaptic neuron.

10.4.1.1. *Architecture of TMM-SNN*

TMM-SNN utilizes a network with three layers. The input layer is used to present a spike pattern, $(\mathbf{x}, c)$, to the network. Here, $\mathbf{x} = [x_1, \ldots, x_i, \ldots, x_m]^T$ is an m-dimensional spike pattern that belongs to class c. $x_i = \{t_i^1, \ldots t_i^g, \ldots, t_i^{G_i}\}$ is a spike train where t_i^g denotes the time of the gth spike generated by the ith input neuron. Each input spike pattern is presented to the network for a duration of 600 milliseconds with a time step of 1 millisecond. These spike patterns presented through the input layer drive the activity in the hidden neurons and the output neurons in the network. The responses of output neurons are used to determine the predicted class for a given spike pattern based on the time to first spike decoding method. The output layer consists of C neurons where C is the total number of classes. Without loss of generality, the description in this section and in Sections 10.4.1.2, 10.4.1.3, and 10.4.1.4 assume a network with K hidden neurons. Figure 10.8 shows the architecture of a TMM-SNN with K hidden neurons.

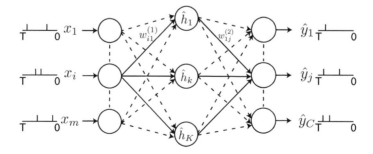

Figure 10.8: Architecture of TMM-SNN.

The spikes generated by the input neurons affect the potential of the hidden neurons which generate a spike when their potential crosses a threshold value. The potential contributed by the ith input neuron at time t is given by

$$\tilde{v}_i(t) = \sum_g \epsilon\left(t - t_i^g\right) \tag{10.19}$$

where $\epsilon(t - t_i^g)$ is the potential contributed by the gth spike at time t. TMM-SNN uses the spike response model to estimate the value of $\epsilon(\cdot)$, which is given by

$$\epsilon(s) = \frac{s}{\tau} \exp\left(1 - \frac{s}{\tau}\right) \tag{10.20}$$

where τ is the time constant of the neuron, which is set to 300 milliseconds for all simulations involving TMM-SNN.

Based on the potential contributed by the input neurons, the potential (v_k^2) of the kth hidden neuron at time t is given by

$$v_k^{(1)}(t) = \sum_i w_{ik}^{(1)} \tilde{v}_i(t) \tag{10.21}$$

where $w_{ik}^{(1)}$ is the weight of the connection between the ith input neuron and the kth hidden neuron. The hidden neuron generates a spike every time its potential crosses its threshold, which is denoted by $\theta_k^{(1)}$. After the neuron generates a spike, its potential is reset to zero and its potential due to subsequent input spikes is computed using Eq. (10.21). The threshold of all hidden neurons is determined by the learning algorithm during training. The spike train generated by the kth hidden neurons is denoted by $\hat{h}_k = \{\hat{t}_k^1, \ldots, \hat{t}_k^g, \ldots, \hat{t}_k^{G_k^{(1)}}\}$ where $\hat{t}_k^g$ denotes the gth spike generated by the kth hidden neuron. $G_k^{(1)}$ represents the number of spikes generated by the kth hidden neuron. Similar to hidden neurons, output neurons are also modeled using the spike response model. Therefore, the potential contributed by the kth hidden neuron to the output neurons at time t is given by

$$\tilde{v}_k^{(2)}(t) = \sum_{g \in \{1,\ldots,G_k^{(1)}\}} \epsilon\left(t - \hat{t}_k^g\right) \tag{10.22}$$

Based on the potential contributed by the hidden neurons, the potential of the jth output neuron at time t is given by

$$v_j^{(2)}(t) = \sum_k w_{kj}^{(1)} \tilde{v}_k^{(2)}(t) \tag{10.23}$$

where $w_{ik}^{(2)}$ is the weight of the connection between the kth hidden neuron and the jth output neuron. The output neuron generates a spike every time its potential crosses the threshold, which is given by $\theta_j^{(2)}$. The threshold for all output neurons is set to one. The spike train generated by the output neurons is denoted by $\hat{y}_j = \{\hat{t}_j^1, \ldots, \hat{t}_j^g, \ldots, \hat{t}_j^{G_j^{(2)}}\}$, where $\hat{t}_j^g$ denotes the gth spike generated by the jth output neuron. The superscript in $G_k^{(1)}$ and $G_k^{(2)}$ is used to differentiate between the number of spikes generated by neurons in the hidden layer and output layer, respectively.

Given the response of output neurons, the predicted class ($\hat{c}$) is determined using the time to first spike decoding method, given by

$$\hat{c} = \underset{j}{\arg\min}\, \hat{t}_j^1 \tag{10.24}$$

10.4.1.2. *Normalized membrane potential learning rule*

The NMP learning rule updates the weight of a connection between two neurons based on the information present in the current input spike pattern and the knowledge acquired by the network from previously learnt spike patterns. It estimates the information present in the current input spike pattern based on the fraction of unweighted membrane potential that is contributed by the presynaptic neuron to the postsynaptic neuron. The current weight of a synapse is used as an estimate of the existing knowledge of the network.

Next, the NMP learning rule is described for the ith neuron in the input layer and kth neuron in the hidden layer of the TMM-SNN (see Figure 10.8). The normalized membrane potential (η_{ik}) contributed by the ith presynaptic neuron to the kth postsynaptic neuron at time t is given by

$$\eta_{ik}(t) = \frac{\widetilde{v}_i(t)}{\sum_p \widetilde{v}_p(t)}, \quad i \in \{1, \ldots, m\}. \tag{10.25}$$

Using only η_{ik} to update the weight of a synapse may result in a loss of the knowledge acquired by the network from previously learnt spike patterns. To avoid this problem, the NMP learning rule updates the weight of a synapse based on the difference between η_{ik} and the current weight of the synapse. Furthermore, it only updates the weight of a synapse when η_{ik} is greater than the current weight of the synapse, and, as a result, synapses with higher weights are not updated. This ensures that the input neurons that contributed significantly toward the membrane potential of the kth hidden neuron for the past spike patterns are not altered, thereby protecting the past knowledge stored in the network.

Since TMM-SNN uses the time to first spike decoding method to determine the predicted class, the NMP learning rule is always used at the time of first spike ($\hat{t}_k^1$) generated by the kth output neuron. To summarize, according to the NMP learning rule, the change in the weight (Δw_{ik}^1) of a synapse between the ith input neuron and the kth hidden neuron is given by

$$\Delta w_{ik}^1 = \begin{cases} 0 & w_{ik}^1 \geq \eta_{ik}\left(\hat{t}_k^1\right) \\ \alpha\left(\eta_{ik}\left(\hat{t}_k^1\right) - w_{ik}^1\right) & w_{ik}^1 < \eta_{ik}\left(\hat{t}_k^1\right) \end{cases}, \quad i \in \{1, \dots, m\} \quad (10.26)$$

where α is the learning rate and is set to 0.01 for all experiments with TMM-SNN.

10.4.1.3. *Structure learning stage*

In this subsection, the structure learning stage of the learning algorithm for TMM-SNN is described. In this stage, the learning algorithm uses two different strategies for evolving the number of hidden neurons and for learning weights for the connections between the input neurons and the hidden neurons in the network. It uses a *neuron addition strategy* for adding hidden neurons to the network in line with the complexity of the classification problem. When a new neuron is added to the network, the class label of the current input spike pattern is used as the associated class for the newly added neuron. It uses the *margin maximization strategy for structure learning* to update weights between the input neurons and the hidden neurons such that the interclass margins estimated from the responses of the hidden neurons are maximized. The learning algorithm uses both learning strategies during the first epoch of this stage. After the first epoch, the number of hidden neurons is fixed and only the margin maximization strategy for structure learning is used to update the weights between the input neurons and the hidden neurons in the network.

A particular learning strategy in this stage is selected based on the time of first spikes generated by the winner neurons associated with the class of the current input spike pattern and any other class. The winner neuron (CC) associated with the same class as the current input spike pattern is given by

$$CC = \underset{k, \bar{c}_k = c}{\operatorname{argmin}} \hat{t}_k^1 \quad (10.27)$$

where $\bar{c}_k$ represents the associated class for the kth hidden neuron and c denotes the class label for the current input spike pattern. Similarly, the winner neuron (MC) associated with a different class is given by

$$MC = \underset{k, \bar{c}_k \neq c}{\operatorname{argmin}} \hat{t}_k^1. \quad (10.28)$$

Next, the different learning strategies used in the structure learning stage will be described, assuming a network that has already evolved to K hidden neurons.

(1) *Neuron addition strategy*: The learning algorithm uses this strategy for those spike patterns that contain information that has not been acquired by the network from previously learned spike patterns. It utilizes the time of the first spike generated by the neuron CC to identify those spike patterns that can be learned

accurately by using this strategy. Specifically, a new neuron is added to the network whenever $\hat{t}^1_{CC}$ is greater than a threshold T_a. The associated class for the newly added neuron is assigned using the class label for the current input spike pattern. The criterion for the neuron addition strategy can be expressed as

If $\hat{t}^1_{CC} > T_a$ **Then** add a hidden neuron to the network. (10.29)

Here, T_a is set to a value in the interval $[0, T]$ which can be mathematically expressed as $T_a = \alpha_a T$ where $\alpha_a \in [0, 1]$ is termed as the addition threshold. An appropriate range for setting α_a is $[0.4, 0.55]$. Refer to [42] for more details regarding the impact of α_a on the performance of TMM-SNN.

To accurately capture the information present in the current input spike pattern, the weights and threshold of the newly added neuron are initialized such that it fires precisely at $T/3$. For this purpose, the weight of the connection between the ith input neuron and the newly added neuron is initialized using the normalized membrane potential (Eq. 10.25) at $T/3$ for the current input spike pattern, given by

$$w^{(1)}_{i(K+1)} = \eta_{i(K+1)}(T/3), \qquad i \in \{1, \ldots, m\} \tag{10.30}$$

Based on this initial value of weights, the threshold of the newly added neuron is initialized as

$$\theta_{K+1} = \sum_i w^{(1)}_{i(K+1)} \tilde{v}_i(T/3). \tag{10.31}$$

(2) *Margin maximization strategy for structure learning*: The learning algorithm uses this strategy to update the weights of hidden neurons when the interclass margin is lower than a certain threshold (T_m) for a given spike pattern. Here, the interclass margin is computed as

$$\Upsilon^{(1)} = \hat{t}^{(1)}_{MC} - \hat{t}^{(1)}_{CC}. \tag{10.32}$$

Based on the definition of the interclass margin, the criterion for this strategy is given by

If $\Upsilon < T_m$ **then** update the weights of hidden neurons (10.33)

T_m is set to a value in the interval $[0, (T - T/3)]$. A value higher than $(T - T/3)$ is not recommended as the parameters for a newly added neuron are initialized such that it fires at $T/3$. An intuitive method to choose T_m is by setting its value based on the following equation:

$$T_m = \alpha_m \left(T - \frac{T}{3} \right) \tag{10.34}$$

where α_m is termed as the margin threshold and is always set to a value in the interval [0, 1]. See [42] for more details.

It may be observed from Eq. (10.32) that the interclass margin depends only on the spike times of the neurons CC and MC. Therefore, the learning algorithm maximizes the margin by only updating weights of the neurons CC and MC. The updated values of weights of these neurons are computed using the NMP learning rule Eq. (10.25) and are given by

$$\left. \begin{aligned} w_{i(CC)}^1 &= w_{i(CC)}^1 + \Delta w_{i(CC)}^1 \\ w_{i(MC)}^1 &= w_{i(MC)}^1 - \Delta w_{i(MC)}^1 \end{aligned} \right\}, \quad i \in \{1, \dots, m\}. \tag{10.35}$$

The update equation described above forces the neuron CC to fire sooner and delays the spike generated by the neuron MC, thereby resulting in a higher interclass margin. The learning strategy for maximizing the margin is used for multiple epochs during the structure learning stage until the average interclass margin across all training samples converges to a maximum value.

To summarize, the pseudo-code for the structure learning stage of TMM-SNN is given in Algorithm 10.1.

Algorithm 10.1 Pseudo-code for the structure learning stage

   Evolving loop (Epoch 1)
1: **for** each training spike pattern **do**
2:    **if** $\hat{t}_{CC}^1 > T_a$ **then**
3:       Add a neuron
   Iterative loop (Epoch 1 until convergence)
4: **for** each training spike pattern **do**
5:    **if** $(\hat{t}_{MC}^1 - \hat{t}_{CC}^1) < T_m$ **then**
6:       Update weights of the neurons CC and MC

10.4.1.4. *Output weights learning stage*

The structure learning stage helps determine the appropriate number of hidden neurons required for a particular classification problem. At the end of the structure learning stage, the parameters for hidden neurons are fixed and the connections between the hidden neurons and the output neurons are randomly initialized. In this stage, the learning algorithm updates the weights of the connections between the hidden neurons and the output neurons to maximize the interclass margins based on the responses of output neurons. For this purpose, the winner neurons associated with the same class as the current input spike pattern (CC) and a different class (MC) are estimated according to the times of spikes generated by the output neurons, given as

$$CC = \arg_j (j = c) \tag{10.36}$$

$$MC = \underset{j, j \neq c}{\operatorname{argmin}} t_j^{(2)}. \tag{10.37}$$

Based on the times of spikes generated by the output neurons CC and MC, the interclass margin is computed as

$$\Upsilon^{(2)} = t_{MC}^{(2)} - t_{CC}^{(2)}. \tag{10.38}$$

In this stage, the learning algorithm only updates weights of the output neurons CC and MC because only these neurons determine the interclass margin (Eq. (10.38)). Furthermore, connections from only those hidden neurons are updated that are associated with the same class as the class label for the current input spike pattern. The required change in the weight is determined based on the unweighted membrane potential contributed by the hidden neuron at the time of the first spike generated by the output neuron. Based on this, the change in weight for the connection between the kth hidden neuron and the jth output neuron is given by

$$\Delta w_{kj}^{(2)} = \begin{cases} \alpha \left(\tilde{v}_k^{(2)} (t_j^{(2)}) \right) & \bar{c}_k = c \\ 0 & \bar{c}_k \neq c \end{cases} \tag{10.39}$$

Based on Eq. (10.39), the updated weights for the output neurons CC and MC are given by

$$\left. \begin{aligned} w_{k(CC)}^{(2)} &= w_{k(CC)}^{(2)} + \Delta w_{k(CC)}^{(2)} \\ w_{k(MC)}^{(2)} &= w_{k(MC)}^{(2)} - \Delta w_{k(MC)}^{(2)} \end{aligned} \right\}, \quad k \in \{1, \ldots, K\} \tag{10.40}$$

The update rule in Eq. (10.40) forces the output neuron associated with the correct class to fire sooner and delays the spikes generated by the neurons associated with the other class (MC). This results in an increase in average margin based on the responses of output neurons. To summarize, the pseudo-code for the structure learning stage of TMM-SNN is given in Algorithm 10.2.

Algorithm 10.2 Pseudo-code for the output weights learning stage

---

    Iterative loop (Epoch 1 until convergence)
1: **for** each training spike pattern **do**
2:     **if** $(\hat{t}_{MC}^2 - \hat{t}_{CC}^2) < T_m$ **then**
3:         Update weights of the neurons CC and MC

10.4.2. *Online Meta-Neuron-Based Learning Algorithm*

In this section, we will describe the online meta-neuron based learning algorithm for a two-layered SNN with a meta-neuron. The architecture of the SNN with a meta-neuron is inspired by the concept of heterosynaptic plasticity that occurs on a tripartite synapse [3] in the brain. A tripartite synapse is a junction between a presynaptic neuron, a postsynaptic neuron and an astrocyte cell. A single astrocyte cell can be simultaneously connected to multiple tripartite synapses, [43] which allows this cell to modulate plasticity on a given synapse based on nonlocal information present in other synapses. Similar to an astrocyte cell, the meta-neuron is also connected to all presynaptic neurons and can access all the information transmitted in the two-layered network. Based on both the local and global information available to the meta-neuron, a meta-neuron-based learning rule has been developed that updates weights in the network to produce precise shifts in the spike times of output neurons. The meta-neuron based learning rule is then used to develop an online meta-neuron-based learning algorithm (OMLA) that can be used to learn from input spike patterns in one shot.

In the next two sections, we provide a description of the architecture for OMLA and its learning algorithm, respectively.

10.4.2.1. *Spiking neural network with a meta-neuron*

The architecture of the SNN with a meta-neuron consists of two layers with an arbitrary number of neurons in each layer. But, to support easier understanding, let us consider a network with m presynaptic neurons and a single postsynaptic neuron. The presynaptic neurons in the network are also connected to a meta-neuron, which allows this neuron to access the information present in spikes generated by the presynaptic neurons. Furthermore, the meta-neuron has access to the global information in the network in the form of synaptic weights between pre- and postsynaptic neurons. Figure 10.9 shows the architecture of the SNN with a meta-neuron.

The first layer in the SNN is used to present m-dimensional spike patterns, $\mathbf{x} = \{x_1, \ldots, x_i, \ldots, x_m\}$, to the network. Each spike pattern is presented to the network for a duration of time T, which is termed as the simulation interval of a single spike pattern. Here, $x_i = \{t_i^{(1)}, \ldots, t_i^{(g)}, \ldots, t^{(G_i)}\}$ is a spike train with G_i spikes, which are generated by the ith presynaptic neuron. The unweighted postsynaptic potential (PSP) resulting from the gth spike generated by the ith presynaptic neuron at time t is denoted by $\epsilon(t - t_i^{(g)})$, which has been modeled using the spike response function [5] given by

$$\epsilon(s) = \frac{s}{\tau} \exp\left(1 - \frac{s}{\tau}\right) \qquad (10.41)$$

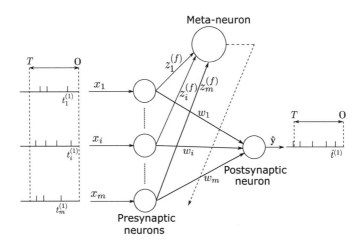

Figure 10.9: Architecture of the two-layered SNN with a meta-neuron.

where τ is the time constant of the neuron and is set to 3 ms for all simulations involving SNN with a meta-neuron. Depending on the PSP contributed by the presynaptic neurons, the PSP (v) of the postsynaptic neuron at time t is computed as

$$v(t) = \sum_i \sum_g w_i \epsilon \left(t - t_i^{(g)} \right) \qquad (10.42)$$

where w_i is the weight of the connection between the ith presynaptic neuron and the postsynaptic neuron. The postsynaptic neuron generates a spike whenever its potential crosses a certain threshold, which is denoted by θ. After generating a spike, the potential of the neuron is reset to zero. The output of the postsynaptic neuron is denoted by $\hat{y} = \{\hat{t}^{(1)}, \dots, \hat{t}^{(f)}, \dots\}$. The aim of the learning algorithm for the SNN with a meta-neuron is to accurately capture the relationship between the input spike patterns and the desired output spike patterns. For this purpose, the weights of the postsynaptic neuron are updated individually for each output spike generated by this postsynaptic neuron. Suppose that $t^{(f)}$ represents the desired spike time of the fth spike generated by the postsynaptic neuron; then the weights of the neuron are updated such that it spikes precisely at $t^{(f)}$.

The postsynaptic neuron will generate a spike at $t^{(f)}$ when its potential is equal to θ at $t^{(f)}$. Therefore, the weights of the postsynaptic neuron should be updated such that the resulting change in potential ($\Delta v^{(f)}$) is equal to

$$\Delta v^{(f)} = \theta - v^{(f)}. \qquad (10.43)$$

By definition, only the presynaptic spikes in the interval $\Gamma = [\hat{t}^{(f-1)}, t^{(f)}]$ will have an impact on the time of the fth output spike generated by the postsynaptic neuron. Therefore, the weights of the postsynaptic neuron are updated such that

$$\sum_i \sum_{t_i^{(g)} \in \Gamma} \Delta w_i \epsilon (t^{(f)} - t_i^{(g)}) = \Delta v^{(f)} \tag{10.44}$$

where Δw_i represents the change in weight of the connection between the ith presynaptic neuron and the postsynaptic neuron.

For a particular output spike, the value of Δw_i is estimated based on the contribution of the ith presynaptic neuron toward $\Delta v^{(f)}$. For this purpose, the meta-neuron uses both the local and global information in the network to estimate a weight sensitivity modulation factor $(M_i^{(f)})$ for each connection between the pre- and postsynaptic neurons. It is used to estimate the proportion of $\Delta v^{(f)}$ that is contributed by the ith presynaptic neuron.

Based on $\Delta v^{(f)}$ (Eq. (10.43)) and $M_i^{(f)}$, the weight of the connection between the ith presynaptic neuron and the postsynaptic neuron is updated as

$$\Delta w_i = M_i^{(f)} \frac{\Delta v^{(f)}}{\sum_{t_i^{(g)} \in \Gamma} \epsilon (t^{(f)} - t_i^{(g)})}, \qquad i \in \{1, \ldots, m\}. \tag{10.45}$$

Here, $M_i^{(f)}$ is computed by the meta-neuron as the proportion of its PSP at $t^{(f)}$ that is contributed by the ith presynaptic neuron, given by

$$M_i^{(f)} = \frac{\sum_{t_i^{(g)} \in \Gamma} z_i^{(f)} \epsilon (t^{(f)} - t_i^{(g)})}{\sum_i \sum_{t_i^{(g)} \in \Gamma} z_i^{(f)} \epsilon (t^{(f)} - t_i^{(g)})}, \qquad i \in \{1, \ldots, m\} \tag{10.46}$$

where $z_i^{(f)}$ is the weight of the connection between the ith presynaptic neuron and the meta-neuron. The meta-neuron estimates its weights by comparing the information present in a given input spike pattern with the knowledge stored in the corresponding synaptic weights. While updating the weights due to a given output spike, the weight of the connection between the ith presynaptic neuron and the meta-neuron is given by

$$z_i^{(f)} = \begin{cases} u_i^{(f)}(t^{(f)}) - w_i & \text{if } u_i^{(f)}(t^{(f)}) > w_i \\ 0 & \text{otherwise.} \end{cases} \tag{10.47}$$

Here, $u_i^{(f)}$ represents the information present in the input spike pattern generated by the ith presynaptic neuron. It is termed as the normalized PSP contributed by the ith presynaptic neuron at $t^{(f)}$, given by

$$u_i^{(f)}(t^{(f)}) = \frac{\sum_{t_i^{(g)} \in \Gamma} \epsilon (t^{(f)} - t_i^{(g)})}{\sum_i \sum_{t_i^{(g)} \in \Gamma} \epsilon (t^{(f)} - t_i^{(g)})}, \qquad i \in \{1, \ldots, m\}. \tag{10.48}$$

It is evident from Eq. (10.47) that the weights between a given presynaptic neuron and the meta-neuron are initialized to zero when the normalized PSP induced by the particular presynaptic neuron for the current input spike pattern at $t^{(f)}$ is lower than w_i. This implies that the weight sensitivity modulation factor will also be zero for these presynaptic neurons, and hence, their weights will not be updated. This selective update mechanism of the meta-neuron based learning rule is similar to the selective plasticity exhibited by astrocyte cells in the brain.

The general idea behind computing $M_i^{(f)}$ using Eq. (10.46) is to induce a higher change in the weight of the neurons that contributed higher PSP to the postsynaptic neuron, and vice versa. Additionally, this also ensures that $\sum_i M_i^{(f)} = 1$, which guarantees that the change in weight will alter the PSP of the postsynaptic neuron at $t^{(f)}$ by $\Delta v^{(f)}$, thereby making sure that it fires precisely at $t^{(f)}$.

The meta-neuron based learning rule (Eq. (10.45)) is a general learning rule that can be used to perform a one-shot weight update in a network such that the spike times of the postsynaptic neuron are precisely shifted. This renders the meta-neuron based learning rule suitable for online learning.

10.4.2.2. *Online meta-neuron-based learning algorithm*

The online meta-neuron-based learning algorithm (OMLA) is developed for a two-layered SNN described in Section 10.4.2.1. It learns from the input spike patterns in an online manner, i.e., each spike pattern is presented to the network only once. The predicted class for a given spike pattern is determined based on the output neuron that spikes first. For this purpose, the learning algorithm updates the synaptic weights in the network to ensure that the output neuron associated with the correct class generates the first spike at the target firing time (T_{ID}). T_{ID} is set to a fixed time instant in the simulation interval. For the other class neurons, the target firing time is set to $T + \delta$, which implies that the other class neurons should not generate any spike within the simulation interval.

OMLA utilizes the meta-neuron-based learning rule to update the weights and evolve the network in an online manner. For every spike pattern, it chooses one of three learning strategies, namely a neuron addition strategy, a delete spike pattern, and a parameter update strategy. The appropriate learning strategy is chosen based on the information present in the network and the knowledge present in the input spike pattern.

To learn effectively in an online manner, OMLA stores past spike patterns that were learned by adding a neuron to the network (neuron addition strategy). While adding neurons for subsequent spike patterns, these pseudo-inputs (spike patterns in the meta-neuron memory) are used by the learning algorithm for better approximation of the past knowledge stored in the network.

Without loss of generality, it is assumed that the network has K output neurons which were added to the network while learning the spike patterns $\mathbf{X}_1, \ldots, \mathbf{x}_h, \ldots, \mathbf{x}_K$. At this stage, the meta-neuron's memory consists of these

K spike patterns that were used to add the K neurons. The learning algorithm is described below for the current input spike pattern **x** from class c that is presented to the network for learning. The description below uses CC (CC implies correct class) to represent the output neuron from class c that has minimum latency. Suppose that c_j represents the class associated with the jth output neuron; then CC is given by

$$CC = \operatorname*{argmin}_{j,c_j=c} \hat{t}_j^{(1)}. \tag{10.49}$$

Similarly, MC is used to represent the neuron from any other class that has minimum latency and is given by

$$MC = \operatorname*{argmin}_{j,c_j \neq c} \hat{t}_j^{(1)}. \tag{10.50}$$

Since the learning algorithm only uses the first spike to determine the predicted class, the following description represents $\hat{t}_j^{(1)}$ and $t_j^{(1)}$ as $\hat{t}_j$ and t_j, respectively. Similarly, normalized PSP contributed by the ith presynaptic neuron is represented by u_i instead of $u_i^{(1)}$. Next, the different learning strategies in OMLA are described in detail.

- **Neuron addition strategy**: In this strategy, a new neuron is added to the network to learn the information present in an input spike pattern that contains a significant amount of new information. For this purpose, the learning algorithm considers the interval between T_{ID} and $\hat{t}_{CC}$. A high value of this interval ($T_{ID} \ll \hat{t}_{CC}$) implies that the knowledge stored in the network is not enough to closely approximate the information present in the current input spike pattern. A fixed time instant ($T_n \in [T_{ID}, T]$) is used as a threshold for $\hat{t}_{CC}$ to develop a heuristic criterion for this strategy, which is given by

$$\textbf{If } \hat{t}_{CC} < T_n \tag{10.51}$$

$$\textbf{Then } \text{a neuron is added to the network} \tag{10.52}$$

where T_n is given by

$$T_n = \alpha_n T + (1 - \alpha_n) T_{ID}. \tag{10.53}$$

Here, α_n is termed as the novelty threshold and is always set to a value in the range [0.7, 1]. See [30] for more details.

The weights of the connections between the ith presynaptic neuron and the output neuron are initialized according to the normalized PSP (Eq. (10.48)) contributed by the ith presynaptic neuron at T_{ID}. Hence, the weight of the connection between the ith presynaptic neuron and the newly added neuron is given by

$$w_{i(K+1)} = u_i(T_{ID}) \tag{10.54}$$

Based on the initial value of weights, the threshold of the newly added neuron is given by

$$\theta_{(K+1)} = \sum_i \sum_g w_{i(K+1)} \epsilon (T_{ID} - t_i^{(g)}) \tag{10.55}$$

The initialization of weights and threshold in this manner ensures that the newly added neuron fires precisely at T_{ID}. After adding a new neuron, the learning algorithm considers the responses of this neuron on pseudo-inputs (past spike patterns in meta-neuron memory) representing past knowledge stored in the network. These pseudo-inputs are used to update the weights of the newly added neuron such that it accurately approximates the past knowledge stored in the network.

Let us assume that $\hat{t}_{K+1}^{[h]}$ is the time of the first spike generated by the newly added neuron for the hth spike pattern in the meta-neuron memory. When $\hat{t}_{K+1}^{[h]}$ is closer to $\hat{t}_h^{[h]}$, the weights of the newly added neuron are updated such that it fires late for samples from class c_h. For this purpose, a fixed time duration T_m is used to develop a criterion for updating the weights of the newly added neuron, given as

$$\textbf{If } (\hat{t}_{K+1}^{[h]} - \hat{t}_h^{[h]}) < T_m, \quad h \in \{1, \ldots, K\}, c_h \neq c_{K+1} \tag{10.56}$$

$$\textbf{Then } \text{update the weights of the } (K+1)^{th} \text{ neuron} \tag{10.57}$$

where T_m is given by

$$T_m = \alpha_m (T - T_{ID}). \tag{10.58}$$

Here, α_m is termed as the margin threshold and is always initialized to a value in the interval [0, 1]. A network trained with a value of α_m closer to 0 may not generalize well on unseen spike patterns due to lower interclass margins. Conversely, a network trained with a value of α_m closer to 1 may not be able to accurately approximate the relationship between the input spike patterns and the desired output. Based on the experimental analysis of OMLA, it was concluded that a suitable range for setting α_m is [0, 0.3]. For details of the experimental analysis, please refer to the work [30]. All results in this chapter on the performance of OMLA use a value of 0.3 for α_m.

The weights of the newly added neuron are updated using the meta-neuron based learning rule and the desired time of the first spike $(\hat{t}_{K+1}^{[h]})$ for the hth spike pattern in meta-neuron memory is given by

$$\hat{t}_{K+1}^{[h]} = \hat{t}_h^{[h]} + T_m \tag{10.59}$$

• **Delete spike pattern strategy**: In this strategy, the learning algorithm deletes a spike pattern when a correct class neuron fires close to T_{ID}. This indicates that the current input spike pattern doesn't contain novel information with regard to the knowledge stored in the network. This prevents OMLA from over-fitting and hence performs better on unseen spike patterns. For this strategy, OMLA uses a fixed time instant $T_d \in [T_{ID}, T]$ to develop a heuristic criterion, which is given by

$$\textbf{If } \hat{t}_{CC} < T_d \& (\hat{t}_{MC} - \hat{t}_{CC}) \geq T_m \tag{10.60}$$

$$\textbf{Then } \text{the current input spike pattern is deleted} \tag{10.61}$$

where T_d is given by

$$T_d = \alpha_d T + (1 - \alpha_d) T_{ID}. \tag{10.62}$$

Here, α_d is set to 0.25 for all simulations. See [30] for more details.

- **Parameter update strategy**: The learning algorithm uses this strategy for learning when the criteria for both of the above-mentioned strategies are not satisfied. The goal of this learning strategy is to update the weights of the neuron CC such that it fires closer to T_{ID}. Furthermore, the weights of the neuron MC are updated such that there is a higher time difference between $\hat{t}_{CC}$ and $\hat{t}_{MC}$. The weights of the neuron CC are updated using the meta-neuron based learning rule only when $\hat{t}_{CC}$ is higher than T_d. In this case, the desired time of the first spike (t_{CC}) of the neuron CC for the current input spike pattern (**x**) after the weight update is given by

$$t_{CC} = \hat{t}_{CC} - \alpha_s \hat{t}_{CC} \tag{10.63}$$

where α_s is termed as the learning rate and is always set to a value in the interval $[0, 0.1]$.

To improve the interclass margin between $\hat{t}_{CC}$ and $\hat{T}_{MC}$, the weights of the neuron MC are updated using the meta-neuron based learning rule. For this purpose, the desired time of the first spike for MC is given by

$$\hat{t}_{MC} = t_{CC} + T_m \tag{10.64}$$

The three learning strategies together allow OMLA to learn input spike patterns in one shot. The pseudo-code for OMLA is given in Algorithm 10.3. The next section presents the architecture and the learning algorithm for the SEFRON classifier.

10.4.3. *Synaptic Efficacy Function-Based Neuron (SEFRON)*

In this section, we will describe the STDP-based learning algorithm to train a single output neuron classifier with a time-varying weight models. A spiking neuron with time-varying weight models is referred to as SEFRON (Synaptic Efficacy Function based neuRON). The architecture of the SEFRON classifier has two layers (input

---

Algorithm 10.3 Pseudo-code for online meta-neuron based learning algorithm

---

1: **for** each training spike pattern **do**
2:      $\hat{t}_{CC} \leftarrow$ spike time of same class neurons with minimum latency
3:      $\hat{t}_{MC} \leftarrow$ spike time of different class neurons with minimum latency
4:      **if** $\hat{t}_{CC} > T_n$ **then**
5:          Add a neuron
6:      **else if** $(\hat{t}_{CC} \leq T_d)$ & $(\hat{t}_{MC} - \hat{t}_{CC}) \geq T_m$ **then**
7:          Delete the spike pattern
8:      **else**
9:          **if** $\hat{t}_{CC} > T_d$ **then**
10:              Update the CC neuron
11:          **if** $(\hat{t}_{MC} - t_{CC}) < T_m$ **then**
12:              Update the MC neuron

---

and output). The normalized form of STDP is used to train the classifier. Training an SNN with time-varying weight models is not exactly the same as training an SNN with constant weight models. The weight update (single value) determined for a given input pattern must be embedded in a function before updating the time-varying weights.

10.4.3.1. *Architecture of SEFRON*

SEFRON has two layers. Real-valued inputs are converted into spike patterns using some encoding scheme. In SEFRON, the first layer is considered the spike input layer and the second layer is considered the spike output layer. The input and output neurons are connected by the time-varying weights. The architecture of SEFRON with population encoding is shown in Figure 10.10

In a SEFRON classifier, let θ be the firing threshold. The postsynaptic potential $v(t)$ increases or decreases for every presynaptic spike. The output neuron fires a postsynaptic spike $\hat{t}$ when the postsynaptic potential $v(t)$ crosses its firing threshold θ.

$$\hat{t} = \left\{ t | v(t) = \theta \right\} \tag{10.65}$$

Here, the postsynaptic potential $v(t)$ of the output neuron is determined as

$$v(t) = \sum_{i \in \{1,m\}} \sum_{r \in \{1,q\}} w_i^r(s_i^r).\epsilon(t - s_i^r).H(t - s_i^r) \tag{10.66}$$

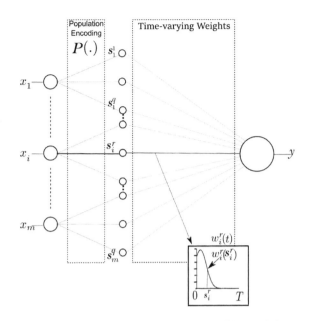

Figure 10.10: Architecture or multiclass SEFRON with population encoding.

where $H(t)$ represents a Heaviside step function and $\epsilon(t)$ is the spike response function, given below [28]:

$$\epsilon(t) = \frac{t}{\tau}.exp\left(1 - \frac{t}{\tau}\right) \tag{10.67}$$

The term $w_i^r\left(s_i^r\right)$ is the momentary weight and is obtained by sampling the time-varying weight function $w_i^r(t)$ at the instant s_i^r as shown in Figure 10.10. $w_i^r(t)$ is the time-varying weight between the rth RF neuron of the ith input feature and the output neuron. The time-varying function $w_i^r(t)$ is also set to $[0, T]$ms.

10.4.3.2. *Learning rule to train SEFRON*

In SEFRON's learning rule, the error between the 'actual' postsynaptic spike time $(\hat{t}_a)$ and the 'reference' postsynaptic spike time $(\hat{t}_{rf})$ is minimized using a modified STDP rule. The steps of SEFRON's learning rule are briefly explained. First, the STDP rule is used to determine the fractional contribution of presynaptic spikes $u_i^r(\hat{t})$ for a given postsynaptic spike time $\hat{t}$. Next, $u_i^r(\hat{t})$ is used to determine the postsynaptic potential due to the fractional contribution $V_{STDP}(\hat{t})$. Next, the error function is defined as the difference in the ratio of θ to $V_{STDP}(\hat{t})$ at the reference and actual postsynaptic spike times. Finally, the error is embedded in a Gaussian distribution function centered at the current presynaptic spike time to update the time-varying weight.

The general STDP learning rule in Eq. (10.18) is used in a normalized form to compute the fractional contribution $u_i^r(\hat{t})$ of the presynaptic spike s_i^r for a given postsynaptic spike $\hat{t}$. The fractional contribution $u_i^r(\hat{t})$ is calculated as

$$u_i^r(\hat{t}) = \begin{cases} \dfrac{\delta w(\hat{t} - s_i^r)}{\sum_{i=1}^{m} \sum_{r=1}^{q} \delta w(\hat{t} - s_i^r)} & \text{for all } s_i^r \leq \hat{t} \\ 0 & \text{for all } s_i^r > \hat{t} \end{cases} \tag{10.68}$$

For classification problems, only the first postsynaptic spike is important. Therefore the presynaptic spikes fired after the first postsynaptic spike are ignored. Hence, A_- is assumed to be 0 in the SEFRON's learning rule. The term $u_i^r(\hat{t})$ is independent of variable A_+ and depends only on the plasticity window τ_+. The sum of $u_i^r(\hat{t})$ is equal to 1.

$$\sum_{i=1}^{m} \sum_{r=1}^{q} u_i^r(\hat{t}) = 1 \tag{10.69}$$

The fractional contribution indicates the influence of a presynaptic spike in firing a postsynaptic spike. A higher value of $u_i^r(\hat{t})$ indicates that the presynaptic spike at s_i^r has more influence in firing an output spike at $\hat{t}$. This is the characteristic of the STDP learning rule, where the presynaptic spikes closer to the postsynaptic spike will have higher weight update.

$V_{\text{STDP}}(\hat{t})$ is determined using $u_i^r(\hat{t})$. $V_{\text{STDP}}(\hat{t})$ is interpreted as the postsynaptic potential at $\hat{t}$ if the fractional contribution from the STDP rule $u_i^r(\hat{t})$ is used instead of the weight $w_i^r(s_i^r)$. $V_{\text{STDP}}(\hat{t})$ is determined by replacing $w_i^r(s_i^r)$ in Eq. (10.66) with $u_i^r(\hat{t}_r)$:

$$V_{\text{STDP}}(\hat{t}) = \sum_{i=1}^{m} \sum_{r=1}^{q} u_i^r(\hat{t}) . \epsilon(\hat{t} - s_i^r) . H(t - s_i^r) \tag{10.70}$$

It must be noted that $V_{\text{STDP}}(\hat{t})$ is not always equal to the firing threshold (θ) (except in the ideal case). The variations in the input data and the weight $w_i^r(s_i^r)$ may have caused the difference. The overall strength (γ) is used to adjust the difference between $V_{\text{STDP}}(\hat{t})$ and θ. γ is the overall strength required by all the connections to make the firing possible at time $\hat{t}$ if $u_i^r(\hat{t})$ is used to determine the postsynaptic potential.

$$\theta = \gamma . V_{\text{STDP}}(\hat{t}) = \gamma . \sum_{i=1}^{m} \sum_{r=1}^{q} u_i^r(\hat{t}) . \epsilon(\hat{t} - s_i^r) . H(t - s_i^r) \tag{10.71}$$

where the overall strength γ is calculated as

$$\gamma = \frac{\theta}{V_{\text{STDP}}(\hat{t})} . \tag{10.72}$$

In supervised learning, a reference signal is used to move the actual output toward the desired value. In SEFRON, the reference signal and actual outputs are the reference postsynaptic spike time $(\hat{t}_{rf})$, and the actual postsynaptic spike time $(\hat{t})$, respectively. The error between $\hat{t}_{rf}$ and $\hat{t}$ is used to update the time-varying weights in SEFRON. The error between $\hat{t}_{rf}$ and $\hat{t}$ is defined using the overall strength required to fire a postsynaptic spike at $\hat{t}_{rf}$ and $\hat{t}$.

$$err = \gamma_{rf} - \gamma_a = \frac{\theta}{V_{STDP}(\hat{t}_{rf})} - \frac{\theta}{V_{STDP}(\hat{t}_a)} \tag{10.73}$$

where γ_{rf} and γ_a are the overall strengths required to fire a postsynaptic spike at the reference and actual postsynaptic spike times, respectively.

This error err is used to determine the weight update. It can be noted by comparing Eqs. (10.66) and (10.71) that the momentary weight is equal to the product of overall strength and fractional contribution for the ideal case. ($w_i^r(s_i^r) = \gamma . u_i^r(\hat{t})$). Hence, multiplying the error err by the fractional contribution for the reference postsynaptic spike time $u_i^r(\hat{t}_{rf})$ ensures that the weight is updated in a directions toward the ideal momentary weight. This indicates that subsequently the actual postsynaptic spike time $(\hat{t}_a)$ also moves in a directions toward the reference postsynaptic spike time $(\hat{t}_{rf})$.

Two steps are involved in determining the time-varying weight update. First, the single-value weight update is determined using err. Next, that single value is embedded in a time-varying function to determine the time-varying weight update. Let $\triangle w_i^r(s_i^r)$ be the single-value weight update. $\triangle w_i^r(s_i^r)$ is determined by multiplying err by $\hat{t}_{rf}$:

$$\triangle w_i^r(s_i^r) = \lambda . u_i^r(\hat{t}_{rf}) . err, \tag{10.74}$$

where λ is the learning rate and is usually set to a smaller value.

The single-value weight update $\triangle w_i^r(s_i^r)$ is computed for a given input pattern. Next, $\triangle w_i^r(s_i^r)$ is embedded in a time-varying function. The time-varying function should ensure that the weight update is similar to other input patterns that are similar to the current pattern. Hence, a Gaussian function is used to embed the weight update. The weight update $\triangle w_i^r(s_i^r)$ at the presynaptic spike time s_i^r is embedded in a time-varying function $g_i^r(t)$ as

$$g_i^r(t) = \triangle w_i^r(s_i^r) . exp\left(\frac{-(t - s_i^r)^2}{2\sigma^2}\right), \tag{10.75}$$

where σ is the efficacy update range. σ determines the temporal neighborhood region affected by the weight update. A smaller value for σ updates smaller temporal neighbours. Hence, more variation in the data distributions can be captured. On the other hand, an infinite value for σ updates all the weights in the interval and subsequently will result in a constant function. This constant function is similar to a constant weight model.

The time-varying weight $w_i^r(t)$ is updated by adding $g_i^r(t)$ to $w_i^r(t)$.

$$w_i^r(t)_{\text{new}} = w_i^r(t)_{\text{old}} + g_i^r(t). \tag{10.76}$$

It can be noted that the updated $w_i^r(t)_{\text{new}}$ may have both positive and negative values. This imitates the GABA-switch phenomenon observed in a biological neuron.

10.4.3.3. SEFRON for the classification problem

Only the first actual postsynaptic spike $\hat{t}$ is used for the classification task and the subsequent postsynaptic spikes are ignored. In the case of no postsynaptic spike firing, the firing time of the postsynaptic spike is taken as the end of the simulation time.

Let $\hat{t}_b$ be the classification boundary referred to as the boundary spike time. The output class label for an input pattern is determined by the sign of the difference between $\hat{t}$ and $\hat{t}_b$. If $\hat{t}$ is fired before $\hat{t}_b$ it belongs to class 1, otherwise it belongs to class 2.

Initialization: In SEFRON, the first sample from the training dataset is used to initialize $w_i^r(t)$ and θ. Let $\hat{t}_d^1$ and $\hat{t}_d^2$ be the desired postsynaptic spike time for class 1 and class 2, respectively. The overall strength γ required to make the firing possible is assumed to be 1 for the first sample. Hence θ is set to the value of $V_{\text{STDP}}(\hat{t}_d)$ using Eq. (10.71).

$$\theta = \sum_{i=1}^{m} \sum_{r=1}^{q} u_i^r(\hat{t}_d).\epsilon(\hat{t}_d - s_i^r).H(\hat{t}_d - s_i^r). \tag{10.77}$$

Here, $\hat{t}_d$ is the desired firing time of the first sample. $\hat{t}_d$ can be either $\hat{t}_d^1$ or $\hat{t}_d^2$. It can be noted from Eq. (10.65) and (10.66) that the postsynaptic potential at $\hat{t}_d$ must be equal to the firing threshold for the first sample to make the postsynaptic firing possible.

$$\theta = v(\hat{t}_d) = \sum_{i=1}^{m} \sum_{r=1}^{q} w_i^r(s_i^r).\epsilon(\hat{t}_d - s_i^r).H(\hat{t}_d - s_i^r). \tag{10.78}$$

It can be noted by comparing Eqs. (10.77) and (10.78), that the initial momentary weight $w_i^r(s_i^r)$ must be equal to $u_i^r(\hat{t}_d)$. Using this similarity, the time-varying weight is initialized by embedding $u_i^r(\hat{t}_d)$ in a Gaussian distribution function.

$$w_i^r(t)_{\text{initial}} = u_i^r(\hat{t}_d).exp\left(\frac{-(t - s_i^r)^2}{2\sigma^2}\right). \tag{10.79}$$

During training, only the reference postsynaptic spike time is required to be determined to update the weights. The desired postsynaptic spike time is used as the reference postsynaptic spike time. $\hat{t}_{rf} = \hat{t}_d^1$ for samples from class 1 and $\hat{t}_{rf} = \hat{t}_d^s$ for samples from class 2, respectively.

10.5. Performance Evaluation

In this section, the performance of SpikeProp, SWAT, SEFRON, TMM-SNN, and OMLA has been evaluated and compared using 10 benchmark datasets from the UCI machine learning repository [44]. The results for all the algorithms were evaluated on the same training and testing splits. Table 10.1 shows details of the different datasets. All the experiments were conducted in a MATLAB 2019a environment using a 64-bit Windows 10 operating system. Table 10.2 shows the results of a performance evaluation for all the learning algorithms used for the comparison.

From Table 10.2, it can be observed that all the learning algorithms except SWAT have similar performances for simple multiclass classification problems such as Iris, Wine, and Acoustic Emission. SWAT performs 5–7% lower than the best performing algorithm. Similarly, a comparable performance is obtained for all the learning algorithms excluding SWAT on simple binary problems such as breast cancer and Echocardiogram. The performance of SWAT is 2–4% lower than that of the best performing algorithm.

For low-dimensional binary classification problems with high interclass overlap such as Mammogram and PIMA, the evolving learning algorithms TMM-SNN and OMLA achieve the best performance due to their evolving nature. The performance of SEFRON and SpikeProp is similar to one another and is 2–4% lower than the performance of the best performing algorithm. SWAT has the highest error

Table 10.1: Description of the dataset used for validation.

Dataset	No. Features	No. Classes	No.Samples Training	Testing
Iris	4	3	75	75
Wine	13	3	60	118
Acoustic emission	5	4	62	137
Breast cancer	9	2	350	333
Echo-cardiogram	10	2	66	65
Mammogram	9	2	80	11
Liver	6	2	170	175
PIMA	8	2	384	384
Ionosphere	34	2	175	176
Hepatitis	19	2	78	77

Table 10.2:   Performance comparison of UCI datasets.

Dataset	Method	Architecture	Training Accuracy (%)	Testing Accuracy (%)
Iris	SpikeProp	4-25-10-3	97.2(1.9)	96.7(1.6)
	SWAT	4-24-312-3	96.7(1.4)	92.4(1.7)
	TMM-SNN	4-24-(4-7)-3	97.5(0.8)	97.2(1.0)
	OMLA	4-24-(5-7)	97.9(0.7)	97.9(0.7)
Wine	SpikeProp	13-79-10-3	99.2(1.2)	96.8(1.6)
	SWAT	13-78-1014-3	98.6(1.1)	92.3(2.4)
	TMM-SNN	13-78-3-3	100(0)	97.5(0.8)
	OMLA	13-78-(3-6)	98.5(1.0)	97.9(0.7)
Acoustic Emission	SpikeProp	5-31-10-4	98.5(1.7)	97.2(3.5)
	SWAT	5-30-390-4	93.1(2.3)	91.5(2.3)
	TMM-SNN	5-30-(4-7)-4	97.6(1.3)	97.5(0.7)
	OMLA	5-30-(4-9)	99.2(0.8)	98.3(1.0)
Breast Cancer	SpikeProp	9-55-15-2	97.3(0.6)	97.2(0.6)
	SWAT	9-54-702-2	96.5(0.5)	95.8(1.0)
	TMM-SNN	9-54-(2-8)-2	97.4(0.3)	97.2(0.5)
	OMLA	9-54-2	97.4(0.4)	97.8(0.4)
	SEFRON	9-55-1	98.3(0.8)	96.4(0.7)
Breast Cancer	SpikeProp	9-55-15-2	97.3(0.6)	97.2(0.6)
	SWAT	9-54-702-2	96.5(0.5)	95.8(1.0)
	TMM-SNN	9-54-(2-8)-2	97.4(0.3)	97.2(0.5)
	OMLA	9-54-2	97.4(0.4)	97.8(0.4)
	SEFRON	9-55-1	98.3(0.8)	96.4(0.7)
Echocardiogram	SpikeProp	10-61-10-2	86.6(2.5)	84.5(3.0)
	SWAT	10-60-780-2	90.6(1.8)	81.8(2.8)
	TMM-SNN	10-60-(2-3)-2	86.5(2.1)	85.4(1.7)
	OMLA	10-60-(6-10)	89.6(1.5)	86.3(0.9)
	SEFRON	10-61-1	88.6(3.9)	86.5(3.3)
Mammogram	SpikeProp	9-55-10-2	82.8(4.7)	81.8(6.1)
	SWAT	9-54-702-2	82.6(2.1)	78.2(12.3)
	TMM-SNN	9-54-(5-7)-2	87.2(4.4)	84.9(8.6)
	OMLA	9-54-(14-20)	88.6(2.0)	85.5(4.1)
	SEFRON	9-55-1	92.8(5)	82.7(10)
Liver	SpikeProp	6-37-15-2	71.5(5.2)	65.1(4.7)
	SWAT	6-36-468-2	74.8(2.1)	60.9(3.2)
	TMM-SNN	6-36-(5-8)-2	74.2(3.5)	70.4(2.0)
	OMLA	6-36-(12-15)	69.9(2.3)	67.7(1.8)
	SEFRON	6-37-1	91.5(5.4)	67.7(1.3)
PIMA	SpikeProp	8-49-20-2	78.6(2.5)	76.2(1.8)
	SWAT	8-48-702-2	77.0(2.1)	72.1(1.8)

(Continued)

Table 10.2: *(Continued)*

Dataset	Method	Architecture	Training Accuracy (%)	Testing Accuracy (%)
	TMM-SNN	8-48-(5-14)-2	79.7(2.3)	78.1(1.7)
	OMLA	8-48-20	78.6(1.7)	77.9(1.0)
	SEFRON	8-49-1	78.4(2.5)	77.3(1.3)
Ionosphere	SpikeProp	34-205-25-2	89.0(7.9)	86.5(7.2)
	SWAT	34-204-2652-2	86.5(6.7)	90.0(2.3)
	TMM-SNN	34-204-(23-34)-2	98.7(0.4)	92.4(1.8)
	OMLA	34-204-(19-25)	94.0(1.7)	93.5(0.5)
	SEFRON	34-205-1	97.0(2.5)	88.9(1.7)
Hepatitis	SpikeProp	19-115-15-2	87.8(5.0)	83.5(2.5)
	SWAT	19-114-1482-2	86.0(2.1)	83.1(2.2)
	TMM-SNN	19-114-(3-9)-2	91.2(2.5)	86.6(2.2)
	OMLA	19-114-12	89.8(2.9)	87.4(2.4)
	SEFRON	19-115-1	94.6(3.5)	82.7(3.3)

rate among all the learning algorithms. Its performance is 6–7% lower than that of the best performing algorithm, which indicates that it's not able to accurately identify the discriminative features of classes with high interclass overlap. For the low-dimensional binary classification problem of Liver, TMM-SNN is the best performing algorithm. SEFRON, OMLA, and SpikeProp have similar performance which are 3–5% lower than the performance of TMM-SNN. SWAT has the highest error rate. Its performance is 10% lower than the performance of TMM-SNN.

The performances of the different learning algorithms have also been studied for high-dimensional datasets such as Ionosphere and Hepatitis. For both of these datasets, the best performance was achieved using TMM-SNN and OMLA whose performances were comparable to one another. Furthermore, in the case of the Hepatitis dataset, all the other algorithms had similar performances, which is 3–5% lower than the best performing learning algorithm. However, for the Ionosphere dataset, the performance of other algorithms exhibited higher variability. In this case, the performances of SEFRON and SWAT are similar to one another and are 2–4% lower than the performances of the best performing algorithm. SpikeProp has the highest error rate among all the learning algorithms for the Ionosphere dataset. Its performance is 6–7% lower than the performances of TMM-SNN and OMLA.

Overall, it can be observed that the evolving learning algorithms of TMM-SNN and OMLA allow them to closely approximate the relationship between the input spike patterns and the desired outputs for the datasets used in the evaluation. SEFRON and SpikeProp are the next better-performing algorithms in most cases whereas SWAT has the highest error rate for most problems.

10.6. Summary and Future Directions

Recently, SNNs have gained a lot of traction due to their biological plausibility and energy efficiency. This chapter focuses on the fundamentals of SNNs in a supervised learning framework to provide an effective starting point for new researchers.

Compared to traditional deep neural networks, deep spiking neural networks are in a nascent stage. In a deep neural network, the errors associated with output neurons are backpropagated to the input layer to update network parameters for minimizing the errors. Biologically inspired learning rules for SNNs provide a mechanism for learning in shallow networks, which alleviates the need for back-propagation. These approaches include SNNs that contain multiple layers but only a single layer has learned parameters [28, 30]. Other layers are used for encoding, feature extractions or other pre-processing steps [45, 46]. To enable backpropagation of errors in deep SNNs, biological learning rules have been combined with gradient descent [47, 48]. However, using gradient descent in SNNs is a challenging problem due to the discontinuity in the response of spiking neurons at the time of spike. To overcome this issue, researchers have developed techniques that replace the output of a spiking neuron with an approximate continuous function [49, 50] or use a proxy to estimate the derivative [51, 52]. Furthermore, silent neurons in SNNs resulting from weight updates during training lead to a sparser forward propagation, which impedes computation of gradient. This could lead to a failure of the training process. This is usually tackled by proper weight initialization or converting a pre-trained deep neural network to SNNs [53, 54].

Despite the above challenges in SNNs, they have been used for many applications. A review of different SNNs for image classification problems is presented in [23]. The inherent temporal input and output in SNNs make them well suited for spatiotemporal processing, thereby increasing their usage in new application areas. This capability of SNNs has been utilized in automatic speech recognition (ASR) where their performance is closer to that of deep neural networks [55–57]. Studies on time series forecasting using SNNs have also shown promising results [58–60]. Several studies have also used SNNs for reinforcement learning [61, 62] but further research is required in this direction. Recently, many techniques have been developed for the explainability of machine learning tools but this is yet to be explored in SNNs. The biological proximity of SNNs might help improve our understanding of the brain.

Another interesting direction involving SNNs is their hardware realization, which has been accelerated by the availability of neuromorphic chips [63, 64] that enable realization of arbitrary SNN architectures in hardware. These chips enable faster deployment of SNNs for edge computing due to their lower energy needs and offer tremendous benefits for areas such as autonomous driving, industrial robotics, etc.

References

[1] W. Maass, Noisy spiking neurons with temporal coding have more computational power than sigmoidal neurons, *Institute of Theoretical Computer Science, Technische Universität Graz, Austria, Technical Report* (1999).

[2] H. Markram, W. Gerstner and P. J. Sjöström, *Spike-Timing-Dependent Plasticity: A Comprehensive Overview*, (Frontiers Media SA (2012)).

[3] A. Araque, V. Parpura, R. P. Sanzgiri and P. G. Haydon, Tripartite synapses: glia, the unacknowledged partner, *Trends Neurosci.*, **22**(5), 208–215 (1999).

[4] J. Gautrais and S. Thorpe, Rate coding versus temporal order coding: a theoretical approach, *Biosystems*, **48**(1–3), 57–65 (1998).

[5] S. M. Bohte, J. N. Kok and H. La Poutré, Error-backpropagation in temporally encoded networks of spiking neurons, *Neurocomputing*, **48**, 17–37 (2002).

[6] A. L. Hodgkin and A. F. Huxley, A quantitative description of membrane current, and its application to conduction, and excitation in nerve, *J. Physiol.*, **117**(4), 500–544 (1952).

[7] E. M. Izhikevich, Simple model of spiking neurons, *IEEE Trans. Neural Networks*, **14**(6), 1569–1572 (2003).

[8] R. B. Stein, A theoretical analysis of neuronal variability, *Biophys. J.*, **5**(2), 173–194 (1965).

[9] R. B. Stein, Some models of neuronal variability, *Biophys. J.*, **7**(1), 37–68 (1967).

[10] W. M. Kistler, W. Gerstner and J. Hemmen, Reduction of the Hodgkin-Huxley equations to a single-variable threshold model, *Neural Comput.*, **9**(5), 1015–1045 (1997).

[11] W. Gerstner, Time structure of the activity in neural network models, *Phys. Rev. E*, **51**(1), 738–758 (1995).

[12] T. V. P. Bliss and T. Lømo, Long-lasting potentiation of synaptic transmission in the dentate area of the anaesthetized rabbit following stimulation of the perforant path, *J. Physiol.*, **232**(2), 331–356 (1973).

[13] D. O. Hebb, *The Organization of Behavior: A Neuropsychological Theory*, vol. 63, John Wiley & Sons, New York (1949).

[14] M. Tsodyks and H. Markram, The neural code between neocortical pyramidal neurons depends on neurotransmitter release probability, *PNAS*, **94**(2), 719–723 (1997).

[15] J. S. Dittman, A. C. Kreitzer and W. G. Regehr, Interplay between facilitation, depression,, and residual calcium at three presynaptic terminals, *J. Neurosci.*, **20**(4), 1374–1385 (2000).

[16] K. Ganguly, A. F. Schinder, S. T. Wong and M. M. Poo, GABA itself promotes the developmental switch of neuronal GABAergic responses from excitation to inhibition, *Cell*, **105**(4), 521–532 (2001).

[17] S. W. Lee, Y. B. Kim, J. S. Kim, W. B. Kim, Y. S. Kim, H. C. Han, C. S. Colwell, Y. W. Cho and Y. I. Kim, GABAergic inhibition is weakened or converted into excitation in the oxytocin, and vasopressin neurons of the lactating rat, *Mol. Brain*, **8**(1), 1–9 (2015).

[18] X. Lin, X. Wang and Z. Hao, Supervised learning in multilayer spiking neural networks with inner products of spike trains, *Neurocomputing*, **237**, 59–70 (2017).

[19] S. B. Shrestha and Q. Song, Adaptive learning rate of SpikeProp based on weight convergence analysis, *Neural Networks*, **63**, 185–198 (2015).

[20] B. Schrauwen and J. Van Campenhout, Extending SpikeProp. In *International Joint Conference on Neural Networks*, vol. 1, IEEE, pp. 471–475 (2004).

[21] Y. Xu, X. Zeng, L. Han and J. Yang, A supervised multi-spike learning algorithm based on gradient descent for spiking neural networks, *Neural Networks*, **43**, 99–113 (2013).

[22] H. Mostafa, Supervised learning based on temporal coding in spiking neural networks, *IEEE Trans. Neural Networks Learn. Syst.*, **29**(7), 3227–3235 (2018).

[23] A. Tavanaei, M. Ghodrati, S. R. Kheradpisheh, T. Masquelier and A. Maida, Deep learning in spiking neural networks, *Neural Networks*, **111**, 47–63 (2019).

[24] F. Ponulak and A. Kasiński, Supervised learning in spiking neural networks with resume: sequence learning, classification and spike shifting, *Neural Comput.*, **22** 2), 467–510 (2010).

[25] A. Taherkhani, A. Belatreche, Y. Li and L. P. Maguire, Multi-DL-ReSuMe: multiple neurons delay learning remote supervised method. In *2015 International Joint Conference on Neural Networks (IJCNN)*, IEEE, pp. 1–7 (2015).

[26] M. Zhang, H. Qu, X. Xie and J. Kurths, Supervised learning in spiking neural networks with noise-threshold, *Neurocomputing*, **219**, 333–349 (2017).

[27] I. Sporea and A. Grüning, Supervised learning in multilayer spiking neural networks, *Neural Comput.*, **25**(2), 473–509 (2013).

[28] A. Jeyasothy, S. Sundaram and N. Sundararajan, SEFRON: a new spiking neuron model with time-varying synaptic efficacy function for pattern classification, *IEEE Trans. Neural Networks Learn. Syst.*, **30**(4), 1231–1240 (2019).

[29] J. J. Wade, L. J. Mcdaid, J. A. Santos and H. M. Sayers, SWAT: a spiking neural network training algorithm for classification problems, *IEEE Trans. Neural Networks*, **21**(11), 1817–1830 (2010).

[30] S. Dora, S. Suresh and N. Sundararajan, Online meta-neuron based learning algorithm for a spiking neural classifier, *Inf. Sci.*, **414**, 19–32 (2017).

[31] S. Thorpe and J. Gautrais, Rank order coding. In *Computational Neuroscience: Trends in Research,* Springer US, pp. 113–118 (1998).

[32] S. G. Wysoski, L. Benuskova and N. Kasabov, On-line learning with structural adaptation in a network of spiking neurons for visual pattern recognition. In S. D. Kollias, A. Stafylopatis, W. Duch and E. Oja (eds.) *Artificial Neural Networks — ICANN 2006. ICANN 2006. Lecture Notes in Computer Science*, vol. 4131, Springer, Berlin, Heidelberg, pp. 61–70 (2006).

[33] S. G. Wysoski, L. Benuskova and N. Kasabov, Evolving spiking neural networks for audiovisual information processing, *Neural Networks*, **23**(7), 819–835 (2010).

[34] S. G. Wysoski, L. Benuskova and N. Kasabov, Fast, and adaptive network of spiking neurons for multi-view visual pattern recognition, *Neurocomputing*, **71**(13), 2563–2575 (2008).

[35] N. Kasabov, K. Dhoble, N. Nuntalid and G. Indiveri, Dynamic evolving spiking neural networks for on-line spatio-, and spectro-temporal pattern recognition, *Neural Networks*, **41**, 188–201 (2013).

[36] S. Dora, K. Subramanian, S. Suresh and N. Sundararajan, Development of a self-regulating evolving spiking neural network for classification problem, *Neurocomputing*, **171**, 1216–1229 (2016).

[37] S. Dora, S. Ramasamy and S. Sundaram, A basis coupled evolving spiking neural network with afferent input neurons. In *International Joint Conference on Neural Networks*, pp. 1–8 (2013).

[38] S. Dora, S. Suresh and N. Sundararajan, A sequential learning algorithm for a Minimal Spiking Neural Network (MSNN) classifier. In *International Joint Conference on Neural Networks*, pp. 2415–2421 (2014).

[39] S. Dora, S. Suresh and N. Sundararajan, A sequential learning algorithm for a spiking neural classifier, *Appl. Soft Comput.*, **36**, 255–268 (2015).

[40] M. Zhang, H. Qu, A. Belatreche, Y. Chen and Z. Yi, A highly effective, and robust membrane potential-driven supervised learning method for spiking neurons, *IEEE Trans. Neural Networks Learn. Syst.*, **30**(1), 123–137 (2019).

[41] A. Mohemmed, S. Schliebs, S. Matsuda and N. Kasabov, Span: spike pattern association neuron for learning spatio-temporal spike patterns, *Int. J. Neural Syst.*, **22**(04), 1250012, 2012.

[42] S. Dora, S. Sundaram and N. Sundararajan, An interclass margin maximization learning algorithm for evolving spiking neural network, *IEEE Trans. Cybern.*, pp. 1–11 (2018).

[43] M. M. Halassa, T. Fellin, H. Takano, J.-H. Dong and P. G. Haydon, Synaptic islands defined by the territory of a single astrocyte, *J. Neurosci.*, **27**(24), 6473–6477 (2007).

[44] D. Dua and C. Graff, UCI machine learning repository (2017).

[45] M. Beyeler, N. D. Dutt and J. L. Krichmar, Categorization, and decision-making in a neurobiologically plausible spiking network using a STDP-like learning rule, *Neural Networks*, **48**, 109–124 (2013).

[46] A. Tavanaei, T. Masquelier and A. S. Maida, Acquisition of visual features through probabilistic spike-timing-dependent plasticity. In *International Joint Conference on Neural Networks*, pp. 307–314 (2016).

[47] A. Tavanaei and A. Maida, BP-STDP: approximating backpropagation using spike timing dependent plasticity, *Neurocomputing*, **330**, 39–47 (2019).

[48] Y. Bengio, T. Mesnard, A. Fischer, S. Zhang and Y. Wu, STDP-compatible approximation of backpropagation in an energy-based model, *Neural Comput.*, **29**(3), 555–577 (2017).

[49] J. H. Lee, T. Delbruck and M. Pfeiffer, Training deep spiking neural networks using backpropagation, *Front. Neurosci.*, **10**, 508 (2016).

[50] E. O. Neftci, C. Augustine, S. Paul and G. Detorakis, Event-driven random back-propagation: enabling neuromorphic deep learning machines, *Front. Neurosci.*, **11**, 324, 2017.

[51] S. B. Shrestha and G. Orchard, Slayer: spike layer error reassignment in time, *Adv. Neural Inf. Process. Syst.*, **31**, 1412–1421 (2018).

[52] E. O. Neftci, H. Mostafa and F. Zenke, Surrogate gradient learning in spiking neural networks, *IEEE Signal Process. Mag.*, **36**, 61–63 (2019).

[53] B. Rueckauer, I.-A. Lungu, Y. Hu, M. Pfeiffer and S.-C. Liu, Conversion of continuous-valued deep networks to efficient event-driven networks for image classification, *Front. Neurosci.*, **11**, 682 (2017).

[54] D. Neil, M. Pfeiffer and S.-C. Liu, Learning to be efficient: algorithms for training low-latency, low-compute deep spiking neural networks. In *Proceedings of the 31st Annual ACM Symposium on Applied Computing*, pp. 293–298 (2016).

[55] Z. Pan, Y. Chua, J. Wu, M. Zhang, H. Li and E. Ambikairajah, An efficient, and perceptually motivated auditory neural encoding, and decoding algorithm for spiking neural networks, *Front. Neurosci.*, **13** (2019).

[56] J. Wu, E. Yılmaz, M. Zhang, H. Li and K. C. Tan, Deep spiking neural networks for large vocabulary automatic speech recognition, *Front. Neurosci.*, **14**, 199 (2020).

[57] M. Dong, X. Huang and B. Xu, Unsupervised speech recognition through spike-timing-dependent plasticity in a convolutional spiking neural network, *PLoS One*, **13**(11), e0204596 (2018).

[58] G. Sun, T. Chen, Z. Wei, Y. Sun, H. Zang and S. Chen, A carbon price forecasting model based on variational mode decomposition and spiking neural networks, *Energies*, **9**(1), 54, 2016.

[59] S. Kulkarni, S. P. Simon and K. Sundareswaran, A spiking neural network (SNN) forecast engine for short-term electrical load forecasting, *Appl. Soft Comput.*, **13**(8), 3628–3635 (2013).

[60] D. Reid, A. J. Hussain and H. Tawfik, Financial time series prediction using spiking neural networks, *PLoS One*, **9**(8), e103656 (2014).

[61] F. Zhao, Y. Zeng and B. Xu, A brain-inspired decision-making spiking neural network, and its application in unmanned aerial vehicle, *Front. Neurorob.*, **12**, 56 (2018).

[62] N. Frémaux, H. Sprekeler and W. Gerstner, Reinforcement learning using a continuous time actor-critic framework with spiking neurons, *PLoS Comput. Biol.*, **9**(4), e1003024 (2013).

[63] M. Davies, N. Srinivasa, T.-H. Lin, G. Chinya, Y. Cao, S. H. Choday, G. Dimou, P. Joshi, N. Imam, S. Jain, *et al.*, Loihi: a neuromorphic manycore processor with on-chip learning, *IEEE Micro*, **38**(1), 82–99 (2018).

[64] F. Akopyan, J. Sawada, A. Cassidy, R. Alvarez-Icaza, J. Arthur, P. Merolla, N. Imam, Y. Nakamura, P. Datta, G.-J. Nam, *et al.*, TrueNorth: design and tool flow of a 65 mW 1 million neuron programmable neurosynaptic chip, *IEEE Trans. Comput. Aided Des. Integr. Circuits Syst.*, **34**(10), 1537–1557 (2015).

Chapter 11

Fault Detection and Diagnosis Based on an LSTM Neural Network Applied to a Level Control Pilot Plant

Emerson Vilar de Oliveira*, Yuri Thomas Nunes†, Mailson Ribeiro Santos‡ and Luiz Affonso Guedes¶

Federal University of Rio Grande do Norte—UFRN, Department of Computer Engineering and Automation—DCA
**emersonvilar@ufrn.edu.br*
†*yuri.tpinheirog@gmail.com*
‡*mailsonribeiro@ufrn.edu.br*
¶*affonso@dca.ufrn.br*

This chapter presents a fault detection and diagnosis (FDD) approach for industrial processes that is based on Recurrent Neural Networks. More specifically, a Long Short-Term Memory (LSTM) neural network architecture is used. A set of experiments using real pilot-scale plant data is performed to analyze the performance of this FDD approach. To evaluate the robustness of the proposed approach, special attention is given to the influence of the LSTM neural network hyper-parameter on the accuracy of fault detection and diagnosis activities. To compare the performance of the LSTM, the same FDD approach using the traditional multilayer perceptron (MLP) neural network architecture is evaluated. The obtained results indicate that the LSTM-based approach has better performance than the MLP-based approach under the same conditions.

11.1. Introduction

The demand for improved operational safety of industrial process operations has led to the development and application of several fault detection and diagnosis (FDD) approaches [1–3].

FDD solutions are considered to be critical assets for the safe operation of industrial processes. For example, they play an important role in preventing accidents in industry. Thus, it is necessary to carefully evaluate and validate these solutions before implementation in real industrial processes. Therefore, it is quite common to adopt simulation and implementation strategies in small-scale prototypes to validate FDD strategies.

Regarding simulation-based benchmarks for FDD, the Tennessee Eastman Process (TEP) benchmark is widely used in the literature [4–7]. Eastman Chemical Company developed this benchmark to provide a simulator for a real chemical process [8]. The TEP is mainly applied in the evaluation of process control and monitoring methods. Another well-known benchmark for FDD is the DAMADICS (Development and Application of Methods for Actuator Diagnosis in Industrial Control Systems), which provides simulated data from faulted control valves in a water evaporation process [9].

In contrast, few works in the literature use fault data from real processes to validate FDD strategies. This may be due to the difficulty to safely obtain or generate fault scenarios in real processes. Thus, small-scale processes (called pilot processes here) are considered to be a good trade-off between simulation and real industrial processes in the FDD context [10, 11].

Concerning the approaches used to carry out FDD, techniques based on machine learning (ML) are the most prominent in the literature [12–15]. Among these ML-based approaches, those that use neural networks stand out [16–23]. However, a great number of these works use the classical multilayer perceptron (MLP) neural networks.

This chapter aims to evaluate the performance of a FDD approach based on a recurrent neural network. The neural network for the FDD strategy adopted a Long Short-Term Memory (LSTM) architecture. In addition, the neural network is performed on data acquired by a pilot process. The pilot process is a two-tank level control system with coupled tanks. We pay particular attention to the influence of the neural network hyper-parameters on the performance of the FDD system. For comparison purposes, we also evaluate the performance of an MLP-based approach. Accuracy and confusion matrices are used to evaluate the performance of both the neural network approaches.

The rest of this chapter is organized as follows. The main concepts of FDD, MLP, and LSTM neural networks are presented in Section 11.2 and Section 11.3, respectively. The proposed architecture for the FDD is presented in Section 11.4. The experimental setup of the experiments is presented in Section 11.5. The results of performance evaluation of LSTM-based and MLP-based FDD are presented in Section 11.6. Finally, our conclusions are outlined in Section 11.7.

11.2. Fault Detection and Diagnosis

In the last few decades, FDD techniques applied to the industrial process operation monitoring context have received a great deal of attention. In addition, there has recently been an increasing number of studies, demonstrating the relevance of this

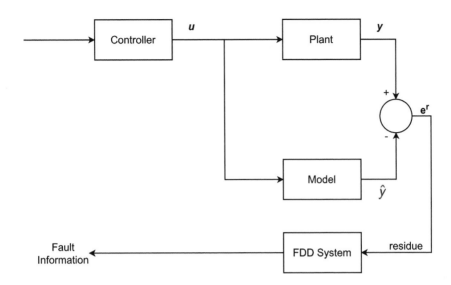

Figure 11.1: General structure of a quantitative model for FDD.

area of research [24]. This interest is mainly due to the expanding complexity of industrial process operations to meet market requirements, increase production, improve continuity, and develop process reliability under stricter environmental and safety restrictions [11]. For example, human operator faults cause about 70% to 90% of accidents in an industrial environment [25, 26].

Fault detection and fault classification are FDD tasks. While fault detection detects whether a fault has occurred, fault classification determines the type of fault that has occurred. The type of fault is useful information for process monitoring [27].

FDD methods can be classified into three groups: quantitative model-based methods, qualitative model-based methods, and data-based methods [25]. Model-based methods are generally developed based on physical knowledge of the process. In quantitative models, process operation knowledge is expressed as mathematical functions that map the system's inputs to outputs. Figure 11.1 shows the general structure of a quantitative model. In contrast, in qualitative model equations, these relationships are expressed as qualitative functions that are centered on different process units. Figure 11.2 shows the general structure of a qualitative model. Meanwhile, data-based approaches use only historical data of the process variables from industrial processes in operation [25]. Figure 11.3 shows the general structure of a data-based model for the FDD problem.

Figure 11.4 presents a tree-based classification of FDD methods. It is important to note that the approach that is adopted in this chapter can be classified as quantitative data-based, using neural networks for FDD.

One of the main concepts for diagnosing faults in the operation of a process is the definition of what a fault is. A fault can be expressed in general terms as a

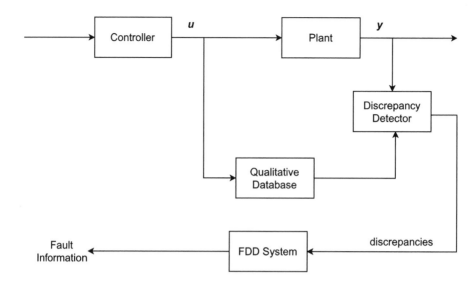

Figure 11.2:   General structure of a qualitative model for FDD.

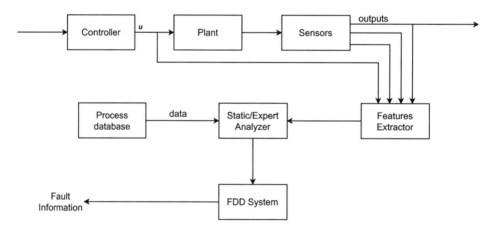

Figure 11.3:   General structure of a data-based model for the FDD problem.

deviation from the behavior of the process concerning the range of acceptable values for a set of variables or calculation parameters [28]. Figure 11.5 shows a controlled process system and indicates the different sources of faults that are present in it.

Based on Figure 11.5, it is possible to basically categorize three classes of faults or malfunctions: parameter faults, structural faults, and faults in actuators and sensors. Parameter faults are observed when a disturbance enters the process through one or more external variables, such as a change in the concentration value of the reagent in the supply of a reactor. Structural faults refer to changes in the process itself that occur due to a serious equipment fault, such as a broken or

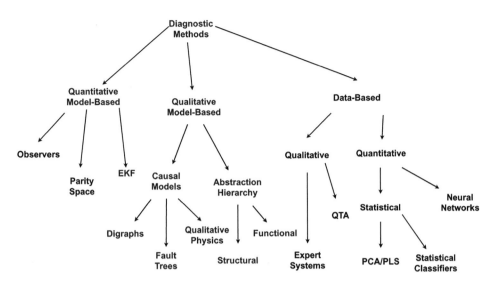

Figure 11.4: Classification of fault detection and diagnosis methods [25].

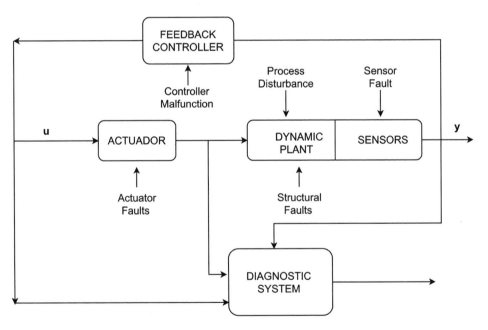

Figure 11.5: A general diagnostic framework [25].

leaking pipe. This type of malfunction results in a change in the flow of information between several variables. Finally, faults in actuators and sensors can occur due to a constant component fault, or with a positive or negative bias. A fault in one of these instruments can cause the plant's state variables to deviate beyond the limits acceptable by the process, which can cause a serious malfunction [25].

11.3. Artificial Neural Networks

This section will outline the concept of a neural network. First, non-recurrent architecture neural networks are briefly discussed. Second, concepts about recurrent neural networks are described. Finally, the LSTM network is presented in detail.

11.3.1. *Multilayer Perceptron Neural Networks*

The behavior of the human brain inspired the concept of the artificial neural network. The human brain has billions of processing structures called neurons. Each of these neurons makes connections to hundreds of other neurons via synapses. Neurons consist of a body (soma), axon, and dendrites. The dendrites receive other neurons' stimuli. The neuron sends an action through the axon towards the synapses. This happens by a chemical reaction. The synapses then spread the information to the connected dendrites. A neuron network made up of billions of these structures can quickly process complex information [29, 30].

The perceptron is the simplest form of an artificial neural network and is composed of only one neuron. The perceptron works by adjusting weights and bias to model a function that describes two linearly separable classes. This structure can classify the inputs into two groups [29]. A perceptron layer is necessary to classify three or more classes. However, these classes must continue to be linearly separable to improve the perceptron results.

Perceptrons are interesting objects for the study of neural networks. However, most real-world problems do not obey the linearity criterion that limits them. Due to these limitations, perceptrons are unproductive in solving this kind of problem. A single perceptron is not able to model complex functions. MLPs are a more robust structure that is capable of real-world problem modeling. MLP is a network composed of more than one layer of chained perceptrons. Figure 11.6 shows an abstract representation of the architecture of an MLP neural network.

In Figure 11.7 each circle (or node) represents a perceptron (or neuron). The arrows at the beginning are the inputs, while the arrows at the end are the outputs. The internal arrows indicate the transfer of information between the layers. Each MLP neuron does a linear operation on the inputs. It starts with a multiplication of the neuron inputs by the layer weights. All of these multiplication results are then summed. A bias is added to this sum to complete the linear operation. Equation (11.1) shows the mathematical computation applied to an MLP neuron.

$$y = \left(\sum_{i=1}^{n} w_n x_n \right) + b \tag{11.1}$$

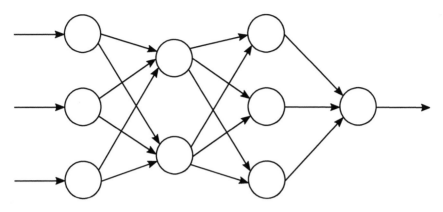

Figure 11.6: Abstract MLP neural network architecture representation.

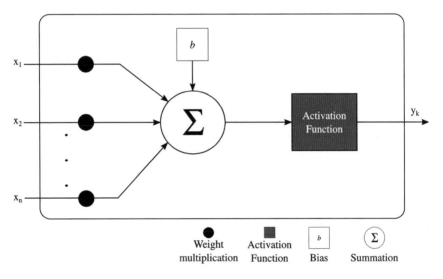

Figure 11.7: Abstract MLP neuron representation.

Here x_n denotes the input values, w_n denotes the respective layer weight to the input value, b is the bias value, and y is the neuron output. Figure 11.7 shows an abstract MLP neuron representation that is associated with a generic activation function.

Here, $x_1, x_2, \ldots, x_n$ are the neuron inputs and b is the bias value as presented in Eq. (11.1). The filled circle represents the input multiplication over the respective weight. The summation is the uppercase Greek letter *sigma*. The filled box is a generic activation function representation. Finally, the neuron output is y to the kth neuron in a layer.

All of the information in an MLP flows through the perceptrons at the input to the output layer. This kind of network is called a feed-forward network. Depending on the network's size, the number of associated weights can be considerable. These weights need adjustments over the network training to fit the problem as desired. The backpropagation algorithm is the most common method to adjust the weight values. This algorithm starts the weights of each neuron with a random and usually low value. As mentioned, all of the information flows from the input to the output of the network. The backpropagation algorithm returns errors over the layers, from the end to the beginning. These errors are responsible for indicating how much to adjust the weights. This iteration continues until the outputs have the desired values. This means that the error has a low value. Given an activation function, a partial derivative calculates the output error about the desired value. This operation generates an error gradient, which is calculated for each k neuron in an MLP-based neural network [29].

11.3.2. *Recurrent Neural Networks*

Feed-forward neural networks, such as the MLP, do not have a cycle in their structure. This happens because of the characteristic of information transport being straightforward through the layers. This information transference occurs from the beginning to the end of the network. Thus, these networks are not able to weigh new information with the already present information. This feature means that feed-forward networks have no memory.

Unlike conventional MLPs, recurrent neural networks (RNNs) use information obtained from feedback cycles. These explicit feedback cycles can happen through one or more neurons. Usually, internal states are responsible for the information forwarded over the network. These elements are changed according to the new inputs. Even with the changes, the past states information continues to have an amount of relevance. Consequently, the RNN features a structure that represents a memory. Figure 11.8 shows two representations of common RNN architectures.

In Figure 11.8(a), it is possible to see explicit feedback from one neuron output to every other neuron in the layer. In addition, it is possible to observe that there is no feedback to itself. Meanwhile, Figure 11.8(b) shows an RNN structure with explicit feedback from the neuron only to itself. In a multi-layer recurrent network, the feedback can be from one to every other neuron inner layer or from the last layer to the first [30]. The memory feature of the RNN is helpful for problems that not only depend on the current input but also have a time dependency on the data [29].

11.3.3. *Long Short-Term Memory Recurrent Neural Networks*

LSTM is a type of RNN. It was originally proposed by the authors of [31] to mitigate the problem resulting from explicit information feedback. The feedback associated with the backpropagation algorithm can bring annoying difficulties. These kinds of

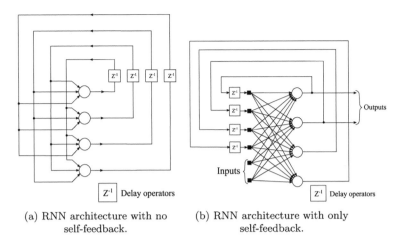

(a) RNN architecture with no self-feedback. (b) RNN architecture with only self-feedback.

Figure 11.8: Abstract RNN representations.

behaviors are usually present in common RNNs [31]. Among these problems, the most well-known are the vanishing gradients and blow-up. Vanishing gradients can make the network lose the fitting capacity. Then, it can take an unworkable amount of time to assimilate the necessary time dependence. Although the result may yet not work as expected, the gradient blow-up may generate an undesirable oscillation over the neural weight values [31]. To overcome these problems, LSTM neurons have internal states and functions. These internal functions work with the neuron input to produce the new state values. The value of the internal state of the neurons is updated at each algorithm time step. This sophisticated structure can keep information from past inputs for longer, while keeping the recent entries relevant. Figure 11.9 represents an LSTM neuron.

In Figure 11.9, it is possible to see the LSTM inputs and outputs (states), activation functions, and gates. At a specific time t, the LSTM has three inputs: the information source x_t, and the two past time instant recurrent states, h_{t-1} and c_{t-1}. These states are the hidden state and cell state. The cell outputs are the current time cell state c_t and hidden state h_t. The output y_t is equal to the hidden state h_t. If the cell belongs to the last network layer, then the hidden state h_t is the final output y_t. If the cell belongs to an internal layer, then it serves only as h_{t-1} to the forward layer. Moreover, in Figure 11.9, the gates are highlighted as *Forget Gate, Input Gate, Cell Gate, Cell Update*, and *Output Gate* whose features are described in the following subsections.

11.3.3.1. *Forget gate*

This component of the LSTM neuron has the work of forgetting information retained by past states, if necessary. Figure 11.10 shows the forget gate in the LSTM cell.

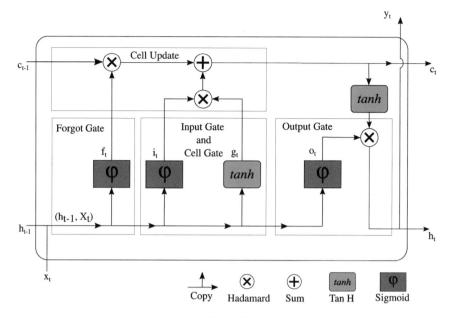

Figure 11.9: LSTM cell representation.

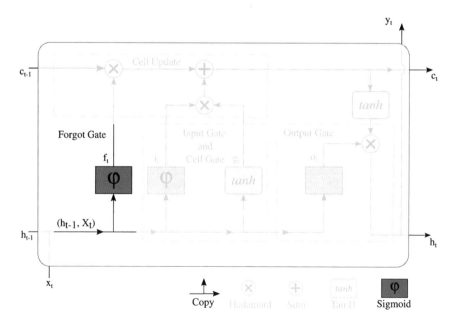

Figure 11.10: Forget gate localization in an LSTM cell representation.

From Figure 11.10, it is possible to observe that two of the cell inputs, h_{t-1} and x_t, are joined and then go through the Sigmoid activation function φ. Equation (11.2) shows the mathematical process used by the forget gate [32].

$$f_t = \varphi(W_{if}x_t + b_{if} + W_{hf}h_{(t-1)} + b_{hf}), \qquad (11.2)$$

where x_t is the neuron input at the current time t, and h_{t-1} is the hidden state at the previous time instant. The matrices $W_{if} \in \mathbf{R}^{H \times X}$ and $b_{if} \in \mathbf{R}^X$ are the weights and bias in the input of the forget gate (input forget, "if"). The matrices $W_{hf} \in \mathbf{R}^{H \times H}$ and $b_{hf} \in \mathbf{R}^H$ are the weights and bias for the hidden states in the forget gate (hidden forget, "hf"). The variable H is the number of neurons in the network and X is the number of inputs. Finally, the Greek letter φ is the Sigmoid activation function and f_t is the forget gate output.

11.3.3.2. *Input gate and cell gate*

The input gate and the cell gate decide how much of the new input information is inserted into the network. Figure 11.11 shows the input gate in the left and the cell gate in the right of the LSTM cell.

Figure 11.11 shows that the initial combination of the inputs h_{t-1} and x_t passes through two different activation functions. For the input gate, the activation function is a Sigmoid. For the cell gate, it is the Hyperbolic Tangent activation function.

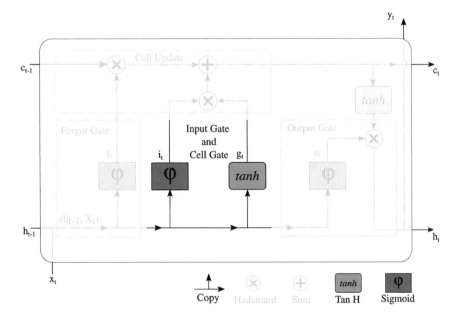

Figure 11.11: Input gate and cell gate localization in an LSTM cell representation.

Equations (11.3) and (11.4) show the respective mathematical operations done by the input and cell gates [32].

$$i_t = \varphi(W_{ii}x_t + b_{ii} + W_{hi}h_{(t-1)} + b_{hi}), \tag{11.3}$$

$$g_t = tanh(W_{ig}x_t + b_{ig} + W_{hg}h_{(t-1)} + b_{hg}) \tag{11.4}$$

where x_t is the neuron input at the current time t, and h_{t-1} is the hidden state at the previous time instant. For the input gate, the matrices $W_{ii} \in \mathbf{R}^{H \times X}$ and $b_{ii} \in \mathbf{R}^X$ are the weights and bias in the input of the input gate (input input, "ii"). The matrices $W_{hi} \in \mathbf{R}^{H \times H}$ and $b_{hi} \in \mathbf{R}^H$ are the weights and bias for the hidden states in the input gate (hidden input, "hi"). The Greek letter φ is the Sigmoid activation function, and i_t is the input gate output. For the cell gate, matrices $W_{ig} \in \mathbf{R}^{H \times X}$ and $b_{ig} \in \mathbf{R}^X$ are the weights and bias in the input of the cell gate (input cell, "ig"[1]). The matrices $W_{hg} \in \mathbf{R}^{H \times H}$ and $b_{hg} \in \mathbf{R}^H$ are the weights and bias for the hidden states in the cell gate (hidden cell, "hg"). Another activation function is the hyperbolic tangent, represented by *tanh*. The g_t is the cell gate output. The variable H is the number of neurons in the network and X is the number of inputs for both equations.

11.3.3.3. *Cell update and cell state*

Cell update is the set of operations accomplished to calculate the new cell state value. The cell state is the internal layer state that is propagating through the neurons. It has the function of loading the information resulting from the internal operations in the same layer of neurons. Figure 11.12 shows the cell update in the LSTM cell.

From Figure 11.12, it is possible to see the element-wise multiplication (Hadamard) between cell states in the past instant c_{t-1} with the output of the forget gate f_t. This value is summing to the result from the element-wise multiplication between the input gate i_t and cell gate g_t outputs. Equation (11.5) shows the mathematical processing done in the cell update [32].

$$c_t = f_t * c_{(t-1)} + i_t * g_t \tag{11.5}$$

The $*$ symbol is the Hadamard multiplication. The output of the operations results in the current cell state value c_t, which is one of the inputs to the next LSTM cell.

11.3.3.4. *Output gate and hidden state*

The output gate works for the processing part of the information that will serve as the output of the network y_t. The hidden state is the element that carries information

---

[1]In this case, the letter g was used to not be confused with the letter c used for the cell state.

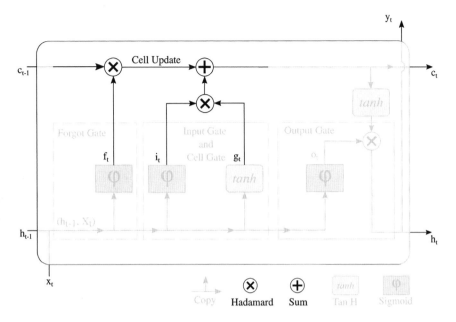

Figure 11.12: Cell update localization in an LSTM cell representation.

from previous moments through the network layers. Figure 11.13 shows the output gate in the LSTM neuron.

Figure 11.13 shows the output gate processing the information coming from the initial combination (x_t, h_{t-1}) through a Sigmoid activation function. The hidden state results from an element-wise multiplication of the output gate output o_t and the cell update output c_t passed by a tangent hyperbolic activation function. Equation (11.7) shows the mathematical processing done in output gate and how to obtain the current hidden state value [32].

$$o_t = \varphi(W_{io}x_t + b_{io} + W_{ho}h_{(t-1)} + b_{ho}), \tag{11.6}$$

$$h_t = o_t * tanh(c_t) \tag{11.7}$$

where x_t is the neuron input at the current time t, and h_{t-1} is the hidden state at the previous time instant. The matrices $W_{io} \in \mathbf{R}^{H \times X}$ and $b_{io} \in \mathbf{R}^{X}$ are the weights and bias in the input of the output gate (input-output, "io"). The matrices $W_{ho} \in \mathbf{R}^{H \times H}$ and $b_{ho} \in \mathbf{R}^{H}$ are the weights and bias for the hidden states in the output gate (hidden output, "ho"). The variable H is the number of neurons in the network and X is the number of inputs. The Greek letter φ is the Sigmoid activation function and o_t is the forget gate output. The hyperbolic tangent activation function is represented by *tanh*. As mentioned, if the neuron belongs to an internal/hidden layer, then the current h_t is the output network y_t.

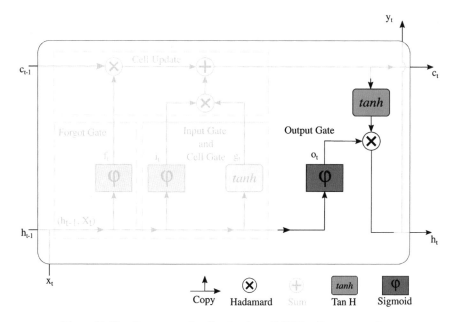

Figure 11.13: Output gate localization in an LSTM cell representation.

In the original proposal from LSTM, there is a truncation factor associated with the gradient calculation. As research on LSTM advances and new variations are proposed, this factor has changed. Some works show better convergence in the network training and the storage of information with a complete calculation of these gradients [33]. This kind of modification features the **Vanilla LSTM**. The Vanilla LSTM is popular among researchers and is an often-used variation [32].

11.3.3.5. *Batch normalization*

This approach uses the methodology that was originally proposed in [34], which uses a batch normalized LSTM to classify the faults generated by an industrial process simulator TEP [8]. As mentioned, it used an LSTM neural network attached to a *Batch Normalization* (BN) procedure. The BN aims to improve the train iterations of the model. This procedure standardizes the activation functions using the mean and standard deviation estimates in each network layer. Assuming a neural network with $K^{(k)}$ layers and a mini-batch of size $M^{(m)} > 1$, each mini-batch instance m is composed of the activation values from the respective layer k. Thus, the BN methodology calculates the mean and standard deviation for each mini-batch instance activation. Then, the mean and standard deviation parameters of the whole layer are estimated [35]. These parameters are $\hat{E}(\mathbf{h})$ and $\hat{Var}(\mathbf{h})$, respectively. According to the authors [34], their main contribution is to apply the BN to the recurrent term $W_{hi}h_{(t-1)}$. They assert that the normalization of the recurrent LSTM term instead of the $W_{ii}x_t$ term improves the LSTM's memory and convergence. Equation (11.8) defines the batch normalization operation.

$$BN(\mathbf{h}; \eta, \rho) = \rho + \eta \odot \frac{\mathbf{h} - \hat{E}(\mathbf{h})}{\sqrt{\hat{Var}(\mathbf{h}) + \epsilon}} \tag{11.8}$$

where $\mathbf{h} \in \mathbf{R}^H$ is the mini-batch vector with size $M^{(m)} > 1$. In the proposed methodology, each set of recurrent hidden states $W_{hi}h_{(t-1)} \in \mathbf{R}^{H \times H}$ are the mini-batch instances. The symbols $\rho \in \mathbf{R}^H$ and $\eta \in \mathbf{R}^H$ are learnable parameter vectors of the normalized feature's mean and standard deviation. ϵ is a constant mini-batch regularization parameter for numerical stability, and $\odot$ is the element-wise multiplication. Following the original notation [34], $\rho = 0$, to avoid unnecessary redundancy and over-fitting, simplifying the BN input to $BN(\mathbf{h}; \eta)$.

11.4. LSTM-Based Approach to FDD

In contrast to the trend present in the literature, the approach presented in [34] does not use a combination of two techniques, such as "feature extraction" + "classification", to solve the FDD problem. Instead, the model directly receives a set of multi-variable faults and returns as output the pertinence scores for each fault class. The inputs feed the BN-LSTM, applying the normalization on the hidden states recurrent terms. After these computations, the BN-LSTM output feeds a fully connected layer. This last step resizes the network output, and then a **LogSoftmax** function is applied to transform the network output in pertinence probabilities for each class. To optimize the gradients, we chose the **Adam** algorithm [36]. To optimize the loss function, we chose the **Negative Log-Likelihood Loss** algorithm.

The source code to implement the proposed methodology is available online.[2] The code is written in the Python programming language using the framework for machine learning *PyTorch*.

Figure 11.14 presents a block diagram of the LSTM-based FDD approach that we have adopted in this study. The Fault Classifier module corresponds to an LSTM/MLP neural network. This module receives the sensor data in the current instant and $J - 1$ delays (Z^{J-1}) for each variable, represented by x_t and $x_{t-1}, \ldots,$ x_{t-J+1}, respectively. These data are the basis of the fault classification task. The classifier output indicates the detected faults, which are represented by $y_1, y_2, \ldots, y_C$.

Figure 11.15 shows the processes that are made in the Fault Classifier module. It is possible to see the fault classification sequence from the window sample generation to the *LogSoftMax* layer output, as mentioned earlier in this section.

---

[2]https://github.com/haitaozhao/LSTM_fault_detection.

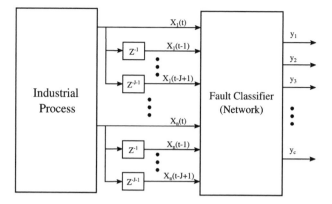

Figure 11.14:   Representation diagram of the fault classification methodology.

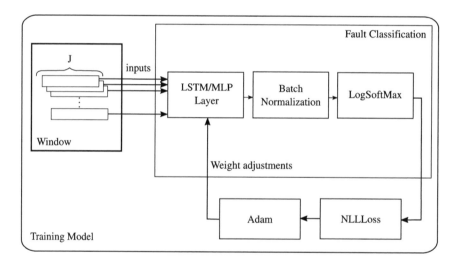

Figure 11.15:   Flowchart describing the Fault Classifier module process.

11.4.1. *The Pilot Plant: PiPE*

The level control pilot plant was developed by *De Lorenzo of Brazil* and named as PiPE, which is an acronym for *Pilot Plant Experiment*. It was specially designed to study process control. It has four process variables: pressure, temperature, flow rate, and level, which are defined by the input vector $S = (u, t, f, y)$ [37].

Figure 11.16 shows a photo of the pilot plant and Figure 11.17 shows its schematic diagram. Regarding instruments and equipment, the pilot plant is composed of a panel with a programmable logic controller (PLC) and an electrical system to plant control; two pressurized vessels, one acrylic made and another

Figure 11.16:   Photograph of the pilot plant [38].

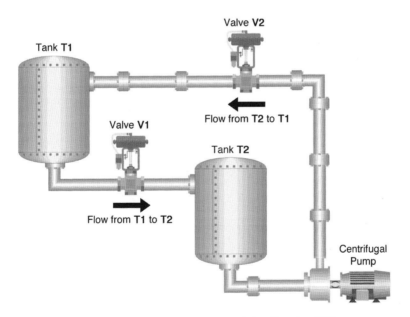

Figure 11.17:   Schematic diagram of the pilot plant [38].

made of stainless steel, named $T1$ and $T2$, respectively; a centrifugal re-circulation pump controlled by a frequency inverter; a heating and heat exchange system; two valves, named $V1$ and $V2$; and sensors for temperature, pressure, flow rate, and level [38]. In addition, this pilot plant has a transducer from a physical to an electrical signal, this signal is processed by the PLC; a terminal bus; and a supervisory control and data acquisition (SCADA) for parameter configuration and process operation visualization.

The pilot plant works with the two tanks, $T1$ and $T2$, connected by a piping system that allows a flow between them. The fluid flows from $T1$ to $T2$ using gravitational force because $T1$ is at a level higher than $T2$ in relation to the ground level. From $T2$ to $T1$, the liquid flows by the pressure generated by a centrifugal pump.

The pilot plant was originally designed for process control. To carry out the fault detection and diagnosis studies that are proposed in this chapter, a fault set was introduced. Consequently, the produced faults were grouped into three fault groups: actuator, sensor, and structural. Each fault group has different intensity levels for the same type of fault. Table 11.1 shows the faults with their respective description.

The actuator fault group has six faults associated with the levels of pump off-set: $+2\%, +4\%, +8\%, -2\%, -4\%,$ and -8%. The sensor fault group also has six faults associated with the levels of off-set. In the structural fault group, there are two levels of drain opening. These openings simulate a physical leak in tank $T1$. In addition to the tank leaks, four levels are struck for valve $V1$ and three are struck for $V2$.

Table 11.1: Set of generated faults.

Group	Fault	Description
Actuator	F1	+2% off-set
	F2	+4% off-set
	F3	+8% off-set
	F4	−2% off-set
	F5	−4% off-set
	F6	−8% off-set
Sensor	F7	+2% off-set
	F8	+4% off-set
	F9	+8% off-set
	F10	−2% off-set
	F11	−4% off-set
	F12	−8% off-set
Structural	F13	100% of tank leak
	F14	66% of tank leak
	F15	30% of stuck valve V1
	F16	50% of stuck valve V1
	F17	85% of stuck valve V1
	F18	100% of stuck valve V1
	F19	25% of stuck valve V2
	F20	50% of stuck valve V2
	F21	75% of stuck valve V2

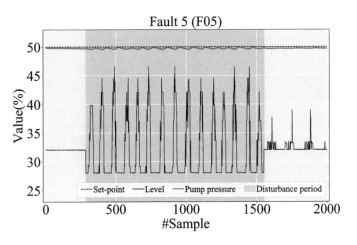

Figure 11.18: Fault $F5$ scenario.

Here, the data are only used as a reference to the pilot plant control. To make this control, we used a multistage fuzzy controller, which was developed on the software **JFuzZ** [39]. The communication between the SCADA system and the PLC was realized by the OPC (OLE for process control) protocol [40], which collects data from the level of tank $T1$ (y), reference (r, set-point defined by the user), and pressure (u, control pump signal) to compose the vector $x = (r, y, u)$. The sample time used in all experiments was 100 ms.

Figure 11.18 shows a fault scenario associated with the occurrence of an F5-type fault. In this fault scenario, it is possible to note that the pressure variable is quite affected, while the level variable is little impacted.

Figure 11.19 shows a fault scenario associated with the occurrence of an F8-type fault. In this fault scenario, the level and pump pressure variables change considerably. Furthermore, there is a high noising region at the end of the fault occurrence. This kind of behavior is not present in the previous scenario.

Figure 11.20 shows a fault scenario associated with the occurrence of an F18-type fault. This fault scenario is more similar to the fault scenario presented in Figure 11.18.

11.5. Experimental Setup

This section presents the setup of the experiments. We explain the criteria for the fault scenario selection in this section, which composes the data for the network training and validation. We also present the selected values for the network hyper-parameter variation. The variation of these values aims to evaluate the hyper-parameters' impact on the FDD system. Finally, some training details are shown.

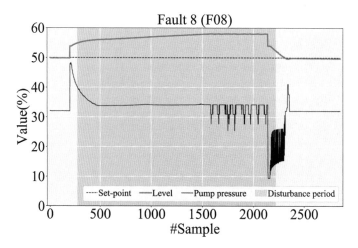

Figure 11.19: Fault *F*8 scenario.

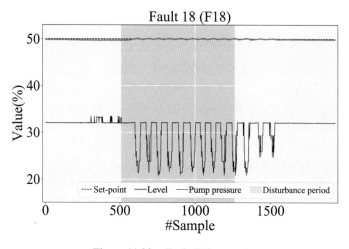

Figure 11.20: Fault *F*18 scenario.

11.5.1. *Fault Selection for Training and Validation*

To train and validate the LSTM neural network models, a pair of faults in each fault group was selected. The least dissimilar fault pairs in each fault group were chosen to compose the training and validation sets. The dissimilar criteria that we used was the mean of the Euclidean distance between the variables operating in different faults.

The Euclidean distance for two variables is defined by Eq. (11.9), where $v_{F_a}^i$ and $v_{F_b}^i$ correspond to the ith process sample when subjected to *fault a* and *fault b*, respectively. N is the number of samples in each fault considered in the analysis. The pair of faults is more different from each other when the distance value is bigger.

Table 11.2: Fault selection.

Subgroup	Combination	Dissimilarity
Actuator Positive	F01 ↔ F02	61.30
(+2%, +4%, +8%)	F01 ↔ F03	**46.45**
	F02 ↔ F03	51.89
Actuator Negative	F04 ↔ F05	**82.57**
(−2%, −4%, −8%)	F04 ↔ F06	114.28
	F05 ↔ F06	156.03
Sensor Positive	F07 ↔ F08	**75.75**
(+2%, +4%, +8%)	F07 ↔ F09	427.42
	F08 ↔ F08	356.74
Sensor Negative	F10 ↔ F11	**72.98**
(−2%, −4%, −8%)	F10 ↔ F12	282.43
	F11 ↔ F12	236.93
Structural Tank leakage	F13 ↔ F14	**122.48**
Structural V1	F15 ↔ F16	226.43
(30%, 50%, 84%, 100%)	F15 ↔ F17	428.27
	F15 ↔ F18	436.50
	F16 ↔ F17	212.47
	F16 ↔ F18	219.92
	F17 ↔ F18	**50.41**
Structural V2	F19 ↔ F20	**41.15**
(25%, 50%, 75%)	F19 ↔ F21	75.15
	F20 ↔ F21	83.50

$$D\left(v^i_{F_a}, v^i_{F_b}\right) = \sqrt{\Sigma^N_{i=1}\left(v^i_{F_a} - v^i_{F_b}\right)^2}. \tag{11.9}$$

Table 11.2 summarizes the fault selection procedure. The subgroup column shows a new grouping of the faults into subgroups based on conceptual similarities. At the remaining columns, the dissimilarity metric is listed for each pair combination in each subgroup.

For both dissimilarity tests and subsequent evaluations, 600 samples of each fault were used. This value was chosen because of the sample files in the fault datasets. The number of input samples for the model varies according to the size of the input size. Equation (11.10) shows the calculation made for the number of model input samples. Here, 600 is the total number of samples at each fault, J is the input size, and Q_e is the number of inputs to the model.

$$Q_e = 600 - (J - 1). \tag{11.10}$$

Then, based on the least dissimilarity criterion shown in Table 11.2, the faults selected for training are $F01$, $F04$, $F07$, $F10$, $F13$, $F17$, and $F19$. The ones that form the validation fault group are faults $F03$, $F05$, $F08$, $F11$, $F14$, $F18$, and $F20$, respectively.

11.5.2. *LSTM Neural Network Architecture Selection*

To carry out the performance evaluation of the LSTM-based FDD approach, a set of hyper-parameters was considered. The selected hyper-parameters were the number of network inputs, J, and the number of neurons in the LSTM neural network layer, HS. The selected values for J and HS were the following:

- $J = 3, 5, 7, 10$.
- $HS = 20, 30, 40, 50, 60$.

The choice of these values was based on the behavior of the selected fault set. For each value of J, all values of HS were tested, resulting in a total of 20 different combinations of hyper-parameter pair values.

The performance metric that was chosen for model evaluation was the accuracy or correctness in the fault classification task. The experiment consists of training 100 models with the same hyper-parameters and extracting the performance metrics obtained by each of them. At the end of the experiment, each architecture has 100 accuracy values obtained from the trained models for 50 periods each. It should be noted that the choice of an exhaustive validation test for various combinations of hyper-parameter values (J and HS) aims to decrease randomness in the LSTM/MLP neural network training process.

11.6. Results

This section presents the main results obtained using the LSTM-based FDD approach. Here, the influence of the LSTM neural network hyper-parameter values on the solution performance is evaluated and discussed. For better interpretation, the obtained results are presented using box-plots and a confusion matrix indicating the accuracy values obtained in the fault classification tasks. To better analyze the LSTM-based FDD approach performance, the same FDD solution using an MLP neural network was also performed and evaluated. The results obtained with the two network approaches are presented in this section.

11.6.1. *Results Using the LSTM-based FDD Approach*

Figure 11.21(a,b) presents box-plots of the accuracy distribution of the validation group by varying the network input size (J) and LSTM layer size (HS), respectively.[3]

---

[3]The graphics of the type of box-plot presented in Figure 11.21(a,b) highlight the following information: (i) the horizontal lines at the ends are the maximum and minimum values; (ii) the box top-line delimits the first quartile and the bottom-line is the third quartile, composed of the distribution inter-quartile distance; (iii) the inner box line is the median distribution value; (iv) the filled point inner box is the mean; and (v) the unfilled points are the outliers.

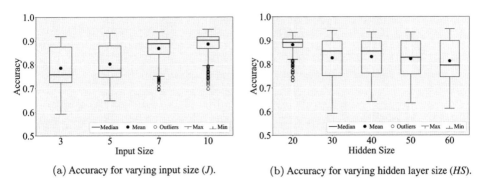

(a) Accuracy for varying input size (J).   (b) Accuracy for varying hidden layer size (HS).

Figure 11.21: Box-plot of the accuracy values for varying hyper-parameters.

From Figure 11.21(a), it is possible to observe that the scenarios with input sizes equal to 7 and 10 ($J = 7$ and $J = 10$) showed more consistent behavior in their distributions, considering all possible network sizes (HS). The mean and median accuracy values are much closer than the remaining scenarios and the inter-quartile distance is smaller, which indicate a smaller variation in the accuracy value. In addition, they have value outliers below the box, which means that low accuracy values are uncommon. The highlight of Figure 11.21(b) is the value of hidden size equal to 20, which has characteristics similar to the evaluation of the input size.

Figure 11.22 shows the behavior of all combinations between the hyper-parameters of the LSTM neural network in isolation from J. In this figure's graphics, a reference line with an accuracy value of 0.95 is given as a visual guide.

To carry out a more detailed performance evaluation, the hyper-parameter values of the LSTM neural network were updated as $J = 7$ and $HS = 20$. This hyper-parameter configuration presents accuracy values with average (0.88), median (0.90), variance (0.05), and maximum (0.93) close to the 0.95 reference. Associated with these accuracy values, this hyper-parameter combination has a lower computational complexity than combinations such as $J = 10 - HS = 30$ and $J = 10 - HS = 50$, which both have averaging accuracy values around *0.89*. A confusion matrix was then used to evaluate the classification accuracy obtained for each fault group. This experiment assesses the model generalization capacity when trained for a specific fault and validated against another with similar behavior in the same subgroup.

Figure 11.23 shows the accuracy confusion matrix obtained for the fault classification task using the LSTM neural network configuration setup that was given previously.[4] In this case, given a confusion matrix (M_C), its elements ($M_C(i, j)$)

---

[4]The row index of the matrix refers to the predict label from the neural network. The column index of the matrix refers to the actual label of the data. The integer number in the labeled cells is the count of samples of the column label classified as the row label. The percentage in the labeled cells

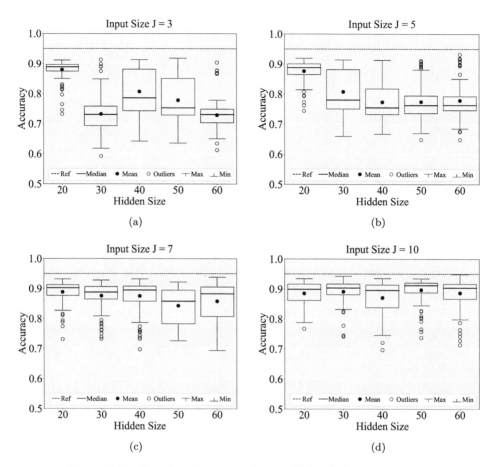

Figure 11.22: Box-plot of accuracy values combining the hyper-parameters.

represent how many times the model classified the i-th fault as the j-th fault. Thus, it is possible to note that faults $F08$ and $F11$ neither produce false positives nor false negatives. The faults $F03$ and $F05$ also obtained good accuracy values for the fault classification task (95.62% and 97.91%, respectively). In contrast, the faults $F14$, $F18$, and $F20$ had lower accuracy values (85.69%, 88.55%, and 72.73%) and the highest error rates. For example, fault $F18$ was erroneously classified as fault $F20$ in 123 samples out of 594. In general, the evaluated model presented a final accuracy value of 91.49%, that is considered quite adequate.

---

is the percentage of the number of samples in this cell over the total samples. The last row presents the percentage of correctly classified samples of the column label. The last column represents the percentage of the correct predictions of the row label. The element of the last row and last column is the overall accuracy of the model.

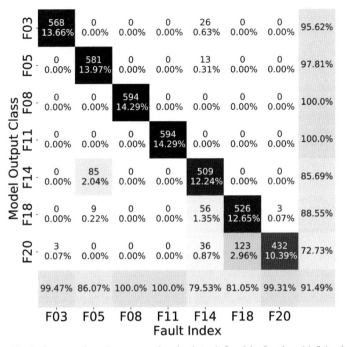

Figure 11.23: Confusion matrix using test and train data defined in Section 11.5.1 with the LSTM classifier.

Regarding the pilot plant, the results corroborate that some fault groups are easier classified. For instance, faults within the actuator and sensor group achieve higher accuracy and low misclassification. Although the structural group has a higher misclassification count, it still presents a good accuracy.

11.6.2. *Results Using MLP-Based FDD Approach*

Figure 11.24(a,b) presents box-plots of the accuracy distribution of the validation group varying the network input size (J) and MLP layer size (HS), respectively. From Figure 11.24(a), it is possible to see that all of the input size scenarios show an undesirable behavior in their distributions, considering all possible network sizes (HS). The mean and median accuracy values are lower and closer to 0.6 value. The inter-quartile distance is also small, which indicates a lesser variation in the accuracy around this value. They also have values outliers above the box, which means that high accuracy values are uncommon. The boxes in Figure 11.21(b) have similar characteristics to the evaluation of the input size variation.

Figure 11.25 shows the behavior of all combinations between the hyper-parameters of the MLP neural network in isolation from J. In this figure's graphics, a reference line with an accuracy value of 0.75 (0.2 less than in the LSTM analysis) is presented as a visual guide.

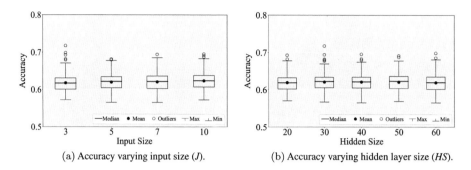

(a) Accuracy varying input size (*J*).   (b) Accuracy varying hidden layer size (*HS*).

Figure 11.24:   Box-plot of the accuracy values for varying hyper-parameters.

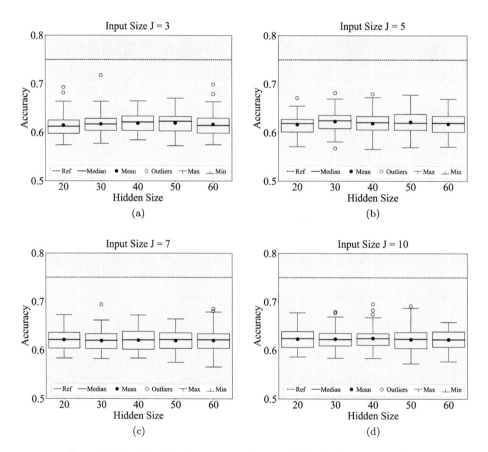

Figure 11.25:   Box-plot of accuracy values combining the hyper parameters.

For a more detailed performance evaluation, the hyper-parameter values of the MLP network were kept the same as those of the LSTM ($J = 7$ and $HS = 20$). This hyper-parameter configuration presents accuracy values with average (0.63) and median (0.63). These values are considerably far from those obtained in the

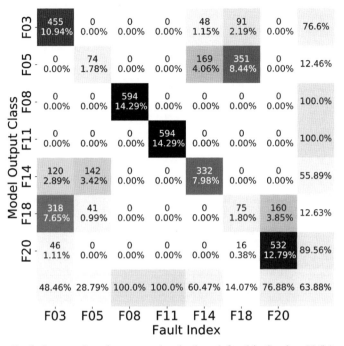

Figure 11.26: Confusion matrix using test and train data defined in Section 11.5.1 with the MLP classifier.

results with the LSTM network. As previously done, the confusion matrix present in the Figure 11.26 shows the classification accuracy obtained for each fault group.

Figure 11.26 shows the accuracy confusion matrix obtained for the fault classification task using the MLP neural network configuration setup that was used previously. In this case, it is possible to note that the faults $F08$ and $F11$ produce neither false positives nor false negatives, as in the LSTM results. The fault $F20$ obtained a reasonable accuracy value for the fault classification task (89.56%). The faults $F03$ and $F14$ obtained a low accuracy value for the fault classification task (76.6% and 55.89%, respectively), but above those of the remaining faults. The faults $F05$ and $F18$ had the lowest accuracy values (12.46% and 12.63%) and the highest error rates. For example, fault $F18$ was erroneously classified as fault $F05$ in 351 samples out of 594. In general, the MLP evaluated model presented a final accuracy value of 63.88%, which is considered to be a low value when compared with that obtained with the LSTM neural network.

11.7. Conclusion

In this chapter, the LSTM-based FDD approach performance was analyzed and compared to the same approach using an MLP layer. The pilot plant data are a noticeable aspect of this study. The pilot plant has the characteristics found in industrial systems, such as industrial instrumentation (sensors and actuators) and inherent nonlinearity. Reducing the gap to a real industrial process, the FDD approach performance addressed in this chapter is evaluated in more realistic scenarios than simulation.

The performance evaluation of the LSTM-based FDD approach shows that it has an excellent performance for fault detection and a good performance for classification tasks. It is, however, relevant to highlight that although fault classification is a more complex task than fault detection, fault detection alone is good enough in many real industrial process operations. Among the groups of faults, the actuator faults were easier to be classified.

Another point to be highlighted is the distribution behavior of the accuracy values concerning the variation of the input size and the size of the LSTM network used. The change in accuracy indicates the need to find a specific combination between hyper-parameters to obtain a model with higher general accuracy, given the behavior observed in the obtained results.

Our future work will analyze neural network-based approaches with incremental learning techniques, which will enable new fault patterns to be learned without losing the previously acquired fault knowledge.

References

[1] H. Yu, F. Khan and V. Garaniya, Nonlinear Gaussian belief network based fault diagnosis for industrial processes, *J. Process Control*, **35**, 178–200 (2015).

[2] S. Zhou, J. Zhang and S. Wang, Fault diagnosis in industrial processes using principal component analysis and hidden Markov model. In *Proceedings of the 2004 American Control Conference*, vol. 6, pp. 5680–5685, IEEE (2004).

[3] S. Verron, T. Tiplica and A. Kobi, Fault diagnosis of industrial systems by conditional Gaussian network including a distance rejection criterion, *Eng. Appl. Artif. Intell.*, **23**(7), 1229–1235 (2010).

[4] S. Yin, S. X. Ding, A. Haghani, H. Hao and P. Zhang, A comparison study of basic data-driven fault diagnosis and process monitoring methods on the benchmark Tennessee Eastman process, *J. Process Control*, **22**(9), 1567–1581 (2012). ISSN 0959-1524. doi: https://doi.org/10.1016/j.jprocont. 2012.06.009. URL http://www.sciencedirect.com/science/article/pii/S0959152412001503.

[5] M. F. D'Angelo, R. M. Palhares, M. C. C. Filho], R. D. Maia, J. B. Mendes and P. Y. Ekel, A new fault classification approach applied to Tennessee Eastman benchmark process, *Appl. Soft Comput.*, **49**, 676–686 (2016). ISSN 1568-4946. doi: https://doi.org/10.1016/j.asoc.2016.08.040. URL http:// www.sciencedirect.com/science/article/pii/S1568494616304343.

[6] X. Gao and J. Hou, An improved SVM integrated GS-PCA fault diagnosis approach of Tennessee Eastman process, *Neurocomputing*, **174**, 906–911 (2016). ISSN 0925-2312. doi: https://doi.org/10.1016/j.neucom.2015.10.018. URL http://www.sciencedirect.com/science/article/pii/S0925231215014757.

[7] N. Basha, M. Z. Sheriff, C. Kravaris, H. Nounou and M. Nounou, Multiclass data classification using fault detection-based techniques, *Comput. Chem. Eng.*, **136**, 106786 (2020).

ISSN 0098-1354. doi: https://doi.org/10.1016/j.compchemeng.2020.106786. URL http://www.sciencedirect.com/science/article/pii/S0098135420300090.

[8] J. Downs and E. Vogel, A plant-wide industrial process control problem, *Comput. Chem. Eng.*, **17**(3), 245–255 (1993). ISSN 0098-1354. doi: https://doi.org/10.1016/0098-1354(93) 80018-I. URL http:// www.sciencedirect.com/science/article/pii/009813549380018I. Industrial challenge problems in process control.

[9] M. Bartyś, R. Patton, M. Syfert, S. de las Heras and J. Quevedo, Introduction to the DAMADICS actuator FDI benchmark study, *Control Eng. Pract.*, **14**(6), 577–596 (2006). ISSN 0967-0661. doi: https://doi.org/ 10.1016/j.conengprac.2005.06.015. URL http://www.sciencedirect.com/ science/article/pii/S0967066105001796. A Benchmark Study of Fault Diagnosis for an Industrial Actuator.

[10] B. S. J. Costa, P. P. Angelov and L. A. Guedes, A new unsupervised approach to fault detection and identification. In *2014 International Joint Conference on Neural Networks (IJCNN)*, pp. 1557–1564, IEEE (2014). doi: 10.1109/IJCNN.2014.6889973.

[11] C. G. Bezerra, B. S. J. Costa, L. A. Guedes and P. P. Angelov, An evolving approach to unsupervised and real-time fault detection in industrial processes, *Expert Syst. Appl.*, **63**, 134–144 (2016). ISSN 0957-4174. doi: https://doi.org/10.1016/j.eswa.2016.06.035. URL http:// www.sciencedirect.com/science/article/pii/S0957417416303153.

[12] M. Chow, P. M. Mangum and S. O. Yee, A neural network approach to real-time condition monitoring of induction motors, *IEEE Trans. Ind. Electron.*, **38**(6), 448–453 (1991). doi: 10.1109/41.107100.

[13] A. Malhi and R. Gao, PCA-based feature selection scheme for machine defect classification, *IEEE Trans. Instrum. Meas.*, **53**, 1517–1525 (2005). doi: 10.1109/TIM.2004.834070.

[14] Y. Wang, Q. Ma, Q. Zhu, X. Liu and L. Zhao, An intelligent approach for engine fault diagnosis based on Hilbert–Huang transform and support vector machine, *Appl. Acoust.*, **75**, 1–9 (2014). ISSN 0003-682X. doi: https:// doi.org/10.1016/j.apacoust.2013.07.001. URL https://www.sciencedirect. com/science/article/pii/S0003682X13001515.

[15] D. Pandya, S. Upadhyay and S. Harsha, Fault diagnosis of rolling element bearing with intrinsic mode function of acoustic emission data using APF-KNN, *Expert Syst. Appl.*, **40**(10), 4137–4145 (2013). ISSN 0957-4174. doi: https://doi.org/10.1016/j.eswa.2013.01.033. URL https://www.sciencedirect.com/science/article/pii/S0957417413000468.

[16] Ł. Jedliński and J. Jonak, Early fault detection in gearboxes based on support vector machines and multilayer perceptron with a continuous wavelet transform, *Appl. Soft Comput.*, **30**, 636–641 (2015).

[17] S. Heo and J. H. Lee, Fault detection and classification using artificial neural networks, *IFAC-PapersOnLine*, **51**(18), 470–475 (2018).

[18] Z. Chen, C. Li and R.-V. Sanchez, Gearbox fault identification and classification with convolutional neural networks, *Shock Vib.*, **2015**, 390134 (2015).

[19] K. B. Lee, S. Cheon and C. O. Kim, A convolutional neural network for fault classification and diagnosis in semiconductor manufacturing processes, *IEEE Trans. Semicond. Manuf.*, **30**(2), 135–142 (2017).

[20] G. Tian, Q. Zhou and L. Du, Deep convolutional neural networks for distribution system fault classification. In *2018 IEEE Power Energy Society General Meeting (PESGM)*, pp. 1–5, IEEE (2018). doi: 10.1109/PESGM. 2018.8586547.

[21] D. Dey, B. Chatterjee, S. Dalai, S. Munshi and S. Chakravorti, A deep learning framework using convolution neural network for classification of impulse fault patterns in transformers with increased accuracy, *IEEE Trans. Dielectr. Electr. Insul.*, **24**(6), 3894–3897 (2017).

[22] M. Hemmer, H. Van Khang, K. G. Robbersmyr, T. I. Waag and T. J. Meyer, Fault classification of axial and radial roller bearings using transfer learning through a pretrained convolutional neural network, *Designs*, **2**(4), 56 (2018).

[23] C. Liu, G. Cheng, X. Chen and Y. Pang, Planetary gears feature extraction and fault diagnosis method based on VMD and CNN, *Sensors*, **18**(5), 1523 (2018).

[24] R.-E. Precup, P. Angelov, B. S. J. Costa and M. Sayed-Mouchaweh, An overview on fault diagnosis and nature-inspired optimal control of industrial process applications, *Comput. Ind.*, **74**, 75–94 (2015). ISSN 0166-3615. doi: https://doi.org/10.1016/j.compind.2015.03.001. URL http://www.sciencedirect.com/science/article/pii/S0166361515000469.

[25] V. Venkatasubramanian, R. Rengaswamy, K. Yin and S. N. Kavuri, A review of process fault detection and diagnosis, Part I: quantitative model-based methods, *Comput. Chem. Eng.*, **27**(3), 293–311 (2003). ISSN 0098-1354. doi: https://doi.org/10.1016/S0098-1354(02)00160-6. URL http://www.sciencedirect.com/science/article/pii/S0098135402001606.

[26] P. Wang and C. Guo, Based on the coal mine's essential safety management system of safety accident cause analysis, *Am. J. Environ. Energy Power Res.*, **1**(3), 62–68 (2013).

[27] L. Yin, H. Wang, W. Fan, L. Kou, T. Lin and Y. Xiao, Incorporate active learning to semi-supervised industrial fault classification, *J. Process Control*, **78**, 88–97 (2019). ISSN 0959-1524. doi: https:// doi.org/10.1016/j.jprocont.2019.04.008. URL https://www.sciencedirect.com/science/article/pii/S095915241930277X.

[28] D. M. Himmelblau, *Fault Detection and Diagnosis in Chemical and Petrochemical Processes*. vol. 8, Elsevier Science Ltd. (1978).

[29] B. Coppin, *Artificial Intelligence Illuminated*. Jones and Bartlett illuminated series, Jones and Bartlett Publishers (2004). ISBN 9780763732301. URL https://books.google.com.br/books?id=LcOLqodW28EC.

[30] S. Haykin, *Neural Networks: A Comprehensive Foundation*. Prentice-Hall (2007).

[31] S. Hochreiter and J. Schmidhuber, Long short-term memory, *Neural Comput.*, **9**(8), 1735–1780 (1997).

[32] K. Greff, R. K. Srivastava, J. Koutník, B. R. Steunebrink and J. Schmidhuber, LSTM: a search space odyssey, *IEEE Trans. Neural Networks Learn. Syst.*, **28**(10), 2222–2232 (2016).

[33] A. Graves and J. Schmidhuber, Framewise phoneme classification with bidirectional LSTM and other neural network architectures, *Neural Networks*, **18**(5–6), 602–610 (2005).

[34] H. Zhao, S. Sun and B. Jin, Sequential fault diagnosis based on LSTM neural network, *IEEE Access*, **6**, 12929–12939 (2018).

[35] S. Ioffe and C. Szegedy, Batch normalization: accelerating deep network training by reducing internal covariate shift, *arXiv preprint arXiv:1502.03167* (2015).

[36] D. P. Kingma and J. Ba, Adam: a method for stochastic optimization, *arXiv preprint arXiv:1412.6980* (2014).

[37] A. Marins, Continuous process workbench. Technical manual. DeLorenzo Brazil, Brazil (2009).

[38] B. Costa, P. Angelov and L. A. Guedes, A new unsupervised approach to fault detection and identification. In *2014 International Joint Conference on Neural Networks (IJCNN)*, IEEE (2014). doi: 10.1109/IJCNN.2014. 6889973.

[39] B. S. J. Costa, C. G. Bezerra and L. Guedes, Java fuzzy logic toolbox for industrial process control. In *Proceedings of the 2010 Brazilian Conference on Automatics (CBA), Brazilian Society for Automatics (SBA)*, pp. 207–214, SBA (2010).

[40] J. Liu, K. W. Lim, W. K. Ho, K. C. Tan, A. Tay and R. Srinivasan, Using the OPC standard for real-time process monitoring and control, *IEEE Software*, **22**(6), 54–59 (2005).

Chapter 12

Conversational Agents: Theory and Applications

Mattias Wahde* and Marco Virgolin†

*Department of Mechanics and Maritime Sciences,
Chalmers University of Technology, 412 96 Göteborg, Sweden,
*mattias.wahde@chalmers.se
†marco.virgolin@chalmers.se*

In this chapter, we provide a review of conversational agents (CAs), discussing chatbots, intended for casual conversation with a user, as well as task-oriented agents that generally engage in discussions intended to reach one or several specific goals, often (but not always) within a specific domain. We also consider the concept of embodied conversational agents, briefly reviewing aspects such as character animation and speech processing. The many different approaches to representing dialogue in CAs are discussed in some detail, along with methods for evaluating such agents, emphasizing the important topics of accountability and interpretability. A brief historical overview is given, followed by an extensive overview of various applications, especially in the fields of health and education. We end the chapter by discussing the benefits and potential risks regarding the societal impact of current and future CA technology.

12.1. Introduction

Conversational agents (CAs), also known as intelligent virtual agents (IVAs), are computer programs designed for natural conversation with human users, either involving informal chatting, in which case the system is usually referred to as a *chatbot*, or with the aim of providing the user with relevant information related to a specific task (such as a flight reservation), in which case the system is called a *task-oriented agent*. Some CAs use only text-based input and output, whereas others involve more complex input and output modalities (for instance, speech). There are also so-called embodied conversational agents (ECAs) that are typically equipped with an animated visual representation (face or body) on-screen. Arguably the most important part of CAs is the manner in which they represent and handle dialogue. Here, too, there is a wide array of possibilities, ranging from simple template-matching systems to highly complex representations based on deep neural networks (DNNs).

Among the driving forces behind the current, rapid development of this field is the need for sophisticated CAs in various applications, for example, in healthcare, education, and customer service; see also Section 12.7. In terms of research, the development is also, in part, driven by high-profile competitions such as the Loebner prize and the Alexa prize, which are briefly considered in Sections 12.5 and 12.6. Giving a full description of the rapidly developing field of CAs, with all of the facets introduced above, is a daunting task. Here, we will attempt to cover both theory and applications, but we will mostly focus on the representation and implementation of dialogue capabilities (rather than, say, issues related to speech recognition, embodiment, etc.), with emphasis on task-oriented agents, particularly applications of such systems. We strive to give a bird's-eye view of the many different approaches that are, or have been, used for developing the capabilities of CAs. Furthermore, we discuss the ethical implications of CA technology, especially aspects related to interpretability and accountability. The interested reader may also wish to consult other reviews on CAs and their applications [1–5].

12.2. Taxonomy

The taxonomy used here primarily distinguishes between, on the one hand, *chatbots* and, on the other, *task-oriented agents*. Chatbots are systems that (ideally) can maintain a casual dialogue with a user on a wide range of topics, but are generally neither equipped nor expected to provide precise information. For example, many (though not all) chatbots may give different answers if asked the same specific question several times (such as "Where were you born?"). Thus, a chatbot is primarily useful for conversations on everyday topics, such as restaurant preferences, movie reviews, sport discussions, and so on, where the actual content of the conversation is perhaps less relevant than the interaction itself: a well-designed chatbot can provide stimulating interactions for a human user, but would be lost if the user requires a detailed, specific answer to questions such as "Is there any direct flight to London on Saturday morning?".

Task-oriented agents, on the other hand, are ultimately intended to provide clear, relevant, and definitive answers to specific queries, a process that often involves a considerable amount of database queries (either offline or via the internet) and data processing that, with some generosity, can be referred to as *cognitive processing*. This might be a good point to clear up some confusion surrounding the taxonomy of CAs, where many authors refer to all such systems as chatbots. In our view, this is incorrect. As their name implies, chatbots do just that: *chat*, while task-oriented agents are normally used for more serious and complex tasks.

While these two categories form the basis for a classification of CAs, many other taxonomic aspects could be considered as well, for example, the input and output modalities used (e.g., text, speech, etc.), the applicability of the agent (general-purpose or domain-specific), whether or not the agent is able to self-learn, and so on [4]. One such aspect concerns the representation used, where one frequently sees a division into rule-based systems and systems based on artificial intelligence (AI), by which is commonly meant systems based on deep neural networks (DNNs) [6]. This, too, is an unfortunate classification in our view; first of all, the field of AI is much wider in scope than what the current focus on DNNs might suggest: for example, rule-based systems, as understood in this context, have played, and continue to play, a very important part in the field. Moreover, even though many so-called rule-based agents are indeed based on *handcrafted* rules, there is nothing preventing the use of machine learning methods (a subfield of AI), such as stochastic optimization methods [7] or reinforcement learning [8], in such systems. The name *rule-based* is itself a bit unfortunate, since a *rule* is a very generic concept that could, at least in principle, even be applied to the individual components of DNNs. Based on these considerations, we will here suggest an alternative dichotomy, which will be used alongside the other classification given above. This alternative classification divides CAs (whether they are chatbots or task-oriented agents) into the two categories *interpretable* systems and *black box* systems. We hasten to add that *interpretable* does not imply a lack of complexity: in principle, the behavior of an interpretable CA could be every bit as sophisticated as that of a black box (DNN) CA. The difference is that the former are based on transparent structures consisting of what one might call *interpretable primitives*, i.e., human-understandable components such as IF–THEN–ELSE rules, sorting functions, or AIML-based statements (see Section 12.4.1.1), which directly carry out high-level operations without the need to rely on the concerted action of a huge number of parameters as in a DNN.

As discussed in Sections 12.5.3 and 12.8, this is a distinction that, at least for task-oriented agents, is likely to become increasingly important in the near future: CAs are starting to be applied in high-stakes decisions, where interpretability is a crucial aspect [9], not least in view of the recently proposed legislation (both in the EU and the USA) related to a user's right to an explanation or motivation, for example, in cases where artificial systems are involved in bank credit decisions or clinical decision-making [10]. In such cases, the artificial system must be able to explain its reasoning or at least carry out its processing in a manner that can be understood by a human operator.

12.3. Input and Output Modalities

Textual processing, which is the focus of the sections below, is arguably the core functionality of CAs. However, natural human-to-human conversation also involves aspects such as speech, facial expressions, gaze, body posture, and gestures, all of which convey subtle but important nuances of interaction beyond the mere exchange of factual information. In other words, interactions between humans are *multimodal*.

Aspects of multimodality are considered in the field of *embodied conversational agents* (ECAs; also known as *interface agents*) that involve an interface for natural interaction with the user. This interface is often in the form of an animated face (or body) shown on-screen, but can also be a physical realization in the form of a *social robot* [16–18]. Figure 12.1 gives some examples; the three left panels show agents with a virtual (on-screen) interface, whereas the rightmost panel shows the *social robot* iCAT. Here, we will focus on virtual interfaces rather than physical implementations such as robots.

12.3.1. *Nonverbal Interaction*

Humans tend to anthropomorphize systems that have a life-like shape, such as an animated face on-screen [19]. Thus, a user interacting with an ECA may experience better rapport with the agent than would be the case for an interaction with an agent lacking a visual representation, and the embodiment also increases (in many, though not all, cases) the user's propensity to trust the agent, as found by Loveys et al. [20]. Some studies show that certain aspects of an ECA, such as presenting a smiling face or showing a sense of humor, improve the experience of interacting with the agent [21, 22], even though the user's personality is also a relevant factor when assessing the quality of interaction. For example, a recent study by ter Stal et al. on ECAs in the context of eHealth showed that users tend to prefer ECAs that are similar to themselves regarding age and sex (gender) [23]. Other studies show similar results regarding personality traits such as extroversion and

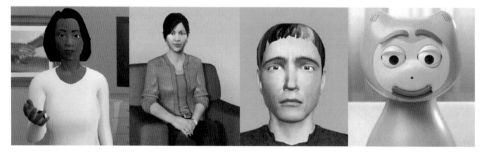

Figure 12.1: Three examples of ECAs and one social robot (right). From left to right: Gabby [11, 12], SimSensei [13], Obadiah [14], and iCAT [15] (Royal Philips / Philips Company Archives). All images are reproduced with kind permission from the respective copyright holders.

introversion [24, 25]. Additional relevant cues for human–agent interaction include gaze [26, 27], body posture [28], and gestures [29, 30], as well as the interaction between these expressive modalities [28].

Another point to note is that human likeness is not a prerequisite for establishing rapport between a human user and an ECA [31]. In fact, to some degree, one may argue that the opposite holds: Mori's *uncanny valley* hypothesis [32] states essentially that artificial systems that attempt to mimic human features in great detail, when not fully succeeding in doing so, tend to be perceived as eerie and repulsive. This hypothesis is supported by numerous studies in (humanoid) robotics, but also in the context of virtual agents [33]. What matters from the point of view of user–agent rapport seems instead to be that the appearance of an ECA should match the requirements of its task [34], and that the ECA should make use of several interaction modalities [31].

Conveying emotions is an important purpose of facial expressions. Human emotions are generally described in terms of a set of basic emotions. Ekman [35] defined six basic emotions, namely anger, disgust, fear, happiness, sadness, and surprise, a set that has later been expanded by others to cover additional basic emotions as well as linear combinations thereof [36]. Emotions can be mapped to facial expressions via the facial action coding system (FACS) [37, 38] that, in turn, relies on so-called action units (AUs), which are directly related to movements of facial muscles (as well as movements of the head and the eyes). For example, happiness can be modelled as the combination of AU6 (*cheek raiser*) and AU12 (*lip corner puller*). Emotion recognition can also be carried out using black box systems such as DNNs [39], trained end to end: these systems learn to predict the emotion from the image of a face, without the need to manually specify how intermediate steps should be carried out [40]. State-of-the-art facial emotion recognition systems typically achieve 80 to 95% accuracy over benchmark datasets [41].

Emotions are also conveyed in body language [42], albeit with greater cultural variation than in the case of facial expressions. ECAs equipped with cameras (especially depth cameras [43]) can be made to recognize body postures, gestures, and facial expressions (conveying emotional states), and to react accordingly. Gesture recognition, especially in the case of hand gestures, helps to achieve a more natural interaction between the user and the ECA [44]. Furthermore, the combination of audio and visual clues can be exploited to recognize emotions by multimodal systems [45, 46].

12.3.2. *Character Animation*

Methods for character animation can broadly be divided into three categories. In *procedural animation*, the poses of an animated body or face are parameterized, using underlying skeletal and muscular models (rigs) [47] coupled with inverse kinematics. In procedural *facial* animation, [48] every unit of sound (phoneme) is mapped to a corresponding facial expression (a *viseme*). Animations are then built in real time, either by concatenation or by blending, a process that allows full control over the animated system but is also computationally demanding and may struggle to generate life-like animations. In *data-driven animation*, the movement sequences are built by stitching together poses (or facial expressions) from a large database. Many different techniques have been defined, ranging from simple linear interpolations to methods that involve DNNs [49, 50]. Finally, *motion capture-based animation* and *performance-based animation* methods [51] map the body or facial movements of a human performer onto a virtual, animated character. This technique typically generates very realistic animations, but is laborious and costly. Moreover, the range of movements of the virtual character is limited by the range of expressions generated by the human performer [52]. Several frameworks have been developed for animating ECAs. An example is the SmartBody approach of Thiebaux et al. [53] that makes use of the behavior markup language (BML) [54] to generate animation sequences that synchronize facial motions and speech.

12.3.3. *Speech Processing*

Speech processing is another important aspect of an ECA or, more generally, of a *spoken dialogue system* (SDS)[1]. CAs handle incoming information in a step involving *natural language understanding* (NLU; see also Figure 12.4). In cases where speech (rather than just text) is used as an input modality, NLU is preceded by *automatic speech recognition* (ASR). The ASR step may provide a more natural type of interaction from the user's point of view, but it increases the complexity of the implementation considerably, partly because of the inherent difficulty in reliably recognizing speech and partly because spoken language tends to contain aspects that are not generally present in textual input (e.g., repetition of certain words, the use of interjections such as "*uh*," "*er*," and so on, as well as noise on various levels).

The performance of ASR can be measured in different ways: a common measure is the word error rate (WER), defined as

$$\text{WER} = \frac{S + I + D}{N}, \tag{12.1}$$

where N is the number of words in the reference sentence (the ground truth), and S, I, and D are, respectively, the number of (word) substitutions, insertions, and deletions required to go from the hypothesis generated by the ASR system to the

---

[1] An SDS is essentially a CA that processes speech (rather than text) as its input and output.

reference sentence. It should be noted, however, that the WER does not always represent the true ASR performance accurately, as it does not capture the semantic content of an input sentence. For example, in some cases, several words can be removed from a sentence without changing its meaning whereas in other cases, a difference of a single word, e.g., omitting the word *not*, may completely change the meaning. Still, the WER is useful in *relative* performance assessments of different ASR methods.

With the advent of deep learning, the accuracy of ASR has increased considerably. State-of-the-art methods for ASR, where DNNs are used for both phoneme recognition and word decoding, generally outperform [55] earlier systems that were typically based on hidden Markov models (HMMs). For DNNs, WERs of 5% or less (down from around 10–15% in the early 2010s) have been reported [56, 57], implying performance on a par with, or even exceeding, human performance. However, it should be noted that these low WERs generally pertain to low-noise speech in benchmark datasets, such as the LibriSpeech dataset, which is based on audio books [58]. In practical applications with noisy speech signals, different speaker accents, and so on, ASR performance can be considerably worse [59].

Modern text-to-speech (TTS) synthesis, which also relies on deep learning to a great degree, generally reaches a high level of naturalness [60, 61], as measured (subjectively) using the five-step mean opinion score (MOS) scale [62]. The requirements on speech output vary between different systems. For many ECAs, speech output must not only transfer information in a clear manner but also convey emotional states that, for example, match the facial expression of the ECA. It has been demonstrated that the pitch of an ECA voice influences the agent's perceived level of trustworthiness [63]. Similar results have been shown for ECAs that speak with a happy voice [64].

Finally, with the concept of *augmented reality*, or the still more ambitious concept of *mixed reality*, even more sophisticated levels of embodiment are made possible [65], where the embodied agent can be superposed onto the real world for an immersive user experience. This approach has recently gained further traction [66] with the advent of wearable augmented reality devices such as Microsoft's Hololens and Google Glass.

12.4. Dialogue Representation

A defining characteristic of any CA is the manner in which it handles dialogue. In this section, dialogue representation is reviewed for both chatbots and task-oriented agents, taking into consideration the fact that chatbots handle dialogue in a different and more direct manner than task-oriented agents.

12.4.1. *Chatbots*

Chatbots can be categorized into three main groups by the manner in which they generate their responses. Referring to the alternative dichotomy introduced in Section 12.2, the first two types, namely *pattern-based chatbots* and *information-retrieval chatbots*, would fall into the category of interpretable systems, whereas the third type, *generative chatbots*, are either of the interpretable kind or the black box variety, depending on the implementation used; those that make strong use of DNNs would clearly fall into the black box category.

12.4.1.1. *Pattern-Based chatbots*

The very first CA, namely Weizenbaum's ELIZA [67] belongs to a category that can be referred to as *pattern-based* chatbots[2]. This chatbot, released in 1966, was meant to emulate a psychotherapist who attempts to gently guide a patient along a path of introspective discussions, often by transforming and reflecting statements made by the user. ELIZA operates by matching the user's input to a set of patterns and then applying cleverly designed rules to formulate its response. Thus, as a simple example, if a user says "I'm depressed," ELIZA could use the template rule (I'm 1) → (I'm sorry to hear that you are 1), where 1 indicates a single word, to return "I'm sorry to hear that you are depressed." In other cases, where no direct match can be found, ELIZA typically just urges the user to continue. For example, the input "I could not go to the party" can be followed by "That is interesting. Please continue" or "Tell me more." ELIZA also ranks patterns, such that, when several options match the user's input, it will produce a response based on the highest-ranked (least generic) pattern. Furthermore, it features a rudimentary short-term memory, allowing it to return to earlier parts of a conversation to some degree.

More modern pattern-based chatbots, some of which are discussed in Section 12.6, are often based on the Artificial Intelligence Markup Language (AIML) [68], an XML-like language developed specifically for defining template-matching rules for use in chatbots. Here, each pattern (user input) is associated with an output (referred to as a *template*). A simple example of an AIML specification is

```
<category>
 <pattern> I LIKE *</pattern>
 <template>I like <star/> as well</template>
<\category>
```

---

[2]This type of chatbot is also commonly called *rule-based*. However, one might raise the same objections to that generic term as expressed in Section 12.2, and therefore the more descriptive term *pattern-based* will be used instead.

With this specification, if a user enters "I like tennis," the chatbot would respond by saying "I like tennis as well." AIML has a wide range of additional features, for example, those that allows it to store, and later retrieve, variables (e.g., the user's name). A chatbot based on AIML can also select random responses from a set of candidates, so as to make the dialogue more life-like. Moreover, AIML has a procedure for making redirections from one pattern to another, thus greatly simplifying the development of chatbots. For example, with the specification

```
<category>
  <pattern>WHAT IS YOUR NAME</pattern>
  <template>My name is Alice</template>
<\category>
<category>
  <pattern>WHAT ARE YOU CALLED</pattern>
  <template>
   <srai>WHAT IS YOUR NAME</srai>
  </template>
<\category>
```

the agent would respond "My name is Alice" if asked "What is your name" or "What are you called." As can be seen in the specification, the second pattern redirects to the first, using the so-called *symbolic reduction in artificial intelligence* (`srai`) tag.

12.4.1.2. *Information-retrieval chatbots*

Chatbots of this category generate their responses by selecting a suitable sentence from a (very) large dialogue corpus, i.e. a database of stored conversations. Simplifying somewhat, the basic approach is as follows: The agent (1) receives a user input $\mathcal{U}$; (2) finds the most similar sentence $\mathcal{S}$ (see below) in the associated dialogue corpus; and (3) responds with the sentence $\mathcal{R}$ that, in the dialogue corpus, was given in response to the sentence $\mathcal{S}$.

Similarity between sentences can be defined in different ways. Typically, sentences are encoded in the form of numerical vectors, called *sentence embeddings*, such that numerical measures of similarity can be applied. A common approach is to use TF-IDF [69] (short for *term frequency—inverse document frequency*), wherein each sentence is represented by a vector whose length equals the number of words[3] (N) available in the dictionary used. The TF vector is simply the frequency of occurrence of each word, normalized by the number of words in the sentence. Taken alone, this measure tends to give too much emphasis to common words such

---

[3]Usually after stemming and lemmatization, i.e., converting words to their basic form so that, for example, *cats* is represented as *cat*, *better* as *good*, and so on.

as "the," "is," and "we," which do not really say very much about the content of the sentence. The IDF for a given word w is typically defined as

$$\text{IDF} = \log \frac{M}{M_w}, \tag{12.2}$$

where M is the total number of sentences (or, more generally, documents) in the corpus and M_w is the number of sentences that contain w. Thus, IDF will give high values to words that are infrequent in the dialogue corpus and therefore likely to carry more relevant information about the contents of a sentence than more frequent words. The IDF values can be placed in a vector of length N that, for a fixed dialogue corpus, can be computed once and for all. Next, given the input sentence $\mathcal{U}$, a vector $q(\mathcal{U})$ can be formed by first generating the corresponding TF vector and then performing a Hadamard (element-wise) product with the IDF vector. The vector $q(\mathcal{U})$ can then be compared with the corresponding vector $q(\sigma_i)$ for all sentences σ_i in the corpus, using the vector (dot) product, and then extracting the most similar sentence S by computing the maximum cosine similarity as

$$S = \text{argmax}_i \left(\frac{q(\mathcal{U}) \cdot q(\sigma_i)}{\|q(\mathcal{U})\| \|q(\sigma_i)\|} \right). \tag{12.3}$$

The chatbot's response is then given as the response $\mathcal{R}$ to S in the dialogue corpus. An alternative approach is to directly retrieve the response that best matches the user's input [70].

Some limitations of the TF-IDF approach are that it does not take into account (1) the order in which the words appear in a sentence (which of course can have a large effect on the semantic content of the sentence) and (2) the fact that many words have synonyms. Consider, for instance, the two words *mystery* and *conundrum*. A sentence containing one of those words would have a term frequency of 1 for that word, and 0 for the other, so that the two words together give zero contribution to the cosine similarity in Equation (12.3). Such problems can be addressed using *word embeddings*, which are discussed below. Another limitation is that TF-IDF, in its basic form, does not consider the *context* of the conversation. Context handling can be included by, for example, considering earlier sentences in the conversation [71].

To overcome the limitations of TF-IDF, Yan et al. proposed an information-retrieval chatbot where a DNN is used to consider context from previous exchanges, and rank a list of responses retrieved by TF-IDF from the least to most plausible [72]. Other works on information-retrieval chatbots via DNNs abandon the use of TF-IDF altogether, and focus on how to improve the modeling of contextual information processing [73–75]. An aspect that is common to different types of DNN-based chatbots (of any kind), and incidentally also task-oriented agents, is the use of *word embeddings*. Similar to sentence embeddings, an embedding e_w of a word w is

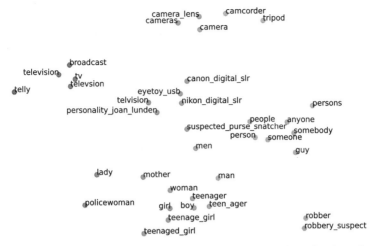

Figure 12.2: Projection obtained with t-SNE [80] of almost forty 300-dimensional word embeddings from word2vec [81]. The projection mostly preserves the embedding proximity, as similar words are clustered together. A notable exception is `suspected_purse_snatcher`, which is in the center of the plot and far from `robber` and `robbery_suspect`, in the bottom right. Note the presence of misspelled words from natural text, such as `telvision` and `televsion`.

a vectorial representation of w, i.e., $e_w \in \mathbb{R}^d$. DNNs rely on word embeddings in order to represent and process words and can actually learn the embeddings during their training process [76–79]. Typically, this is done by incorporating an $N \times d$ real-valued matrix Ω within the structure of the DNN as a first layer, where N is the number of possible words in the vocabulary (or, for long words, word-chunks) and d is the (predetermined) size of each word embedding. Ω is initialized at random. Whenever the network takes some words $w_i, w_j, w_k, \ldots$ as the input, only the corresponding rows of Ω, i.e., the embeddings $e_{w_i}, e_{w_j}, e_{w_k}, \ldots$ become active and pass information forward to the next layers. During the training process, the parameters of the DNN, which include the values of Ω and those of each e_{w_i}, are updated. Ultimately, each word embedding will capture a particular meaning. For example, Mikolov et al. [78] famously showcased that arithmetic operations upon DNN-learned word embeddings can be meaningful:

$$e_{\text{King}} - e_{\text{Man}} + e_{\text{Woman}} \approx e_{\text{Queen}}. \qquad (12.4)$$

As an additional example, Figure 12.2 shows a word cloud obtained by applying dimensionality reduction to a few dozen 300-dimensional word embeddings. As can be seen, embeddings of words with similar syntax or semantics are clustered together.

We remark that there are other ways than training DNNs to build word embeddings, resulting in word embeddings that carry information of another nature. Some of these methods are focused, e.g., on statistical occurrences of words within document classes [82, 83], or on word–word co-occurrences [84, 85]. Moreover, word embeddings can be used as numerical word representations in other systems, e.g., in evolutionary algorithms, to obtain human-interpretable mathematical expressions representing word manipulations [86].

12.4.1.3. *Generative chatbots*

While chatbots in the two previous categories rely on existing utterances, either in the form of pre-specified patterns or retrieved from a dialogue corpus, generative chatbots instead *generate* their responses using statistical models, called *generative models* or, specifically when one intends to model probability distributions over language (e.g., in the form of what words are likely to appear after or in between some other words), *language models*. Currently, this field is dominated by black box systems realized by DNNs trained on large amounts of data.

An important neural network model that is used at the heart of several generative chatbots is the *sequence to sequence* model (seq2seq) [86]. Figure 12.3 shows a simplified representation of seq2seq. Given a sequence of general tokens (in this case, words), seq2seq returns a new sequence of tokens, typically by making use of recurrent neural networks. Generally speaking, these networks operate by taking as input, one by one, the tokens that constitute a given sequence; processing each token; and producing an output that, crucially, depends on both the token processing and the outputs produced so far. Depending on the task, the training process of these systems can be based on the feedback of interacting users (a feedback that can be as simple as just indicating whether answers are *good* or *bad*) or on reference output text, such as known translations, answers to questions, or phrases where some words are masked and need to be guessed.

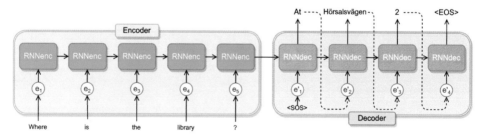

Figure 12.3: Simplified representation of seq2seq, unfolded over time. Each token of the input sentence "Where is the library?" is transformed into an embedding and fed to the recurrent neural network called the *encoder* (RNN$_{enc}$). This information is passed to the recurrent neural network responsible for providing the output sentence, called the *decoder* (RNN$_{dec}$). Note that each output token is routed back in the decoder to predict the next output token. The special tags <SOS> and <EOS> identify the start and end of the sentence, respectively.

One of the first uses of seq2seq to realize (part of the conversational capability of) chatbots can be attributed to Vinyals and Quoc [88], who showed that even though seq2seq was originally proposed for machine translation, it could be trained to converse when provided with conversation corpora (e.g., movie subtitles [89]). Today, seq2seq is a core component in several state-of-the-art generative chatbots: MILABOT [90] from the Montreal Institute for Learning Algorithms, Google's Meena [91], and Microsoft's XiaoIce[4] [92].

Another recent and popular component of DNNs useful for generating language is the *transformer* [93, 94]. Like recurrent neural networks, the transformer is designed to process sequential data, but it is different in that it does not need to parse the sequence of tokens in a particular order. Rather, the transformer leverages, at multiple stages, an information retrieval-inspired mechanism known as *self-attention*. This mechanism makes it possible to consider context from any other position in the sentence[5]. Broadly speaking, self-attention is capable of scoring, for each token (or better, for each embedding), how much contextual focus should be put on the other tokens (embeddings), no matter their relative position. For example, in the phrase *"Maria left her phone at home"*, the token "her" will have a large attention score for "Maria," while *"home"* will have large attention scores for *"left"* and "at." In practice, self-attention is realized by matrix operations, and the weights of the matrices are optimized during the training process of the DNN, just like any other component.

Transformers owe much of their popularity in the context of natural language processing to BERT (Bidirectional Encoder Representations from Transformers), proposed by Devlin et al. [79]. At the time of its introduction, BERT outperformed other contenders on popular natural language processing benchmark tasks of different nature [97], at times by a considerable margin. Before tuning the DNN that constitutes BERT to the task at hand (e.g., language translation, question answering, or sentiment analysis), pre-training over large text corpora is carried out to make the system learn what words are likely to appear next to others. Specifically, this is done by (1) collecting large corpora of text; (2) automatically masking out some tokens (here, words); and (3) optimizing the model to infer back the masked tokens. As mentioned above, when trained enough, the self-attention mechanism is capable of gathering information on the most important context for the missing tokens. For example, when the blanks need to be filled in *"Maria _ _ phone at home,"* a well-tuned self-attention will point to the preceding token *"Maria"* to help infer *"her,"* and point to *"at"* and *"home"* to infer *"left."* In particular, when trained to

---

[4]Note that XiaoIce is a large system that includes many other functionalities than chatting.

[5]The concept of (self-)attention is not a transformer-exclusive mechanism; in fact, it was firstly proposed to improve recurrent neural networks [95, 96].

guess the token at the end of the sequence, transformer-based DNNs are proficient at *generating* language. At inference time, they can take the user's utterance as the initial input.

Today's state-of-the-art DNNs for language modeling use a mix of (advanced) recurrent neural networks and transformers. Notable examples include ALBERT [98], XLNet [99], and the models by OpenAI, GPT2, and GPT3 [100, 101]. The latter two in particular contain hundreds of billions of parameters, were trained on hundreds of billions of words and are capable of chatting quite well even in so-called *few-* or *zero-shot* learning settings, i.e., when a very limited number of examples or no examples at all, respectively are used to tune the model to chatting. For the readers interested in delving into the details of DNNs for language modeling, we refer to the recent surveys by Young et al. [102] and Otter et al. [103].

12.4.2. *Task-Oriented Agents*

As mentioned in Section 12.2, the role of task-oriented agents is to engage in fact-based conversations on specific topics, and they must thus be able to give precise, meaningful, and consistent answers to the user's questions. Here, we will review such agents, following the alternative dichotomy from Section 12.2, where agents are classified as either interpretable systems or black box systems. The use of this dichotomy is particularly important here, since task-oriented agents are responsible for reaching concrete goals and may be deployed in sensitive settings (for example, medical or financial applications; see also Section 12.7) where transparency and accountability are essential.

Figure 12.4 shows the so-called *pipeline model*, in which the various stages of processing are shown as separate boxes. In this model, the first and last steps, namely ASR and speech synthesis, can be considered to be peripheral, as many

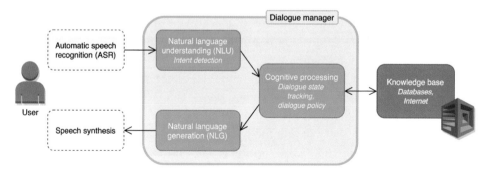

Figure 12.4: The pipeline model for CAs. The first and last steps (ASR and speech synthesis; see also Section 12.3) can, to some degree, be considered as external from the core components, shown in green. It should be noted that there are different versions of the pipeline model, with slightly different names for the various components, but essentially following the structure shown here.

agents operate in a completely text-based fashion. Turning to the core elements, shown in green in Figure 12.4, one can view the processing as taking place in three stages: First, in a step involving *natural language understanding* (NLU) the CA must identify precisely *what* the user said, or rather what the user *meant*; hence the notion of *intent detection*. Next, in a step that one may refer to as *cognitive processing* [104], the agent executes its *dialogue policy*, i.e., undertakes the actions needed to construct the knowledge required for the response, making use of a *knowledge base* in the form of an offline database, or via the internet or cloud-based services. A key factor here is to keep track of context, also known as *dialogue state*. Finally, the CA formulates the answer as a sentence in the process of *natural language generation* (NLG).

While the pipeline model offers a clear, schematic description of a task-oriented agent, it should be noted that not all such agents fall neatly into this model. Moreover, in the currently popular black box systems, the distinction between the stages tends to become blurred, as research efforts push toward requiring less and less human specification of how the processing should take place; see also Subsection 12.4.2.2.

12.4.2.1. *Interpretable dialogue systems*

The simplest examples of interpretable, task-oriented agents are the so-called *finite-state* systems [105], where the dialogue follows a rigid, predefined structure, such that the user is typically required to provide information in a given sequence. For example, if the CA is dealing with a hotel reservation, it might first ask the user "Which city are you going to?" then "Which day will you arrive?" and so on, requiring an answer to each question in sequence. In such a system the dialogue initiative rests entirely with the CA, and the user has no alternative but to answer the questions in the order specified by the agent. In addition, finite-state systems can be complemented with the capability of handling *universal commands* (such as "Start over"), which the user might give at any point in the conversation.

Even with such features included, however, CAs based on the finite-state approach are generally too rigid for any but the most basic kinds of dialogues; for example, in the case of a natural conversation regarding a reservation (flight, hotel, restaurant, etc.), the user may provide the required information in different orders, sometimes even conveying several parts of the request in a single sentence (e.g., "I want to book a flight to Paris on the 3rd of December"). Such aspects of dialogue are handled, to a certain degree, in *frame-based* (or *slot-filling*) systems, such as GUS [106], where the dialogue is handled in a more flexible manner that allows *mixed initiative*, i.e. a situation where the control over the dialogue moves back and forth between the agent and the user. Here, the agent maintains a so-called *frame* containing several *slots* that it attempts to fill by interacting with the user who may provide the information in any order (sometimes also filling more than one slot

Slot	Question
DEPARTURE CITY	*Where are you traveling from?*
ARRIVAL CITY	*Where are you going to?*
DEPARTURE DATE	*What day would you like to travel?*
DEPARTURE TIME	*What time would you like to leave?*

Figure 12.5: An example of a frame for a flight-reservation system. The frame contains a set of slots, each with an associated question. Note that only some of the required slots are shown in this figure.

Rule
QUERY → *{is there, do you have}*
VEHICLE → *{a car (available), any car (available)}*
PRICELIMIT → *{for less than, under, (priced) below}*
PRICE → *{*NUMBER *(dollars)}*
NUMBER → *{50, 100, 150, 200, 300, 500}*
TIMERANGE → *{a day, per day, a week, per week}*

Figure 12.6: An example of a simple semantic grammar for (some parts of) a car rental dialogue.

with a single sentence). Figure 12.5 shows (some of the) slots contained in a frame used in a flight-reservation system.

In a single-domain frame-based system, the agent's first step is to determine the intent of the user. However, in the more common multi-domain systems, this step is preceded by a *domain determination* step where the agent identifies the overall topic of discourse [105]. Intent detection can be implemented in the form of explicit, hand-written rules, or with the use of more sophisticated *semantic grammars* that define a set of rules (involving phrases) that form a compact representation of many different variations of a sentence, allowing the CA to understand different user inputs with similar meaning.

As a simple (and partial) example, consider a CA that handles car rentals. Here, a suitable semantic grammar may contain the rules shown in Figure 12.6, so that the sentences "Is there any car available for less than 100 dollars per day?" and "Do you have a car priced below 300 a week?" would both be identified as instances of QUERY–VEHICLE–PRICELIMIT–PRICE–TIMERANGE. Semantic grammars can be built in a hierarchical fashion (see, for example, how NUMBER is part of PRICE in the example just described), and can be tailored to represent much more complex features than in this simple example [107]. The output of frame-based systems (i.e., the NLG part in Figure 12.4) is typically defined using a set of predefined templates. Continuing with the car rental example, such a template could take the form "Yes, we have a <VEHICLETYPE> available at <NUMBER> dollars per day," where <VEHICLETYPE> and <NUMBER> would then be replaced by the appropriate values for the situation at hand.

The frame-based approach works well in situations where the user is expected to provide several pieces of information on a given topic. However, many dialogues involve other aspects such as, for example, frequently switching back and forth between different domains (contexts). Natural dialogue requires a more advanced and capable representation than that offered by frame-based systems and typically involves identification of *dialogue acts* as well as *dialogue state tracking*. Dialogue acts [108] provide a form of categorization of an utterance, and represent an important first step in understanding the utterance [109]. For example, an utterance of the form "Show me all available flights to London" is an instance of the COMMAND dialogue act, whereas the possible response "OK, which day to you want to travel?" is an instance of CLARIFY, and so on. Dialogue act *recognition* has been approached in many different ways [110], reaching an accuracy of around 80–90%, depending on the dataset used. Dialogue state tracking, which is essentially the ability of the CA to keep track of context, has also been implemented in many ways, for example using a set of state variables (as in MIT's JUPITER system [111]) or the more general concept of *information state* that underlies the TrindiKit and other dialogue systems [112]. Dialogue state tracking has also been the subject of a series of competitions; see the work by Williams et al. [113] for a review.

For the remainder of this section, the systems under consideration reach a level of complexity such that their interpretability is arguably diminished, yet they still make use of high-level, interpretable primitives and are most definitely far from being complete black boxes. Thus, going beyond finite-state and frame-based systems, several methods have been developed that incorporate more sophisticated models of the user's beliefs and goals. These methods can generally be called *model-based* methods [114] (even though this broad category of methods also goes under other names, and involves somewhat confusing overlaps between the different approaches). Specifically, in *plan-based* methods [115, 116], such as Ravenclaw [117], which are also known as belief-desire-intention (BDI) models, the CA explicitly models the goals of the conversation and attempts to guide the user toward those goals. *Agent-based* methods [118] constitute another specific example. They involve aspects of both the plan-based and information state approaches, and extend those notions to model dialogue as a form of cooperative problem-solving between agents (the user and the CA), where each agent is capable of reasoning about its own beliefs and goals but also those of the other agent. Thus, for example, this approach makes it possible for the CA not only to respond to a question literally, but also to provide additional information in anticipation of the user's goals [119].

Even though there is no fundamental obstacle to using a data-driven, machine learning approach to systems of the kind described above, these methods are often referred to as *handcrafted* as this is the manner in which they have most often been built. Moreover, these methods generally maintain a single, deterministic description of the current state of the dialogue. There are also methods that model dialogue in a probabilistic, statistical way and which can be seen as extensions of the information-state approach mentioned above. The first steps toward such systems model dialogue as a Markov decision process (MDP) [120], in which there is a set of states (S), a set of actions (A), and a matrix of transition probabilities (P) that models the probability of moving from one given state to another when taking a specific action $a \in A$. Any action a resulting in state s is associated with an immediate reward $r(s, a)$. There is also a dialogue policy π, specifying the action that the agent should take in any given situation. The policy is optimized using reinforcement learning so as to maximize the expected reward. Levin et al. [121] provide an accessible introduction to this approach. The MDP approach, which assumes that the state s is observable, is unable to deal with the inevitable uncertainty of dialogue, whereby the user's goal, the user's last dialogue act, and the dialogue history, which together define the dialogue state, cannot be known with absolute certainty [122]. Therefore, systems that take into account the inherent uncertainty in conversation (including ASR uncertainty) have been proposed in the general framework of partially observable Markov decision processes (POMDPs). Rather than representing a single state, a POMDP defines a distribution over all possible dialogue states, referred to as the *belief state*. A difficult problem with MDPs and, to an even greater degree, POMDPs, is the fact that their representation of dialogue states is very complex. This, in turn, results in huge state spaces and therefore computational intractability. Much work on POMDPs, therefore, involves various ways of coping with such problems [123]. Young et al. provide a review of POMDPs for dialogue [124].

12.4.2.2. *Black box dialogue systems*

Black box task-oriented agents are essentially dominated by the field of DNNs. For these CAs, many of the aspects that were described before for DNN-based chatbots still apply. For example, DNN-based task-oriented agents also represent words with embeddings, and rely on DNN architectures such as recurrent or convolutional ones [125], as well as transformer-based ones [126, 127]. There are other types of DNNs used for task-oriented systems, such as memory networks [128, 129] and graph convolutional networks [130, 131]. However, delving into their explanation is beyond the scope of this chapter.

Normally, the type of DNN used depends on what stage of the agent the DNN is responsible for. In fact, black box systems can often be framed in terms of the pipeline model (Figure 12.4), where NLU, NLG, dialogue policy, etc., are modeled somewhat separately. Even so, the DNNs responsible for realizing a black box task-oriented agent are connected to, and dependent on, one another, so as to allow the flow of information that makes end-to-end information processing possible. An emerging trend in the field, as we mentioned before, is to make the agent less and less dependent on human design, and instead increase the responsibility of the DNNs to automatically learn how to solve the task from examples and interaction feedback.

Wen et al. [125] proposed one of the first DNN-based task-oriented agents trained end-to-end, namely a CA for restaurant information retrieval. To collect the specific data needed for training the system, the authors used a *Wizard-of-Oz* approach [132], scaled to a crowd-sourcing setting, to gather a large number of examples. In particular, one part of Amazon Mechanical Turk [133] workers were instructed to act as normal users asking information about restaurants and food. The other part, i.e., the *wizards of Oz*, were asked to play the role of a perfect agent by replying to all inquiries using a table of information that was provided beforehand. Alternatively, since training from examples requires large corpora to be collected beforehand, reinforcement learning can be used [134].

Some works attempt to improve the way these black box systems interface with the knowledge base. Typically, the DNN that is responsible for the dialogue policy chooses the information retrieval query deemed to be most appropriate. Dhingra et al. [135] have shown, however, that one can include mechanisms to change the lookup operation so as to use *soft* queries that provide multiple degrees of truth, ultimately making it possible to obtain a richer signal that is useful to improve training. Madotto et al. [136] instead looked at improving the scalability of the systems to query large knowledge bases, by essentially having the DNNs assimilate information from the knowledge base within the network parameters at training time. This improves information retrieval speed because querying the external knowledge base normally takes longer than inferring the same information from within a DNN. However, this also means that some degree of re-training is needed when the information in the knowledge base is changed.

There are many more works on DNN-based task-oriented agents that deal with different aspects for improvement. For instance, a problem is that a DNN responsible for NLG can learn to rely on specific information retrieved from the knowledge base in order to generate meaningful responses, to such an extent that changes to the knowledge base can lead to unstable NLG. This problem is being tackled in ongoing research aimed at decoupling NLG from the knowledge base [137, 138]. Another interesting aspect concerns incorporating training data from multiple domains, for situations where the data that are specific to the task at hand are scarce [139]. Finally, we refer to the works by Bordes et al. [129], Budzianowski et al. [140], and Rajendran et al. [141] as examples where datasets useful for training and benchmarking this type of CA are presented.

Evaluation of conversational agents

Objective & automatic scoring metrics	Categorization & organization of human feedback	Evaluation of societal implications
Accuracy, precision, recall, perplexity, BLEU, ROUGE, #utterances, avg. phrase length, ...	Overall satisfaction, sensibleness, specificity, coherence, proactivity, SUS, SASSI, PARADISE, ...	Governmental regulations, (lack of) evaluation tools, privacy concerns, risks, ethics, black-box systems, ...

Figure 12.7: Schematic view of the different levels at which CAs can be evaluated, mirroring the organization of Section 12.5.

12.5. Evaluation of Conversational Agents

Evaluation of CAs is a very much an open topic of research. Current systems are still far from achieving seamless, human-like conversation capabilities [142, 143]. Understanding how best to measure such capabilities represents an important endeavor to advance the state-of-the-art. There are many different evaluation criteria, aimed at different levels of the human-agent interaction. Firstly in this section, a brief introduction on low-level metrics used to evaluate general language processing is given. Next, moving on to a higher-level of abstraction, evaluation metrics that address the quality of interaction with CAs, in a more general setting, and in more detail for the case of ECAs, are considered. Last but not least, evaluation systems that delve into broad implications and ethics are described. Figure 12.7 summarizes these different aspects of evaluation.

12.5.1. *Low-level Language Processing Evaluation Metrics*

On a low level, when developing the capabilities of a CA to process utterances, retrieve information, and generate language, traditional metrics for general pattern recognition like *precision* and *recall* represent useful metrics for evaluation. For example, for a CA employed in a psychiatric facility, one may wish the agent (or a component thereof) to assess whether signs of depression transpire from the interaction with the patient: In such a case, maximizing recall is important. In practice, traditional metrics such as precision and recall are employed across several types of benchmark problems, e.g., to evaluate sentiment analysis [144], paraphrase identification [145], question answering [146], reading comprehension [49], and also gender bias assessment [147]. The *general language understanding evaluation* (GLUE) benchmark [97], and its successor SuperGLUE [148], provide a carefully picked collection of datasets and tools for evaluating natural language processing systems, and maintain a leaderboard of top-scoring systems.

Alongside traditional scoring metrics, the field of natural language processing has produced additional metrics that are useful to evaluate CAs in that they focus on words and n-grams (sequences of words) and are thus more directly related to language. A relevant example of this is the bilingual evaluation understudy (BLEU) scoring metric. Albeit originally developed to evaluate the quality of machine translation [149], BLEU has since been adopted in many other tasks, several of which are of relevance for CAs, e.g., summarization and question answering. For the sake of brevity, we will only describe how BLEU works at a high level. In short, BLEU can be seen as related to precision and is computed by considering how many n-grams in a candidate sentence (e.g., produced by a CA) match n-grams in reference sentences (e.g., high-quality sentences produced by humans). The n-grams considered are normally of length 1 to 4. Matches for longer n-grams are weighted exponentially more than matches for smaller n-grams. In addition, BLEU includes a penalty term to penalize candidate sentences that are shorter than reference sentences. We refer the reader interested in the details of BLEU to the seminal work by Panineni et al. [149]. A metric similar to BLEU, but with the difference that it focuses on recall rather than precision, is *recall-oriented understudy for gisting evaluation* (ROUGE), which is reviewed in the seminal works by Lin et al. [150, 151].

12.5.2. *Evaluating the Quality of the Interaction*

The evaluation of the quality of interaction requires human judgment. In this context, researchers attempt to find the aspects that define a good interaction with an agent in order to obtain a better understanding of how CAs can be built successfully. This section is divided into one general part on conversational capabilities and one part on embodiment.

12.5.2.1. *General CAs*

The work by Adiwardana et al. of Google Brain proposes to categorize human evaluation into *sensibleness* and *specificity* [91]. Evaluating sensibleness means to assess whether the agent is able to give responses that make sense in context. Evaluating specificity, instead, involves determining whether the agent is effectively capable of answering with specific information, as opposed to providing vague and empty responses, a strategy often taken to avoid making mistakes. Interestingly, the authors found that the average of sensibleness and specificity reported by users correlates well with *perplexity*, a low-level metric for language models that represents the degree of uncertainty in token prediction.

The Alexa Prize competition represents an important stage for the evaluation of CAs [152]. To rank the contestants, Venkatesh et al. defined several aspects, some of which require human assessment, and some of which are automatic [153].

For example, one aspect is *conversational user experience*, which is collected as the overall rating (in the range 1, 5) from users that were given the task of interacting with the CAs during the competition. Another aspect, *coherence*, was set to be the number of sensible responses over the total number of responses, with humans annotating sensible answers. Other aspects were evaluated with simple metrics, e.g., *engagement* as the number of utterances, and *topical breadth* and *topical depth* as the number of topics touched in the conversation (identified with a vocabulary of keywords) and the number of consecutive utterances on a certain topic, respectively. Venkatesh et al. also attempted to find a correlation between human judgment and automatic metrics, but only small correlations were found.

The recent survey by Chaves and Gerrosa [154] reports on further research endeavors to elucidate the aspects that account for the perception of successful and engaging interactions with CAs. These aspects include, for example, *conscientiousness*: how aware of and attentive to the context the CA appears to be; *communicability*: how transparent the CA's interaction capabilities are, e.g., for the user to know how to best query the agent [155]; *damage control*: how capable the CA is to recover from failure, handle unknown concepts, etc [156]. Some apparent qualities can actually be perceived to be negative, when excessive. CAs that take too much initiative constitute a clear example, as they can be perceived as intrusive or frustrating, or even give the feeling of attempting to exercise control over the user [157, 158].

Aspects of the perception of the interaction are collected using standardized questionnaires (involving, for example, the Likert scale [159]), which can be relatively general and can be applied beyond CAs, such as the *system usability scale* (SUS) [160], or specific to the human–CA interaction, including particular focuses such as evaluation of speech recognition, as done by the *subjective assessment of speech system interfaces* (SASSI) [161]. A notable organizational framework of user feedback that applies well to task-oriented CAs is the *paradigm for dialogue system evaluation* (PARADISE) [162]. PARADISE links the overall human-provided rating about the quality of interaction to the agent's likelihood of success in completing a task and the cost of carrying out the interaction. Task success is based on pre-deciding what the most important building blocks of the interaction are, in the form of attribute–value pairs (e.g., an attribute could be *departing station*, and the respective values could be *Amsterdam, Berlin, Paris*, etc.). With this organization of the information, confusion matrices can be created, useful for determining whether the CA returns the correct values for interactions regarding certain attributes. The cost of the interactions, i.e., how much effort the user needs to invest to reach the goal, consists of counting how many utterances are required in total, and how many are needed to correct a misunderstanding. Finally, a scoring metric is obtained by a linear regression of the perceived satisfaction as a function of task success statistics and interaction costs.

Recently, in an effort to provide consistent evaluations and to automate human involvement, Sedoc et al. proposed ChatEval [163], a web application aimed at standardizing comparisons across CAs. To use ChatEval, one uploads (the description and) the responses of a CA to a provided set of prompts. As soon as they are uploaded, the responses are evaluated automatically with low-level metrics such as average response length, BLEU score, and cosine similarity over sentence embeddings between the agent's response and the ground-truth response [164]. Optionally, by paying a fee one can make ChatEval automatically start a human-annotation task on Amazon Mechanical Turk, where users evaluate the responses of the agent in a standardized way.

12.5.2.2. *Evaluation of embodiment*

When embodiment comes into play, alongside aspects that are general to the interaction with CAs such as conversational capabilities in both chat and task-oriented settings, or handling of intentional malevolent probing, ECAs can be evaluated in terms of *visual look* and *appearance personalization options* [165]. Another aspect of evaluation considers whether the (E)CA exhibits (interesting) *personality traits*. ECAs are arguably at an advantage in this context compared to non-embodied CAs, because they can enrich their communication with body language and facial expressions.

Since ECAs can leverage nonverbal interaction, they can engage the user more deeply at an emotional level. In this setting, emotional ECAs can be evaluated by comparison with non-emotional ones [166], in terms of aspects such as *like-ability, warmth, enjoyment, trust, naturalness of emotional reactions, believability,* and so on.

Evaluation of embodiment can also be carried out in terms of opposition with the absence of embodiment, or in terms of physical embodiment vs. virtual embodiment, the latter type of comparison being more popular. In one such study [167], it was found that people evaluate (at different levels) the interaction with a physical ECA (specifically, Sony's Aibo [168]) and a prototype robot (by Samsung, called April) more positively than the interaction with a virtual version of the same ECA. A similar study has been carried out using a physical and virtual ECA to interact during chess games [169]. At the same time, other studies have instead recorded that physical ECAs are no better than virtual ECAs. For example, it was found that whether a task-oriented ECA is physical or virtual results in no statistical differences between two very different tasks: persuading the user to consume healthier food and helping to solve the Towers of Hanoi puzzle [170]. Last but not least, as mentioned before in Section 12.3, an *excess* of embodiment (particularly so when embodiment attempts to be too human-like) can actually worsen the quality of the perceived interaction. Aside from the uncanny valley hypothesis [32, 171], another valid reason for this is that more sophisticated embodiments can lead to bigger expectations on conversational capabilities that leave the user more disappointed when those expectations are not met [172].

Much uncertainty about the benefits of using physical or virtual ECAs is still present, since both the ECAs involved and the methods used for their evaluations vary widely in the literature, from adopting questionnaires on different aspects of the interaction to measuring how long it takes to complete a puzzle. For further reading on the evaluation of ECAs, we refer to Granström and House [173] and Weiss et al. [174].

12.5.3. *Evaluating Societal Implications*

With CAs becoming ever more advanced and widespread, it is becoming increasingly clear that their societal impact must be evaluated carefully before they are deployed. In fact, failures of CAs from a societal and ethical standpoint have already been recorded. Microsoft's chatbot *Tay* for Twitter is an infamous example [175]: The agent's capability to learn and mimic user behavior was exploited by Twitter trolls, who taught the agent to produce offensive tweets, forcing a shutdown of the agent. Moreover, it is not hard to imagine that a lack of regulations and evaluation criteria for the safe deployment of CAs in sensitive societal sectors can lead to a number of unwanted consequences. While some general regulations might exist [10], for many societal sectors the evaluation tools required to ensure safe and ethical use of CAs are still largely missing.

Healthcare is one among several sectors where the adoption of CAs could bring many benefits, e.g., by helping patients to access care during a pandemic [176] or supporting pediatric cancer patients who must remain in isolation during part of their treatment [177]. However, many risks exist as well [178]. For example, safeguarding patient privacy is crucial: it must be ensured that a CA does not leak sensitive patient information. Ethical and safety implications regarding the circumstances and conditions under which a CA is allowed to operate in a clinic must also be carefully assessed. Examples of questions in this domain are: "In what context is it ethical to have patients interacting with a CA rather than a human?"; "Is informing about health complications a context where an agent should be allowed to operate?" "Is it safe to use CAs for patients who suffer from psychiatric disorders?" "Would it be acceptable to introduce disparities in care whereby wealthier patients can immediately access human doctors, while the others must converse with agents first?" Evaluation tools to answer these questions have yet to be developed.

Last but not least, it is essential to note that the use of black box CAs comes with additional risks, especially in cases where such CAs are involved in high-stakes decisions, where one can instead argue in favor of more transparent and accountable systems [9]. The field of *interpretable AI* involves methods for developing such inherently transparent systems. The closely related, and perhaps more general, notion of *explainable AI* (XAI) [179, 180] considers (post hoc) approaches for attempting to explain the decisions taken by black box systems [9] as well as methods for improving their level of explainability [181].

With transparent systems originating from interpretable AI, a sufficient understanding of the system's functionality to guarantee safe use can generally be achieved. For black box CAs, however, one should be careful when applying methods for explaining their decision-making to the specific case of evaluating their *safety*. This is so since explanations for black box systems can, in general, only be specific (also referred to as *local* [179]) to the particular event under study. In other words, given two events that are deemed to be similar and for which it is expected that the CA should react similarly, this might not happen [9]. Furthermore, the possibility of understanding the workings of agent components derived using machine learning is key to spotting potential biases hidden in the (massive amounts of) data [179, 180] used when training such components. With black box systems, it is simply harder to pinpoint potential damaging biases before the system has been released and has already caused damage [9, 182].

12.6. Notable Conversational Agents

To some degree, this section can be considered a historical review of CAs, but it should be observed that the set of CAs that have gained widespread attention is very much dominated by chatbots rather than task-oriented agents: even though some task-oriented systems are mentioned toward the end of the section, for a complete historical review the reader is also advised to consider the various systems for task-oriented dialogue presented in Subsection 12.4.2. Moreover, this section is focused on dialogue capabilities rather than the considerable and concurrent advances in, say, speech recognition and the visual representation of CAs (embodiment).

The origin of CAs can be traced back to the dawn of the computer age when, in 1950, Turing reflected on the question of whether a machine can think [183]. Noting that this question is very difficult to answer, Turing introduced *the imitation game*, which today goes under the name *the Turing test*. In the imitation game, a human interrogator (C) interacts with two other participants, a human (A) and a machine (B). The participants are not visible to each other, so that the only way that C can interact with A and B is via textual conversation. B is said to have passed the test if C is unable to determine that it is indeed the machine.

Passing the Turing test has been an important goal in CA research (see also below) even though, as a measure of machine intelligence, the test itself is also controversial; objections include, for example, suggestions that the test does not cover all aspects of intelligence, or that successful imitation does not (necessarily) imply actual, conscious thinking[6].

As computer technology became more advanced, the following decade saw the introduction of the first CA, namely the chatbot ELIZA [67] in 1966; see also Subsection 12.4.1.1. The most famous incarnation of ELIZA, called DOCTOR, was implemented with the intention of imitating a Rogerian psychoanalyst. Despite its relative simplicity compared to modern CAs, ELIZA was very successful; some users reportedly engaged in deep conversations with ELIZA, believing that it was an actual human, or at least acting as though they held such a belief.

In 1972, ELIZA was followed by the PARRY chatbot that, to a great degree, represents its opposite: instead of representing a medical professional, PARRY was written to imitate a paranoid schizophrenic and was used as a training tool for psychiatrists to learn how to communicate with patients suffering from this affliction. The semblance of intelligence exhibited by both ELIZA and PARRY can be derived, to a great degree, from their ability to deflect the user's input, without actually giving a concrete, definitive reply to the user. Predictably, ELIZA has actually met PARRY in several conversations [184], which took place in 1972 over the ARPANet, the predecessor to the internet.

At this point, it is relevant to mention the Loebner prize, which was instituted in the early 1990s. In the associated competition, which is an annual event since 1991, the entrants participate in a Turing test. A 100,000 USD one-time prize (yet to be awarded) is offered for a CA that can interact with (human) evaluators in such a way that it is deemed indistinguishable from a real human in terms of its conversational abilities. There are also several smaller prizes. The Loebner competition is controversial and has been criticized in several different ways, for example on the grounds that it tends to favor deception rather than true intelligence. Nevertheless, the list of successful entrants does offer some insight into the progress of CA development.

A.L.I.C.E [185], a somewhat contrived abbreviation of Artificial Linguistic Internet Computer Entity, was a pattern-based chatbot built using AIML (see Section 12.4.1.1). Its first version was released in 1995, followed by additional versions a few years later. Versions of A.L.I.C.E. won the Loebner competition several times in the early 2000s.

Two other notable chatbots are Jabberwacky and its successor Cleverbot. Jabberwacky was implemented in the 1980s, and was released on the internet in 1997,

---

[6]It should be noted, in fairness, that Turing did address many of those objections in his paper, and that he did not intend his test to be a measure of machine consciousness.

whereas Cleverbot appeared in 2006. These chatbots are based on information retrieval [186] and improve their capabilities (over time) automatically from conversation logs: every interaction between Cleverbot and a human is stored, and can then be accessed by the chatbot in future conversations. Versions of Jabberwacky won the Loebner competition in 2005 and 2006. Cleverbot rose to fame when, in 2011, it participated in a Turing test (different from the Loebner competition) in India, and was deemed 59.3% human, which can be compared with the average score of 63.3% for *human* participants. Another chatbot for which similar performance has been reported is Eugene Goostman. In two Turing tests [187], one in 2012 marking the centenary of the birth of Alan Turing and one in 2014, organized in Cambridge on the occasion of the 60th anniversary of his death, this chatbot managed to convince 29% (2012) and 33% (2014) of the evaluators that it was human. Claims regarding the intellectual capabilities of these chatbots have also been widely criticized.

Another recent AIML-based chatbot is Mitsuku [188], which features interactive learning and can perhaps be considered a representative of the current state-of-the-art in pattern-based chatbot technology. Mitsuku has won the Loebner competition multiple times (more than any other participant) in the 2010s. Implemented in a scripting language called ChatScript [189], the chatbot Rose and its two predecessors Suzette and Rosette have also won the Loebner competition in the 2010s.

The 2010s also saw the introduction of CAs used as personal assistants on mobile devices, starting with the launch of SIRI (for Apple's iPhone) in 2011 and rapidly followed by Google Now in 2012, as well as Amazon's Alexa and Microsoft's Cortana a few years later[7]. These CAs, which also generally feature advanced speech recognition, combine chatbot functionality (for everyday conversation) with task-oriented capabilities (for answering specific queries). In this context, it is relevant to mention again the Alexa prize [152]; introduced in 2016, this contest does not focus on the Turing test. Instead, the aim is to generate a CA that is able to converse "coherently and engagingly" on a wide range of current topics, with a grand challenge involving a 20-minute conversation of that kind [190].

In 2020, Google Brain presented Meena [91], a new DNN-based generative chatbot the architecture of which was optimized with evolutionary algorithms. With human evaluation recorded in percentage and based on the average of sensibleness and specificity (see Section 12.5.2), Meena was found to outperform chatbots such as XiaoIce, DialoGPT, Mitsuku, and Cleverbot, with a gain of 50% compared to XiaoIce and 25% compared to Cleverbot (the best after Meena).

---

[7]SmarterChild, a CA released in the early 2000s on instant messenger networks, can perhaps be seen as a precursor to SIRI.

12.7. Applications

This section provides a review of recent applications of CAs, focusing mainly on task-oriented agents. We have attempted to organize applications into a few main subtopics, followed by a final subsection on other applications. However, we make no claims regarding the completeness of the survey below; in this rapidly evolving field, new interesting applications appear continuously. The description below is centered on results from scientific research. There are also several commercial products that are relevant, for example general-purpose CAs such as Apple's Siri, Amazon's Alexa, and Microsoft's Cortana, and CA development tools such as Google's DialogFlow, Microsoft's LUIS, IBM's Watson, and Amazon's Lex. However, these products will not be considered further here.

12.7.1. *Health and Well-Being*

Arguably one of the most promising application areas, health and well-being is a central topic of much CA research [3, 191]. This application area is not without controversy, however, due to ethical considerations such as safety and respect for privacy [178].

With the continuing rise in human life expectancy, especially in developed countries, the fraction of elderly people in the population is expected to rise dramatically over the coming decades, an undoubtedly positive development but also one that will exacerbate an already strained situation for the healthcare systems in many countries. Thus, a very active area of research is the study of CAs (and, especially, ECAs) for *some* (noncritical) tasks in elderly care. Examples include CAs that monitor medicine intake [192], interact with patients regarding their state of health (e.g., during cancer treatment) [193], or provide assistance and companionship [194–196], a case where social robots, such as Paro by Shibata et al. [197] (see also Hung et al. [198]), also play a role.

Mental health problems affect a large portion of the worldwide population. Combined with a shortage of psychiatrists, especially in low-income regions, these diseases present a major challenge [199]. CAs are increasingly being applied in the treatment of mental health problems [199–201], generally with positive results, even though most studies presented so far have been rather preliminary and exploratory in nature, rarely involving full, randomized controlled trials. Moreover, issues beyond the CA functionality and performance, such as legal and ethical considerations, must also be addressed [178, 200] carefully and thoroughly before CAs can be applied fully in the treatment of mental health problems (or, indeed, in any form of healthcare). Several tasks can be envisioned for CAs applied to mental health problems. A prominent example is intervention in cases of anxiety and depression, using CAs such as Woebot [202] that applies cognitive behavioral therapy (CBT).

Another important application is for the treatment of post-traumatic stress disorder (PTSD), where the anonymity offered by a CA interaction (as opposed to an interaction with a human interviewer) may offer benefits [203].

CAs can also be used in lifestyle coaching, discouraging harmful practices such as smoking [204] or drug abuse [205], and promoting healthy habits and lifestyle choices involving, for example, diet or physical exercise [206]. An example of such a CA is Ally, presented by Kramer et al. [207], which was shown to increase physical activity measured using step counts. A related application area is self-management of chronic diseases, such as asthma and diabetes. In the case of asthma, the kBot CA was used for helping young asthma patients manage their condition [208]. Similarly, Gong et al. [209] proposed Laura, which was tested in a randomized controlled trial and was shown to provide significant benefits.

Another important application, where spoken dialogue is crucial, is to provide assistance to people who are visually impaired, with the aim of improving social inclusion as well as accessibility to various services [210, 211].

CAs may also play an important role in assisting medical professionals, for example, in scheduling appointments, in providing information to patients, as well as in dictation. A survey of 100 physicians showed that a large majority believe that CAs could be useful in administrative tasks, but less so in clinical tasks [212]. Still, some CAs, such as Mandy by Ni et al. [213], aim to provide assistance to physicians in primary care, for example, in basic interaction with patients regarding their condition.

12.7.2. *Education*

Education is another field where CAs have been applied widely. Most of the educational applications reported below rely on interpretable CAs (e.g., based on AIML [214]); however, black box CAs have also been investigated (e.g., using seq2seq [215]). A natural application of CAs in the education domain is to provide a scalable approach to knowledge dissemination. Massive open online courses are a clear example, since one-to-one interaction between teacher and student is not feasible in these cases. In such settings, the course quality can be improved by setting up CAs that can handle requests from hundreds or thousands of students at the same time [216]. For instance, Bayne et al. proposed Teacherbot [217]. This pattern-based CA was created to provide teaching support over Twitter for a massive open online course that enrolled tens of thousands of students. Similarly, a CA in the form of a messaging app was created to provide teaching assistance for a large course at the Hong Kong University of Science and Technology [218].

Even though CAs can improve the dissemination of education, their effectiveness in terms of learning outcomes and engagement capability strongly depends on the specific way in which they are implemented, and the context in which they are proposed. For example, AutoTutor was found to compare favorably when contrasted with classic textbook reading in the study of physics [219]. On the other hand, the AIML-based CA Piagetbot (a successor of earlier work, Freudbot [220]) was not more successful than textbook reading when administered to psychology students [221]. More recently, Winkler et al. proposed Sara [222], a CA that interacts with students during video lectures on programming. Interestingly, equipping Sara with voice recognition and structuring the dialogue into sub-dialogues to induce scaffolding were found to be key mechanisms to improve knowledge retention and the ability to transfer concepts. Beyond providing an active teaching support, CAs have also been used to improve the way education is conducted, e.g., as an interface for course evaluation [223], and related logistics aspects, e.g., by providing information about the campus [224–226].

Linking back to and connecting with the previous section on health and well-being, educational CAs have also been applied to provide learning support to visually impaired adults [227] and deaf children [228]. Moreover, a particularly sensitive context of care where CAs are being investigated is the education of children with autism. For example, an AIML-based virtual ECA called Thinking Head was adopted to teach children with autism (6 to 15 years old) about conversational skills and dealing with bullying [229]. Similarly, the ECA Rachel [230] was used to teach emotional behavior. More recently, ECAs have also been used to help teenagers with autism learn about nonverbal social interaction [231, 232]. Alongside speech recognition, these ECAs include facial features tracking in order to provide cues on smiling, maintaining eye contact, and other nonverbal aspects of social interaction.

For more reading on this topic, we refer to the works by Johnson et al. [233], Kerry et al. [234], Roos [214], Veletsianos and Russell [235], and Winkler and Söllner [216].

12.7.3. *Business Applications*

The rise of e-commerce has already transformed the business landscape and it is a process that, in all likelihood, will continue for many years to come. Currently, e-commerce is growing at a rate of 15–20% per year worldwide, and the total value of e-commerce transactions is more than 4 trillion US dollars. Alongside this trend, many companies are also deploying CAs in their sales and customer service. It has been estimated that CA technology will be able to answer up to 80% of users' questions, and provide savings worth billions of dollars [236].

Research in this field is often centered on customer satisfaction. For example, Chung et al. [237] considered this issue in relation to customer service CAs for luxury brands, whereas Feine et al. [238] studied how the customer experience can be assessed using sentiment analysis, concluding that automated sentiment analysis can act as a proxy for direct customer feedback. An important finding that must be taken into account when developing customer service CAs is that customers generally prefer systems that provide a quick and efficient solution to their problem [239], and that embodiment does not always improve users' perception of the interaction [172]. Another useful design principle is to use a tiered approach, where a CA can refer to a human customer service agent in cases where it is unable to fulfill the customer's request [240]. As in the case of other applications, the development of CAs for business applications is facilitated by the advent of relevant datasets in this case involving customer service conversations [241].

12.7.4. *Tourism and Culture*

CAs are becoming increasingly popular means to improve and promote tourism. In this context, a verbal interaction with a CA can be useful to provide guidance at the airport [242], assist in booking recommendations [243, 244], and adapt tour routes [245]. To improve portability, oftentimes these CAs are implemented as text-based mobile apps [245–247], sometimes making use of social media platforms [248].

Several CAs have been designed specifically to provide guidance and entertainment in museums and exhibits. Gustafson et al. built August, an ECA consisting of a floating virtual head, and showcased it at the Stockholm Cultural Centre [249]; Cassell et al. set up MACK, a robot-like ECA, at the MIT Media Lab [250]; Traum et al. proposed Ada and Grace, two more ECAs, employed at the Museum of Science of Boston [251]; and Kopp et al. studied how the visitors of the Heinz Nixdorf Museums Forum interacted with Max, a full-body human-like virtual ECA [252]. Seven years after the introduction of Max, Pfeiffer et al. compiled a paper listing the lessons learned from using the ECA [253]. Beyond queries about the venue, tourists were found to ask about Max's personal background (e.g., "Where are you from?") and physical attributes (e.g., "How tall are you?"), but often insult and provoke the agent, overall testing the human-likeness of the CA's reactions. For the interested reader, the short paper by Schaffer et al. [254] describes key steps toward the development of a technical solution to deploy CAs in different museums.

While the previous works were targeted on a specific museum or venue, CulturERICA can converse about cross-museum, European cultural heritage [255]. As in the case of tourism, many museum-guide CAs are implemented as mobile apps, or as social media messaging platform accounts, for mobility [256, 257].

For the reader interested in a similar application, namely the use of CAs in libraries, we refer to the works by Rubin et al. [258] and Vincze [259].

12.7.5. *Other Applications*

There are many more and wildly different applications where CAs can be beneficial. For example, CAs are being investigated to aid legal information access. Applications of this kind include legal guidance for couple separation and child custody [260], as well as immigration and banking [261]. DNN-based CAs are also being investigated to summarize salient information from legal documents in order to speed up the legal process [262].

Research is also being conducted regarding the role of CAs in vehicles, and especially so in the realm of self-driving cars [263]. Since vehicles are becoming increasingly autonomous, CAs can act as driver assistants in several ways, from improving passenger comfort by chatting about a wide range of activities, possibly unrelated to the ride (e.g., meetings, events), to assessing whether the driver is fit to drive, and even commanding the driver to take back vehicle control in case of danger [264, 265].

Games are another application of relevance for CAs. Beyond entertainment, games are often built to teach and train (so-called *serious games*): in this setting, CAs are used to improve engagement in disparate applications, e.g., guiding children in games about healthy dietary habits [266], teaching teenagers about privacy [267], and training business people as well as police personnel to react appropriately to conflicts and emergencies [268]. Researchers have also investigated the effect of using CAs to help gaming communities grow and bond, by having the community members converse with a CA in a video game streaming platform [269]. Furthermore, CAs themselves represent a gamification element that can be of interest for the media: The BBC is exploring the use of CAs as a less formal and more fun way of reaching a younger audience [270].

Finally, CAs are often proposed across different domains to act as recommender systems [271]. Other than in business and customer service applications, recommender system-like CAs have been developed to recommend music tracks [272], solutions for sustainable energy management [273], and also food recipes: Foodie Fooderson, for example, converses with the user to learn his or her preferences and then uses this information to recommend recipes that are healthy and tasty at the same time [274].

12.8. Future Directions

Over the next few years, many new CAs will be deployed, as much by necessity as by choice. For example, the trend toward online retailing is an important factor driving the development of CAs for customer service; similarly, the ongoing demographic shift in which an increasing fraction of the population becomes elderly implies a need for technological approaches in healthcare, including, but not limited to, CAs; furthermore, the advent of self-driving vehicles will also favor the development of new types of CAs, for example, those that operate essentially as butlers during the trip, providing information and entertainment. The further development of CAs may also lead to a strong shift in the manner in which we interact with AI systems, such that current technology (e.g., smartphones) may be replaced by immersive technologies based on augmented or virtual reality. Just like smartphones have made interaction with screens more natural (touch as opposed to keyboards and smart pencils), we can expect that advanced, human-like CAs will lead to the development of new devices, where looking at a screen becomes secondary, and natural conversation is the primary mode of interaction.

While the current strong focus on black box systems is likely to persist for some time, we also predict that the widespread use of CA technology, especially for task-oriented agents operating in areas that involve high-stakes decision-making as well as issues related to privacy, where accountability and interpretability are crucial, will eventually force a shift toward more transparent CA technologies, in which the decision-making can be followed, explained and, when needed, corrected. This shift will be driven by not only ethical considerations but also legal ones [275].

In the case of chatbots (e.g., Tay; see Subsection 12.5.3), we have already witnessed that irresponsible use of black box systems comes with risks, as these systems are trained based on large corpora of (dialogue) data that may be ridden with inherent biases toward the current majority view, something that could put minority groups at a further disadvantage [276]. This raises an interesting point since one of the supposed advantages of black box systems is that they reduce the need for handcrafting, yet they may instead require more effort being spent in manually curating the datasets on which they rely.

As always, technology itself is neither good nor evil, but can be used in either way; there is a growing fear that CAs might be used unethically, for example, in gathering private conversational data for use in, say, mass surveillance and control. Moreover, as technology already exists for generating so-called deep fakes (such as fake text, speech, or videos, wrongfully attributed to a specific person or group [277–281]), CA technology could exacerbate the problem by allowing the development and deployment of legions of fake personas that are indistinguishable from real persons and that may swarm social networks with malicious intent. Even in cases where intentions are good, the use of CAs may be controversial. For example, affective agents may promote unhealthy or unethical bonding between humans and machines. The research community and policymakers have a strong collective responsibility to prevent unethical use of CA technology. Tools must be developed for evaluating not only the functionality but also the *safety* and *societal impact* of CAs. As mentioned in Subsection 12.5.3, this is a nascent field where much work still remains to be done.

CAs will most likely become a game-changing technology that can offer many benefits, provided that the issues just mentioned are carefully considered. This technology may radically change the manner in which we interact with machines, and will hopefully be developed in an inclusive manner allowing, for example, disadvantaged groups the same access to online and digital services as everyone else. Because of the transformative nature of this technology, making specific long-term predictions is very difficult. Thus, we end this chapter by simply quoting Alan Turing [183]: "We can only see a short distance ahead, but we can see plenty there that needs to be done."

References

[1] J. Lester, K. Branting and B. Mott, Conversational agents, *The Practical Handbook of Internet Computing*, pp. 220–240 (2004).

[2] J. Masche and N.-T. Le, A review of technologies for conversational systems. In *International Conference on Computer Science, Applied Mathematics, and Applications*, pp. 212–225. Springer (2017).

[3] L. Laranjo, A. G. Dunn, H. L. Tong, A. B. Kocaballi, J. Chen, R. Bashir, D. Surian, B. Gallego, F. Magrabi, A. Y. Lau, et al., Conversational agents in healthcare: a systematic review, *J. Am. Med. Inf. Assoc.*, **25**(9), 1248–1258 (2018).

[4] S. Diederich, A. B. Brendel and L. M. Kolbe, Towards a taxonomy of platforms for conversational agent design. In *14th International Conference on Wirtschaftsinformatik (WI2019)*, pp. 1100–1114 (2019).

[5] R. Bavaresco, D. Silveira, E. Reis, J. Barbosa, R. Righi, C. Costa, R. Antunes, M. Gomes, C. Gatti, M. Vanzin, et al., Conversational agents in business: a systematic literature review and future research directions, *Comput. Sci. Rev.*, **36**, 100239 (2020).

[6] Y. LeCun, Y. Bengio and G. Hinton, Deep learning, *Nature*, **521**(7553), 436–444 (2015).

[7] M. Wahde, *Biologically Inspired Optimization Methods: An Introduction* (WIT Press, 2008).

[8] R. S. Sutton and A. G. Barto, *Reinforcement Learning: An Introduction* (MIT Press, 2018).

[9] C. Rudin, Stop explaining black box machine learning models for high stakes decisions, and use interpretable models instead, *Nat. Mach. Intell.*, **1**(5), 206–215 (2019).

[10] B. Goodman and S. Flaxman, European Union regulations on algorithmic decision-making, and a "right to explanation", *AI Mag.*, **38**(3), 50–57 (2017).

[11] P. M. Gardiner, K. D. McCue, L. M. Negash, T. Cheng, L. F. White, L. Yinusa-Nyahkoon, B. W. Jack and T. W. Bickmore, Engaging women with an embodied conversational agent to deliver mindfulness and lifestyle recommendations: a feasibility randomized control trial, *Patient Educ. Couns.*, **100**(9), 1720–1729 (2017).

[12] B. W. Jack, T. Bickmore, L. Yinusa-Nyahkoon, M. Reichert, C. Julce, N. Sidduri, J. Martin-Howard, Z. Zhang, E. Woodhams, J. Fernandez, et al., Improving the health of young African American women in the preconception period using health information technology: a randomised controlled trial, *Lancet Digital Health*, **2**(9), e475–e485 (2020).

[13] D. DeVault, R. Artstein, G. Benn, T. Dey, E. Fast, A. Gainer, K. Georgila, J. Gratch, A. Hartholt, M. Lhommet, et al., SimSensei Kiosk: a virtual human interviewer for healthcare decision support. In *Proceedings of the 2014 International Conference on Autonomous Agents, and Multi-agent Systems*, pp. 1061–1068 (2014).

[14] M. Ochs, C. Pelachaud and G. McKeown, A user-perception based approach to create smiling embodied conversational agents, *ACM Trans. Interact. Intell. Syst.*, **7**(1), 1–33 (2017).

[15] A. van Breemen, X. Yan and B. Meerbeek, iCat: an animated user-interface robot with personality. In *Proceedings of the Fourth International Joint Conference on Autonomous Agents, and Multiagent Systems*, pp. 143–144 (2005).

[16] I. Leite, C. Martinho and A. Paiva, Social robots for long-term interaction: a survey, *Int. J. Social Rob.*, **5**(2), 291–308 (2013).

[17] T. Belpaeme, J. Kennedy, A. Ramachandran, B. Scassellati and F. Tanaka, Social robots for education: a review, *Sci. Rob.*, **3**(21), eaat5954 (2018).

[18] S. M. Anzalone, S. Boucenna, S. Ivaldi and M. Chetouani, Evaluating the engagement with social robots, *Int. J. Social Rob.*, **7**(4), 465–478 (2015).

[19] N. Epley, A. Waytz, S. Akalis and J. T. Cacioppo, When we need a human: motivational determinants of anthropomorphism, *Social Cognit.*, **26**(2), 143–155 (2008).

[20] K. Loveys, G. Sebaratnam, M. Sagar and E. Broadbent, The effect of design features on relationship quality with embodied conversational agents: a systematic review, *Int. J. Social Rob.*, pp. 1–20 (2020).

[21] C. Creed and R. Beale, User interactions with an affective nutritional coach, *Interact. Comput.*, **24**(5), 339–350 (2012).

[22] P. Kulms, S. Kopp and N. C. Krämer, Let's be serious, and have a laugh: can humor support cooperation with a virtual agent? In *International Conference on Intelligent Virtual Agents*, pp. 250–259. Springer (2014).

[23] S. ter Stal, M. Tabak, H. op den Akker, T. Beinema and H. Hermens, Who do you prefer? The effect of age, gender, and role on users' first impressions of embodied conversational agents in eHealth, *Int. J. Hum.-Comput. Interact.*, **36**(9), 881–892 (2020).

[24] A. M. von der Pütten, N. C. Krämer and J. Gratch, How our personality shapes our interactions with virtual characters-implications for research, and development. In *International Conference on Intelligent Virtual Agents*, pp. 208–221. Springer (2010).

[25] A. Cerekovic, O. Aran and D. Gatica-Perez, How do you like your virtual agent?: Human-agent interaction experience through nonverbal features, and personality traits. In *International Workshop on Human Behavior Understanding*, pp. 1–15. Springer (2014).

[26] K. Ruhland, C. E. Peters, S. Andrist, J. B. Badler, N. I. Badler, M. Gleicher, B. Mutlu and R. McDonnell, A review of eye gaze in virtual agents, social robotics, and HCI: behaviour generation, user interaction, and perception. In *Computer Graphics Forum*, vol. 34, pp. 299–326 (2015).

[27] T. Pejsa, S. Andrist, M. Gleicher and B. Mutlu, Gaze, and attention management for embodied conversational agents, *ACM Trans. Interact. Intell. Syst.*, **5**(1), 1–34 (2015).

[28] L. Marschner, S. Pannasch, J. Schulz and S.-T. Graupner, Social communication with virtual agents: the effects of body, and gaze direction on attention, and emotional responding in human observers, *Int. J. Psychophysiol.*, **97**(2), 85–92 (2015).

[29] C. Pelachaud, Studies on gesture expressivity for a virtual agent, *Speech Commun.*, **51**(7), 630–639 (2009).

[30] A. Sadeghipour and S. Kopp, Embodied gesture processing: motor-based integration of perception, and action in social artificial agents, *Cognit. Comput.*, **3**(3), 419–435 (2011).

[31] K. Bergmann, F. Eyssel and S. Kopp, A second chance to make a first impression? How appearance, and nonverbal behavior affect perceived warmth and competence of virtual agents over time. In *International Conference on Intelligent Virtual Agents*, pp. 126–138. Springer (2012).

[32] M. Mori, K. F. MacDorman and N. Kageki, The uncanny valley [from the field], *IEEE Rob. Autom. Mag.*, **19**(2), 98–100 (2012).

[33] A. Tinwell, M. Grimshaw, D. A. Nabi and A. Williams, Facial expression of emotion and perception of the uncanny valley in virtual characters, *Comput. Hum. Behav.*, **27**(2), 741–749 (2011).

[34] K. Keeling, S. Beatty, P. McGoldrick and L. Macaulay, Face value? Customer views of appropriate formats for embodied conversational agents (ECAs) in online retailing. In *Proceedings of the 37th Annual Hawaii International Conference on System Sciences, 2004*, pp. 1–10. IEEE (2004).

[35] P. Ekman, Basic emotions. In *Handbook of Cognition, and Emotion*, pp. 45–60. John Wiley & Sons (1999).

[36] C. M. Whissell, The dictionary of affect in language. In *The Measurement of Emotions*, pp. 113–131. Elsevier (1989).

[37] C.-H. Hjortsjo, *Man's Face and Mimic Language* (Studentlitteratur 1969).

[38] P. Ekman and W. V. Friesen, *Facial Action Coding Systems* (Consulting Psychologists Press 1978).

[39] S. Li and W. Deng, Deep facial expression recognition: a survey, *IEEE Trans. Affective Comput.*, 2020), doi: 10.1109/TAFFC.2020.2981446.

[40] B. C. Ko, A brief review of facial emotion recognition based on visual information, *Sensors*, **18**(2), 401 (2018).

[41] D. Mehta, M. F. H. Siddiqui and A. Y. Javaid, Facial emotion recognition: a survey, and real-world user experiences in mixed reality, *Sensors*, **18**(2), 416 (2018).

[42] M. Coulson, Attributing emotion to static body postures: recognition accuracy, confusions, and viewpoint dependence, *J. Nonverbal Behav.*, **28**(2), 117–139 (2004).

[43] T. D'Orazio, R. Marani, V. Renè and G. Cicirelli, Recent trends in gesture recognition: how depth data has improved classical approaches, *Image Vis. Comput.*, **52**, 56–72, (2016).

[44] S. S. Rautaray and A. Agrawal, Vision based hand gesture recognition for human computer interaction: a survey, *Artif. Intell. Rev.*, **43**(1), 1–54 (2015).

[45] S. E. Kahou, X. Bouthillier, P. Lamblin, C. Gulcehre, V. Michalski, K. Konda, S. Jean, P. Froumenty, Y. Dauphin, N. Boulanger-Lewandowski, et al., EmoNets: multimodal deep learning approaches for emotion recognition in video, *J. Multimodal User Interfaces*, **10**(2), 99–111 (2016).

[46] H. M. Fayek, M. Lech and L. Cavedon, Evaluating deep learning architectures for speech emotion recognition, *Neural Networks*, **92**, 60–68 (2017).

[47] M. Gillies and B. Spanlang, Comparing, and evaluating real time character engines for virtual environments, *Presence: Teleop. Virt. Environ.*, **19**(2), 95–117 (2010).

[48] J. Serra, O. Cetinaslan, S. Ravikumar, V. Orvalho and D. Cosker, Easy generation of facial animation using motion graphs. In *Computer Graphics Forum*, vol. 37, pp. 97–111. Wiley Online Library (2018).

[49] S. Zhang, X. Liu, J. Liu, J. Gao, K. Duh and B. Van Durme, ReCoRD: bridging the gap between human, and machine commonsense reading comprehension, *arXiv preprint arXiv:1810.12885* (2018).

[50] K. Lee, S. Lee and J. Lee, Interactive character animation by learning multi-objective control, *ACM Trans. Graphics,* **37**(6), 1–10 (2018).

[51] T. Weise, S. Bouaziz, H. Li and M. Pauly, Realtime performance-based facial animation, *ACM Trans. Graphics,* **30**(4), 1–10 (2011).

[52] P. Edwards, C. Landreth, E. Fiume and K. Singh, Jali: an animator-centric viseme model for expressive lip synchronization, *ACM Trans. Graphics,* **35**(4), 1–11 (2016).

[53] M. Thiebaux, S. Marsella, A. N. Marshall and M. Kallmann, Smartbody: behavior realization for embodied conversational agents. In *Proceedings of the 7th International Joint Conference on Autonomous Agents, and Multiagent Systems,* vol. 1, pp. 151–158 (2008).

[54] S. Kopp, B. Krenn, S. Marsella, A. N. Marshall, C. Pelachaud, H. Pirker, K. R. Thorisson and H. Vilhjalmsson, Towards a common framework for multimodal generation: the behavior markup language. In *International Workshop on Intelligent Virtual Agents*, pp. 205–217. Springer (2006).

[55] V. Këpuska and G. Bohouta, Comparing speech recognition systems (Microsoft API, Google API, and CMU Sphinx), *Int. J. Eng. Res. Appl.*, **7**(03), 20–24 (2017).

[56] C.-C. Chiu, T. N. Sainath, Y. Wu, R. Prabhavalkar, P. Nguyen, Z. Chen, A. Kannan, R. J. Weiss, K. Rao, E. Gonina, et al., State-of-the-art speech recognition with sequence-to-sequence models. In *2018 IEEE International Conference on Acoustics, Speech, and Signal Processing (ICASSP)*, pp. 4774–4778. IEEE (2018).

[57] D. S. Park, W. Chan, Y. Zhang, C.-C. Chiu, B. Zoph, E. D. Cubuk and Q. V. Le, Specaugment: a simple data augmentation method for automatic speech recognition, *arXiv preprint arXiv:1904.08779* (2019).

[58] V. Panayotov, G. Chen, D. Povey and S. Khudanpur, Librispeech: an ASR corpus based on public domain audio books. In *2015 IEEE International Conference on Acoustics, Speech, and Signal Processing (ICASSP)*, pp. 5206–5210 (2015).

[59] D. Amodei, S. Ananthanarayanan, R. Anubhai, J. Bai, E. Battenberg, C. Case, J. Casper, B. Catanzaro, Q. Cheng, G. Chen, et al., Deep speech 2: end-to-end speech recognition in English, and Mandarin. In *International Conference on Machine Learning*, pp. 173–182 (2016).

[60] A. Oord, Y. Li, I. Babuschkin, K. Simonyan, O. Vinyals, K. Kavukcuoglu, G. Driessche, E. Lockhart, L. Cobo, F. Stimberg, et al., Parallel wavenet: fast high-fidelity speech synthesis. In *International Conference on Machine Learning*, pp. 3918–3926 (2018).

[61] M. Bińkowski, J. Donahue, S. Dieleman, A. Clark, E. Elsen, N. Casagrande, L. C. Cobo and K. Simonyan, High fidelity speech synthesis with adversarial networks, *arXiv preprint arXiv:1909.11646* (2019).

[62] R. C. Streijl, S. Winkler and D. S. Hands, Mean opinion score (MOS) revisited: methods, and applications, limitations, and alternatives, *Multimedia Syst.*, **22**(2), 213–227 (2016).

[63] A. C. Elkins and D. C. Derrick, The sound of trust: voice as a measurement of trust during interactions with embodied conversational agents, *Group Decis. Negot.*, **22**(5), 897–913 (2013).

[64] I. Torre, J. Goslin and L. White, If your device could smile: people trust happy-sounding artificial agents more, *Comput. Hum. Behav.*, **105**, 106215 (2020).

[65] M. Anabuki, H. Kakuta, H. Yamamoto and H. Tamura, Welbo: an embodied conversational agent living in mixed reality space. In *CHI'00 Extended Abstracts on Human Factors in Computing Systems*, pp. 10–11 (2000).

[66] I. Wang, J. Smith and J. Ruiz, Exploring virtual agents for augmented reality. In *Proceedings of the 2019 CHI Conference on Human Factors in Computing Systems*, pp. 1–12 (2019).

[67] J. Weizenbaum, Eliza–a computer program for the study of natural language communication between man, and machine, *Commun. ACM*, **9**(1), 36–45 (1966).

[68] R. Wallace, The elements of AIML style, *Alice AI Foundation*, **139** (2003).

[69] G. Salton and C. Buckley, Term-weighting approaches in automatic text retrieval, *Inf. Process. Manage.*, **24**(5), 513–523 (1988).

[70] A. Ritter, C. Cherry and W. B. Dolan, Data-driven response generation in social media. In *Proceedings of the 2011 Conference on Empirical Methods in Natural Language Processing*, pp. 583–593 (2011).

[71] X. Zhao, C. Tao, W. Wu, C. Xu, D. Zhao and R. Yan, A document-grounded matching network for response selection in retrieval-based chatbots, *arXiv preprint arXiv:1906.04362* (2019).

[72] R. Yan, Y. Song and H. Wu, Learning to respond with deep neural networks for retrieval-based human-computer conversation system. In *Proceedings of the 39th International ACM SIGIR conference on Research, and Development in Information Retrieval*, pp. 55–64 (2016).

[73] R. Lowe, N. Pow, I. Serban and J. Pineau, The Ubuntu dialogue corpus: a large dataset for research in unstructured multi-turn dialogue systems. In *Proceedings of the 16th Annual Meeting of the Special Interest Group on Discourse and Dialogue*, pp. 285–294, Prague, Czech Republic (2015). Association for Computational Linguistics.

[74] X. Zhou, D. Dong, H. Wu, S. Zhao, D. Yu, H. Tian, X. Liu and R. Yan, Multi-view response selection for human-computer conversation. In *Proceedings of the 2016 Conference on Empirical Methods in Natural Language Processing*, pp. 372–381 (2016).

[75] Y. Wu, W. Wu, C. Xing, C. Xu, Z. Li and M. Zhou, A sequential matching framework for multi-turn response selection in retrieval-based chatbots, *Comput. Ling.*, **45**(1), 163–197 (2019).

[76] Y. Bengio, R. Ducharme, P. Vincent and C. Jauvin, A neural probabilistic language model, *J. Mach. Learn. Res.,* **3**, 1137–1155 (2003).

[77] H. Schwenk, Continuous space language models, *Comput. Speech Lang.,* **21**(3), 492–518 (2007).

[78] T. Mikolov, W.-t. Yih and G. Zweig, Linguistic regularities in continuous space word representations. In *Proceedings of the 2013 conference of the North American Chapter of the Association for Computational Linguistics: Human Language Technologies*, pp. 746–751 (2013).

[79] J. Devlin, M.-W. Chang, K. Lee and K. Toutanova, BERT: pre-training of deep bidirectional transformers for language understanding. In *Proceedings of the 2019 Conference of the North American Chapter of the Association for Computational Linguistics: Human Language Technologies,* vol. 1 (Long, and Short Papers), pp. 4171–4186, Minneapolis, Minnesota (2019). Association for Computational Linguistics.

[80] L. v. d. Maaten and G. Hinton, Visualizing data using t-SNE, *J. Mach. Learn. Res.,* **9**, 2579–2605 (2008).

[81] T. Mikolov, K. Chen, G. Corrado and J. Dean, Efficient estimation of word representations in vector space, *arXiv preprint arXiv:1301.3781* (2013).

[82] S. T. Dumais, G. W. Furnas, T. K. Landauer, S. Deerwester and R. Harshman, Using latent semantic analysis to improve access to textual information. In *Proceedings of the SIGCHI Conference on Human Factors in Computing Systems*, pp. 281–285 (1988).

[83] T. K. Landauer, P. W. Foltz and D. Laham, An introduction to latent semantic analysis, *Discourse Processes,* **25**(2–3), 259–284 (1998).

[84] K. Lund and C. Burgess, Producing high-dimensional semantic spaces from lexical co-occurrence, *Behav. Res. Methods Instrum. Comput.,* **28**(2), 203–208 (1996).

[85] R. Collobert, Word embeddings through Hellinger PCA. In *Proceedings of the 14th Conference of the European Chapter of the Association for Computational Linguistics*, Citeseer (2014).

[86] L. Manzoni, D. Jakobovic, L. Mariot, S. Picek and M. Castelli, Towards an evolutionary-based approach for natural language processing. In *Proceedings of the 2020 Genetic, and Evolutionary Computation Conference*, GECCO '20, pp. 985–993, New York, NY, USA (2020). Association for Computing Machinery. ISBN 9781450371285.

[87] I. Sutskever, O. Vinyals and Q. V. Le, Sequence to sequence learning with neural networks. In *Proceedings of the Advances in Neural Information Processing Systems,* pp. 3104–3112, (2014).

[88] O. Vinyals and Q. Le, A neural conversational model, *arXiv preprint arXiv:1506.05869* (2015).

[89] J. Tiedemann, News from OPUS–a collection of multilingual parallel corpora with tools, and interfaces. In *Recent Advances in Natural Language Processing*, vol. 5, pp. 237–248, (2009).

[90] I. V. Serban, C. Sankar, M. Germain, S. Zhang, Z. Lin, S. Subramanian, T. Kim, M. Pieper, S. Chandar, N. R. Ke, et al., A deep reinforcement learning chatbot, *arXiv preprint arXiv:1709. 02349* (2017).

[91] D. Adiwardana, M.-T. Luong, D. R. So, J. Hall, N. Fiedel, R. Thoppilan, Z. Yang, A. Kulshreshtha, G. Nemade, Y. Lu, et al., Towards a human-like open-domain chatbot, *arXiv preprint arXiv:2001.09977* (2020).

[92] L. Zhou, J. Gao, D. Li and H.-Y. Shum, The design, and implementation of XiaoIce, an empathetic social chatbot, *Comput. Ling.,* **46**(1), 53–93 (2020).

[93] A. Vaswani, N. Shazeer, N. Parmar, J. Uszkoreit, L. Jones, A. N. Gomez, L- . Kaiser and I. Polosukhin, Attention is all you need. In *Proceedings of the Advances in Neural Information Processing Systems,* pp. 5998–6008 (2017).

[94] T. Wolf, J. Chaumond, L. Debut, V. Sanh, C. Delangue, A. Moi, P. Cistac, M. Funtowicz, J. Davison, S. Shleifer, et al., Transformers: state-of-the-art natural language processing. In

Proceedings of the 2020 Conference on Empirical Methods in Natural Language Processing: System Demonstrations, pp. 38–45 (2020).

[95] D. Bahdanau, K. Cho and Y. Bengio, Neural machine translation by jointly learning to align, and translate. In *3rd International Conference on Learning Representations, ICLR 2015* (2015).

[96] M.-T. Luong, H. Pham and C. D. Manning, Effective approaches to attention-based neural machine translation. In *Proceedings of the 2015 Conference on Empirical Methods in Natural Language Processing*, pp. 1412–1421 (2015).

[97] A. Wang, A. Singh, J. Michael, F. Hill, O. Levy and S. Bowman, GLUE: a multi-task benchmark, and analysis platform for natural language understanding. In *Proceedings of the 2018 EMNLP Workshop BlackboxNLP: Analyzing, and Interpreting Neural Networks for NLP*, pp. 353–355, Brussels, Belgium (2018). Association for Computational Linguistics.

[98] Z. Lan, M. Chen, S. Goodman, K. Gimpel, P. Sharma and R. Soricut, ALBERT: a lite BERT for self-supervised learning of language representations, *arXiv preprint arXiv:1909.11942* (2019).

[99] Z. Yang, Z. Dai, Y. Yang, J. Carbonell, R. R. Salakhutdinov and Q. V. Le, XLNet: generalized autoregressive pretraining for language understanding. In *Proceedings of the Advances in Neural Information Processing Systems,* pp. 5753–5763 (2019).

[100] A. Radford, J. Wu, R. Child, D. Luan, D. Amodei and I. Sutskever, Language models are unsupervised multitask learners, *OpenAI Blog*, **1**(8), 9 (2019).

[101] T. B. Brown, B. Mann, N. Ryder, M. Subbiah, J. Kaplan, P. Dhariwal, A. Neelakantan, P. Shyam, G. Sastry, A. Askell, et al., Language models are few-shot learners, *arXiv preprint arXiv:2005.14165* (2020).

[102] T. Young, D. Hazarika, S. Poria and E. Cambria, Recent trends in deep learning based natural language processing, *IEEE Comput. Intell. Mag.*, **13**(3), 55–75 (2018).

[103] D. W. Otter, J. R. Medina and J. K. Kalita, A survey of the usages of deep learning for natural language processing, *IEEE Trans. Neural Networks Learn. Syst.,* **32**(2, 604–624 (2020).

[104] M. Wahde, A dialogue manager for task-oriented agents based on dialogue building-blocks, and generic cognitive processing. In *2019 IEEE International Symposium on Innovations in Intelligent Systems, and Applications (INISTA)*, pp. 1–8 (2019).

[105] D. Jurafsky and J. H. Martin, *Speech, and Language Processing,* 2nd edn. (Prentice-Hall, 2009).

[106] D. G. Bobrow, R. M. Kaplan, M. Kay, D. A. Norman, H. Thompson and T. Winograd, GUS, a frame-driven dialog system, *Artif. Intell.*, **8**(2), 155–173 (1977).

[107] W. Ward, S. Issar, X. Huang, H.-W. Hon, M.-Y. Hwang, S. Young, M. Matessa, F.-H. Liu and R. M. Stern, Speech understanding in open tasks. In *Speech, and Natural Language: Proceedings of a Workshop Held at Harriman,* New York, February 23–26 (1992).

[108] H. Bunt, Context, and dialogue control, *Think Q.*, **3**(1), 19–31 (1994).

[109] A. Stolcke, K. Ries, N. Coccaro, E. Shriberg, R. Bates, D. Jurafsky, P. Taylor, R. Martin, C. V. Ess-Dykema and M. Meteer, Dialogue act modeling for automatic tagging, and recognition of conversational speech, *Comput. Ling.*, **26**(3), 339–373 (2000).

[110] Z. Chen, R. Yang, Z. Zhao, D. Cai and X. He, Dialogue act recognition via crfattentive structured network. In *The 41st International ACM SIGIR Conference on Research & Development in Information Retrieval*, pp. 225–234 (2018).

[111] V. Zue, S. Seneff, J. R. Glass, J. Polifroni, C. Pao, T. J. Hazen and L. Hetherington, JUPITER: a telephone-based conversational interface for weather information, *IEEE Trans. Speech Audio Process.*, **8**(1), 85–96 (2000).

[112] S. Larsson and D. R. Traum, Information state, and dialogue management in the TRINDI dialogue move engine toolkit, *Nat. Lang. Eng.*, **6**(3–4), 323–340 (2000).

[113] J. D. Williams, A. Raux and M. Henderson, The dialog state tracking challenge series: a review, *Dialogue Discourse*, **7**(3), 4–33 (2016).

[114] J.-G. Harms, P. Kucherbaev, A. Bozzon and G.-J. Houben, Approaches for dialog management in conversational agents, *IEEE Internet Comput.*, **23**(2), 13–22 (2018).

[115] P. R. Cohen and C. R. Perrault, Elements of a plan-based theory of speech acts, *Cognit. Sci.*, **3**(3), 177–212 (1979).

[116] J. Allen, G. Ferguson and A. Stent, An architecture for more realistic conversational systems. In *Proceedings of the 6th International Conference on Intelligent User Interfaces*, pp. 1–8 (2001).

[117] D. Bohus and A. I. Rudnicky, The RavenClaw dialog management framework: architecture, and systems, *Comput. Speech Lang.*, **23**(3), 332–361 (2009).

[118] N. Blaylock, Towards tractable agent-based dialogue. PhD thesis, University of Rochester, Rochester, New York (2005).

[119] M. F. McTear, Spoken dialogue technology: enabling the conversational user interface, *ACM Comput. Surv.*, **34**(1), 90–169 (2002).

[120] E. Levin, R. Pieraccini and W. Eckert, Using Markov decision process for learning dialogue strategies. In *Proceedings of the 1998 IEEE International Conference on Acoustics, Speech, and Signal Processing, ICASSP'98 (Cat. No. 98CH36181)*, vol. 1, pp. 201–204, (1998).

[121] E. Levin, R. Pieraccini and W. Eckert, A stochastic model of human-machine interaction for learning dialog strategies, *IEEE Trans. Speech Audio Process.*, **8**(1), 11–23 (2000).

[122] S. Young, J. Schatzmann, K. Weilhammer and H. Ye, The hidden information state approach to dialog management. In *2007 IEEE International Conference on Acoustics, Speech, and Signal Processing-ICASSP'07*, vol. 4, pp. IV-149–IV-152 (2007).

[123] S. Young, M. Gašić, S. Keizer, F. Mairesse, J. Schatzmann, B. Thomson and K. Yu, The hidden information state model: a practical framework for POMDP-based spoken dialogue management, *Comput. Speech Lang.*, **24**(2), 150–174 (2010).

[124] S. Young, M. Gašić, B. Thomson and J. D. Williams, POMDP-based statistical spoken dialog systems: a review, *Proc. IEEE*, **101**(5), 1160–1179 (2013).

[125] T.-H. Wen, D. Vandyke, N. Mrkšić, M. Gašić, L. M. Rojas-Barahona, P.-H. Su, S. Ultes and S. Young, A network-based end-to-end trainable task-oriented dialogue system, pp. 438–449 (2017).

[126] P. Budzianowski and I. Vulić, Hello, it's GPT-2–How can I help you? Towards the use of pre-trained language models for task-oriented dialogue systems, *arXiv preprint arXiv:1907.05774* (2019).

[127] Y. Gou, Y. Lei and L. Liu, Contextualize knowledge bases with transformer for end-to-end task-oriented dialogue systems, *arXiv preprint arXiv:2010.05740v3* (2020).

[128] J. Weston, S. Chopra and A. Bordes, Memory networks, *CoRR* abs/1410.3916 (2015).

[129] A. Bordes, Y.-L. Boureau and J. Weston, Learning end-to-end goal-oriented dialog. In *International Conference of Learning Representations (ICLR)* (2017).

[130] T. N. Kipf and M. Welling, Semi-supervised classification with graph convolutional networks. In *International Conference on Learning Representations* (2017).

[131] S. Banerjee and M. M. Khapra, Graph convolutional network with sequential attention for goal-oriented dialogue systems, *Trans. Assoc. Comput. Linguist.*, **7**, 485–500 (2019).

[132] J. F. Kelley, An iterative design methodology for user-friendly natural language office information applications, *ACM Trans. Inf. Syst.*, **2**(1), 26–41 (1984).

[133] K. Crowston, Amazon mechanical turk: a research tool for organizations, and information systems scholars. In eds. A. Bhattacherjee, and B. Fitzgerald, *Shaping the Future of ICT Research. Methods, and Approaches*, pp. 210–221, Berlin, Heidelberg (2012). Springer Berlin Heidelberg.

[134] B. Liu, G. Tur, D. Hakkani-Tur, P. Shah and L. Heck, End-to-end optimization of task-oriented dialogue model with deep reinforcement learning. In *NIPS Workshop on Conversational AI* (2017).

[135] B. Dhingra, L. Li, X. Li, J. Gao, Y.-N. Chen, F. Ahmed and L. Deng, Towards end-to-end reinforcement learning of dialogue agents for information access, pp. 484–495 (2017).

[136] A. Madotto, S. Cahyawijaya, G. I. Winata, Y. Xu, Z. Liu, Z. Lin and P. Fung, Learning knowledge bases with parameters for task-oriented dialogue systems, *arXiv preprint arXiv:2009.13656* (2020).

[137] D. Raghu, N. Gupta and Mausam, Disentangling language, and knowledge in task-oriented dialogs. In *Proceedings of the 2019 Conference of the North American Chapter of the Association for Computational Linguistics: Human Language Technologies*, vol. 1 (Long, and Short Papers), pp. 1239–1255 (2019).

[138] C.-S. Wu, R. Socher and C. Xiong, Global-to-local memory pointer networks for task-oriented dialogue. In *International Conference on Learning Representations* (2019).

[139] L. Qin, X. Xu, W. Che, Y. Zhang and T. Liu, Dynamic fusion network for multi-domain end-to-end task-oriented dialog, *arXiv preprint arXiv:2004.11019* (2020).

[140] P. Budzianowski, T.-H. Wen, B.-H. Tseng, I. Casanueva, S. Ultes, O. Ramadan and M. Gašić, MultiWOZ—a large-scale multi-domain wizard-of-oz dataset for task-oriented dialogue modelling, *arXiv preprint arXiv:1810.00278* (2018).

[141] J. Rajendran, J. Ganhotra, S. Singh and L. Polymenakos, Learning end-to-end goal-oriented dialog with multiple answers. In *Proceedings of the 2018 Conference on Empirical Methods in Natural Language Processing*, pp. 3834–3843, Brussels, Belgium (2018).

[142] E. Luger and A. Sellen, "Like having a really bad PA" the gulf between user expectation, and experience of conversational agents. In *Proceedings of the 2016 CHI Conference on Human Factors in Computing Systems*, pp. 5286–5297 (2016).

[143] H. J. Levesque, *Common Sense, the Turing Test, and the Quest for Real AI* (MIT Press, 2017).

[144] R. Socher, A. Perelygin, J. Wu, J. Chuang, C. D. Manning, A. Y. Ng and C. Potts, Recursive deep models for semantic compositionality over a sentiment treebank. In *Proceedings of the 2013 Conference on Empirical Methods in Natural Language Processing*, pp. 1631–1642 (2013).

[145] W. B. Dolan and C. Brockett, Automatically constructing a corpus of sentential paraphrases. In *Proceedings of the Third International Workshop on Paraphrasing (IWP2005)* (2005).

[146] P. Rajpurkar, J. Zhang, K. Lopyrev and P. Liang, SQuAD: 100,000+ questions for machine comprehension of text. In *Proceedings of the 2016 Conference on Empirical Methods in Natural Language Processing*, pp. 2383–2392, Austin, Texas (2016). Association for Computational Linguistics.

[147] J. Zhao, T. Wang, M. Yatskar, V. Ordonez and K.-W. Chang, Gender bias in coreference resolution: evaluation, and debiasing methods. In *Proceedings of the 2018 Conference of the North American Chapter of the Association for Computational Linguistics: Human Language Technologies*, pp. 15–20 (2018).

[148] A. Wang, Y. Pruksachatkun, N. Nangia, A. Singh, J. Michael, F. Hill, O. Levy and S. Bowman, SuperGLUE: a stickier benchmark for general-purpose language understanding systems. In *Proceedings of the Advances in Neural Information Processing Systems*, pp. 3266–3280 (2019).

[149] K. Papineni, S. Roukos, T. Ward and W.-J. Zhu, BLEU: a method for automatic evaluation of machine translation. In *Proceedings of the 40th annual meeting of the Association for Computational Linguistics*, pp. 311–318 (2002).

[150] C.-Y. Lin, ROUGE: a package for automatic evaluation of summaries. In *Text Summarization Branches Out*, pp. 74–81 (2004).

[151] C.-Y. Lin and F. J. Och, Automatic evaluation of machine translation quality using longest common subsequence, and skip-bigram statistics. In *Proceedings of the 42nd Annual Meeting of the Association for Computational Linguistics (ACL-04)*, pp. 605–612 (2004).

[152] The Alexa prize. https://developer.amazon.com/alexaprize. Accessed: December (2020).

[153] A. Venkatesh, C. Khatri, A. Ram, F. Guo, R. Gabriel, A. Nagar, R. Prasad, M. Cheng, B. Hedayatnia, A. Metallinou, et al., On evaluating, and comparing open domain dialog systems, *arXiv preprint arXiv:1801.03625* (2018).

[154] A. P. Chaves and M. A. Gerosa, How should my chatbot interact? A survey on social characteristics in human–chatbot interaction design, *Int. J. Hum.-Comput. Interact.*, pp. 1–30 (2020).

[155] J. Hill, W. R. Ford and I. G. Farreras, Real conversations with artificial intelligence: a comparison between human–human online conversations, and human–chatbot conversations, *Comput. Hum. Behav.*, **49**, 245–250 (2015).

[156] T. J.-J. Li, I. Labutov, B. A. Myers, A. Azaria, A. I. Rudnicky and T. M. Mitchell, Teaching agents when they fail: end user development in goal-oriented conversational agents. In *Studies in Conversational UX Design*, pp. 119–137. Springer (2018).

[157] W. Duijvelshoff, Use-cases, and ethics of chatbots on Plek: a social intranet for organizations. In *Workshop on Chatbots and Artificial Intelligence* (2017).

[158] E. Tallyn, H. Fried, R. Gianni, A. Isard and C. Speed, The Ethnobot: gathering ethnographies in the age of IoT. In *Proceedings of the 2018 CHI Conference on Human Factors in Computing Systems*, pp. 1–13 (2018).

[159] R. Likert, A technique for the measurement of attitudes, *Arch. Psychol.*, **22**(140), 55 (1932).

[160] J. Brooke, SUS: a "quick, and dirty" usability scale. In *Usability Evaluation in Industry*, p. 189. CRC Press (1996).

[161] K. S. Hone and R. Graham, Towards a tool for the subjective assessment of speech system interfaces (SASSI), *Nat. Lang. Eng.*, **6**(3–4), 287–303 (2000).

[162] M. A. Walker, D. J. Litman, C. A. Kamm and A. Abella, PARADISE: a framework for evaluating spoken dialogue agents, *arXiv preprint cmp-lg/9704004* (1997).

[163] J. Sedoc, D. Ippolito, A. Kirubarajan, J. Thirani, L. Ungar and C. Callison-Burch, ChatEval: a tool for chatbot evaluation. In *Proceedings of the 2019 Conference of the North American Chapter of the Association for Computational Linguistics (Demonstrations)*, pp. 60–65, (2019).

[164] C.-W. Liu, R. Lowe, I. Serban, M. Noseworthy, L. Charlin and J. Pineau, How NOT to evaluate your dialogue system: an empirical study of unsupervised evaluation metrics for dialogue response generation. In *Proceedings of the 2016 Conference on Empirical Methods in Natural Language Processing*, pp. 2122–2132, Austin, Texas (2016). Association for Computational Linguistics.

[165] K. Kuligowska, Commercial chatbot: performance evaluation, usability metrics, and quality standards of embodied conversational agents, *Professionals Center for Business Research*, **2** (2015).

[166] M. d. O. Meira and A. d. P. Canuto, Evaluation of emotional agents' architectures: an approach based on quality metrics, and the influence of emotions on users. In *Proceedings of the World Congress on Engineering*, vol. 1, pp. 1–8 (2015).

[167] K. M. Lee, Y. Jung, J. Kim and S. R. Kim, Are physically embodied social agents better than disembodied social agents?: The effects of physical embodiment, tactile interaction, and people's loneliness in human–robot interaction, *Int. J. Hum. Comput. Stud.*, **64**(10), 962–973 (2006).

[168] Aibo. https://us.aibo.com/. Accessed: December (2020).

[169] A. Pereira, C. Martinho, I. Leite and A. Paiva, iCat, the chess player: the influence of embodiment in the enjoyment of a game. In *Proceedings of the 7th International Joint Conference on Autonomous Agents, and Multiagent Systems,* vol. 3, pp. 1253–1256 (2008).

[170] L. Hoffmann and N. C. Krämer, Investigating the effects of physical, and virtual embodiment in task-oriented, and conversational contexts, *Int. J. Hum. Comput. Stud.*, **71**(7–8), 763–774 (2013).

[171] L. Ciechanowski, A. Przegalinska, M. Magnuski and P. Gloor, In the shades of the uncanny valley: an experimental study of human–chatbot interaction, *Future Gener. Comput. Syst.*, **92**, 539–548 (2019).

[172] M. S. B. Mimoun, I. Poncin and M. Garnier, Case study—embodied virtual agents: an analysis on reasons for failure, *J. Retail. Consum. Serv.*, **19**(6), 605–612 (2012).

[173] B. Granstrom and D. House, Modelling, and evaluating verbal, and non-verbal communication in talking animated interface agents. In *Evaluation of Text, and Speech Systems*, pp. 65–98. Springer (2007).

[174] B. Weiss, I. Wechsung, C. Kühnel and S. Möller, Evaluating embodied conversational agents in multimodal interfaces, *Comput. Cognit. Sci.*, **1**(1), 6 (2015).

[175] G. Neff and P. Nagy, Talking to bots: symbiotic agency, and the case of Tay, *Int. J. Commun.*, **10**, 17 (2016).

[176] U. Bharti, D. Bajaj, H. Batra, S. Lalit, S. Lalit and A. Gangwani, Medbot: conversational artificial intelligence powered chatbot for delivering tele-health after COVID-19. In *2020 5th International Conference on Communication, and Electronics Systems (ICCES)*, pp. 870–875. IEEE (2020).

[177] M. Ligthart, T. Fernhout, M. A. Neerincx, K. L. van Bindsbergen, M. A. Grootenhuis and K. V. Hindriks, A child, and a robot getting acquainted-interaction design for eliciting self-disclosure. In *Proceedings of the 18th International Conference on Autonomous Agents, and Multi Agent Systems*, pp. 61–70 (2019).

[178] D. D. Luxton, Ethical implications of conversational agents in global public health, *Bull. World Health Organ.*, **98**(4), 285 (2020).

[179] A. Adadi and M. Berrada, Peeking inside the black-box: a survey on explainable artificial intelligence (XAI), *IEEE Access*, **6**, 52138–52160 (2018).

[180] R. Guidotti, A. Monreale, S. Ruggieri, F. Turini, F. Giannotti and D. Pedreschi, A survey of methods for explaining black box models, *ACM Comput. Surv.*, **51**(5), 1–42 (2018).

[181] P. Angelov and E. Soares, Towards explainable deep neural networks (xDNN), *Neural Networks*, **130**, 185–194 (2020).

[182] 600,000 images removed from AI database after art project exposes racist bias. https://eur02.safelinks.protection.outlook.com/?url=https%3A%2F%2Fhyperallergic.com%2F518822%2F600000-images-removed-from-ai-database-after-art-project-exposes-racist-bias%2F&data=04%7C01%7Cangelov%40live.lancs.ac.uk%7C40fce153c9a14096f12408da038fdb9c%7C9c9bcd11977a4e9ca9a0bc734090164a%7C0%7C0%7C637826213638828385%7CUnknown%7CTWFpbGZsb3d8eyJWIjoiMC4wLjAwMDAiLCJQIjoiV2luMzIiLCJBTiI6Ik1haWWiLCJXVCI6Mn0%3D%7C3000&sdata=hVcTGsdRMIqzOoRH0%2Bh6VRx8Nasf9%2BjO6sH4%2Fhl72WY%3D&reserved=0. Accessed: December (2020).

[183] A. M. Turing, Computing machinery and intelligence, *Mind*, **59**(236), 433–460 (1950).

[184] Log of conversations between Eliza and Parry. https://eur02.safelinks.protection.outlook.com/?url=https%3A%2F%2Fdatatracker.ietf.org%2Fdoc%2Fhtml%2Frfc439&data=04%7C01%7Cangelov%40live.lancs.ac.uk%7C40fce153c9a14096f12408da038fdb9c%7C9c9bcd11977a4e9ca9a0bc734090164a%7C0%7C0%7C637826213638984582%7CUnknown%7CTWFpbGZsb3d8eyJWIjoiMC4wLjAwMDAiLCJQIjoiV2luMzIiLCJBTiI6Ik1haWWiLCJXVCI6Mn0%3D%7C3000&sdata=Dv6p4xXmz%2B70sELqMuiG7oTN7bj%2FSQDMoLz%2BMitIbvw%3D&reserved=0. Accessed: December (2020).

[185] R. S. Wallace, The anatomy of ALICE. In *Parsing the Turing Test*, pp. 181–210. Springer (2009).

[186] Cleverbot. http://www.cleverbot.com. Accessed: December (2020).

[187] H. Shah, K. Warwick, J. Vallverdú and D. Wu, Can machines talk? Comparison of ELIZA with modern dialogue systems, *Comput. Hum. Behav.*, **58**, 278–295 (2016).

[188] Mitsuku. http://www.pandorabots.com. Accessed: December (2020).

[189] Chatscript. https://sourceforge.net/projects/chatscript. Accessed: December (2020).

[190] A. Ram, R. Prasad, C. Khatri, A. Venkatesh, R. Gabriel, Q. Liu, J. Nunn, B. Hedayatnia, M. Cheng, A. Nagar, E. King, K. Bland, A. Wartick, Y. Pan, H. Song, S. Jayadevan, G. Hwang and A. Pettigrue, Conversational AI: the science behind the Alexa Prize, *arXiv preprint* (2018). URL http://arxiv.org/abs/1801.03604.

[191] J. L. Z. Montenegro, C. A. da Costa and R. da Rosa Righi, Survey of conversational agents in health, *Expert Syst. Appl.*, **129**, 56–67 (2019).

[192] A. Fadhil, A conversational interface to improve medication adherence: towards AI support in patient's treatment, *arXiv preprint arXiv:1803.09844* (2018).

[193] A. Piau, R. Crissey, D. Brechemier, L. Balardy and F. Nourhashemi, A smartphone chatbot application to optimize monitoring of older patients with cancer, *Int. J. Med. Inform.*, **128**, 18–23 (2019).

[194] Y. Sakai, Y. Nonaka, K. Yasuda and Y. I. Nakano, Listener agent for elderly people with dementia. In *Proceedings of the 7th ACM/IEEE International Conference on Human-Robot Interaction*, pp. 199–200 (2012).

[195] R. Yaghoubzadeh, M. Kramer, K. Pitsch and S. Kopp, Virtual agents as daily assistants for elderly or cognitively impaired people. In *International workshop on intelligent virtual agents*, pp. 79–91. Springer (2013).

[196] S. Nikitina, S. Callaioli and M. Baez, Smart conversational agents for reminiscence. In *2018 IEEE/ACM 1st International Workshop on Software Engineering for Cognitive Services (SE4COG)*, pp. 52–57. IEEE (2018).

[197] T. Shibata, T. Mitsui, K. Wada, A. Touda, T. Kumasaka, K. Tagami and K. Tanie, Mental commit robot, and its application to therapy of children. In *2001 IEEE/ASME International Conference on Advanced Intelligent Mechatronics*, vol. 2, pp. 1053–1058. IEEE (2001).

[198] L. Hung, C. Liu, E. Woldum, A. Au-Yeung, A. Berndt, C. Wallsworth, N. Horne, M. Gregorio, J. Mann and H. Chaudhury, The benefits of and barriers to using a social robot PARO in care settings: a scoping review, *BMC Geriatr.*, **19**(1), 232 (2019).

[199] H. Gaffney, W. Mansell and S. Tai, Conversational agents in the treatment of mental health problems: mixed-method systematic review, *JMIR Ment. Health*, **6**(10), e14166 (2019).

[200] A. N. Vaidyam, H. Wisniewski, J. D. Halamka, M. S. Kashavan and J. B. Torous, Chatbots, and conversational agents in mental health: a review of the psychiatric landscape, *Can. J. Psychiatry*, **64**(7), 456–464 (2019).

[201] E. Bendig, B. Erb, L. Schulze-Thuesing and H. Baumeister, The next generation: chatbots in clinical psychology, and psychotherapy to foster mental health–a scoping review, *Verhaltens-therapie*, pp. 1–13 (2019).

[202] Woebot. https://woebothealth.com. Accessed: December (2020).

[203] G. M. Lucas, A. Rizzo, J. Gratch, S. Scherer, G. Stratou, J. Boberg and L.-P. Morency, Reporting mental health symptoms: breaking down barriers to care with virtual human interviewers, *Front. Rob. AI*, **4**, 51 (2017).

[204] O. Perski, D. Crane, E. Beard and J. Brown, Does the addition of a supportive chatbot promote user engagement with a smoking cessation app? An experimental study, *Digital Health*, **5**, 2055207619880676 (2019).

[205] R. Bhakta, M. Savin-Baden and G. Tombs, Sharing secrets with robots? In *EdMedia+ Innovate Learning*, pp. 2295–2301. Association for the Advancement of Computing in Education (AACE) (2014).

[206] A. Fadhil and S. Gabrielli, Addressing challenges in promoting healthy lifestyles: the AI-chatbot approach. In *Proceedings of the 11th EAI International Conference on Pervasive Computing Technologies for Healthcare*, pp. 261–265 (2017).

[207] J.-N. Kramer, F. Künzler, V. Mishra, S. N. Smith, D. Kotz, U. Scholz, E. Fleisch and T. Kowatsch, Which components of a smartphone walking app help users to reach personalized step goals? Results from an optimization trial, *Ann. Behav. Med.*, **54**(7), 518–528 (2020).

[208] D. Kadariya, R. Venkataramanan, H. Y. Yip, M. Kalra, K. Thirunarayanan and A. Sheth, kBot: knowledge-enabled personalized chatbot for asthma self-management. In *2019 IEEE International Conference on Smart Computing (SMARTCOMP)*, pp. 138–143. IEEE (2019).

[209] E. Gong, S. Baptista, A. Russell, P. Scuffham, M. Riddell, J. Speight, D. Bird, E. Williams, M. Lotfaliany and B. Oldenburg, My diabetes coach, a mobile app-based interactive conversational agent to support type 2 diabetes self-management: randomized effectiveness-implementation trial, *J. Med. Internet Res.*, **22**(11), e20322 (2020).

[210] S. M. Felix, S. Kumar and A. Veeramuthu, A smart personal AI assistant for visually impaired people. In *2018 2nd International Conference on Trends in Electronics, and Informatics (ICOEI)*, pp. 1245–1250. IEEE (2018).

[211] J. P. Bigham, M. B. Aller, J. T. Brudvik, J. O. Leung, L. A. Yazzolino and R. E. Ladner, Inspiring blind high school students to pursue computer science with instant messaging chatbots. In *Proceedings of the 39th SIGCSE Technical Symposium on Computer Science Education*, pp. 449–453 (2008).

[212] A. Palanica, P. Flaschner, A. Thommandram, M. Li and Y. Fossat, Physicians' perceptions of chatbots in health care: cross-sectional web-based survey, *J. Med. Internet Res.*, **21**(4), e12887 (2019).

[213] L. Ni, C. Lu, N. Liu and J. Liu, Mandy: towards a smart primary care chatbot application. In *International Symposium on Knowledge, and Systems Sciences*, pp. 38–52. Springer (2017).

[214] S. Roos, Chatbots in education: a passing trend or a valuable pedagogical tool? Dissertation (2018).

[215] K. Palasundram, N. M. Sharef, N. Nasharuddin, K. Kasmiran and A. Azman, Sequence to sequence model performance for education chatbot, *Int. J. Emerg. Technol. Learn.*, **14**(24), 56–68 (2019).

[216] R. Winkler and M. Söllner, Unleashing the potential of chatbots in education: a state-of-the-art analysis. In *Academy of Management Annual Meeting (AOM)* (2018).

[217] S. Bayne, Teacherbot: interventions in automated teaching, *Teach. Higher Educ.*, **20**(4), 455–467 (2015).

[218] D. E. Gonda and B. Chu, Chatbot as a learning resource? Creating conversational bots as a supplement for teaching assistant training course. In *2019 IEEE International Conference on Engineering, Technology, and Education (TALE)*, pp. 1–5. IEEE (2019).

[219] A. C. Graesser, S. Lu, G. T. Jackson, H. H. Mitchell, M. Ventura, A. Olney and M. M. Louwerse, AutoTutor: a tutor with dialogue in natural language, *Behav. Res. Methods Instrum. Comput.*, **36**(2), 180–192 (2004).

[220] B. Heller, M. Proctor, D. Mah, L. Jewell and B. Cheung, Freudbot: an investigation of chatbot technology in distance education. In *EdMedia+ Innovate Learning*, pp. 3913–3918. Association for the Advancement of Computing in Education (AACE) (2005).

[221] B. Heller and M. Procter, Conversational agents, and learning outcomes: an experimental investigation. In *EdMedia+ Innovate Learning*, pp. 945–950. Association for the Advancement of Computing in Education (AACE) (2007).

[222] R. Winkler, S. Hobert, A. Salovaara, M. Söllner and J. M. Leimeister, Sara, the lecturer: improving learning in online education with a scaffolding-based conversational agent. In *Proceedings of the 2020 CHI Conference on Human Factors in Computing Systems*, pp. 1–14 (2020).

[223] T. Wambsganss, R. Winkler, M. Söllner and J. M. Leimeister, A conversational agent to improve response quality in course evaluations. In *Extended Abstracts of the 2020 CHI Conference on Human Factors in Computing Systems*, pp. 1–9 (2020).

[224] S. Ghose and J. J. Barua, Toward the implementation of a topic specific dialogue based natural language chatbot as an undergraduate advisor. In *2013 International Conference on Informatics, Electronics, and Vision (ICIEV)*, pp. 1–5. IEEE (2013).

[225] B. R. Ranoliya, N. Raghuwanshi and S. Singh, Chatbot for university related FAQs. In *2017 International Conference on Advances in Computing, Communications, and Informatics (ICACCI)*, pp. 1525–1530. IEEE (2017).

[226] M. Dibitonto, K. Leszczynska, F. Tazzi and C. M. Medaglia, Chatbot in a campus environment: design of LiSA, a virtual assistant to help students in their university life. In *International Conference on Human-Computer Interaction*, pp. 103–116. Springer (2018).

[227] M. N. Kumar, P. L. Chandar, A. V. Prasad and K. Sumangali, Android based educational chatbot for visually impaired people. In *2016 IEEE International Conference on Computational Intelligence, and Computing Research (ICCIC)*, pp. 1–4. IEEE (2016).

[228] R. Cole, D. W. Massaro, J. d. Villiers, B. Rundle, K. Shobaki, J. Wouters, M. Cohen, J. Baskow, P. Stone, P. Connors, et al., New tools for interactive speech, and language training: using animated conversational agents in the classroom of profoundly deaf children. In *MATISSE-ESCA/SOCRATES Workshop on Method, and Tool Innovations for Speech Science Education* (1999).

[229] M. Milne, M. H. Luerssen, T. W. Lewis, R. E. Leibbrandt and D. M. Powers, Development of a virtual agent based social tutor for children with autism spectrum disorders. In *The 2010 International Joint Conference on Neural Networks (IJCNN)*, pp. 1–9. IEEE (2010).

[230] E. Mower, M. P. Black, E. Flores, M. Williams and S. Narayanan, Rachel: design of an emotionally targeted interactive agent for children with autism. In *2011 IEEE International Conference on Multimedia, and Expo*, pp. 1–6. IEEE (2011).

[231] H. Tanaka, H. Negoro, H. Iwasaka and S. Nakamura, Embodied conversational agents for multimodal automated social skills training in people with autism spectrum disorders, *PLoS One*, **12**(8), e0182151 (2017).

[232] M. R. Ali, Z. Razavi, A. A. Mamun, R. Langevin, B. Kane, R. Rawassizadeh, L. Schubert and M. E. Hoque, A virtual conversational agent for teens with autism: experimental results and design lessons, *arXiv preprint arXiv:1811.03046v3* (2020).

[233] W. L. Johnson, J. W. Rickel, J. C. Lester, et al., Animated pedagogical agents: face-to-face interaction in interactive learning environments, *Int. J. Artif. Intell. Educ.*, **11**(1), 47–78 (2000).

[234] A. Kerry, R. Ellis and S. Bull, Conversational agents in e-learning. In *International Conference on Innovative Techniques, and Applications of Artificial Intelligence*, pp. 169–182. Springer (2008).

[235] G. Veletsianos and G. S. Russell, Pedagogical agents. In *Handbook of Research on Educational Communications, and Technology*, pp. 759–769. Springer (2014).

[236] M. Adam, M. Wessel and A. Benlian, AI-based chatbots in customer service, and their effects on user compliance, *Electron. Mark.*, pp. 1–19 (2020).

[237] M. Chung, E. Ko, H. Joung and S. J. Kim, Chatbot e-service, and customer satisfaction regarding luxury brands, *J. Bus. Res.*, **117**, 587–595 (2020).

[238] J. Feine, S. Morana and U. Gnewuch, Measuring service encounter satisfaction with customer service chatbots using sentiment analysis. In *14th Internationale Tagung Wirtschaftsinformatik (WI2019)*, pp. 1115–1129 (2019).

[239] M. Dixon, K. Freeman and N. Toman, Stop trying to delight your customers, *Harv. Bus. Rev.*, **88**(7/8), 116–122 (2010).

[240] J. Cranshaw, E. Elwany, T. Newman, R. Kocielnik, B. Yu, S. Soni, J. Teevan and A. Monroy-Herń, andez, Calendar.help: designing a workflow-based scheduling agent with humans in the loop. In *Proceedings of the 2017 CHI Conference on Human Factors in Computing Systems*, pp. 2382–2393 (2017).

[241] M. Hardalov, I. Koychev and P. Nakov, Towards automated customer support. In *International Conference on Artificial Intelligence: Methodology, Systems, and Applications*, pp. 48–59. Springer (2018).

[242] V. Kasinathan, M. H. Abd Wahab, S. Z. S. Idrus, A. Mustapha and K. Z. Yuen, AIRA chatbot for travel: case study of AirAsia. In *Journal of Physics: Conference Series*, vol. 1529, p. 022101. IOP Publishing (2020).

[243] I. Nica, O. A. Tazl and F. Wotawa, Chatbot-based tourist recommendations using model-based reasoning. In *20th International Configuration Workshop*, pp. 25–30 (2018).

[244] A. V. D. Sano, T. D. Imanuel, M. I. Calista, H. Nindito and A. R. Condrobimo, The application of AGNES algorithm to optimize knowledge base for tourism chatbot. In *2018 International Conference on Information Management, and Technology (ICIMTech)*, pp. 65–68. IEEE (2018).

[245] M. Casillo, F. Clarizia, G. D'Aniello, M. De Santo, M. Lombardi and D. Santaniello, CHAT-Bot: a cultural heritage aware teller-bot for supporting touristic experiences, *Pattern Recognit. Lett.*, **131**, 234–243 (2020).

[246] A. I. Niculescu, K. H. Yeo, L. F. D'Haro, S. Kim, R. Jiang and R. E. Banchs, Design, and evaluation of a conversational agent for the touristic domain. In *Signal, and Information Processing Association Annual Summit, and Conference (APSIPA), 2014 Asia-Pacific*, pp. 1–10. IEEE (2014).

[247] R. Alotaibi, A. Ali, H. Alharthi and R. Almehamdi, AI chatbot for tourist recommendations: a case study in the city of Jeddah, Saudi Arabia, *Int. J. Interact. Mobile Technol.*, **14**(19), 18–30 (2020).

[248] A. M. M. Kyaw, Design, and development of a chatbot for recommending tourist attractions in Myanmar. Information Management Research Reports, AIT (2018).

[249] J. Gustafson, N. Lindberg and M. Lundeberg, The August spoken dialogue system. In *Sixth European Conference on Speech Communication, and Technology* (1999).

[250] J. Cassell, T. Stocky, T. Bickmore, Y. Gao, Y. Nakano, K. Ryokai, D. Tversky, C. Vaucelle and H. Vilhjalmsson, MACK: media lab autonomous conversational kiosk. In *Proceedings of Imagina*, vol. 2, pp. 12–15 (2002).

[251] D. Traum, P. Aggarwal, R. Artstein, S. Foutz, J. Gerten, A. Katsamanis, A. Leuski, D. Noren and W. Swartout, Ada, and grace: direct interaction with museum visitors. In *International Conference on Intelligent Virtual Agents*, pp. 245–251. Springer (2012).

[252] S. Kopp, L. Gesellensetter, N. C. Krämer and I. Wachsmuth, A conversational agent as museum guide–design, and evaluation of a real-world application. In *International Workshop on Intelligent Virtual Agents*, pp. 329–343. Springer (2005).

[253] T. Pfeiffer, C. Liguda, I. Wachsmuth and S. Stein, Living with a virtual agent: seven years with an embodied conversational agent at the Heinz Nixdorf Museums Forum. In *Proceedings of the Re-Thinking Technology in Museums 2011-Emerging Experiences*, pp. 121–131, (2011).

[254] S. Schaffer, O. Gustke, J. Oldemeier and N. Reithinger, Towards chatbots in the museum. In *mobileCH@ Mobile HCI* (2018).

[255] O.-M. Machidon, A. Tavčar, M. Gams and M. Dugulean¢a, CulturalERICA: a conversational agent improving the exploration of European cultural heritage, *J. Cult. Heritage*, **41**, 152–165 (2020).

[256] S. Vassos, E. Malliaraki, F. dal Falco, J. Di Maggio, M. Massimetti, M. G. Nocentini and A. Testa, Art-bots: toward chat-based conversational experiences in museums. In *International Conference on Interactive Digital Storytelling*, pp. 433–437. Springer (2016).

[257] G. Gaia, S. Boiano and A. Borda, Engaging museum visitors with AI: the case of chatbots. In *Museums, and Digital Culture*, pp. 309–329. Springer (2019).

[258] V. L. Rubin, Y. Chen and L. M. Thorimbert, Artificially intelligent conversational agents in libraries, *Library Hi Tech,* **28**(4), 496–522 (2010).

[259] J. Vincze, Virtual reference librarians (chatbots), *Library Hi Tech News,* **34**(4), 5–8, (2017).

[260] K. S. B. Agreda, E. D. B. Fabito, L. C. Prado, M. H. G. Tebelin and V. Benil-daEleonor, Attorney 209: a virtual assistant adviser for family-based cases, *J. Autom. Control Eng.*, **1**(3), 198–201 (2013).

[261] M. Queudot, É. Charton and M.-J. Meurs, Improving access to justice with legal chatbots, *Stats*, **3**(3), 356–375 (2020).

[262] G. Shubhashri, N. Unnamalai and G. Kamalika, LAWBO: a smart lawyer chatbot. In *Proceedings of the ACM India Joint International Conference on Data Science, and Management of Data*, pp. 348–351. Association for Computing Machinery (2018).

[263] G. Lugano, Virtual assistants, and self-driving cars. In *2017 15th International Conference on ITS Telecommunications (ITST)*, pp. 1–5. IEEE (2017).

[264] E. Okur, S. H Kumar, S. Sahay and L. Nachman, Audio-visual understanding of passenger intents for in-cabin conversational agents. In *Second Grand-Challenge, and Workshop on Multimodal Language (Challenge-HML)*, pp. 55–59, Seattle, USA (2020). Association for Computational Linguistics.

[265] E. de Salis, M. Capallera, Q. Meteier, L. Angelini, O. Abou Khaled, E. Mugellini, M. Widmer and S. Carrino, Designing an AI-companion to support the driver in highly autonomous cars. In *International Conference on Human-Computer Interaction*, pp. 335–349. Springer (2020).

[266] A. Fadhil and A. Villafiorita, An adaptive learning with gamification & conversational UIs: the rise of CiboPoliBot. In *Adjunct Publication of the 25th Conference on User Modeling, Adaptation, and Personalization*, pp. 408–412 (2017).

[267] E. Berger, T. H. Sæthre and M. Divitini, PrivaCity. In *International Conference on Informatics in Schools: Situation, Evolution, and Perspectives*, pp. 293–304. Springer (2019).

[268] J. Othlinghaus-Wulhorst and H. U. Hoppe, A technical, and conceptual framework for serious role-playing games in the area of social skill training, *Front. Comput. Sci.*, **2**, 28 (2020).

[269] J. Seering, M. Luria, C. Ye, G. Kaufman and J. Hammer, It takes a village: integrating an adaptive chatbot into an online gaming community. In *Proceedings of the 2020 CHI Conference on Human Factors in Computing Systems*, pp. 1–13 (2020).

[270] B. Jones and R. Jones, Public service chatbots: automating conversation with BBC news, *Digital Journalism*, **7**(8), 1032–1053 (2019).

[271] D. Jannach, A. Manzoor, W. Cai and L. Chen, A survey on conversational recommender systems, *arXiv preprint arXiv:2004.00646* (2020).

[272] Y. Jin, W. Cai, L. Chen, N. N. Htun and K. Verbert, MusicBot: evaluating critiquing-based music recommenders with conversational interaction. In *Proceedings of the 28th ACM International Conference on Information, and Knowledge Management*, pp. 951–960 (2019).

[273] U. Gnewuch, S. Morana, C. Heckmann and A. Maedche, Designing conversational agents for energy feedback. In *International Conference on Design Science Research in Information Systems, and Technology*, pp. 18–33. Springer (2018).

[274] P. Angara, M. Jiménez, K. Agarwal, H. Jain, R. Jain, U. Stege, S. Ganti, H. A. Müller and J. W. Ng, Foodie fooderson a conversational agent for the smart kitchen. In *Proceedings of the 27th Annual International Conference on Computer Science, and Software Engineering*, pp. 247–253 (2017).

[275] A. Jobin, M. Ienca and E. Vayena, The global landscape of AI ethics guidelines, *Nat. Mach. Intell.*, **1**(9), 389–399 (2019).

[276] E. Bender, T. Gebru, A. McMillan-Major and S. Shmitchell, On the dangers of stochastic parrots: can language models be too big?. In *Proceedings of the 2021 ACM Conference on Fairness, Accountability, and Transparency (FAccT '21)*, pp. 610–623, (2021).

[277] D. I. Adelani, H. Mai, F. Fang, H. H. Nguyen, J. Yamagishi and I. Echizen, Generating sentiment-preserving fake online reviews using neural language models, and their human-and machine-based detection. In *International Conference on Advanced Information Networking, and Applications*, pp. 1341–1354. Springer (2020).

[278] A. Bartoli, A. De Lorenzo, E. Medvet, D. Morello and F. Tarlao, "Best dinner ever!!!": automatic generation of restaurant reviews with LSTM-RNN. In *2016 IEEE/WIC/ACM International Conference on Web Intelligence*, pp. 721–724. IEEE (2016).

[279] A. Bartoli and E. Medvet, Exploring the potential of GPT-2 for generating fake reviews of research papers. In *6th Fuzzy Systems, and Data Mining (FSDM)*, Xiamen, China (2020).

[280] T. T. Nguyen, C. M. Nguyen, D. T. Nguyen, D. T. Nguyen and S. Nahavandi, Deep learning for deepfakes creation, and detection: a survey, *arXiv preprint arXiv:1909.11573v2* (2020).

[281] M. Westerlund, The emergence of deepfake technology: a review, *Technol. Innov. Manag. Rev.*, **9**(11), 39–52 (2019).

Index